Footprint Tanzania

Lizzie Williams
1st edition

*I have two skins, one to lie on and one to cover myself with;
the earth and the sky.*

Masai proverb

Tanzania Highlights

See colour maps at back of book

1 Serengeti National Park
The endless plains are trampled by over 3 million large animals during the annual migration

2 Ngorongoro Crater
The largest caldera with the highest density of lion in the world

3 Lake Manyara National Park
A diversity of habitats that support flamingo, elephant and tree-climbing lion

4 Arusha
Unashamed safari capital of Tanzania and closest town to the parks of the northern circuit

5 Mount Meru
Tanzania's second tallest mountain with the Arusha National Park at its base

6 Mount Kilimanjaro
Climb Africa's highest peak to see the sun rise over the 'roof of Africa'

7 Gombe Stream National Park
Track chimpanzees at this important research centre started by Jane Goodall

8 Pemba Island
World class scuba diving in the coral gardens and reefs

Bukoba
Musoma
Tarime
Lake Victoria
Muleba
KAGERA
MARA
Nansio
Bunda
RWANDA
Ngara
Mwanza
Biharamulo
Geita
MWANZA
1 Serengeti National Park
BURUNDI
Shinyanga
Kibondo
SHINYANGA
Nzega
KIGOMA
Gombe Stream National Park
Kasulu
Singida
Kigoma
Tabora
Uvinza
Kaliua
Manyoni
TABORA
Lagosa (Mugambo)
Mpanda
Sitalike
RUKWA
Inyonga
Ikola
Lake Tanganyika
Rungwa
Kipili
Lake Rukwa
RD CONGO
Sumbawanga
MBEYA
Lake Rukwa
Ngomba
Makongolosi
Nuzi
Chimala
Mbeya
Iyayi
Vwawa
Tukuyu
Njombe
Kyela
Ikombe
ZAMBIA
Lake Nyasa
Manda
Lituhi
MALAWI
Liuli
N
0 km 50
0 miles 50

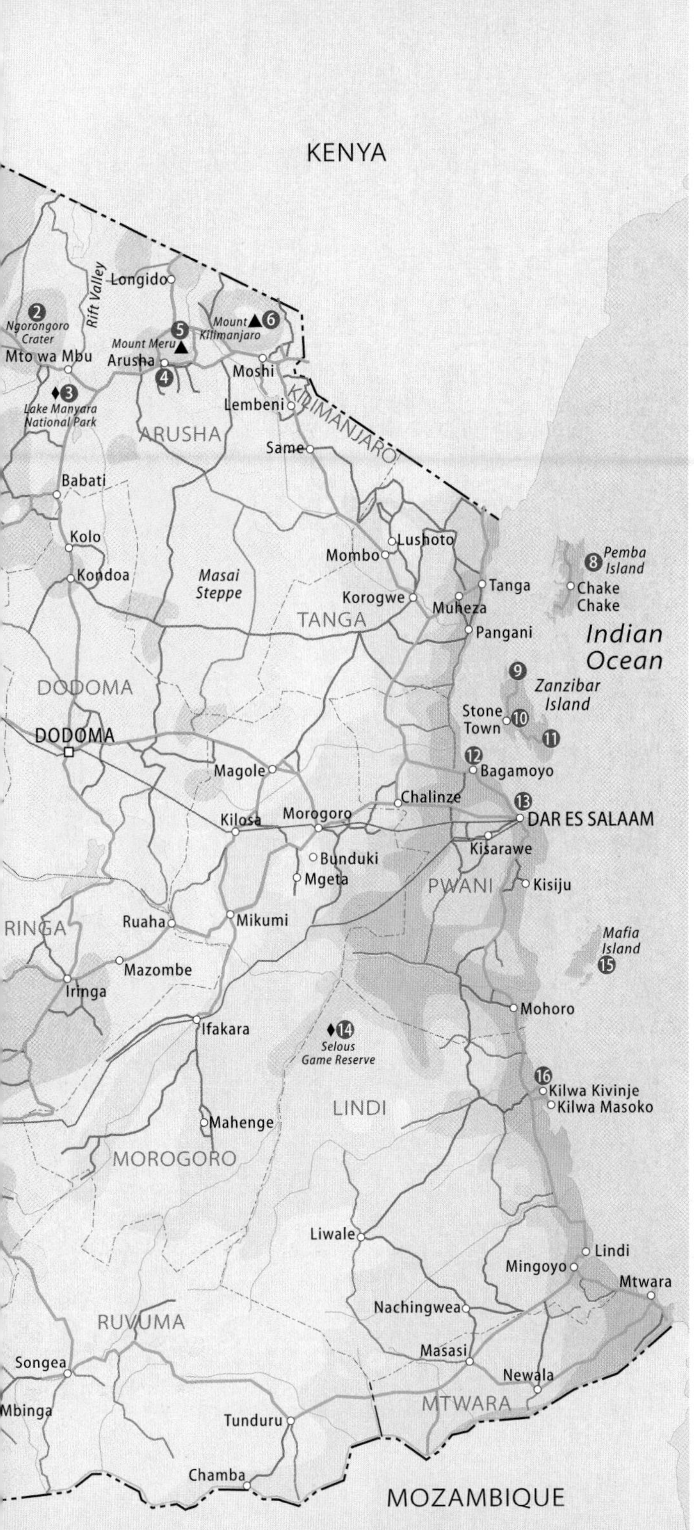

9 Zanzibar north coast beaches
Rustic resorts and hammocks beneath palm trees next to the crystal clear Indian Ocean

10 Stone Town
A World Heritage Site for its intriguing alleyways, Arabian houses and importance to Swahili culture

11 Zanzibar east coast beaches
Fabulous swathes of pristine beach and top class resorts

12 Bagamoyo
Historical town with Arabic architecture and once the home of the German East Africa Company

13 Dar es Salaam
The largest city in Tanzania and a lively, balmy, humid sea port

14 Selous Game Reserve
Vast and wildly remote, this is the biggest game park in the world

15 Mafia Island
The new Mafia Island Marine Reserve protects many species of marine life

16 Kilwa
The atmospheric ruins of a 13th-century city located in a mangrove-fringed bay

Status symbol

Zanzibar's ornately carved wooden doors were designed before the rest of the house and the building was constructed around them. The greater the wealth and social position of the owner of the house, the larger and more elaborately carved his front door.

Introduction

Tanzania's natural environment and geographical features make it one of the most exciting places to visit in Africa. It is serious about protecting its natural inheritance and almost a quarter (23%) of its varied landscape has been allocated to game reserves and national parks that are home to a staggering range of African animals. The town of Arusha is the safari capital of East Africa, from where thousands of minibuses depart all year round to visit the vast plains of the Serengeti, the birthplace of man at the Olduvai Gorge, the natural beauty of Lake Manyara, and the animal-stuffed Ngorongoro Crater. The Serengeti National Park and Ngorongoro Conservation Area are World Heritage Sites and, along with the Masai Mara in neighbouring Kenya, this important ecosystem contains over three million large mammals, which move around the plains on a continuous annual migration – singularly the world's biggest natural movement of large animals. In contrast to the flat plains, Tanzania has a couple of very tall mountains: Mount Meru and Mount Kilimanjaro. Thousands of people every year fulfil their lifetime ambition of climbing to the top of Kili and the experience is the pinnacle of outdoor adventure. It's the third tallest – and the most visited – mountain in the world and the only seriously big one you can literally walk up. The country also has a long coastline steeped in a Swahili culture that has been alive since the first dhows arrived on the trade winds from Asia. A walk through the narrow, twisting passageways of Zanzibar's capital, Stone Town, reveals beautiful Arabian architecture and a fragile Islamic way of life. Zanzibar and the other islands of Pemba and Mafia offer excellent opportunities for diving, snorkelling, fishing, sailing and even swimming with dolphins around their world-class coral reefs. Here are some of the best beaches in the world; where it is impossible not to relax in the dazzling sun next to the warm and azure Indian Ocean.

1 *In many of Tanzania's lesser known parks, such as Tarangire National Park, you will feel like you have the wilderness all to yourself.* ▸▸ *See page 242.*

2 *Traditional white-sailed dhows play an integral part in Swahili life on the coast.* ▸▸ *See page 79.*

3 *Mount Meru dominates Arusha National Park and from the top you can see the snows of Kilimanjaro.* ▸▸ *See page 224.*

4 *Tanzania's varied landscapes and climate make it a great source of fresh produce, traditionally sold in the open markets, like this one in Stone Town, Zanzibar.* ▸▸ *See page 143.*

5 *The glorious Indian Ocean is a playground for tourists but it also provides a living for many fishermen and seaweed harvesters.* ▸▸ *See page 171.*

6 *Tanzania's popular colourful buses criss cross the country on sometimes appalling roads, but still manage to offer efficient services.* ▸▸ *See page 29.*

7 *The beautiful Lake Natron is in the north of the Ngorongoro Conservation Area. The Masai graze their cattle on the surrounding plains.* ▸▸ *See page 251.*

8 *Chimpanzees live in the tangled jungle of Gombe Stream National Park on the shores of Lake Tanganyika.* ▸▸ *See page 311.*

9 *A young herder near Lake Manyara; cattle are the central feature of life for the Masai.* ▸▸ *See page 248.*

10 *Outside the Ngorongoro Conservation Area near Ol Doinyo Lengai; this is the heart of Masailand.* ▸▸ *See page 251.*

11 *The sun-baked plains of the Serengeti are the scene of the greatest wildlife shows on earth.* ▸▸ *See page 262.*

12 *The tallest mountain in Africa, Mount Kilimanjaro dominates Tanzania's landscape and tourist industry.* ▸▸ *See page 201.*

Market day, Iringa
In the chilly highlands of Southwest Tanzania, Iringa has great views of the surrounding countryside and a fruit and veg market you'll find it impossible to leave empty handed.

Contents

Northern Circuit Game Parks

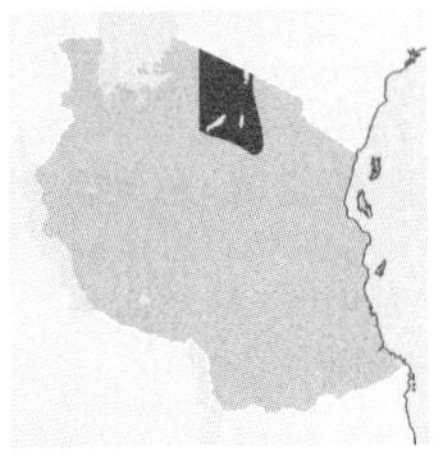

Around Lake Victoria

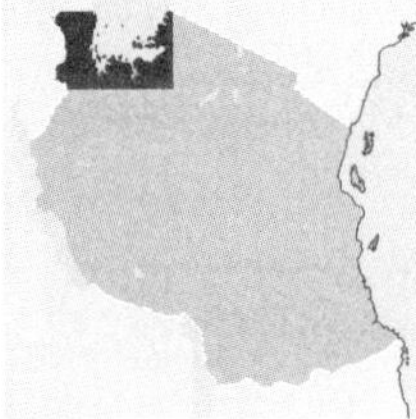

Central Region

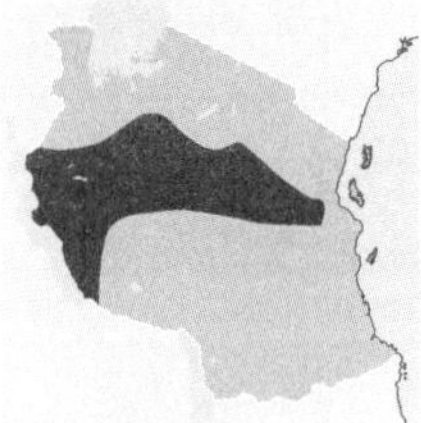

Southwest Tanzania

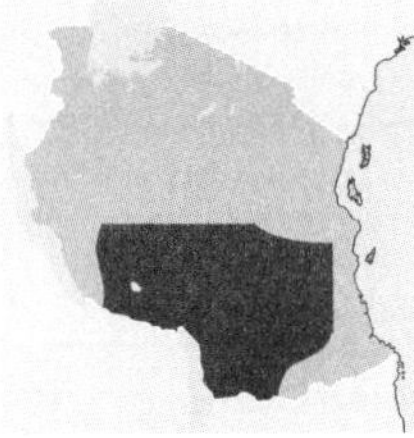

Background

Footnotes

Essentials

Footprint features

Planning your trip

Where to go

Tanzania is a country of enormous diversity. Four times the size of the United Kingdom, 23% (or roughly one million sq km) of its land mass is dedicated to national parks and game reserves. Tanzania has perhaps the best wildlife in East Africa and most people visit in pursuit of the Big Five. The **Selous Game Reserve** is the biggest in Africa (it's bigger than Denmark) and supports large elephant populations, while **Serengeti National Park** is where the annual wildebeest migration begins. The lodges are not as luxurious as in other regions of Africa, but they are improving, and some first-rate small establishments that match the luxury of lodges in southern Africa are beginning to appear on the safari circuit. With the exception of the **Ngorongoro Crater**, which gets rather overrun with pop-up minibuses, the great game areas of Tanzania are less crowded than those in, say, Kenya or South Africa. Snow-capped **Mount Kilimanjaro** is Africa's highest mountain and **Lake Victoria** to the west is Africa's largest freshwater lake. Tanzania's coastal attractions include palm-fringed, white sandy beaches and coral reefs surrounding the off-shore islands, some of which drop off forming steep underwater cliffs that plunge to depths of over 600 m, while **Zanzibar** evokes romantic images of narrow winding streets in Stone Town, fragrant spices and glorious beaches.

With so many parks and itineraries to choose from, safaris to Tanzania are often divided into groups of game parks or circuits. Some of the circuits are of course more travelled than others. Tanzania's northern circuit alone easily attracts the majority of tourists. But the northern circuit's fame and popularity means that other equally stunning but less well-known locations remain little-visited. The southern circuit contains the Selous Game Reserve. None of these circuits is a complete itinerary in itself, nor is it set in stone. Rather, they are regional suggestions for travellers wishing to explore a certain part of the country, or for return visitors to travel somewhere new.

The northern circuit (7 days) This is an extremely popular route as it includes the best known of the national parks in Tanzania. All the safari operators offer combinations of a few or all of the following parks, and how long you go for depends on how many parks you want to visit. Popular routes take in **Lake Manyara National Park, Ngorongoro Crater Conservation Area** (with **Olduvai Gorge**) and the **Serengeti National Park**. The **Tarangire National Park**, as a dry season retreat for many animals, is a splendid game viewing opportunity and is also located in the north of the country, as are Mkomazi and Umba game reserves. To see Ngorongoro Crater and Lake Manyara you will need, absolute minimum, 3 days and 2 nights. To see these two plus Serengeti you will need 4 days and 3 nights, and if you add Tarangire to these three you will need 6 days and 5 nights. Also allow for one night's accommodation in Arusha before and at the end of your safari.

Game and beach safari (14-21 days) Tanzania's mainland coast is not very developed for tourists, but there are good beaches and accommodation at Pangani and Bagamoyo and there are a few resorts on the outskirts of Dar es Salaam. However, it's a different story on Zanzibar, where there are fine tropical coastlines, beach resorts and many watersports on offer. Most visitors choose the popular option of combining the game park experience with time on Zanzibar. For this you really need a week in the Arusha region to visit the northern circuit, and another week to explore and relax on Zanzibar. To save time, the easiest option is to fly between these two destinations. An absolute minimum time to spend on Zanzibar is 3 days/nights. This gives enough time to see Stone Town and get across to either the north or east coasts for a day or two on the beach. There are also a number of other major attractions in northern Tanzania. In particular, keen climbers and walkers visit the area to climb **Mount Kilimanjaro** and **Mount Meru** in **Arusha National Park**. You will need an additional 3 days to climb Meru, and an extra week to climb Kilimanjaro.

The grand tour (28 days and more) If you have additional time, all the above can be seen and you have the option of exploring some of the more remote regions. Along the mainland coast are the historical and atmospheric towns of **Bagamoyo** and **Kilwa**, which can be visited on very long day trips or overnight trips from **Dar es Salaam**. A day or two is warranted in Dar itself if you are heading to Zanzibar by ferry. Two parks that are reasonably easy to access from the city are **Mikumi National Park** reached from the paved road through Morogoro, and **Saadani National Park**, which is now easier to get to via the paved road to Bagamoyo and then 60 km of sandy track. The main attractions in the southern region – the **Selous Game Reserve** (and adjacent Udzungwa National Park) and **Ruaha National Park**, have unspoiled atmospheres that reflect their remote locations. Visiting these parks requires long journeys by road from Dar es Salaam (it is possible to go part of the way to Selous by train). The easiest, but most expensive, access is by air to the airstrips at the camps. The parks in the west include two famous chimpanzee sanctuaries, **Gombe Stream National Park** and **Mahale Mountains National Park**. Both are difficult to access and again the best way to get there is to fly. Nine other parks and reserves – Ibanda, Rumanyika Orugundu, Burigi, Biharamulo, Moyowosi, Kigosi, Ugalla River, Uwanda and Katavi Plains – are all miles from anywhere, with no accommodation to speak of. Travellers to these parks tend to have a specific objective for their visit and make a well-organized, self-sufficient camping trip in their own vehicle, or have an excursion expensively arranged by a safari company.

When to go

Situated just south of the equator, Tanzanian temperatures average between 25-30C°. The hottest season is January-February and the coldest month is August. Humidity varies, being high along the coastal strip and on Zanzibar but much lower in the interior highlands. There are long rains, *masika*, from March to May and short rains, *mvuli*, fall from October to December. In addition there are frequently heavy rains in the south of Tanzania from December until April. On the coast high temperatures are cooled by ocean breezes so it is rarely overpoweringly hot, although humidity levels peak just before the rains arrive and it can become unbearably uncomfortable. Away from the coast, it is much drier and the rains are a little kinder.

 On peaks above 1,500 m the climate is cooler with permanent snow on the highest peaks such as Kilimanjaro where nightime temperatures drop well below zero.

In terms of avoiding the rains, the best time to visit is between May and October, but Tanzania has much to offer all year around. The wildebeest migration in the Serengeti occurs in June and July. If you are planning a trekking holiday the best months are May to September. Travelling by road, especially in the more remote areas or through the national parks, is easier during the dry months, as road conditions deteriorate significantly in the rainy seasons. March, April and May can be months of heavy rain making travel on unsealed roads difficult. Even in these months, however, there is an average of 4-6 hours of sunshine each day. Finally, bear in mind that malaria peaks during the rainy seasons, when the mosquitoes are prolific.

Most of the lodges drop their rates significantly, sometimes by as much as 50%, during low season from the beginning of April to the end of June.

Tour operators

UK overland truck safari operators
Dragoman, T01728-861133, www.dragoman.co.uk.
Encounter, T01728-861133, www.encounter.co.uk.
Exodus Travels, T020-8772 3822, www.exodus.co.uk.
Explore, T0125-239448, www.explore.co.uk.
Kumuka Expeditions, T020-7937 8855, www.kumuka.com.
Oasis Overland, T01963-363400, www.oasisoverland.co.uk.
Phoenix Expeditions, T01509-881341, www.phoenix-expeditions.co.uk.

Specialist tour operators
UK
Abercrombie & Kent, T0800-5547016, www.abercrombiekent.com.

Tanzania tourism

The Tanzanian tourism industry concentrates primarily on the safari tourism in the national parks, as well as Kilimanjaro and Zanzibar. The country receives around half a million tourists each year, of which around 20,000 climb Kilimanjaro. 60% visit the country on a package tour and almost all spend at least some time on safari with a tour operator. The average tourist spends US$127 per day and the turnover from these tourists amounts to nearly US$700 million each year which represents almost 25% of Tanzania's Gross Domestic Product. Tourism offers employment to about 300,000 people. There are about 150 safari companies in Tanzania, of which over 100 are concentrated in Arusha, the nearest town to the national parks.

Acacia Adventure Holidays, T020-7706 4700, www.acacia-africa.com.
Africa Travel Centre, T0845-4501520, www.africatravel.co.uk.
African Odyssey, T01242-224482, www.africanodyssey.co.uk.
Alpha Travel/Ranger Safaris, T020-8423 0220, www.rangersafaris.com.
Africa Travel Resource, T01306-880770, www.africatravelresource.com.
Footprint Adventures, T01522-804929, www.footprint-adventures.co.uk.
Global Village, T0870-999484, www.globalvillage-travel.com.
Hoopoe Safaris, T01923-255462, www.hoopoe.com.
Safari Consultants, T01787-228494, www.safari-consultants.co.uk.
Safari Drive, T01488-71140, www.safaridrive.com.
Sherpa Expeditions, T020-8577 2717, www.sherpa-walking-holidays.co.uk.
Somak, T020-8423 3000, www.somak.co.uk.
Steppes Africa, T01285-650011, www.steppesafrica.co.uk.
Tanzania Odyssey, T020-7471 8780, www.tanzaniaodyssey.com.
Tanzania Safari Specialists, T01452-8662288, www.tanzaniasafaris.info.

Europe

Jambo Tours, Germany, T029-3579191, www.jambotours.de.

North America

Adventure Centre, T0800-2288747, www.adventure-centre.com.
Africa Adventure Company, T800-8829453, T954-4918877, www.africa-adventure.com.
Distant Horizons, T800-3331240, T562-9838828, www.distant-horizons.com.
Legendary Adventure Co, T303-4131182, www.legendaryadventure.com.
Hoopoe Safaris, T800-4083100, www.hoopoe.com.

Africa
Africa Travel Co, T021-5568590, www.africatravelco.com.
Easy Travel & Tours Ltd, T0744-748602151/T0744-748400141, www.easytravel.co.tz
Wild Frontiers, T011-7022035, www.wildfrontiers.com. Offer a full range of safaris throughout Tanzania. Have a fleet of 4x4 landcruisers based in Arusha. Also organise Kilimanjaro climbs.
Wild Things Safaris, T0748-479427 www.wildthingsafaris.com.

Australia and New Zealand
Classic Safari Company, T1300-130218, www.classicsafaricompany.com.au.
Peregrine Travel, T303-96638611, www.peregrine.net.au.

For Tanzania-based operators, see Activities and tours listings throughout the guide.

Finding out more

The **Tanzania Tourist Board**, has its offices in the IPS Building, 3rd Floor, Samora Av/ Azikiwe St, Dar es Salaam, T022-2111244-5, www.tanzaniatouristboard.com. Contact them in advance and they will send you a brochure. The **Tourist Information Office** for drop in visitors is at the Matasalamat Bldg, Samora Av, Dar es Salaam, T022-2131555. It's open Mon-Fri 0900-1700, and Sat 0900-1200. The staff can make reservations at any of the larger hotels in Tanzania and national park lodges (payment in foreign currency only) but they can't help you with budget accommodation. It's better to book national park lodges through a travel agency or tour operator, as they may offer special deals. Brochures and maps can also be picked up from the tourist offices in Zanzibar and Arusha (see pages 133 and 214). **Tanzania National Parks (TANAPA)** has an office in Arusha, T027-2503471, www.tanzaniaparks.com (see page 214).

Useful websites

www.africaonline.com Comprehensive website covering news, sport and travel all over Africa.
www.marineparktz.com Information about Tanzania's marine parks and reserves. Lots of colourful marine life.
www.tanzania-web.com Useful destination and tourism website.
www.intotanzania.com Profiles of parks and attractions by region, hotel reviews, travel advice.
www.go2africa.com Full accommodation and safari booking service for East Africa, with useful practical information.
www.zanzibar.web.com General information about Zanzibar.
www.tanzania.org Includes geographical and general information for travellers in English and Italian.
www.overlandafrica.com Sells a variety of overland tours throughout East Africa.
www.zanzibartourism.net Official site for tourist information for Zanzibar in English, German and French.

Language

Tanzania is a welcoming country and the first words that you will hear and come to know is the **Swahili** (also called Kiswahili) greeting Jambo – hello, often followed by Hakuna matata – no problem! There are a number of local languages but most people in Tanzania, as in all East Africa, speak Swahili and some **English**. Swahili is the official language of Tanzania and is taught in primary schools. English is generally used in business and is taught in secondary schools. Only in the very remote rural regions, will you find people that only speak in their local tongues. A little Swahili goes a long way, and most Tanzanians will be thrilled to hear visitors attempt to use it. Although Swahili is a Bantu language in structure and origin, its vocabulary draws on a variety of sources including Arabic and English. On the coast, it is a little more grammatically developed. In other parts of the country, a more simplified version is spoken. Since the language was originally written down by the British colonists, words are pronounced just as they are spelt. ›› *See also Useful Swahili words and phrases, page 382.*

Disabled travellers

Wheelchairs are very difficult to accommodate on public road transport, so you will probably need to come to Tanzania on an organised tour or in a rented vehicle. With the exception of the most upmarket hotels there are few designated facilities for disabled travellers. A few of the game park lodges have ground floor bedrooms, in contrast to most hotels where the bedrooms are upstairs and there are no lifts. Safaris should not pose too much of a problem given that most of the time is spent in the vehicle, and wheelchair-bound travellers may want to consider a camping or tented safari which provides easy access to a tent at ground level. Most operators are accommodating, and being disabled should not deter you from visiting Tanzania.

Gay and lesbian travellers

Homosexuality is illegal in Tanzania so extreme discretion is advised. Gay clubs and bars are conspicuous by their absence.

Student travellers

There are generally no discounts for students in Tanzania and student rates advertised for museums and parks will usually only apply to local residents. There are a few hostels affiliated to the YHA network, though you do not need to produce a card to either stay there or hope for a discount.

Travelling with children

Tanzania has a great appeal for children: animals and safaris are very exciting, especially when they catch their first glimpse of an elephant or lion. However, small kids may get bored driving around a hot game park or national park all day if there is no animal activity. At some game lodges children are not permitted at all whereas others are completely child-friendly. If you travel in a group, think about the long hours inside the vehicle sharing cramped space with other people. Noisy and bickering children may annoy your travel mates and scare the animals away. But on a more positive note, there are usually young person's discounts for national park entry fees and some accommodation rates. Many travel agencies organize family safaris that are especially designed for couples travelling with children. There are also considerable discounts on accommodation at the beach for children, especially in the family orientated resorts of Zanzibar, when often under-12s get a sizeable reduction and under-6s go free. Many hotels have either specific family rooms or adjoining rooms suitable for families. This is always worth asking about when booking accommodation. Disposable nappies, formula milk powders, and puréed foods, are only available in major cities and they are expensive, so you may want consider bringing enough of these with you. It is important to remember that children have an increased risk of gastro-enteritis, malaria and sunburn and are more likely to develop complications, so care must be taken to minimize risks. See Health, page 44, for more details.

Women travellers

Tanzania does not have a high record of sexual crime and tourists are unlikely to be targeted. It is a relatively safe country for women to travel in, but always keep vigilant, especially for petty theft, and follow the usual common sense about avoiding travelling alone after dark and avoiding quiet places. Women may experience unwanted attention from men, but this can usually be dealt with if you are assertive. Women should be aware that the coast, and in particularly Zanzibar, is largely Islamic. It's fine to lie on the beaches in Zanzibar, as these are at tourist resorts (although see guidelines on page 141), but in local villages and in Stone Town, remember to cover up in loose fitting and non-revealing clothing so you don't cause offence. Non-Islamic women generally are not welcome around mosques.

Working in the country

Whilst there is a fairly large expatriate community in Dar es Salaam working in construction, telecommunications and the import/export industry, there are few opportunities for travellers to obtain casual paid employment in Tanzania and it is illegal for a foreigner to work there without an official work permit. A number of NGOs and Voluntary Organizations can arrange placements for volunteers, usually for periods ranging from six months to two years, see www.volunteerafrica.org.

Before you travel

Visas and immigration

Visas are required by all visitors except citizens of the Commonwealth (excluding citizens of the UK, Australia, Canada, India and Nigeria who do require visas), Republic of Ireland and Iceland. Citizens of neighbouring countries do not normally require visas.

It is straightforward to get a visa at the point of entry (ie border crossing or airport) and many visitors find this more convenient than going to an embassy. Visas are issued at the following entry points: Namanga, Tunduma, Sirari, Horohoro, Kigoma port, Dar es Salaam International Airport, Kilimanjaro International Airport, Zanzibar Harbour and Zanzibar Airport. Visas are paid for in US$, Euros or UK£.

Visas obtained from Tanzanian Embassies require two passport photographs and are issued in 24 hours. All visa costs have now been set at US$50 or €50. Visitors who do not need a visa are issued with a visitor's pass on arrival, valid for 1-3 months. Your passport must be valid for a minimum of six months after your planned departure date from Tanzania; this is a requirement whether you need a visa or not.

It is worth remembering that there is an agreement between Tanzania, Kenya and Uganda that allows holders of single entry visas to move freely between all three countries without the need for re-entry permits. Also remember that although part of Tanzania, Zanzibar has its own immigration procedures and you are required to show your passport on entry and exit to the islands.

Visas can be extended at the **Immigration Headquarters**, Ohio/Ghana Av, Dar es Salaam, uhamiaji@intafrica.com, T022- 2118637/40/43. Mon-Fri, 0730-1530. There are also immigration offices in Arusha and Mwanza (see pages 238 and 282). You will be asked to show proof of funds (an amount of US$1000 or a credit card should be sufficient) and your return or onward airline ticket. Occasionally, independent travellers not on a tour may be asked for these at point of entry.

Resident status for people permanently employed in Tanzania can be arranged after arrival. Your employer will need to vouch for you, and the process can take several weeks. Information on residence permits can be found at www.tanzania.go.tz. Because of Tanzania's two-tiered price system for residents and non-residents, resident status does give certain privileges (lower rates on air flights, in hotels, and game park entry fees).

Tanzanian embassies and consulates abroad

Belgium, 363 Av Louise, 1050 Brussels, T02-6406500, tanzania@skynet.be.
Canada, 50 Range Rd, Ottawa, Ontario KIN 8J4, T613-232 1500, tzottawa@synapse.net.
France, 13 Av Raymond, Pointcare, 75116 Paris, T01-53706366, tanzanie@infonie.fr.
Germany, Theaterplatz 26, 5300 Bonn 2, T0228-3580514, balozi@tanzania-gov.de.
Italy, Via Cesare, Beccaria 88, 00196 Rome, T06-36005234, tanzarep@pcg.it.
Japan, 21-9, Kamiyoga 4, Chome Setagaua-Ku, Tokyo 158, T03-34254531-3, tancon@user.africaoline.co.ke.
Kenya, Continental House, Harambee Av/ Uhuru Highway, Nairobi, T02-331056/7, tanzania@users.africaonline.co.ke.
Mozambique, Ujamaa House, Av Marites Da Machava 852, Maputo, T01-490110-3, ujamaa@zebra.eum.mz.
South Africa, 845 Goont Av, Arcadia, 0007, Pretoria, T012-3424371/93, tanzania@cis.co.za.
Sweden, Oxtorgsgatan 2-4, 103-89 Stockholm, T08-244870, mailbox@tanemb.se.
Switzerland, 47 Av Blanc, CH, 1201 Geneva, T022-7318920, mission.tanzania@itu.ch.
Uganda, 6 Kagera Rd, Kampala, T041-257357, tzrepkla@imul.com.
UK, Tanzania House, 3 Stratford Pl, London W1C 1AS, T020-7569 1470, www.tanzania-online.gov.uk.

US, 2139 R Street NW Washington D.C. 20008, T202-939-6125, www.tanzaniaembassy-us.org.

Zambia, Ujamaa House, No 5200, United Nations Av, 10101 Lusaka, T01-227698, tzreplsk@zamnet.zm.

Zimbabwe, Ujamaa House, 23 Baines Av, Harare, 04-721870, tanrep@icon.co.zw.

Customs and duty free

There is now no requirement to change currency on entry. A litre of spirits or wine and 200 cigarettes can be taken in duty free. There is no duty on any equipment for your own use (eg laptop computers or cameras). Narcotics, pornography and firearms are prohibited. Duty is payable on fax machines, TVs, video recorders and other household electrical items. The CITES (Convention on International Trade in Endangered Species of Wild Fauna and Flora) Convention was established to prevent trade in endangered species. Attempts to smuggle controlled products can result in confiscation, fines and imprisonment. International trade in elephant ivory, sea turtle products and the skins of wild cats, such as leopard, is illegal. Casual vendors and small stalls can offer prohibited products – sea-shells can be a particular problem. Whilst you may legally buy curios made from animal products in Tanzania, you are unlikely to be permitted to take it out of the country or get it into your own country.

Vaccinations

Visitors to Tanzania require a valid yellow fever vaccination certificate. You may not be asked for it on entry into Tanzania but you will certainly be asked for it on exit. Most neighbouring countries and your home country will want to know that you have been vaccinated for yellow fever as Tanzania is classed as a high risk region. The following other vaccinations are recommended: typhoid, poliomyelitis, tetanus, hepatitis A and B, BCG (against tuberculosis), meningitis, and rabies. Children should in addition be protected against whooping cough, mumps, measles and diphtheria, and teenage girls if they haven't already had it, should be given the rubella (German measles) vaccination. ➡ *See also Health section, page 44.*

What to take

Light cotton clothing is best, with a fleece or woollen clothing for evenings. Also take something to change into at dusk – long sleeves and trousers help ward off mosquitoes (remember to bring insect repellant too), which are at their most active in the evening. During the day you will need a hat, sunglasses, and high factor sun cream. Modest dress is advisable for women, particularly on the coast, where men too should avoid revealing shoulders. Tanzania is a great place to buy sarongs (known in East Africa as kikois), which in Africa are worn by both men and women and are ideal for covering up quickly. Footwear should be airy because of the heat; sandals or canvas trainers are ideal. Trekkers will need comfortable walking boots, and if you are climbing Kilimanjaro, ones that have been worn in.

Insurance

Before departure, it is vital to take out comprehensive travel insurance. There are a wide variety of policies to choose from, so shop around. At the very least, the policy should cover medical expenses, including repatriation to your home country in the event of a medical emergency. If you are going to be active in Tanzania, ensure the policy covers whatever activity you will be doing (for example trekking or diving). If you do have something stolen whilst in Tanzania, report the incident to the nearest police station and ensure you get a police report and case number. You will need these to make any claim from your insurance company. Tanzania is covered by the **Flying Doctors' Society of Africa**, based at Wilson Airport in Nairobi. For an annual tourist fee of US$50, it offers free evacuation by air to a medical centre or hospital. This may be worth considering if you are visiting more remote regions, but is not necessary if visiting the more popular parks in the north as adequate provision is made in the case of an emergency. The income goes back into the service and the **African Medical Research Foundation (AMREF)** behind it; membership/information on T+254 (0)2-501301-3, www.amref.org.

Money

Currency

The Tanzanian currency is the **Tanzanian Shilling (TSh)**, not to be confused with the Kenyan and Uganda Shilling which are different currencies. Notes currently in circulation are TSh 200, 500, 1,000, 5,000 and 10,000. Coins are TSh 50, 10 and 20 but these are hardly worth anything and are rarely used. The currency has suffered from extensive depreciation since 1983 when the exchange rate was TSh9 = US$1. At the time of writing the exchange rate was US$1 = TSh1,120. In current conditions, it will probably continue to depreciate at around 7% a year. Visitors can take in any amount of foreign currency, there is no currency declaration, but the import and export of Tanzanian currency is illegal. It is a good idea to bring your money in a mixture of cash and travellers' cheques, with perhaps a credit card as a back up. The good old greenback is the most useful, though the larger banks accept British pounds or Euros. Bring some foreign currency in small denomination notes and to keep at least US$30 in cash (US$25 if flying out from Zanzibar) to pay for departure tax when you leave. Also, try and bring newer notes – because of the prevalence of forgery, many banks and bureaux de change do not accept US dollar bills printed before 1995.

Changing money

The government has authorized bureaux de change known as forex bureaux to set rates for buying foreign currency from the public. Forex bureaux offer faster service than banks and although the exchange rates are only nominally different, the bureaux usually offer a better rate on travellers' cheques. They will also sell foreign currency up to US$3,000 to bona fide travellers (you need to produce an international airline ticket). However, because of the high prevalence of forged US bank notes in East Africa, it is always better to bring them from your home country. In the state-owned and other large private hotels, rates are calculated directly in dollars, and must be paid in foreign currency. Airline fares, game park entrance fees and other odd payments to the government (such as the US$30 airport international departure tax) must also be paid in foreign currency. Only at the very cheap hotels can you pay in local currency. You should pay all hotel bills other than the room rate (such as meals and drinks) in local currency – the rate used to convert the bill into dollars is usually markedly inferior to bureaux rates. Do not be tempted to deal on the black market – there's a high chance you'll get ripped off and the street rate is no different from the bureau rate anyway. Note that lower denomination dollar bills attract a lower exchange rate than higher denomination ones.

Credit cards and travellers' cheques

These are now accepted by large hotels, airlines, major tour operators and travel agencies, but of course will not be taken by small hotels, restaurants and so on. Many banks refuse to exchange travellers' cheques without being shown the purchase agreement – that is, the slip issued at the point of sale that in theory you are supposed to keep separately from your travellers' cheques. Travellers' cheques are now accepted as payment for park entry fees by Tanzania National Parks, as well as cash. In any town of a reasonable size you will be able to use an ATM. It is possible to buy travellers' cheques from **Rickshaw Travel**, the sole American Express Agents in

 Tanzania, in Dar es Salaam (see page 74), on presentation of an American Express card, paying with a personal cheque.

Cost of travelling

In first-rate luxury lodges and tented camps expect to pay in excess of US$150 per night for a double rising to US$500 per night per person in the most exclusive establishments. There are half a dozen places aimed at the very top of the range tourist or honeymooner that charge nearer US$1000 per person per night. For this you will get impeccable service, cuisine and decor in fantastic locations either in the parks or on the coast. In 4-5 star hotels and lodges expect to spend US$150-200 a day. Careful tourists can live reasonably comfortably on US$60 a day staying in the mid-range places, though to stay in anything other than campsites on safaris, they will have to spend a little more for the cheapest accommodation in the national parks. Budget travellers can get by on US$20 using cheap guest houses and going on a basic camping safari. However, with additional park entry fees and related costs organized camping safari costs can exceed US$280 for a three-day trip and climbing Mount Kilimanjaro is an expensive experience whatever your budget. The cost of living and favourable exchange rate in Tanzania is attractive to tourists spending US$s, British pounds and Euros. A bottle of water costs around US$0.50, a soda US$0.30, and a beer US$1. Commodities such as camera film, chocolate, and toiletries are on the expensive side as they are imported but are readily available. Restaurants vary widely from side-of-the-road local eateries where a simple meal of chicken and chips will cost no more than US$2-3 to the upmarket restaurants in the cities and tourists spots that can charge in excess of US$60 for two people with drinks.

Getting there

Air → *See also Airport information, page 24 and Transport in Dar es Salaam, page 74.*

The majority of travellers arrive in Tanzania through **Dar es Salaam Airport** (see page 50). There are also direct international flights to **Kilimanjaro Airport** (between Arusha and Moshi, see page 186) and to **Zanzibar** (see page 132). It is not generally cheaper to arrange a return to Nairobi and a connecting return flight to Dar es Salaam. But for travellers who are only visiting the northern parks, it is easier to fly to Nairobi, given that Arusha is only 273 km to the south of Nairobi, and enter Tanzania through the Namanga land border from Kenya. There are regular shuttle buses between Nairobi and Arusha. Nairobi is served by more airlines than Dar es Salaam so air fares are more competitively priced. There is a departure tax of US$30 (US$25 from Zanzibar) on all international flights leaving Tanzanian airports but is usually included in the price of the ticket.

From Europe **British Airways** has three direct flights a week from Heathrow to **Dar es Salaam** and flying time is 9 hr 40 min. Currently the best options from Europe are with **KLM** from Schiphol, which has daily flights to Dar. Flights will cost upwards of €1000 in High season (July-end March) and €750 in low season. **Air Tanzania** has suspended its service to London. They currently fly between Dar es Salaam and South Africa, Dubai, Zambia, and Uganda. To **Kilimanjaro** (Arusha/Moshi), there are flights with **Egypt Air, Ethiopian Airlines** and **KLM** who touch down on the way to Dar es Salaam. To **Zanzibar, Gulf Air** and **KLM** have direct flights. Travel agents can arrange economical fares from Europe, typically for fixed arrival and departure dates, and for stays of a week or longer. Fares depend on the season.

From North America There are no direct flights to Tanzania from the US, so you will have to fly via Europe.

From Australia and New Zealand There are no direct flights to Tanzania from Australasia – your best bet is to fly to South Africa and change there.

From South Africa **South African Airways** and **Air Tanzania** have plenty of direct flights from Johannesburg. From Cape Town, you'll have to change in Johannesburg.

Airlines

Air Tanzania, T022-2117500 (Tanzania), www.airtanzania.com
British Airways, T0870-8509850 (UK), www.britishairways.com
Kenya Airways, T01784-888222 (UK), www.kenya-airways.com
KLM, T0870-5074074 (UK), www.klm.com
South African Airways, T011-9785313 (South Africa), www.flysaa.com

Discount flight agents

UK and Ireland
Bridge the World, T0870-4432399, www.bridgetheworld.com
Flightbookers, T0870-0107000, www.ebookers.com
Flight Centre, T0870-4990040, www.flightcentre.co.uk
STA Travel, T0870-1600599, www.statravel.co.uk
Trailfinders, T020-7938 3939, www.trailfinders.co.uk
Travelbag, T0870-9001351, www.travelbag.co.uk

North America
Air Brokers International, T01-800883-3273, www.airbrokers.com
STA Travel, T1800-7814040, www.statravel.com
Travel Cuts, T1866-2469762 (Canada), www.travelcuts.com
Worldtek, T1800-2421723, www.worldtek.com

Australia and New Zealand
Flight Centre, T133-133, www.flightcentre.com.au
Skylinks, T02-9234277, www.skylink.com.au
STA Travel, T1-300733035 (Australia), T09-3099723 (New Zealand), www.statravel.com.au
Travel.com.au, T02-9246000, www.travel.com.au

Rail

→ *See also Transport in Dar es Salaam, page 75.*

Train services are fairly reliable, and there are two companies operating in Tanzania. The first is the **Tanzania Railway Corporation's** Central Line, www.trctz.com, that runs between Dar es Salaam and both Kigoma and Mwanza. If arriving into Tanzania by ferry from Zambia you are most likely to connect with the train at Kigoma. The second is the **Tazara** (Tanzania and Zambia Railway Authority) railway line which runs from Kapiri Mposhi in Zambia and runs through the south of Tanzania via Mbeya, Iringa and Morogoro to Dar es Salaam. For prices and timetables visit www.tazara.co.tz.

Road

If you are **driving**, border crossings between Tanzania and its neighbours can be laborious or simple, depending on your preparation and the state of your vehicle's paperwork. You will require a Carnet de Passage issued by a body in your own country (such as the Automobile Association), vehicle registration, and you will also be required to take out third party insurance for Tanzania from one of the insurance companies who have kiosks at the border posts. Travelling in a car registered in Kenya requires leaving the vehicle log book with the Kenyan customs, and keeping a photocopy for the Tanzanian side. Tanzania charges US$65 for the car (multiple entry valid for three months) and car insurance US$34 per month.

From Kenya The main road crossing is at Namanga, about halfway along the road between Arusha and Nairobi. As this border receives thousands of tourists on safari each week en route between the Kenyan and Tanzanian parks (see page 39), it is reasonably quick and efficient. There are also regular shuttle buses connecting the two cities, which takes about 4 hr on fairly good roads all the way. The shuttle services pick up and drop off at the major hotels in Nairobi and Arusha and cost in the region of US$25 each way. A cheaper alternative is to do the journey in stages by taking a minibus from Ronald Ngala Road in Nairobi to Namanga, crossing the border on foot, then catching another minibus to Arusha. This will take a little longer than the shuttle, but will cost half the price. Other crossings are at Lunga Lunga, see page 103, between Mombasa and Dar es Salaam on a recently improved road. There are daily through buses between the two cities. Public buses and minibuses (*dala-dalas*) frequent the quieter border crossings at Taveta, between Moshi and Voi, at Isebania, and between Kisuma and Musoma.

Other neighbouring countries Travellers entering Tanzania from **Malawi** will pass through the Songwe border southeast of Mbeya. There are bus services between Lilongwe and Dar es Salaam, and services between Lilongwe, Mzuzu and Mbeya depart several times each week. Overland transport to Tanzania from **Mozambique** is fairly limited, as there are currently no bridges over the Ruvuma River. There is a passenger ferry at Kilambo (south of Mtwara) and several other ferry crossings at larger towns and junctions. However, foreigners must pass through Kitaya to the south of the Kilambo ferry to get their passport stamped out of Tanzania. There is a good bus link to the border with **Rwanda** at Rusomo. This is roughly 170 km on a fairly good road from Rwanda's capital of Kigali which is served by regular minibuses. There is a bus leaving very early each day from Ngala 10 km from the border post on the Tanzania side and arriving at Mwanza in the evening. From **Uganda** there is crossing at Mutakulu, northwest of Bukoba. Buses connect Kampala to Bukoba several times a week. There are buses to the border with **Zambia** at Nakonde, see page 348. You have to walk between the border posts (or use a bicycle-taxi) to Tunduma where there are buses to Mbeya.

Sea

From Kenya there have been in the past boats from Mombasa to Tanga, Zanzibar and Dar es Salaam. However these services have not been running in recent years. A US$5 port tax is applied to all ferry tickets departing from Tanzanian ports. From Burundi there is in theory a lake ferry to Kigoma from Bujumbura, every Monday. However at the time of writing this was currently suspended, though the service may resume at any time. From Mpulungu (Zambia) there is a weekly ferry to Kigoma on Friday that arrives in Kigoma on Sunday (see page 318 for further details). From Nkhata Bay (Malawi) there is a ferry to Mbamba Bay on Tuesday, though this is a very erratic service and should not be counted on.

Touching down

Airport information

Dar es Salaam International Airport is 15 km west of the city, T022-2842402. There are foreign exchange bureaux, but limited hotel bookings or car hire facilities so you should go directly to your hotel to arrange these things. Flight information is virtually impossible to obtain by telephone at the airport. Contact the airline direct. (Airline offices are listed under Dar es Salaam, page 74, and Arusha, page 237.) Phone cards

Touching down

Electricity 230 volts (50 cycles). The system is notorious for power surges. Computers are particularly vulnerable so take a surge protector plug (obtainable from computer stores) if you are using a laptop. New socket installations are square 3-pin but do not be surprised to encounter round 3-pin (large), round 3-pin (small) and 2-pin (small) sockets in old hotels – a multi-socket adaptor is essential. Some hotels and businesses have back-up generators in case of power cuts, which are more common in the rainy season.
IDD 000. **Country code** 255.
Opening hours Most offices will start at 0800, lunch between 1200-1300, finish business at 1700, Mon-Fri; 0900-1200 on Sat. Banking hours are Mon-Fri, 0830-1530, and Sat 0830-1130.
Time Three hours ahead of GMT.
Weights and measures Metric.

are available from shops just outside the airport and cost US$3. There are public telephones in the terminal buildings. Some of the more upmarket hotels can arrange a shuttle service to and from the airport, which must be booked in advance. There are private buses (*dala-dala*), which cost about US$1 but are very crowded and only leave when they are full. A taxi to town will cost US$15-20 depending on your destination. It takes about 30 min to drive from the airport to the ferry terminal in the city.

Kilimanjaro International Airport is halfway between Arusha and Moshi, about 40 km from each, T027-2502223. The **Air Tanzania** offices in Arusha and Moshi can organize a shuttle bus (US$3) out to the airport 2 hrs before the scheduled flight departure, and the buses meet the incoming flights. If you are using one of the other airlines, the only option is to take a taxi between the airport and Moshi or Arusha, which should cost around US$12, or arrange for one of the tour operators to meet you.

Zanzibar International Airport is 4 km southwest of Stone Town, T024-2230213. On arrival you will be badgered by the taxi drivers. Ask inside the airport what you should pay for a taxi to take you the short distance into town, which will help with bargaining once outside. A taxi should cost in the region of US$6-10, or alternatively there are buses and *dala-dala* to town for less than US$1. Some of the more upmarket hotels and resorts offer free airport pick ups, so it always worthwhile asking. There is a small bank at the airport immediately before you exit the baggage retrieval area. It does not accept travellers' cheques but will change US dollars, pounds sterling, Euros and some other hard currencies. The rates are OK, but are better at the forex bureaux in Stone Town.

Local customs and laws

Calling a **policeman** 'sir' is customary in Tanzania. If you do get in trouble with the law or have to report to the police – for any reason – always be exceptionally polite, even if you are reporting a crime against yourself. The Tanzania police generally enjoy their authoritative status and to rant and rave and demand attention will get you absolutely nowhere. Importing or possession of drugs and guns is prohibited and punished severely. Penalities for possession of any drugs will be extremely harsh. Homosexual activity is unlawful so great discretion is advised. Also, in the Muslim areas, any public display of affection for anyone else is ill advised. Police have arrested tourists canoodling on the beaches of Zanzibar in the past. For petty offences (driving without lights switched on, for example) police will often try to solicit a bribe, masked as an

How big is your footprint?

The point of a holiday is, of course, to have a good time, but if it's relatively guilt-free as well, that's even better. Perfect ecotourism would ensure a good living for local inhabitants, while not detracting from their traditional lifestyles, encroaching on their customs or spoiling their environment. Perfect ecotourism probably doesn't exist, but everyone can play their part. Here are a few points worth bearing in mind:

- Think about where your money goes, and be fair and realistic about how cheaply you travel. Try and put money into local people's hands; drink local beer or fruit juice rather than imported brands and stay in locally-owned accommodation wherever possible.
- Haggle with humour and not aggressively. Remember that you are likely to be much wealthier than the person you're buying from.
- Think about what happens to your rubbish. Take biodegradable products and a water bottle filter. Be sensitive to limited resources like water, fuel and electricity.
- Help preserve local wildlife and habitats by respecting rules and regulations, such as sticking to footpaths, not standing on coral and not buying products made from endangered plants or animals, see boxes pages 38 and 42.
- Don't treat people as part of the landscape; they may not want their picture taken. Ask first and respect their wishes.
- Learn the local language and be mindful of local customs and norms. It can enhance your travel experience and you'll earn respect and be more readily welcomed by local people.
- And finally, use your guidebook as a starting point, not the only source of information. Talk to local people, then discover your own adventure.

'on the spot' fine. Establish the amount being requested, and then offer to go to the police station to pay, at which point you will be released with a warning. For any serious charges, immediately contact your embassy or consulate. Finally, be careful where you point your camera when near government buildings.

It is customary to **tip** around 10% for good service and this is greatly appreciated by hotel and restaurant staff, most of whom receive very low pay. Some of the more upmarket establishments may add a service charge to the bill. It is also expected that you tip safari guides, and if you are climbing Kilimanjaro, porters too. What you give rather depends on the level of service you have received and the enjoyment of your tour. A tip of roughly US$10-15 a day for drivers and guides is about right, but remember excessive tipping can make it difficult for the next customer. If in any doubt, ask the company that you booked the tour through for advice on how much to tip.

Responsible tourism

Increasing awareness of the environmental impact of travel and tourism has led to a range of advice and information services as well as spawning specialist travel companies who claim to provide 'responsible travel' for clients. This is an expanding field and the veracity of claims needs to be verified in many cases. The following organizations and publications can provide useful information and contacts for ethical tourism companies.

Conservation organizations

International

CARE International, T+44 (0)20-7934 9334, www.careinternational.org.uk, works to improve the economic conditions of people living in developing countries.

Responsible Travel, www.responsibletravel.com, is an excellent website offering links to alternative, responsible holidays around the world.

Street Kids International (SKI), based in Toronto, Canada, www.streetkids.org. If you feel the need to do something constructive to help street children, consider making a donation here rather than to begging children directly. SKI run the **Kuleana project** in Mwanza that supports the street kids. Another worthwhile project is **Makombozi**, www.mkombozi.org, which helps the estimated 800 street children living in Arusha and Moshi by providing, through donations, food, medical supplies, clothes, bedding and school equipment.

Tourism Concern, T+44 (0)20-7133 3330, www.tourismconcern.org.uk, works with communities in destination countries to reduce social and environmental problems connected to tourism.

Conservation in Tanzania

Tanzania Wildlife Protection Fund, PO Box 1994, Dar es Salaam, T022-2866377.

Wildlife Conservation Society of Tanzania, PO Box 70919, Dar es Salaam, wcst@africaonline.co.tz.

African Wildlife Foundation, www.awf.org.

Frontier Tanzania, www.frontier.ac.uk.

Safety

In August 1998 there was a bomb blast at the American Embassy on the main road through an ocean-side residential suburb. The outrage, which killed 10 people and coincided with a similar bomb blast in Kenya, was attributed to an Islamic extremist group in Afghanistan led by Saudi-born/Osama bin Laden. Though there is not thought to be a terrorist group active and resident in Tanzania, you should be aware of the global terrorist threat which can make developing countries with a significant tourist industry possible targets. There has been political unease and violence on Zanzibar in the past during elections, but this is not targetted specifically at tourists.

Aside from this, domestic crime has meant that Tanzania has become less safe for travellers in recent years and it is no longer rare for people to have a trip marred by theft. Visitors on tours or who are staying in upmarket hotels are generally very safe. Otherwise, it is sensible to take reasonable precautions by not walking in deserted unlit areas at night, and by avoiding places of known risk during the day. Petty theft and snatch robberies can be a problem, particularly in the urban areas. Don't wear jewellery or carry cameras in busy public places. Bum-bags are also very vulnerable as the belt can be cut easily. Day packs have also been known to be slashed, their entire contents drifting out on to the street without the wearer knowing. Carry money and any valuables in a slim belt under clothing.

Always lock room doors at night as noisy fans and air-conditioning can provide cover for sneak thieves. Be wary of being distracted whilst in a parked vehicle – always keep car doors locked. You also need to be vigilant of thieves on public transport and guard your possessions fiercely.

Crime and hazardous road conditions make travel by night dangerous. Car-jacking has occurred in both rural and urban areas. The majority of these attacks have occurred on the main road from Dar es Salaam to Zambia, between Morogoro and Mikumi National Park. Travellers are advised not to stop between populated areas, and to travel in convoys whenever possible.

It's not only crime that may affect your personal safety; you must also take safety precautions when visiting the game reserves and national parks. If camping, it is not advisable to leave your tent or banda during the night. Wild animals wander around the camps freely in the hours of darkness, and a protruding leg may seem like a tasty take-away to a hungry hyena. This is especially true at organised campsites, where the local animals have got so used to humans that they have lost much of their inherent fear of man. Exercise care during daylight hours too – remember wild animals can be dangerous.

Getting around

Air → *See also Transport in Dar es Salaam, page 74.*

There is talk that in the next couple of years the three East African countries of Tanzania, Kenya and Uganda will establish a single air space over these three countries which would mean that regional flights could become considerably faster, cheaper and more frequent. **Air Tanzania** (it changed its name from Air Tanzania Corporation in 2002) has a limited schedule of domestic flights. The state-owned carrier has suffered from severe financial and operating difficulties, meaning that flights are cancelled and the schedules changed all the time. Often there are delays of several hours for a flight and a whole day needs to be allocated to a leg of air travel. Air Tanzania has daily flights scheduled to Zanzibar, Mwanza and Kilimanjaro. The private companies are better, especially **Precision Air** which has flights from Kilimanjaro, Dar es Salaam, Tabora, Kigoma, Mwanza, Bukoba and Zanzibar and also connects with Nairobi. The smaller companies, **Zan Air** and **Coastal Air** run flights between Dar es Salaam, Zanzibar, Arusha and to the various smaller regional airports and national park airstrips such as Grumeti, Mafia, Lake Manyara, Pemba, Ruaha, Rubondo, Selous, Seronera, and Tanga. These airlines use small 6 or 12 seater planes and have frequent scheduled flights but will only fly with the required minimum of passengers, though sometimes this is only 2 people. Again there are frequent delays and cancellations on these services, though between the three airlines there is extensive air coverage of the country.

Airlines

Air Tanzania, ATC Bldg, Ohio St, Dar es Salaam, T022-2117500, www.airtanzania.com. 2 daily flights from Dar to Zanzibar (25 min) at 0900 and 1600, a daily flight to Kilimanjaro (55 min) at either 0910 or 2000 depending on the day of the week, and 2 daily flights to Mwanza (1 hr 30 min) at 0700 and 1600.
Precision Air, Dar es Salaam, T022-2130800, www.precisionairtz.com. Sample one way fares are Kilimanjaro-Dar-Zanzibar, from US$170; Mwanza-Dar, from US$150; Kigoma-Dar, US$175.
Coastal Air, Dar es Salaam, T022-2117969-60, www.coastal.cc.
Zan Air Zanzibar, T024-2233670, www.zanair.com. Sample fares are Arusha-Selous, from US$310; Arusha-Ruaha, from US$490; Selous-Dar es Salaam, from US$120; Selous-Zanzibar, from US$130; Selous-Ruaha, from US$270; Ruaha-Zanzibar, from US$300; Ruaha-Dar es Salaam, from US$300.

Air charter

There are several companies that offer small planes for air charter, especially between the parks and islands, and have flights most days of the week. These can work out to be economical for groups of 6-12. Alternatively, these same companies often have spare seats on certain charter flights and sell these to individuals for between US$50 and US$100.
Tanzanair, Dar es Salaam Airport, T022-2843131-3, info@tanzanair.com, Royal Palm Hotel sales office, Ohio St, Dar es Salaam, T022-2113151-2, reservations@tanzanair.com, www.tanzanair.com.
Other companies at Dar es Salaam Airport include: **Flightlink**, T022-2843073, **Sky Aviation**, T022-2844410, **Tanzania Government Flight**, T022-2138638, and **Zantas Air**, T022-2137181; and at Zanzibar Airport: **Twin Wings Air Ltd**, T024-2230747, sbc@zanzinet.com.

Bus → *See also Transport in Dar es Salaam, page 75.*

There is now an efficient network of privately-run buses across the country. On good sealed roads buses cover 50-80 km per hour. On unsealed or poorly maintained roads they will average only 20 km per hour. Larger buses give a considerably more comfortable ride than minibuses and have more space for luggage, and are to be recommended on safety grounds as well. If you are taking a shorter journey (Dar-Morogoro or Mwanza-Musoma, say), the bus will leave when full. You can join an almost full bus, and leave promptly for an uncomfortable journey, either standing or on a makeshift gangway seat. Or you can secure a comfortable seat and wait until the bus fills, which can take 1-2 hrs on a less busy route. On the larger and more travelled routes (Dar-Arusha, Dar-Mbeya, Dar-Mombasa in Kenya) there is now a choice of 'luxury', 'semi-luxury' and 'ordinary' and fares vary by a few dollars. The difference between them is that the 'luxury' and 'semi-luxury' buses often have a/c and only take the amount of people the buses are designed to seat. On the 'ordinary' services, the buses are usually older, carry additional standing passengers, and stop more frequently en route making the journey considerably slower. Fares on all buses are very reasonable – roughly US$2 per 100 km on the ordinary buses, rising to US$4 per 100 km on the luxury buses. On a 'luxury' bus the fare from Arusha to Dar es Salaam (a journey of 650 km or 8 hrs) is around US$22, on a semi-luxury bus it's US$14, and on an ordinary bus US$9. On the main routes it is possible to book ahead at a kiosk at the bus stand and this is wise rather than turning up at the departure time on the off-chance. Consistently recommended is **Scandinavian Express**, which has its own terminal in Dar es Salaam, T022-2850847, www.scandinaviangroup.com. They are very popular so book ahead when possible, the offices throughout the country issue computerized tickets, and you can choose your seat on screen. Buses are speed limited, luggage is securely locked up either under the bus or in overhead compartments, and complimentary video, drinks, sweets and biscuits are offered.

Car

Driving is on the left side of the road. The key roads are in good condition, and there has been considerable road-building going on in Tanzania in recent years thanks to foreign aid. The best roads are the tarmac ones from Dar es Salaam to Zambia and Malawi, Dar es Salaam to Arusha and the new tarred road from Arusha to the Ngorongoro Crater. If you are making a long journey you can book a seat at kiosks run

> *If you are driving yourself, your home driving licence, with English translation if necessary, is accepted.*

by the bus companies at the bus stations. Away from the main highways, however, the majority of roads are bad and hazardous. Most of the minor roads are unmade gravel with potholes: there are many rough stretches and they deteriorate further in the rainy season. Road conditions in the reserves and national parks of Tanzania are extremely rough. During the rainy season, many roads are passable only with four-wheel drive vehicles.

Car hire If you are planning to visit some of the national parks and don't want to go on an organized safari, hiring a car becomes a necessity. Car hire is not as well organized in Tanzania as it is in Kenya. There are fewer companies (although this is changing) and they are more expensive. Also, many of the vehicles are poorly maintained and you may find it difficult to hire a car without a driver. The hire charge for this will depend on where you get the vehicle from. It can be as high as US$80-120 a day, plus US$1 per km, plus at least US$10 a day for the driver. On safari, you will have to pay the park entrance fees for the car and the driver and although it will work out expensive this method does allow for greater flexibility than an organized safari. Most of the tour and travel agents listed in the book will be able to arrange vehicle hire.

Dala-dala

Called *dala-dala*, it is said, because they charged a dollar, although this seems a high sum, these are local private buses and passenger vehicles using Toyota (or other) minibuses. On Zanzibar they are also made from small trucks. Tanzania banned these vehicles until 1985, and road transport was a state monopoly. However, inability to provide enough buses (Dar es Salaam required 250 minimum, and was down to 60 in 1980) led to unseemly fights to get on, huge queues, and many commuters were resigned to walking up to 20 km a day. State corporations and private firms tended to provide their own buses for staff. Liberalization of transport is an enormous improvement and these days the small buses are by the far largest method of urban and rural transport. *Dala-dala* are cheap, US$0.20 for any length of journey. However they get very crowded and there is often a squeeze to get on. But fellow travellers will be very helpful in directing you to the correct *dala-dala* if you ask (most have a sign indicating their route and destination on the front), will advise on connections, fight on your behalf to try to get you a seat and tell you when to get off at your destination.

Hitchhiking

In the western sense (standing beside the road and requesting a free ride) this is not an option. However, truck drivers and many private motorists will often carry you if you pay, and if you are stuck where there is no public transport you should not hesitate to approach likely vehicles on this basis.

Rail → *See also Transport in Dar es Salaam, page 75.*

Train services are fairly reliable. There are two railway companies operating in Tanzania. **Tazara** is the name of the Tanzania-Zambia Railway Authority and the trains run from Dar es Salaam, southwest to Zambia (see Getting there above). The other service is the **Tanzania Railway Corporation**, T022-2117833, www.trctz.com, which operates services between Dar es Salaam and Kigoma with a branch line to Mwanza. The Northern line service to Tanga and Moshi has been discontinued. There are four classes of travel; first class compartment sleeping 2, second class compartment sleeping 6, second class sitting, and third class sitting. All cabins on Tanzanian trains are sexually segregated unless you book the whole cabin.

Sea and lake ferries

The ferries are reliable and pleasant. Between Dar es Salaam and Zanzibar there are several sailings each day on modern hydrofoils and an older ferry (see page 77 for details). On **Lake Victoria**, the main sailings are between Mwanza and Bukoba (see pages 281 and 289), though small islands and some other lakeside towns are served. On **Lake Tanganyika** boats go from Kigoma to various small ports south (see page 318). Fares for non-residents greatly exceed those for residents, though they are not overly expensive. On **Lake Nyasa** (also known as Lake Malawi) there is a boat going from the northern port of Itungi to Mbamba Bay, the last Tanzanian port on the east shore (see page 340). The cost of travel varies between US$40 per 100 km for first class hydrofoil travel to US$2 per 100 km for third class on a steamer.

Taxis
Hotels and town centre locations are well served by taxis, some good and some very run-down but serviceable. It is wise to sit in the back if there are no front seat belts. Hotel staff, even at the smallest locations, will rustle up a taxi even when there is not one waiting outside. If you visit an out-of-town centre location, it is wise to ask the taxi to wait – it will normally be happy to do so for benefit of the return fare. Up to 1 km should cost US$1. A trip to the outskirts of Dar es Salaam such as the university (13 km) would be US$7.50. There is a bargaining element: none of the cabs have meters, and you should establish the fare (*bei gani?* – how much?) before you set off.

Tuk tuks
These motorised 3-wheel buggies are starting to feature in many of Tanzania's cities and are cheap and convenient. The driver sits in the front whilst 2-3 passengers can sit comfortably on the back seat. They are still quite a novelty and as yet there are few around, but the idea is catching on quickly and in the future they should offer a service that is at least half the price of regular taxis. They do not, however, go very fast so for longer journeys stick to taxis.

Maps

The best map and travel guide store in the UK is **Stanfords**, 12-14 Long Acre, Covent Garden, London WC2 9LP, T020-783 61321, www.stanfords.co.uk, with branches in Manchester and Bristol. The **Michelin Map of Africa**; Central and South, www.michelin-travel.com, covers Tanzania in detail. The **Map Studio**, T0860-105050, www.mapstudio.co.za, produces a wide range of maps covering much of Africa.

Sleeping

There is a wide range of accommodation on offer from top-of-the-range lodges and tented camps that charge US$150-1000 per couple per day, to mid-range safari lodges and beach resorts with double rooms with a/c and bathroom for around US$25-100, and budget options for under US$10 a day, which may be a simple bed, shared toilet and washing facilities, and have an irregular water supply. Generally accommodation booked through a European agent will be more expensive than if you contact the hotel or lodge directly.

Low season in Tanzania is from the beginning of April to the end of June, when most room rates drop considerably. Some places close during this period.

Hotels
Tanzania's hoteliers are embracing the age of the internet, and an ever increasing number can take a reservation by email or through their websites. At the top end of the market, Tanzania now boasts some accommodation options that would rival the luxurious camps in South Africa – intimate safari camps with unrivalled degrees of

Accommodation price codes

L	over US$150	D	US$10-20
A	US$100-150	E	US$5-10
B	US$50-100	F	under US$5
C	US$20-50		

Prices refer to the cost of a double room including tax, not including service charge or meals unless otherwise stated.

comfort and service in stunning settings. The beach resorts too have improved considerably in recent years, and there are some highly luxurious and romantic beach lodges, spas and hotels on the islands that again are in commanding positions. At the budget end there's a fairly wide choice of cheap accommodation but it is always a good idea to look at a room before deciding to ensure it's clean and everything works. (Make sure your luggage will be locked away securely especially in shared accommodation.) At the very bottom of the budget scale are numerous basic lodgings in all the towns that cost under US$5. For this you get a bare room with a bed and door that may or may not lock. Unless these are exceptionally secure or good value, they are generally not recommended and are often simply rooms attached to a bar that more often than not are rented by the hour. Generally, however, even rooms at the cheaper end of the scale usually have fans or air-conditioning and hot water (check that mosquito nets are provided).

Most town and city hotels tend to be bland with poor service, but increasingly, much nicer options are opening outside the major towns. For instance, many guest houses have opened up on coffee farms around Arusha. In some areas, Stone Town on Zanzibar being the prime example, there is the opportunity to sleep in some historical and atmospheric hotels. Here, even the cheaper establishments are beautiful old houses decorated with fine antiques and Persian carpets, with traditional Zanzibar four-poster beds swathed in mosquito nets.

For the more expensive hotels, the airlines, and game park entrance and camping fees, a system operates where tourists are charged approximately double the local rate and this must be paid in foreign currency and not TSh. In the cheaper hotels you should get away with paying in TSh but always ask before checking in.

Note that the word 'hotel' (or in Swahili, *hoteli*) means food and drink only, rather than lodging. It would be better to use the word 'guest house' (*guesti*).

Camping

Away from the campsites in the national parks and game reserves, camping in Tanzania is fairly limited to the road that runs from Kenya all the way to Malawi in the south. This is part of the great African overland route and each year thousands of independent overlanders travel in either direction. Campsites have sprung up along this route to accommodate the vehicles and campers and some are very good; indeed better than what is on offer in the national parks. The better ones have bars and restaurants, simple sleeping huts for those that don't want to camp, guards for tents and vehicles, and clean ablution blocks with plenty of hot water. In Dar es Salaam there are several campsites that, for a small fee, will allow you to park your vehicle safely for a few days whilst you go to Zanzibar. If you are travelling overland in your own vehicle, we strongly advise you not to bush or free camp at the side of the road. We have heard too many stories about people being robbed in the middle of the night.

National park accommodation

All safari companies offer basically the same safari but at different prices, depending on what accommodation you want. If camping, the companies provide the equipment, if staying in a lodge safari, you will have to spend considerably more. Either way, you are likely to have the same sort of game viewing experiences.

Park lodges vary and may be either typical hotels with rooms and facilities in one building or individual bandas or rondavels (small huts) with a central dining area. Some of the larger ones in the parks of the northern circuit are enormous impersonal affairs with little atmosphere that were built some decades ago, though comfort and service is good.

Camping in public campsites is more atmospheric but facilities are very basic. The Serengeti campsites, for example, have nothing more than a long drop loo, but sleeping here at night is really exciting: the campsites are unfenced and are frequent haunts of hyena and lion. Many of the camps advertise hot running water for showers. This is accurate when the sun is out, otherwise the water may be cold. Be careful about leaving items outside your tent. Many campsites have troupes of baboons nearby that can be a nuisance and a hyena can chew through something as solid as a saucepan. If you are camping on your own, you will almost always need to be totally self-sufficient with all your own equipment. The campsites usually provide running water and firewood.

A luxury tented camp is really the best of both worlds – the comfort of extremely high facilities and service combined with sleeping closer to the animals. They are usually built with a central dining and bar area, are in stunning well designed locations, and each tent will have a thatched roof to keep it cool inside, proper beds, and veranda and they will often have a small bathroom at the back with solar-heated hot water. The added benefit is that they are usually fairly small with just a few tents, so safari experience is intimate and professional.

Eating

Food

Cuisine on mainland Tanzania is not one of the country's main attractions. There is a legacy of uninspired British catering (soups, steaks, grilled chicken, chips, boiled vegetables, puddings, instant coffee). Tanzanians are largely big meat eaters and a standard meal is *nyama choma* – roasted beef or goat meat, usually served with a spicy relish, although some like it with a mixture of raw peppers, onions and tomato known as *kachumbari.* The main staple or starch in Tanzania is *ugali,* a mealie porridge eaten all over Africa. Small town hotels and restaurants tend to serve a limited amount of bland processed food, omelette or chicken and chips, and perhaps a meat stew but not much else. Asian eating places can be better, but are seldom of a high standard. There is a much greater variety in the cities and the tourist spots; both Dar es Salaam and Zanzibar in particular (with its exquisite coastal seafood) do a fine line in eateries. The Swahili style of cooking features aromatic curries using coconut milk, fragrant steamed rice, grilled fish and calamari, and delicious bisques made from lobster and crab. A speciality is *halau*, a sweet dessert made from almonds. Larger resorts offer breakfast, lunch and dinner buffets for their all inclusive guests, some of which can be excellent. Vegetarians are catered for, and fruit and vegetables are used frequently, though there is a limited choice of dishes specifically made for vegetarians on menus and you may have to make special requests. The service in Tanzanian restaurants can be somewhat slower than you are used to and it can take hours for something to materialize from a kitchen. Rather than complain just enjoy the laid-back pace and order another beer.

Restaurant price codes

ΨΨΨ	Expensive	above US$10
ΨΨ	Mid-range	US$5-10
Ψ	Cheap	under US$5

There is a variety of food on most menus; for example fish and seafood can be 2-3 time more expensive than a basic curry or stew, and some restaurants offer more courses than basic main dishes, plus additional extras such as alcoholic drinks. Restaurants and cafés are divided where possible into three simple price grades for a meal of at least 1 main course with either soft drinks or beers.

Various dishes can be bought at temporary roadside shelters from street vendors who prepare and cook over charcoal. It's pretty safe, despite hygiene being fairly basic, because most of the items are cooked or peeled. **Savouries** include: barbecued beef on skewers (*mishkaki*), roast maize (corn), samosas, kebabs, hard-boiled eggs and roast cassava (looks like white, peeled turnips) with red chilli-pepper garnish. **Fruits** include: oranges (peeled and halved), grapes, pineapples, bananas, mangoes (slices scored and turned inside-out), paw-paw (*papaya*) and water melon.

Most food is bought in open air markets. In the larger towns and cities these are held daily, and as well as fresh fruit and vegetables sell eggs, bread and meat. In the smaller villages, markets are usually held on one day of the week. Markets are very colourful places to visit and as Tanzania is very fertile, just about any fruit or vegetable is available.

Drink

Local beers (lager) are decent and cheap, around US$1.20 for a 700 ml refundable bottle. Brands include Kilimanjaro and Safari lager. There is a wide variety of imported lagers from Kenya, South Africa and Europe, but these are around three times the price. Imported **wines** are on the expensive side: US$6-8 in a supermarket and US$10-12 in a restaurant for a European or South African label. Tanzanian wines produced by the White Fathers at Dodoma, **Bowani Wine**, are reasonable. Wines made by the **National Milling Corporation** are undrinkable. **Soft drinks** are mainly limited to colas, orange, lemon, pineapple, ginger beer, tonic and club soda. Like beer, you have to give the bottle back when you've finished. Fresh juices are common and quite delicious. **Bottled water** is widely available and safe. **Coffee**, when fresh ground, is the local Arabica variety with a distinctive, acidic flavour. In the evenings, particularly, but all day at markets, bus and railway stations there are traditional Swahili coffee vendors with large portable conical brass coffee pots with charcoal braziers underneath. The coffee is sold black in small porcelain cups, and is excellent. They also sell peanut crisp bars and sugary cakes made from molasses. These items are very cheap and are all worth trying. On the coast chai (**tea**) is drunk in small glasses; black with lots of sugar.

Holidays and festivals

New Year's Day 1 January; **Zanzibar Revolution Day** (Zanzibar only) 12 January; **CCM Foundation Day** 5 February; **Union Day** 26 April; **Mayday Workers' Day** 1 May; **Farmers' Day** 7 July; **Peasants' Day** 8 August; **Prophet's Birthday** 10 September; **Independence Day** 9 December; **Christmas Day** 25 December;

Boxing Day 26 December. **Good Friday, Easter Monday, Id-ul-Fitr** (end of Ramadan), **Id-ul-Haji** (Festival of Sacrifice), **Islamic New Year,** and **Prophet Mohammad's Birthday** are other holidays that vary from year to year. Muslim festivals are timed according to local sightings of the various stages of the moon. Christian holidays will not be observed by all Muslims and vice versa. There are a number of annual festivals held on Zanzibar each year including the Zanzibar Cultural Festival, the Zanzibar International Film Festival of the Dhow Countries, and the Sauti za Busara Swahili Music and Cultural Festival. For information on these see page 156, or visit www.ziff.or.tz.

Shopping

Tanzania has several interesting craft items for sale including Makonde and ebony wood carvings, soapstone carvings, musical instruments, basket ware and textiles. Masai crafts such as beaded jewellery, decorated gourds and spears are available to buy in northern Tanzania as well as the red checked Masai blankets. *Mkeka* are plain, straw-coloured mats woven from sisal by craftsmen in Karatu, near the Ngorongoro Crater. The women of Mafia Island make more colourful *mkeka* from dried and twisted palm fronds. In Zanzibar, you can find old tiles, antique bowls, and the famous carved wooden Zanzibar chests. Brightly coloured sarongs called *kangas* are worn by women all over Tanzania. They're sold in pairs and emblazoned with a traditional proverb. Woven with vertical stripes, *kikois* are similar but are traditionally worn by the men. You can pick up bags of Zanzibar spices direct from the market. Tanzania is the world's only source of tanzanite (www.tanzanites.net), a semi-precious stone found in the open mines around Arusha. The deep blue of Tanzanite is magnificent, ranging from ultramarine to a light purplish blue. Fakes abound, so if you're going to invest in one of Tanzania's largest exports, be sure to do it right. Don't buy from dealers on the street – most licensed curios shops and jewellers stock different grades, cuts, and colours.

Sport and activities

Tanzania has good opportunities to get active, and trekking, cycling or horse or camel riding safaris are popular alternatives to being ferried around in zebra-camouflaged vehicles in the national parks. Diving, snorkelling and deep sea fishing are favourite pastimes on the coast and climbing Mount Kilimanjaro remains a popular challenge. Details about local operators are given in the activities and tours listings of each section.

Birdwatching

Apart from all the animals, Tanzania also boasts a fine selection of birds with 1117 recorded species of which 26 are endemic to Tanzania. Birdwatching is a popular pastime and can easily be combined with game viewing. Apart from the national parks, good spots for birdwatching include the Umsambara Mountains and the foothills of Kilimanjaro. Most tour operators will be able to arrange safaris particularly aimed at birdwatchers. Alternatively visit **www.tanzaniabirding.com**.

Climbing

Tanzania's numerous parks and reserves (see page 39) offer many climbing options for the avid explorer. Although Kilimanjaro tops the list as Africa's most famous – and highest – mountain, Tanzania boasts many other mountain ranges and attractive peaks. Most of the country's mountains and volcanoes

are in the north and east of the country. They vary from the dramatic crater of **Mount Meru** and the active volcano of **Ol Doinyo Lengai** to tamer options like the **Usambara Mountains** and comparatively gentle slopes of the **Crater Highlands**. Tour operators and trekking companies will happily put together an itinerary that suits your preferences. It is advisable, especially when climbing at higher altitudes, to take things slowly and allow your body to acclimatize. There are no mountaineering
or outdoor outfitters in Tanzania, so when preparing for a trek in the country, bear in mind that you'll need to bring most of your own gear. Sleeping bags, good hiking boots, many layers, and waterproof outer clothing is essential for keeping warm and comfortable at high altitudes. Bring a few refillable plastic water bottles and a good day pack as well – although porters will carry the heavier equipment, you'll want to have a few things easily available throughout the day. For climbers on Kilimanjaro, the Kilimanjaro Guides Cooperative Society runs a small shop inside the Marangu Gate of the national park, where you can pick up a few things before you start your climb. But these items are usually expensive and it is far better to arrive prepared. Tour operators offering climbs are listed in the relevant chapters.

Diving

Undoubtedly one of East Africa's greatest tourism assets is the vast areas of fringing coral reef that stretch south from the equator hugging the coastline and surrounding islands. These huge living coral formations, which in the past were a mariner's worst nightmare, have now become the playground for the tourist and house at least 3,000 different species of marine animals and plants. El Niño has been to blame for much of the coral bleaching and damage to many top reefs of East Africa but the positive signs of regrowth are definitely in place, and for divers the visible damage shouldn't detract from the splendour and abundance of the fish life. The **best time to dive** in Tanzania is between October and April before the long rains and subsequent river outflows affect visibility but check individual locations in this section for more details. Plankton blooms are reasonably common and can reduce the visibility drastically. Out of season many dive centres/resorts close (Swahili Divers, Pemba, boast excellent visibility year round and do not close). The diving conditions surrounding the islands are more reliable and the waters generally clearer than off the mainland. Average visibility in the diving season ranges between 10-30 m increasing to 20-40 m around Pemba and Mafia islands. The Northeast Monsoon wind (*Kaskazi*) blows from November to March and can affect diving conditions along the coast of Pemba during January.

Equipment

If you are a qualified diver and have your own kit, take it. All dive centres mentioned in this section have both din and A-Clamp fittings and will give discounts when you bring your own. Prior to departure, check your baggage allowance with the airlines and see if you can come to some arrangement for extra weight. Water temperature varies between 24°C (September) and 30°C+ (March) depending on time of year. Most dive centres hire 3 mm wetsuits, which are fine if you are an occasional diver and don't get cold quickly. If you do, then bring your own 5 mm one-piece wetsuit. If you do not have your own equipment everything is available for hire.

New divers

The warm waters and colourful reefs provide an exciting training ground for first-timers wishing to explore the underwater realm. Most dive centres run PADI courses up to Divemaster level. BSAC, NAUI, CMAS and SSI centres also exist but are not as common. Five-day entry level courses include theory, pool sessions and four or five ocean training dives, or a one-day *One Ocean Diving* on Zanzibar also offers 'Discover Scuba' option if you just want to experience a one-off dive for fun. They also give the option of doing the theory and pool section of the course at home, before completing the dive part of the course on arrival, allowing more time on Zanzibar for additional diving. Medical questionnaires must be completed prior to a course; medical certificates might be

Diving jargon

BSAC British Sub Aqua Club.
CMAS Confédération Mondiale des Activités Subaquatique.
Coral garden An area of pristine coral with much variety and high concentration.
Drop offs Where a coral reef or shelf descends into the depths.
IANTD International Association for Nitrox and Trimix Divers; specializes in courses for technical diving.
NAUI National Association of Underwater Instructors (SA)
Nitrox Oxygen enriched air.
Negative entries Entering the water without any air in your buoyancy jacket in order to enable rapid descent and to avoid strong surface currents and potential shark excitement.
PADI Professional Association of Dive Instructors (international).
Visibility How far you can see underwater – measured horizontally.

required. Costs average US$50 per dive, though if you book more than one dive at a time costs come down. The beginner's PADI Open Water course takes 4-5 days and costs US$320-500 depending on marine park fees, day excursions including lunch, and whether you get to keep the expensive training manual after the course. Check with your dive centre for local marine hazards.

Mainland sites

The main diving areas of Tanzania are found on the islands of Pemba, where there are dramatic drop offs, and Zanzibar and Mafia where there are fringing reefs and coral gardens. On the mainland, local divers recommend the offshore islands around Dar es Salaam, though mainland reefs accessible from Tanga and Dar have been damaged through the illegal practice of dynamite fishing, which, through slack policing, is still a problem today. However, if you are not visiting Pemba or Zanzibar and need to get wet, there are a number of memorable dive sites around Dar worth a dip or two. Of particular note is **Ferns Wall**, which is on the seaward side of Fungu Yasin Reef, where you'll find large barrel sponges, gorgonian fans and 2-m long whip corals. Reef sharks are often spotted here. Because of its depth this site is for advanced divers only. Another favourite is **Mwamba**, a unique reef comprising large fields of pristine brain, rose and plate corals. Although slightly further out, **Big T** reef is a must dive for the experienced diver but only on a calm day. **Latham Island**, southwest of Dar, is an area surrounded by deep water where big game fish and elusive schools of hammerheads can be found. It can only be dived with a very experienced skipper who knows the area.

Dive centres DiveMaxx, Bahari Beach Hotel/Silver Sands Hotel, T022-2650231, divemaxx@twiga.com. Contact: Jens Kruuse.

Zanzibar *p*

Zanzibar has a fair amount to offer as far as diving is concerned. October-November are the best diving months with clearer visibility and calm conditions. From Stone Town there are a number of dive sites with pristine coral gardens and a proliferation of marine life. **Murogo Reef** has probably some of the most beautiful coral on the whole East African coast. **Turtle's Den** is another favourite; this site actually lives up to its name with as many as 10 turtles seen in one 45-minute dive. **Boribo Reef** is classed as the best for larger pelagics by many advanced divers but is far from shore and minimum numbers are required. On the north coast, **Leven Banks** is popular with advanced divers as it lies near the deep water of the Pemba Channel and is home to big shoals of

Tanzanian authorities are now waking up to need to protect the marine environment and several areas have been set aside for marine conservation, funded through conservation agencies and tourism. These include: Mesali Island (off Pemba), Chumbe Island (off Stone Town) and the whole of Mafia Island.

How big is your flipper?

All divers should be aware of the potential threat they pose to reefs and should help to sustain this delicate ecosystem by doing a few simple things. These diving tips are adapted from the Marine Conservation Society 'Coral Code'. For further information visit www.mcsuk.org or contact the Communications Officer, T01989-566017.

- ✔ Review your skills. If you haven't dived for a while, practise in the pool or sandy patch before diving around the reef.
- ✔ Choose your operator wisely. Report irresponsible operators to relevant diving authorities (PADI, NAUI, SSI).
- ✔ Control your fins. Deep fin kicks around coral can cause damage.
- ✔ Practise buoyancy control. Through proper weighting and practice, you should not allow yourself or any item of your equipment to touch any living organism.
- ✖ Never stand on the reef. Corals can be damaged by the slightest touch. If you need to hold on to something, look for a piece of dead coral or rock.
- ✖ Avoid kicking up sand, which can smother corals and other reef life.
- ✖ Know your limits. Don't dive in conditions beyond your skills.
- ✖ Do not disturb or move things around (eg for photography)
- ✖ Do not collect or buy shells or any other marine curios (eg dried pufferfish)
- ✖ Do not feed fish
- ✖ Do not ride turtles or hold on to any marine animal as this can easily cause heart attacks or severe shock to the creature.

jacks and trevally. Famous for remote 'holiday brochure style' beaches and colourful reefs, the east coast diving is the most talked about on Zanzibar. **Mnemba Island**, reached from Nungwi or Matemwe, has a wide range of sites varying in depth with exciting marine life. Great for snorkelling. **Pungu Wall**, East Mnemba, is a recommended dive for experienced divers looking for sharks, rays and groupers. This site can only be dived in calm conditions. On the south coast, at **Kizimkazi**, there is a growing industry springing up around large resident pods of humpbacked and bottlenose dolphins. (Marine biologists assess these dolphins as being very stressed by the uncontrolled jostling and chasing of boat operators. They advise that if you snorkel with these dolphins you exercise respect, restraint and common sense. Splashy water entries and boat drivers in hot pursuit will only drive them away.) See box on page 160 for dive sites off Zanzibar.

Dive centres **Stone Town**: Zanzibar Dive Centre/One Ocean, T024-2238374, T0742-750161 (mob), www.zanzibaroneocean.com. **Matemwe**: Matemwe Bungalows, T0747-425788 (mob), www.matemwe.com. **Nungwi**: Ras Nungwi Beach Hotel, T024-2233767, www.rasnungwi.com.

Pemba *p182*

Known as the Emerald Isle for its lush vegetation and idyllic setting, Pemba is most definitely the jewel in East Africa's dive-site portfolio. On the more chartered west coast the deep waters of the Pemba Channel have conspired to create dramatic walls and drop-offs, where glimpses of sharks and encounters with eagle rays, manta rays, Napoleon wrasse, great barracuda, tuna and kingfish are the norm. Visibility can range from 6 m in a plankton bloom to 60 m, though 20 m is classed as a bad day and 40 m is average. Some of the coral has been affected by El Niño, but Pemba remains a world-class diving destination.

There are a few dive centres on Pemba – for barefoot luxury try remote Manta Reef Lodge. However, to appreciate Pemba's magical diversity fully, take the liveaboard option and dive the east coast, for this is the territory of the schooling hammerheads. It would be impossible to single out the best dive sites; they are all simply breathtaking. On Mesali Island and the surrounding reefs, the West Coast is a protected marine park and entrance of US$5 must be paid to dive or snorkel there. See box on page 182 for dive sites from Pemba.

Dive centres Dive 7/10, luxury outfit based at Fundu Lagoon, T024-2232926, www.fundulagoon.com. **Manta Reef Lodge**, specific diving lodge at Tumbe, T0747-423930 (mob), www.mantareeflodge.com. **Swahili Divers**, The Old Mission Lodge, Chake Chake, T024-2452786, www.swahilidivers.com. Highly recommended for the budget traveller.

Mafia Island *p105*

The diving around Mafia can be described as a 'shallow Pemba with more fish' – beautiful reefs and spectacular fish life. **Jino Pass** and **Dindini Wall** are two sites to the northeast of Chole Bay. Both reefs have flat tops at 8 m dropping vertically in a spectacular wall to 25 m with a sandy bottom. Whip corals 2-3 m long grow out from the walls. There are a couple of interesting (if tight) swim-throughs and a long tunnel cave at 20 m on 'Dindini Wall'. Impressive sightings include huge malabar, potato and honeycomb groupers, giant reef rays, green turtles, great barracuda, kingfish, bonito, shoals of bluefin trevalley and snappers in their thousands. On the eastern entrance to Chole Bay lies **Kinasi Pass**. There is a recommended drift dive in the Pass but it must be dived on an incoming tide and is for experienced divers only if diving on a spring tide. The Pinnacle in the centre of the mouth of the Pass is a good opportunity to see large rays, groupers, eagle rays and jacks. Best dived on slack or gentle incoming tide and you will need an experienced guide to find the site.

Dive centres Pole Pole Bungalow resort, T022-2601530 (Dar es Salaam booking office), www.polepole.com. **Kinasi Lodge**, T032-2238220, www.mafiaisland.com. Both these are luxury resorts.

Safaris

The parks and game reserves of Tanzania are without rival anywhere in the world. Some are world famous, such as Serengeti, Ngorongoro and Kilimanjaro, have excellent facilities and receive many visitors. Many others rarely see tourists and make little or no provision in the way of amenities for them. The differences between a 'national park' and a 'game reserve' depends on the access by local people. In national parks the animals have the parks to themselves. In game reserves the local people, in particular pastoralists such as the Masai, are allowed rights of grazing. Game reserves are often found adjoining national parks and have usually been created as a result of local pressure to return some of the seasonal grazing lands to pastoralists.

It is essential to tour the parks by vehicle and walking is prohibited in most. So you will either have to join an organized tour by a safari company, or hire (or have) your own vehicle. Being with a guide is best; without one you will miss a lot of game, and not get to the most promising viewing locations.

Going on safari – can be a most rewarding experience. However, it is something to be prepared for, as it will almost certainly involve a degree of discomfort and long journeys. Some of the roads in Tanzania can be very exhausting. The unsealed roads are bumpy and dusty, and it will be hot. It is also important to remember that despite the expert knowledge of the drivers, they cannot guarantee that you will see any animals. When they do spot one of the rarer animals, however, watching their pleasure is almost as enjoyable as seeing the animal itself. To get the best from your safari, approach it with humour, look after the driver as well as you are able (a disgruntled driver will quickly ruin your safari), and do your best to get on with, and be considerate to, your fellow travellers.

The rules of the national parks are really just common sense and are aimed at visitor safety and conservation (see page 42). The parks are open from 0600-1900 and at other times driving in the parks is not permitted. The speed limit is 50 kph but you will probably want to go much slower most of the time.

Overland truck safaris are another way of exploring Tanzania by road although they demand a little more fortitude and adventurous spirit. The compensation is usually the camaraderie and life-long friendships that result from what is invariably

Park fees

Park permit entry fees
(In any period of 24 hours, or part thereof. Children under 5, free entry.)

Kilimanjaro
Adult US$60
Child 5-16 years US$5

Serengeti
Adult US$50
Child 5-16 years US$10

Arusha, Tarangire and Lake Manyara
Adult US$35
Child 5-16 US$10

Katavi, Mikumi, Ruaha, Rubondo and Udzungwa National Parks
Adult US$20
Child 5-16 years US$5

Gombe Stream
Adult US$100
Child 5-16 years US$20
Child under 5 Free

Mahale
Adult US$80
Child 5-16 US$30

Vehicle entry to parks
Up to 2,000 kg US$40 (foreign)
Tsh 10,000 (Tanzanian)
2,000-3000 kg US$150 (foreign)
Tsh 25,000 (Tanzanian)

Camping permit
(In any period of 24 hours, or part thereof. Fees as of Jan 2006.)
Established campsites
Adult US$30
Child 5-16 US$5

Special campsites
Adult US$50
Child 5-16 US$10

Guide fees
Service of official guide US$10
(outside his working hours) US$15
Walking safaris guides US$20

Special sport fishing fees
Applicable only to Gombe, Mahale and Rubondo Island National Parks (sport fishing allowed between 0700 and 1700 only)
Adult US$50
Child 5-16 US$25
Child under 5 years Free

Hut, hostel and rest house fees
(rates per head per night)

Kilimanjaro National Park: Mandara, Horombo and Kibo US$50
Meru - Miriakamba and Saddle US$20
Other huts - Manyara, Ruaha, Mikumi etc US$20
Hostels - Marangu, Manyara, Serengeti, Mikumi, Ruaha and Gombe Stream (strictly for organized groups with permission of park wardens in charge) US$10
Rest houses - Serengeti, Ruaha, Mikumi, Arusha, Katavi US$30
Rest house - Gombe Stream US$20

Rescue fees
Mounts Kilimanjaro and Meru: The park shall be responsible for rescue between the point of incident to the gate on any route. The climber will take care of other expenses from gate to KCMC or other destination as he/she chooses.
The rates are payable per person for trip US$20

National parks

Tanzania's 13 national parks and 1 conservation area together hold a population of over 4,000,000 wild animals.

Name	Area (sq km)
Arusha	137
Gombe Stream	52
Katavi	2,253
Kilimanjaro	756
Lake Manyara	320
Mahale Mountains	1,613
Mikumi	3,230
Ngorongoro Crater	2,288
Ruaha	12,950
Rubondo	457
Saadani	300
Serengeti	14,763
Tarangire	2,600
Udzungwa Mountains	1,000

Game reserves

In addition, there are 14 game reserves few of which have any tourist facilities.

Name	Area (sq km)
Biharamulo	1,300
Burigi	2,200
Ibanda	200
Kizigo	4,000
Lukwika-Lumesule	600
Maswa	2,200
Mkomazi	1,000
Moyowosi	6,000
Rumanyika-Orugundu	800
Rungwa	9,000
Selous	55,000
Ugalla	5,000
Umba River	1,500
Uwanda	5,000

See colour map page 396

a real adventure, as you go to places that more luxurious travellers will never visit. The standard overland route most commercial trucks take through East Africa (in either direction) is a two-week circuit from Nairobi into Uganda to see the mountain gorillas via some of the Kenyan national parks, then crossing into Tanzania to Arusha for the Ngorongoro Crater and Serengeti, before heading south to Dar es Salaam, for Zanzibar, and then driving though southern Tanzania via the Mikumi National Park to Malawi. The overland operators are listed under Tour operators (see page 14).

There are also huge number of companies offering safaris which are listed in the relevant chapters. Safaris can be booked either at home or once in Tanzania – if you go for the latter it may be possible to obtain substantial discounts. If you elect to book in Tanzania avoid companies offering cheap deals on the street – they will almost always turn out to be a disaster and may appear cheap because they do not include national park entrance fees. At the tourist office in Arusha there is a blacklist of unlicensed operators and people with convictions for cheating tourists. Safaris do not run on every day of the week. In the low season you may also find that they will be combined. If you are on a four-day safari you can expect to join another party. This can be awkward as the 'six-dayers' will already have formed into a cohesive group and you may feel that you are an outsider.

Food and drink

Standards at lodges and tented sites are the same as at normal hotels. Camping safaris usually have a cook. Food is wholesome and surprisingly varied. You can expect eggs, bacon and sausages and toast for breakfast, salads at midday and meat/pasta in the evening with perhaps a fruit salad for desert. Companies will cater for vegetarians, and you must tell the cooks if you have specific allergies. Insects are a fact of life and despite valiant attempts by the cook it is virtually impossible to avoid flies (as well as moths at night) alighting on plates and uncovered food. Notwithstanding this, hygiene standards are high.

Game viewing rules and regulations

- **Keep on the well-marked roads and tracks** Off-road driving is harmful because smoke, oil and destruction of the grass layer cause soil erosion. Do not drive through closed roads or park areas. Do not try and persuade your driver to go off road to get closer to the animals. It is mandatory to enter and exit the parks through the authorised gates.
- **For your own safety, stay in your vehicle at all times** In all the parks that are visited by car, it is forbidden to leave the vehicle except in designed places, such as picnic sites or walking trails.
- **Stick to the parks' opening hours** It is usually forbidden to drive from dusk to dawn unless you are granted a special authorisation. At night you are requested to stay at your lodge or campsite.
- **Never harass the animals** Make as little noise as possible. For wildlife photography, silence is golden. Your vehicle serves as a blind or hide, since animals usually will not identify it with humans. Never chase the animals and always give way, they have right of way under any circumstances.
- **Do not feed the animals** The food you provide might make them ill. More importantly, this practice alters their behaviour patterns and can result in aggression when they do not get what they want. This is especially true of baboons. If camping at night in the parks, ensure that the animals cannot gain access to any food you are carrying.
- **Do not throw any litter, used matches and cigarette butts** This not only increases fire risk in the dry season, but also some animals will eat whatever they find.
- **Do not disturb other visitors** They have the same right as you to enjoy nature. If you discover a stopped vehicle and you want to check what they are looking at, never hinder their sight nor stop within their photographic field. If there is no room for another car, wait patiently for your turn, the others will finally leave and the animals will still be there. If there is a group of vehicles most drivers will take it in turns to occupy the prime viewing spot. Always turn the engine off when you are watching game up close.
- **Do not speed** The speed limit is usually 50 kmph. Speeding damages road surfaces, increases noise and raises the risk of running over animals.
- **Wild animals are dangerous** Wild animals' reactions are unpredictable. Don't expose yourself to unnecessary risks and stay inside your car. Severe accidents can happen due to an excess of confidence.
- **Do not take or purchase anything that is a bi-product of an animal** Most curio shops no longer sell any items manufactured with animal materials, though on rare occasions you might be approached by someone trying to sell such products (ostrich eggs, for example). Never buy anything, it is an offence and if caught you will be heavily fined.
- **In marine parks** Stick to the same rules as above. Do not take or harm coral, shells, starfish or any other living organisms, as it is illegal and hazardous for their ecosystems. Also, do not buy any shells or other products made from living things. This promotes looting in reefs around the protected areas. Line and bait fishing is allowed in certain regions but not in the Marine Parks. Harpoons are forbidden everywhere.

Game drives

There are usually two game drives each day. The morning drive sets off at about 0700 and lasts until midday. The afternoon drive starts at about 1600 and lasts until the park closes (1830-1900). In addition you may have an early morning drive which will mean getting up well before dawn (about 0500).

Safari costs

Safaris vary in cost and duration. On the whole you get what you pay for. Obviously the longer you spend actually in the parks, rather than just driving to and from them, the better. The costs will also vary enormously depending on where you stay and how many of you there are in a group. For an all inclusive **tented camp** or **lodge safari** the cost will average out at about US$150-250 per person per day, though at the very top end of the scale, staying in the most exclusive tented camps and lodges and flying between destinations, expect to pay US$500-600 per day. At the lower end of the market, a **camping safari** using the basic national park campsites is about US$80-100 per person per day. These rates include park entrance fees, cost of vehicle and driver, and food.

Tipping

How much you should tip the driver on safari can be a tricky decision. It is best to enquire from the company at the time of booking what the going rate is. As a rough guide you should perhaps allow about US$10-15 per adult per night (half this for a child). Always try to come to an agreement with other members of the group and put the tip into a common kitty. Again remember that wages are low and there can be long lay-offs during the low season. Despite this there is also the problem of over- or excessive tipping which can cause problems for future clients. If you are on a camping safari and have a cook, give all the money to the driver and leave him to sort out the split.

Transport

It is worth emphasizing that most parks are some way from departure points. If you go on a three-day safari, you will often find that at least one day is taken up with travelling to and from the park – leaving you with a limited amount of time in the park itself. You will be spending a lot of time in a vehicle. On most safaris these will almost certainly be a Landrover, Landcruiser or minibus accommodating 6-8 people. Leg room can be very limited. They will have a viewing point through the roof (the really upmarket ones will also have a sun shade). In practice this means that only three-four people can view out through the roof at any one time – passengers usually take turns to stick their heads and cameras out of the top.

What to take

Room is very limited in the vehicles and you will be asked to limit the amount you bring with you. There is very little point in taking too much clothing – expect to get dirty, particularly during the dry season when dust can be a problem. Try to have a clean set of clothes to change into at night when it can also get quite cold. Loose clothing and sensible footwear is best. Few companies provide drinking water and it is important to buy enough bottles to last your trip before you set off. It is surprising how much you get through and restocking is not easy.

The other important items are binoculars, a camera with a telephoto lens (you will not get close enough to the animals without one) and plenty of film. Take twice as much as you think you will need. Film can be purchased at the lodges but it will cost you three times as much.

You may also wish to take a more detailed field guide. The Collins series is particularly recommended. The drivers are usually a mine of information. Take a notebook and pen – it is good fun to write down the number of species of animals and birds that you have spotted (anything over 100 is thought to be pretty good).

See page 33 for safari accommodation options and page 232 for 'How to organize a safari'.

Safaris to Serengeti NP, Ngorongoro Conservation Area, Lake Manyara, Tarangire and Arusha NPs are best arranged from Arusha (see page 232). For trips to Mikumi and Ruaha NPs and Selous Game Reserve arrangements are best made in Dar es Salaam (see page 74).

Spectator sports

In large towns the main activities will be **soccer** matches. Fixtures tend to be arranged, or postponed, at short notice so check the daily press. There are also **cricket** matches over weekends (predominantly a pursuit of the Asian community), and **golf**, **tennis** and **squash** tournaments are held at clubs but are open to the public. Many world class runners have come from Tanzania and every year, a torch called the *uhuru* or freedom torch is lit on Mount Kilimanjaro and then carried across the country by runners to celebrate independence. Occasional **sailing** regattas are held at the yacht clubs in Dar es Salaam and Tanga. **Track and field** meetings are staged, the Mount Meru marathon is an annual event in June, as is the Zanzibar marathon held in November, and there are boxing tournaments. For details see local press.

Health

See your GP or travel clinic at least six weeks before your departure for general advice on travel risks, malaria prophylaxis and vaccinations. Make sure you have travel insurance (the **Flying Doctors** based at Wilson Airport in Nairobi covers Tanzania, see page 20), get a dental check (especially if you are going to be away for more than a month), know your own blood group and if you suffer a long-term condition such as diabetes or epilepsy make sure someone knows or that you have a Medic Alert bracelet/necklace with this information on it. Few medical facilities are available outside the big towns.

Health risks

Malaria is present in almost all of Tanzania and can cause death within 24 hours. If you have any flu-like symptoms (lethargy, headaches, fever; or, more seriously, develop fits) go to a doctor and ask for a malaria blood test as soon as possible. Have a low index of suspicion because it is very easy to write off vague symptoms, which may actually be malaria. (On your return home if you suffer any of these symptoms, get tested as soon as possible, even if any previous test proved negative, the test could save your life.) You can help to avoid getting malaria by trying to avoid being bitten by the mosquitos that carry the disease. Cover up in the evenings and at night, use a repellent and sleep under mosquito nets dipped in permethrin, an insect repellent. You should also consult your doctor before leaving about adequate anti-malarial drugs and be aware that you may have to start taking these at least a week before you leave in order to be covered when you get to Tanzania.

Diarrhoea is common and although it should be short lasting, go to the doctor if it persists beyond two weeks, or if there is blood or you are in pain. Ciproxin (Ciprofloxacin) is a useful antibiotic for bacterial traveller's diarrhoea that can be obtained by private prescription in the UK. If this has no effect after 24 hrs then the diarrhoea is likely to be viral (in which case there is little you can do apart from keep yourself rehydrated and wait for it to settle on its own). The key treatment with all diarrhoeas is rehydration. Oral Rehydration Salts (ORS) in ready-made sachets or can be made up by adding a teaspoon of sugar and a half teaspoon of salt to a litre of clean water.

There are a number of ways of purifying water. Dirty water should first be strained through a filter bag and then boiled or treated. Bringing water to a rolling boil at sea level is sufficient to make the water safe for drinking, but at higher altitudes you have to boil the water for a few minutes longer to ensure all microbes are killed. There are sterilizing methods that can be used and there are proprietary preparations containing chlorine (eg Puritabs) or iodine (eg Pota Aqua) compounds.

Chlorine compounds generally do not kill protozoa (eg Giardia). There are a number of water filters now on the market available in personal and expedition size. They work either on mechanical or chemical principles, or may do both. Make sure you take the spare parts or spare chemicals with you and do not believe everything the manufacturers say.

If you go **diving** make sure that you are fit do so. The British Sub-Aqua Club (BSAC), Telford's Quay, South Pier Rd, Ellesmere Port, Cheshire CH65 4FL, UK, T01513-506200, www.bsac.com, can put you in touch with doctors who do medical examinations. Protect your feet from cuts, beach dog parasites (larva migrans) and sea urchins. Check that the dive company know what they are doing, have appropriate certification from BSAC or Professional Association of Diving Instructors (PADI), Unit 7, St Philips Central, Albert Rd, St Philips, Bristol, BS2 0TD, T0117-3007234, www.padi.com, and that the equipment is well maintained.

Altitude sickness can strike from about 3,000 m upwards and in general is more likely to affect those who ascend rapidly and those who over-exert themselves. Teenagers are particularly prone. On reaching heights above 3,000 m, heart pounding and shortness of breath, especially on exertion, are almost universal and a normal response to the lack of oxygen in the air. Acute mountain sickness, on the other hand, takes a few hours or days to come on and presents with heachache, lassitude, dizziness, loss of appetite, nausea and vomiting. Insomnia is common and often associated with a suffocating feeling when lying down in bed. You may notice that your breathing tends to wax and wane at night and your face is puffy in the mornings – this is all part of the syndrome. If the symptoms are mild, the treatment is rest, painkillers (preferably not aspirin-based) for the headaches and anti-sickness pills for vomiting. Should the symptoms be severe and prolonged it is best to descend to a lower altitude immediately and reascend, if necessary, slowly and in stages. The symptoms disappear very quickly with even a few 100 m of descent. Other problems experienced at high altitude are sunburn, excessively dry air causing skin cracking, sore eyes (it may be wise to leave your contact lenses out) and sore nostrils. Treat the latter with Vaseline. Do not ascend to high altitude if you are suffering from a bad cold or chest infection and certainly not within 24 hours following scuba diving.

Schistosomiasis (bilharzia) occurs in the freshwater lakes of Tanzania and can be contracted from a single swim. If you have swum or waded through snail infested water you may notice a local itch soon after, fever after a few weeks and much later diarrhoea, peeing blood, abdominal pain and spleen or liver enlargement. A single drug cures this disease but it can do damage to your liver, so get yourself checked out as soon as possible if you have any of these symptoms, or alternatively avoid swimming in any freshwater areas, there is no guarantee that they will not be contaminated, no matter what local advice you receive.

Keeping in touch

Internet

Internet cafés and email facilities offered in small business centres have mushroomed in all the major towns. The cost of access has fallen considerably to around US$0.50-1 per hr. Access is not super-quick but neither is it painfully slow and services are improving all the time. Most urban centres with their own server keep costs low but in more out of the way places where a satellite connection is relied upon, the price per hr is two or three times higher. Many hotels and guest houses also offer internet access to their guests.

Media

Tanzania has two English daily newspapers, Daily News and the Guardian, as well as several Swahili dailies. An excellent regional paper, The East African, published in Nairobi, comes out weekly and has good Tanzanian coverage. The Kenyan daily, The Nation, is a high quality source of regional and international news. There are two government operated radio stations. Radio Tanzania on 1442 KHZ MW broadcasts in Swahili. The External Service at 1204 MW has programmes in English. News bulletins tend to contain a lot of local coverage. BBC World Service can be received on radios with short waveband reception. World Service is now also available via an FM relay in Mwanza (Radio Free Africa 89.8 FM), Arusha (Radio 5 Arusha 105 FM) and Dar es Salaam (BBC/IPP 101.4 FM), and the reception is better than on short-wave. In 1994 television channel ITV began to transmit with a mixture of locally produced Swahili items and international programmes. There are now several local stations, and many hotels have satellite TV. This is usually DSTV (Digital Satellite Television), South African satellite TV, with several channels.

Post

Postal system is fairly reliable. Airmail takes about two weeks to destinations in Europe and North America. Buy stamps at the hotel or at a postcard shop, post offices are crowded and chaotic. However, items have been known to go missing so post anything of personal value through the fast post service known as EMS; a registered postal service available at all post offices. DHL has offices in the major cities, as do TNT and Fedex in Dar es Salaam. Packages to Europe take three working days, to North America, five days.

Telephone

In most towns there is an efficient international service from the Telecoms office. These are usually within the post office or nearby. Connections are quick and about a third of the price of a call through hotels, which are expensive for phone calls and faxes. The recent installation of new telephone exchanges as part of a privatization initiative has led to a radical change of telephone numbers, involving new area codes and the addition of a 2 before most existing numbers, resulting in seven-digit numbers. In case of difficulties, the **Tanzania Telecommunications Company Ltd (TTCL)** enquiry number in Dar es Salaam is T022- 2110055, www.ttcl.co.tz. Tanzanian mobile telephone numbers start with 07. If you have international roaming it is possible to use your mobile or you can buy a local Sim card. Top-up cards for the pay-as-you-go mobile providers are available just about everywhere.

Dar es Salaam

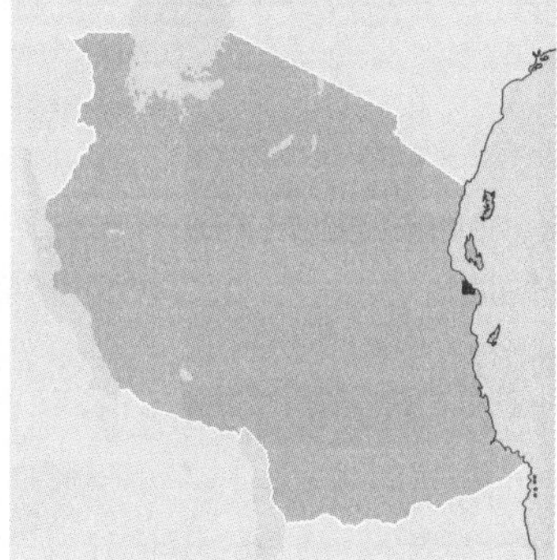

Footprint features

Introduction

Meaning 'haven of peace' in Arabic, having grown into a frantic East African city these days, Dar es Salaam is hardly peaceful, but it's very much a vibrant and balmy place with a lot of atmosphere. The city dates from 1857 and was successively under the control of Zanzibar, Germany and Britain before self-determination, and these influences have all left their mark. During German occupation in the early 20th century, it was the centre of colonial administration and the main contact point between the agricultural mainland and the world of trade and commerce in the Indian Ocean and the Swahili Coast. Remnants of colonial presence, both German and British, can still be seen in the landmarks and architecture around the city. Today it is the largest city in Tanzania, and has grown rapidly since independence in 1961, roughly trebling in size. Dar's bustling harbour is the country's main port, and its industrial area produces products for export and use throughout the country.

Rather incomprehensibly, the official capital of Tanzania was transferred from Dar to the city of Dodoma, 480 km to the west of Dar, in 1973. While some government bodies and the main parliamentary sittings are in Dodoma, many of the government agencies, large corporations and foreign embassies have shown their reluctance to move by staying right where they are in Dar. It remains the principal city and commercial hub of Tanzania, it is home to Tanzania's major international airport, and tourists are most likely to pass through the city as it is the springboard for excursions to Zanzibar.

★ Don't miss

1 **National Museum and Botanical Gardens** For Leakey fossils, one of George V's cars, a wooden bicycle and gardens, now restored, that were first laid out in the German period, page 58.

2 **Cricket** If it is the weekend, take in some cricket at the Gymkhana Club off Ocean Road, pages 60 and 73.

3 **Makumbusho Village Museum** See examples of traditional dwellings and displays of dancing from around Tanzania, page 61.

4 **Kigamboni** Take the ferry across the harbour mouth and wander along the coast, where you will find a noticeable lack of bustle, the odd small bar and restaurant, and access to swimming in the sea, page 61.

5 **North coast beaches and Mwenge** Take a trip out for the day to the beaches 20-25 km to the north for R&R and snorkelling, page 63. On the way visit the craft and curio market at Mwenge, page 72.

6 **Kisarawe and Pugu Hills Forest Reserve** Take a trip, only 30 km out of the city, to this peaceful hill town and coastal forest nature trail, page 64.

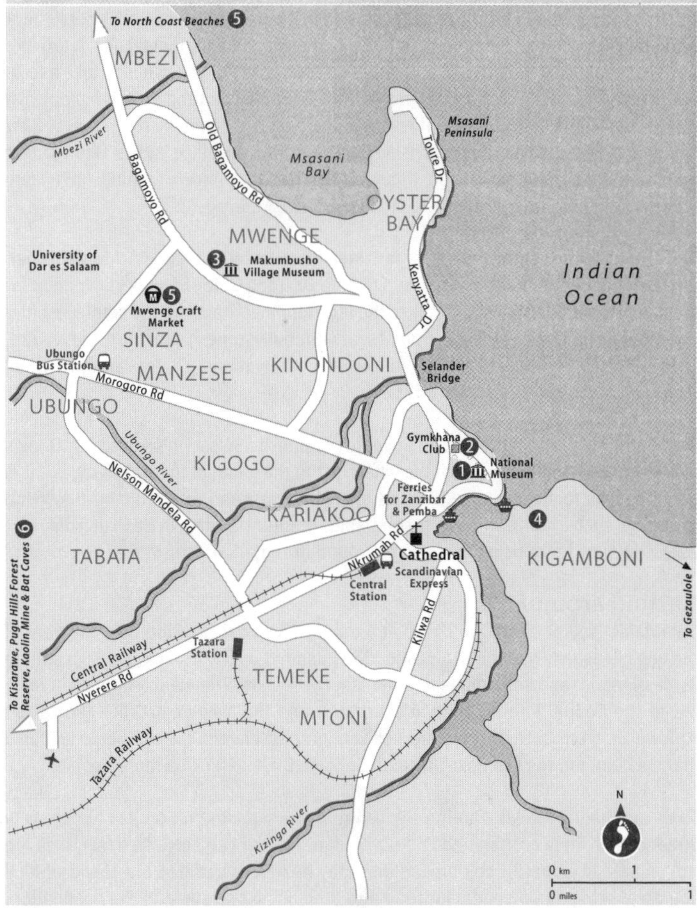

Ins and outs → *Phone code: 022. Colour map 1, grid B6. Population 2,500,000*

Altitude: sea level
Area: approx 90 sq km.
Position: 6°50'S 39°12'E

Getting there

Air International and domestic flights depart from **Dar es Salaam International Airport**, along Nyerere (formerly Pugu) Rd, 13 km from the city centre, flight information T022-2844562. The airlines have desks at the airport and there is a range of facilities (see page 24). For those international visitors requiring a visa for Tanzania, the visa desk is just before immigration at international arrivals. To get from the airport to the city, *dala-dala* and minibuses run regularly, are cheaper than regular taxis, but are crowded and there can be a problem with luggage, which will normally have to be accommodated on your knees. Taxis are the better option and cost US$8-12, depending on your skill at bargaining. If in any doubt ask someone in the airport what you should pay before approaching the taxi drivers outside. » *For airline office details, see page 74.*

Bus The main bus station for up-country travel is on Morogoro Rd in the Ubungo area, 6 km to the west of the centre. It is well organized and modern with cafés and shops and ticket offices on the main road outside. It is also reasonably secure as only ticket holders and registered taxi drivers are allowed inside; nevertheless watch out for pick pocketing. For a few shillings you can hire a porter with a trolley for luggage. A taxi into the city should cost around US$3. Outside on Morogoro Rd, you can also take a local bus or *dala-dala* to the centre, though again these are crowded and there is a problem if you are carrying a large amount of luggage. The best bus company recommended for foreigners, **Scandinavian Express** (see page 29), has an office at the Ubungo Bus Station where all their buses stop, though it also has a downtown terminal on Nyerere Rd where all their services start and finish. » *For details see page 75.*

Rail Trains to the central regions of Tanzania (the Dar-Tabora-Kigoma/Mwanza line), run from the Central Railway Station, Sokoine Dr, T022-2110600. It is convenient for most hotels and is only a short walk to the ferry terminal. Trains for the southwest (the Dar-Mbeya-Zambia line) leave from Tazara Station some 5 km from the centre, T022-2865187, www.tazara.co.tz for online reservations. There are plenty of *dala-dala* and a taxi costs about US$4. » *For details see page 75.*

Sea Ferries leave from the jetty on Sokoine Dr opposite St Joseph's Cathedral. Dhows and motorized boats leave from the wharf just to the south of the boat jetty, but it is now illegal for foreigners to take dhows along the coast and you would be ill-advised to arrange such a journey. The ferry companies request payment in US$ cash only and each company has a ticket office on or around the wharf. » *For details see page 77.*

Getting around

Dala-dalas (see page 30) are cheap at around US$0.20 for any journey. The front of the vehicle usually has the two destinations painted on the bonnet or a sign stating its destination, and sometimes another stating the fare. The main terminals in town are at the Central Railway Station (Stesheni) and the New Post Office (Posta) on Azikiwe St. From both, if there are not enough passengers, the *dala-dala* will also make a detour to the Old Post Office on Sokoine Drive to pick up more people.

Taxis are readily available in the city centre and are parked up on just about every street corner. They cost around US$1-2 per km. Any car can serve as a taxi, they are not painted in a specific colour, and they may be new or battered but serviceable. If you are visiting a non-central location and there is no taxi stand at the destination, you can always ask the driver to wait or come back and pick you up at an allotted time. These days most of Dar's taxi drivers have cell phones, so it is easy enough to get the number and call the driver when you want to be picked up. Taxis do not have meters so always negotiate taxi fares before setting off on your journey.

Tuk tuks (see page 31) are still quite a novelty in Dar and as yet there are few around, but the idea is catching on quickly and in the future they should offer a service that is at least half the price of regular taxis. They don't go very fast, though, so for longer journeys stick to taxis.

Tourist offices

Tanzania Tourist Board, IPS Building, 3rd Fl, Samora Av/Azikiwe St, T022-2111244-5, www.tanzaniatouristboard.com. If you contact them in advance they will post out brochures. The **Tourist Information Office** (for drop-in visitors), Matasalamat Bldg, Samora Av, T022-2131555. Open Mon-Fri 0900-1700, and Sat 0900-1200. The office has a limited range of glossy leaflets about the national parks and other places of interest, a noticeboard with out-of-date railway and lake ferry timetables and fares, a (not too good) map of the city and, sometimes, a 1:2,000,000 scale map of Tanzania. The staff can also make reservations at any of the larger hotels in Tanzania and national park lodges (payment in foreign currency only) but they can't help you with budget accommodation. However, it's generally better to book the larger resort hotels and national park lodges through a travel agency or tour operator as they may offer special deals. There are two free publications available from some hotels and travel agencies; the bi-monthly *Dar es Salaam Guide*, which has transport timetables and good articles about destinations and sights in the city; and the monthly *What's Happening in Dar es Salaam*. The latter is better for information about upcoming events.

Climate

The hottest months are Dec to the end of Mar, when the Indian Ocean is warm enough to swim in at night. The long rains are from Mar to May and the short rains in Nov and Dec. The best season is Jun-Oct, although there is sun all the year round, even during the rains, which are short and heavy and bring on intense humidity.

Background

Zanzibar period 1862-1886

The name Dar es Salaam means 'Haven of Peace' and was chosen by the founder of the city, Seyyid Majid, Sultan of Zanzibar. The harbour is sheltered, with a narrow inlet channel protecting the water from the Indian Ocean. An early British visitor in 1873, Frederic Elton, remarked that "it's healthy, the air clear – the site a beautiful one and the surrounding country green and well-wooded."

Despite the natural advantages it was not chosen as a harbour earlier, because of the difficulties of approaching through the narrow inlet during the monsoon season and there were other sites, protected by the coral reef, along the Indian Ocean coast that were used instead. However, Majid decided to construct the city in 1862 because he wanted to have a port and settlement on the mainland, which would act as a focus for trade and caravans operating to the south. Bagamoyo (see page 82) was already well established, but local interests there were inclined to oppose direction from Zanzibar, and the new city was a way of ensuring control from the outset.

Construction began in 1865 and the name was chosen in 1866. Streets were laid out, based around what is now Sokoine Drive running along the shoreline to the north of the inner harbour. Water was secured by the sinking of stone wells, and the largest building was the Sultan's palace. An engraving from 1869 shows the palace to have been a substantial two-storey stone building, the upper storey having sloping walls and a crenellated parapet, sited close to the shore on the present-day site of Malindi Wharf. In appearance it was similar in style to the fort that survives in Zanzibar (see page 146). To the southwest, along the shore, was a mosque and to the northwest a group of buildings, most of which were used in conjunction with trading activities. One building that survives is the double-storeyed structure now known as the Old Boma, on the corner of Morogoro Road and Sokoine Drive. The Sultan used it as an official residence for guests, and in 1867 a western-style banquet was given for the British, French, German and American consuls to launch the new city. Craftsmen and slaves were brought from Zanzibar for construction work. Coral for the masonry was cut from the reef and nearby islands. A steam tug was ordered from Germany to assist with the tricky harbour entrance and to speed up movements in the wind-sheltered inner waters. Economic life centred on agricultural cultivation (particularly coconut plantations) and traders who dealt with the local Zaramo people as well as with the long-distance caravan traffic.

Dar es Salaam suffered its first stroke of ill-luck when Majid died suddenly in 1870, after a fall in his new palace, and he was succeeded as Sultan by his half-brother, Seyyid Barghash. Barghash did not share Majid's enthusiasm for the new settlement, and indeed Majid's death was taken to indicate that carrying on with the project would bring ill-fortune. The court remained in Zanzibar. Bagamoyo and Kilwa predominated as mainland trading centres. The palace and other buildings were abandoned, and the fabric rapidly fell into decay. Nevertheless the foundation of a Zaramo settlement and Indian commercial involvement had been established.

Despite the neglect, Barghash maintained control over Dar es Salaam through an agent (*akida*) and later a governor (*wali*) and Arab and Baluchi troops. An Indian customs officer collected duties for use of the harbour and the Sultan's coconut plantations were maintained. Some commercial momentum had been established, and the Zaramo traded gum copal (a residue used in making varnishes), rubber, coconuts, rice and fish for cloth, ironware and beads. The population expanded to around 5,000 by 1887, and comprised a cosmopolitan mixture of the Sultan's officials, soldiers, planters, traders, and shipowners, as well as Arabs, Swahilis and Zaramos, Indian Muslims, Hindus and a handful of Europeans.

German period 1887-1916

In 1887 the German East African Company under Hauptmann Leue took up residence in Dar es Salaam. They occupied the residence of the Sultan's governor whom they succeeded in getting recalled to Zanzibar, took over the collection of customs dues and, in return for a payment to the Zaramo, obtained a concession on the land. The Zaramo, Swahili and Arabs opposed this European takeover, culminating in the Arab revolt of 1888-1889, which involved most of the coastal region as well as Dar es Salaam. The city came under sporadic attack and the buildings of the Berlin Mission, a Lutheran denomination located on a site close to the present Kivokoni ferry, were destroyed. When the revolt was crushed, and the German government took over responsibility from the German East Africa Company in 1891, Dar es Salaam was selected as the main centre for administration and commercial activities.

The Germans laid out a grid street system, built the railway to Morogoro, connected the town to South Africa by overland telegraph, and laid underwater electricity cables to Zanzibar. Development in Dar es Salaam involved the construction of many substantial buildings, and most of these survive today. In the quarter of a century to 1916, several fine buildings were laid out on Wilhelms Ufer (now Kivukoni Front), and these included administrative offices as well as a club and a casino. Landing steps to warehouses, and a hospital, were constructed on the site of the present Malindi Wharf and behind them the railway station. Just to the south of Kurasini Creek was the dockyard where the present deep-water docks are situated. A second hospital was built at the eastern end of Unter den Akazien and Becker Strasse, now Samora Avenue. The Post Office is on what is now Sokoine Drive at the junction with Mkwepu Street. A governor's residence provided the basis for the current State House. The principal hotels were the *Kaiserhof*, which was demolished to build the *New Africa Hotel*, and the *Burger Hotel*, razed to make way for the present Telecoms building. The area behind the north harbour shore was laid out with fine acacia-lined streets and residential two-storey buildings with pitched corrugated-iron roofs and first-floor verandas, and most of these survive. Behind the east waterfront were shops and office buildings, many of which are still standing.

British period 1916-1961

In the 45 years that the British administered Tanganyika, public construction was kept to a minimum on economy grounds, and business was carried on in the old German buildings. The governor's residence was damaged by naval gunfire in 1915, and was remodelled to form the present State House. In the 1920s, the Gymkhana Club was laid out on its present site behind Ocean Road, and Mnazi Moja ('Coconut Grove') established as a park. The Selander Bridge causeway was constructed, and this opened up the Oyster Bay area to residential construction for the European community. The Yacht Club was built on the harbour shore (it is now the customs post) and behind it the Dar es Salaam Club (now the Hotel and Tourism Training Centre), both close to the present *Kilimanjaro Hotel*.

As was to be expected, road names were changed, as well as those of the most prominent buildings. Thus Wilhelms Ufer became Azania Front, Unter den Akazien became Acacia Avenue, Kaiser Strasse became City Drive. Other streets were named after explorers Speke and Burton, and there was a Windsor Street. One departure from the relentless Anglicization of the city was the change of Bismarck Strasse to Versailles Street – it was the Treaty of Versailles in 1918 that allocated the former German East Africa to the British.

The settling by the various groups living in the city into distinctive areas was consolidated during the British period. Europeans lived in Oyster Bay to the north of the city centre, in large Mediterranean-style houses with arches, verandas and gardens surrounded by solid security walls and fences. The Asians lived either in tenement-style blocks in the city centre or in the Upanga area in between the city and Oyster Bay, where they built houses and bungalows with small gardens. African families built Swahili-style houses, initially in the Kariakoo area to the west of the city. Others were accommodated in government bachelor quarters provided for railway, post office and other government employees. As population increased, settlement spread out to Mikocheni and along Morogoro Road and to Mteni to the south.

Independence 1961-present

For the early years of independence Dar es Salaam managed to sustain its enviable reputation of being a gloriously located city with a fine harbour, generous parklands with tree-lined avenues (particularly in the Botanical Gardens and Gymkhana area), and a tidy central area of shops and services. New developments saw the construction of high-rise government buildings, most notably the Telecoms building on the present Samora Avenue, the *New Africa Hotel*, the massive cream and brown Standard Bank Building (now National Bank of Commerce) on the corner of Sokoine Drive and Maktaba Street, and the *Kilimanjaro Hotel* on a site next to the Dar es Salaam Club on Kivukoni Front.

But with the Arusha Declaration of 1967 (see page 359), many buildings were nationalized and somewhat haphazardly occupied. The new tenants of the houses, shops and commercial buildings were thus inclined to undertake minimal repairs and maintenance. In many cases it was unclear who actually owned the buildings. The city went into steady decline, and it is a testament to the sturdy construction of the buildings from the German period that so many of them survive. Roads fell into disrepair and the harbour became littered with rusting hulks.

The new government changed the names of streets and buildings, to reflect a change away from the colonial period. Thus Acacia became Independence Avenue, the *Prince of Wales Hotel* became the *Splendid*. Later names were chosen to pay tribute to African leaders – Independence Avenue changed to Samora, and Pugu Road became Nkrumah Street. President Nyerere decided that no streets or public buildings could be named after living Tanzanians, and so it was only after his death that City Drive was named after Prime Minister Edward Sokoine.

Old Dar es Salaam was saved by two factors. First, the economic decline that began in the 1970s (see page 363) meant that there were limited resources for building new modern blocks for which some of old colonial buildings would have had to make way. Second, the government decided in 1973 to move the capital to Dodoma. This didn't stop new government construction entirely, but it undoubtedly saved many historic buildings.

In the early 1980s, Dar es Salaam reached a low point, not dissimilar from the one reached almost exactly a century earlier with the death of Sultan Majid. In 1992 things began to improve. Colonial buildings have now been classified as of historical interest and are to be preserved. Japanese aid has allowed a comprehensive restoration of the road system. Several historic buildings, most notably the Old Boma on Sokoine Drive, the Ministry of Health building on Luthuli Road and the British Council headquarters on Samora Avenue, have been restored or are undergoing restoration. Civic pride is returning. The Askari Monument has been cleaned up and the flower beds replanted, the Cenotaph Plaza relaid, pavements and walkways repaired and the Botanical Gardens restored. Very usefully, new signposts are a feature throughout the city, which not only clearly show the street names but places of interest, hotels, and major institutions such as banks or embassies. The main road into Dar es Salaam – the 109 km branch road off the Arusha-Mbeya road that neatly dissects the middle of the country – was for years a ribbon of potholed and broken tar. But this too has been upgraded into super-smooth highway thanks to foreign aid.

Sights

The best way to discover the heart of Dar es Salaam is on foot and we have suggested two half-day walks that take in most of the historic buildings. An alternative is to join a guided walking tour. ⓘ *Morning walks through the old town of 2½ hours cost US$30 adult, US$10 child, discounts for groups, and include tastings of Swahili, Arab and Indian foods. Enquire at the tourist office for a recommendation of a tour operator.*

Walking tour of the old town

A walking tour (about half a day) of the historic parts of old Dar es Salaam might start at the **Askari Monument** at the junction of Samora Avenue and Azikwe Street. Originally on this site was a statue to Major Hermann von Wissmann, the German explorer and soldier, who suppressed the coastal Arab Revolt of 1888-1889 (see page 83) and went on to become governor of German East Africa in 1895-1896. This first statue erected in 1911 depicted a pith-helmeted Wissmann, one hand on hip, the other on his sword, gazing out over the harbour with an African soldier at the base of the plinth draping a German flag over a reclining lion. It was demolished in 1916 when the British occupied Dar es Salaam, as were statues to Bismarck and Carl Peters. The present bronze statue, in memory of all those who died in the First World War, but principally dedicated to the African troops and porters, was unveiled in 1927. The statue was cast by Morris Bronze Founders of Westminster, London, and the sculptor was James Alexander Stevenson (1881-1937), who signed himself 'Myrander'. There are two bronze bas-reliefs on the sides of the plinth by the same sculptor, and the inscription, in English and Swahili, is from Rudyard Kipling.

Proceeding towards the harbour, on the left is the *New Africa Hotel* on the site where the old *Kaiserhof Hotel* stood. The *New Africa* was once the finest building in Dar es Salaam, the venue for the expat community to meet for sundowners. The terrace outside overlooked the Lutheran church and the harbour, while a band played in the inner courtyard. Across Sokoine Drive, on the left is the **Lutheran cathedral** with its distinctive red-tiled spire and tiled canopies over the windows to provide shade. Construction began in 1898. Opposite is the **Cenotaph**, again commemorating the 1914-1918 war, which was unveiled in 1927 and restored in 1992.

Turning left along Kivukoni Front, there is a fine view through the palm trees across the harbour. Just past Ohio Street, on the shore side, is the **Old Yacht Club**. Prior to the removal of the club to its present site on the west side of Msasani Peninsula in 1967, small boats bobbing at anchor in the bay were a feature of the harbour. The Old Yacht Club buildings now house the harbour police headquarters.

Opposite the Old Yacht Club is the site of the German Club for civilians, which was expanded to form the **Dar es Salaam (DSM) Club** in the British period. It used to have a spacious terrace and a handsome bar. On the first floor are rooms that were used for accommodation, with verandas facing inward and outside stone staircases. Evelyn Waugh once stayed here. At the time of writing the building was being refurbished as part of the new *Kimpinski Kilimanjaro Hotel*.

Further along Kivukoni Front is the first of an impressive series of German government buildings. The first two, one now the High Court, and the other the present Magistrates' Court on the corner of Luthuli Road, were for senior officials. In between is the old **Secretariat**, which housed the governor's offices. On the other corner of Luthuli Road is the German Officers' Mess, where some gambling evidently took place as it became known as the **Casino**. These buildings are exceptional, and it is a tribute to the high quality construction of the German period that they have survived, with virtually no maintenance for the past 30 years. Construction was completed in 1893. On the high ground further along Kivukoni Front is the site of the first European building in Dar es Salaam, the **Berlin Mission**. It was constructed in 1887, extensively damaged in the 1888-1889 uprising and demolished in 1959 to make way for a hotel, which, in the event, was not constructed.

The eastern part of the city resembles an eagle's head (it is said the Msasani Peninsula is one of the eagle's wings). At the tip of the eagle's beak was a pier, just where the fish market (see page 59) stands today, constructed in the British period for the use of the governor. This was just a little further round the promontory from the present ramp for the ferry that goes over to Kigamboni. Past Magogoni Street is the **Swimming Club** (see page 73), constructed in the British period and now mostly used by the Asian community.

Following Ocean Road, on the left is the present **State House**, with a drive coming down to gates. This was the original German governor's residence. It had tall, Islamic-style arches on the ground floor rather similar to those in the building today, but the upper storey was a veranda with a parapet and the roof was supported on cast-iron columns. The building was bombarded by British warships in 1914 and extensively damaged. In 1922 it was rebuilt and the present scalloped upper-storey arches added, as well as the tower with the crenellated parapet.

The **German Hospital** is further along Ocean Road with its distinctive domed towers topped by a clusters of iron spikes. It is an uneasy mixture of the grand (the towers) and the utilitarian (the corrugated-iron roofing). It was completed in 1897 and was added to during the British period with single-storey, bungalow-style wards to the rear.

Turning left past the baobab tree down Chimera Road and taking the left fork, Luthuli Road leads to the junction with Samora Avenue. Here stood the statue of Bismarck, a replica of the celebrated Regas bust. The area either side of this boulevard, one of the glories of Dar es Salaam in the German era, was laid out as an extensive park. The flamboyant trees and *oreodoxa* (Royal Palms) still border it.

The first Director of Agriculture, Professor Stuhlmann, began laying out the **Botanical Gardens** in 1893. The building to house the Agriculture Department as well as the Meteorological Station and the Government Geographer lies just to the southwest and was completed in 1903. It has recently been restored. By that time the gardens were well established, Stuhlmann using his position as Chief Secretary from 1900-1903 to channel resources to their development. The gardens became the home of the Dar es Salaam Horticultural Society, which still has a building on the site, and have recently undergone some rehabilitation with most of the exhibits now labelled. It is one of the few places in the world to see the coco-de-mer palm tree apart from the Seychelles.

To the left of the gardens is **Karimjee Hall**, built by the British and which served as the home of the Legislative Council prior to independence. It then became the home of the National Assembly, the Bunge. In the same area is the original **National Museum** (see page 58), a single-storey stone building with a red-tiled roof and arched windows constructed as the King George V Memorial Museum in 1940, changing its name in 1963. A larger, modern building was constructed later to house exhibits, and the old building was used as offices.

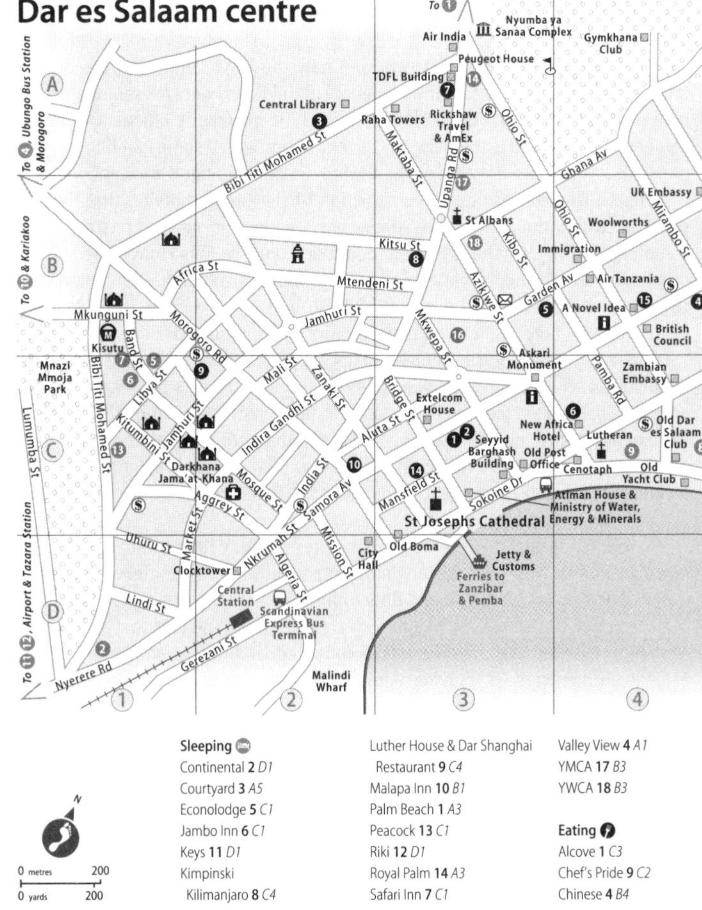

Turning left down Shaaban Robert Street, on the other side of Sokoine Drive, in a crescent behind the Speaker's Office is the first school built in Dar es Salaam (1899) by the German government. It was predominantly for Africans, but also had a few Indian pupils, all children of state-employed officials (*akidas*). Walking west down Sokoine Drive you return to the *New Africa Hotel*.

Walking tour of the City

A second half-day walking tour might begin at the *New Africa Hotel* and proceed west along Sokoine Street past the National Bank of Commerce building on the right. On the corner with Mkwepa Street is the German **Post Office** completed in 1893. Although the façade has been remodelled to give it a more modern appearance, the structure is basically unchanged. Just inside the entrance is a plaque to the memory of members of the Signals Corps who lost their lives in the First World War in East Africa. There are some 200 names listed with particularly heavy representation from South Africa and India whose loyalty to the British Empire drew them into the conflict.

On the opposite corner to the Post Office is the site of the old customs headquarters, the **Seyyid Barghash Building**, constructed around 1869. The building on the corner with Bridge Street is the modern multi-storey Wizaraya Maji, Nishati na Madim (Ministry of Water, Energy and Minerals), which is on the site of the old Customs House. Next door, sandwiched between the ministry building and Forodhani Secondary School, is the **White Fathers' House** – called **Atiman House**. It is named after a heroic and dedicated doctor Adrian Atiman, who was redeemed from slavery in Niger by White Father missionaries, educated in North Africa and Europe, and who worked for decades as a doctor in Tanzania until his death, circa 1924. Atiman House was constructed in the 1860s in the Zanzibar period and is the oldest surviving house in the city, excluding administrative buildings. It was built as a residence for the Sultan of Zanzibar's Dar es Salaam wives, and sold by the Sultan to the White Fathers in 1922. In the visitors' parlour are two extremely interesting old photographs of the waterfront at Dar es Salaam as it was in German colonial times.

City Garden **5** *B4*
Cynics Café & Wine Bar **7** *A3*
Debonairs & Steers **15** *B4*
Garden Food Court at Haidery Plaza **8** *B3*
L'Epidor **2** *C3*
Planet Bollywood **10** *C2*
Sawasdee **6** *C4*
Sichaun **3** *A2*
Sno-cream **14** *C3*

Bars & clubs
Club Billicanos **16** *B3*

Continuing along Sokoine Drive to the west, the next building is **St Joseph's Roman Catholic Cathedral**. Construction began in 1897 and took five years to complete. St Joseph's remains one of the most striking buildings in Dar es Salaam, dominating the harbour front. It has an impressive vaulted interior, shingle spire and a fine arrangement of arches and gables. Next to the cathedral was Akida's Court.

On the corner of Morogoro Road is Dar's oldest surviving building, the **Old**

 Boma dating from 1867. It was built to accommodate the visitors of Sultan Majid and features a fine Zanzibar door and coral-rag walls. On the opposite corner is the **City Hall**, a very handsome building with an impressive façade and elaborate decoration.

On the corner of Uhuru Street is the **Railway Station**, a double-storey building with arches and a pitched-tile roof, the construction of which began in 1897. Between the station and the shore was the site of the palace of Sultan Majid and of the hospital for Africans constructed in 1895 by Sewa Haji, but which was demolished in 1959.

Turning right in front of the railway station leads to the **Clocktower**, a post-war concrete construction erected to celebrate the elevation of Dar es Salaam to city status in 1961. A right turn at the Clocktower leads along Samora Avenue and back to the Askari Monument.

There are other notable buildings in the City. On Mosque Street is the ornate **Darkhana Jama'at-Khana** of the Ismaili community, three storeys high with a six-storey tower on the corner topped by a clock, a pitched roof and a weathervane.

There are several other mosques, two (**Ibaddhi Mosque** and **Memon Mosque**) on Mosque Street itself (clearly signposted and stringed with coloured lights used for religious occasions), one on Kitumbini Street, one block to the southwest of Mosque St, (a **Sunni mosque** with an impressive dome), and there are two mosques on Bibi Titi Mohamed Street, the **Ahmadiyya mosque** near the junction with Pugu Road and the other close by. On Kitsu Street, there are two Hindu temples, and on Upanga Road is a grand Ismaili building decorated with coloured lights during festivals.

St Alban's Church on the corner of Upanga Road and Maktaba Street was constructed in the interwar period. St Alban's is a grand building modelled on the Anglican church in Zanzibar. This is the Anglican Church of the Province of Tanzania, and was the Governor's church in colonial times. The **Greek Orthodox church**, further along Upanga Street, was constructed in the 1940s. **St Peter's Catholic Church**, off the Bagamoyo Road, was constructed in 1962, and is in modern style with delicate concrete columns and arches.

★ National Museum

ⓘ *0930-1800. Shabaan Robert St next to the Botanical Gardens, between Sokoine Dr and Samora Av. Entry US$3. Student US$2.*

The National Museum opened in 1940 in the former King George V Memorial Museum building next to the Botanical Gardens. King George V's car can still be seen in the newer wing, which was built in front of the old museum in 1963. The museum is in a garden where a few peacocks stroll and where there is a sculpture in memory of victims of the American Embassy bombing. Created in 2004 by US artist Elyn Zimmerman, it comprises a group of six related geometric forms that surround a granite-rimmed pool. Their flatness and thinness, as well as their striking silhouettes and outlines, were inspired by shapes used in traditional African art, shields and other objects including Tanzanian stools, which Zimmerman said greatly influenced her work. Very interestingly, the very same artist designed the World Trade Centre Memorial in 1993, after a bomb set by terrorists exploded on the site of the World Trade Centre in New York. That sculpture was a cenotaph to an attack that predated both the August 7, 1998 bombings in Dar es Salaam and Nairobi, and the September 11, 2001 attacks in New York. Zimmerman's 1993 sculpture was destroyed in the 2001 attack at the World Trade centre.

The museum has excellent ethnographic, historical and archaeological collections. The old photographs are particularly interesting. Traditional craft items, head-dresses, ornaments, musical instruments and witchcraft accoutrements are on display. Artefacts representing Tanzanian history date from the slave trade to the post-colonial period. Fossils from Olduvai Gorge kept there include those of Zinjanthropus – sometimes referred to as Zinj or 'nutcracker man' – the first of a new

Casuarina cones

A particularly fine set of casuarina trees can be found along Ocean Road in Dar es Salaam. Strangely, they are also found in Australia. Quite unlike most other trees in East Africa, the theory is that the seed-bearing cones were carried by the cold tidal currents from the west coast of Australia into the equatorial waters flowing west across the Indian Ocean to the shore of Tanzania and then north along the East African coast in the Somalia current, eventually germinating after a journey of about 10,000 km.

group of hominid remains collectively known as *Australopithecus boisei*, discovered by Mary Leakey. The coastal history is represented by glazed Chinese porcelain pottery and a range of copper coins from Kilwa. One of the more unusual exhibits is a bicycle in working order made entirely of wood. The museum also regularly stages exhibitions – see press for details.

West towards Kariakoo

The area to the northwest of India Street, on either side of Morogoro Road, was an Asian section of the city in the colonial period, and to a large extent still is. Buildings are typically several storeys high, the ground floor being given over to business with the upper storeys being used for residential accommodation. The façades are often ornate, with the name of the proprietor and the date of construction prominently displayed. Two superb examples on Morogoro Road, near Africa Street, are the premises of **M Jessa**. One was a cigarette and tobacco factory and the other a rice mill.

Further to the west is the open Mnazi Mmoja (coconut grove) with the **Uhuru Monument** (dedicated to the freedom that came with independence). The original Uhuru monument is a white obelisk with a flame – the Freedom Torch. A second concrete monument, designed by R Ashdown, was erected to commemorate 10 years of independence. This was enlivened with panels by a local artist. On the far side of the space is **Kariakoo**, laid out in a grid pattern and predominantly an African area. It become known as Kariakoo during the latter part of the First World War when African porters (the carrier corps, from which the current name is derived) were billeted there after the British took over the city in 1916. The houses are in Swahili style. The colourful **market** in the centre and the shark market on the junction of Msimbazi and Tandamuti Streets are well worth a visit but watch out for pickpockets.

Fish market and Banda Beach

At the point of the eagle's beak, where the ferry leaves for Kivukoni, is the **Integrated Fish Market Complex**. A fish market has been on this site since time immemorial, but it was extensively expanded when a new fish market was built in 2002 with funding from the Japanese government. There are zones for fish cleaning, fish frying, one for shellfish and vegetables, another for firewood and charcoal, an auction hall for wholesale vendors and buyers, and a maintenance area for the repair of boats, fishing nets and other tools of the trade. The complex is one of a kind and provides employment for 100 fishermen catering to thousands of daily shoppers. As you can imagine, this is an extremely smelly place. Fresh fish can be bought here and there is an astonishingly wide variety of seafood from blue fish, lobster, red snapper, to calamari and prawns. Be warned though, the vendors are quite aggressive and you'll need to haggle hard. You can also buy ice here to pack the fish. *Mzizima* is the name of the old fishing village that existed somewhere between State House and Ocean Road Hospital before Seyyid Majid founded Dar es Salaam in 1862. This stretch of

Tingatinga Art

It is easy enough to recognize Tingatinga paintings for their powerful images and vivid colours. Canvasses are crowded with exaggerated figures of birds, fish and all manner of African creatures, with giant heads and eyes, that roam rainbow landscapes and brilliant seas. Detailed traditional village life or hospital and markets scenes take on an almost cartoon appearance. It's a style of pop art and is considered to be the only indigenous painted art of East Africa. The custom of painting on walls using natural pigments had been in existence in Africa for centuries, but it wasn't until the arrival of the Europeans that African painters were encouraged to produce canvasses.

Tingatinga art was created in the dusty back streets of Dar es Salaam by Edward Tingatinga in the late 1960s. Born in 1937 in the Tanga region of southern Tanzania, he went to Dar in 1959 in search of work. After attempting several jobs, he worked on building sites and began painting murals on the walls. He then progressed to boards and canvasses and used an enamel bicycle paint that is especially glossy. He sold his paintings underneath a baobab tree at the Morogoro Stores in Oyster Bay which attracted the rich Europeans. He took on several young apprentices and taught them his unique style. Tragically, in 1972, only four years into his discovery of art, he was shot dead by police who accidentally mistook his car for the getaway car in a local robbery. But his students continued to use the Tingatinga style and took on more apprentices. The Tingatinga Art Cooperative Society was established six years after his death, and is still going strong today in Oyster Bay. There are presently around 60-70 artists working here; most are illiterate and come from poor backgrounds, but have been accepted by the cooperative for their artistic skills. One of them is Daudi Tingatinga, Edward's son, who was only two when his father died. He continues to paint in memory of his father. In 1997, a Swedish customer introduced the art to a gallery in Stockholm and exhibitions appeared in other European cities. This instigated a TSh60 million donation to build the gallery and workshop at Oyster Bay. After 25 years underneath a baobab tree, Tingatinga got its own home and Edward Tingatinga would no doubt have been impressed by the success of his legacy. Since then the art has also been exhibited in Japan where it has been reproduced on traditional Japanese kimonos.

ⓘ *The Tingatinga Arts Cooperative is at the Morogoro Stores in Oyster Bay, off Haile Selassie Rd, near the Hotel Karibu. There is a gallery of paintings for sale and more stalls outside on the street. Open daily 0900-1800.*

sand was always known as **Banda Beach**, a well-known place for sittin' on the dock of the bay. Fishing boats, mostly lateen-sailed *ngalawas*, are beached on the shore.

Gymkhana Club

Further along Ocean Road, past State House and the hospital, are the grounds of the **Gymkhana Club**, which extend down to the shore. Amongst other sports practised here (see page 73) is golf, and there is an 18-hole course featuring what are called 'browns' as opposed to 'greens'. There were various cemeteries on the shore side of the golf course, a European cemetery between the hospital and Ghana Avenue, and a Hindu crematorium beyond.

Nyumba ya Sanaa Complex

ⓘ *Junction of Ohio St, Ali Mwinyi Rd and Bibi Titi Mohammed St, northwest of the Royal Palm Hotel, T022-2131727, www.catgen.com/sanaa. Open daily 0830-1730.*

This art gallery has displays of paintings in various styles including oil, watercolour and chalk, as well as carvings and batiks. You can see the artists at work, and there is also a café on site. The centre was started by a nun and the present building was constructed with help from a Norwegian donation in the early 1980s.

Oyster Bay

At the intersection of Ocean Road and Ufukoni Road on the shore side is a rocky promontory which was the site of European residential dwellings constructed in the interwar period by the British. These are either side of Labon Drive (previously Seaview Road). Continuing along Ocean Road is Selander Bridge, a causeway over the Msimbazi Creek, a small river edged by marsh that circles back to the south behind the main part of the city. Beyond Selander Bridge, on the ocean side, is **Oyster Bay**, which became the main European residential area in the colonial era (Rita Hayworth had a house here), and today is the location of many diplomatic missions. There are many spacious dwellings, particularly along Kenyatta Drive, which looks across the bay. The area in front of the (now closed) *Oysterbay Hotel* is a favourite place for parking and socializing in the evenings and at weekends, particularly by the Asian community. Ice cream sellers and barbecue kiosks have sprung up on the shore in the last few years.

! In spite of, or perhaps because of, the grand houses and embassies, Oyster Bay has acquired a reputation for armed robberies and car jacking, even in daylight hours.

Excursions from Dar

★ Makumbusho Village Museum

ⓘ *Bagamoyo Rd, about 9 km from the city centre, on the right-hand side of the road just before the African Sky Hotel, T022-2700437, www.homestead.com/villagemuseum. Open daily 0930-1900, US$1, Tanzanians and all children free, still photos US$2.50, video or cine US$10. Taxis cost about US$4.50 from the city centre, or dala-dala from the New Post Office (Posta) heading towards Mwenge, which pass the entrance. Ask for Makumbusho bus stop or get off when you see the tall African Sky Hotel and walk back a few metres.*

The museum gives a compact view of the main traditional dwelling styles of Tanzania, with examples of artists and craftsmen at work. There are constructions of tribal homesteads from 18 ethnic groups with examples of furnished dwelling huts, cattle pens, meeting huts and, in one case, an iron-smelting kiln. On Saturday and Sunday, from 1600 to 1800, and occasionally during the week, there are performances from a dance troupe with performers recruited from all over Tanzania. It's worthwhile having a guide to explain on the origin of the dances, which end with a display of tumbling and acrobatics. There is a café, and an unusual compound, the Makumbusho Social Club, to which the public is welcome, with its small, corrugated-iron, partly open-sided huts, each named after one of Tanzania's game parks.

★ Kigamboni

The beaches on Kigamboni are the best close to the city and, like on the beaches to the north, the resorts here (see Sleeping page 67) are popular with day visitors especially at the weekends. The Kigamboni ferry (which takes cars) leaves from the harbour mouth, close to the fish market, just before Kivukoni Front becomes Ocean Road, at regular intervals during the day, crossing the mouth of the harbour to Kigamboni. The ferry runs from 0600-midnight and costs US$0.90 per vehicle and US$0.25 per person. Foot

Msasani Peninsula

Msasani Bay
Oyster Bay
Msimbazi Bay
MSASANI PENINSULA
REGENT ESTATE
KINONDONI
HANNA NASIF
Masaki St
Toure Drive
Haile Selassie Rd
Mahando St
Mwaya
Chole Rd
Chake Chake Rd
Msasani Rd
Yacht Club
Msasani Slipway
Arcade Shopping Complex
Old Bagamoyo Rd
Shopper's Plaza
Kimweri Av
Tinga Tinga Arts Co-op & Morogoro Stores
Oyster Bay Hotel (Closed) & Shopping Centre
Ghuba Rd
Guinea Rd
Uganda Av
Drive-Inn-Cinema
Ursino St
Rashidi Trawawa Rd (Formerly Morocco Rd)
Bagamoyo Rd
Pol
Alibin Said Rd
Karume Rd
Catholic
Little Theatre
Bongoyo Rd
Mkwawa Rd
Kaunda Rd
Ali Hasan Mwinyi Blvd
Kenyatta Drive
Tunisia Rd
Kinondoni Rd
Baptist
Lutheran
US Embassy & Mayfair Plaza
To Makumbusho Village Museum, Bagamoyo, Mwenge & North Coast Beaches
To Town Centre
A B C D E
1 2 3

Sleeping
Karibu **2** *C2*
Q Bar & Guest House **1** *C2*
Sea Cliff **4** *A3*

Eating
Addis in Dar **1** *D1*
Azuma **2** *B2*
Coral Ridge Spur **7** *A3*
Fishmonger **7** *A3*
Hot (In Africa) **10** *C2*
Java Lounge **7** *A3*
La Dolce Vita **13** *D3*
L'Arca Di Noe' **12** *D2*
La Trattoria Jan **14** *C2*
Lilylike House **6** *D2*
Manchu Wok **7** *A3*
Mashua Bar & Grill **2** *B2*
Oyster Bay Grill **8** *C2*
Seacliff Village **7** *A3*
Shooter's Grill **3** *D2*
Simona **18** *C1*
Sweet Eazy **8** *C2*
The Pub **2** *B2*
The Terrace **2** *B2*
Turquoise **7** *A3*

passengers can walk directly on to the ferry from the city side and at Kigamboni taxis and *dala-dala* can be picked up that follow the beach road for several km to where most of the more accessible resorts are. The hotels such as *Ras Kutani* and the *Protea Amani Beach Hotel* are further along this road, around 30 km from the ferry and you will need to organize transport with these lodges to reach them if not driving yourself.

The small town of Kigamboni itself spreads up from where the ferry docks and is the site of Kivukoni College, which provided training for CCM (see page 360) party members, but has now been turned into a school and a social science academy. Just before the college, which faces across the harbour to Kivukoni Front, is the Anglican church and a free-standing bell. The Anglican church was formerly a Lutheran church. The Lutheran church, a fine modern building, lies 500 m into Kigamboni. On the Indian Ocean shore side there are several small enterprises making lime by burning cairns of coral.

The two Kigamboni ferries each carry 15 vehicles and 400 people on a crossing that takes 10 min and costs US$0.25. In total some 30,000 people use the ferries each day.

Gezaulole

ⓘ *Part of the Cultural Tourism Programme operated from Arusha. Further details can be obtained from the Tanzanian tourist information centre in Arusha, T027-2503840-3, www.infojep.com/culturaltours. Brochures for each project can be downloaded from the website.*

The coastal village of Gezaulole lies 13 km or half an hour's drive southeast of the ferry at Kigamboni, reachable by *dala-dala*. This was chosen as one of the first Ujamaa villages, part of an ultimately unsuccessful settlement policy of the early 1970s, in which people from many areas of the country were relocated to form agricultural communes (see page 360). In earlier days it was a Zaramo settlement, who gave the village the name Gezaulole, which means 'Try and See' in the Kizaramo language. Today the community has an active role in a cultural tourism programme that offers walks through the village and on the beach, short trips on a local dhow, and visits to an old slave depot and a 400-year-old mosque. It is possible to stay with a local family, though it is easy enough to reach on a day trip. Inexpensive and tasty local meals are available and can be taken with one of the families even if you are not staying for the night. Locally-made handicrafts are also for sale. Profits from the programme go towards buying equipment for the local school.

★ Northern beaches

ⓘ *To get to either beach a taxi from the city will cost in the region of US$12. To get to Kuncuchi by public transport take a dala-dala from the New Post Office (Posta) in the city to Mwenge about 10 km along the Bagomoyo Rd, then swap to one heading to Kunduchi (clearly signposted on the bonnet of the vehicle). Both rides will cost US$0.20. To get to Mbezi, take the same Kunduchi dala-dala from Mwenge, and at the sign for the White Sands Hotel on the Bagamoyo Road a couple of km before the Kunduchi turn off, ask to get off (look out for the Kobil service station). At this junction you can catch a bicycle taxi for US$0.50 or a tuk-tuk, US$1, the couple of km to the hotels. Do not walk along this road, there have been mugging incidents.*

The shore close to Dar es Salaam is not particularly good for swimming. The best beaches are at **Kunduchi**, some 25 km north of the city, and **Mbezi Beach,** 20 km north of the city. These beaches are separated by a lagoon but both are accessed along side roads off the Bagamoyo Rd and are easily reached by good tarmac roads. Most of the hotels and resorts along the coast here (see page 67) permit day visits to enjoy the facilities and beaches though some charge a fee of US$1-5 for the day. It is worth paying the fee to use the hotels' private (and guarded) beaches – the stretches of beach between the hotels should not be visited unaccompanied, people have been mugged here. Some also charge an extra fee if you bring your own food and drink. This is because many Indian families bring full-on picnics for a day on the beach and the hotel benefits little from selling food and drink. Most have restaurants and bars with bands playing at weekends and public holidays and some offer a variety of excursions to nearby islands and windsurfing. Snorkelling is a bit hit and miss because sometimes the water is not very clear, especially during the rainy seasons. The hotels that offer day visits include: *Silver Sands Hotel*, *Kunduchi Beach Hotel*, *Bahari Beach Hotel*, *Jangwani Sea Breeze Lodge* and *White Sands Hotel*.

There is a good beach on the uninhabited **Bongoyo Island**, 2 km north of Msasani Peninsula. The island is a marine reserve popular for diving and snorkelling and on the island are a few short walking trails, good beaches, and simple seafood meals are available. A popular destination for a day trip from Dar es Salaam, boats take 30 minutes, cost US$7 and leave from *The Slipway* on Msasani Peninsula at 0930,1130, 1330 and 1530, each time returning approximately one hour later. A similarly good beach, but no facilities, are to be found on **Mbudya Island**, 4 km north of Bongoyo Island. Boat rides are available from *White Sands Hotel*, *Jangwani Sea Breeze Lodge*, and *Bahari Beach Hotel*.

★ Kisarawe and Pugu Hills Forest Reserve

ⓘ *Follow the airport road to the south of the city. Buses to Kisarawe leave from Narungumbe St (next to the Tanzania Postal Bank on Msimbazi St in Kariakoo) about once an hour and cost US$1. To get to Pugu, turn left at the Agip petrol station in Kisarawe and the track into the reserve is a little further along on the right. It's 3 km from Kisarawe and if you're driving you'll need a 4x4 vehicle.*

In the peaceful rural hill town of Kisarawe it is hard to believe that you are just 32 km southwest from the hustle and bustle of Dar es Salaam. During the colonial period Kisarawe was used by European residents of the capital as a kind of hill station to escape from the coastal heat. It receives a higher rainfall than Dar because of a slightly increased elevation. There is little to see in the town itself but the surrounding countryside is very attractive, in particular the nearby rainforest at Pugu Hills Forest Reserve about 3-4 km from the centre of Kisarawe town. It constitutes one of the few remaining parts of a coastal forest, which 10 million years ago extended from Mozambique to northern Kenya. It was gazetted as a reserve in 1954, at which time it stretched all the way to Dar's international airport and was home to many big game animals, including lions, hippos and elephants. Since then the natural growth of the metropolis, as well as the urban demand for charcoal (coupled with the lack of alternative sources of income), has seen a large reduction in the forested area. In the past few years a concerted effort has been made to counter this process and a nature trail has been established in order to encourage people to visit the area. Although Pugu contains flora and fauna which are unique to the forests of this district, you are unlikely to come across many animals in the forest; but it is a very beautiful spot and the perfect tonic for those in need of a break from Dar es Salaam. Most visitors spend the night in the new lodge here (*Pugu Hills*), though you can visit just for the day but still need to make a reservation for this with the lodge (see page 68).

Pugu Kaolin Mine and the Bat Caves

A further 3-4 km on from the Pugu Hills Reserve is Pugu Kaolin mine, which was established by the Germans in the early 1900s. Kaolin is a type of fine white clay that is used in the manufacture of porcelain, paper and textiles. The deposits here at Pugu are reputed to be the second largest in the world and should the market for it pick up, the mining of kaolin will clearly constitute a further threat to the survival of the remaining rainforest. If you continue through the mine compound you come to a disused railway tunnel, 100 m long and German built (the railway was re-routed after the discovery of kaolin). On the other side of this are a series of man-made caves housing a huge colony of bats. In the early evening at around 1800 or 1900 (depending on the time of year) the bats begin to fly out of the caves for feeding. It is a remarkable experience to stand in the mouth of the caves surrounded by the patter of wings as vast numbers of bats come streaming past you.

Sleeping

As far as top-grade accommodation is concerned, hotels in Dar es Salaam have improved in recent years and there is excellent international standard accommodation in the city centre, Msasani Peninsula and on the beaches to the north and south of the city. The lower end of the market is reasonable value, although it is always sensible to check the room and the bathroom facilities and enquire what is provided for breakfast. Also check on the security of any parked vehicle. Bear in mind that it is possible to negotiate lower rates, especially if you plan to stay a few days. Most upmarket hotels will ask visitors to pay in foreign exchange – this really makes no difference but just check the rates in TShs and US$S against the current exchange rate, and make a fuss if you are charged more than the US$ equivalent of the TSh rate. Increasingly more and more establishments are accepting credit cards, but this often incurs a commission of around 8-15%. In the middle and lower range it is usually possible to pay in TSh, and this is an advantage if money is changed at the favourable bureau rate. VAT at 20% was officially introduced in 1998 and is added to all service charges, though this is usually included in the bill.

City centre and Msasani Peninsula

maps p56 and p62

L Royal Palm, Ohio St, T022-2112416, www.moevenpick-hotels.com. Part of the Moevenpick chain (but used to be a Sheraton) this hotel has conference and banqueting facilities, a shopping arcade and recreation centre, an outdoor swimming pool and lovely gardens. The 251 rather gloomy rooms are all a/c and have mod cons except tea/coffee-making facilities; the best are at the rear. There's a British Airways office and several restaurants, see Eating, coffee shop and bakery, and wireless internet access. They will also store luggage for you.

L-A Kimpinski Kilimanjaro, Kivukoni Front. Occupying a commanding position in the centre of the city overlooking the harbour. At the time of writing this was being completely rebuilt (but should be open August 2005) and promises 5-star standards on completion. A large 5-storey building enclosed with blue glass which will feature a number of bars and restaurants and top class facilities. Reports are welcome.

A The Courtyard, Ocean Rd, T022-2130130, www.contitrades.com/courtyard.html. A quality small hotel with good facilities, a bit more character than some of the larger hotels and with excellent food and service. Standard, superior and deluxe rooms, with a/c, TV and minibar, business centre, wireless internet, bar, restaurant, and swimming pool.

A Hotel Sea Cliff, northern end of Msasani Peninsula on Toure Dr, T022-2600380-7, www.hotelSeaCliff.com. Stylish hotel with whitewashed walls and thatched *makuti* roofing set in manicured grounds. 107 spacious and modern a/c rooms, most with ocean view, and 20 more units in garden cottages, all with satellite TV. Coral Cliff and Ngalawa bars, Little Indian restaurant, coffee shop, health club, gift shop, casino, bowling alley, shopping centre. One of the most luxurious hotels in Dar with all the trimmings and reasonably priced.

A-B Palm Beach, 305 Ali Hassan Mwinyi Rd, opposite the junction with Ocean Rd, T022-2130985, www.pbhtz.com. Stylish art deco hotel, completely refurbished, a little away from the centre of town. Cool and modern decor, 32 rooms, wireless internet access, airy bar and restaurant, and a popular beer garden with barbecue.

For an explanation of the sleeping and eating price codes used in this guide, see inside the front cover. Other relevant information is found in Essentials pages 31-34.

B Hotel Karibu, Haile Selassie Rd, T022-2602946, www.hotelkaribu.com. Oyster Bay area. Well run, newly refurbished hotel with swimming pool, *Malaika* restaurant with Indian and Chinese (see Eating), 49 rooms with balconies and a/c, satellite TVs and fridges.

B Peacock Hotel, Bibi Titi Mohamed St, T022-2120334-40. Well run and centrally located modern hotel with 69 rooms with a/c and TV in a tower block. The restaurant in the basement is a windowless air-conditioned cell, but the food is passable and good value. Great views of downtown Dar from the bar on the top floor. The unmistakable building was recently 'cocooned' in blue glass to make it cooler inside.

B-C Valley View Hotel, on the corner of Congo St and Matumba A St, T022-2184556, www.valley-view.co.tz. The neat white and stone building has 41 slightly dated rooms with a/c, TVs, fridge, 24 hr room service. Buffet breakfast. A bit out of the way, off Morogoro Rd, a turning opposite United Nations Rd, about 1 km from the intersection with Bibi Titi Mohamed St.

C Continental, 159 Nkrumah St, T022-2114894, cohotel@kicheko.com. Old-fashioned and gloomy but functional hotel, some rooms a/c, patio bar, cheap restaurant, shop. Useful for the railway station. Rates are US$20-30 per room including basic breakfast.

C Luther House Hotel, Sokoine Dr, T022-2121735, luther@simbanet.net, behind the Lutheran church on the waterfront. Central and in considerable demand, so it's necessary to book. Simple freshly painted rooms with basic shower and loo, and fans that work only slowly. The *Dar Shanghai* Chinese restaurant is on the ground floor (see Eating), no alcohol.

C Q Bar and Guest House, off Haile Selassie Rd, behind the Morogoro Stores, Msasani Peninsula, T022-22120334, qbar@hotmail.com. 20 comfortable, if a little noisy, rooms in a smart 4 storey block. All have a/c, fridge, bathroom, cool tiled floors, Tingatinga paintings on the walls. Also 6 dorm beds for US$12 each. The bar and restaurant has 3 pool tables, big screen for watching sport, and plenty of draft beer and cocktails (see Eating). Separate dining room for guests only on the 2nd floor, breakfast included.

C Riki Hotel, Kleist Sykes St, west of Mnazi Mmoja Park, T022-2181802, rikihotel@raha.com. 40 rooms in a smart white block several storeys high, comfortable a/c rooms with bathrooms. Restaurant with very good à la carte food, bar and shops, 24-hr bureau de change. Will arrange a free pick up from the airport.

C-D Econolodge, corner of Libya St and Band St, T022-2116048-50, www.econolodgetz.com. A plain but functional place with sparsely furnished but clean self-contained rooms, the cheaper ones have fans, the more expensive have a/c. Small TV lounge. Price includes continental breakfast. The cheapest double is US$19.

D Jambo Inn, Libya St, T022-2114293, T0743-800790 (mob). Centrally located reasonable budget option with reliable hot water and working fans, the 28 rooms are self-contained. Rates are as low as US$15 for a double and for a little more you can get a/c. The affordable restaurant serves Indian food (no booze), fresh juice and ice cream; if you are staying in the hotel you get 10% off meals. Internet café downstairs.

D Keys, Uhuru St, near Mnazi Moja, T022-2183033, www.keys-hotels.com. Sister hotel to Keys in Moshi, also a tour agent and can arrange most activities including the Kilimanjaro climb. Simple self-contained rooms with fans, small restaurant serving local *nyama choma* and some international dishes, friendly and helpful set up.

D-E Safari Inn, Band St, T022-2119104, safari-inn@mailcity.com. Very central, similar to the nearby *Jambo Inn,* fairly simple but sound, 40 rooms, though only 3 with a/c, in a square concrete block, continental breakfast included, no restaurant. Doubles are US$15 and a single is US$9.

D-E YWCA, corner of Azikiwe St and Ghana Av, T022-2121196, ywca.tanzania@africaonline.co.tz, and the **YMCA**, T022-2122439, are one block apart across Maktaba St. (The YWCA is above the Tanzania Post Bank on Azikiwe St). Traditionally both offer simple and cheap accommodation but at the time of writing both were undergoing major structural renovations. We would be happy to get reports from anyone who visits after these have been completed.

E Malapa Inn, Wmumba St, beyond Mnazi Moja Park, T022-2180043. Very, very basic, but clean sheets on the beds, mosquito nets and fans. Have self-contained cubicles with loo (no toilet seats) and shower. Basic bread and eggs for breakfast, tea, coffee and soft drinks, rooms are US$7.

North of Dar

Note It is unsafe to walk along the beach between the northern hotels. The hotels' private beaches are watched by security guards and at the end of the beaches are signs warning guests of the danger of mugging – take heed.

L **Kunduchi Beach**, Kunduchi, T022-2650413, kunduchi@raha.com. Recently completely renovated to very high standards, very elegantly decorated modern rooms with a/c, TV and minibar, a mixture of African and Islamic-style architecture and decor for main service areas. Bar, pool bar, excellent restaurants, swimming pool, charming beach with palms and flowers, live music on Sun and public holidays, watersports facilities and trips to off-shore islands.

A **African Sky**, 10 km north of the city on the Bagomoyo Rd, Kijitonyama, part of the Millennium Towers shopping centre, T022-2774588, www.africanskyhotels.com. Dar's newest hotel opened at the end of 2004 in a glass tower block with ultra modern decor and facilities. Its 60 rooms have a/c, satellite TV, internet access, the executive suites are twice the size of the standard rooms, and the junior suites have an extra spare bedroom, both for only US$20 more. Swimming pool, gym, 2 restaurants and bars, the Famous Butcher's Grill (see Eating). Rather uniquely, the rooms at the back the hotel overlook the World War II cemetery, with its head stones arranged in semi-circles amongst neat gardens.

A **Bahari Beach**, Kunduchi, T022-2650352, www.twiga.ch/tz/bahari.htm. Self-contained accommodation in thatched rondavaals with a/c and TV. There's a large bar and restaurant area under high thatched roofing (limited menu but good food). Swimming pool with bar, band at the weekends and public holidays, traditional dancing Wed night, sandy beach, garden surroundings, gift shop, tour agency, and watersports centre. Rates include English breakfast.

A **Beachcomber Hotel**, Mbezi Beach, T022-2647772-4, www.beachcomber.co.tz. Newish, if not rather concrety development, a/c rooms with TV, minibar and phone, Swahili decor, health club with sauna, steambath and massage, watersports facilities and dive school offering 4-day PADI open water courses, free shuttle between the hotel and airport.

A **Jangwani Sea Breeze Lodge**, Mbezi Beach, T022-2647215, www.jangwani.com. 34 a/c rooms with TVs and en suite bathrooms. Swimming pool set in pretty gardens with lots of flowering shrubs, right on the beach. Watersports, restaurant, informal bar, barbecues and live music at the weekends. Dutch and German spoken. Can organize a day tour to Bagamoyo with a guide. *Sealion Charters* is based here at the curio shop, Joseph can organize boat trips and makes and sells rather exquisite furniture made from old dhows.

A **White Sands**, Mbezi Beach, T022-2647620-6, www.hotelwhitesands.com. 88 sea-facing rooms in thatched villas with TVs, a/c and minibar, and 28 new apartments for short and long term lets. Swimming pool, gym, beauty centre, watersports including a dive school, **Sea Breeze Marine Ltd,** T0744-783241 (mob), that offers courses. Several restaurants, one off which (Indian) is superb, and bars. There is a waterpark adjacent to the hotel with slides and pools. Free shuttle service into the city.

C-E **Silver Sands**, Kunduchi, T022-2650231, www.silversands.co.tz. Pleasant old hotel with restaurant, bar, and basic accommodation, some rooms have fans and are cheaper than those with a/c. The weekends attract a number of day visitors when a band plays on the terrace, the food is good and not badly priced. There is also a campsite with a well-maintained ablutions block and it is possible to pitch your tent right on the beach. Car parking is US$2 per night and you can leave a vehicle here while you make a trip to Zanzibar.

South of Dar

L **Protea Hotel Amani Beach**, 30 km south from the Kigamboni ferry, or air transfers can be arranged from Dar by the resort, T0744-410033 (mob), www.proteahotels.com for online information and reservations. Quality South African hotel chain, with a/c, en suite rooms in individual whitewashed cottages decorated with African art and with garden terraces and hammocks where breakfast is delivered. Swimming pool, tennis courts, horse riding, restaurant, bar, conference facilities, TVs. Set in 40 acres of tropical woodlands around a wide bay. Rates are from US$200 per person full board.

L **Ras Kutani Beach Resort**, T022-2134802, www.raskutani.com. Across Kigamboni ferry and 28 km further south, 2-hr road journey or a short charter flight from Dar es Salaam arranged by the resort. This resort is small and intimate with only 12 luxurious cottages, beautifully decorated, in a superb location on a hill overlooking the ocean and the wide arch of white sandy isolated beach and freshwater lagoon. Windsurfing, swimming pool, water-sports and fishing available but not diving. All rates are full board and are in the region of US$200 per person, resident rates are considerably lower with specials on weekdays.

B **Sunrise Beach Resort**, on Kipepeo Beach near the village of Mjimwema, 7 km south of the Kigamboni ferry, T022-2820862, www.sunrisebeachresort.co.tz. Smart 2-storey bandas with balconies and bathrooms, thatched restaurant and bar, sun loungers on the beach, watersports including jet skiing, and quad bikes (4-wheel motorbikes) available for hire.

C-E **Kipepeo**, on Kipepeo Beach next to the Sunrise Beach Resort (above), near the village of Mjimwema, 7 km south of the Kigamboni ferry, T022-2820877, www.kipepeovillage.com. 20 beach huts built on stilts in a grove of coconut palms with en suite bathrooms. Plenty of space for vehicles and camping (separate hot showers). Overlanders can leave vehicles for a small daily fee while they go to Zanzibar. Very good food and drinks are served on the beach or at the beach bar. A relaxed and affordable option close to the city. Camping US$4 per person, huts from US$65 including full English breakfast. Recommended.

D-E **Mikadi Beach**, T022-2820485, 2 km from the Kigamboni ferry. Popular campsite in a grove of coconut palms, right on the beach. Secure parking, simple ablutions, some double bandas, very good bar that gets busy at the weekends. For a small fee you can park vehicles here whilst you visit Zanzibar.

Pugu Hills *p64*

B-E **Pugu Hills**, T0744 565 498 (mob), www.puguhills.com. In the Pugu Hills Reserve, 35 km to the south of Dar (see page 64). 4 smart bamboo huts erected above the forest floor on poles, with hardwood floors and Swahili furnishings, swimming pool, fabulously rustic restaurant offers 4 dishes per day including one vegetarian, plus snacks, lovely nature trails through the forest, can also arrange visits to a local cattle market, camping available.

Eating

Most of the hotels, including those on the beach out of town, have restaurants and bars. While the city centre has a fair amount of good places to eat, many of these are only open during the day, cater for office workers and do not serve alcohol. The best places for dinner and evening drinks are out of the centre on the Msasani Peninsula.

City centre and Msasani Peninsula
maps p56 and p62

TTT **Addis in Dar**, 35 Ursino St, off Migombani St/Old Bagamoyo Rd in the Oyster Bay area, near the site of the new US Embassy, T0741-266299 (mob). Small and charming Ethiopian restaurant with an outside terrace. Open 1200-1430, 1800-2300, closed on Sun. It is wise to drop in and book ahead.

TTT **Alcove**, T022-2137444, Samora Av. Very good Indian food, also some Chinese, usually busy at weekends, recommended is the spicy crab bisque. Open daily for dinner except Mon. Sat and Sun lunch too.

TTT **Azuma**, 1st floor at The Slipway, Msasani Peninsula, T022-2600893. Japanese and Indonesian restaurant, authentic cuisine, good views over the bay. Very good sushi, if you book ahead, the chef will come out from the kitchen and prepare food at your table. Open daily for dinner, except Mon, Sat and Sun lunch too.

TTT **Malaika**, ground floor of Karibu Hotel, Haile Selassie Rd, Oyster Bay, T022-2602946. Very good quality Indian, Chinese and continental cuisine, recently refurbished, also a dance floor and an outside beer garden with a tandoori oven, regular special offers such as family discounts, Indian live band, buffets from US$11.

TTT **Serengeti** (open daily) and **Tradewinds** (closed Sun) at the Royal Palm Hotel, Ohio St, T022-2112416. Both are upmarket, reservations are recommended and you need to dress up. At the Serengeti there are themed nights every day of the week: Mediterranean on Mon, Italian on Tue, Oriental on Wed, seafood menu on Thu, popular fondue night on Fri, Tex-Mex on Sat and Indian on Sun. Tradewinds is good for steaks as well as seafood, fine wines cigars and whiskies.

ΨΨΨ **Fishmonger**, upstairs at the Sea Cliff Village Food Court, Msasani Peninsula, T0744-304733. Excellent fish and seafood from US$9-20, nice outdoor terrace, though the only non-fishy options are 3 chicken dishes, 1 steak and 1 vegetarian option.

ΨΨΨ **Hot (in Africa)**, off Haile Selassie Rd, behind Hotel Karibu, Msasani Peninsula, T0748-839607. Afro-European food, some of the most inventive cuisine in Dar, traditional roast lunches on a Sun, very trendy decor and a good atmosphere.

ΨΨΨ **Istana**, Ali Hassan Mwinyi Rd, opposite Caltex petrol station, a few km out of the city on the Bagamoyo Rd, T022-2761348. Specializes in Malaysian cuisine, (the name means palace in Malay). Theme nights throughout the week, Chinese on Tue, meat grill Wed, satay buffet on Thu, etc. Specialities include *roti canai*, puffed bread filled with meat, chicken and apples and served with hot curries. All you can eat buffets start from US$7. Open kitchen, tables in the garden, play area with staff to look after children.

ΨΨΨ **L'Arca di Noe'**, Kimweri Av, Msasani Peninsula, T0741-601282. Italian pastas, seafood, pizzas, range of desserts, wide selection of wines, pleasant atmosphere. On Wed night is an all you can eat buffet featuring 26 different pastas and sauces, and on Thu you get a free glass of wine with every pizza ordered. Closed Tue.

ΨΨΨ **Mashua Bar and Grill**, at The Slipway, Msasani Peninsula, T022-2600893. Grills, burgers, salads and pizza, ocean views, open evenings only. Live music and dancing on Thu.

ΨΨΨ **Mediterraneo**, Kawe Beach off Old Bagomoyo Rd, midway between the city and the northern beaches, T0744-812567. Italian pastas, salads and Chinese, occasional live music and Swahili-style buffets. On Sat afternoon there is a barbecue from 1200-2000. Overlooks the ocean, a good place for kids.

ΨΨΨ **Oyster Bay Grill**, Oyster Bay Shopping Centre, Msasani Peninsula, T022-2660131. Very elegant and some of the best food in Dar specializing in steak, seafood and fondue. Average price with wine US$25 per head, much more if you go for the lobster thermidor. Huge range of international wines, whisky and cigar bar, jazz music, outside terrace and more formal fancy tables inside. Accepts credit cards. Open daily 1800-2300.

ΨΨΨ **The Pub**, at The Slipway, Msasani Peninsula, T022-2600893. International food, mainly French and Italian in an English-style pub setting, also serves burgers, sandwiches and grills, draft beer and there are good Sun roast lunch specials.

ΨΨΨ **Sawasdee**, top floor of New Africa Hotel, Azikwe St, T022-2117050. Exceptionally good and very authentic Thai food, wonderful harbour views, buffet on Tue and Fri, US$14.

ΨΨΨ **Simona Restaurant**, Kimweri Av, Msasani Peninsula, T022-2666935. Italian and Croatian cuisine, plus seafood, rather cavernous interior, live music on Fri and Sat, good selection of European wine, open 1000-2300, closed Sun.

ΨΨΨ **The Terrace**, at The Slipway, Msasani Peninsula, T0741-608564 (mob). Italian cuisine and barbecued grills and seafood. The seafood platter for 2 goes for US$25. Moorish painted arches and outside dining area. Closed Sun.

ΨΨΨ **Turquoise**, Sea Cliff Village Food Court, Msasani Peninsula, T022-2600979. Very good authentic Turkish cuisine, meze and kebabs, healthy vegetarian dishes, homemade desserts and Turkish sweets.

ΨΨ **Chef's Pride Restaurant**, virtually opposite Jambo Inn hotel, on road between Lubya St and Jamhuri St. Good food at excellent prices, fast service – Italian, Chinese, Indian and local dishes available. Closed evenings.

ΨΨ **Chinese Restaurant**, basement of NIC Bldg, Samora Av. Good standard of inexpensive Chinese cuisine, also African and some continental dishes. This restaurant has been going some 30 years.

ΨΨ **City Garden Restaurant**, corner of Garden Ave and Pamba Rd, T022-2127707. African, Indian and western meals, buffets at lunchtime, excellent juices, tables are set in garden, good service and consistently popular especially at lunchtime with office workers. Highly recommended.

ΨΨ **Coral Ridge Spur**, Sea Cliff Village Food Court, Msasani Peninsula. Imported South African steak and ribs chain, geared up for families with a play area, Wild West themed decor, big portions, help-yourself salad bar. The meat is good but if you have eaten at a Spur elsewhere in Africa there's no surprises.

ƚƚ **Garden Food Court**, on the 2nd floor of the Haidery Plaza, Kisutu St. Here is the **Red Onion**, a fairly formal Indian and Pakistani restaurant serving good value lunchtime buffets for US$6; **Natasha Spiced Chicken** for barbecued fast food; and the **Coffee Bud** for snacks and drinks. Food can be taken out of each restaurant and eaten on the outside terrace. Open daily 1100-2300.

ƚƚ **Java Lounge**, Sea Cliff Village Food Court, Msasani Peninsula, T0748-467149. Very good service, trendy outdoor wooden deck, large range of cocktails and 20 different coffees, good breakfasts and light meals.

ƚƚ **La Dolce Vita**, Toure Dr, Msasani Peninsula, T022-2668212. Open-air, pleasant atmosphere under thatched roofing. Pizza and Italian food though also unusually some Ethiopian dishes and ostrich meat. Lively atmospheric bar. Open daily 1100-2300.

ƚƚ **L'Epidor**, Samora Av. Coffee shop and bakery serving very good sandwiches made from French or pitta bread with imaginative fillings, cappuccino and fresh juice, croissants, pastries, salads. Open 0700-1900, closed Sun.

ƚƚ **La Trattoria Jan**, Kimweri Av, Msasani Peninsula, T0741-282969 (mob). Excellent Italian cuisine, ice creams, open air seating at the rear, pleasant atmosphere and good value too. The pizzas are some of the best in town, take-away available.

ƚƚ **Lilylike House**, Kimweri Av, Msasani Peninsula, T0741-360098 (mob). More of a café than a restaurant but nevertheless wonderful sizzling dishes and a full range of Chinese cuisine.

ƚƚ **Manchu Wok**, Sea Cliff Village, Msasani Peninsula, T022-2600963. Chinese and Indonesian food prepared by a chef from Nepal, very modern take-away counter in the Sea Cliff Food Court, can eat at the tables outside.

ƚƚ **Q Bar and Guest House**, Haile Selassie Rd, Msasani Peninsula, T0744-282474. Open daily from 1700 until late, happy hour 1700-1900, Fri is shooters' night with various tots for TSh1000. The bar has 3 pool tables, big screen for watching sport, pub grub, and plenty of draft beer and cocktails. Live music on Fri and Sat is 1970s soul night. Also has accommodation (see under sleeping).

ƚƚ **Shooter's Grill**, 86 Kimweri Av, Namanga, T0744-304733. Very good steaks, ladies get a free glass of wine on Wed and men get a free beer with every T-bone steak sold on a Thu. Live music on Sun, good atmosphere.

ƚƚ **Sichuan Restaurant**, Bibi Titi Mohamed St, T022-2150548. Excellent and authentic Chinese restaurant where Chinese people eat (which is always a good sign); most main course dishes are around US$4 and there is a large range to choose from including plenty of vegetarian options.

ƚƚ **Sweet Eazy**, Oyster Bay Shopping Centre, Toure Drive, Msasani Peninsula, T0745-754074. Cocktail bar and restaurant, African and Thai cuisine. Open daily until midnight, happy hour 1700-1900 and all night on Fri, jazz band on Sat.

ƚ **Cynics' Café and Wine Bar**, in the TDFL building opposite the Royal Palm Hotel. Fresh pastries, salads, sandwiches, wine by the glass, beer and coffee, only opens weekdays and closes at 1800 except for Fri when it stays open until 2100.

ƚ **Dar Shanghai**, behind the Swiss Air office in Luther House, Sokoine Dr, T022-2134397. Chinese and Tanzanian menus, not brilliant food in a canteen style atmosphere but quick and filling, no booze but soft drinks.

ƚ **Debonair's and Steer's**, corner of Ohio St and Samora Av. Quality South African chains. Debonair's serves pizza and salads, while Steer's offers burgers, ribs and chips. Also in the complex is Hurry Curry, an Indian takeaway, Chop Chop, Chinese, and a coffee shop. Eat at plastic tables in a/c.

ƚ **Jambo Inn**, Libya St. Excellent cheap Indian menu, huge inflated chapattis like air-cushions, also Chinese and European dishes, outside and inside dining areas.

ƚ **Planet Bollywood**, corner Morogoro Rd/ Samora Av. Cheap pizzas, burgers and ice cream, though small portions and not terribly authentic fare.

ƚ **Sno-cream**, Mansfield St. An old-fashioned ice cream parlour serving excellent ice cream, done out in Disney style. Incredibly elaborate sundaes with all the trimmings.

North of Dar

ƚƚƚ **The Famous Butcher's Grill**, African Sky Hotel, Ali Hassan Mwinyi Rd, Kijitonyama, 9 km out of the city towards Kunduchi, T022-2774588. High quality South African steak restaurant chain that dishes up probably the best steaks in Dar. Excellent cuts of dry and wet aged beef (although most meat is actually imported from Australia), melt in the mouth fillets, T-bones and rumps accompanied by flavoursome sauces. Try the cheese and champagne sauce. Also serves local fish; red snapper with shrimp and mushroom sauce. All accompanied by imported spirits and wines. Expect to pay around US$60 for 2 with drinks.

Bars and clubs

There are few nightclubs as such in Dar, though many of the hotels and restaurants mentioned above crank it up late in the evening with live music or a DJ, especially at weekends when tables are cleared away for dancing. Some discos are in attractive outdoor settings. Those hotels and restaurants that have regular discos are notably **Jangwani Sea Breeze Lodge**, **White Sands** and **Bahari Beach** hotels on the northern beaches, the **Malaika Restaurant** at Hotel Karibu and the **Q bar** on the Msasani Peninsula.

California Dreamer, next to Las Vegas Casino on corner of Upanga Rd and Ufokoni Rd. Bright and busy disco during the week and packed at weekends. Entry US$4, girls free before 2300 during the week.

Club Billicanos, Mkwepu St, T022-2120605. Far and away the most popular club in Dar es Salaam, it's obviously had mega-dollars poured into it, has been imaginatively designed and has all the lighting and other effects you'd expect from a world-class night club. Drink prices are reasonable, the place is fully a/c. Open every night until around 0400, entry US$3 per person or US$4 for a couple.

Entertainment

Cinema

Europeans and visitors seldom visit the cinema, which is a pity as the general audience reaction makes for an exciting experience. Programmes are announced in the newspapers or at www.darcinemas.com. The cinemas show mostly Indian, martial arts or adventure films. Entrance is about US$1. The following are the most popular: **Empire**, Maktaba St, opposite the Post Office; **Empress**, Samora Av; **New Chox**, Nkrumah St; **Odeon**, Zaramo St.

The most up-to-date, showing Hollywood or Bollywood films, is the **Drive-Inn-Cinema**, New Bagamoyo Rd, on the way to Mwenge, which has 3 regular a/c cinema screens as well as a drive-in, T022-2773053 (answering machine for schedules).

The **British Council**, Ohio St, T022-2116574 has fairly regular film shows on Wed, and the **Alliance Française**, Maktaba St, opposite the New Africa Hotel shows films from time to time.

Casinos

Las Vegas Casino, T022-2116512, corner of Upanga Rd and Ufukoni Rd. Roulette, poker, blackjack, vingt-et-un and slot machines. There are also casinos at the **New Africa Hotel**, T022-2119752, and **Hotel Sea Cliff**, T022-2600380.

Music

Live music Concerts of classical music by touring artists are presented by the **British Council**, the **Alliance Française** and occasionally other embassies. African bands and artists and Indian groups play regularly at the hotels and restaurants especially at the weekends. Look for announcements in the *Dar es Salaam Guide*, and *What's Happening in Dar es Salaam*.

Theatre

Little Theatre, Haile Selassie Rd, off Ali Hassan Mwinyi Rd, next door to the Protea Apartments, T0748-607060 (mob), daressalaamplayers@raha.com, presents productions on an occasional basis, perhaps half a dozen a year, usually drama and comedy and one musical a year, very popular, particularly the Christmas pantomime.

British Council, Ohio St, occasionally presents productions. Check announcements in the papers.

Shopping

There are shops along Samora Av (electrical goods, local clothing, footware) and on Libya St (clothing and footwear). Supermarkets, with a wide variety of imported foods and wines, are on Samora Av between Pamba Av and Azikawe St, on the corner of Kaluta St and Bridge St, opposite Woolworth's on Garden Av, in Shopper's Plaza and in the Oyster Bay

Hotel shopping mall. A popular location for purchase of fruit and vegetables is the market on Kinondoni Rd, just north of Msimbuzi Creek. The Namanga shops are at the corner of old and new Bagamoyo Rd, and are basically a bunch of stalls selling household supplies and food; there's a good butcher's towards the back. Manzese Mitumba Stalls, Morogoro Rd, Manzese, has great bargains for second-hand clothing. Ilala Market, on Uhuru St, sells vegetables, fresh and dried fish, and second-hand clothing. Fresh fish and seafood can be bought at the Fish Market on Ocean Rd just past the Kigamboni ferry.

Shopping centres and department stores

Haidery Plaza, at the corner of Upanga Rd and Kisutu St in the city centre. A small shopping centre that as well as shops has an internet café and a food court on the upper level.

Mayfair Plaza, opposite TMJ Hospital, Old Bagomoyo Rd, Oyster Bay, www.mayfairplaza.co.za. New in 2004 this centre has a number of quality shops including upmarket clothes and shoe shops, a Kodak film processing shop, jewellers, dry cleaners, banks, pharmacies and a branch of **Shoprite**, a South African supermarket chain, plus coffee shops and a food court. (Very close to the new US Embassy, the shopping centre was once the site of a petrol station. When the embassy was being built, it was discovered that the petrol station was owned by Iranians, and because of this the US government felt compelled to buy it and turn the site into something else!)

Oyster Bay Hotel shopping centre. Has a supermarket, internet café, gift and art shops, and photo developers.

Sea Cliff Hotel shopping centre. Has a branch of the excellent bookshop A Novel Idea (see below), a French bakery, and a good shop upstairs called Mswumbi that sells fresh coffee beans. Here are more 'day rooms' for rent - contact the Sea Cliff Hotel.

Shoppers' Plaza, Old Bagamoyo Rd, on the Msasani Peninsula, has a good variety of shops including a large supermarket and The Arcade, nearby, has a travel agency, boutiques, hairdresser, nail technician, glass and framing shop, and restaurants.

The Slipway complex, on the Msasani Peninsula, facing Msasani Bay. Expensive, high quality goods can be found here. There's another branch of Shoprite, an internet café, a craft market, a hair and beauty salon, several restaurants, and a branch of Barclay's Bank with an ATM. There are also a few 'day rooms' – bedrooms that are only let out during the day for people who have returned to Dar from safari and are not flying out until the evening. To book these contact **Coastal Air**, T022-2600893, slipway@coastal.cc.

Woolworths, in the New PPF Towers building on Ohio St, is the only department store in Dar es Salaam, a South African clothing store very similar to the UK's *Marks & Spencer*.

Bookshops

Secondhand books can be found at the stalls on Samora Av, on Pamba St (off Samora), on Maktaba St and outside Tancot House, opposite Luther House. Most of these also sell international news magazines such as *Time*, *Newsweek*, *New African*, etc.

A Novel Idea, T022-2601088, www.anovelidea-africa.com. The best bookshop in Dar by far. There are branches at The Slipway on Msasani Peninsula, at the Hotel Sea Cliff, and on the corner of Ohio St and Samora Av. This is perhaps the most comprehensive bookshop in East Africa with a full range of new novels, coffee table books, maps and guide books.

Other bookshops are the **Tanzanian Bookshop**, Indira Gandhi St, leading from the Askari Monument and **Tanzania Publishing House**, Samora Av, but both have only limited selections.

Curios and crafts

Traditional crafts, particularly wooden carvings, are sold along Samora Av to the south of the Askari Monument. Good value crafts can be purchased from stalls along Ali Hassan Mwinyi Rd near the intersection with Haile Selassie Rd and, in particular, at **Mwenge**, along Sam Njoma Rd, close to the intersection with Ali Hassan Mwinyi Rd. This is the best place for handicrafts in Dar es Salaam, and for ethnographia from all over Tanzania and further afield (notably the Congo). There are a large number of shops and stalls offering goods at very reasonable prices and you can watch the carvers at work. The market is 10 km or about half an hour's journey from the town centre towards the northern beaches, easily reached by *dala-dala* (destination: Mwenge). It is just around the corner from the *dala-dala* stand.

More expensive, quality modern wood products can be obtained from **Domus**, in the Slipway complex, which also houses **The Gallery**, also selling wood products as well as other items such as paintings by local artists. There is also a craft market here selling tablecloths, cushions and beadwork, and a **Tingatinga** art workshop.

Activities and tours

Athletics

Meetings at the National Stadium, Mandela Rd to the south of the city.

★ Cricket

Almost entirely a pursuit of the Asian community. There are regular games at:
Gymkhana Club, off Ghana Av;
Annadil Burhani Cricket Ground, off Aly Khan Rd;
Leaders Club, Dahomey Rd, off Ali Hassan Mwinyi Rd; and
Jangwani Playing Fields, off Morogoro Rd, in the valley of Msimbazi Creek, at weekends.

Fishing

Marine fishing can be arranged through many of the hotels on the beaches.

Fitness

The Fitness Centre, off Chole Rd on Msasani Peninsula, T022-2600786. A gym with weights and also aerobics and yoga classes.
Millenium Health Club, Mahando St, at the north end of Msasani Peninsula, T022-2602609. Has a gym, aerobics, sauna and beauty parlour.
There are also gyms at the **Hotel Sea Cliff** and **White Sands Hotel**.
Running **Hash House Harriers** meet at 1730 on Mon afternoons T0744-874083 (mob), or details from British Council, Ohio St, T022-2116574.

Golf

Gymkhana Club, Ghana Av, T022-2120519. Only guests are only permitted to play golf at the club. Costs are US$22 for 18 holes, you can hire very good quality clubs and shoes for an extra US$9, and a caddie is around US$5 with a tip. Here, because of a shortage of water, you will be playing on browns not greens.

Sailing

Yacht Club, Chole Rd on Msasani Peninsula, T022-2600136. Visitors can obtain temporary membership. The club has been going since 1933 and organizes East Africa's premier sailing event, the Dar to Tanga (and back) Yacht Race every Dec.

Soccer

The main African pursuit, followed by everyone from the President and the Cabinet down. Matches are exciting occasions with radios throughout the city tuned to the commentary. Terrace entrance is around US$1 (more for important matches). It is worth paying extra to sit in the stand. There are 2 main venues:
National Stadium, Mandela Rd to the south of the city; and
Karume Stadium, just beyond the Kariakoo area, off Uhuru St. There are two divisions of the National league, and Dar es Salaam has two representatives – **Simba** and **Young Africans** (often called Yanga) – and there is intense rivalry between them. Simba, the best-known Tanzanian club, have their origins in Kariakoo and are sometimes referred to as the 'Msimbazi Street Boys' – they have a club bar in Msimbazi St. Initially formed in the 1920s as 'Eagles of the Night', they changed their name to 'Sunderland FC' in the 1950s. After independence all teams had to choose African names and they became Simba. www.simbasportsclub.com for more information on the team.

The national team **Taifa Stars** play regularly at the National Stadium, mostly against other African teams.

Swimming

Many of the larger hotels have swimming pools that charge a small fee for non-guests.
Swimming Club, Ocean Rd near Magogoni St. This is the best place to swim in the sea. Otherwise the best sea beaches are some distance to the north and south of the city.
Water World, next to White Sands Hotel at Mbezi Beach. Has several different water slides and games for children. Open Wed, Fri-Sun, entrance US$3 adults, US$2.50 children.
Wet 'n' Wild, Kunduchi Beach, T022- 2650326. This is an enormous new complex largely,

though not exclusively, for children. There are 7 swimming pools with 22 water slides, 2 are very high and one twists and turns for 250 m. There is an area for younger children, tennis and squash courts, go- karting, an internet café, hair and beauty parlour, fast food outlets and a main restaurant, and also facilities for watersports on the open ocean, including windsurfing and fishing trips; there is even a qualified diving instructor.

Tour operators

A variety of companies offer tours to the game parks, the islands (Zanzibar, Pemba, Mafia) and to places of historical interest (Kilwa, Bagamoyo). It is well worth shopping around as prices (and degrees of luxury) vary. It is important to find an operator that you like, offers good service, and does not pressure you into booking something.

Alone with Nature, Pamba House St, T022-2110159.
Bon Voyage Travel, Ohio St St, T022-2117833, www.bonvoyagetz.com.
Cordial Tours, Indira St/Mkwepu St, T022-2136259, www.cordialtours.com.
Cruxton Travel, Extelecom Bldg, 8th Flr, Samora Av, T022-2134235.
Delvims Travel International, Sukari House, Ground Flr, Ohio St/Sokoine Dr, T022-2122215.
Easy Travel & Tours, Raha Tower, Bibi Titi Mohamed St, T022-2121747, www.easytravel.co.tz.
Ebony Tours & Safaris, Hotel Karibu, Haile Selassie Rd, T022-2601457, www.ebony-safaris.com.
Emslies Travel Ltd, NIC Investment House, 3rd Flr, Samora Av, opposite Royal Palm Hotel, T022-2114065, www.emsliestravel.biz.
Fortune Travels & Tours Ltd, Jamhuri St, T022-2138288, www.fortunetz.com.
Gogo Safaris, Bagamoyo Rd, T022-2114719.
Hakuna Matata, The Arcade, Old Bagamoyo Rd, T022-2700230.
Hima Tours & Travel, Simu St, behind Mavuno House, T022-2111083, www.himatours.com.
Hippo Tours & Safaris, Ohio St, T022-2128662, www.hippotours.com.
Hit Holidays, Bibi Titi Mohamed St (near Rickshaw Travel), T022-2119624, www.hittours.co.tz.
Holiday Africa Tours & Safaris, TDFL Bldg, Ohio St, T022-2111357/8.
Interline Travel & Tours, NIC Life House, Sokoine Dr/Ohio St, T022-2137433.
Kearsley Travel and Tours, Kearsley House, Indira Gandhi St, T022-2115026-30, www.kearsley.net.
Leopard Tours, Haidery Plaza, Upanga Rd/ Kisutu St, T022-2119750/4-6, www.leopard-tours.com.
Lions of Tanzania Safari & Tours, Peugeot House, Bibi Titi Mohamed Rd, T022-2128161, www.lions.co.tz.
Luft Travel & Cargo Ltd, GAK Patel Bldg, Maktaba St, T022-2110672.
Mako Tours & Safaris, Nkrumah St, T0748-588838 (mob), www.makosafaris.com.
Planet Safaris, Ohio St, adjacent to the Royal Palm Hotel, T022-2137456, www.planetsafaris.com.
Reza Travel & Tours, Jamhuri St, opposite Caltex Station, T022-2134458/68, reza@rezatravel.com.
Rickshaw Travel (American Express Agents), Royal Palm Hotel, Ohio St, T022-2114094, www.rickshawtravels.com.
Selous Safaris, DT Dobie Bldg, Nkrumah St, T022-2134802, www.selous.com.
Skylink Travel & Tours, TDFL Bldg, Ohio St, opposite Royal Palm Hotel, T022-2115381, airport, T022-2842738, Mayfair Plaza, T022-2773983, www.skylinktanzania.com.
Sykes, Indira Ghandi St, T022-2115542, www.sykestravel.com.
Takims Holidays Tours and Safaris, Mtendeni St, T022-2110346-8, T022-2110346, www.takimsholidays.com.
A Tent with a View Safaris, Samora Av, T022-2110507, www.saadani.com, www.selouslodge.com.
Travel Link, New Red Cross Building, Morogoro Rd, T022-2127242, www.tanzaniatravellink.com.
Walji's Travel Bureau, Zanaki St/Indira Ghandi St corner, T022-2110321, www.waljistravel.com.
Wild Thing Safaris, corner of Makunganya St and Simu St, above TNT, T0748-888188 (mob), www.wildthingsafaris.com.

Transport

Air

For air charter operators see page 28.
Air Tanzania, T022-2117500, www.air tanzania.com, has 2 daily flights from Dar to

Zanzibar (25 min) at 0900 and 1600, a daily flight to **Kilimanjaro** (55 min) at either 0910 or 2000 depending on the day of the week, and 2 daily flights to **Mwanza** (1 hr 30 min) at 0700 and 1600.
Coastal Air, T022-2117969-60, www.coastal.cc, has a scheduled service from Dar to **Arusha** (2 hr 30 min) daily 0900. This service continues on to the **Serengeti**. To **Kilwa** (1 hr) via **Mafia Island** (30 min). **Pemba** (1 hr) daily 1400. **Ruaha** (3 hr) Mon, Thu and Sat via **Selous** (30 min). There's another daily flight to the Selous at 1430 which stops at all the camps. **Tanga** (1 hr 30 min) daily 1400. To **Zanzibar** (20 min) daily 0615, 0730, 0900, 1230, 1400, 1645, and 1745 (US$55).
Precision Air, T022-2130800/2121718, www.precisionairtz.com, flies to **Mwanza** (2 hr) daily 0810. To **Tabora** (2 hr) and **Kigoma** (3 hr 15 min) daily except Thu 1335. To **Zanzibar** (20 min) daily 0650 and 1320. There are additional flights to Zanzibar on Thu and Fri at 0830, and on Mon, Tue, Wed, Sat and Sun 1100. To **Arusha** (1 hr 15 min) daily 0820. To **Shinyanga** (2 hr) and **Mwanza** (3 hr) on Mon, Wed, Thu, Fri, and Sun 1330. To **Kilimanjaro** (1 hr 15 min) daily 1800.

Airline offices Air India, Bibi Titi Mohamed St, opposite Peugeot House, T022-2152642-4. Air Tanzania, ATC Bldg, Ohio St, T022-2117500, www.airtanzania.com. British Airways, based at the Royal Palm Hotel, Ohio St, T022- 2113820-2, www.britishairways.com. Egypt Air, Matsalamat Bldg, Samora Av, T022-2113333. Emirates, Haidery Plaza, Kisutu St, T022-2116100-3, www.emirates.com. Ethiopian Airlines, TDFL Bldg, Ohio St, T022-2117063-5. Gulf Air, Raha Towers, Bibi Titi Mohamed St/Maktaba St, T022-2137852-6, www.gulfairco.com. Kenya Airways, Peugeot House, Upanga Rd, T022-2119376, www.kenya-airways.com. KLM, Peugeot House, Upanga Rd, T022-2113336, www.klm.com. Oman Air, airport, T022-2135660. South Africa Airways, airport, T022-2117044-7, www.flysaa.com. Swiss Air, Luther House, Sokoine Dr, T022-2118870-3. Yemenia Airways, TDFL Bldg, Ohio St, T022-2126032.

Train

The Central Railway Station is off Sokoine Dr at the wharf end of the city at the corner of Railway St/Gerezani St, T022-2117833, www.trctz.com. This station serves the passenger line that runs through the central zone to **Kigoma** on Lake Tanganyika and **Mwanza** on Lake Victoria.

The Tazara Railway Station is at the junction of Mandela Rd and Nyerere Rd, about 5 km from the city centre, T022-2865187, www.tazara.co.tz. You can book train tickets online. It is well served by *dala-dala* and a taxi from the centre costs about US$4. This line runs southwest to Iringa and **Mbeya** and on to **Tunduma** at the Zambia border. It is a broader gauge than the Central and Northern Line.

Express trains go all the way to **New Kapiri Mposhi** in Zambia and this journey takes 40-50 hrs. The local trains, which stop at the Zambian border, are a little slower, and take approximately 23 hrs to get to Mbeya. First class cabins on both trains contain 4 berths and second class 6.

Bus

The main bus station is Ubungo Bus Station on Morogoro Rd, 6 km from the city centre, which can be reached by bus, *dala-dala* or taxi. Outside on the road is a long line of booking offices. Recommended for safety and reliability is Scandinavian Express, which has its own terminal on Nyerere Rd at the corner of Msimbazi St (taxi from the city centre approximately US$2), though all buses also stop at the Ubungo bus station, T022-2850847, www.scandinaviangroup.com. There is a small airport-style arrival and departure lounge at the terminal with its own restaurant. Buses are speed limited, luggage is securely locked up either under the bus or in overhead compartments, and complimentary video, drinks, sweets and biscuits are offered. Buses depart daily for **Arusha** 0830 and 0915 (US$20 luxury service, US$14 standard), journey time 8 hrs, **Iringa** 0815, 1015 and 1345 (US$8.50), 7 hrs, **Mbeya** 0645 and 0745 (US$14), 12 hrs, **Tanga** 0830 and 1430 (US$6.50), 6 hrs, and **Dodoma**, 0915 and 1100 (US$8.50), 4 hrs. International destinations include **Mombasa** and **Nairobi** in Kenya, **Kampala** in Uganda and **Lusaka** in Zambia.

Car hire

Car hire can be arranged through most of the tour operators. Alternatively try:

The *dala-dalas* of Dar es Salaam

Ownership of one or more minibuses, or *dala-dalas*, remains a favourite *mradi* (income-generating project) for Dar es Salaam's middle class and, judging by the numbers squeezed into their interiors and the speed at which they travel between destinations, those returns are handsome. Realizing that they can't monitor the number of passengers using their buses, the *dala-dala* owners stipulate how much they expect to receive at the end of the day from the 'crew' they hire to operate the vehicle; anything left over constitutes the crew's wages.
It is a system that appears to work to everyone's advantage other than that of the passenger, who suffers the consequent overcrowding and the suicidal driving as *dala-dala* competes with *dala-dala* to arrive first and leave fullest.

In a forlorn attempt to reduce the number of accidents, the Tanzanian government passed a law in early 1997 requiring all public service vehicles to install governors restricting speeds to under 80 kph. However, *dala-dala* and coach operators soon worked out ways to override them, or simply disconnected them completely, and within weeks the drivers were proceeding with their old reckless abandon.

The basic crew of each *dala-dala* is made up of two people: the driver (clearly picked for the ability to drive fast rather than well) and the turnboy (in Dar slang *Mgiga debe* – literally 'he who forces things into a tin can'), whose job it is to collect money and issue tickets, harangue passengers who fail to make room for one more, as well as to entertain the remainder of the bus with hair-raising acrobatic stunts hanging from the door of the bus (there is at least one *Mpiga debe* currently working in Dar who has just one leg – it's not hard to imagine how he lost the other one).
Supplementing this basic crew at either end of the journey is a tout, who bawls out the intended destination and route, attempting to attract or, if necessary, intimidate people (at times this stretches to actual manhandling of passengers) into entering his *dala-dala*. He is paid a fixed amount for each bus that he touts for. In addition, when business is slow, there are people who are paid a small amount to sit on the bus pretending to be passengers in order to give the impression that it is fuller than it actually is to the potential passenger, who will then enter the *dala-dala*, assuming it will be leaving sooner than the next one along.

The *dala-dala* network radiates from three main termini in the town centre, **Posta** at *Minazi Mirefu* ('Tall palm trees') on the Kivukoni Front opposite the old Post Office; **Stesheni**, close to the Central Railway Station; and **Kariakoo**, around the Uhuru/Msimbazi Street roundabout for destinations south and at the central market for those in the north. From each of these you can catch *dala-dalas* to destinations throughout Dar es Salaam, although the four main routes are along Ali Hassan Mwinyi to Mwenge (for the Makumbusho Village Museum, Mwenge handicrafts market and the university); along the Kilwa Road to Temeke, Mtoni and Mbagala (these take you to the Salvation Army); to Vingunguti via Kariakoo and Ilala (for the Tazara Railway Station); and along the Morogoro Road to Magomeni, Manzese and Ubongo. For a *dala-dala* going to the airport ask for *Uwanja wa Ndege at Minazi Miretu*.

Avis, www.avis.com, in the TDFL building, opposite the Royal Palm Hotel, Ohio St, run by Skylink Travel & Tours, T022-2115381, airport, T022-2842738, Mayfair Plaza, T022-2773983, www.skylinktanzania.com. New branch to open at the Kilimanjaro Kempiski Hotel. Specialist company in Tanzania, also has offices in Mwanza and Arusha.
Business Rent a Car, 16 Kisutu St, T022-2122852, www.businessrentacar.com.
Green Car Rentals, Nkrumah St, T022-2183718, www.greencars.co.tz. **Hertz**, Royal Palm Hotel, T022-2112967, www.hertz.com.

Sea

All ticket offices of the ferry companies with services to **Zanzibar** and **Pemba** are on Sokoine Dr adjacent to the jetty. Ignore the touts who may follow you to the offices to claim credit and take commission. The companies themselves advise travellers to completely ignore them and it is easy enough to book a ticket on your own.

Most ferries are fast and comfortable hydrofoils or catamarans that take on average 90 min, and the tourist fare is fixed at US$40 one way (including port tax) for all companies. The slow overnight boat back from Zanzibar operated by Flying Horse is US$20. Payment for ferry tickets is strictly in US$ cash. Companies no longer accept TCs.

The following companies offer services to **Zanzibar and Pemba**:
Azam Marine, T022-2123324, www.azam-marine.com. Australian-built Seabus catamarans that take 1 hr 40 min to Zanzibar. They depart daily at 0800, 1115, 1330, 1400 and 1600. From Zanzibar to Dar, ferries depart at 0700, 0930, 1330 and 1630. On Tue and Fri they also operate a service from Dar es Salaam to Pemba via Zanzibar at 0730 which arrives in Zanzibar at 0855, departs again at 1000 and arrives in Pemba at 1205. The return boat is also on Tue and Fri and departs Pemba at 1230, arrives in Zanzibar at 1435, departs again at 1630 and arrives in Dar at 1755.
Sea Express, T022-2110217, www.sea-express.net, daily ferry from Dar at 0730 which arrives in Zanzibar at 0915, leaving Zanzibar for the return at 1615. On Mon, Wed, Fri and Sun the ferry continues from Zanzibar (departing at 1000) to Pemba where it arrives at 1200, beginning its return from Pemba at 1300. Dar es Salaam to Zanzibar US$40, to Pemba US$65.
Sea Star, T022-2139996, fast service to Zanzibar that takes 1 hr 30 min, departs Dar at 1030. The return leaves Zanzibar at 0700.
Flying Horse (aka Africa Shipping Corporation), T022-2124507, outward journey to Zanzibar departs at 1230 and takes 2 hrs, the overnight return from Zanzibar departs 2200. For some this return journey is inconvenient as passengers are not let off at Dar es Salaam until 0600, when Customs open. However, tourists are accommodated in comfortable, fully carpeted, a/c compartments, and provided with mattresses to sleep on until 0600. A good option for budget travellers as the fare is only US$20 each way and you save on accommodation for one night.

Directory

Banks

All the banks listed have ATMs, though some may only accept Visa cards. **Standard Chartered**, in the Plaza on Sokoine Dr near Askari Monument, and at International House on corner of Garden Av and Shaaban Robert St. **Barclay's**, TDFL Building, Ohio St, and at the Slipway. **CitiBank**, Peugeot House, Upanga Rd. **National Bank of Commerce**, Samora Av and corner of Sokoine Dr and Azikiwe St. Bank hours are 0830-1500 on weekdays and 0830-1130 on Sat.

Embassies and consulates

You can usually be sure that diplomatic missions will be open in the mornings between 0900 and 1200. Some have afternoon opening, and some do not open every day. Even when a mission is officially closed, the staff will usually be helpful if something has to be done in an emergency.
Austria, Samora Av, T022-2112900. **Belgium**, 5 Ocean Rd, T022-2112688. **Burundi**, 1007 Lugalo Rd, T022-2117615. **Canada**, 38 Mirambo St, Garden Av, T022-2112831-5, dslam@ dfait-maeci.gc.ca. **Denmark**, Ghana Av, T022-2113887-8. **Egypt**, 24 Garden Av, T022- 2113591. **Finland**, Mirambo St/ Garden Av, T022-2119170. **France**, 34 Ali Hassan Mwinyi Rd, T022-2666021-3. **Germany**, Umoja House, Garden Av/Mirambo St, T022-2117409-15, www.daressalam.diplo.de. **Ireland**, 353 Toure Dr, T022-2602355. **Italy**, 316 Lugalo Rd, T022-2115935/6. **Japan**, 299

Ali Hassan. Mwinyi Rd, T022-2115827/9. **Kenya**, Plot 1018 Upanga Rd, T022-2701747. **Malawi**, 6th Fl, NIC Life House, Samora Av, T022-2113240-41. **Mozambique**, 25 Garden Av, T022-2116502. **Netherlands**, New ATC Bldg, Ohio St, 2nd Fl, T022-2118566. **Norway**, 160 Mirambo St, T022-2113366. **Rwanda**, 32 Ali Hassan Mwinyi Rd, T022-2115889. **South Africa**, 1338 Mwaya Rd, Oyster Bay, T022- 2601800. **Spain**, 99B Kinondoni Rd, T022- 2666936. **Sudan**, 64 Ali Hassan Mwinyi Rd, T022-2117641. **Sweden**, Extelcoms Bldg, Samora Av, T022-2111265. **Switzerland**, 79 Kinondoni Rd, T022-2666008/9. **Uganda**, Extelcom Bldg, Samora Av, T022-2117646/7, 0830-1600. **UK**, Umoja House, Garden Av, T022-2110101. **USA**, 25 Msasani Rd, off Kinondoni Rd, T022-2666010/5. **Zambia**, Ohio St/Sokoine Dr, T022-2118481-2. **Zimbabwe**, NIC Life House, 6th Flr, Sokoine Dr, T022-2116789.

Foreign exchange bureaux

These are to be found in almost every street, and are especially common in the area between Samora Av and Jamhuri St. They are usually open 0900-1700 Mon-Fri and 0900-1300 on Sat. Some are also open on Sun morning. Rates vary and it is worth shopping around. Tanzania's sole agent for *American Express* is **Rickshaw Travel**, at the Royal Palm Hotel, T022-2114094, www.rickshaw travels.com, who will issue TCs to card-holders. Open weekdays and Sat and Sun mornings. **Western Union** money transfer is available at the Tanzanian Postal Bank, on Samora Av, and at the General Post Office on Azikiwe St.

Internet

There are hundreds of internet cafés all over the city centre and you will not have a problem accessing your email. The cost of internet access has fallen considerably over the last few years, and is available for less than US$0.50 per hour, although it is usually quite slow. Some places offer additional services such as printing or scanning.

Libraries

Alliance Française, behind Las Vegas Casino, T022-2131406, library facilities, French TV news, occasional concerts and recitals, open Mon-Fri, 1000-1800. **British Council**, on the corner of Ohio St and Samora Av, T022- 2116574-6. Has an excellent library, with reference, lending, newspapers and magazines. **National Central Library**, Bibi Titi Mohamed Rd, near the Maktaba St intersection, T022-2150048/9.

Medical services

Hospitals The main hospital is **Muhimbili Hospital**, off United Nations Rd, northwest of the centre towards Msimbazi Creek, T022-2151298. **Oyster Bay Medical Clinic**, follow the signs along Haile Selassie Rd, T022-2667932, is an efficient and accessible small private medical centre. **Aga Khan Hospital**, Ocean Rd at the junction with Ufukoni Rd, T022-2115151-3. All these hospitals are well equipped and staffed. See also **Flying Doctors Society of Africa**, page 20. **Pharmacies** In all shopping centres, and small dispensaries are also found in the main residential areas.

Post

The **main post office** is on Azikiwe St, and it's here that you will find the poste restante. There's a small charge for letters collected. Other offices are on Sokoine Dr, behind the bus stand on Morogoro Rd; and Libya St. Post offices are generally crowded. **Courier services**: There are several branches of the major courier companies around town which will collect. **DHL** at DHL House, 12B Nyerere Rd, T022-2861000/4, www.africa.dhl.com. **Fedex**, T022-2123112. **TNT**, T022-2124585.

Telephone

International calls and faxes can be made from the telecommunications office near the main post office on Simu St. There are also many private telephone/fax offices all over town. Hotels will usually charge up to 3 times the actual cost.

Useful addresses

Immigration Corner of Ohio St and Garden Av, T022-2112174, open Mon-Fri, 0730-1530. **Police** The main police station is on Gerazani St near the railway station, T022-2115507. Also stations on Upanga Rd on the city side of Selander Bridge, T022-2120818; on Ali Hassan Mwinyi Rd at the junction with Old Bagamoyo Rd (Oyster Bay), T022-2667322/3; and at the port T022-2116287. For emergencies, police, ambulance and fire brigade, T112.

Coastal Tanzania

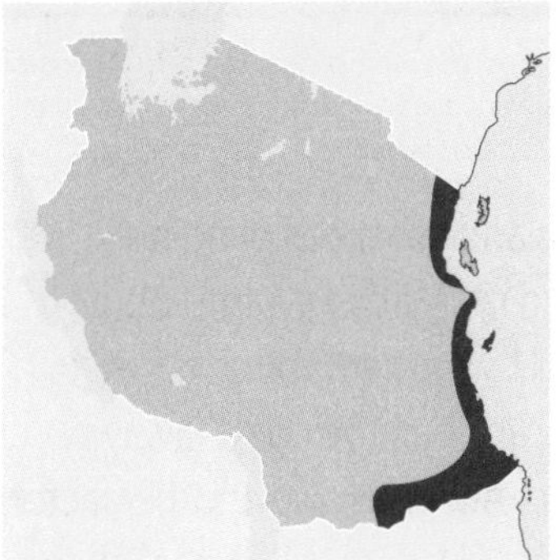

Footprint features

Introduction

The 800 km of the Tanzanian mainland coast has blindingly white beaches, coconut groves and mangrove swamps, but much of it is virtually undiscovered by modern tourism. Generally overlooked in favour of Zanzibar, the coast (away from Dar es Salaam) is rarely visited. Access is also another factor as the roads to the north and south of Dar are still in poor shape in many places. With little development of any kind (tourist or otherwise), the coast has just a few farming and fishing villages dotted along its shoreline with nearby coral reefs and natural lagoons. Yet there are vivid reminders of the Swahili past to be found and the coast has a bloody and fascinating history. Palatial remnants of Persian and Omani kingdoms still remain and ancient mosques dating from the 12th century testify to the far-reaching roots of Islam. Bagamoyo was the last point reached by slave caravans before shipment and fortified houses still stand, as does the tree under which they were brought to be sold. There is also the fading grandeur of Tanga in the north, and the relatively undiscovered island of Mafia, location of the newly-gazetted marine park and a wonderful place for scuba diving. Towards the Mozambique border there is the historic ruined city of Kilwa.

Things are beginning to change, however, and there is now a clutch of upmarket beach resorts and a new road from Dar es Salaam to Bagamoyo has recently been completed thanks to an EU grant. In the future this part of Tanzania could attract many more visitors.

★ Don't miss

1 **Bagamoyo** Explore the historic ruined town on a guided tour for an informative insight into the history of the Swahili coast, page 82.

2 **Saadani National Park** Newly gazetted, this is the only game park with an ocean frontage – if you're lucky you may spot animals on the beach, page 89.

3 **Pole Pole Bungalow Resort** Meaning 'slowly-slowly' in Kiswahili, this resort on Mafia Island is one of the top beach resorts in the world. Here you will get the sense that you have the whole island – and Indian Ocean – to yourself, page 107.

4 **Kilwa** Take an adventurous excursion to the south coast and explore these 13th-century ruined settlements surrounded by mangrove swamps and glorious beaches; another testament to the Swahili civilization, page 108.

5 **Swahili cuisine** Enjoy the coastal cooking, especially the seafood: fish and prawn curries are laced with coconut milk and game fish include red snapper and tuna.

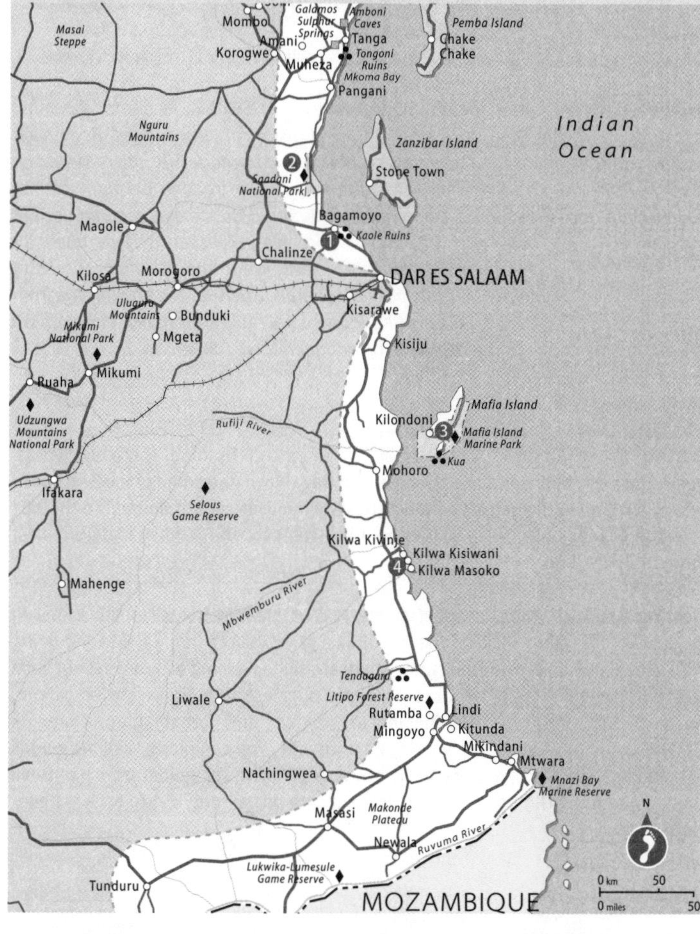

North coast

Travel along the coast has improved over the last few years thanks to some ongoing major road building supported by foreign aid to promote the coastal region. There has been major resurfacing work around Kilwa and from Dar es Salaam to Bagamoyo there is a new tar road. North of the Bagamoyo however, the road deteriorates into a sandy track, and access to the coastal towns of Tanga and Pangani is easiest from the inland road. From Dar this goes the 109 km to the junction at Chalinze before heading north to Moshi and Arusha, off which are roads that go back towards the coast. There is also good access along this route from Dar to Mombasa in Kenya and the journey can easily be made in a day by bus. To the south from Dar es Salaam to the Mozambique border is a road that is so bad that it is only passable in the dry season and then only in a 4x4 vehicle, though buses still attempt this route. Flights connect Dar es Salaam, and in some cases Zanzibar, to Tanga and Mafia Island.

The islands of the Zanzibar Archipelago are covered in the next chapter. Mafia Island, on the other hand, which is not part of the archipelago and is administered from mainland Tanzania is covered in this chapter.

Bagamoyo

→ *Phone code: 023. Colour map 1, grid B5. www.bagamoyo.com.*

Bagamoyo, whose name means 'bury my heart' in Swahili, is one of the most fascinating towns in East Africa. With a host of historical associations, Bagamoyo was recently designated as Tanzania's seventh World Heritage Site and is the oldest town in Tanzania. The town has seen Arab and Indian traders, German colonial government and Christian missionaries and although Bagamoyo is no longer the busy port city that it once was, Tanzania's Department of Antiquities is working to revitalize it and maintain dozens of ruins. It is quite possible to make a very interesting day trip from Dar es Salaam (the journey only takes an hour), although an overnight stay at one of the resorts is recommended. ▸▸ *For Sleeping, Eating and other listings, see pages 89-91.*

Altitude: sea level
Position: 6°20'S 38°30'E

Ins and outs

Getting there About 70 km north of Dar es Salaam by road, there are several *dala-dala* a day between Dar es Salaam and Bagamoyo and some of the Bagomoyo hotels offer a shuttle service to their guests. From Dar get a *dala-dala* to the bus stand at Mwenge and swap to another to Bagamoyo. The journey shouldn't cost more than US$1.50.

Getting around There is not a single taxi at present but all destinations in Bagamoyo are within walking distance. It is a good idea to hire a guide and being with a local person provides security. There are signs warning of muggers, but local residents suggest this is to boost the guide business. It is as well to be careful, however. Mr. Pazi runs the **Bagamoyo Tourism and Rehabilitation Network (BATREN)** and he is presently working on a website. You can pick one of his guides at either the Holy Ghost Mission or Livingstone's church. The guides have been well trained and bring Old Bagamoyo to life. Expect to pay around US$10 for a 3-4 hour walking tour.

History

The coastal area opposite Zanzibar was first settled by fishermen and cultivators. Towards the end of the 18th century, 12 or so Muslim diwans arrived to settle, build dwellings and establish their families and retinues of slaves. These diwans were all related to Shomvi la Magimba from Oman. They prospered through levying taxes whenever a cow was slaughtered, or a shark or other large fish caught, as well as on all salt produced at Nunge, about 3 km north of Bagamoyo.

Bagamoyo's location as a mainland port close to Zanzibar led to its development as a centre for caravans and an expansion of commerce in slaves and ivory soon followed. Although the slave trade officially ended in 1873, slaves continued to be sold and traded in Bagamoyo until the end of the 19th century. During this time, it was not uncommon to see hundreds of slaves walking through the streets of Bagamoyo chained together by the neck. There was also growing trade in sun-dried fish, gum copal and the salt from Nunge. Copra (from coconuts) was also important, and was used to make soap. A boat-building centre was established, which supplied craft to other coastal settlements.

In 1880 the population of the town was around 5,000 but this was augmented by a substantial transient population in residence after completing a caravan or undertaking preparations prior to departure. The numbers of those temporarily in town could be considerable. In 1889, after the slave trade had been suppressed, significantly reducing the numbers passing, it was still recorded that 1,305 caravans, involving 41,144 people, left for the interior.

The social composition of the town was varied. There were the initial Muslim Shomvi and the local Zaramo and Doe. Among the earliest arrivals were Hindus from India, involving themselves in administration, coconut plantations and boat-building. Muslim Baluchis, a people based in Mombasa and Zanzibar, and for the most part mercenary soldiers, also settled and were involved in trade, financing caravans and land-owning. Other Muslim sects were represented, among them the Ismailis who settled in 1840 and by 1870 numbered 137. A handful of Sunni Muslims from Zanzibar established shops in Bagamoyo, some Parsees set up as merchants, and a small group of Catholic Goans was engaged in tailoring and retailing.

In 1888 the German East Africa Company signed a treaty with the Sultan of Zanzibar, Seyyid Khalifa, which allowed the company to collect customs duties along the coast. The Germans rapidly made their presence felt by ordering the Sultan's representative (the Liwali) to lower the Sultan's flag and, on being refused, they axed down the flag-pole. Later in the year a dispute between a member of the company and a townsman culminated in the latter being shot. The Usagara trading house of the company was beseiged by irate townspeople, 200 troops landed from the *SS Moewe*, and over 100 local people were killed.

Further resentment was incurred when the Germans set about registering land and property, demanding proof of ownership. As this was impossible for most residents there was widespread fear that property would be confiscated.

One of the diwans, Bomboma, organized local support. They enlisted the help of Bushiri bin Salim al-Harthi who had earlier led Arabs against the Germans in Tabora. Bushiri had initial success. Sections of Bagamoyo were burned and Bushiri formed up in Nzole about 6 km southwest of the town ready for an assault. The German government now felt compelled to help the company and Hermann von Wissmann was appointed to lead an infantry force comprising Sudanese and Zulu troops. Admiral Denhardt, commanding the German naval forces, played for time by initiating negotiations with Bushiri whose demands included being made governor of the region from Dar es Salaam up to Pangani, payment of 4,000 rupees a month (about US$10,000 in present-day values), and the right to keep troops.

By May 1889 Wissmann had consolidated his forces and built a series of fortified block houses. He attacked Nzole and Bushiri fled. The alliance of the diwans and

Mangroves

Up and down the coast of East Africa you will come across stretches of mangrove forests. Ecologically these can be described as evergreen saline swamp forests and their main constituents are the mangroves Rhizophora, Ceriops and Bruguiera. These are all described as viviparous, that is the seeds germinate or sprout when the fruits are still attached to the parent plant. Mangrove forests support a wide range of other plants and animals including a huge range of birds, insects and fish.

Economically mangrove forests are an important source of building poles, known on the coast as *boriti*, which were once exported in large quantities to the Arabian Gulf. Their main property is that they are resistant to termite attack. Mangrove bark is also used as a tanning material and charcoal can be obtained from mangrove wood. As with so many natural resources in East Africa, care needs to be taken in the use of mangrove forests. Their over-exploitation could lead to the delicate balance that is found in the forests being upset, with serious consequences for these coastal regions.

Bushiri weakened, and in June the Germans retook Saadani and in July, Pangani. Bushiri was captured and executed at Pangani in December. Bomboma, and another of the diwans leading the resistance, Marera, were also both executed, and other diwans were deposed and replaced by collaborators who had assisted the Germans.

It was now clear that the German government intended to extend their presence and, in October 1890, rights to the coast were formally purchased from the Sultan of Zanzibar for 4 million German marks.

In early 1891 German East Africa became a formal colony, but in April it was decided to establish Dar es Salaam as the capital. Commercial activity in Bagamoyo revived, and in the last decade of the century rebuilding began with the construction of new stone buildings including a customs house and the Boma, which served as an administrative centre.

The caravan trade resumed and there was a further influx of Indians together with the arrival of Greeks who established a European hotel. William O'Swald, the Hamburg trading company, arrived and the company Hansing established vanilla plantations at Kitopeni and Hurgira. An important Koran school was established in the town. Yet, despite these developments Bagamoyo was destined for steady decline: its harbour was unsuitable for deep draught steamships and no branch of the railway was built to serve the port. The ending of the German rule further reduced commercial presence in the town, and the last century saw Bagamoyo decline steadily, lacking even a sealed road to link it to Dar es Salaam. These days, thanks to the new tar road from Dar es Salaam tourism has boomed considerably and there are now a number of good quality beach resorts.

Sights

★ Old Bagamoyo

On the south approach to the town, on the road from Kaole, is the fully restored **Old Fort** (sometimes referred to as the Old Prison). It is the oldest surviving building in Bagamoyo having been started by Abdallah Marhabi around 1860, and extended and strengthened by Sultan Baghash after 1870, and then by the German colonialists. It was used as a police post until 1992. Initially one of its functions was to hold slaves until they could be shipped to Zanzibar. It is said there is an underground passage through which the slaves were herded to dhows on the shore, although this passage is not apparent today. It's a particularly handsome building, whitewashed, three storeys high, and with buttresses and battlements and an enclosed courtyard. Today it is the local headquarters to the Department of Antiquities and you can visit it, no fee.

Off to the right on the path to *Badeco Beach Hotel* is the **German cemetery** with some 20 graves dating from 1889/1890, and most are of Germans killed during the uprising led by Bushiri in those years (see page 83). A German deed of freedom for a slave is reproduced on a tree. The cemetery is well tended, surrounded by a coral wall. In the grounds of the *Badeco Beach Hotel* is the site of the tree reputedly used by the German administration for executions. The site is marked by a plaque.

Continuing along India Street on the left is an old two-storey building, **Liku House**, with an awning supported by slender iron columns and a central double door. This served as the first administrative headquarters for the Germans from 1888 until the Boma was completed in 1897. Emin Pasha stayed there in 1889.

The **Boma** is an impressive two-storey building topped by crenellations, constructed in a U-shape. There are pointed arches on the first floor and rounded arches on the ground floor. This was the German administrative centre from 1897, and it currently serves as the headquarters for the district commissioner. The building is

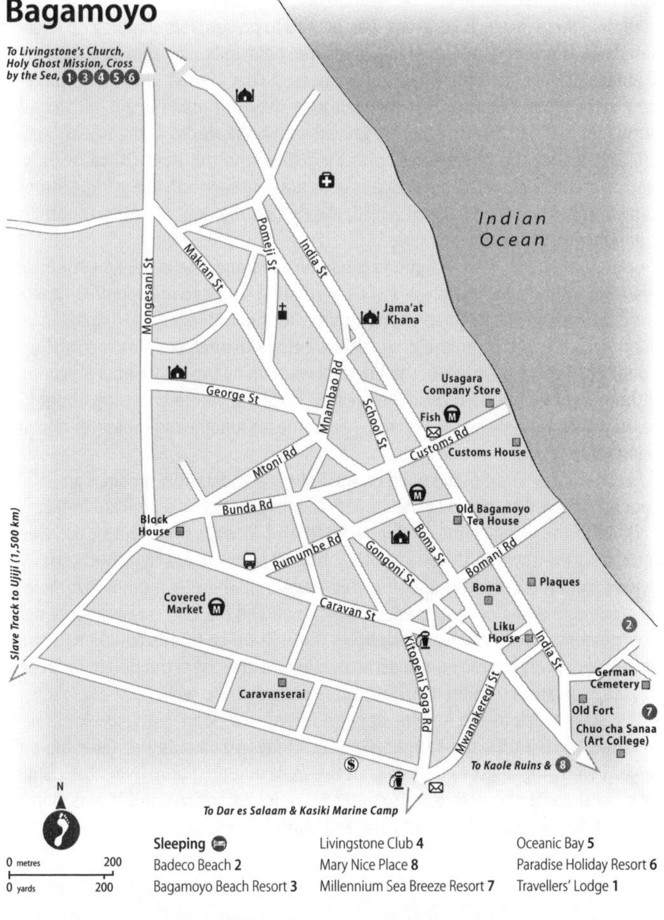

undergoing some restoration, and it is possible to look round. On the inland side of the building is a well constructed by Sewa Haji.

On the shore side is a semi-circular levelled area on which was a monument with brass commemorative plaques erected by the Germans. With the fall of Bagamoyo to the British, the monument was razed and replaced with the present construction which commemorates the departure of Burton and Speke to Lake Tanganyika from nearby Kaole in 1857. The old German plaques have been reset in the walls which support the levelled area, on the shore side. To the left is an Arabic two-storey building fronted by six columns, a fretted veranda and curved arch windows, said to be the **Old Bagamoyo Tea House**, and thought to be one of the oldest buildings in the town, constructed by Abdallah Marhabi in 1860. In front of the Boma is the **Uhuru Monument**, celebrating Tanzania's independence in 1961, and a bandstand.

Continuing north along India Street there is a particularly fine residential house on the right with columns and arched windows just before Customs Road. This leads down to the **Customs House**, built in 1895 by Sewa Haji and rented to the Germans. It is a double-storey lime-washed building with an open veranda on the first floor, buttresses and arched windows. It looks on to a walled courtyard and is currently undergoing restoration. Opposite the Customs House are the ruins of the **Usagara Company Store** built in 1888 with the arrival of the German commercial presence. The unusual construction had stone plinths on which were mounted cast-iron supports for the timber floor, raised to keep the stores dry. The cast-iron supports have cups surrounding them in which kerosene was poured to prevent rats climbing up to eat the stored grain. At one end of the building is a tower, held up by a tree growing through it.

Halfway down Customs Road is the covered **Fish Market** with stone tables for gutting fish. When not used for this purpose they are marked out with chalk so informal games like checkers can be played with bottle-tops. At the top of Customs Road, just before the intersection with India Street is the **Post Office**, with a fine carved door and a blue-painted upstairs veranda. Further north along India Street is a series of Arabic buildings, one of which, the first on the right after the square to the left, is being restored as a hotel.

Continuing north, on the right, is the **Jama'at Khana**, the Ismaili mosque, which dates from 1880, double-storeyed with a veranda and carved doors. On the right beyond the mosque is the hospital, now part of Muhimbili Teaching Hospital in Dar es Salaam, which is based on the original Sewa Haji Hospital, constructed in 1895. On the death of Sewa Haji in 1896, the hospital was run by the Holy Ghost Mission, and then from 1912 by the Germans. The present hospital, where goats loll about in the covered walkways between the wards, has some handsome old buildings and some more modern blocks.

At the northern end of the town on the right is a substantial **mosque** and Muslim school with curved steps up to the carved door over which is a delicate fretted grill.

Close to the intersection of Sunda Road and Mongesani Street at the western approach to the town is the white **Block House**, constructed in 1889 by Hermann Wissman during the Bushiri uprising (see page 83). There is a mangrove pole and coral stone roof and an outside ladder, which enabled troops to man the roof behind the battlements. The walls have loopholes through which troops could fire, standing on low internal walls, which doubled as seating, to give them the height to fire down on their adversaries. Behind the Block House is a disused well.

The **slave track** to the interior departed from this point – a 1,500 km trail that terminated at Ujiji on Lake Tanganyika. Off Caravan Street is the **Caravanserai**, a courtyard with single-storey buildings at the front and a square, two-storey building with a veranda at the centre (the corner of which is collapsing). It was here that preparations were made to fit out caravans to the interior.

Bagamoyo Art College

The Bagamoyo Art College, also known as the Chuo cha Sanaa is a school for the arts where music, drama, dance and painting are taught. The college, established in 1981, is the most famous art institute in Tanzania and one of very few training institutions in Africa offering practical training in the arts. Most students are Tanzanian, but there are several from Europe, America and the Far East. Students learn traditional Tanzanian drumming, sculpture, carving and painting, as well as acting and stage management. Other courses cover instrument manufacture, music improvization, and dance. The main buildings are located along the road to Kaole to the south of Bagamoyo. They are a mixture of a Viking house and a traditional African home, recently constructed with help from a Swedish Aid Project, and are very impressive. The main building has a Greek-style open amphitheatre, with proscenium stage covered by a 15-m high thatched canopy. The amphitheatre stage backs on to a second theatre area, which is roofed and enclosed. Attached to the stage are workshops and offices. Students can be observed in the area round the dormitories practising their skills. Visitors are welcome to observe the training.

At weekends there are entertainments including music, dance and drama performed by the Bagamoyo Players. They are well attended and the atmosphere is excellent. The players do not only perform but are also teachers at the college. There are 24 teachers for 45 students. Ask at the college for times and programmes. There is an annual arts festival that usually is held in Bagamoyo in the last week of September, which includes performances, exhibitions and workshops.

ⓘ *Bagamoyo College of Arts, T023-2440032, www.college-of-arts.org*.

Livingstone's Church

This is a simple construction with a tin roof, curved arch windows and wooden benches. Its formal name is the Anglican Church of the Holy Cross. Above the entrance is the sign 'Through this door Dr David Livingstone passed', referring to the fact that his body was kept in the church prior to it being returned to England.

Cross by the Sea

There's a monument in green marble surmounted by a cross on the path leading to the sea from Livingstone's Church. It marks the spot where, in 1868, Father Antoine Horner of the French Holy Ghost Fathers crossed from Zanzibar (where they had operated a mission since 1860) and stepped ashore to establish the first Christian church on the mainland.

Holy Ghost Mission

Opposite the path to the Cross by the Sea is **Mango Tree Drive**, which was established in 1871 as the approach to the Mission. A statue of the Sacred Heart, erected in 1887, stands in front of the **Fathers' House** which was begun in 1873 – the third storey finally added in 1903. In 1969 the building was taken over by MANTEP as a training centre for educational management.

Behind the Fathers' House is the **First Church**, construction of which started in 1872. It comprises a stone tower topped with arches with a cross at the centre and crosses on the pediments at each corner. The main building is a simple rectangular structure with a tin roof, unusually behind and to the side of the tower so that the tower sits at one corner.

It was here on 24 February 1874 that the body of David Livingstone was brought by the missionary's African followers, Sisi and Chuma, who had carried their master 1,500 km from Ujiji. Speke, Burton, Grant, Stanley, Peters, Emin Pasha and Wissmann all visited the church at one time or another.

Following the path to the right of the First Church is a cemetery where the early missionaries are buried. Further down this path is a small shrine built by freed slaves in 1876 with the sign 'Salamnus Maria' picked out in flowers. A great baobab tree, planted in 1868, stands to the side of the the First Church. At the base can be seen the links of the chain where Mme de Chevalier, a mission nurse, tethered her donkey.

The **New Church**, constructed of coral blocks, begun in 1910 and completed in 1914, stands in front of the First Church. A small iron cross commemorates the centenary, in 1968, of the Holy Ghost Mission in Bagamoyo.

The **Mission Museum** is housed in the **Sisters' Building**. The displays present a history of Bagamoyo and there are relics and photographs from the slave period. One intriguing exhibit is the uniform, presented by HA Schmit in 1965, that he wore during the East African Campaign under von Lettow (see page 356). Adjacent to the museum is a **craft workshop** with *Ufundi* ('craftsmen') picked out in flowers.

One of the main activities of the Holy Ghost Mission was to purchase slaves and present them with their freedom. A certificate of freedom was provided by the German authorities. These freed slaves had originally been captured hundreds of kilometres away in the hinterland, and the Mission undertook to rehabilitate them in **Freedom Village** just to the north of the main Mission buildings.

Kaole Ruins → *Colour map 1, grid B5.*

The Kaole Ruins are 5 km south of Bagamoyo, along the road past Chuo Cha Sanaa (Bagamoyo Art College), on the coastal side of the present-day village of Kaole. The site consists of the ruins of two mosques and a series of about 30 tombs, set among palm trees. Some of the tombs have stone pillars up to 5 m high. The older of the two mosques ('A' on the site plan) dates from some time between the third and fourth centuries AD and is thought to mark one of the earliest contacts of Islam with Africa, before the main settlement took place. The remains of a vaulted roof constructed from coral with lime mortar can be seen, which formed the *mbirika* at the entrance. Here ceremonial ablutions took place, taking water from the nearby well. There is some buttressing with steps that allowed the muezzin access to the roof to call the faithful to prayer. The recess (*kibula*) on the east side, nearest to Mecca, has faint traces of an inscription on the vaulting.

It is quite possible to walk to the ruins, but it's a good idea to take a guide for security.

The stone pillars that mark some of the tombs were each surmounted by a stone 'turban' and the remains of some of these can be seen on the ground. Delicate porcelain bowls with light green glaze were set in the side of the pillars and the indentations can be seen. The bowls, identified as celadon made in China in the 14th century and the main indication of the likely age of the structure, have been removed for safekeeping to the National Museum in Dar es Salaam. Some of the tombs have frames of dressed coral and weathered obituary inscriptions. Bodies would have been laid on the right side, with the face toward Mecca.

Mosque 'B' is of later construction and has been partially restored. It is similar to the triple-domed mosque at Kilwa Kisiwani (see page 110) in style, and it is thought that the builder may well have been the same person.

The community that gave rise to these ruins would have been founded during the Muslim period AD 622-1400. The first Muslim colonies were established from AD 740 by sea-borne migrations from the Persian Gulf down the East African coast as far as Sofala, the area round the Zambezi River. The settlement at Koale would have traded mangrove poles (see page 84), sandalwood, ebony and ivory. It is suggested that Koale might have had several hundred inhabitants. The dwellings would have used timber in their construction and would therefore have been less durable than the all-stone mosques and tombs. As they were on more fertile soil inland, they rapidly became overgrown when the dwellings collapsed. The settlement went into gradual decline as the shore became more densely packed with mangroves, making its use by dhows difficult, and commercial activity shifted to Bagamoyo.

★ Saadani National Park → *Colour map 1, grid B5.*  » p90

About 70 km north of Bagamoyo, Saadani was gazetted as a National Park in 2003 and it is the only national park in East Africa with ocean frontage. Some of the animals come down to the beach, especially in the early morning, and you may see elephants frolicking in the sand and sometimes even venturing into the crashing surf, and this makes Saadani one of the more special and unique parks to visit in Tanzania. Its boundaries have been expanded to include land north of the Mligaji, which contains the only permanent elephant population in the area, as well as sable antelope. It also incorporates the Zaraninge forest, noted for its variety of indigenous vegetation and animal and birdlife, and land south of the Wami river. The total protected area now covers over 1000 sq km and the park headquarters are based at Mkwaja Ranch. It has plentiful game including giraffe, hartebeest, waterbuck, wildebeest, eland, buffalo, hippo, crocodile, reedbuck, black and white colobus monkey and warthog. Also present but harder to see are lion, leopard, elephant, sable antelope, greater kudu and the Beisa oryx. To the north of the reserve is a green turtle breeding beach and the only lodge in the park, *A Tent With a View Safari Lodge* (see Sleeping) has started its own turtle hatchery to help conserve this endangered species. A particular highlight are the thousands of flamingos found in the salt marshes in the Wami River estuary. There is also an extensive range of bush, river and sea birds.

Ins and outs

Generally the park is accessible all year round, but the access roads are sometimes impassable during Apr-May. The best game viewing is in Jan-Feb and from Jun-Aug. Charter flights can be arranged through the lodge from Zanzibar or Dar es Salaam and there is a possibility of scheduled flights in the future. Fares are expensive, however, and start from US$300 from/to Dar each way and US$200 from/to Zanzibar. To get there by road used to be very difficult, but thanks to the new tar road to Bagamoyo, the park is only 60 km north of Bagamoyo on a sand track. *A Tent with a View Safaris* operate a shuttle car service between Dar and Sadaani for US$150 each way. Alternatively many of the resorts in Bagamoyo offer good value day trips by boat or vehicle. The entrance fee to the reserve is US$20 per day.

Sleeping and eating

Bagamoyo *p82, map p85*

Bagamoyo is in a glorious location, with a splendid, curved, palm-fringed beach. There are a few beach hotel rooms around town, and it is advisable to book as they are increasingly becoming popular with European holiday makers and residents from Dar. Currently the hotels are all good value and most offer full board package rates. For restaurants and bars, the hotels are your best bet but there are some snack bars near the covered market on Caravan St.

L **Lazy Lagoon Island**, private luxury island off the coast, a 20-min boat ride across the water from a jetty close to Mbegani Fisheries (a private airstrip is nearby), 8 km east of Bagamoyo. Bookings through *Foxes of Africa*, Dar es Salaam, T022-2440194, www.tanzaniasafaris.info. A beautiful thatch and wood construction on a perfect swathe of beach, 12 bandas with en suite bathrooms, swimming pool, spacious lounge and restaurant area linked to the rooms by a nature trail through the indigenous forest.

Price includes all meals, seafood is a speciality and dining is outside with an exceptional view of the lights of Bagamoyo in the distance. Snorkelling, kayaking, windsurfing and sailing, fishing and boat trips cost extra.

A-B **Livingstone Club**, T023-2440059/80, www.livingstone-club.com. Fairly new complex 2 km to the north of town. 40 a/c rooms with fridge and minibar in 10 brick cottages with thatched roofs in lovely gardens. The restaurant has an international menu. Facilities include a swimming pool, tennis courts, watersports and it is possible to arrange local excursions. 10% discount if you book online. Rates for a double are bed and breakfast US$95, half board US$120, full board US$140. Italian spoken.

B **Millennium Sea Breeze Resort**, adjacent to Bagamoyo Art College, T023-2440201/3, www.millennium.co.tz. Accommodation in attractive double storey thatched rondavaals with wrought iron staircases, big beds, satellite TV, minibar. Set in pleasant grounds, with a swimming pool, extensive buffets for lunch and dinner, and 2 bars. Dhow trips available. Full and half board rates available.

B **Oceanic Bay Hotel**, T023-2440181, www.oceanicbay.com. Very smart new establishment built in 2003 with 40 a/c rooms in double-storey thatched and whitewashed buildings, all of them with satellite TV, room service, minibar and veranda with beach view, internet café, Olympic size swimming pool, beach bar, restaurant, German spoken.

B **Paradise Holiday Resort**, 1 km north of Bagamoyo, T023-2440000, www.paradise resort.net. 83 a/c rooms in double thatched whitewashed building with own bathrooms and satellite TV. Swimming pool, 2 restaurants and bars, tennis, volleyball and basketball courts, gym, children's playground and watersports are available. Can also arrange trips to Saadani National Park. Good all round family resort.

C **Bagamoyo Beach Resort** (sometimes called 'Gogo'), at the north end of town – continue along India St, T023-2440083, www.bagamoyo.org/bagbeach.htm. French management, a/c or fans, hot water showers, most of the 22 rooms are comfortable but the style is a little uninspired with tin roofs and concrete walls. There are a few traditional- style rooms with thatched roofs, but not facing the ocean. Simple restaurant, plus pleasant open-air bar with thatched roof overlooking beach. Sports facilities include windsurfing, snorkelling, diving, golf, tennis and volleyball.

C **Kasiki Marine Camp**, approximately 7 km east of Bagamoyo along the road to Dar es Salaam, T0744-278590 (mob) , www.bagamoyo.org/kasiki.htm. Quiet resort with 6 bungalows, the price includes breakfast, or full board accommodation at twice the cost, US$58 B&B/US$108 full board. The restaurant specializes in Italian cuisine and you can buy items such as home-made pesto from the Italian chef. Can organize boat trips, watersports and fishing, and there are massages and fitness classes on offer.

C **Travellers' Lodge**, at north end of town on India St, T023-2440077, www.bagamoyo.com/travellers-lodge. Good value small bungalows with shared facilities, or pleasant, traditional thatched-style self-contained rooms, with a/c or fans. Excellent bar, restaurant serving plenty of seafood, watersports. Camping is available in the grounds.

C-E **Badeco Beach Hotel**, T023-2440018, www.badecobeachhotel.com. Glorious location right on the beach at south end of town, small, with 15 rooms, 9 self-contained, in thatched bandas. The garden is planted with bougainvillaea. Small restaurant, but has an excellent and imaginative seafood menu, open air disco at the weekend. Room rates are US$15-30 including breakfast, camping available.

D-E **Mary Nice Place**, maryniceplace@yahoo.com. Several clean rooms, some with shower/toilet, budget accomodation, about 200 m from Bagamoyo College of Arts near the police station, no beach view. The owner Mary Chibwana is a teacher at the college and a member of the Bagamoyo Players.

Saadani National Park *p89*

L **A Tent with a View Safari Lodge**, bookings through *A Tent with a View Safaris*, in Dar, T022-2110507, www.saadani.com. This is the

For an explanation of the sleeping and eating price codes used in this guide, see inside the front cover. Other relevant information is found in Essentials pages 31-34.

only lodge in the park with 8 tented bandas with en suite bathrooms, elegantly perched on stilts individually spaced out along the beach and large balconies with hammocks, decorated in bright colours. Activities include walking safaris through the bush and on the beach, birdwatching by canoe on the Mafue River, game drives and a boat safari on the Wami River. A cultural tour offers an opportunity to meet the local fishing community in Saadani village. There are 2 rates: US$175 per person per night sharing full board, with the option of paying for activities separately depending on what you want to do, or US$265 per person per night sharing including all safari activities.

Shopping

Bagamoyo *p82, map p85*
There are some small general and pharmacy stores on School St. The covered market on Caravan St is excellent for fruit, vegetables, meat and dried fish. Fresh fish at fish market on Customs Rd. There is a curio stall with crafts on sale at the **Badeco Beach Hotel**, and some of the other resorts have curio shops.

Activities and tours

Bagamoyo *p82, map p85*
Marine fishing can be arranged through Badeco Beach Hotel and there is a full range of watersports available and most of the resorts. **Football matches** at ground on road to Kaole, south of town.

Transport

Bagamoyo *p82, map p85*
Bus Several *dala-dala* a day leave from the bus stand opposite the covered market on Caravan St. To **Dar es Salaam** costs US$3 and takes 1-2 hrs.

Directory

Bagamoyo *p82, map p85*
Banks Foreign exchange bureaux: there are none at present in Bagamoyo. The National Microfinance Bank on Dar es Salaam Rd, opposite the post office will change money as will the resorts, though these tend to offer poor exchange rates. National Bank of Commerce is off the road to Dar es Salaam to south of town (follow the sign) which has an ATM. Increasingly, many of the resorts are accepting credit cards. **Post office** Customs Rd. **Medical services** Hospital, Bagamoyo District, located on India St. **Useful addresses** Police: at intersection of Caravan St and Boma St at south end of town.

Tanga and around

→ *Phone code: 027. Colour map 1, grid B5.*

Tanga is Tanzania's second biggest seaport and third largest town. It is an attractive place with a sleepy ambiance and many fine German and Asian buildings in its centre. It has a natural deep water harbour and was briefly the German colonial capital following the treaty between the Sultan of Zanzibar and the German East Africa Company. Much of its wealth came from the sisal plantations in the hinterland but with the advent of alternative rope-making fibres this industry has fallen into decline, adversely affecting the region. Nearby places of interest include the enormous Amboni limestone caves, the Shirazi ruins at Tongoni, dating from the 10th century, and offshore coral gardens, consisting of three reefs, Mwamba Wamba, Mwamba Shundo and Fungu Nyama. The Usambara Hills are worth a detour, Lushoto and Amani can be visited either on the way to Tanga, or when travelling to Kilimanjaro and Arusha, and Pangani, on the coast south of Tanga, makes for a decent beach holiday destination. ▸▸ *For Sleeping, Eating and other listings, see pages 99-103.*

Tanga

▸▸ pp99-103

The centre of Tanga (meaning 'sail' in Kiswahili) is a congested grid of roads centred around the bustling market. The buildings along Market Street are old and traffic stained, but the street is a hive of activity of small traders, food kiosks and women carrying bunches of vegetables. There are a number of interesting colonial buildings around Market Street and Independence Avenue. Most are in a poor state of repair, but it's a relaxing and easy walk around the tree lined streets, and easy to imagine that Tanga was very grand in its heyday. It's a very friendly place and lots of men on bicycles bumping in and out of the pot holes will take time to say *jambo*. Further out of town on Hospital Road towards the Yacht Club, are the quieter and more sedate leafy suburbs of the more upmarket residential area, where the large houses look out into the bay from a hill. There are good views to uninhabited Toten Island out in the bay, especially when the tide is low and the yellow sandstone cliffs of the island are exposed.

Altitude: Sea Level
Position: 5°5'S 39°2'E

Ins and outs

Getting there There are scheduled air services between Tanga and Dar es Salaam, Pemba and Zanzibar. Now that passenger rail services between Dar es Salaam and Tanga have been terminated, the only land route to Tanga is by road. Bus services or *dala-dala* take 4-6 hrs from Dar es Salaam and 1-3 hrs from the Kenyan border. ▸▸ *See Transport page 102 for further details.*

Getting around Taxis, buses and *dala-dala* can be found in Uhuru Park. However, most of Tanga is within walking distance. Taxis are advisable after dark. Bikes can be hired at several places including Kiboko campsite and restaurant on Bombo St.

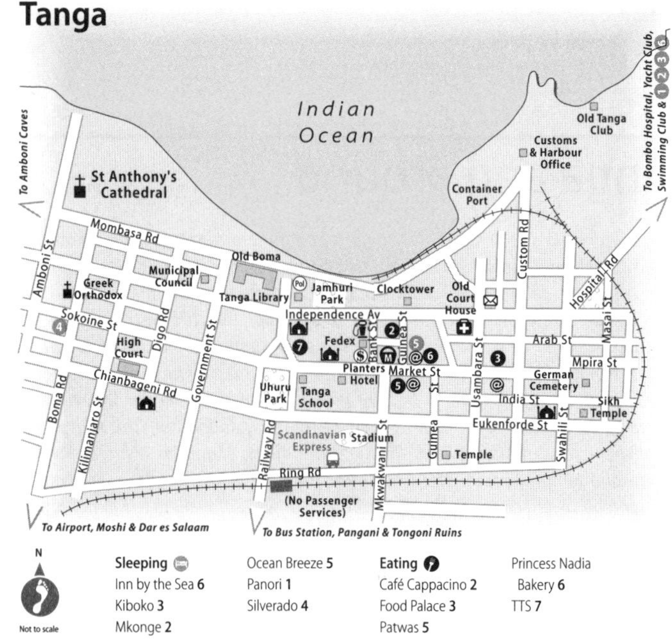

History

Carl Peters and the German East Africa Company arrived in 1885 and in 1888 leased a 16-km wide strip from the Sultan of Zanzibar along the entire coast of what is now Tanzania, between the Ruvuma and the Umba rivers. The Germans appointed agents (calling them *Akidas*), though they were often not of the same tribe as the people they administered, to collect taxes and enforce law and order.

With the advent of European settlement and trade, Somalis arrived, trading in cattle but seldom intermarrying. Islanders from the Comoros also settled here.

Agriculture in the Usambara area expanded and, with the construction of the railway to Moshi, Tanga became a flourishing port. Tanga was the site of a substantial reversal for the British during the First World War. Allied troops, including 8,000 Indian soldiers, found it difficult to disembark through the mangrove swamps and were repulsed by the well-organized German defence and some hostile swarms of bees that spread panic among the attackers. Over 800 were killed and 500 wounded, and the British abandoned substantial quantities of arms and supplies on their withdrawal.

After the eventual German withdrawal from Tanga, the German population was steadily replaced by Greek plantation owners. Tanga's prosperity declined with the collapse in sisal prices in the late 1950s and the large estates were nationalized in 1967. Some have now been privatized, and sisal has made a modest recovery.

The African groups in the Tanga area, excluding those in the coastal belt, number six. The **Pare** who now live in the Pare Hills came originally from the Taveta area of Kenya in the 18th century. The **Zigua** inhabited the area south of Tanga and have a reputation for aggression: Bwana Heri attacked and defeated the force of the sultan of Zanzibar in 1882. The **Nguu** clan to the west occupy the Nguu Hills and the **Ruvu** clan inhabit the Pangani islands. The **Shambaa** are around the Lushoto area and are closely allied with the **Bondei** who occupy the area between Tanga and Pangani.

Sights

The open space in the centre of town is **Uhuru Park**, originally named Selous Square after the celebrated naturalist and hunter (see box, page 324). At the junction of the square with Eukenforde Street are the German buildings of **Tanga School**, the first educational establishment for Africans in Tanzania.

On Market Street to the east of Uhuru Park is **Planters Hotel**. This once grand wooden building is now virtually derelict, but is reputed to have seen wild times as Greek sisal plantation owners came into town for marathon gambling sessions at which whole estates sometimes changed hands. It was an ornate building with arches, columns and plinths. The ground floor had a bar with a huge antique corner cabinet full of miniatures.

Proceeding north across Independence Avenue leads to the **Tanga Library**, originally the King George VI Library. The west wing was opened in 1956 and the east wing in 1958 by the then governor, Sir Edward Twining. There is a courtyard behind with cloisters and Moorish arches. To the west is the **Old Boma**, a substantial structure in typical style. Opposite the Boma is a building from the German period with keyhole-style balustrades. Further to the west down Mombasa Road leading down to the shore is **St Anthony's Cathedral**, a modern 1960s octagonal building with a free-standing bell tower, a school and various mission buildings. On Boma Road there is a small, white **Greek Orthodox church**.

Following Independence Avenue back east you reach the **Clocktower** and the **Post Office**. To the west of the Clocktower is the German Monument in marble, decorated with an eagle and oak leaves, dedicated to the 18 who died in 1889 during the Arab Revolt led by Bushiri (see page 83) and listing the five German naval vessels, under the command of Admiral Denhart, supporting Major Hermann Wissmann on the ground.

Just to the east of the Clocktower are some ruins thought to be part of the fortifications built during the First World War. On the corner of Independence Avenue and Usambara Street is the **Old Court House**, dating from the German period. Today it has been fully restored and serves as the Tanga Medical Hospital. It is a fine, double-fronted building with a Mangalore tiled roof, offices on the mezzanine level, a fluted façade and fretwork over the windows.

Opposite the Court House is **Tanga Ropeworks** where you can see examples of the ropes and twine made from sisal, known as 'white gold' in the 1950s. The **German Cemetery** is on Swahili Street and contains the graves of 16 Germans and 48 Askaris killed in the action of 4-5 November 1914. One of the Askaris is listed as *sakarini* ('crazy drunk'). Also buried here is Mathilde Margarethe Scheel (1902-1987), known as 'Mama Askari', who looked after the welfare interests of the African soldiers of the Schutztruppe (see box, page 357) after Tanganyika became a British protectorate. Crossing over the railway line along Hospital Road to Ocean Drive is the old Tanga Club of the British period. Further east of the centre, the **Bombo Hospital** is a handsome German building, with a three-storey central block, a first-floor veranda overlooking the ocean, a Mangalore tile roof and a gatehouse, now serving as a pharmacy.

Excursions from Tanga

Amboni Caves → *Colour map 1, grid B5.*

ⓘ *Open 0900-1600. The caves are 6 km to the north of Tanga on the road to Lunga Lunga at the Kenyan border. They are badly signposted. The best way to get there is to cycle. It's a good way to meet the local people, the birds are numerous and you might spot a dikdik. Bikes can be hired in town for about US$1 an hour. Tours can be arranged through the Amboni Culture & Guiding Promoters, 1st Floor Majestic Cinema Building, Mkwakwani Rd, T0748-502899 (mob). Kassim and Tegani are very experienced guides and they will cycle with you to the caves. Before entering the mouth of the cave, you are required to write your name in the official record book, which is kept in the tour guide's office. All visitors entering the caves are recorded, in the event of someone becoming lost.*

Formed during the Jurassic Age some 150 million years ago, when reptiles were dominant on land, these natural limestone caves extend over a wide area, lying mostly underground, accessed through openings in the gorges of the Mkilumizi River and the Sisi River. They form the most extensive cave system in East Africa (estimated at over 230 sq km) and there are chambers up to 13 m high with stalactites and stalagmites. A German-Turkish survey in 1994 found that there are 10 separate cave systems, and the longest cave was 900 m. Only one of the caves is used for guided tours.

The location is of great religious significance to local people and offerings to ensure fertility are made in one of the shrines. There are many legends associated with the caves, including beliefs that they form a 400-km underground passage to the foothills of Mount Kilimanjaro. The main cave, known as *Mabavu*, is said to be the home of the Snake God. The Digo people were reputed to dispose of unwanted albino babies in a section of the caves known as the Lake of No Return. The caves were used by the Mau Mau as a refuge during the troubles in Kenya. A guide will escort you round the caves, illuminating the chamber with a burning torch. The caves are home to many thousands of bats (called *popo* in Kiswahili) – watching the '*popo flight*', when the bats fly out of the cave entrance at sunset, is popular.

Warning: take your own powerful torch and go in pairs using a guide. There have been fatalities when people have explored the caves on their own.

On the way back to Tanga you can stop at the **Galamos Sulphur Springs**, 3 km from the caves off the Tanga-Mombasa road. Discovered by a local Greek sisal planter, Christos Galamos, the springs are hot and sulphurous and are said to relieve arthritis and cure skin ailments. A small spa was erected, but it has now fallen into

The legend of the Shirazi migration

Ali ben Sultan Hasan of Shiraz in Persia (now Iran) had a dream in AD 975 in which a rat with jaws of iron devoured the foundations of his house. He took this as a sign that his community was to be destroyed. The court in Shiraz ridiculed the notion but his immediate family and some other followers resolved to migrate. They set out in seven *dhows* from the nearby port of Bushehr and sailed through the mouth of the Persian Gulf, into the Indian Ocean. There they were caught in a great storm and separated, making landfalls at seven different points on the East African coast where they settled. Among these were Zanzibar, Tongoni and Kilwa.

disrepair. It is still possible to bathe in the springs, however. From Amboni village, the guide will take you to the Ziggi river. Here children will look after your bicycles and you can pay a small fee to cross the river by canoe. The springs are on the other side.

Tongoni Ruins → *Colour map 1, grid B5.*

ⓘ *20 km south of Tanga on the road to Pangani about 1 km off the road. Buses or dala-dala from Tanga cost about US$1 and will take up to 1 hr. A return taxi will cost about US$15; ask the driver to wait for you.*

The Tongoni Ruins date from the Shirazi period (see box) and the settlement was started at the end of the 10th century. The community would have been similar to that at Kaole (see page 88), but it was almost certainly larger. There are 40 tombs, some with pillars, and the remains of a substantial mosque. The mosque is of the type found along the north part of the East African coast. There is a central *musalla* (prayer room) with arches leading to aisles (*ribati*) at each side. The mosque is constructed of particularly finely dressed, close-grained coral, especially on the lintel of the *kibula,* the side of the building that faces towards Mecca. The roofs were coral on mangrove rafters. There are depressions in the pillars where there were porcelain bowls, all apparently removed during the German period. It is said that Tongoni was founded by Ali ben Sultan Hasan at much the same time as he established the settlement at Kilwa (see page 108). There are Persian inscriptions at Tongoni that would seem to establish a link with Shiraz.

Muheza → *Phone code: 027. Colour map 1, grid B5.*

A sprawling, bustling town, 35 km west of Tanga along a good road, Muheza provides a link between the coastal beaches and the lush, cool Usambara Mountains. Access to the Amani Nature Reserve is from here (see below) and although part of the Usambara Mountains, which are dealt with in the North to Moshi chapter (see page 186), Amani is in the eastern mountains and accessed from the Tanga side. Muheza district is a relatively cosmopolitan area of Tanzania, a result of the influx of workers for the now defunct sisal industry. The town is being improved under a government urban renewal programme that has already produced a new bus stand and market (market days Thursday and Sunday). There is a post office and bank, but there are no money-changing facilities. There are a few basic guest houses in town and one hotel, *The Ambassador*, outside which is the terminal for **Scandinavian Express** (buses stop here en route between Dar and Tanga and Mombasa), but accommodation is very primitive and there are better options in either Tanga, Korogwe to the west, or Amani.

Magila

ⓘ *Approximately 6 km to the southwest of Muheza. From Muheza cross the railway line, head south past the football ground and take the next right.*

The small town of Magila is the original site of the Anglican mission church (1876) and hospital (1884), buildings that survive today. Close by are two **waterfalls**, fed by a natural reservoir at the top of Margoroto mountain. It takes about two hours to reach the reservoir from Magila (ask around for the best paths to take) and there are excellent views across the plains towards Tanga. There are no guesthouses in Magila.

Amani → *Colour map 1, grid B5.*

▸▸ p100

ⓘ *To get there, you will need to make a connection at Muheza on the road linking Tanga to the Dar es Salaam to Moshi highway. There is a bus that leaves Muheza at around 1400 each day for the 25-km trip to Amani, which takes about an hour and costs US$0.50. In the mornings the bus leaves Amani when full, usually around 0800. The reserve charges a one-off fee of US$14 per person entry.*

More information on the mountains and forests in this region can be found at www.tfcg.org, the website for the Tanzania Forest Conservation Group.

The Amani Nature Reserve, part of the Eastern Usambara Mountains, is 25 km from Muheza on a dirt road that most of the year requires a 4x4 vehicle as it is steep and winding in places. In 1898, the Germans established an agricultural research institute here that was the envy of Africa. With the twin benefits of the north railway from Tanga to Moshi and the Amani Institute, the Usambara area flourished under settler farming. By 1914, 40,000 ha were under sisal, 80,000 ha under rubber and 14,000 ha under cotton, as well as extensive areas of tobacco, sugar, wheat and maize. One of the great lessons of farming in Africa is that crops have to be carefully adapted to local conditions. Amani tested soils, experimented with insecticides and developed new varieties. After 1914, Amani turned its hand to the war effort, developing a local quinine for use against malaria from cinchona bark and manufacturing chocolate, tooth-powder, soap and castor oil.

In 1997 the Nature Reserve was established to protect the biodiversity of the flora and fauna of the sub-montane rainforests of the East Usambara Mountains. This joint venture of the Tanzanian and Finnish governments seeks to protect an area whose biological significance in terms of plant and animal diversity has been compared to the Galapagos Islands. There are, for instance, three endemic bird species, the Usambara alethe, Naduk eagle owl and the Usambara weaver. The rainforests also provide the water supply for 160,000 people in Tanga.

The total area of the Amani Nature Reserve is 8,380 ha, which includes 1,065 ha of forests owned by private tea companies under the management of the East Usambara Tea Company. It also includes the Amani Botanical Garden, established in 1902, which has over 460 plant species and is one of the largest botanical gardens in Africa. Amani also has a medical research centre run by the Tanzanian government. Birdlife and small animals such as monkeys abound. It is excellent hiking country.

The reserve's information centre is housed in the recently rehabilitated old German Station Master's house in the small settlement of Sigi which is also the entrance gate to the reserve. A small resthouse has also been constructed nearby. The East Usambara Catchment Forest Project has made efforts to strengthen the villagers' rights to manage their own forests, and pilot farm forestry activities have been set up in a number of

The African violet was discovered in the East Usambara Mountains in 1892 by Baron von Saint Paul, hence the name in latin, saintpaulia ionantha. The star-shaped flowers come in every shade of blue, pink and red.

villages in an effort to improve local land husbandry. A dozen forest trails have been established, including three driving routes. The East Usambara Conservation Area Management Programme created and maintains the nature trails, as well as training guides in an effort to encourage village collaboration and conservation efforts. Short or long walks can be arranged, and the guides are very knowledgeable about local species, bird and insect life and uses for traditional plants. It is worth trying to buy a copy of the guidebook to the East Usambaras written by Graham Mercer.

Pangani → *Phone code: 027. Colour map 1, grid B5. Position: 5° 25' S, 38° 58' E.*

» *pp100-103*

Pangani village, 52 km south of Tanga, is located at the point where the Pangani River empties itself into the Indian Ocean. The river passes through the north side of the village, separating the old buildings and the present-day market from the farms and small houses on the south side. The river itself has a car and passenger ferry that runs from early morning to 1800. Pangani has good beaches and is a fine location for a quiet beach holiday. There are some handsome old Arab houses, though these are in poor repair.

Ins and outs

The best approach to Pangani is along the unpaved road from Tanga. The road is fine in the dry season but becomes slippery in the wet. Much of it goes through a vast sisal plantation. The beach resorts lie off this road between the two towns. There are regular buses from Tanga. There is another road from Muheza that goes directly southeast to Pangani across country for 45 km. This was used as the access road

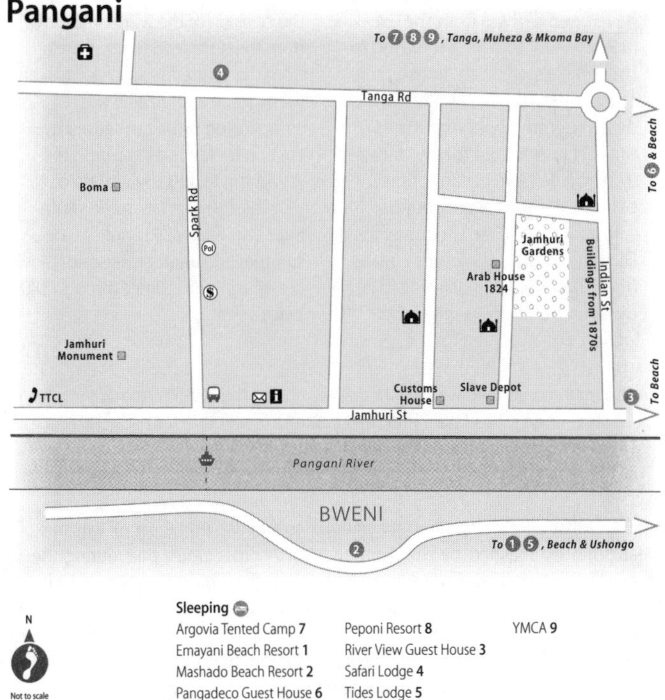

Sleeping
Argovia Tented Camp **7**
Emayani Beach Resort **1**
Mashado Beach Resort **2**
Pangadeco Guest House **6**
Peponi Resort **8**
River View Guest House **3**
Safari Lodge **4**
Tides Lodge **5**
YMCA **9**

Rhapta

Around AD 100 an anonymous merchant, born in Egypt, compiled a guide written in Greek for merchants and sailors with details of all the trade routes and ports known in the ancient world. The book was named Periplus Maris Erythraei, or 'Voyage around the Red Sea'. In Periplus the lost port of Rhapta is mentioned, but scholars remain uncertain as to its exact location. Rhapta was described as the most southerly port along the East African coastline, then known as Azania. Details were given of the trade carried out with Azania – the sale of swords, spears, axes and glassware in exchange for cowrie shells, ivory, tortoiseshell and cinnamon. The inhabitants of Rhapta were described as being of great stature, pirates or tillers of the soil, inhabiting the whole coastline, with many local chiefs.

According to Ravenstein (1898), the name 'Rhapta' was believed to have been derived from the Greek or Arab verb 'to sew' – referring to the 'small sewn boats' in use there. The early Portuguese sailors describe Arab boats with the timbers lashed together with coir (rope made from coconut fibre), carrying cargoes of coconuts.

In about AD 50 the Greek merchant Diogenes describes a journey inland from Rhapta to lakes believed to be the source of the Nile and to the 'Mountains of the Moon', which could refer to Mt Kilimanjaro or even the Rwenzori Mountains in Uganda. His findings were marked on the maps of the ancient geographer Ptolemy, considered until the 15th century, to be the great authority on the Nile's origin and course. Prior to his death in 1984, archaeologist Neville Chittick argued that Rhapta was in the region of Kilwa or the Rufiji delta, and that the island of Menouthias, mentioned by Ptolemy in the 2nd century AD, was the nearby island of Mafia. Other researchers, such as James Kirkman, suggest Rhapta was near Dar es Salaam or Lamu; and several place it at Pangani, with the island Menouthias being either Zanzibar or Pemba.

Rhapta was said to be near the end of the known world. This was because ships were hampered in sailing further south by the Doldrums, a windless zone in the Indian Ocean caused by the collision of the winter monsoon from the north and the trade winds from the south. Ancient Egyptian and Greek trade with Azania was complicated by delays caused by waiting for favourable winds, the return trip taking a minimum of 16 months. By contrast, trading with India was relatively simple as the summer and winter monsoons blow in opposing directions, through 180°, twice a year.

when the main coast road was washed away during the El Niño floods several years ago, but since then it has fallen into disrepair and is suitable for high clearance 4x4s only. There is no public transport along this route.

History

Swahili for 'distribute' or 'arrange', it comes as no surprise that Pangani was one of the earliest ports established by the Arab settlers. A prosperous port during the 19th century, the community was ruled by an Arab Liwali, five Shirazi Jumbes and a network of Akidas. Indian traders financed parties under Akidas to collect ivory and rhinoceros horn in the interior, and there was some trading in slaves. The town prospered as the trade in ivory and slaves flourished. It was at Pangani that Bushiri, leader of the Arab revolt of 1888-1889, was finally captured and executed (see page 83).

The mouth of the Pangani River is crossed by a sand bar. This provided shelter for dhows, and prevented them from being pursued by steam vessels when the slave trade was being suppressed after 1873. However, it also meant that vessels of deeper draught could not use the port. Traffic drifted steadily to the newer facilities at Tanga, subsequently accelerated by the railway linking Tanga to Dar es Salaam and Moshi.

In 1930 the population was around 1,500 but the substantial houses on the north side of the river, built largely by slave labour, have fallen into disrepair. The economy of the town shifted to reliance on the sisal plantations, Pangani being served by shallow-draught steamers, but sisal declined drastically in price with the advent of synthetic fibres in the mid-1950s. There are still many coco-palms and some fishing.

Sights

The old **Customs House**, originally built in 1916 as the post office, and the old **CCM Building** are both fine structures, unfortunately in poor repair. Next to the Customs House is the old slave depot, built around 1850 and still largely intact, with some characteristic carved doors and remnants of whipping posts. It is also thought that there are underground tunnels and pits that lead to the river, along which weak slaves were taken to be washed out to sea. Just by the ferry is a plaque recording the capture of Pangani by the British on 23 July 1916, and the **Uhuru** or **Jamhuri Monument**, celebrating independence. The **Boma** is also a handsome building. Built in 1810, it is said that slaves were buried alive to strengthen the foundations. The distinctive roof was added in the German period. It is now the District Commissioner's Office and some of the original carved doors remain.

Across the river by ferry (US$0.10, US$3 cars) is the village of **Bweni**. From the hill behind the village are fine views of Pangani and of the Indian Ocean. There is a luxurious hotel here, though it is currently closed (see Sleeping). It is possible to hire a boat, through the Pangani Coast Cultural Tourism Programme (see Activities, page 102), to travel up the river (around US$4 per hour for a boat taking up to 10 people). There are many birds, best seen at dusk, and crocodiles further upstream. You will also see local fishermen in dugout canoes and vast coconut plantations beside the river. Men climb the trees to collect coconuts or the sap from cut branches – used to make *mnazi*, an alcoholic drink.

Mkoma Bay

This is a tranquil area about 3 km north of Pangani on the road to Tanga. There are several places to stay, all set in attractive, well-kept gardens with good sea views at the edge of a small cliff. Steps lead down to the beach, which is quiet but a little rocky in places and does not have the brilliant white sands found elsewhere. Along the coral shoreline in the area known as Mkomo and Mwanaunguja, the **fossilized remains of dinosaurs** have been found found, estimated to be 200-300 million years old. Three **offshore islands** can be visited (Marve Mdogo, Mwamba Marve and Mazivi) and there is sport fishing and snorkelling, although the quality of the latter can be disappointing in the rainy seasons when the water is not clear. Boats can be arranged through the resorts.

Sleeping

Tanga *p92, map p92*

C Mkonge (sometimes known as the *Sisal (Mkonge) Hotel*), is about 1 km east from the centre along Hospital Rd, which leads into Ocean Dr, T027-2643440, mkongehotel@kaributanga.com. Set in grounds by the sea, in what was designed as Amboni Park, there are lovely views over the bay and vervet monkeys play in the gardens. Completely refurbished to very high standards in 2004, the staff are excellent, credit cards are accepted, and this is easily the best place to stay in town. The 49 rooms have a/c, are a very reasonable US$55, there's a good bar and restaurant, and a swimming pool. It's worth coming here just to eat in the lovely surroundings (see Eating).

C **Panori Hotel**, east of the centre, south of Hospital Rd, in a quiet area beyond the Yacht Club and the other hotels, T027-2646044, panori@africaonline.co.tz. Colonial-style building with new wing added in 1997 (though there is nothing new about any of the furnishings); rates vary so ask to see a selection of rooms, some have a/c and TV. Indian and international food in an attractive open banda restaurant and bar built around a mango tree. Well run and comfortable.

C **Silverado Hotel**, Boma Rd, T027-2646054. Reasonably new hotel with 9 modern rooms, with en suite bathrooms, cable TV, fridge and phone. Rates include breakfast and there's a small terrace restaurant and bar. Only street parking available.

E **Inn by the Sea**, close to *Mkonge* on Ocean Dr, T027-2644614. The 24 rooms have a/c or fans, mosquito nets. Price includes breakfast but there is no restaurant or bar (Muslim owned). A good location on cliffs overlooking the harbour. Rather neglected in recent years but clean and has secure parking.

E **Ocean Breeze**, just off Independence Av, T027-2644545. Superb value, this is easily the best budget in town in a neat and fairly modern block, lots of rooms but fills up quickly and is deservedly popular. Self-catering rooms with mosquito nets and cool tiled floors cost US$7. Restaurant with curries, grilled chicken and fish.

F **Kiboko**, Bombo St, in the residential area to the north of Ocean Dr, T027-2644929, jda-kiboko@bluemail.ch. Run by a very nice Swiss man who is a fantastic chef, this is better known as a great place to eat (see Eating), but you can camp here too and rent a tent. The camping rate of US$4 includes breakfast, immaculate ablution block, bike hire. 12 rooms are planned.

Amani *p96*

D **Sigi Resthouse**, near to the Amani Forest Information Centre, T027-2646907, usambara@twiga.com. Very comfortable triple rooms with mosquito nets and en suite showers and toilets in a new smart white wooden block. Serves fresh produce and can make arrangements for guided forest walks. Also camping for US$3.

E **Emau Hill Camp**, to get here go through Amani Nature Reserve and out the other side and follow the road for a few km, turn right at the sign for Emau Hill (4x4 only), email ahead to get directions, tukae@tukae.org. This is a mission post and school that offers some accommodation in rooms or in 3 tented bandas for US$4 per person or you can pitch a tent. Small bar and food is available. Lovely forested spot, along the border of the plot is a winding creek, lots of bushbabies and birds in the trees.

Pangani *p97, map p97*

The better accommodation options are on the beaches to the north and south of town. There are, however, a few budget places in town itself – useful if you are arriving late.

L **Mashado Beach Resort**, T027-25507702. A luxury hotel on the hill south of the river ferry. Has 40 a/c rooms with en suite bathrooms, a swimming pool and has its own private airstrip. However, despite its plushness the hotel has become a bit of a folly since it was built in the mid-1990s and has twice now gone bust and closed. The reason is that it is not a beach resort at all and is built on the top of the cliff. The new owners are in the process of reinventing the place as an upscale fishing lodge.

E **Pangadeco Guest House**, near the beach at the east end of town, T0748-369066 (mob). Very simple and run-down rooms for little more than US$5 a double, no fans or mosquito nets, dubious sheets, you need to give notice of meals required well in advance, the bar is ok though and you can walk to the beach.

E **River View Guest House**, Jamhuri St, just east of the old slave depot, (no phone). Very basic, shared bathrooms with cold water, rooms have fans but no nets, food available, nice river view as the name suggests.

E **Safari Lodge**, Tanga Rd, straight up the road from the ferry, T027-2630013. Reasonable budget option in town, the 6 rooms are US$7-10 depending on size, breakfast of eggs and bread included, tatty

For an explanation of the sleeping and eating price codes used in this guide, see inside the front cover. Other relevant information is found in Essentials pages 31-34.

but clean, simple local meals and cold beers are available on the thatched terrace outside, friendly service, and a good place to meet the locals.

Beaches

To get to the two upmarket beach resorts south of Pangani you will need to go to the village of Ushomo, a 40-min taxi ride from the ferry at Pangani. Here the beaches are excellent and largely free of tourists.

B Argovia Tented Camp, 4 km north of Pangani at Mkoma Bay, T027-2630000, or through Moshi office, T027-2753531, www.argovia-lodge.com. Whitewashed buildings decorated with antiques, beautifully furnished tents or cheaper bandas, all have en suite bathrooms with hot water and flush toilets, mosquito nets. There's also a safety deposit box, swimming pool, well-stocked bar, restaurant offering excellent but quite expensive western food (US$5-15) and they accept credit cards. Can organize day trips to the Amboni Caves for US$50 and a walking tour of Pangani for US$15.

B Emayani Beach Resort, 17 km south of Pangani across the ferry, the lodge is signposted from the junction of the Muheza and Tanga roads, reservations, Arusha T027-2640755, www.emayanilodge.com. Thatched resort on the beach, bungalows with en suite bathrooms have verandas with ocean views, surrounded by coconut trees. B&B or half board rates, considerable discounts for children, friendly cocktail bar, breakfast US$5, 4-course set dinner each night for US$12 or à la carte menu, watersports, lots of boats for fishing and snorkelling, and can arrange Zanzibar day trips, 3 hr each way.

B The Tides Lodge, 16 km south of Pangani, follow signs for Ushongo Beach and Tides Lodge, T027-2640844, www.thetideslodge.com. Transfers can be arranged from Pangani for US$16. Intimate lodge with 7 comfortable thatched and brightly painted bandas with en suite bathrooms, romantic bar and restaurant lit by lamplight. Seafood is a speciality. Arranges snorkelling trips to the nearby islands and sunset cruises on the Pangani River. There is an airstrip and Coastal Air will stop here on request en route between Tanga and Pemba.

C-F Peponi Resort, further north from Mkoma Bay, 15 km north of Pangani at Kigombe village, T0748-202962 (mob), www.peponiresort.com. Thatched bandas with 2-5 beds, en suite bathrooms; for a group of 4+ accommodation can work out about US$10 pp. Includes continental breakfast. Advisable to book in advance, rates are negotiable for longer stays. Good restaurant and pleasant bar that can get especially lively if there is a crowd. Camping US$4. Game fishing in the Pemba Channel on the resort's own dhow, snorkelling trips can also be arranged, wild pigs have been known to come into the resort at night.

F YMCA, on the same road towards the beach as Argovia, T027-2630044. Very basic and pretty dilapidated, 3 s/c double rooms, extra beds can be added, no hot water, sparodic running water, nets and fans, also camping. Serves fish or beans with rice, *ugali* or chips, for approximately US$2.50. Nevertheless it's in a fine setting overlooking Mkoma Bay's beach.

Eating and drinking

Tanga *p92, map p92*

TTT Kiboko, Bombo St, T027-2644929. With a good local reputation, the kitchens here are immaculate and very modern, and the tables are surrounded by a flowering garden. Inventive dishes of kingfish, red snapper, prawns and calamari. Open daily, dinner only.

TTT Mkonge Hotel, on Ocean Dr, T027-2643440. Fantastic setting overlooking the town and bay and set in lovely gardens. Dine inside in a dark wood dining room or outside on the terrace. Serves up very good grills and salads, or try the excellent prawn curry, and there's a full bar and some wines.

TTT Yacht Club, Ocean Dr. Day membership US$2, for which you can use the bar and restaurant. There is no cash payment and instead you need to buy a book of tickets to pay for things as you go along. Very large menu, good seafood, well stocked bar. A real expat hangout, but entertaining nonetheless, and the service is excellent. Dining tables are spread out on lovely stone terraces overlooking the bay.

TT Ocean Breeze Hotel, just off Independence Av, T027-2644545. Terrace restaurant serves excellent curries, grilled chicken and fish and cold beer, popular and busy and the outside area is lively for a few drinks in the evening.

Café Cappuccino, Guinea St. Good and varied coffees, as the name suggests, fresh juices and milk, snacks, though in a grim cafeteria environment with a huge painting of Mecca on the wall.

Patwas Restaurant, off Market St just south of market. Well run, with snacks of egg-chop (Scotch egg), meat chop, kebabs, samosas. Excellent ice-cold drinks: lemon, mango, pineapple, papaya, lassi, milkshakes, locally made grapefruit crush and ginger beer. Recommended – just beware the roadkill cuisine.

Food Palace, Market St, look for the red corrugated roof. Serves grills, curries, ice cream and fruit juices. The Indian food is cheap and superb for around US$3 a plate plus extra for rice and naan bread. There's no alcohol and the restaurant is closed during Ramadan, but if you bring your own beer you are permitted to drink it at the outside tables. Good value and highly recommended.

Princess Nadia Bakery, on Market St, in a yellow building. Recommended for fresh bread and pastries.

TTS, on northwest corner of Uhuru Park. Very cheap snacks and local dishes in a white building with wraparound veranda.

Pangani *p97, map p97*

Along the river front are many small food stalls, where you can get items such as chapatti, omelette and rice very cheaply, otherwise, look to the hotels.

Activities and tours

Tanga *p92, map p92*

Cricket Aga Khan Club, behind the *Aga Khan School* off Swahili St, south of the railway line.

Sailing Yacht Club, Ocean Dr. Day membership is US$2 for which you can use the facilities such as bar and restaurant (see under eating).

Soccer The soccer stadium is on the intersection of Eukenforde St and Mkwakwani St. You will need to consult the *Daily News*, or a local enthusiast, for fixtures.

Swimming Swimming Club, on Ocean Dr before the *Yacht Club*, T027-2646618. There is also a bar that serves basic food. Also try **Mkonge Hotel**, see above, US$4.

Tennis and squash Aga Khan Club (see Cricket above) and at the **Tanga Club** off Ocean Dr.

Pangani *p97, map p97*

Pangani Coast Cultural Tourism Programme, Jamhuri St (or Harbour Rd), next to the post office, T027-2642611, tourinfo@habari.co.tz. This programme is co-ordinated by Mr Sekibaha who has been the district cultural officer for 20 years. On offer are walks through the town to local farms, coconut plantations and homes, river cruises to the mangrove swamps and fishing with local fishermen. Can also arrange bicycle hire, snorkelling and other excursions. The programme is supported by the Dutch development organization, SNV, and profits are used for development projects, particularly in education. Further details can be obtained from the Tanzanian tourist information centre in Arusha, T027-2503840-3, www.infojep.com/culturaltours. Brochures for each project can be downloaded from the website.

Transport

Tanga *p92, map p92*

Air

Coastal Air, T022-2117969-60, Tanga Airport office T027-2646548, www.coastal.cc. Flights from **Dar** depart daily at 1400 and arrive in Tanga at 1535 (US$100) via **Zanzibar**, (1430; US$80) and **Pemba** (1515; US$55). The return flight departs from Tanga daily at 1600, and arrives in Pemba at 1630, Zanzibar 1710, and Dar at 1735.

Road

Bus and *dala-dala* leave from the bus station south of the town on the other side of the railway track for **Dar es Salaam** from 0800, the trip takes 4-6 hrs and a regular bus costs US$6 and a luxury one US$10. For **Moshi** the bus takes 4-6 hrs and costs US$6. To

For an explanation of the sleeping and eating price codes used in this guide, see inside the front cover. Other relevant information is found in Essentials pages 31-34.

Pangani buses take 2-3 hrs and cost US$1, and there are several departures a day to **Lushoto** 3-4 hrs, US$3. The **Scandinavian Express** office is on Ring Rd between the railway station and stadium, T027-2644337, www.scandinaveangroup.com. There are through buses from Tanga to **Mombasa** that take 4 hr, daily 1300, US$10. This returns from Mombasa at 1245. Very usefully these drop off at **Diani Beach** to the south of Mombasa. The roads are unmade dirt roads until the Amboni Sisal Estates, where tarmac begins, although there are some potholes developing. The **border crossing at Lunga Lunga** is quick and efficient. Daily buses to **Dar** depart at 0730 and 1330, 4-6 hrs, US$12.

Sea

Boat Dhows operate from Tanga. You will need to ask if any are sailing at the port. Routes to and from Tanga are not sailed that frequently and remember foreigners are not allowed to use dhows as transport between the mainland and the islands along the coast. In the past there have been ferries to **Pemba**, but this does not seem to be the case these days, though it is worth asking around locally in case this service resumes.

Pangani *p97, map p97*

Bus The only regular bus services are from **Tanga**. Buses depart from the main stand at Tanga at around 0800, 1200 and 1400 and cost US$1.50. Although it is only 52 km, the road is very bumpy and buses may take over 3 hrs depending on the season. The bus will drop off outside the beach resorts between Tanga and Pangani. None of them are more than 1 km off the road. The bus stand in Pangani is on Jamhuri St opposite the ferry. There are no buses from Bweni on the other side of the river.

Directory

Tanga *p92, map p92*

Banks Exim Bank, Market St, near *Planters Hotel*. **Courier services** Fedex has an office on Customs Rd down from the Exim Bank. **Internet** Globe Net Works on Market St, Impala Internet, Market St or at Internet Cavern, Garden St , $0.50 for 1 hr. **Post** Post office on Independence Av near Msambara St. **Libraries** Tanga library off Independence Av near the Old Boma. **Medical services** Bombo Hospital on Ocean Dr to east of town centre, T027-2644390. Dr Patel's clinic at the town end of Hospital Rd has been recommended by a traveller. **Useful addresses** Police off Independence Av near Tanga library.

Pangani *p97, map p97*

Banks The only bank in Pangani does not change money. **Telephone** Telephone calls may be made from the TTCL shop just west of the Jamhuri Monument.

South coast

The inaccessible south coast receives few visitors. However, if you have the patience, or can go by plane, you will be well rewarded. Off the coast is the island of Mafia, which now is partially protected as the Mafia Island Marine Park. It's an idyllic setting and a paradise for scuba divers and snorkellers and, with its stunning lodges, a haven for those at the luxury end of the market. Further south is the town of Kilwa, with the small island of Kilwa Kisiwani just off the mainland. This is the location of the intriguing Kilwa ruins and although very remote worth the trouble to get to. Further south still are the towns of Lindi and Mtwara, best known for their Makonde carvings. They receive very few visitors because they are so isolated and they are very difficult to get to. The main coastal road to the south of Dar es Salaam is fairly good for the first 150 km or so, but after this it deteriorates to a very simple track that requires a 4x4 and is totally impassable in the rains.

Mafia Island

→ *Phone code: 023. Colour map 1, grid B6. 7°45'S 39°50'E.*

Mafia, the southernmost of the islands along the coast, is a wonderful little island at the centre of the largest marine park in East Africa. At around 20 km long and 8 km wide, it's a real sleepy backwater, a remnant of the old Swahili coast and a place to visit now if you want to see how Zanzibar was 30 years ago. Unlike Zanzibar and Pemba which, along with a number of smaller islands, form the semi-autonomous state of Zanzibar, Mafia is politically an integral part of mainland Tanzania. The inhabitants are mainly fishermen but other industries involve the coconut palms and cashew nut tree plantations. Geographically, as well as politically, the island, with its central areas covered with bush and light woodland and its plantations, is much more like the mainland in character than the other islands. The coast is generally lined with palm trees, but there are not the sweeping sandy beaches like those of Zanzibar. Here the shoreline is generally narrow and mangrove forests are widespread so it's not primarily a beach destination. It is, however, an excellent diving destination. The recent gazetting of Mafia Island Marine Park – the largest protected area in the Indian Ocean – which includes surrounding villages in its conservation efforts means that the millions of fish and coral species that thrive in the warm waters around Mafia are fully protected. ▸▸ *For Sleeping, Eating and other listings, see pages 107-108.*

Ins and outs

Getting there Flights from Dar es Salaam take 30-40 mins and there are now several operators offering 3-4 flights per week. By sea, there are irregular services out of Dar. ▸▸ *See Transport, page 108, for further details.*

Getting around The airport is about 12 km from the lodges at the southern tip of the island around Chole Bay. The lodges will collect you in their vehicles. There are no taxis on the island; indeed there are few vehicles of any sort. Mafia has no public transport system. The upmarket lodges and hotels ferry their guests around the island, and budget travellers have the option of walking, hitch-hiking – which can involve lengthy waits – or hiring a bicycle. Enquire at **New Lizu Hotel** in Kilindoni.

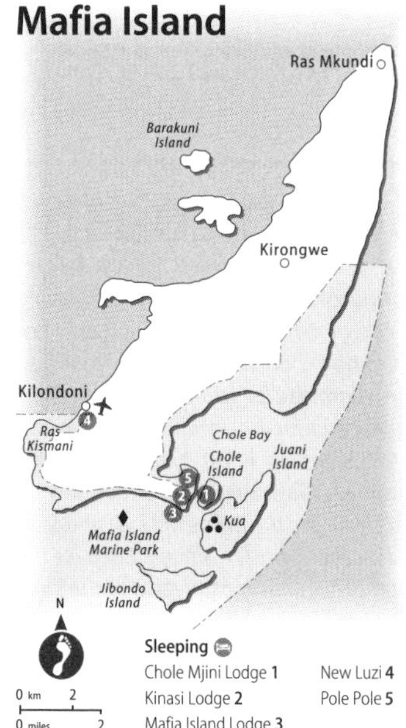

History

There is evidence of foreign, probably Shirazi, settlers on Mafia from as early as the 8th or 9th century. From the 12th to the 14th century it was an important settlement and the remains of a 13th-century mosque have been found at Ras Kismani, at the southwestern point of the island. By the 16th century, when the Portuguese arrived, it had lost much of its importance and was part of the territory ruled by the king of Kilwa. There is little left of the site of the settlement of the 12th to 14th century, although old coins and pieces of pottery are still found occasionally, particularly to the south of Kilindoni where the sea is eating away at the ruins. On the nearby island of Juani can be found extensive ruins of the town of Kua. The town dates back to the 18th century and the five mosques go back even further to the 14th century. In 1829 the town was sacked by Sakalava cannibals from Madagascar who invaded, destroyed the town and dined on the inhabitants.

From the beginning of the 19th century traders from all over the world had been plying these coastal waters. 'Americani' cloth proved itself to be perhaps the most popular of all the traded goods among the resident population. The trading of goods and of slaves was soon to be followed by the interest of European politics but it was not until the end of the century that this affected territorial rights. Under the treaty of 1890, Mafia, along with Zanzibar and Pemba, were initially allotted to the British sphere. However, it was later agreed that Mafia should go to Germany in exchange for some territory on the southern border, which was allocated to the British Territory of Nyasaland (now Malawi). The island was therefore included in the purchase of the coastal strip from Sultan Seyyid Ali and the German flag was raised in 1890.

The name Mafia is derived from the Arab word morfieyeh, which means a group, and refers to the archipelago.

The Germans established a headquarters at Chole and in 1892 a resident officer was posted here together with a detachment of Sudanese troops. A large two-storey boma was constructed with various other buildings such as a gaol. The site seemed ideal with good anchorage for dhows, but with the opening of a regular coastal steamship service a deeper harbour was needed and the headquarters were moved to Kilindoni in 1913.

During the First World War it became clear that Mafia represented an extremely useful base from which attacks could be launched. In particular the British needed a base from which to attack the SS *Königsberg*, which was wreaking havoc up and down the East African coast. In January 1915 a British expeditionary force under Colonel Ward landed on the island at Kisimani and the islands were captured with little resistance. A garrison of about 200 troops remained on the island. The *Königsberg* had been damaged and gone into the mouth of the River Rufiji for repairs. The delta, with its many creeks and maze of streams, proved the perfect hiding place. It was important that the British should find and destroy the ship before any further damage could be done. In 1915 a British warplane was assembled on Mafia, took off from there, spotted the ship and boats then went into the delta to destroy it. This was the first use of aerial reconnaissance in warfare. The wrecked remains of the crippled boat could be seen until 1979 when it finally sank out of sight into the mud.

For a short period the islands were under military rule, and were later administered by Zanzibar. In 1922 the islands were handed over by the government of Zanzibar to become part of the Tanganyika Territory under the United Nations Mandate.

These days, the coconut industry is particularly important and Mafia has the largest coconut factory in East Africa at Ngombeni Plantation. It produces copra (dried kernels), oil, coir yarn and cattle cake. More recently, geological surveys have shown that the Mafia Deep Offshore Basin, an area of 75,000 sq km, contains deposits of oil and gas. Exploration has already started and, given the extreme poverty of many of the people on the island, the onset of employment opportunities has given a renewed sense of optimism to Mafia's inhabitants – ecological concerns notwithstanding.

Sights

Kilondoni

Kilondoni is the main town and a refreshingly simple place. The only road is flanked on either side for a kilometre or so by classic Swahili buildings with carved doors and in the centre of town there is a small market. Whilst dhows remain commonplace to this day all along the East Coast of Africa, the huge ocean-going *jahasi* are increasingly rare. Here on the beach at Kilondoni there are usually three or four of

The legend of Ras Kismani

The town of Ras Kismani was originally settled by the Sakalava from Madagascar. The townspeople built a large ship, and when it was completed they invited the local people of Kua to a feast. During the celebrations, the Sakalava seized several children and laid them on the sand in the path of the ship as it was launched.

The Kua people planned revenge at their leisure. Seven or eight years later they invited the Sakalava of Ras Kismani to attend a wedding at Kua. The celebrations were in a special room beneath a house. Gradually the hosts left, one by one, until only an old man was left to entertain the guests. As he did so, the door was quietly bricked up, and the bodies remain to this day. A message was sent to the headman at Ras Kismani that the account was now squared. Within a month, Ras Kismani was engulfed by the sea.

these giant boats, which are still in service providing an essential means of trade with the mainland. This working beach-front at Kilondoni is one of the highlights of a visit to Mafia. On the shore you can watch the construction of boats 20-25 m in length and weighing up to 100 tonnes. Timbers are prepared by hand and the frame of the boat is made from naturally V-shaped forked branches of trees.

Ruins at Kua

ⓘ *Local fishermen will take you to Kua for US$2.*

The largely 18-century ruins of the town of Kua are on Juani Island to the south of Mafia Island. The remains are tucked away inconspicuously on the western side of the island covering a large area of about 14 ha. In 1955, when the site was cleared of bush, one observer stated that he believed that these ruins were 'potentially the Pompeii of East Africa'. However, the remains still require a lot of work on them to bring them up to anything like that standard. There are several houses, one of which was clearly double-storeyed. Beneath the stairs leading to the upper level is a small room in which slaves could be confined for punishment. Under the building is the *haman* (bathroom), with a vaulted ceiling of curved coral blocks. A soil pipe runs from the remains of an upper room to a pit below. Two mosques and a series of tombs, some with pillars, are nearby. The evidence suggests that the town did not have a protective wall and that the inhabitants were mainly involved in agricultural pursuits on the island rather than in sea-trading.

Kua is also famous for the supposed curative properties of its milk.

There is also a cave on the island formed by the action of the sea. The water streaming out of the cave as the tide turns is reputed to cure *baridi yabis* ('cold stiffness' – rheumatism) and other ailments. The cure is not effective, however, unless the hereditary custodian of the cave is paid a fee and the spirits of the cave appeased by an offering of honey, dates or sugar.

Nororo Island

Nororo is a small island 12 km off the north coast of Mafia with a fishing community of about 50 local boats. There are two small *hotelis* selling rice, *ugali* and fish and it's possible to camp on the beach in a thatched shelter.

Baracuni Island

This is a beautiful small island with fine beaches about 12 km off the northwest coast of Mafia and an hour's sailing from Nororo. It's used as a base for fishing dhows. You need to have your own food, water and tent if you want to stay.

Mafia Island Marine Park

ⓘ *Park fee of US$10 per day. All the lodges (see Sleeping below) have dive schools and rent out equipment. Note that during Apr-Sep the monsoon winds blow too hard, making it impossible to dive outside the lagoon and leading to a deterioration in visibility.* ▸▸ *See also Diving, page 39.*

To protect an internationally significant ecosystem, the Mafia Island Marine Park (the first in Tanzania) was opened in July 1995. The project is backed by the World Wildlife Fund which contributes human and financial resources for its development and maintenance. Here you can experience some of the best deep-sea diving in Tanzania. There is something here for everyone from the most experienced diver to those who want to snorkel in the shallower pools. The coral gardens off Mafia are marvellous – wonderfully vivid fish, shells, sponges, sea cucumber and spectacular coral reefs. Two of the most beautiful reefs are the Okuto and Tutia reefs around Juani and Jibondo Islands, a short distance from Chole Bay. About 1 km off Mafia's coastline there is a 200-m deep contour along the seabed of the Indian Ocean. The depth contributes to the wide variety of sea life. Due to its position alongside the barrier, the island is the meeting place of large oceanic fish and the the vast variety of fish common to the Indian Ocean coral reefs. There are over 400 species of fish in the park. Mafia Island and some of the uninhabited islands around are also traditional breeding sites for the green turtle. Sadly you would be very lucky to see these as the local population is now close to being wiped out – they are killed both as adults for their meat and as eggs. Another threatened species is the dugong, which lives in sea grass such as that found between Mafia and the Rufiji delta. Because of their strange shape, early sailors thought they had breasts (giving rise to the legend of the mermaid.) This strange beast is protected by law, but hunting continues.

Sleeping

Mafia Island *p104, map p104*

There are only 5 places to stay on the whole island. Note that both Pole Pole and Chole Mjini close during rainy season from the beginning of Apr to the end of May.

L **Chole Mjini Lodge**, on the 1 sq km Chole Island, UK reservations, T+ 44 (0)1306-880770, www.africatravelresource.com. The lodge has been developed by Jean and Ann de Villiers with the prime intention of using money earned to help the local people on the island. The lodge is truly eco-sensitive, built by local people using local materials, and revenues have helped to establish a school and medical centre on the island. Chole is part of the Mafia Island Marine Park, so there is an additional park fee of US$10 per day. The 7 rooms are actually treehouses, built partially on stilts, most with private bathrooms with long-drop toilets, solar heated water for the showers, and balconies. There is a restaurant and bar area, the meals being primarily seafood, and snorkelling and diving are on offer. Rates vary seasonally from US$140-320.

★ L **Pole Pole Bungalow resort**, T022-2601530 (Dar es Salaam booking office), www.polepole.com. Voted as one of the world's top 25 eco-lodges by Travel & Leisure magazine and one of the top 10 world's secret beaches by the *Times* newspaper. Ten bungalows on stilts with wide verandas face the Mafia Island Marine Park and the islands of Chole, Juani and Jibondo. The decor is stunning with hard wood floors and mahogany furniture and linen imported from Italy. This is a beautiful and remote spot and there's a dive school on site. US$175 per person sharing but the rates are full board and include boat trips to the nearby coves and islands.

L **Kinasi Lodge**, 100 m up the beach from Mafia Lodge, T023-2238220, www.mafiaisland.com. Set up on a hillside

For an explanation of the sleeping and eating price codes used in this guide, see inside the front cover. Other relevant information is found in Essentials pages 31-34.

above the bay, on the site of an old cashew plantation, the lodge has a dozen rooms arranged around a stylish central dining and lounge area. Its beach is not quite as nice as its rivals but it has a beautiful main complex with old coastal traditional decor, and a small library, bar, patio and dining room. It accommodates 20 people, has en suite bathrooms with hot water and mosquito nets. There's no a/c but it does have a swimming pool, can arrange diving and other watersports, and massages are available. Rates are US$160 per person.

B **Mafia Island Lodge**, reservations Dar es Salaam, T022-2116609, www.mafialodge.com. Recently refurbished and in a lovely setting overlooking Chole Bay, there are 40 rooms here all with a/c. There's a nice bar and restaurant, the food is good but a bit unvaried, and the lodge has its own beach. Windsurfing boards and Hobicats for rent. There is also a small diving centre run by a divemaster (dives US$50 per person with all equipment, plus oxygen facilities with a DAN oxygen provider for safety, PADI and NAUI courses).

E **The New Lizu Hotel**, T023-2402683. A very basic guest house in the centre of Kilondoni with simple rooms with fans for about US$5. It is aimed at the resident market, so don't expect anywhere near a Western level of comfort or facilities, but the place is friendly and there is a bar, restaurant and disco at weekends. This really is the only choice for budget travellers.

Activities and tours

Fishing

Fishing is at its best from Sep-Mar when the currents and the northeast monsoon (*kaskazi*) give rise to an enormous variety of fish. When the south monsoon (*kusi*) blows during the rest of the year fishing can be rather sparse. 'Big game' fish that can be caught in the area include marlin, shark, kingfish, barracuda and red snapper.

Game fishing, diving and other boat excursions can be arranged at **Chole Mjini Lodge**, **Pole Pole**, and **Kinasi Lodge**. Guests are taken out with an experienced skipper. Kinasi Lodge is a member of the International Game Fishing Association and has weighing facilities. It also holds a fishing competition every Feb.

Transport

Air

Coastal Air, T022-2117969-60, www.coastal.cc, has a daily scheduled service that departs **Dar** at 1500 (30 min; US$70) and **Zanzibar** at 1400 (1½ hr; US$100). It returns from Mafia at 1700. Another daily service connecting Mafia with all the camps in the **Selous**, departs the Selous at 1400, and Mafia at 1500 (1hr; US$120). They will also run a daily service between Mafia and **Kilwa**, if there are enough takers, leaving Mafia at 1545 (35 min; US$70) and Kilwa at 1630 on the return to Mafia.

Kilwa → *Colour map 1, grid B6. 9°0'S 39°0'E.*

Of exceptional historical interest, Kilwa is a group of three settlements magnificently situated on a mangrove-fringed bay dotted with numerous small islands. It grew up as a gold trade terminus and when its fortunes faded some magnificent ruins were left behind. These are said to be some of the most spectacular on the East African coast but which today are giving themselves slowly to the encroaching jungle and the relentless cycles of the tide. Once an important centre of Swahili culture and civilization, the baked limestone, coral blocks, the fig tree roots growing through the windows and a few shattered tiles give witness to many years' habitation here. If Kilwa was in Kenya the place would be full of tourists – it is an extraordinarily rewarding place to visit. As it is, it gets just a handful of visitors each week. » *For Sleeping, Eating and other listings, see pages 112-113.*

Ins and outs

Getting there The road from Dar es Salaam to Kilwa is part tar, part dirt. There is now a new bridge over the Rufiji river so there is no more hassle with catching ferries or buses waiting overnight at the crossing. The road from Dar to the bridge is good tar as far as Mazomora but from here the road is potholed tar and the journey is slow and uncomfortable. Journey time: 12 to 20 hours, depending on the weather. ▸▸ *See Transport, page 113, for further details.*

Getting around The town is split between **Kilwa Kisiwani** (Kilwa on the Island), 2 km offshore; **Kilwa Kivinje** (Kilwa of the Casuarina Trees) on the mainland; and **Kilwa Masoko** (Kilwa of the Market), which was built as an administrative centre on a peninsula and is the site of the main present-day town. There is a superb beach within a stone's throw from Kilwa Masako centre and another, even better, one a few miles north of the town (ask for *Masako pwani*).

History

Kilwa Kisiwani contains the ruins of a 13th-century city of the Shirazi civilization, which is well preserved and documented. The town was founded at the end of the 10th century by Shirazis (see box, page 95), and flourished with the core of commercial activity based on the trade of gold from Sofala (in present-day Mozambique). It grew to be the largest town on the south coast and prospered to the extent that Kilwa could maintain an independent status with its own sultan and coinage.

The large stone town that grew up thrived and the architecture was striking. The largest pre-European building in equatorial Africa was located here – the Husuni Kubwa. However, Kilwa's fortunes were reversed in the 14th century. Vasco da Gama was said to have been impressed by the buildings of Kilwa and in 1505 a large Portuguese fleet arrived and took the town by force. Their aim was to take control of the Sofala gold trade and they did this by erecting a garrison and establishing a trading post in the town from where they set up a gold trade link with the interior. Without the gold trade the Shirazi merchants were left with little to keep the wealth growing and the town quickly went into decline. Having taken over the gold trade, and thus triggering the decline of the town, the Portuguese decided there was little point in staying in Kilwa, now an outpost that was expensive to maintain. So they withdrew from Kilwa and continued the gold trade from further afield.

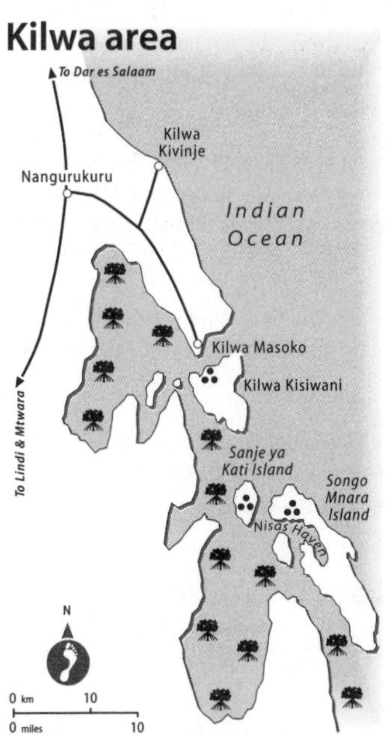

Deprived of the main source of income, the town continued to decline. In 1589 disaster struck when a nearby tribe, the Zimba, attacked the town, killing and eating many of the inhabitants. In the 17th century, with the arrival of the Oman Arabs, Kilwa began to revive and many of the buildings were taken over by the sultans as palaces. The slave trade (see page 353) made a significant impact on this area and Kilwa Kivinje on the mainland flourished from the caravan route from the interior, which terminated at the port.

Sights

★ Kilwa Kisiwani

ⓘ Small dhows in the harbour at Kilwa Masoko will take you across the 2 km channel for US$7. However, it is necessary first to get a permit to visit the site (approximately US$2) from the Cultural Centre at the district headquarters, which is on the road leading to the harbour. They can also organize a half-day boat trip for US$10 (the boat will take up to six people). There are 2 guides on the island who will take you through the ruins, giving some background information on the buildings, for a negotiable fee of around US$3.50. Allow at least half a day for your visit.

'One Thousand Years of East Africa' by John Sutton is highly recommended further reading (available in Dar es Salaam from the museum bookshop).

Gereza Fort The original Gereza was built in the 14th century. The one standing there today was built by the Omani Arabs in the 19th century on the site of the original on the orders of the Imam of Muscat. It is a large square building built of coral set in lime. The walls, with circular towers at the northeast and southwest corners, are very thick and it has an impressive entrance of fine wood carving.

Great Mosque (Friday Mosque) This mosque is said to have been built in the 12th century and is probably the largest of this period on the east coast. It was excavated between 1958 and 1960 and parts of it have been reconstructed. The oldest parts that remain are outer sections of the side walls and the north wall. The façade of the *mihrab* (the aspect that points towards Mecca) is dated from around 1300. The domed chamber was supposed to have been the sultan's prayer room. The water tanks and the slabs of stone were for rubbing clean the soles of the feet before entering the mosque.

Great House The large single-storey building is said to have been the residence of the sultan, and the remains of one of the sultans are said to reside in one of the four graves found within its walls. The building is an illustration of the highly developed state of building and architectural skills in this period with examples of courtyards, reception rooms, an amphitheatre that is unique to this part of the world, latrines, kitchens and cylindrical clay ovens.

Small Domed Mosque About 150 m southwest of the Great House, this is without doubt the best preserved of all the buildings in Kilwa. It is an ornamental building with beautiful domes. The long narrow room on its east side is thought once to have been a Koran school.

House of Portico Little remains of this once large building. There are portico steps on three of its sides from where it gets its name and its doorway has a decorated stone frame.

Makutini Palace (Palace of Great Walls) This large, fortified building is believed to date from the 15th century. It is to the west of the Small Domed Mosque and is roughly triangular in shape. Its longest wall, which ran along the coast, is in ruins. Within the complex is the grave of one of the sultans.

Jangwani Mosque The ruins of this stone building are concealed under a series of mounds to the southeast of the Makutini Palace. This mosque was unique for having ablution water jars set into the walls just inside the main entrance.

Malindi Mosque This mosque to the east of the Gereza Fort was said to have been built and used by immigrants from Malindi on the Kenya coast.

Husuni Kubwa This building is thought to be the largest pre-European building in equatorial Africa. It is between 1-2 km to the east of the main collection of ruins on top of a steep cliff. It is certainly an exceptional construction with over 100 rooms and a large conical dome that reaches about 30 m above the ground. The mosque has 18 domes on octagonal piers, separated by high barrel vaults. The piers are decorated with bowls of white porcelain set in the plaster.

Husuni Ndogo This is a smaller version of Husuni Kubwa separated from it by a small gully. It is said to have been built in the 15th century with walls 1 m thick and towers in the corners.

Kilwa Kivinje

About 29 km north of Kilwa Masoko, Kilwa Kivinje is an attractive historical trading centre whose heyday was during the slave trading times of the 18th and 19th centuries, but which remained the district headquarters up until 1949. It retains many interesting old buildings dating back to the 19th century as well as the colonial period and is somewhat reminiscent of Bagamoyo. A handsome old boma on the shore dates from the German period, as does the covered market. Several fine, though rather dilapidated, houses stand along the main street. There is an old mosque in the centre, and to the east of the town is a cemetery with tombs and pillars. The town can be reached by *dala-dala*, heading for Manguruturu, costing about US$1. There are half a dozen or so each day.

Songo Mnara and offshore islands

Songo Songo is an island about 25 km northeast of Kilwa Kivinje, protected by a reef, lying close to the site of a large natural gas field in a Lower Cretaceous sandstone reservoir. The Songo Songo gas field contains unusually dry petrogenic gas, which is 97% methane. From 2003 the Songas Project has been operational and the gas is being extracted from the gas field and piped to Dar es Salaam to fuel a power station that was until recently fuelled by more expensive oil. Songo Songo, Jewe Island and the surrounding smaller islands are an important marine bird breeding site. Access is by dhow, and there is usually at least one service each day transporting the gas employees, which takes around three hours each way, arranged in Kilwas Kivinje.

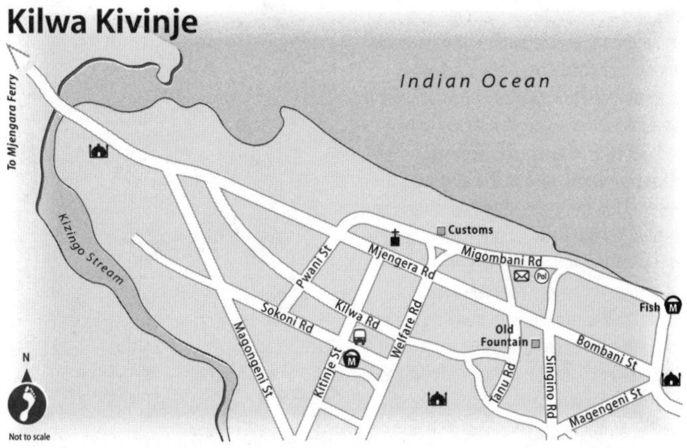

About 10 km south of Kilwa Kiswani there is another group of islands. To get there you must hire a motorized dhow in Kilwa Masoko (US$20 for up to six people). The ruined buildings at **Songo Mnara** are exceptional. The settlement is surrounded by the remains of a wall and the main mosque is distinguished by herringbone stonework and it has a double row of unusually high arches at one end. The Sultan's Palace, with its high walls, is extensive and was evidently at least two storeys high. The doorways, faced with slender stonework, are particularly fine. The building to the east of the palace has a room with a vaulted roof and porcelain bowls are set into the stonework. There are three other smaller mosques, two of which abut the surrounding wall. Fragments of porcelain and earthenware abound, and some relics have been identified as Egyptian, dating from the 14th and 15th centuries.

About 3 km southwest of Songo Mnara is an area known as **Sanje Majoma**, which also contains the ruins of a number of once-beautiful houses, complete with courtyards and stone arches. **Sanje ya Kati** is a nearby uninhabited island, which was once settled by the Shanga people who are now extinct. In the 13th century they were considered a force to be reckoned with and strongly resisted foreign control. There are ruins of oblong-shaped houses estimated to date from the 14th to 15th century.

Sleeping and eating

Kilwa Masoko *p111, map p111*

A **Kilwa Lodge**, also known as Kilwa Ruins Beach Resort, bookings through *Family Travel & Tour Services Ltd*, Dar es Salaam, T022-2772215, www.kilwalodge.co.za. Full board, 6 tents and 2 beach cottages with en suite bathrooms, mosquito nets and wooden decks. Restaurant serves seafood and vegetarian options, bar. Can organize birdwatching, fishing, scuba diving and guided boat trips to Kilwa Kisiwani.

B **Kilwa Seaview Resort**, T023-2402542, www.kilwa.net. Set up on a cliff overlooking the Kilwa Masoko Bay. The restaurant and bar has a natural palm thatched roof, built around an old baobab tree. Rooms with bathrooms are in stone bandas, all with views over Kilwa Kisiwani. There's a good beach with fronded shades and a beach shower, as well as a swimming pool, and separate campsite with ablution block (US$5 per night). Activities include day trips to Kilwa Kivinje, and there are several fishing boats and dhows to be rented out with all fishing equipment.

C-E **Upepo Pwani**, east to the airstrip, T0748-500402 (mob), www.kilwa-safari.com. Twin-bedded bandas with mosquito nets, shared showers and toilets, full board rates, good restaurant where everyone eats together, bar, campsite with cooking area. Bandas are US$50, camping US$3 and tents can be hired for US$3, nice spot surrounded by palms, very friendly owners and good value. Recommended.

C **Kilwa Dreams**, next to Upepo Pwani. This is a new development that has just opened. It is run by a Danish man and currently offers 3 bungalows, each with a bathroom and fan and accommodating 3 people. There are plans to add a further 7 bungalows over

Kilwa Masoko

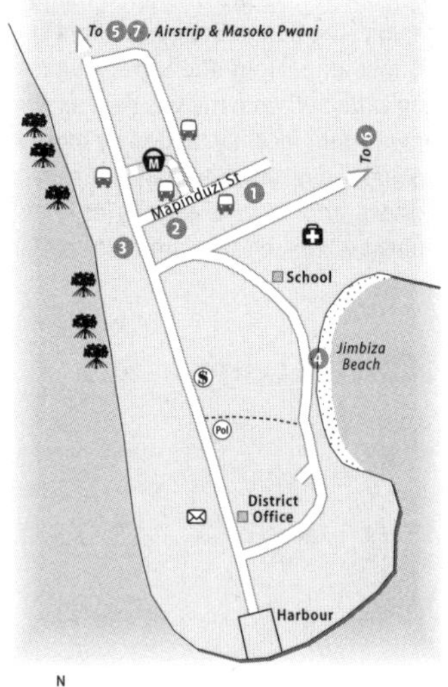

Sleeping
Hilton Guest House & Restaurant **1**
Kilwa Dreams **5**
Kilwa Guest House **2**
Kilwa Lodge **4**
Kilwa Seaview Resort **6**
New Mjaka Guest House **3**
Upepo Pwani **7**

time. There is a restaurant and the facility will offer fishing and boat trips and possibly diving in future.

F Hilton Guest House, Mapinduzi St, T0748- 677921 (mob). Simple rooms with fan, with or without bathrooms, a bit run down and dingy but all less than US$5. There is a restaurant adjoining the guest house offering local dishes and breakfast and the fish here is good.

F Kilwa Guest House, Mapinduzi St. Similar to the Hilton, simple but basic rooms with fans cost US$3.

F New Mjaka Guest House, on right of road that leads from main Mangurukivu Rd to the market. Fans, only single rooms, though 2 people could probably fit on the ¾ sized beds, clean and tidy though running water can be a problem, local food served.

Transport

Kilwa Masoko *p111, map p111*

Air

Coastal Air, T022-2117969-60, www.coastal.cc, has a scheduled daily flight between Kilwa and **Dar** (2 hr; US$110) via **Mafia** (45 min; US$70). It departs Dar at 1500, and departs Kilwa 1630. A charter is a possibility, particularly for groups.

Road

Bus Direct to Kilwa from the Ubungo Bus Station in **Dar**, at 0500 (13 hrs), around US$10. Confirm exact departure time and book a ticket the day before you travel. Return from Kilwa at 0500 daily. Alternatively take one of the numerous buses heading for destinations south of Kilwa, such as Mtwara, Lindi or Nachingwea. These leave Dar between 0700 and 0900. Again it is advisable to book at least a day in advance. Seats closer to the front are recommended as the going is rough. This bus will drop you off at **Nangurukuru**, a village 12 km from Kilwa Masoko, from where you have to transfer to a minibus or pickup to complete the journey (US$1). In order to travel south to **Lindi**, **Mtwara** or **Masasi** you have to catch buses coming from Dar at Nangurukuru. They start arriving from about 1400 onwards. The journey takes 5 hrs minimum as the road is poor. You'll be lucky to get a seat. There are numerous minibuses/pickups between Kilwa **Kivinje** and **Kilwa Masoko** daily.

Lindi

Phone code: 023. Colour map 1, grid C6. Population: 40,000. 9°58'S 39°38'E.

Despite the fact that Lindi translates from Ki Mwera (a local language) as 'a pit latrine', the place still has a great deal of charm, albeit faded. It was an important port for early traders and travellers, and the Arab influence is visible. The centre has many attractive colonial buildings, but poor communications and the collapse of the Groundnut Scheme (see page 358), one site for which was at nearby Nachingwea, have hampered development. Since the opening of the deep-water harbour at Mtwara in 1954, Lindi's harbour, too shallow for modern ships, is only used by local fishing boats, and the quay is slowly crumbling away. Around Lindi Bay there are several attractive beaches fringed with palm trees. ▸▸ *For Sleeping, Eating and other listings, see page 118.*

Ins and outs

Getting there The airstrip is at Kikwetu about 25 km north of town but at present there are no commercial flights. The only way to get there is by road, perhaps breaking your journey at Kilwa as the daily bus journey from Dar takes anything up to 2 days depending on road conditions and buses may not run at all during the rainy season – the road from Kilwa to Lindi can be impassable after heavy rains. Seek advice on the road condition before travelling, there is no accommodation en route should you get stuck. On the plus side, the road is under construction from both south and north and should be sealed within 1 to 2 years but the worst part of the road, covering a distance of about 100km in the middle, still has no contract to seal it, so the road improvement scheme will only partially assist travellers on route. The drive between Kilwa and Lindi can take over 12 hours depending on the road condition. » *See Transport, page 118, for further details.*

Getting around Lindi itself is a very compact town and most of the places of interest are within walking distance. *Dala-dalas* can be caught at the market, the bus stand or along the main streets (Kawawa, Market and Mchinga roads).

Background

Initial settlement was by Shirazi migrants (see page 95). Being the main seaport for Lake Nyasa (now Lake Malawi), it was a destination for slave caravans from the interior in the 19th century. The only remnant of this Omani Arab period is the massive round tower on the beach side of the stadium.

The colonial German powers chose Lindi as the administrative headquarters of the Southern Province, a huge administrative area, which encompassed the whole of the south of Tanganyika right across to Lake Nyasa at the end of the 19th century. A Custom House and store for the German East African Company were constructed close to the remains of the fort, These, and other buildings of the colonial period, are now very dilapidated. One German building, the police station, is still in use, it's easily identifiable by its solid build and ornamental finishes. The German Boma is disappearing behind the trees growing out of it.

Lindi has a long history as a trading port for ivory, beeswax and mangrove poles. Rock salt is extensively mined nearby. Its advantages were the comparatively easy approach along the Lukuledi River valley and the relative proximity of Mozambique, source of much of the produce.

There are fine examples of Asian-inspired architecture along Market and Kawawa roads, dating from when the town used to support an Asian community trading in grain, sisal and cashew nuts.

There are ornamental decorative finishes on some of the buildings, especially the mosques, such as those on Makongoro Street facing the stadium. The modest mosque next to the bus station possesses a wonderful elaborately carved and colourful door. Lindi is now essentially a Muslim town and the Muslim Brotherhoods or *tariqa* are quite active. You are likely to hear, if not see, noisy celebrations at night on feasts such as *maulid*, the commemoration of the Prophet's birth. It involves Quran school teachers and their students singing in turn, drumming, lots of incense, and possibly deep-breathing exercises known to Muslim mystics as *dhikr*. If you want to see a *maulid*, dress modestly and exercise discretion. Other rather high-pitched drums heard at night are for girls' initiation ceremonies or spirit possession dances – no contradiction for the local brand of Islam.

Sights

The present centre of town around the bus stand dates from the British period. The historic centre of the town between Kawawa Road and the beach is now a poor area with a reputation for rampant witchcraft. Here the last descendant of the once-dominant Jamalidini family, of Mombasa origins, lives in a mud hut on a waterlogged compound. Several of the newer houses resemble pillboxes made of cement or breeze-blocks or occasionally mud and wattle.

Lindi has a large football stadium and its team is in Tanzania's 1st division, worth watching if you get the opportunity.

The beach doubles as a boulevard and football pitch in the evenings, and sometimes you can see the fishermen unloading their catch which includes octopus, kingfish and sharks (caught outside the bay). Their catch of the day is for sale after dark at the bus stand, freshly cooked. The beach by the town is also good for swimming, but you are likely to be closely observed by the townspeople.

Mitema

There are several excellent beaches around Lindi Bay, the best probably at Mitema, 4 km north of the town, just a 10-minute drive from the centre. This is where Lindi's few expatriates go swimming. The long beach, often deserted, is sheltered by palms and closed off at each end by rocks and enormous baobab trees. Occasionally you may meet a herd boy with his goats or a couple of Lindi's Asian traders in their four-wheel drive vehicles. The ground is a bit rocky at low tide and the waves are high in the evening but it makes an enjoyable excursion – if you don't have your own transport make arrangements with *dala-dala* operators at the bus stand.

Kitunda and 'ngambo'

Many of Lindi's residents come from 'ngambo', which means 'the other shore', and in Lindi it refers to the peninsula across the bay, Kitunda being the beachside village. For a negligible fare, and at approximately half-hour intervals from Lindi harbour until 1800, you can take a wooden motorboat ferry to Kitunda. Here the water is clearer than at Lindi though mangroves make swimming difficult at low tide. You can hire a dugout very cheaply from a local fisherman to paddle along the shore or across the bay. Take the owner along for safety. Locals can show you around the hill behind the village. You will be shown many edible plants and odd animals such as *ndandanda*, a small wedge-shaped fish with large eyes at the top of its head that uses its fins for crawling and jumping in shallow water. The sisal and coconut estates here are in terminal decline and there are the remains of a railway and jetty jutting out over the water, a good vantage point for swims at high tide. Across the hill to the south lie the villages of **Mwitingi**, once the home of Arab plantation owners, and **Shuka**, where locals catch sharks.

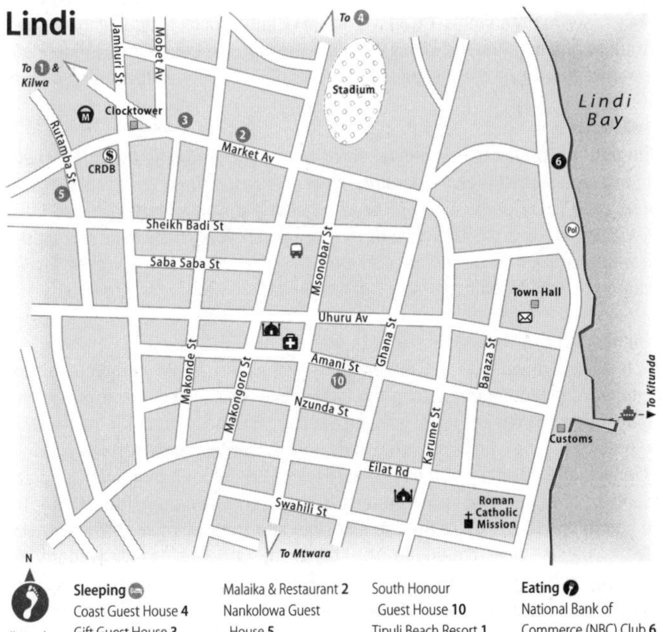

Kikwetu

Kikwetu is a breezy promontory 25 km north of Lindi, the location of the town's **airfield** and also of the last sisal estate to close in the area. It closed in 1999 after 100 years of production because sisal, used as coarse fibre for sackcloth and ropes, is no longer profitable. Hidden among the large fields is the manager's mansion, from where there are excellent views. There is regular transport to the airport – to see the mansion, a 20-minute walk away from the roadside village, ask for *kambi* and the locals will show you. There are reports that South Africans may buy the estate, so it could yet have a future.

Kisiwa cha popo

This small island in Lindi Bay is famed for its large bat population. Chiroptera fanciers can take a boat trip to the island where the trees are heavy with sleeping bats hanging from the branches during the day. You may also see crocodiles if you take a boat ride south across the Lukuledi River estuary to the other side of Lindi Bay.

Litipo Forest Reserve

ⓘ *Litipo is 30 km west of Lindi, just north of Rutamba. To get here you really need your own vehicle as there are no buses. Although only 30 km or so, the journey takes at least 3 hrs. To get into the reserve, go along the road leading to Tandangogoro village and take one of the paths leading north that go into the reserve. To get more information about Litipo it may be worth asking the forest reserve officer who is usually stationed at Rutamba.*

There are numerous little-known forest reserves dotted throughout Tanzania, including many that exist to help preserve some of the remaining patches of coastal rainforest that millions of years ago covered the whole coastal area. Several of these reserves are in Lindi district, the most accessible of which is west of Litipo. The reserve here consists of a patch of rainforest lying between two small lakes. Litipo Forest Reserve covers an area of 999 ha. It is a beautiful spot and although you are unlikely to see many animals the area is rich in visible birdlife, including the red-tailed ant thrush, African pitta and Livingstone's flycatcher. On the nearby Rondo Plateau the spotted ground thrush, the green-headed oriole and green barbet are also found.

Tendaguru

ⓘ *The natural resources administration of Lindi (Mali Asili) will be able to help to arrange a visit, something only possible in the dry season. This geological site is quite remote, so a fossil enthusiast will need at least 3 days for getting there, looking around and getting back. As elephants may be present you'll need to be accompanied by a game warden. You should also be self-sufficient as there are no facilities, although you may be able to arrange accommodation with local villagers.*

The richest African deposit of the Late Jurassic strata is found in Tendaguru. The Natural History museums in London and Berlin both boast complete dinosaur skeletons from Tendaguru, among the largest ever discovered. Bernhard Sattler, a German mining engineer who was prospecting in the region for minerals and semi-precious stones, first uncovered fossil remains in 1907. Between 1909 and 1913, W Janensch and E Hennig of the Natural History Museum of Berlin uncovered about 225,000 kg of bones and, using porters, transported them along footpaths – there were no roads – for 70 km to the coast at Lindi and shipped them to Europe. British palaeontologists later continued the research, undertaking excavations from 1925-1929. Post-independence, smaller research investigations have been carried out with the permission of the Tanzanian authorities. Many bones remain under the ground and fragments can be seen at the sites of previous digs. The beds consist of

Cashew nuts

Cashew nuts are the main export product in the Lindi, Mtwara and Kilwa regions of Tanzania. They grow on massive trees, rarely more than 10 m tall, but with sprawling, shady crowns, which line many of the streets in these districts. They supply elephant repellent, poison, furniture varnish, high-voltage liquor and, of course, nuts. Two properties combine to make the fruit so versatile. First, cashew nuts come attached to cashew apples, a tasty, brightly coloured fruit which is easily fermented. Second, between the shell and the kernel, cashew nuts contain a noxious oil strong enough to cause serious wounds. Hence the use of cashew nuts to drive off elephants: the animals detest the smell of the burning oil.

The oil makes the shelling of cashew nuts difficult and the shelled nuts expensive. The trick is to burn the shells and the oil of the nuts, but not the kernels, by roasting them quickly and then as quickly extinguishing the fire. If people do this in their back yards in old gasoline drums, the kernels end up spotty, half raw, half charred. Nuts like these are sold cheaply in the countryside and sometimes in Dar. Better quality ones, shelled in factories, are much more expensive, and a mere handful might cost more than a meal.

Tanzania's cashew shelling industry has not fared very well. Most of the nuts are exported raw and shelled in India. In Tanzania, the state-owned cashew marketing board tried to introduce industrial processing of the nuts. Factories have been opened and closed at various times in Mtwara, Nachingwea and Dar es Salaam. At present, only the one in Dar is working efficiently.

Cashew trees are not indigenous to Africa. They entered Tanzania from Mozambique, where they had arrived from Brazil, a fringe benefit of Portuguese colonialism. For a long time, Mozambique (then Portuguese East Africa) was the only African cashew nut exporter, the nuts being sent to Goa, Portugal's colonial possession in India, for processing. In Tanzania, efforts to build up production only started in the late 1940s, British reluctance to support cashew production being partly due to colonial officials' fear of drunkenness among Africans – cashew apples make a good raw material for distilling illicit spirits.

In the 1940-60s, cashew nuts helped to improve the economic situation of one of the poorest parts of Tanzania where, until then, grain had been the main export crop. But from the early 1970s, the spread of a tree disease, low producer prices, and the effects of the 'villagization' policy combined to almost destroy cashew production. Villagization separated cultivators from their plots and occasionally even involved the cutting down of trees in order to construct the villages, while disease caused yields to dwindle to almost nothing.

Production was revived only at the end of the 1990s, when people were again free to live where they chose, and it was discovered that if sulphur was sprayed on the leaves, it protected the trees against disease. It has been rising since. In the 1999/2000 season, prices to farmers for Tanzanian cashew nuts hit an all-time high because of a poor harvest in India, the world's largest cashew supplier. The southern regions had a bumper harvest, and for the year 2000 cashew nuts became Tanzania's top foreign-currency earning cash crop.

three strata of terrestrial marls alternating with marine sandstone interbeds. Remains of the giant vegetarian, long-necked sauropod, *Brachiosaurus brancai*, named after the museum's director at the time and measuring 22 m long by 12 m high, and the spiny-plated stegosaurus, *Kentrurosaurus aethiopicus*, 4.8 m long by 1.7 m high, both of which were found here, are now on display in Berlin.

Sleeping

Lindi *p113, map p115*

There is a very poor choice of accommodation in Lindi and most is in cheap local guest houses, none of which is especially good.

D **Malaika Hotel**, Market Av, T023-2202717. Good clean self-contained rooms, with fans and mosquito nets. Price includes breakfast. In Lindi it seems like the hotels mostly have single beds and this is one of the few places with double rooms. Also has a restaurant with a good value menu of mainly rice dishes and snacks. It's the best restaurant in town.

E **Coast Guest House**, about 500 m north of ferry on beach, T023-2202496. Fans and mosquito nets in single rooms. Run down but in a good location amongst palm trees on the beach.

E **Gift Guest House**, near *Malaika Hotel* on Market Av, T023-2202462. New and clean, decent-sized rooms, fans and nets.

E **Nankolowa Guest House**, Rutamba St, signposted from the Clocktower. New and well furnished, good value, self-contained double rooms, single rooms have shared toilet. Price includes large breakfast, and they serve other good meals on request, after a long wait.

F **South Honour Guest House**, Amani St, 3 blocks back from the ferry. Fans, nets, simple, bucket showers, agreeable staff, very cheap (about US$2.50). There are a number of similar guest houses around the bus stand.

F **Tipuli Beach Resort**, 6km north of Lindi on the Kilwa road, T0748-703340 (mob). The only bet for camping (US$4 per car). Quite a nice setting on a cliff overlooking the sea with a path down to the beach. The facilities are basic but clean, food can be made on request and there is a little bar.

Eating

Lindi *p113, map p115*

All of the hotels have restaurants, and there are snack bars around the bus station that serve sweet, milky tea, as well as *maandazi*, *chapattis* and other snacks. Fresh fruit and simple fare can be purchased at the market on Jamhuri St. The fishermen's catch of the day is for sale, freshly cooked, at the bus stand after dark.

National Bank of Commerce (NBC) Club, also called the **Lindi Club**, is a good choice for a beer. A bit dilapidated, but the sea view makes it one of the most pleasant locations. If you give plenty of notice they can cook something basic.

Transport

Lindi *p113, map p115*

Bus

Buses leave from **Dar** at 0600-0900, (14-20 hrs, US$15). The bus to Dar leaves at 0500 from bus stand on Makongoro Rd. The fare to **Kilwa** along the way (approximately US$6). To **Mtwara** buses run fairly frequently (about 4 hrs, US$3). To **Nachingwea** and **Newela** there are daily buses (5-6 hrs, both about US$5); the road rising up to the Makonde plateau is pretty grim.

Directory

Lindi *p113, map p115*

Banks There is now only one bank in town, the CRDB near the clocktower, where travellers' cheques can be cashed. **Post** The post office is on Uhuru Av not far from the ferry. **Medical services** Sokoine Hospital, T023-2202027/8. There is a medical clinic at the corner of Amani St and Msonobar St. **Useful addresses** The police station T023-2202505 is housed in an old German building beside the waterfront, towards the NBC Club.

Mikindani and Mtwara

Mikindani is a sleeping fishing village, but with an interesting history reflected in the few old Arab-style buildings with carved doors and elaborate balconies. Here are the best two places to stay in the region, the Old Boma and 10° South which both offer good value accommodation, excellent food, and trips to the region's local attractions including the Mnazi Bay Marine Reserve. Mtwara, 10 km to the south, is more modern and the administrative town of the south coast region. There is little to see here, though it offers facilities such as a bank and post office and is the immigration office is here if you are planning to cross the border into Mozambique. » *For Sleeping, Eating and other listings, see pages 122-125.*

Mikindani → *Phone code: 023. Colour map 1, grid C6.*  » *pp122-125*

The small town of Mikindani is 11 km to the northwest of Mtwara on the Mtwara to Lindi road. Unlike most towns in this region, Mikindani has managed to retain much of its traditional Arab charm. A very Muslim town, you should dress and act appropriately. It is located beside a sheltered circular lagoon, itself an inlet from the larger Mikindani Bay. The lagoon has made an excellent harbour for the dugout canoes and dhows of local fishermen for centuries and there has been a settlement here for almost 1,000 years. When the Arabs arrived Mikindani grew in prosperity, its importance as a trading centre being greatest in the 15th century. Later, with the arrival of the first Europeans, notably the explorer Dr Livingstone, and with the subsequent ban on slave trade, Mikindani began to decline. There was a revival when the German colonial government briefly made the town the district headquarters in 1890. However, by the 1950s production of groundnuts and oil seed demanded larger ships, for which the port was unsuitable, and Mikindani declined once more.

Mikindani Bay is not suitable for swimming because the water is contaminated.

Sights

Much of the town's traditional character remains. There is an interesting mix of thatched mud houses and Arab-style buildings including several fine two-storey townhouses with elaborate fretwork balconies. Arabs, Portuguese, Germans and British have all occupied the town at different times. The 500-year-old Portuguese fort was used as a slave prison and later bombarded by the British in the First World War. There is an old slave market, now a collection of small art shops, and a fort, dating from the German period and built in 1895, which has been renovated to become a hotel. Most of the other old colonial buildings are in a poor state of repair. Mikindani was the port from which Livingstone departed on his final journey to the interior in 1867 (see page 305) and a house with a fine carved door bears a plaque to mark the site where the explorer is said to have camped.

A walk up the hill behind the Old Boma (see below) will bring you to a very large hole. A witchdoctor saw his lucky chicken scratching in that spot several years ago and ever since has been digging for German gold that he firmly believes is buried there.

Trade Aid

ⓘ *To find out more about this project or to offer either financial or practical help, contact the UK headquarters of the charity at: Trade Aid, Burgate Court, Burgate, Fordingbridge, Hants SP6 1LX, UK, T01425-657774, www.mikindani.com.*

Since 1996 this British charity has been working at Mikindani helping the local people to build and develop a sustainable ecotourist trade and thus alleviate poverty. The old German Boma has been rehabilitated and converted to a very comfortable hotel. Trade Aid has had a number of volunteers from the UK working on the project – often gap year students. The Old Boma is the base for the charity, which actively encourages small businesses within the village. Some of the first ventures include an organic market garden supplying the Old Boma and a tree nursery. So far some 40 jobs have been created in the Boma, and a further 20 in the other ventures. Trade Aid Mikindani also oversees the Danish Schools Project, a group of caring Danish donors who support the education of over 100 local children. They can help organize trips to Msimbati Beach and possibly to other attractions in the future.

Mtwara

→ *Phone code: 023. Colour map 1, grid C6. Population: 80,000. 10°20'S 40°20'E.*

pp123-125

Mtwara is a sizeable town that came to prominence during the British period. It has been a centre for agricultural processing, and there is a factory for shelling and canning the cashew nuts that are grown extensively in the southeast (see box, page 117). Although the town itself is set a little way from the shore, Mtwara boasts a magnificent sheltered harbour. However the port, built in 1948-1954, has never been used to capacity as there is relatively little traffic generated in this economically depressed region. The second deepest port in Africa, it was built as part of the ill-fated scheme to grow and export groundnuts from southern Tanzania, a project that included the construction of a railway from Mtwara to Nachingwea – now dismantled. The scheme was implemented after the Second World War, when the British had taken control of what was then Tanganyika from the Germans, and the groundnuts were expected to make up for post-war food shortages in the United Kingdom and for export to the rest of Europe. There are current plans to dredge and widen the port's entrance channel to facilitate the handling of larger modern vessels.

The town has one site of particular interest, **St Paul's Church**, which houses some remarkable murals of Biblical scenes painted by German priests. There are some **beaches** about 2 km from the town centre good for swimming and diving.

Crossing into Mozambique

Mtwara is close to the border with Mozambique and there is a launch boat that crosses the Ruvuma River (see box page 122 for details). However, for those going to Mozambique visas are only available at the border to Tanzanian nationals; other nationalities need to get one from Dar es Salaam in advance. If crossing the other way, visas are available from the immigration office in Mtwara.

The Mnazi Bay Marine Reserve

ⓘ *The reserve is 22 km along a dirt track from the main road which is in a good state of repair and accessible to all vehicles because of a gas drilling operation on the peninsula. The road is, however, frequented by fairly heavy traffic and is liable to flooding during the wet season. The charge for entering the reserve is US$10 per person for a 24-hr period. There is at present no charge for vehicles. Currently there is only one (not very good) place to stay in the reserve, the Ruvula Sea Safari Lodge (see Sleeping). 10 Degrees South has put on hold its plans to build an eco lodge due to ongoing land ownership disputes in the area. They do, however, offer diving to the reefs in the reserve, operated from their lodge in Mikindani. Trade Aid in Mikindani can also arrange a visit at a cost of US$25 per person (minimum 4 people) to include a driver and cook. A shelter and table are set up on the beach and the price includes lunch.*

Mnazi Bay Marine Reserve was gazetted in 1999 and is similar in status to the Mafia Marine Reserve further up to the coast to the north. It offers superb snorkelling and scuba diving and, as the reef along the coast is not tidal, it is good for swimming at all times of the day. It is 8 km north of the Mozambique border post on the Ruvuma River and 30 km south of Mtwara. The **Msimbati Beach** is a pristine, white sandy beach that shelves steeply. There is a fabulous coral reef lying offshore and turtles are common.

The self-proclaimed 'Sultan of Msimbati', a British eccentric named Leslie Latham Moore, came to these parts after the First World War. He attempted to declare independence from Tanganyika – a situation that was briefly tolerated before he was arrested. The remains of his dilapidated house can still be seen. Geological surveys on **Msimbati Island** in the Ruvuma Basin have shown several oil seeps, some showing characteristics of true degraded crude oil. There is also a gas seep on the island, believed to be of biogenic origin. This basin lies at the southern end of the large East African Karoo Rift System that extends from Somalia. Exploration licences have been granted to the oil companies, and there is a new gas installation offshore.

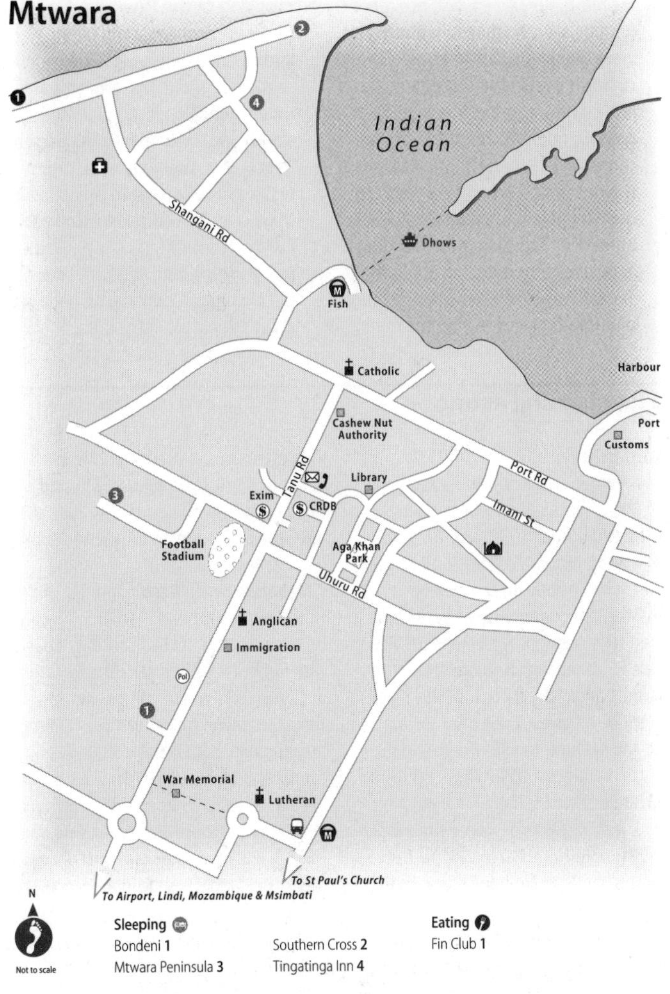

Namuiranga – Kilambo border crossing

From Mozambique, the Mozambique immigration and customs is reached after 126 km along dirt and sand tracks from Mocimboa da Praia. The last petrol station is in Mocimboa da Praia and the next fuel available is in Mtwara on the Tanzanian side. Mozambique immigration is in the settlement of Namuiranga (S10° 32.021 E040° 23.264) and can be slow as they speak no English (only Portuguese and Swahili). They may try to exhort US$2.50 per person for a supposed tax for stamping passports; however this is only for Mozambique citizens and not other nationals. At the time of writing they were building a new immigration and customs post in the settlement and service may improve in future. There are plans to open the border as a major thoroughfare for trade and tourism in the next few years and we were told that funding for a bridge had been agreed with the Japanese. Building is expected to start later in 2005. The Tanzanians are currently in the process of upgrading and sealing the road from Mtwara to the border and there are plans to build an international market at Kilambo to facilitate and develop trade. The track from Namuiranga to the ferry is only 6 km but is atrocious and only passable with a 4x4 in the dry season (in the wet, forget it). Taxis will not venture down the track after heavy rains and people should expect to have to walk from the border post to the ferries. There are, however, many baggage carriers who will carry your luggage down for a fee.

Passenger ferries and mokoro crossing of the Ruvuma Motorized ferries are numerous and often, particularly at weekends. They operate both sides of the river. Mokoros are even more abundant although obviously slower and the amount of luggage and people that can be carried is more restricted. For a mokoro crossing expect to pay around US$2 per person each way. For a motorboat ferry crossing expect to pay anything from US$1.50-4 per person, per crossing, depending on how many other people are in the boat.

Sleeping and eating

Mikindani *p119*
There are three excellent places to stay and eat in Mkindani catering for all budgets.

A-B **The Old Boma**, T0748-360110 (mob), www.mikindani.com. A converted 100-year-old fort, it has 7 standard and superior rooms, the latter having balconies. All have fans, en suite bathrooms, tremendous views, and are furnished with beautiful local-style beds and handicrafts. Rates are US$90-120, and include breakfast. Even if not staying come and eat here, food is superb and set 3-course menus cost US$6. They also stock a good range of wines. There is a swimming pool for use by guests or diners, email facility for guests only. Note that this is a TV-free zone. The hotel can arrange excursions to local attractions such as Mzani Marine Reserve US$70, town tours US$10, and night canoe fishing trips US$20. They also advertise free Swahili language and cookery lessons. Recommended.

C **Makonde Beach Resort**, formely Litingi's Hotel, on a good beach 2 km from the village on the peninsula of Mikindani Bay. It has 15 well-furnished, self-contained bandas with a/c, satellite TV and telephone. Indian-Tanzanian owned, a bit run down but has huge potential. Set in large grounds, camping available US$10 per vehicle. The bar and restaurant has an extensive menu with Indian, Chinese and local dishes from US$3-5, and holds the occasional disco when there's demand. They are in the process of

For an explanation of the sleeping and eating price codes used in this guide, see inside the front cover. Other relevant information is found in Essentials pages 31-34.

Vehicle ferry crossing of the Ruvuma There is now a new vehicle ferry operating and service is reliable. The ferry is located and operated from Tanzania and anyone wishing to cross with vehicles should contact the ferry owners to arrange a suitable time and date. If needed you can take a passenger ferry to the Tanzanian side and travel the 6 km to Kilambo to arrange for the ferry to come and pick you up. The Ruvuma is a tidal estuary and crossings are dictated by tidal conditions (we had to wait 5 days because of neap tides and low seasonal waters from up stream). This is another reason to phone ahead from Mocimboa da Praia to arrange when a crossing can be made. Note there is no cell phone coverage on the Mozambique side. Contact number for the ferry is: +255 (0)744 869357.

Car ferry costs There are two routes taken for crossing the Ruvuma. The short route takes 10 minutes and is only passable at high tides. This crossing for vehicle and passengers costs between US$40-50, receipts are issued. Price may fluctuate due to diesel costs but this range seems to be the norm. The long route takes about 20 minutes and is used during low water. Expect to pay between US$80-90.

Vehicle documentation and fees for border crossing Travel in Mozambique and Tanzania with your own vehicle requires either a Temporary Import Permit or Carnet De Passage. These act as bonds for the vehicle to the respective governments to ensure that the vehicles are not sold and import taxes evaded. The TIP can be arranged at the borders, cost is variable depending on the age and value of the vehicle. Carnets are arranged prior to travel in the country of register of the vehicle. Note the fine for no TIP or Carnet in Mozambique is 1 Million Meticals. There is a US$5 road tax payable on the Tanzanian side and third party vehicle insurance should be arranged for travel in both countries at the nearest large town after the border.

With thanks to David and Kat Horner.

building a restaurant closer to the bandas with conference facilities and swimming pool which is expected to be finished by the time this book comes out.

D 10° South (Ten Degrees), T023-2334053, tendegreessouth@twiga.com. Managed by Martin, an English Marine Biologist, 10° South offers 5 simple but very clean rooms in a pleasant house setting just off of the bay road. The bar, with friendly staff, is probably the most atmospheric place to come to for a drink. Large dining area has comfortable chairs and excellent food, local fish, calamari and a variety of other good western dishes. There's usually a barbecue on Sat evenings. Also sells postcards, stamps and magazines, and you can send mail from here. Eco2 Diving, run by Martin offers PADI dive courses up to instructor level. PADI open water costs US$400, advanced US$300 and recreational dives cost US$40. There is an equipment hire charge of an additional US$15 per day. Dives go to 12 local reefs, and also to the Mnazi Marine Reserve as either day trips or overnighters.

Trade Aid owns a piece of land known as the Yacht Club where it may be possible to pitch a tent. Enquiries should be made at The Old Boma.

Mtwara *p120, map p121*

The hotels offer a limited selection of inexpensive simple meals, with little variety – usually rice with chicken or fish. The best cheap street food is at the fish market, beside the beach, where fresh fish and cassava chips are sold.

C Southern Cross Hotel (also known as Msuma Hotel), T023-2333206. The best place to stay. On the peninsula overlooking the bay in a great setting. Swedish-owned but locally run. The food is OK, with seafood and curry dishes from US$4. The rooms, which are all doubles, are exceptionally clean and spacious

Lip plugs

The origin of the lip plug is not clear, but about 40 years ago it was fairly common to see elderly women in south Tanzania wearing them. One suggestion is that they were introduced to stop the women being taken away as slaves in the slave-raiding days. Others suggest that they were in use long before the slave trade and they were originally purely ornamental. No special rights were associated with the wearing of a plug and there was no religious significance attached to them. They were worn by a variety of ethnic groups and principally among tribes that had originated from what is now Mozambique. The tribes that wore the lip plug most commonly included the Makonde, Mwera, Mukua, Mawiha and Metu.

The procedure that was necessary for the wearing of a lip plug began when a girl was just five or six. One of the older women in the tribe would pierce the girl's upper lip using a thorn and would then thread a blade of grass into it. Three days later another blade of grass would be inserted, this time a little larger. This would be repeated about three times until a millet stalk about the thickness of the little finger would be inserted. A week later a second, thicker stalk would be inserted and would be left in place for about a month. By this time the lip would have healed and from then on a series of lip plugs would be inserted each just a little wider in diameter than the last so that the upper lip would gradually be stretched. The first three plugs usually have a circumference of about 50 mm. The first plug was worn for about two months and the second for about four months. When the third plug was inserted a number of markings would be cut into the girl's face – usually about three vertical lines each side of the eyes. When the girl reached puberty a plug of about 125 mm in circumference would be used and kept in place until the birth of her second child when it would be replaced by a larger one. In Makonde plugs of about 100 mm in diameter were fairly common.

The plugs were mostly made of ebony. They would be hollowed out by the older men of the tribe and often were highly polished. The wearer of the plug could not remove it at any time in public – in fact it would only have been taken out to be washed.

with their own bathroom and fridge. There is also a TV lounge. Service can be slow.

C **Mtwara Peninsula Hotel**, west of town near the football stadium, T023-2333965, T2333638. Run down but adequate, executive rooms have TV and minibar, all rooms a/c with en suite bathrooms. Good restaurant with an extensive menu of seafood, curries and some vegetarian dishes.

E **Bondeni**, Tanu Rd, south of police station. Plain but spacious rooms with fans and mosquito nets. The garden bar has satellite TV and is a good place for a few beers.

E **Tingatinga Inn**, south of the Southern Cross and the headland, T023-2333146. Reasonably neat rooms, shared bathrooms, in a quiet suburb, no restaurant.

Fin Club in Shangani serves good meals and has satellite TV. It is planning to offer accommodation in this area in the future under the name of the Shangani Housing Project and it is currently in the process of looking into converting some old expat houses as guest accommodation in Mtwara as well as Lindi. Check www.shangani.com for further information.

Mnazi Bay Marine Reserve *p120*

D **Ruvula Sea Safari**, on the beach front. Run by Jean Marie, a Belgian, this place is very run down, and has 5 simple bandas sleeping 2 to 3 people, only 1 of which has electricity. Shared bathrooms are in a poor state of repair, with only 1 toilet serviceable and cold water bucket showers only. Dinner costs an expensive US$10 and is mainly chicken and chips or rice. Camping costs US$5 but there are no ablutions or facilities. Security may be an issue as the campsite is unlit and unfenced to the beach. Very expensive for what you get and now overpriced thanks to the gas exploration guys who drink and eat here.

Transport

Mikindani and Mtwara

p119 p120, map p121

Bus

All buses stop at Mikindani en route to Mtwara. Between the two are also regular *dala-dala*. From **Dar** buses leave early in the morning (roughly 24 hrs, US$18). It's about 640 km from Dar along a rough, unsurfaced road and you are advised to break the journey in either Lindi or Kilwa. Buses leave for Dar at 0500 from the bus stand on Market St in Mtwara. Book ticket day before and confirm departure time. Buses to **Masasi** leave fairly frequently (US$4). Regular buses and *dala-dala* to **Lindi** (US$1). *Dala-dala* to **Mnazi Mmoja** (US$2), **Mikindani** (US$0.25).

Sea

This stretch of ocean can be rough – travel sickness tablets are recommended. There is a passenger ferry service between **Dar** and **Mtwara** on the **MV Safari** though this service is constantly disrupted and may not run at all during certain parts of the year. In theory it departs Dar at 1200 on Wed, arrives at Mtwara 24 hrs later and returns on Fri. 1st class US$25, 2nd class US$15 one way, plus US$5 port tax. Enquire at port in Dar or in Mtwara at the ferry office near the market. 1st class includes a bed of sorts, and you can buy meals on the ferry but its still a good idea to take your own food and drink.

Directory

Mtwara *p120, map p121*

Banks You can cash TCs at the recently opened **Exim Bank** on Tanu Rd, and **CRDB**. The latter now also has an ATM. **Post** Post office on Tanu Rd, half-way between *NBC Club* and Port Rd, has phone and fax facilities. **Useful addresses** The **immigration office** is to the south of the *NBC Club* on Tanu Rd, just past the Anglican church. You will need to come here to get a Tanzania visa if crossing from Mozambique. The **police station** is across the road from there.

Tunduru via Makonde Plateau

Travel to the extreme southern district of Tanzania is not for the feint hearted, as the roads that run from the coast to Tunduru are little more than tracks and can become completely impassable in the wet. Accommodation is limited and it is a gruelling bus journey but you will be rewarded by meeting the remote communities on the Makonde Plateau and get good views of the scenic granite Masasi Hills. *» For Sleeping, Eating and other listings, see page 127.*

Newala → *Colour map 1, grid C6.*

This area is occupied by the Makonde people who have three claims to distinction. The first is their exceptional ebony carvings, groups of exaggerated figures, the traditional work related to fertility and good fortune. The second is their spectacular *sindimba* dancing with the participants on stilts and wearing masks. The third is that Makonde women are celebrated throughout Tanzania for their sexual expertise. The best place to experience the atmosphere of the Makonde is to visit Newala, 150 km southwest of Mtwara. The road passes through dense woodland as it climbs up to the plateau from the coast.

The livelihood of the wood carvers is under threat from excessive sawmill logging of the *Mpingo* trees in the region. The carvers now have to cycle distances of 20 km or

Man-eating lions

The sparsely populated district of 20,000 sq km surrounding Tunduru has achieved a certain notoriety for man-eating lions. There are extensive forests and savanna that offer the big cats good cover. In 1986-1987 lions, believed to have come into the region from Mozambique, were reported to have killed 30 people in Tunduru District within one year. Because all the victims were male, women were sent out to work in the fields.

The attacks may have resulted from the shortage of natural prey due to overhunting, which has decimated most of the larger wild mammals in the area. People have been reported to be killing game to eat as they have so few remaining cattle or domestic animals. There has also been macabre speculation that lions acquired the taste for human flesh from eating the victims of the war in nearby Mozambique. Among the victims was a game warden sent to deal with the problem. However, it is also thought that some of the human deaths were in fact paid killings carried out by 'lion men'.

more to obtain supplies of wood. This tree plays both an economic and socio-cultural role in the lives of the villagers. It is used for its medicinal qualities and, traditionally, new-born babies must be bathed in water containing the leaves to ensure they grow up to be strong.

Masasi → *Phone code: 023 Colour map 1, grid C5 Altitude: 440 m.*

The other main Makonde town is Masasi, surrounded by granite hills, some 140 km southwest of Lindi and 190 km west of Mtwara. In 1875 Masasi was selected by Bishop Steere of the Universities Mission to Central Africa as a place to settle freed slaves and it has been an important mission centre since then. Nowadays it is a pretty undistinguished town, although it is strikingly situated between a series of large *gneiss kopjes* (hills). It acts as an important junction for Nachingwea, Tunduru/ Songea, Lindi, Mtwara and Newala and the Makonde Plateau. There are some pleasant walks around town (head towards the *kopjes*) and there is a cave that contains rock paintings nearby.

Lukwika-Lumesule Game Reserve

ⓘ *To get to the reserve, follow the Tunduru road out of Masasi, and at the village of Michiga, there is a left turn to Lukwika-Lumesule. Driving time from Masasi is about 4 hrs and 4WD is essential. The Old Boma in Mikindani offers camping safaris here, and is considering setting up a semi permanent camp.*

The Lukwika-Lumesule Game Reserve is one of the least visited wilderness areas in Africa. About 100 km south of Masasi on the Ruvuvi River, which marks the border with Mozambique, the reserve covers an area of approximately 600 sq km and it adjoins the Niassa Reserve in northern Mozambique though there are no bridges or border crossings, or any facilities for visitors. Herds of elephant migrate across the Ruvuma River on the southern edge of the reserve in September. The reserve is also home to lion, leopard, crocodile, hippo, antelope and numerous bird species. Less well known is the fact that this is one of the reserves in which a Spanish tour company arranges safaris where professional game hunters bring clients for trophy shooting holidays, and it is closed to visitors during the hunting season (July to December).

Tunduru → *Colour map 1, grid C5. Altitude: 701 m. 11°5'S 37°22'E.*

From Masasi to Tunduru you pass through mile after mile of miombo scrub, where monotony is only broken by some impressive *gneiss kopjes* scattered about the countryside for the first few hours after leaving Masasi.

After the journey from Masasi or Songea – over 340 km distance – you'll be pleased to reach Tunduru. Be prepared to pay more for your drinks here. The state of the road you came in on today (along with the state of the one you'll probably be leaving on tomorrow) means that sodas are around twice the normal price. It's a pleasant enough town in its own modest way, attractively situated with fine views over the surrounding undulating countryside, but there's little to keep you here for more than one night – unless you are a gem dealer, for the surrounding area is rich in gemstones, including amethyst, diamonds and sapphires. The population is poor, mostly subsistence farmers growing maize and cashew nuts. Extensive damage is frequently done to crops by wild animals, especially boars, monkeys and elephants.

Sleeping

Newala, Masasi and Tunduru *p125*
There are several very basic guest houses in Newala (near the bus stand), Masasi and Tunduru, none of which stand out and all rooms are very similar. For little more than US$2 you will get a bare room with a bed, bucket of water and shared WC. Some serve food and beer.

Transport

Newala *p125*
Bus Newala is 150 km from Mtwara but you need to stay at least one night in Newala as the bus journey takes 6-7 hrs. There are a few buses a day to and from **Mtwara** that leave in the morning from each (US$3). There is a daily bus to and from **Masasi** that leaves Newala at 0500, arrives in Masasi around 1100 and returns again to Newala in the afternoon.

Masasi *p126*
Masasi is 200 km from Mtwara and there are several buses from Masasi to **Lindi** (about 4 hrs, US$3) and to **Mtwara** daily (5-6 hrs, US$3.50). There is a daily bus to **Newala** that leaves Newala at 0500, arrives in Masasi around 1100 and returns again to Newala in the afternoon. There is usually one bus per day going to **Tunduru** (7-8 hrs, US$6). Travelling along this route by bus from Mtwara to Songea via Masasi will take a minimum of 3 days on very unpleasant roads. There are no direct buses to **Songea** from Mtwara, you have to first go to Masasi and overnight there and then to Tunduru and overnight there, before the final leg to Songea. Be prepared for breakdowns or punctures on all the journeys. The buses are in a sorry state and the roads are atrocious (impassable without a 4x4 during the rainy season). For those travelling across the south it is worth knowing that the average speeds of the buses plying the awful roads are around 25 kph or less.

Tunduru *p127*
There are daily buses from **Masasi** to Tunduru leaving in the morning (US$6, 7-8 hrs). There is at least one bus leaving for **Songea** early every morning at about 0500 (US$7, 10-12 hrs). Try to book a seat in front of the back axle, as this can make a big difference considering the state of the road. There are also *Land Rovers* (ask for *ëgari ndogo*) that do this trip carrying passengers though the cost is slightly more and they are very overcrowded. They are quicker although more uncomfortable than a bus – unless you happen to get a front seat – but they may be the only thing going on a particular day. There are also lorries which take passengers in the back.

Zanzibar and Pemba

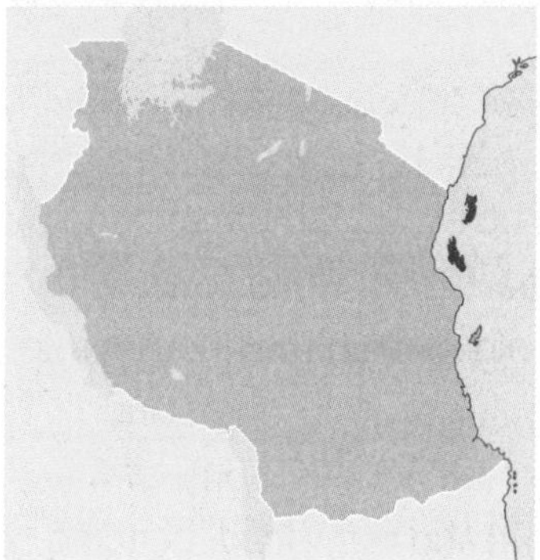

Footprint features

Introduction

The very name Zanzibar conjures up exotic and romantic images. The main town on Zanzibar Island, Stone Town, with its intriguing, winding alleyways, old Arabian townhouses and heaving port, is steeped in history, full of atmosphere and immensely attractive. Zanzibar's coastlines offer some of the best beaches in the world, but sand and surf vary depending on what side of the island you're on. On the east coast, waves break over coral reefs and sand bars offshore, and low tide reveals small pools of starfish. Up north, ocean swimming is much less susceptible to the tides, and smooth beaches and white sand make for dazzling days in the sun. Roads to the southeast coast take visitors through the Jozani Forest, home to Zanzibar's rare red colobus monkeys and a number of other primate and small antelope species. But Zanzibar attracts hundreds of thousands of visitors a year, and to some extent the island has suffered from the consequences of over-zealous mass tourism. In recent years its popularity as a European charter destination has seen the growth of all-inclusive resorts housing tourists on sun, sea and sand holidays, from where visitors experience little of the island outside the compound of their resort.

Quite by contrast, Pemba is hardly visited at all and is infinitely more difficult to get around. The sea around Pemba is dotted with desert islands and is the location of some of the best scuba diving in the Indian Ocean. The Pemba Channel drops off steeply just off the west coast and the diverse species of marine life and coral are exceptional. Unlike Zanzibar, tourism is still in its early stages and a visit here is truly a Robinson Crusoe experience.

★ Don't miss

1 **Forodhani Market** In the evening dine casually on the sumptuous food offered by the numerous outdoor grills and stalls at this market held nightly in front of the Old Fort in Stone Town, pages 148 and 156.
2 **Emerson and Green's Hotel** Kick back and dine on low cushions in the rooftop restaurant of the tallest building in Stone Town, pages 152 and 155.
3 **Festivals** Take in one, such as the Festival of the Dhow Countries or the Film Festival, which uniquely showcase the culture and arts of the Swahili coast, page 156.
4 **Spice tours** Dazzle the senses on a tour to Zanzibar's plantations, where an informative guide will show you the variety of spices that the islands are famous for, page 158.
5 **Mnemba Island** If you are seriously rich, stay here on one of the world's most exclusive private desert islands. It's a top spot for honeymooners and the lodge is one of the most exquisite in the Indian Ocean, page 171.
6 **Scuba diving** Particularly off Pemba, where the Pemba Channel has the best deep water and coral dives on the east African coast, page 182.

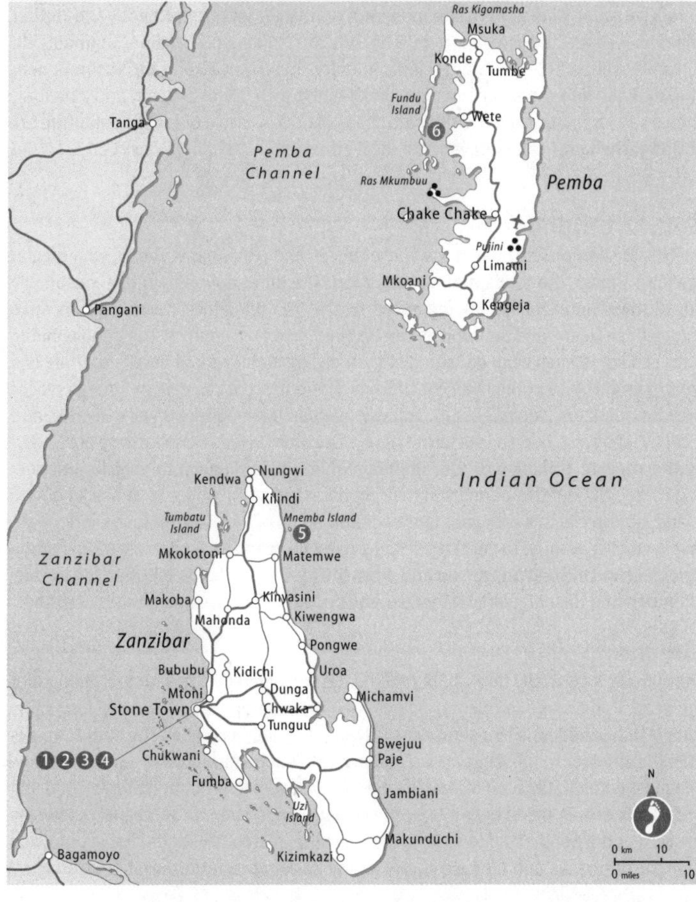

Ins and outs → *Phone code: 024. Colour map 1, grid B6. 6°12'S 39°12'E.*

Getting there

Immigration The islands lie roughly 35 km off the coast of mainland Tanzania. Whilst still part of Tanzania they are administered autonomously and have their own immigration procedures. Therefore you will be asked to show your passport to an immigration official on entry and exit and have it stamped in and out. Likewise your passport is stamped on arrival once back on mainland Tanzania. Note that the agreement between Tanzania, Kenya and Uganda, that allows holders of single entry visas to move freely between all three countries without the need for re-entry permits, also covers travel to Zanzibar. You also require a vaccination certificate for yellow fever to get onto the islands, and this is asked for before you even get onto a ferry or plane. Without one you may not be permitted to travel.

Travel There are frequent ferries between Dar es Salaam and Stone Town on Zanzibar, from big old slow overnight boats to 90-min hydrofoils, and how much you pay depends on level of comfort and how quickly you want to get there. (See Dar es Salaam, page 77, for information.) There are less frequent ferry services between Dar and Mkoani on Pemba, of which almost all stop at Zanzibar en route. **Zanzibar's international airport**, T024-2230213, is 4 km outside of Stone Town and is equipped to receive small planes from the mainland and larger jets from Nairobi and further afield as well as European charter flights. Visitors arriving on Zanzibar from outside Tanzania will be able to obtain a visa on entry. The small **airport at Pemba** is near Chake Chake and the smaller airlines link Pemba with Dar es Salaam and Zanzibar. There is an international airport departure tax of US$25, and a domestic departure tax of US$5 (the latter can is payable in local currency). ⏩ *See also Transport, page 161, for further details.*

Getting around

Public transport on Zanzibar in the way of buses and *dala-dala* is cheap, with regular services, though the roads are not very good. The other option is to use reasonably priced transfers in minibuses organized by the tour operators. If you want to drive yourself cars, jeeps and motorbikes can be hired, and for a group of four people, hiring a car can sometimes work out cheaper than paying for individual transfers. There is a vehicle rental office in the Old Post Office in Stone Town or you can go through one of the tour operators (see page 159). You will need an International Driver's licence, and recently it has also been necessary to have a Zanzibar Driver's Permit. These are issued by the car hire company or tour operator when you arrange your vehicle and cost US$10-20. Without this permit you may get harassed at the police road blocks on the island, so discuss this with your tour operator. Some of the more exclusive lodges are on the smaller islands. To get to these the lodge will organize a boat transfer. On Pemba *dala-dala* and the odd bus run up and down the main roads from early morning to early afternoon and their regularity rather depends on how many people want to use them.

Climate

The climate is generally tropical, but the heat is tempered by a sea breeze throughout the year. The average temperature fluctuates between 25-30°C. There are long rains from March to mid-June and short rains in November and December. The hottest time is after the short rains from December-February, with temperatures up to 34°C at midday. The most comfortable time of year is June-October, with lower temperatures, little rain and plenty of sun, made bearable by the cooling winds from the southeast, known as the *Kusi* or the Southeast Monsoons. From October-March the winds change, blowing from the northeast, and they are known as the *Kaskazi* or the Northeast Monsoons.

Tourist information and maps

The **Zanzibar Tourism Cooperation (ZTC)**, is in Livingstone House about 1 km along the road to Bububu, Stone Town, T024-2238630, www.zanzibartourism.net. They can arrange all tours of the island. The ZTC also has another **Tourist Information Centre**, on Creek Rd, at the north end in the Kikoni district, T024-2233430, which sells maps of the island but otherwise is not terribly helpful. *The Swahili Coast* is a free quarterly publication available from some hotels, tour agencies, a few embassies and airline offices in Dar es Salaam. It lists hotels, restaurants, transport services etc, and features articles about local events on the islands and along the mainland coast.

Zanzibar Island

Zanzibar of the Sultans

Salme Said was the daughter of one of the concubines of Sultan Said, who ruled from 1804 to 1856. Later known as Emily Ruete, she described her life in *Memoirs of an Arabian Princess from Zanzibar* (Princeton: Markus Wiener), from which the following extracts were distilled:

On life at Mtoni Palace

The Palace buildings were arranged round a large courtyard in which roamed a variety of exotic wildlife – peacocks, gazelles, geese, flamingoes and ostriches. One side of the courtyard contained 12 bathhouses, each with two baths 15 ft by 12 ft by 4 ft deep. Platforms, either side of the baths, covered with mats served for rest and prayer areas. The baths were in continual use during waking hours. The older children had riding lessons, twice a day, in the morning and evening. When they were sufficiently competent, each boy was given a horse, and each girl a white donkey. A regular diversion for these children was a ride in the country.

The Sultan's wife occupied the rooms overlooking the sea. The Sultan only spent four nights a week at Mtoni, the rest at the Palace by the promenade in Stone Town. Other palace rooms were occupied by concubines and their children, while the outbuildings housed slaves and eunuchs. In all there were estimated to be about 1,000 people living in and around the palace.

On the shore side was a tower with a vaulted roof and balcony that caught the breeze. Coffee was taken and a telescope offered sightings of approaching vessels and a view of Stone Town to the south. A flagpole on the shore was used to run up messages for the Sultan's ships at anchor in the bay.

On a typical day at the palace in Stone Town

The first set of prayers would begin some time between 0400 and 0530. After these prayers sleep would be resumed until around 0800 when there would be a massage from a slave followed by a bath. At 0900, the children all went to greet their father after which the Sultan would preside over breakfast attended by his wife, relatives and children, but not the concubines. After breakfast small children would play, older children attend lessons, the women engage in conversation or embroidery. The slaves were dispatched to arrange evening visits.

The Sultan would repair to the audience chamber on the first floor. A rather grand entrance was made with an African guard followed by a detail of eunuchs then the Sultan, followed by his sons. All senior notables were expected to attend and the company rose as the Sultan's party entered. Disputes, requests and complaints were dealt with, the Sultan delegating minor matters to his ministers, judges or the senior eunuchs. The business was all transacted verbally and the senior eunuchs recorded the decisions.

At 1300, the second prayers took place, followed by siestas, perhaps a visit to the bathhouse, while fruit and cake were partaken.

Third prayers were at 1600 and were followed by the evening meal, with much the same food being served as for breakfast. During the meal there would usually be organ music or some Taraab.

Fingers were used for eating, and rinsed in bowls of scented water. Sherbet water and coffee were available after the meal. The assembly sat on the floor and ate in silence around a long, low table with the Sultan at the head. A variety of rice dishes, meat and fresh breads and sweetmeats were served onto small dishes.

The fourth prayers were said at 1900 after which the Sultan would conduct a second audience session at which coffee would be served. This was also the time for womenfolk to visit each other, and for men to do likewise, proceeding through the narrow streets of Stone Town accompanied by slaves carrying lanterns. The day concluded with the fifth prayers before bed at around 2200.

On the education of women

School (madresse) for the children of the affluent began at the age of six and continued to 12 or so. Usually all the children of the household would be taught privately by a female teacher in a room in the house, sitting on the floor, on matting. There were a few schools for the children of poorer parents. Children often brought their personal slaves to class with them, and they sat at the back.

The only book would be the Koran, open on a folding wooden book holder. As a result, the Koran would more-or-less all be learnt by heart, but there would be no discussion of the text or its interpretation, which was regarded as irreverent. The girls would be taught the Arabic alphabet first and then reading from sections of the Koran. Except in a few cases, only the boys learned to write. Quill pens and washable ink were used to copy sections of the Koran onto smooth tablets made from a camel's scapula (shoulder-blade). After use the tablets could be scrubbed clean and used again. A little arithmetic was taught, mostly simple addition and subtraction. Classes started at 0700, breakfast was at 0900 and school finished at noon. Discipline was strict, and the teacher used a bamboo cane to punish pupils. Girls learned sewing, embroidery and lace-making from their mothers.

On the role of women

Women in society, as long as they were not concubines or slaves, had equal rights with men. Dress conventions demanded that a woman must be completely veiled except for the eyes when meeting with any male who was not a relative or a slave. Furthermore, a woman was forbidden to speak with a male stranger. This made life very difficult for single women, particularly as this restriction prevented discussions with employees or officials.

Although Islamic law allowed four formal wives, in Zanzibar it was unusual for a man to have more than one wife. There was no restriction on the number of concubines or slaves, which were purchased. Children born to concubines were free, and in the event of the master's death, the concubines, too, became free.

Marriages were arranged. The girl was not allowed to meet with her intended husband, but endeavoured to find out as much as possible about him from relatives. Normally the girl was required to agree to the match, although occasionally the match went ahead against her wishes. Brides tended to be youthful, sometimes as young as nine.

Prior to the wedding, the bride-to-be was required to spend eight days in a darkened room. The marriage ceremony took place in the bride's house. The bride would not be present but would be represented by a male relative.

The best maps available are produced by **The Zanzibar Gallery**, Gizenga St, Stone Town; *Illustrated Zanzibar Map* and *Illustrated Pemba Map*, both have extra information about weather, distances and very usefully, *dala-dala* routes. Each costs around US$2.50 and is available from The Gallery and various other outlets in Stone Town and Dar es Salaam. Try the bookshops in Dar such as *A Novel Idea*, see page 72.

History

The origin of the name Zanzibar is disputed. The Omani Arabs believe it came from *Zayn Zal Barr*, which means 'Fair is the Island'. The alternative origin is in two parts – the early inhabitants of the island were from the mainland and were given the name *Zenj*, a Persian word that is a corruption of *Zangh* meaning negro. The word *bar* meaning 'coast' was added to this to give 'Negro Coast'.

The earliest visitors were Arab traders who brought with them Islam, which has remained the dominant religion on the island. They are believed to have arrived in the eighth century. The earliest remaining building is the mosque at Kizimkazi that dates from about 1100. For centuries the Arabs had sailed with the monsoons down from Muscat and Oman in the Gulf to trade in ivory, slaves, spices, hides and wrought-iron. The two main islands, both of roughly similar size, Unguja (usually known as Zanzibar Island) and Pemba, provided an ideal base, being relatively small islands and thus easy to defend. From here it was possible to control 1,500 km of the mainland coast from present day Mozambique up to Somalia. A consequence of their being the first arrivals was that the Arabs became the main landowners.

In 1832 Sultan Seyyid Said, of the Al Busaid dynasty that had emerged in Oman in 1744, moved his palace from Muscat to Zanzibar. Said and his descendants were to rule there for 134 years. In 1822, the Omanis signed the Moresby Treaty that made it illegal for them to sell slaves to Christian powers in their dominions. To monitor this agreement, the United States in 1836 and the British in 1840 established diplomatic relations with Zanzibar, and sent resident consuls to the islands. The slaving restrictions were not effective and the trade continued to flourish. Caravans set out from Bagamoyo on the mainland coast, travelling up to 1,500 km on foot as far as Lake Tanganyika, purchasing slaves from local rulers on the way, or, more cheaply, simply capturing them. The slaves, chained together, carried ivory back to Bagamoyo. The name Bagamoyo means 'lay down your heart' for it was here that the slaves would abandon hope of ever seeing their homeland again. They were shipped to the slave market in Zanzibar Town, bought by intermediary traders, who in turn sold them on without any restrictions.

All the main racial groups were involved in the slave trade. Europeans used slaves in the plantations in the Indian Ocean islands, Arabs were the main capturers and traders, and African rulers sold the prisoners taken in battle to the traders. Alas, being sold into slavery was not the worst fate that could befall a captive. If a prolonged conflict led to a glut, the Doe tribe from just north of Bagamoyo would run down excess stocks of prisoners by the simple expedient of eating them. Nevertheless, it is the perception of the African population that the Arabs were mainly responsible.

Cloves had been introduced from Southeast Asia, probably Indonesia, prior to the advent of Sultan Seyyid Said. They flourished in the tropical climate on the fertile and well-watered soils on the western areas of both Zanzibar and Pemba islands. Slaves did the cultivation and harvesting and the Sultan owned the plots: by his death in 1856 he had 45 plantations. Other plantations were acquired by his many children, as well as by numerous concubines and eunuchs from the royal harem. In due course cinnamon, nutmeg, black pepper, cumin, ginger and cardamom were all established, their fragrance was everywhere and Zanzibar became known as the 'Spice Islands'. Slaves, spices and ivory provided the basis of considerable prosperity, mostly in the hands of the Arab community, who were the main landowners, and who kept themselves to themselves and did not intermarry with the Africans.

This was not true of a second group that came from the Middle East to settle on the East African coast, the Shirazis (see box page 95). Intermarriage between Shirazis and Africans gave rise to a coastal community with distinctive features, and a language derived in part from Arabic. This became known as Swahili. In Zanzibar the descendants of this group were known as the Afro-Shirazis. They were not greatly involved in the lucrative slave, spice and ivory trades. They cultivated coconuts, fished and became agricultural labourers. Those Shirazis who did not intermarry retained their identity as a separate group.

Two smaller communities were also established. Indian traders arrived in connection with the spice and ivory trade, and, as elsewhere, settled as shopkeepers, traders, skilled artisans, money-lenders, lawyers, doctors and accountants. The British became involved in missionary and trading activities in East Africa while attempting to suppress the slave trade. And when Germans began trading on the mainland opposite Zanzibar, things needed to be sorted out with the Sultan of Zanzibar, who controlled the 10-mile coastal strip that ran for 1,500 km from Mozambique to Somalia. The Germans bought their strip of the coast from the Sultan for £200,000. The British East African Company had been paying the Sultan £11,000 a year for operating in the Kenyan portion. In 1890, Germany allowed Britain to establish a protectorate over Zanzibar in return for Heligoland, a tiny barren island occupied by the British, but strategically placed opposite the mouth of the River Elbe, 50 km from the German coast. In 1895 Britain took over responsibility for its section of the mainland from the British East African Company and agreed to continue to pay the £11,000 a year to the Sultan. The British mainland territory (later to become Kenya), was administered by a Governor, to whom the British representative in Zanzibar, the Resident, was accountable.

The distinctive feature of Zanzibar as a protectorate (Kenya had become a colony in 1920) was recognized in 1926 when the British Resident was made directly responsible to the Colonial Secretary in London. Germany had by this stage lost control of its section of the mainland when, as a result of its defeat in the First World War, the territory was transferred to British control and became Tanganyika.

The colonial period

Further legislation in 1873 had made the slave trade illegal, the slave market in Zanzibar was closed and the Protestant cathedral erected on the site. But slavery lingered on. The trade was illegal, but the institution of slavery existed openly until Britain took over the mainland from the Germans in 1918, and covertly, it is argued, for many years thereafter. Many former slaves found that their conditions had changed little. They were now employed as labourers at low wage rates in the clove plantations. Zanzibar continued to prosper with the expansion of trade in cloves and other spices. The fine buildings that make Zanzibar Stone Town such a glorious place were constructed by wealthy Arab slavers and clove traders, British administrators and prosperous Indian businessmen and professionals. These structures were so soundly built that they have survived for the most part without repairs, maintenance and redecoration from 1964 to the present.

The wealth of the successive Sultans was considerable. They built palaces in the Stone Town and around Zanzibar Island. Islamic law allowed them to have up to four wives, and their wealth enabled them to exercise this privilege and raise numerous children. Until 1911 it was the practice of the Sultan to maintain a harem of around 100 concubines, with attendant eunuchs. The routine was established whereby the Sultan slept with five concubines a night, in strict rotation. The concubines had children, and these were supported by the Sultan.

Social practices changed with the succession of Khalifa bin Harab, at the age of 32, as Sultan in 1911. He was to reign until his death, in 1960, at the age of 81. The harem and concubines were discontinued – apart from anything else, this proved a sensible economy measure. Gradual political reforms were introduced and the practice of Islam was tolerant and relaxed. Social pressures on non-Muslims were minimal. But the office of the Sultan was held in considerable awe. As the Sultan drove each day to spend the afternoon a few kilometres away at his palace on the shore, his subjects would prostrate themselves as he passed. In 1959, when it was suggested that there should be elected members of the Legislative Councils, and Ministers appointed to deal with day-to-day matters of state, the Sultan received numerous delegations saying change was unnecessary and the Sultan should retain absolute power. The present Sultan is still addressed as 'Your Highness' when Zanzibaris visit him.

David Reed, writing for *Readers' Digest* in 1962, described Zanzibar as the "laziest place on earth – once a Zanzibari has caught a couple of fish, he quits for the day, to retire to his bed, or the heavenly chatter of the coffee house". He developed his theme – "Once a clove has been planted, its lethargic owner has only to sit in the shade and watch as its tiny green buds grow into handsome pounds sterling. Even when the market is in the doldrums, a good tree may produce as much as £6 worth of cloves a year for its owner. In better times, it simply rains money on those who sleep below."

Despite these impressions of tropical torpor under a benevolent ruler, however, there were significant tensions. Several small Arab Associations combined to form the Zanzibar National Party (ZNP) in 1955. The leader was Sheikh Ali Muhsin, educated at Makerere University in Uganda with a degree in agriculture. The leadership of the party was Arab, and their main objective was to press for independence from the British without delay. Two African associations, active with small landless farmers and agricultural labourers, formed the Afro-Shirazi Party (ASP) in 1957. The leader was Sheikh Abeid Karume, at one time a school teacher, a popular and charismatic personality, with great humorous skills that he exercised to the full at public meetings.

Although the ZNP tried to embrace all races, the fact was that they were seen as an Arab party, while the ASP represented African interests. Arabs comprised 20% of the population, Africans over 75%. Elections to the Legislative Council in 1955 were organized on the basis of communal rolls – that is, so many seats were allocated to Arabs, so many to Africans, and so on. This infuriated the ZNP who wanted a common electoral roll so that they could contest all seats. They boycotted the Legislative Council. When a ZNP member broke ranks, he was assassinated, and an Arab was executed for his murder. The next elections, in 1957, were held on the basis of a common roll, and the ZNP did not win a single one of the six seats that were contested. ASP took five and the Muslim League one. More damaging, Ali Muhsin insisted on a head-to-head with Karume in the Ngambo constituency, and was soundly beaten, polling less than 25% of the votes cast. ZNP's belief that they could draw broad-based support was very badly dented. In the next four years, the ZNP greatly increased its efforts with youth and women's organizations, and published five daily papers. It was also felt that wealthy Arab landowners and employers flexed their economic muscles to encourage support for ZNP among Africans. ZNP was greatly assisted in 1959 by a split in the ASP. Sheikh Muhammed Shamte, a Shirazi veterinary surgeon with a large clove plantation in Pemba, formed the Zanzibar and Pemba People's Party (ZPPP). Two other ASP members of the Legislative Council joined Shamte, and the ASP was left in a minority with just two seats.

In the run-up to Independence, there were three more elections. In the first, in January 1961, ASP won 10 seats, ZNP took nine and ZPPP was successful in three. A farce ensued in which both ASP and ZNP wooed the three ZPPP members. One supported ASP and the remaining two supported ZNP, creating a deadlock with 11 apiece. In the event, ZNP and ASP formed a coalition caretaker government on the understanding that new elections be held as soon as possible.

For the June 1961 elections a new constituency was created, to make a total of 23 seats. ASP and ZNP won 10 each, and ZPPP three. However, ZPPP had committed

John Okello – drifter who destroyed a dynasty

John Okello was born in Uganda in 1937. There is no record of him having had any early schooling. He left home at the age of 15 and did a variety of jobs while travelling, including work as a domestic servant, a tailor and as a building labourer. Eventually he worked as a mason in Nairobi and went to evening classes where he learnt to read and write. In 1957 he was given a two-year prison sentence for a sexual offence. On his release he travelled to Mombasa, and did some casual building jobs. In 1959 he crossed illegally, at night, in a dhow, to Pemba. While doing odd jobs he attended some ZNP political meetings. Later he began a stone-quarrying business, and joined ASP, campaigning for them in the three elections in the run-up to Independence.

After the third election, Okello moved to Zanzibar Island. The Shamte administration was anxious about the police force containing many African recruits from the mainland, and began to replace them with inexperienced Zanzibaris. It was in this context that John Okello began to form plans to overthrow the government, recruiting mainly from Africans who were not Zanzibaris (including some disaffected former policemen) and who feared that they might be expelled by a pro-Arab government. Okello warned his followers that after Independence all male African babies would be killed, Africans would be ruled as slaves, and 3,000 Africans would be slaughtered in reprisal for the 64 Arabs killed in the 1961 disturbances. By November Okello was having visionary dreams and commanding his men to abstain from sex until after the revolution and not to wear other people's clothes, in order to keep strong. He designed a Field- Marshal's uniform and pennant for himself. Final battle instructions indicated who should be killed (males aged between 18 and 55) and who could be raped (no wives of men killed or detained, and no virgins). The Sultan and three specified politicians were to be killed and the remainder captured. Some of his followers thought that Independence Day, 10 December 1963, would be an appropriate day for the revolution, but Okello thought it would be a pity to spoil the celebrations for the many overseas visitors.

On 12 January 1964, Okello led the crucial attack on Ziwani Police Station which overthrew the government and resulted in the flight of the Sultan into exile. Following this coup Okello pronounced himself Field-Marshal, and for a while assumed the title of Leader of the Revolutionary Government. As a semblance of order was restored, it was clear that Okello was an embarrassment to the ASP Government, and by 11 March he was expelled, resuming his former career of wandering the mainland, taking casual employment, and languishing for spells in prison.

itself to support ZNP, and this coalition duly formed a government. However, ASP had gained a majority of the popular vote (albeit narrowly at 50.6%) and this caused resentment. The improved performance of ZNP in the two elections after the debacle of 1957 was bewildering to ASP. There were serious outbreaks of violence, and these were clearly along racial lines and directed against Arabs. There were 68 deaths of which 64 were Arab.

In 1962 a Constitutional Conference was held at Lancaster House in London, attended by the main figures of the three political parties. A framework was duly thrashed out and agreed, with the Sultan as the constitutional Head of State. The number of seats was increased to 31 and women were given the vote. Elections in 1963 saw ASP gain 13 seats, ZNP 12 and ZPPP six. A ZNP/ZPPP coalition government was formed under the leadership of Muhammed Shamte of ZPPP. Once again ASP had the majority of the popular vote with 54%. Independence was set for later that year, on 10 December.

The old Sultan had died in 1960 and was succeeded by his son Abdullah bin Khalifa, who was to reign for less than three years, dying of cancer in July 1963. His son, Jamshid Bin Abdullah, became Sultan at the age of 34.

The revolution

It has been described as 'the most unnecessary revolution in history'. At 0300 on the night of 12 January 1964, a motley group of Africans, armed with clubs, pangas (long implements with bent, curved blades, swished from side to side to cut grass), car springs, bows and arrows, converged on the Police Headquarters at Ziwani on the edge of Zanzibar Stone Town. There were two sentries on duty. John Okello (see box, page 139) was the leader of the attacking force. He rushed forward, grappled with one of the sentries, seized his rifle and bayonetted him. The other sentry was hit by an iron-tipped arrow. Encouraged, the attackers stormed the building. In a matter of moments the police had fled, and the mob broke into the armoury. Thus armed, they moved on to support other attacks that had been planned to take place simultaneously at other key installations – the radio station, the army barracks, and the gaol. By midday, most of the town was in the hands of Okello's forces.

As the skirmishes raged through the narrow cobbled streets of the historic Stone Town, the Sultan, his family and entourage (about 50 in all) were advised to flee by the Prime Minister and his Cabinet. Two government boats were at anchor off-shore. The Sultan's party was ferried to one of these, and it set off to the northwest to Mombasa, in nearby Kenya. The government there, having gained Independence itself only a month earlier, had no desire to get involved by acting in a way that might be interpreted as hostile by whatever body eventually took control on the island. The Sultan was refused permission to land, and the boat returned southwards down the coast to Dar es Salaam in Tanganyika. From there the party was flown to Manchester and exile in Britain.

Okello began the business of government by proclaiming himself Field-Marshal, Leader of the Revolutionary Government, and Minister of Defence and Broadcasting. Members of the ASP were allocated other ministries, with Abeid Karume as Prime Minister. Meanwhile there was considerable mayhem throughout the islands, as old scores were settled and the African and Arab communities took revenge upon one another. Initial figures suggest that 12,000 Arabs and 1,000 Africans were killed before the violence ran its course.

A trickle of countries, mostly newly independent African states and Soviet regimes recognized the Karume regime fairly promptly. In February 1964 Karume expelled the British High Commissioner and the Acting US Chargé d'Affaires as their countries had not recognized his government.

Army mutinies in Kenya, Tanganyika and Uganda earlier in the year, the presence of British troops in the region and some ominous remarks by the US Ambassador in Nairobi about Communist threats to the mainland from Zanzibar all served to make Karume anxious. He felt vulnerable with no army he could count on, and what he saw as hostile developments all around. He needed some support to secure his position.

On 23 April, Karume and Julius Nyerere signed an Act of Union between Zanzibar and Tanganyika to form Tanzania. Later the mainland political party merged with ASP to form Chama Cha Mapinduzi (CCM), the only legal political party in Tanzania.

The union

The relationship between Zanzibar and the mainland is a mess. It is neither a proper federation nor a unitary state. Zanzibar retains its own President (up to 1995, *ex officio*

Sensitivity to Zanzibar culture

Zanzibar has a relaxed and sympathetic attitude to visitors. However, the islands are predominantly Muslim and as such Zanzibaris feel uncomfortable with some western dress styles. In the towns and villages it is courteous for women to dress modestly, covering the upper arms and body, with dress or skirt hemlines below the knee. Wearing bikinis, cropped tops, vests that reveal bra straps, or shorts causes offence. For men there is no restriction beyond what is considered decent in the west, but walking around the towns bare- chested or with no shoes is considered offensive. Zanzibaris are either very vocal in expressing their offence, or by contrast are too polite to say anything. It is because of the latter that many tourists continue to take this advice unheeded. When on the beach it is acceptable to wear swimwear, but if a fisherman or harvester wanders by, it is polite to cover up. Some tourists sunbathe topless on the beaches – this is hugely insensitive and completely inappropriate. It is worthwhile remembering that whilst you may see other tourists wandering around in inappropriate dress, this doesn't mean that you should do the same. Behave like a responsible tourist and cover up. Other sensitivities to consider are during the holy month of Ramadan when most Muslims fast during daylight hours. It is considered the height of bad manners to eat, drink or smoke in the street or public places at this time. Although alcohol is freely available, drunken behaviour is not regarded with tolerance and is considered offensive by most non-drinking Muslims. Finally, public displays of affection are also considered to be inappropriate.

one of the Vice-Presidents of the Union). It has a full set of ministries, its own Assembly, and keeps its own foreign exchange earnings. Mainlanders need a passport to go to Zanzibar, and cannot own property there. No such restrictions apply to Zanzibaris on the mainland. Despite comprising less than 5% of Tanzania's total population, Zanzibar has 30% of the seats in the Union Assembly. The practice of rotating the Union Presidency between Zanzibar and the mainland meant that from 1985-1995 two of the occupants of the top three posts (the President and one of the two Vice-Presidents) come from Zanzibar. Zanzibar has not paid for electricity supplied by the mainland's hydro-electric power stations for over 15 years.

Despite all these privileges (which annoy the daylights out of many mainlanders) the Zanzibaris feel they have had a rough time since 1964. The socialist development strategy pursued by Tanzania after 1967 has seen living standards fall in Zanzibar. Where once the inhabitants of Zanzibar Town were noticeably better off than the urban dwellers in mainland Dar es Salaam, they now feel themselves decidedly poorer. They consider that if they had been able to utilize their historical and cultural links with oil-rich Oman they would have benefited from substantial investment and development assistance.

The legitimacy of the Act of Union has been called into question – it was a deal between two leaders (one of whom had come to power unconstitutionally) without any of the democratic consultation such a radical step might reasonably require. Separatist movements have emerged, pamphleting sporadically from exile in Oman and Scandinavia, and suppressed by the Tanzanian government. A Chief Minister in Zanzibar, Seif Sharrif Hamad, was dismissed when it was thought he harboured separatist sympathies. Later he was detained for over two years on a charge of retaining confidential government documents at his home.

Sharrif Hamad was the candidate for the Zanzibar Presidency of the Civic United Front (CUF), an already registered party. Support for CUF in the islands prior to the election was very strong but, victorious by a only narrow margin in both the Presidential and Assembly elections, a recount was called, and the incumbent Salim Amour was declared President with 50.2% of the vote (Hamad had 49.8%). CUF and Hamad were incensed at the outcome, and CUF briefly boycotted the Zanzibar Assembly. Political turmoil and outbreaks of violence followed, but CCM kept its position as poll winner. The CCM won further elections in 2000, and again violence flared amid accusations of fraud. Many CUF supporters fled to Kenya after deadly clashes with police. Both parties signed a reconciliation agreement in 2001. Under the ruling pro-union CCM, Zanzibar is set to remain part of Tanzania. But the CUF, which enjoys strong support on Pemba, has called for greater autonomy; some CUF members have called for independence. At the time of writing Tanzania and Zanzibar were preparing for elections in October 2005. Because of the possibility of violence on Zanzibar during elections, you are ill advised to visit during these times.

Stone Town

It may not have a particularly romantic name, but Stone Town is the old city and cultural heart of Zanzibar, where little has changed for hundreds of years. It's a delightfully romantic place of narrow alleys, crumbling mosques, and grand Arab houses with giant brass-studded wooden doors. Most of the buildings were built by the Omani sultans in the 19th century when Zanzibar was one of the most important trading centres in the Indian Ocean. European influences such as balconies and verandas were added some years later. The walls of the houses are made from coralline rock, which is a good building material, but erodes easily. Many of Stone Town's 1900 historical houses have crumbled beyond repair, whilst others have been beautifully renovated. Since Stone Town was deservedly declared a World Heritage Site by UNESCO in 2000, the Stone Town Conservation Authority is working towards restoring the ancient town before these buildings are lost for ever. Most hotel accommodation is in the restored old houses and rooms are decorated with antiques, Persian rugs and the delightful four poster Zanzibarian beds. At least two nights is warranted in Stone Town to soak up the atmosphere, take one or more of the interesting half or full day tours on offer to sights in and around the city, and to learn a little about its fascinating history. ▸▸ *For Sleeping, Eating and other listings, see pages 151-162.*

Greater Stone Town

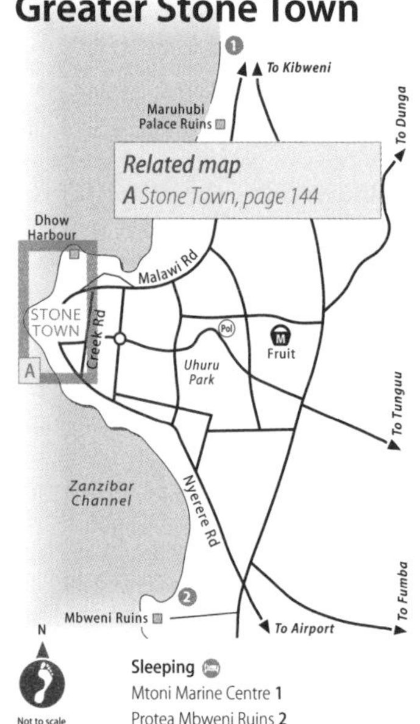

Ins and outs

➔ *See also Ins and outs, page 132.*

Getting there If arriving at the airport, which is 4 km from town, you will be badgered by the many taxi drivers. Ask inside the airport what you should pay for a taxi to take you the short distance into town, which will help with bargaining once outside. A taxi should cost in the region of US$6-10, or alternatively there are buses and *dala-dala* to town for less than US$1. There is a bureau de change in the airport. Some of the more upmarket hotels and resorts offer free airport pick ups, so it always worthwhile asking.

The ferry terminal is in the Malindi area of Stone Town. Many of the hotels are within walking distance of the ferry terminal, or alternatively you can take a taxi directly from the port. The booking offices for the ferries are clustered around the jetty where you will need to reconfirm the date of your return ticket to Dar if you have not already done so when booking the ticket. The dhow harbour is next to the port, but remember it is illegal for foreigners to travel between the mainland and the islands by dhow. » *See also Transport, page 161, for further details.*

Safety

Safety is becoming an increasing concern on Zanzibar. There have recently been several violent robberies, at knifepoint, of tourists even during daylight hours in Stone Town and its environs. There is speculation that the perpetrators are mainland Tanzanians, as Zanzibaris are usually noted for their honesty. Be careful walking after dark, especially in poorly lit areas. Avoid alleyways at night, particularly by the Big Tree on Mizingani Road and the Malindi area near the port. Valuables can usually be left in your hotel safe as an extra precaution. At night use taxis to get back to the hotel, which can be found easily around the major restaurants and nightclubs. Exert caution on quiet beaches. Ignore anyone that might offer you drugs on the street. Drug use is illegal and the police may be watching the drug pushers – you will get into all sorts of serious trouble if caught negotiating with them. Quite surprisingly there is a growing problem of heroin use amongst some young Zanzibaris and there is a concern about how and by whom the drug made its way on to the island. It is not uncommon for travellers in hire cars or motorcycles to be stopped by the police while driving to one of the beaches. The police may try to claim that your papers are not in order – basically they are looking for a small bribe. If you ask for a receipt or suggest that you want to go to the actual police station to pay the fine, they will wave you through.

Sights

The area west of Creek Road is the original Stone Town and a tour of it will take at least a day. But it is such a fascinating place that you could easily spend a week wandering the narrow streets and still find charming and interesting new places.

Creek Road

A good place to start a walking tour is from the **Central Darajani Market** on Creek Road. This was opened in 1904 and remains a bustling, colourful and aromatic place. Here you will see Zanzibarian life carrying on as it has done for so many years – lively, busy and noisy. Outside are long, neat rows of bicycles carefully locked and guarded by their minder while people are buying and selling inside the market. Fruit, vegetables, meat and fish are all for sale here as well as household implements, many of them locally made, clothing and footwear. On Wednesday and Saturday there is also a flea market selling antiques and bric-a-brac. Note that the chicken, fish and meat areas are not for the squeamish – the smell and flies can be somewhat overwhelming.

Returning to Creek Road, after a further 200 m there is a large crossroads. To the left, a dual carriageway leads up to the 1960s developments of Michenzani – ugly concrete flats built by the East Germans during Tanzania's socialist period. To the

A common feature in Stone Town are the 'barazas' – long stone benches built along the outside walls of the houses where men often sit idly gossipping and drinking chai (tea). They also serve as raised walkways when Stone Town gets flooded during the rainy season.

Stone Town

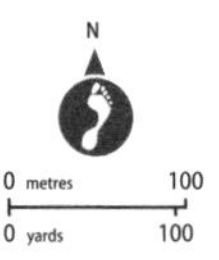

Sleeping
Africa House 1 *D2*
Baghani House 2 *D3*
Beit-al-Amaan 3 *E3*
Chavda 6 *D3*
Clove 7 *C4*
Coco de Mer 8 *D3*
Dhow Palace 9 *D2*
Emerson & Green & Tower Top Restaurant 10 *C4*
Flamingo Guest House 11 *E4*
Florida Guest House 12 *E4*
Garden Lodge Resthouse 13 *E3*
Haven Guest House 14 *E3*
International 16 *C4*
Karibu Inn 17 *D2*
Kiponda 18 *C4*
Lail-Noor Guest House 15 *F5*
Malindi Guest House 20 *A6*
Manch Lodge Vuga 21 *E4*
Marine 22 *A5*
Mazsons 23 *D2*
Pyramid Guesthouse 26 *B5*
St Monica's Hostel 27 *D5*
Spice Inn 29 *C5*
Stone Town Inn 30 *D2*
Tembo 31 *D2*
Vuga 33 *E2*
Zanzibar Serena Inn 36 *D1*

Eating
Archipelago 9 *D2*
Baobab Tree 2 *D4*
Dolphin 7 *D2*
Forodhani Gardens 6 *C2*
La Fenice 5 *D2*
Le Spices Rendez-vous 10 *E2*
Luis Yoghurt Parlour 11 *D3*
Luna Mare 11 *D3*
Mercury's 1 *B4*
Neem Tree 3 *C3*
Pagoda 13 *D2*
Sea View Indian 17 *B4*
Sweet Eazy 4 *C3*

Bars & clubs
Garage Club 8 *D2*

To Dar es Salaam & Pemba
New Dock
Gulf Air
The Big Tree
Oman Air
Mizingani Rd
KIPONDA
Beit-al-Sahel (People's Palace)
Nyumbaya Moto St
FORODHANI
Aga Khan Mosque
Beit-el Ajaib (House of Wonders)
Jamituri (Forodhani) Gardens
Hurumzi St
Changa Bazaar
Orphanage
Old Fort
Zanzibar Dive Centre-One Ocean
Bahari Divers
Mambo Msiige
Gizenga St
Hamamni Persian Baths
Shangani St
Zanzibar Gallery
Bohora Mosque
St Joseph's Catholic Cathedral
Coastal Air
Ras Shangani
SHANGANI
BAGHANI
New M
Kenyatta Rd
Baghani St
Tippu Tip's House
Mathews House
Suicide Alley
Former English Club
Pipalwadi St
Sokomuhogo St
VUGA
Kenyatta Rd
Vuga Rd
National Library & High Court
People's Gardens (Victoria Gardens)
Kaunda Rd
Zanzibar Channel
State House
National Museum
National Museum

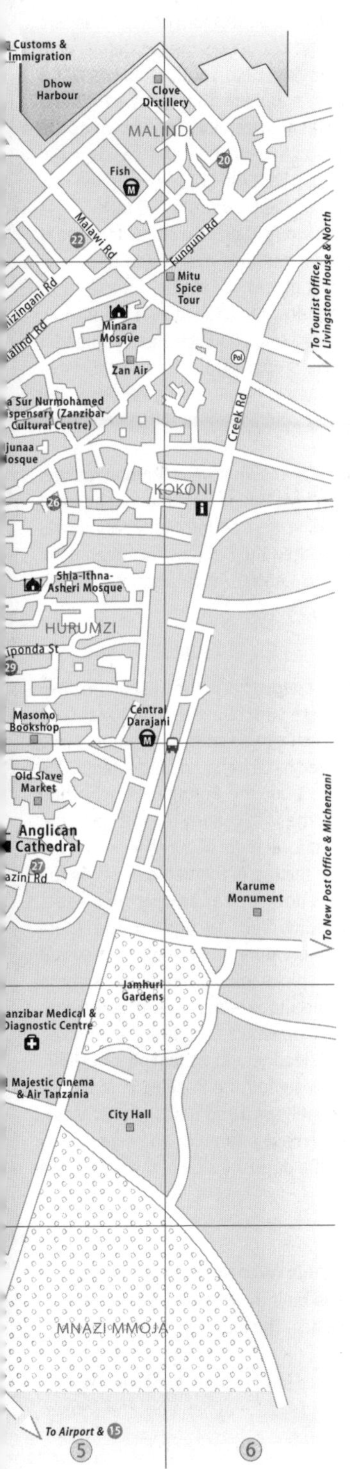

right is New Mkunazini Road, and after about 50 m another right leads into the cathedral courtyard. The building to the left of the entrance to the courtyard is the **Anglican Missionary Hospital**, which is constructed on top of the old slave chambers. The **Anglican Cathedral**, was built in 1887 on the site of the old slave market to commemorate the end of the slave trade. You can pick up guides here who will for a small fee give you a short tour of the slave chambers and cathedral (daily 0800-1800). The altar is on the actual site of the slave market's whipping post. The marble columns at the west end were put in upside down, while the bishop was on leave in the UK. Other points of interest are the stained-glass window dedicated to David Livingstone who was instrumental in the abolition of the slave trade, and the small wooden crucifix said to have been made from the wood of the tree under which Livingstone died in Chitambo in Zambia. If you can, try to go up the staircase of the cathedral to the top of the tower from where you will get an excellent view of the town. There are services in Swahili every Sun, and in English once a month. Also on Creek Road is the **City Hall**, a wonderfully ornate building that has recently been restored.

Western tip

The People's Gardens on Kaunda Rd, also known as the Victoria Gardens, were originally laid out by Sultan Barghash for the use of his extensive harem. The grand pavilion was renovated in 1996 by German aid agencies. Many of the plants in the garden were added in the 1880s by naturalist and British Resident Sir John Kirk. Opposite the gardens and behind a white wall is the **State House**. Originally built as the British Residency, it was designed to complement the earlier Arabic buildings such as the People's Palace. Since independence the building has housed the President's Office. **Note** Photography is not permitted around the State House.

Mathews House is close to *Africa House Hotel*, just to the south of Ras Shangani at the western tip of the town. Before the First World War it was the residence, with characteristic overhanging balconies, of Lloyd Mathews (1850-1901). Mathews was a naval officer who was put in charge of the Sultan's army in 1877 (he was a mere Lieutenant of 27 at the time). Later he became Chief Minister and was known as the 'Strong Man of Zanzibar'. The **Africa House Hotel** is on Suicide Alley and was once the English Club, opened in 1888 (the oldest such club in East Africa), see box page 147. One of the great events at the English Club used to be the New Year's Eve fancy dress ball, when great crowds of dumfounded Zanzibaris would gather to stare at the crazy 'wazungu' (whites) in their costumes. It has been beautifully restored to its former glory and the upstairs terrace bar is one of the best places in Zanzibar for a drink at sunset (see also Sleeping, page 152). A little further down Suicide Alley is **Tippu Tip's House**, named after the wealthy 19th-century slave-trader, which has a splendid carved wooden door and black and white marble steps. Tippu Tip was the most notorious of all slavers and Livingstone's arch-enemy – the latter's report of the massacre at Nyangwe, in the Congo, where Tippu Tip had commercial hegemony, led ultimately to the abolition of the slave trade.

Also at the western tip of the town is the building known now as **Mambo Msiige**, which was built in 1847 and was once owned by a slave trader. It is said that he used to bury slaves alive within the walls of the building and added many thousands of eggs to the mortar to enhance the colour. Since then the building has been used as the headquarters of the Universities Mission to Central Africa and later as the British Consulate.

Old Fort

The Old Fort (also known as the Arab Fort or *Ngome Kongwe*) is in the west of the town next to the House of Wonders (see below). This huge structure was built in 1700 on the site of a Portuguese church, the remains of which can be seen incorporated into the fabric of the internal walls. Its tall walls are topped by castellated battlements. The fort was built by Omani Arabs to defend attacks from the Portuguese, who had occupied Zanzibar for almost two centuries. During the 19th century the fort was used as a prison and in the early 20th century it was used as a depot of the railway that ran from Stone Town to Bububu. It is possible to reach the top of the battlements on the west side and look at the towers. The central area is now used as an open air theatre. On Friday at 1930 film nights are held, and on Tuesday, Thursday and Saturday there is a Zanzibar buffet barbecue with African dance and drums. The fort also houses an art gallery, several small shops selling crafts and spices, plus a tourist information desk. There is also a charming café, with tables in the shade of a couple of large trees.

On the south side of the fort you can take a walk down Gizenga Street (used to be Portuguese Street) with its busy bazaars. This will lead you to **St Joseph's Catholic Cathedral**, designed by Henri Espérandieu, who designed the Basilica in Marseille and loosely based this work on it. The cathedral is well used and holds regular Mass. When not in use, the doors may be closed, in which case entrance can be gained by the back door, through the adjoining convent. On the opposite side of the road is the **Bohora Mosque**.

Beit-el-Ajaib (House of Wonders)

Close to the fort and opposite the Jamituri Gardens, this is Zanzibar's tallest building. It has four storeys surrounded by verandas and was built in 1883 by a British marine engineer for Sultan Barghash and served as his palace. The name 'House of Wonders'

In 1946 Freddie Mercury was born Farokh Bulsara in Stone Town to parents who were Parsee followers of the Zoroastrian faith. His body was cremated at a Zoroastrian funeral ceremony in London in 1992.

Zanzibar under the British – the English Club

The British in Zanzibar (as everywhere) were profoundly insular, and in general reluctant to establish social relations with other communities. This was expressed in the formation of the English Club, which subsequently provoked every other significant community to establish its own club, thereby underscoring the religious and racial divisions in the society.

Although the English Club was formed some time before the turn of the 20th century, it was only in 1907 that it began to look seriously for substantial premises. A suitable building was located in Shangani just back from the shore, which is now the *Africa House Hotel* and, backed by a government loan, the club opened in 1908 on its new site with a restaurant, a committee room that doubled as a library, a bar and a billiards room.

In 1911 the club proposed taking over two rooms in an adjoining building to provide accommodation for out of town members. The government was approached to provide the capital to buy a lease and to refit the rooms. It agreed on condition that the rooms would be made available to the government for officials and their wives, and other visitors needing accommodation in Stone Town.

The Secretary, EWP Thurston, reported that the constitution of the club did not allow Americans or Europeans, and that it was a 'Man's Club', and there were the "strongest social and sanitary reasons against ladies occupying rooms". The government reacted vigorously to the proposed exclusions.

Women were allowed in to use the library in the mornings and between 1800-2000 in the evenings. They were also admitted to take lunch and dinner in the restaurant. As for the Committee's sanitary objections to women using the accommodation, these were dismissed by the government as the "merest bogies of their perfervid imaginations". In April 1912 the club gave way, and the two rooms were added. Later some garages were built on the shore site of the building, and more rooms for women were added above them.

In 1916 the club had plans to demolish a warehouse on the shore and build a swimming pool and squash courts. But the war interfered with these plans and they never went ahead. The space was cleared, however, and became known as 'German Forodhani' (Forodhani means 'customs house' – the German Consulate was nearby) or 'Shagani Steps'. Coloured lights were strung from cast-iron telegraph poles (two can still be seen on the site), and on Tuesday evenings the Sultan's band played a selection of classical and popular music, for the benefit of locals who sat around on the grass and those taking sundowners in the club's veranda bar.

came about because it was the first building on the island to have electricity and even a lift. It has fine examples of door carving. At the entrance are two Portuguese cannons, which date from about the 16th century. In 1896 in an attempt to persuade the Sultan to abdicate, the palace was subjected to a bombardment by the British navy. Inside, the floors are of marble and there are various decorations that were imported from Europe; there are also exhibits from the struggle for independence. The building once served as the local headquarters of Tanzania's political party CCM, but was fully restored in 2002 as the **Museum of History and Culture** ⓘ *Mon-Sat, 0900-1800, US$2*, with several permanent exhibitions on the history of the Swahili Coast.

Zanzibar doors

At last count, there were 560 original carved doors in Zanzibar. When a house was built the door was traditionally the first part to be erected, and the rest of the house built around it. The tradition itself originates from the countries around the Persian Gulf and spread through Afghanistan to Punjab in India where they were reported in the first half of the 12th century. They started to feature in Zanzibar houses in the 15th century, but most of those surviving today were built in the 18-19th centuries. The greater the wealth and social position of the owner of the house, the larger and more elaborately carved his front door. The door was the badge of rank and a matter of great honour amongst merchant society. British explorer Richard Burton remarked in 1872: "the higher the tenement, the bigger the gateway, the heavier the padlock and the huger the iron studs which nail the door of heavy timber, the greater the owner's dignity". Set in a square frame, the door is a double door opening inwards that can be bolted from the inside and locked from the outside by a chain and padlock. Popular motifs in the carvings on the doors include the frankincense tree that denotes wealth, and the date palm that denotes abundance. Some of them feature brass knockers, and many are studded with brass spikes. This may be a modification of the Indian practice of studding doors with sharp spikes of iron to prevent them being battered in by war elephants. In 915 AD, an Arab traveller recorded that Zanzibar island abounded in elephants, and in 1295 Marco Polo wrote that Zanzibar had 'elephants in plenty'. These days there are of course no elephants, and the studs are there merely for decoration. The doors are maintained by the Stone Town Conservation and Development Corporation who keep a photographic record of the doors, and a watchful eye that they are not removed and exported from Zanzibar.

Jamituri (or Forodhani) Gardens

The formal gardens are in front of the House of Wonders and the Old Fort and were once the location for the port's customs sheds before the port was moved in 1936 to the deepwater anchorage. Complete with a bandstand, the gardens are a pleasant place to stroll and watch the young boys diving off the sea wall. Every night the ★ **Forodhani Market** is held here. It sells an extraordinary variety of snacks and seafood cooked on charcoal burners under paraffin lamps. Kebabs, freshly squeezed sugar-cane milkshakes, grilled calamari and prawns, omelettes, chips, pieces of fried fish, mussels, crab claws – everything is quite delicious and very cheap and a night-time wander around the gardens is highly recommended: it is one of the highlights of a visit to Zanzibar. Adjacent to the Jamituri Gardens, there is a building through which the road passes in a tunnel. This is Zanzibar's **Orphanage**, although it has previously been an English Club and an Indian School. Passing through the tunnel, the second building on the right has a plaque on the wall facing that reads: "This building was the British Consulate from 1841 to 1874. Here at different times lived Burton, Speke, Grant and Kirk. David Livingstone lived here and in this house his body rested on its long journey home." If the tide is low enough it is possible to pass down the side of the British Consulate and onto the beach, from where the magnificent houses can be viewed to their best advantage.

The market also attracts many hundreds of Stone Town's cats after the fishy debris.

Beit al-Sahel (People's Palace)

ⓘ *Tue-Sat 1000-1800. US$3.*

The palace on Mizingani Road, north of the House of Wonders, is where the sultans and their families lived from the 1880s until their rule was finally overturned by the revolution of 1964. It was built in the late 1890s for members of the Sultan's family and for his harem. Following the revolution in 1964 it was renamed the People's Palace and was used by various political factions until it was turned into a museum in 1994. There are three floors of exhibits and it is well worth a visit. There is a wide variety of furniture including the Sultan's huge bed. Look out for the formica wardrobe with handles missing – obviously very fashionable at the time. There are good views from the top floor. The palace has grounds that can sometimes be viewed, containing the tombs of Sultan Seyyid Said and his two sons Khaled and Barghash. Heading north from the People's Palace is the Big Tree, which was planted in 1911 by Sultan Khalifa. Today it shelters local dhow builders.

Na Sur Nurmohamed Dispensary

Often called the 'Old Dispensary', this very ornate building is on Mizingani Road, north of the Big Tree. It was built in 1887 by Thaira Thopen, Zanzibar's richest man at the time, to commemorate Queen Victoria's Silver Jubilee. It's one of the most imposing of Stone Town's buildings, with four grand storeys and wrap-around decorative balconies. It served as a dispensary in colonial times and was one of the first buildings to be successfully restored to its former glory and today is the **Stone Town Conservation and Development Corporation**. Inside is a small tourist development known as the Zanzibar Cultural Centre with fixed priced shops, including a jeweller, curio and clothes boutique and a small, very pleasant cheap restaurant with a shady courtyard.

Port and dhow harbour

Further up Mizingani Road is the main port and the dhow harbour which is a lively and bustling part of the Malindi quarter. The deepwater harbour has wharfs piled high with containers, and the landing is most frequently used by boats and hydrofoils from Dar es Salaam and Pemba. Built in 1925, the port remains essentially the 'industrial' end of town, with docks, cargo sheds, and a clove distillery. The dhow harbour is at its busiest in the morning when the dhows arrive and unload their catches, and buyers bargain and haggle over the prices. These days very few dhows cross the Indian Ocean, unlike times gone by when fleets would arrive carrying goods from Arabia and the Orient, returning loaded with slaves, ivory and the produce of the islands' plantations. The best time to see one of these large ocean-going dhows is between December and March, before they return on the south-westerly monsoon. There is still plenty of smaller dhow traffic all year round between Zanzibar and the mainland, most bringing building materials and flour to Zanzibar.

> *Occasionally an enormous ocean-going container ship or cruise liner comes into port and dwarfs the whole town.*

Livingstone House

On Malawi Road, Livingstone's House was built around 1860 for Sultan Majid. It was also used by many missionaries and explorers as a starting point for expeditions into deepest, darkest Africa. Most notably, David Livingstone lived here before beginning his last journey to the mainland in 1866. Since then, it's been a laboratory (among other things) for research into clove production. It is now home to the Zanzibar Tourism Corporation.

Hammani Persian Baths

In the centre of Stone Town on Hammani Street, these baths were built by Sultan Barghash in 1888 for use as public baths and have been declared a protected monument. The building of the baths was overseen by a specialist team brought from

Persia. If you want to have a look inside them ask for the caretaker who will let you in and show you around for a small fee. There is no water there any more, so you have to use your imagination to imagine what it was like in its heyday.

National Museum

ⓘ *Creek Rd, south end of town. Mon-Sat, 0900-1800. US$1 for both buildings.*
The museum is in two buildings and although fairly run down and shabby has some interesting exhibits relating to Zanzibar's history. It was built in 1925 and has relics and exhibits from the sultans, the slave traders and European explorers and missionaries. Livingstone's medicine chest is here and the story of the German battleship the *Königsberg,* sunk during the First World War in the Rufiji Delta (see page 105), is documented. There are also displays of local arts and crafts. If you are 'out of season' for the Spice Tour, it has a most interesting exhibition on clove production. There is a giant tortoise in the grounds of the natural history museum and library next door and a door here, near the junction of Creek Road with Nyerere and Kuanda Roads, is reputedly one of the oldest doors on the island.

Excursions

Changuu Island

ⓘ *You can get there through one of the tour agencies on a half day tour for about US$15, but it is just as easy – and cheaper – to find a boat yourself. Many boats will take you across to the island, and come back at a prearranged time to pick you up for about US$5 per person. Ask around on the beaches in front of the Sea View Indian Restaurant or Tembo Hotel. Just ensure that you only pay when you have been safely deposited back on the mainland. There is also a US$5 landing fee on the island.*

Also known as **Prison Island**, Changuu Island is almost 5 km northwest of Stone Town. It was once owned by an Arab who used it for 'rebellious' slaves. Some years later in 1893 it was sold to General Mathews, a Briton who converted it into a prison. However, it has never actually been used as such and was later converted to serve as a quarantine station in colonial times. The prison is still relatively intact and a few remains of the hospital can be seen including the rusting boilers of the laundry. There is good snorkelling, windsurfing and sailing from the beautiful little beach, though jellyfish can sometimes be a problem. The island is also home to giant tortoises, which are supposed to have been brought over from Aldabra (an atoll off the Seychelles) around the turn of the 20th century. They stand up to a rather staggering 1 m high and could feasibly be hundreds of years old. The tortoises are no longer roaming freely over the island because many were stolen. Now they are kept in a large fenced area. You can buy leaves to feed the tortoises. The *Changuu Island Resort*, is a simple and reasonable café serving cold beers and basic meals like grilled fish and salad and also rents out snorkelling gear.

Chapwani Island

Also known as **Grave Island**, Chapwani Island is a nearby private island with one exclusive lodge on it (see page 154). There is an interesting cemetery with headstones of British sailors and marines who lost their lives in the fight against slavery and in the First World War. The island itself is 1 km long and 100 m wide with a perfect swath of beach on the northern edge. The forested section is home to a number of birds, duikers and a population of colobus monkeys (how they got here is a bit of a mystery).

Kiungani, Mbweni and Chukwani

ⓘ *To the south of town off the airport road near the Protea Mbweni Ruins Hotel.*

The route south of Stone Town will take you past Kiungani where there was once a hostel built in 1864 by Bishop Tozer for released slave boys. A little further on are the ruins of the **Mbweni Settlement**, which was also established for rescued slaves. This was built in 1871 by the Universities Mission to Central Africa. In 1882 St John's Church was built in the same place for the use of the released slaves. There is a fine carved door and a tower. Also at Mbweni is **Kirk House**, which was built by Seyyid Barghash in 1872. Kirk came to Zanzibar as the Medical Officer as part of Livingstone's expedition to the Zambezi. He played an important role in the fight to end the slave trade and in 1873 was appointed His Majesty's Agent and Consul General in Zanzibar. He was also a botanist, introducing to the island a number of plants said to have originated from Kew Gardens, including cinnamon, vanilla, mahogany and eucalyptus. Further south at Chukwani are the **Mbweni Palace Ruins**. This was once a holiday resort of Sultan Seyyid Barghash and it had a wonderful position overlooking the sea. However, it has been totally neglected and as a result is slowly crumbling away. The main palace has completely disappeared, although some of the other buildings do remain and may be toured.

Chumbe Island

ⓘ *The island is a private conservation project and has an all-inclusive resort of the same name (see page 154). A day trip can be booked directly with the park, T024-2231040, www.chumbeisland.com, or through Protea Mbweni Ruins Hotel, US$70 per person including transport, snorkelling equipment, nature trail guides and a picnic lunch.*

Approximately 4 km offshore southwest from the Mbweni Palace ruins lies the **Chumbe Island Coral Park**. This is an important marine park with a wonderful reef of coral gardens that can be viewed from glass-bottomed boats. The reef remains in a pristine state and is shallow (between 1-3 m according to tides). If you swim up to the reef ridge it's possible to spot shoals of barracuda or dolphins.

There are nearly 400 species of fish here: groupers, angelfish, butterfly fish, triggerfish, boxfish, sweetlips, unicornfish, trumpetfish, lionfish, moorish idols, to name but a few. The snorkelling opportunities are excellent but scuba diving is not permitted in the park. There are nature trails through the forest on the island, the home of the rare roseate tern and coconut crab, the largest land crab in the world that can weigh up to 4 kg, and it is now a refuge for the shy Ader's duiker, introduced to the island with the assistance of the World Wide Fund for Nature. There is also an old mosque, and a lighthouse built in 1904.

Sleeping

Accommodation on Zanzibar ranges from town hotels to beach resorts, and from local-style, budget accommodation to 5-star luxury. The decor and furnishings in most are traditional Zanzibar, with antiques and ornate Zanzibari four-poster beds. Bookings can be made directly through the hotel, or through tour operators. Check that the VAT is included in the quoted prices on the hotel tariff. Reservations for the peak seasons (Jul-Sep and Nov-Jan) should be made well in advance. Note that there is often a surcharge over the Christmas and New Year period. At most accommodation children under 18 years get substantial discounts. Most beach resorts offer bungalow-type accommodation and watersports like diving and snorkelling. Some of these are all inclusive, while others give the option of B&B, half board or full board rates. Note that camping is not

For an explanation of the sleeping and eating price codes used in this guide, see inside the front cover. Other relevant information is found in Essentials pages 31-34.

permitted on Zanzibar. As with elsewhere in Tanzania, room rates are quoted in US$, though the smaller budget hotels will often accept TSh. Credit cards are now accepted by all the larger hotels and resorts. If you have not prebooked accommodation in Stone Town, you need to walk around and find a hotel that suits. Young men will tout for business, offering hotels, taxis, spice or other tours. They will usually pounce on you as soon as you get off the ferry. Some can be very aggressive and persistent. A polite 'no thank you' is rarely a successful method to rid yourself of their services. If you have just arrived you could tell the touts that you have already booked hotel accommodation from Dar es Salaam, and if you make your own way to a hotel insist that the management give no commission to any touts who may be following. Other strategies for tout evasion include saying you have been on all the tours, and that you are leaving tomorrow and have already bought the ferry ticket. It is better to deal directly with one of the many tour companies for excursions and organize everything in the confines of their office.

Stone Town *p142, map p144*

L Zanzibar Serena Inn, Shangani St, Shangani Sq, direct lodge number T024-2233051/587, www.serenahotels.com. One of the best hotels in East Africa and a member of Small Luxury Hotels of the World. Stunning restoration of two historic buildings in Stone Town funded by the Aga Khan Fund for Culture to provide a seafront hotel, with 52 luxury rooms and swimming pool. Beautifully decorated with antique clocks, Persian rugs, carved staircases, chandeliers and brass- studded doors. The several restaurants have excellent but pricey menus. Wonderful location with first-class service.

A Africa House, just off Kenyatta Rd, on Suicide Alley, T0747-432340 (mob), www.theafricahouse-zanzibar.com. This used to be the English Club in the pre-independence days and in 2001 was completely restored to its former glory. The building has many archways, studded wooden doors, cool stone floors, and a wide rooftop terrace with a bar which is *the* place on Zanzibar to sit and watch the sunset, sundowner in hand. There are 15 elegantly decorated rooms with a/c and TV, 2 restaurants, internet access, and Pirate's Cove nightclub. Tastefully furnished throughout with antiques, original photographs and paintings by local artists, and the library houses a rare collection of many first editions and antiquarian books. Considerable discounts on room rates during low season (Apr-Jun).

A Emerson and Green, 236 Hurumzi St, behind the House of Wonders, T0747-423266 (mob), www.emerson-green.com. Beautiful individually themed rooms in restored 19th-century houses with old Zanzibari furniture and fittings, original stucco decor, ornate carved doors, and stone baths, lower rooms have a/c. All rooms get a bottle of water and fresh jasmine flowers are scattered on the pillows at bedtime. The highlight here is the spectacular open-sided rooftop restaurant *Tower Top* – no shoes, sit on cushions, not cheap but worthwhile – a really magical experience. This is the second tallest building in Stone Town so the views over the rooftops are quite spectacular.

A Tembo Hotel, opposite the *Fisherman's Restaurant*, Forodhani St, T024-2233005, www.tembohotel.com. This is a fully restored historic building that was the American Consulate in the 19th century. Rooms are decorated with antique furniture and have a/c, satellite TV, and balconies overlooking either the ocean or swimming pool courtyard. Great location on the beach, the food is good, and the staff are very friendly and willing to negotiate over rates.

B Baghani House, one block south of Baghani St off Kenyatta Rd, T024-2235654, baghani@zanzinet.com. A meticulously looked-after private house with 8 rooms with attractive furnishings, a/c, fans, TV. Breakfast is served in the courtyard but there's no restaurant. Rates are slightly more expensive in the high season.

B Chavda, in the heart of Stone Town, off Kenyatta Rd, T024-2232115, chavda@zanzinet.com. A good mid-range establishment in a large restored Arab mansion with 16 large rooms, comfortable and well decorated, if slightly inauthentic. Reasonable restaurant serving international and Chinese food and a good rooftop bar which are both open to non-guests.

B Dhow Palace Hotel, just off Kenyatta Rd, T024-2230304, www.tembohotel.com/

dhowpalace.html. Large rooms with lovely bathrooms, a/c variable effect, fans, fridge, phone, and antique furniture. Central courtyard and a very good rooftop restaurant that is rarely busy.

B International, Kiponda St, T024-2233182, hotelinter@zanlink.com. An imposing black and white townhouse, with 20 comfortable and airy rooms with a/c, fridge, TV, phone, balconies and lovely furnishings. Ground floor and rooftop restaurants, bureau de change. It's near *Emerson's* and *Spice Inn*, and you have to walk through the market, which adds to the atmosphere. Under new management and standards have improved considerably. Try to get a room on the upper floors which offer wonderful views, though be wary of the steep wooden staircase.

B Mazon's Hotel, Kenyatta Rd, Shangani, T024-2233694, mazson@zenjcom.com. 35 rooms with a/c, fridge, TV, rooftop restaurant, all in a lovely whitewashed 19th-century building with wraparound balconies, and pretty gardens with a fountain.

C Beit-al-Amaan, Vuga Rd, opposite Victoria Gardens, T024-2239366. As an alternative to staying in a hotel, this private apartment with a large salon and 6 rooms can be booked for a group or each individual room can be let out, suitable for groups of 2-11 people. Very nicely furnished, each of the rooms have private bathrooms, and there's also shared kitchen with fridge and microwave and large living room. Breakfast is included in the room rate and is served to all the guests in the salon. Friendly and excellent value from US$25-35 per person.

C Clove, Hurumzi St, behind the *House of Wonders*, T0747-484567 (mob), www.zanzibarhotel.nl. This previously run- down hotel was refurbished in late 2003 and is now a good mid-range option. It's in a nice quiet square with an excellent roof bar and restaurant with a sea view. The building itself is quite modern by Stone Town standards, but the interiors have been remodelled to include elements of the more traditional Zanzibari style. Rooms have fridge, fan and bathrooms with hot water.

C Coco de Mer Hotel, between Shangani St and Gizenga St, one block east of Kenyatta Rd, T024-2230852. 10 basic rooms, restaurant, bar, fans, a little frayed around the edges, but in a central location, clean and friendly, rooms go for about US$25.

C Hotel Marine, Malawi Rd, Malindi, diagonally across from port entrance, T024-2232088, hotelmarine@africaonline.co.tz. Three-star, recently renovated establishment near the gates of the main harbour. Comfortable rooms have a/c, satellite TV and en suite bathrooms and are decorated with traditional Zanzibari furniture. The restaurant serves local, Indian and Chinese dishes and there's room service. Note: this is a busy area and the street noise can be obtrusive. Be wary around the port area at night.

C Spice Inn, where Changa Bazaar meets Kiponda St, T024-22307194. An imposing building in the centre of town, with a magnificent veranda overlooking a small square. This used to be very popular with a good atmosphere, but the rooms are rundown, bland, shabby and consequently over-priced, so ask to take a look before you decide; price includes breakfast, some rooms with a/c, shared or private bathroom.

C-D Pyramid Guesthouse, Kokoni St, behind the Ijumaa Mosque near the seafront, T024-2233000, pyramidhotel@hotmail.com. Charming staff, modest accommodation, a mixture of self-contained rooms and dorms for as little as US$10 per person. The rooms vary in size so ask to see a few, simple but recommended. Breakfast is served on the roof and they offer free pick-up from the port or airport.

C-D Stone Town Inn Hotel, a great location opposite the Tembo House Hotel, T0741-334872 (mob). Rooms are airy with traditional furniture and Persian rugs, with or without bathrooms and with a/c or fans, depending on how much you want to pay.

C-D St Monica's Hostel, New Mkunazini St, T024-2230773, cathedral@zanzinet.com. An old building next to the Anglican Cathedral with very clean and comfortable but simple rooms with or without bathrooms, mosquito nets and balconies. Price includes breakfast. Has a restaurant.

C-D Vuga Hotel, near Africa House, T024-2233613, vugahotel@yahoo.com. 4 single, 4 double and 2 triple rooms, with a/c, most are self-contained, but the ones that aren't are good value and include breakfast. Friendly and helpful staff, traditional furniture.

C-E Malindi Guest House, Funguni Bazaar, Malindi St, T024-2230165, www.zanzibarhotels.net/malindi. Excellent value place with a wonderful atmosphere. Central courtyard with plants, plenty of space to relax, clean, prices include breakfast. Recent renovations have created a rooftop coffee shop and bar with views of the harbour and the fisherman landing their catch every morning. Some of the rooms have bathrooms whilst others are dormitories with shared facilities. The only downside is that Malindi is not the safest part of Stone Town after dark – exercise caution if coming home late at night. A double is US$35, a dorm US$15.

D Hotel Kiponda, Nyumba ya Moto St, behind the People's Palace, T024-2233052. Another nicely restored building with simple clean rooms, mosquito nets, some rooms are self-contained, others have spotless shared bathrooms. Central location with good restaurant, sea views, fans. Good value but look at a range of rooms before deciding as they vary in size.

D-E Karibu Inn, next to *Coco de Mer Hotel*, T024-2233058, karibuinn@zanzinet.com. Very popular and deservedly so, one of the best locations in Stone Town tucked away behind the Old Fort, 15 rooms with or without bathrooms, a/c is US$10 extra, fans, double rooms have fridges, also dorms for about US$10 per person, pre-booking is advised as it is frequently used by large overland groups. Excellent management who are very helpful and can organize all activities.

D Manch Lodge Vuga, Stone Town off Vuga Rd, around the corner from the Haven Hotel, T2231918. Friendly, clean, recently repainted. The best rooms on top floor are very spacious. Price includes a huge breakfast.

D-E Garden Lodge Resthouse, Kaunda Rd, in Vuga opposite the National Library/High Court, T024-2233298. Lovely gardens, peaceful and quiet with friendly staff. The rooms on the ground floor are basic and shabby, but cheap, whilst the newer rooms on the first floor are a little better but are tastelessly decorated. There is a combination of twins, triples and a 5-bed dorm, all with shared bathroom. Rates start from US$8.

D-E The Haven Guest House, off Vuga Rd, T024-2232511, havenhouse@hotmail.com. Secure budget place to stay. Rooms with or without bathrooms, plenty of hot water, nets and fans, breakfast included in the price, self-catering kitchen, spotlessly clean and very friendly, owned by Mr Hamed.

E Flamingo Guest House, Mkunazini St, just north of junction with Sokomuhogo St, not far from Vuga Rd, T024-2232850, flamingo guesthouse@hotmail.com. Very good value at around US$10 per person. Simple guest house most with shared showers, a small book exchange and satellite TV in the lobby.

E Florida Guest House, off Vuga Rd, T024-2233136. Has been recommended by some readers, another simple budget guest house but in a noisy location, communal showers, twin rooms, the ones upstairs are quieter and nicer, and 1 room has 4 beds with a/c and TV, that is ideal for a group of friends travelling together.

Outside Stone Town *p150*

L Chapwani Private Island, T+39 (0)51-234974 (central reservations number in Italy), www.chapwaniisland.com. This is an exclusive private island about 10 min from Stone Town by speed boat, offering super-luxury and privacy in only 10 rooms right on the beach in separate reed chalets with four-poster beds. At night there are fantastic views of Stone Town. Seafood is the main feature on the restaurant menu, activities include volley ball, canoeing, and snorkelling. Prices are in the region of US$450 per person. No children.

L Chumbe Island Coral Park, T024-2231040, www.chumbeisland.com. The utmost care has been taken to minimize the environmental impact of this resort; sustainably harvested local materials were used in the construction of the 7 luxury cottages and dining area, there is solar power and composting toilets, and rainwater is collected as the source of fresh water. Recognition of these efforts came when the resort was made the global winner of the British Airways Tourism for Tomorrow Awards in 2000. The emphasis here is very much on the wildlife, coral reefs and ecology of the island and a stay here makes for an interesting alternative to the other beach resorts. Rates from US$200 per person.

L-A (depending on the season) **Protea Hotels Mbweni Ruins Hotel**, south of Stone Town, T024-2235478, www.mbweni.com. Built in the spacious grounds of the ruins of the first Anglican Christian missionary settlement in East Africa. Private beach, pool, garden setting, open-air restaurant under thatch, art gallery, 13 suites with a/c and fans, 4-poster beds, mosquito nets, balconies, free shuttles to Stone Town 5 times a day, candlelit chapel for weddings, organizes various tours around the island.

D **Lail-Noor Guest House**, T024-2234343, www.amaanbungalows.com/lailanoor.htm, 5-min walk from Stone Town along Nyerere Rd, close to the beach. Self-catering bungalows or apartments with cooking facilities aimed at families, mosquito nets, restaurant and bar, free pick-ups from the port and free transfers to *Amaan's Bungalows* at Nungwi. Basic but good value.

Eating

Stone Town *p142, map p144*

There are a few moderate standard eating places in Zanzibar and you will not usually need to reserve a table; and many of them have good, fresh seafood. In recent years many places (especially those serving alcohol) have closed because of complaints by Muslim neighbours. However, most of the hotels have good restaurants and bars, many of which are on rooftops, that are also open to non-guests. During Ramadan it is difficult to get meals in the day time. It is not possible to purchase bottles of spirits in shops any more. Bring your own supply from the mainland if required.

TTT **Baharia**, in the *Serena Inn*. An expensive à la carte restaurant with fantastic food and attentive service in one of the most beautiful of the restored buildings on Zanzibar. It's worth eating here for a treat even if you are not staying. It's very romantic and you need to dress up.

★ TTT **Emerson and Green**, 236 Hurumzi St, behind the House of Wonders, T0747-423266 (mob), www.emerson-green.com. Here you can eat in wonderful surroundings on the rooftop; if you are not staying here you need to book a day ahead as space on the roof is limited. Fixed dinner menus with the emphasis on seafood, expect to pay in the region of US$30 and take all evening to enjoy the excellent food and sumptuous setting.

TTT **Africa House Hotel**, T0747-432340. As well as a bar and disco, there are 2 restaurants at the Africa House. *Tradewinds* is the more formal of the two with very good gourmet cuisine as well as Swahili dishes and seafood, whilst the *Sunset Grill* has an outside terrace, fresh fish dishes and BBQ meat grills. Now the hotel has been renovated the atmosphere and service are excellent.

TT **Hotel Kiponda**, Nyumba ya Moto St, behind the People's Palace, T024-2233052. Another relaxing rooftop restaurant serving speciality seafood dishes and Zanzibar curries in a traditional atmosphere in what was once a sultan's harem.

TT **Pagoda**, has relocated from Funguni to the Shangani area, and is now only a few paces away from *Africa House Hotel*, T024-2234688. Has really excellent spicy Chinese cuisine, generous portions. Go for a beer at the hotel first to watch the sunset.

TT **Archipelago**, Kenyatta Rd, opposite the National Bank of Commerce, T0747-462311 (mob). Open daily for breakfast, lunch and dinner, traditional Swahili dishes, salads, burgers and daily specials. Good coffee and cakes. Outdoor terrace with modern furniture overlooking the harbour.

TT **La Fenice**, on seafront just around the corner from the *Serena*, T024-2250368. Does a good lunch as well as a good dinner, authentic continental and Swahili seafood dishes.

TT **Le Spices Rendez-vous**, Kenyatta Rd, near the High Court, T0747-413062 (mob). Formerly the *Maharaja Restaurant*, it still serves up excellent Indian meals, snacks and seafood. African music and dance on Tue evenings. Prices have risen steeply since the change of ownership. Recommended.

TT **Mercury's**, T024-2233076. Atmospheric wooden outdoor terrace overlooking the harbour, serves pizzas, pasta, seafood barbecue and cocktails with good service. Great place to watch football games on the beach but food is a little overpriced.

TT **Neem Tree Restaurant**, at the Old Fort, T024-2237823. Serves a reasonable buffet of barbecued food and hosts cultural events like *taarab*, Zanzibari traditional drummers. These events usually happen at least twice a week, more in high season. If you do not want to eat, you can still go and watch the entertainment for a smaller fee. We have had mixed reports about this show; in high season when there is quite a crowd of tourists to entertain it is very good, whilst readers have said that in low season only a couple of unenthusiastic drummers appear in their tracksuits and it is not worth the money.

Sea View Indian Restaurant, Mizingani Rd, T024-2232132. A splendid location overlooking the harbour. You can eat inside or out and there is a wide range of food on the menu including delicious and good value curries, freshly cooked on order, but nevertheless service can be slow, and if you want to sit on the balcony you would be advised to book ahead.

Sweet Eazy Restaurant, Forodhani, on the beachfront opposite the National Bank of Commerce, T0747-416736 (mob). A fairly new and popular place with fresh salads, snacks, Swahili and Thai dishes served in lovely gardens almost on the beach. Happy hour 1700-1900. Cocktails, fresh juice, shooters, pool table, live bands, TV for watching sport, open until midnight. Appears to have taken over from the (now closed) *Blues* which used to be the premier bar in the area.

Baobab Tree, New Mkunazini Rd, near the UMCA cathedral. Large thatched roof constructed around the trunk of a baobab tree, open-sided seating area beneath, some meals, snacks, juices, bar.

Dolphin Restaurant, Kenyatta St, T024-2231987. Popular place selling mainly seafood. Nothing special but one of the cheapest places where you can sit down. A sandwich will cost you about US$0.50.

Luis Yoghurt Parlour, Gizenga St, not far from *Africa House Hotel*. Very small place serving excellent local dishes including lassi, yoghurt drinks, milk shakes, fresh fruit juices, spice tea, and fabulous Italian ice cream. Opens 1000-1400 and 1800-2200 Mon-Sat. Closes for long periods in low season while the owner goes away.

Luna Mare, Gizenga St, signposted from the Kenyatta Rd end, T024-2231922. Reasonably-priced Indian and Chinese food and local snacks. Nothing special in canteen-style surroundings but filling fare.

★ **Forodhani Gardens** (also known as *Jamituri*), between the fort and the sea. Here you can get excellent meat or prawn kebabs, lobster, grilled calamari and fish, corn on the cob, cassava and curries all very cheaply. It is very popular with tourists who return night after night, and fun to wander around even if you don't feel hungry. If you're thirsty, try some fresh coconut milk or freshly squeezed sugar cane juice. The 'African Pizza' (*mantabali*) is also well worth a try. You may need to haggle over some of the prices, but you will still come away very full and with change from US$5. Just ensure everything is cooked well and inspect it carefully in the dim light. If it's not ask the vendor to throw it back on the coals for a little longer. After dinner you can also get excellent ice cream from the *Arsenal* ice cream vendor at the north end of the market, who very usefully will also inform you of up-to-date European football results!

Bars and clubs

Africa House Hotel, the most popular bar in the town on a wide marble upstairs terrace which looks out across the ocean. The beers are cold and plentiful although rather expensive, and it is a good place to meet people. Get there early if you want to watch the sun set: seats are quickly taken.

Garage Club, and adjoining **Dharma Lounge**, next to *Fisherman's Restaurant* on Shangani St, opposite Tembo House Hotel, T024-2233626, are the biggest and most popular nightclubs in Stone Town, open Wed-Mon 2200 until the early hours. Modern hi-tec club with a large dance floor and good selection of music, there is a line of taxis outside all night and security guards will accompany you to the closer guest houses and hotels.

Pirate's Cove, in *Africa House Hotel*, T024-2230708, open nightly until late, with state of the art sound and lighting systems and resident DJ. There is live music on Sat nights.

★ Festivals and events

February

Sauti za Busara Swahili Music and Cultural Festival. *Sauti za Busara* means 'songs of wisdom' in Kiswahili, and this annual festival of Swahili music attracts the best musicians and performers in the region. Held in Stone Town, there are concerts (mostly in the Old Fort) of traditional music, from Swahili *taraab* and *ngoma* to more contemporary genres that mix African, Arab and Asian music. Held annually during the **second weekend in Feb**, the 4-day festival attracts talent from all over East Africa with performances in music, theatre and dance. See **Dhow Countries Musical Academy**, www.zanzibarmusic.org, for more information.

Eid al-Haj (also called Eid al-Adha or Eid al-Kebir) is the Islamic festival of the annual pilgrimage, or haj, to Mecca. It is the second major holiday of Islam and a 3-day festival of feasting and celebration in all Muslim communities in Tanzania. For Muslims, this holiday is about sacrifice, faith, and honouring the prophet Ibrahim. Along the Swahili Coast, and the islands of Zanzibar, each family sacrifices a goat or sheep; a third of the meat is given to the poor, another third to family and friends, and the final third is kept by the family to be served in a lavish meal. Any family members or friends who made the pilgrimage to Mecca that year are welcomed home with much rejoicing. During the night there is live Swahili *taraab* music and much rejoicing.

July

Zanzibar International Film Festival of the Dhow Countries celebrates and promotes the unique culture that grew as a result of Indian Ocean trade and the wooden sailing dhow. All nations around the Indian Ocean known as the dhow countries are included in the celebration. Contemporary artists, musicians, cultural troupes, photographers and film makers are showcased and their work promoted, discussed, awarded, and explored. The highlight is the Zanzibar International Film Festival; film screenings take place around Stone Town in various historic landmarks. During the festival, workshops, seminars, conferences and a variety of cultural and arts-related programmes are open to the public, with specific forums to attract and creatively empower women and children. The festival is held every year during the **first 2 weeks of July**. www.ziff.or.tz

Zanzibar Cultural Festival is held throughout the archipelago, many performers from around Africa perform at the annual Zanzibar Cultural Festival but the Swahili culture is mostly represented. Zanzibari *taraab* music and traditional dances are performed by a rich ensemble of cultural troupes and there are exhibits of arts and crafts. Street carnivals in Stone Town, small fairs, and canoe races also take place. On Pemba, the festival marks the annual bull fight, a remnant of Portuguese presence on the islands. The festival is held each year in July, directly after the Zanzibar International Festival of the Dhow Countries. www.ziff.or.tz

November/December

Eid al-Fitr (in Kiswahili also called 'Idi' or 'Sikuku,' which means 'celebration') is the Muslim holiday that signifies the end of the holy month of Ramadan. It is without a doubt the central holiday of Islam, and a major event throughout Tanzania, but especially observed on the coast and Zanzibar. Throughout Ramadan, Muslim men and women fast from sunrise to sunset, only taking meagre food and drink after dark. The dates for Eid al-Fitr vary according to the sighting of the new moon, but as soon as it is observed the fasting ends and four days of feasting and festivities begin. Stone Town is the best place to witness this celebration when the whole of the town takes to the streets.

Zanzibar Marathon and Triathlon take place annually in **early Nov**. Both events have been successful in drawing participants from East Africa, Asia and Europe. Information concerning participation in either of these events can be obtained from: The Secretary, Zanzibar International Marathon Committee, PO Box 1410, Zanzibar, F024-2233448.

O Shopping

Central Darajani Market on Creek Rd, sells mainly fresh fruit and vegetables and meat. However, the shops nearby sell *kikois* and *kangas* (sarongs), wooden chests and other souvenirs. Also try the small shops in the Old Fort, one shop sells only locally handcrafted wooden boxes, many made of fragrant rosewood.

Capital Art Studios, Kenyatta St, sells wonderful black and white photographs of old Zanzibar as well as prints of the Masai and other Tanzanian people. These make great souvenirs and look particularly good when framed in heavy wood.

Masomo Bookshop near the Old Empire Cinema just behind the Central Market, T024-2232652, has a good range of books and also sells Tanzanian and Kenyan newspapers.

The Zanzibar Gallery, Mercury House, reputedly the former home of singer Freddie Mercury, Shangani, T024-2232721, gallery@swahilicoast.com. The beautifully decorated shop boasts the most comprehensive range of books in Zanzibar; guidebooks, wildlife guides, coffee table books and the best of contemporary and historical fiction from the whole of Africa. The CD collection focuses on the best of Swahili music traditions such as *taarab*. Also authentic artworks, antiques, fabrics and textiles from Zanzibar and mainland Africa, and clothes. It also sells excellent postcards taken by the owner's son. Accepts credit cards.

Memories of Zanzibar, opposite the Shangani post office, T024-2239377. Another upmarket shop with quality souvenirs, jewellery, hand bags, cloth, cushions, and books.

Abeid Curio Shop, Cathedral St, opposite St Joseph's Cathedral, T024-2233832. Sells old Zanzibari furniture, clocks, copper and brass.

Activities and tours

In order to maximize your time in Zanzibar it is worth considering going on a tour. All the tour companies listed below offer the following range of tours:

City tour

This includes most of the major sites of Stone Town, such as the market, national museum, cathedral, Beit al-Sahel and Hammani baths. If you are interested in the architecture, this is a good opportunity to learn more about the buildings. Half day, US$15.

Cruises

Safari Blue, T0747- 423162 (mob), www.safariblue.net/xperience. This daily cruise departs from the village of Fumba to the southwest of Stone Town several kilometres beyond the airport; transfers can be arranged. A full day trip around sandbanks, small islands and coral reefs, includes use of top quality snorkelling equipment with guides and instructors, sodas, mineral water and beer, and a seafood lunch of grilled fish and lobster, fruit and coffee. Dolphins can be seen most of the time.

Sabran Jamiil is a traditional 36 ft *jahazi* (ocean going dhow) that has been fully restored and is decorated with Persian cushions, flowing cloth and storm lanterns. Each evening between 1700-1900 she sails along the coast of Stone Town and you can get on at either the Tembo Hotel or the Forodhani Gardens. The views of the city from the water at sunset are gorgeous. The price of US$25 includes drinks and snacks. T0747-417279, www.zanzibarunique.com.

Dolphin tour

Humpback and bottlenose dolphins swim in pods off Kizimkazi Beach on the southwest of the island, and are not always easy to spot. It takes about an hour for the boats to reach Kizimkazi Beach from Stone Town and you are advised to leave early. A dolphin tour includes transport by minibus to Kizimkazi, and transfer to a boat at the beach, a route that easily allows for a visit of Jozani Forest (see above and page 171). Prices and the quality of the boats vary, and many of the small boats do not run to a timetable but wait to fill up, usually accommodating 6-8 tourists. Book this excursion through a tour operator rather than with the touts on the beachfront in Stone Town. From Stone Town, a half day trip is around US$40. Full day including the dolphins in the morning and Jozani Forest in the afternoon is about US$45.

North and east coast tour

All the operators offer transport to the North and East coast beaches, which can be combined with tours. For example, you can be picked up in Stone Town and taken to the East Coast via the **Jozani Forest** (US$35, US$25 if you only go to Jozani and return to Stone Town, see page 171) where the rare red colobus monkey is found. On the way to the North Coast, you have the option of combining a morning Spice Tour and perhaps a visit to the Mangapwani slave caves, and ending the tour by being transferred to the hotels in Nungwi. US$35.

★ Spice tour

For centuries Zanzibar's cloves, nutmeg, cinnamon, pepper and many other spices attracted traders across the Indian Ocean. The exotic spices and fruits are grown in the plantations around Stone Town and there's ample opportunity to dazzle the senses as you taste and smell them and guess what they are. This tour is highly recommended in

The leaves of the neem tree were once used as a cure for malaria and indigestion, the iodine tree produces a deep red sap used to fight infection, while the foaming berries of the soap berry tree were used for centuries as an alternative to soap.

Being dolphin friendly

- ✗ Swimming with the dolphins is not recommended if you are a nervous swimmer. Dolphins are usually found in the open sea, which frequently has a marked swell and you may struggle if you are not a strong swimmer.
- ✗ Loud noises or splashy water entries will scare off the dolphins. If you see a school, ensure that your boatman does not try to chase them at full speed as this will only scare them off.
- ✓ Once you are reasonably close, get the boatman to turn off the engine and slide gently into the water.
- ✓ Swim with your arms along your body and duck/dive/spiral – do interesting things to attract their attention. Dolphins are curious mammals but they are wild. If you are lucky they will surround you and nudge you.
- ✗ Try not to touch them and do not feed them. Given that up to 100 people a day in high season take this excursion, there is debate as to whether it is good or not for the dolphins.

during season, out of season you may get weary of looking at leaves that look very similar. Most tours are by *dala-dala*, the longer ones also include lunch. Guides give detailed descriptions of the various plants. The henna tree produces a dye from its crushed leaves used by women to elaborately decorate their hands and feet in delicate patterns. On the tour you'll have the opportunity to have a body part painted, but with quick-drying Indian ink instead (henna takes all day to dry). The tours last 4 hrs and are offered by various tour operators, though the legendary Mr. Mitu (see page 160) is still the best. Half day, US$25; full day with additional visits to the slave caves and beach at Mangapwani, US$30.

Scuba diving → *See also box next page*

Zanzibar is a great place to go diving. There are 2 recommended diving schools in Stone Town that both offer good value. It is worth noting that the best time for diving in Zanzibar is from Feb till Apr and from Aug through to the end of Nov, allowing you to take advantage of low season hotel rates.
Zanzibar Dive Centre-One Ocean, bottom of Kenyatta Road on the sea front, T024-2238375, 0748-750161 (mob), www.zanzibaroneocean.com. Motorized dhows and custom-built dive boats go to several coral reefs, PADI certificate course US$320 for open-water diving. If you have a scuba certificate, 1 dive including boat trip to the reef costs US$50 and 2 dives US$75, including all equipment hire and lunch. The inexperienced are offered 'fun dives' for US$75, which include 30 mins' instruction of the basics, plus a 12-m deep dive on a coral reef, snorkelling is US$20 a trip, safety highest priority, with fully trained dive masters/instructors. Recommended.
Bahari Divers, next to the National Bank of Commerce on the corner of Shangani and Kenyatta rds, T0748-254786 (mob), www.zanzibar-diving.com. Offer all PADI courses to instructor level and snorkelling using a motorized dhow, German owned; if you book on line there is a 10% discount. PADI Open Water course US$320, single dives US$50, discounts for multiple dives, snorkelling trips with lunch US$20.

Zanzibar Heritage Conservation Park

An alternative to going on a Spice Tour is to visit this park in Jumbi, 12 km southeast of Stone Town. The park is a private enterprise, operated by the very knowledgeable Omar Suleiman, who will show you around the large garden of herbs, fruits and other plants, and also the small museum and aviary. Entrance under US$1, to get there ask a taxi driver to take you to Jumbi as the park is not widely known. There is a small sign on the left of the road as you approach the village.

Tour operators

All these operators offer the tours listed above and others including: historical ruins

★ Stone Town dive sites

Pange Reef The first sandbank west of Stone Town with a maximum depth of 14 m. There is an enormous variety of coral and lots of tropical reef fish such as clown fish, parrot fish, moorish idol and many others. Pange reef is ideal for Open Water Diver courses, as it offers calm and shallow waters. This is also a good spot for night dives, where you may see cuttle fish, squid, crab and other nocturnal life.

Bawe Island Bawe has a reef stretching around it with a maximum depth of 18 m. Here you will find beautiful corals like acropora, staghorn, brain corals and a large variety of reef fish.

Wrecks Wreck diving for all levels: At 12 m *The Great Northern* (built 1870), a British steel cable-laying ship, which sank on New Year's Eve 1902. She has become a magnificent artificial reef and is home to a number of leaf fish, lionfish and morays. Parts of the ship can still be identified and some relics may still be found (though not taken). *The Great Northern* is an ideal wreck for the beginner diver as she is only 12 m below the surface and is also great for snorkelling. The 30 m wreck of the *Royal Navy Lighter*, is home to large schools of rainbow runners, trevally, sweepers, and sometimes reef sharks, best suited for experienced advanced divers. At 40 m a steam sand dredger, *The Penguin*, is only suitable for very experienced deep water divers. Here you can find huge numbers of barracuda, big stingrays and morays.

Murogo Reef Maximum depth 24 m, 25 min from Stone Town by boat. Sloping reef wall with a huge variety of coral and fish. Turtle are often seen here and this is usually the preferred dive site for the Open Water Diver course.

Nyange Reef This reef is the largest of all reefs on the west coast of Zanzibar and contains several dive sites, all of which are unique. A new species of coral has recently been identified on this reef and marine biologists believe it to be endemic to Nyange.

Boribu Reef One of the best dive sites off Zanzibar and huge barrel sponges, large moray eels, pelagic fish and large lobsters are all features of this dive. In season whale sharks pass through. The maximum depth is 30 m.

Thanks to **Zanzibar Dive Centre-One Ocean**, www.zanzibaroneocean.com.

and slave relics, Prison Island. Some are also able to arrange dhow sailing trips to the smaller islands, visits to Pemba, domestic flights, and car and motorbike hire. This is certainly not a comprehensive list, there are so many tour operators to choose from. Alternatively you may be able to book all excursions through your hotel.

Mitu. Mr Mitu is one of Stone Town's most famous and formidable characters and has been running excellent Spice Tours in numerous languages for decades. Contactable at the café next door to the *Ciné Afrique* early in the mornings or in the evenings. Mr Mitu, an elderly Indian (or one of the people he has trained), will take you on a tour visiting the Marahubi Palace, 2 spice plantations, the Kidichi Baths and a 1-hr trip to relax on the beach. They are good value. However, they have become very popular and you may find yourself in a large group of 30 or more. Cost US$10 per person including vegetarian lunch. Bookings are taken the evening before or from 0800 on the day, get there by 0900, depart 0930, return 1300-1600 (depending on if you want to go to the beach or not).

Adventure Afloat, based at the Mbweni Ruins Hotel, T024-2235478, www.mbweni.com.

Anderson's African Adventure, T024-2503361, T0742-402401 (mob).

Centre Island Tours & Travel, office near *Emerson & Green*, T024-2233854, citours@zanzinet.com.

Chema Bros Tours and Safaris, Kenyatta Rd, at the roundabout with Kaunda Rd and Vuga Rd, T024-2233385, chema@zanzinet.com

Classic Tours, c/o *Emerson & Green*, T024-2238127.
Easy Travel and Tours, Malawi Rd, opposite *Hotel Marine*, T024-2235372, www.easytravel.co.tz.
Eco and Culture Tours, opposite *Emerson & Green*, T024-2230366, www.ecoculture-zanzibar.org.
Equator Tours and Safaris, Sokomohogo St, T024-2333722, eqt@zanlink.com.
Exotic Tours and Safaris, T024-2236392-3, www.zanzibarexotictours.com.
Fisherman Tours and Travel, Vuga Rd, T024-2238791/2, reservations@fishermantours.com.
Fernandes Tours and Safaris, T024-2230666, fts@zanlink.com.
Forodhani Car Hire, near the Forodhani Gardens near the Old Fort, T0747-410186.
Hima Tours and Travel, Kiponda St, T024-2237916, www.himatours.com.
Jasfa Tours and Safaris, Shangani Rd, T024-2234027.
Links Tours and Travel, at the port, T024-2234563.
Ocean Tours, opposite the Zanzibar Serena Inn, T024-2233642, www.oceantourszanzibar.com.
Sama Tours, Changa Bazaar St, T024-2233543, samatours@zitec.org.
Simba Tours, T024-2239695, www.simbatours.com.
Sun 'n' Fun Safari Tours, Sea View Restaurant, Shangani Rd, T024-2237381.
Tima Tours and Safaris, Mizingani Rd, T024-2231298, tima@zitec.org.
Tanzania Adventure, Diplomat House, Mianzini, T024-2232119, www.tanzania-adventure.com.
Tropical Tours and Safaris, Kenyatta Rd, Shangani, T024-2230868, tropicalts@hotmail.com.
Zan Tours, Malindi St, T024-2233116, www.zantours.com.

Transport

You can arrange transfers by **minivans** (seating 8 passengers) through most of the tour agencies to get around the island. It will cost an average of about US$10 per person to get out to the beaches in the north or east. You can **hire cars** for about US$40-50 per day, **motorbikes** for US$20-25 per day, and **bicycles** for US$5, from many of the tour operators. Sometimes they also charge a refundable deposit. Ensure all your paperwork is in order if driving.

Air

International airlines that serve Zanzibar are:
Kenya Airways, off Vuga Rd a few metres northeast of the Air Tanzania office, T024-2232041.
Gulf Air, just off Malindi Rd towards the port, T024-2232824.
Oman Air, a block south of Gulf Air in Malindi, T024-2238308.

Several airlines have scheduled services to and from the mainland and Zanzibar airport. Expect to pay in the region of US$55 one way. Some also operate a service between Zanzibar and **Pemba** which is around US$70 one way. Bear in mind that the airline industry is highly changeable, so the following timetables are subject to change.
Air Tanzania, Vuga Rd, T024-2230297, www.airtanzania.com, has flights between **Dar** and Zanzibar daily at 0900 and 1600 which take 25 min. In the opposite direction flights depart from Zanzibar for Dar at 0950 and 1700. These services connect with onward flights in Dar.
Precision Air Dar, T022-2130800/2121718, Zanzibar, Mazons Hotel, T2234521, www.precisionairtz.com. Flights depart **Dar** for Zanzibar (20 min) daily at 0650, 1100 and 1320, and depart Zanzibar for Dar at 1150, 1230 and 1700. There are also daily direct flights between Zanzibar and **Nairobi** (1 hr 45 min) at 0730, which returns from Nairobi at 0945, to **Arusha** (1 hr 10 min) at 1400, returning from Arusha at 1530, and to **Mombasa** (40 min) at 1140, returning from Mombasa at 1555. There are connections to other domestic destinations from Dar.
Coastal Air, reservations, Dar, T022-2117969-60, Zanzibar Airport office T024-2233112, www.coastal.cc, have daily flights from **Dar** to Zanzibar at 0615, 0900, 1230, 1400, 1645, and 1745, and from Zanzibar to Dar, 0640, 1300, 1400, and 1715. The 1400 from Zanzibar continues to **Selous** and costs a further US$130 from Dar. There are also daily return flights to **Arusha**, which depart Zanzibar at 0930 and Arusha at 1215, take approximately 2 hrs and cost US$190

one way. There's also a daily flight from Zanzibar to **Pemba** (30 min) at 1430 that costs US$70. This returns from Pemba to Zanzibar at 1640.

Zan Air, to the west of Malawi Rd, Malindi area, T024-2233670, www.zanair.com, has scheduled daily flights from **Dar** to Zanzibar that depart at 0845, 1515, 1800 and 1815. From Zanzibar to Dar flights depart at 0650, 1300, 1600 and 1730. From Zanzibar to **Pemba**, flights are at 0945 and 1600, returning at 1030 and 1645. They also have 1 daily direct flight between **Arusha** and Zanzibar that departs Arusha at 1415, and departs Zanzibar at 0930.

Bus and dala-dala

Dala-dala, which that are usually converted pickup vans with wooden benches in the back, and regular buses are the cheapest way of getting around the island. It will cost about US$2 to the east or north coasts, but they are hot, dusty and not very comfortable. Most go from the bus station on Creek Rd opposite the market. Buses with lettered codes serve routes in and around Stone Town. A to **Amani**, B to **Bububu**, and U to the **airport**, amongst others. Numbered vehicles go further afield, and tend to leave once a day around noon, returning early the next morning. Bus number 9 goes to **Paje**, **Jambiani** (3 hrs) and **Bwejuu** (4½ hrs), costing about US$3. Other buses from Creek Rd go to **Pwani Mchangani** and **Matemwe** (bus number 1), **Mangapwani** (bus 2), **Fumba** (bus 7), **Makunduchi** and **Kizimkazi** (bus 10), **Nungwi** (bus 16), and **Kiwengwa** (bus 17). There is another bus station, Mwembe Ladu, one block north of the new Post Office about 1½ km east of Stone Town. Bus number 6 from here goes to **Chakwa** (1½ hrs), **Uroa** and **Pongwe**.

Ferry

The booking offices of the ferry companies are on the approach road to the harbour.
Azam Marine, T024-2231655.
Flying Horse, T024-2233031.
Sea Express, T024-2234690.
Sea Star, T0707-2233857 (mob).
Zanzibar Port's Corporation, for general enquiries, T024-2232857.

Directory

Banks There are no ATM facilities in Zanzibar, although Barclay's may offer one soon. **People's Bank of Zanzibar**, T024-22131118/9, behind the fort on Gizenga St. Also a branch at the Airport Terminal, T024-221118/9. **Barclay's**, ZSTC Building, Malawi Rd, Gulioni, T024-2235796. **National Bank of Commerce (NBC)**, Shangani St, T024-2233590. Banks often give an inferior rate compared with the foreign exchange (forex) bureaux, which are also open for longer hours. There are plenty of these all over Stone Town, just ensure you go into an office and do not deal with money changers on the street. **Western Union** money transfer is available from the Tanzanian Postal Bank on Malawi Rd, Malindi area, T024-2231798, open 0830-1800 Mon-Sat. **Visa and Mastercard Assistance Point**, next to Serena Inn, open 0830-1730 Mon-Sat. You can withdraw cash against your credit card. **Post** The new Post Office is outside Stone Town, in Kijangwani, just over 1 km east of the Karume Monument, T024-2231260. Bus A or M from the market will take you there. Poste restante and faxes are held there. The old Post Office is on Kenyatta Rd in the Shangani area, there is a fax machine and they should be able to help with poste restante. Worldwide delivery services available from **DHL**, opposite Serena Inn. **Internet** There are many internet cafés all over Stone Town. Services are particularly good, with fast connections and reasonable prices. Expect to pay around US$0.50 for 1 hr. **Medical services** **Mkunazini Hospital**, near the market, T024-2230076. British trained doctor. Pay fee to register, wait to see doctor then pay for any prescription necessary. Pay again when you go to collect medicine: this may be at the clinic or in a nearby drug-store. **Zanzibar Medical & Diagnostic Centre**, near Majestic Cinema, off Vuga Rd, T024-2233113. **Dr Mehta's Hospital**, Pipalwadi St, Vuga has a 24-hr casualty facility, T024-2230194. **Useful services** **Police**, T024-2230771. **Director of Immigration**, T024-2239148. If you lose your passport whilst on Zanzibar contact the immigration department who will arrange for an emergency travel document to get you back to Dar where the international embassies and high consulates are located.

North to Nungwi

The stretch of coastline immediately to the north of Stone Town was once an area of villas, recreational beaches, and Sultans' out-of-town palaces. This is also the route that was once followed by the Bububu light railway and an iron pipeline that carried domestic water supplies to the town during the reign of Sultan Barghash. Today many of the ruined palaces can be visited, though little of their previous opulence remains and they are fairly overgrown. Nevertheless they offer an interesting excursion off the road to Nungwi. At the northern end of the island are the villages of Nungwi and Kendwa. Until recently these were once sleepy fishing villages hosting a couple of backpacker's lodges, but today the two settlements are almost joined together by a ribbon of hotel development and this is one of the most popular spots on the island for a beach holiday. The party atmosphere along the Nungwi Strip may not appeal to everyone, but there is no denying that this is a wonderful stretch of palm lined beach. Days are warm and sunny, the Indian Ocean is a brilliant blue, and the snorkelling and diving are excellent. » *For Sleeping, Eating and other listings, see pages 166-168.*

Maruhubi Palace ruins

The Maruhubi Palace ruins are about 3 km to the north of the town. They were built in 1882 by Sultan Barghash for his harem of what is said to be one wife and 99 concubines. The Palace was once one of the most impressive residences on the island. Built in the Arabic style, the main house had balustrade balconies, the great supporting columns for which can still be seen. From here you can imagine him looking out over his beautiful walled gardens, which are believed to have been inspired by the Sultan's 1875 visit to Richmond Park in London. An overhead aqueduct and lily-covered cisterns (or 'pleasure ponds') can also be seen on the site and are evidence of the extensive Persian Baths. On the beach are the remains of a fortified *seble* or reception area, where visiting dignitaries would have been welcomed. The palace was almost completely destroyed by a fire in 1899, the site is now very overgrown, and marble from the baths has long since been stolen.

Mtoni Palace ruins

Shortly after the Marahubi Palace, just before the small BP oil terminus, are the ruins of the earlier Mtoni Palace. Shortly before he relocated his court from Muscat to Zanzibar in 1840, Sultan Seyyid constructed the Royal Palace at Mtoni as his primary residence. The palace was abandoned by 1885, in favour of more modern residences built by Sultan Barghash (see Maruhubi Palace, above) and quickly fell into disrepair. Use as a storage depot in World War I caused further damage and now only the walls and part of the roof remain. The site, sadly, is sandwiched between commercial premises and the small BP oil refinery. There have been suggestions that the remaining shell be converted into a Museum of Maritime and Industrial History, but this looks some considerable way away from fruition.

Around 3km North of Mtoni, to the left hand side of the road is **Kibweni Palace**. This fine whitewashed building is the only Sultan's Palace on the island to remain in public use, accommodating both the President and state visitors.

Zanzibar had the first steam locomotive in East Africa that ran on a tiny two foot gauge and carried the Sultan to and from his summer palace in the 1880s. The train became notorious for setting the countryside alight.

Maviko ya Makumbi

As you walk along the beach you will see mounds of what look like stones, known locally as 'Heaps of Stones', but which are in fact deposits of coconut husks. Each Heap of Stones belongs to a family or sometimes an individual, and some are 60 years old, passed down from one generation to the next. They are made into coir and then used to make ropes, matting and decorations. The coconuts are buried in the mud for 3-6 months, which accelerates the decay of unwanted parts of the coconut, leaving the coir (the sea water helps to prevent insect infestation). The coir is then hammered to separate it out from the vegetable matter.

If you see a group of women working on the Maviko ya Makumbi, make sure you request permission before taking a photograph.

Persian Baths at Kidichi

ⓘ *The baths are 1 km north of Kibwenii. Take a right hand turn opposite a small filling station, along a rough dirt road. Follow the track for 4 km out through the clove and coconut plantations.*

Built on the highest point of Zanzibar Island by Sultan Seyyid Said in 1850, they were for his wife who was the grand-daughter of the Shah of Persia, Fatah Ali, and are decorated in ornamental Persian stucco work. The remarkably preserved baths have a series of domed bathhouses with deep stone baths and massive seats. This is quite a contrast to the plain baths nearby at **Kizimbani**, which were built within Said's clove tree and coconut plantation. Persian poetry inscribed inside the baths at Kidichi has been translated (approximately) as "Pleasant is a flower-shaped wine/With mutton chops from game/Given from the hands of a flower-faced server/At the bank of a flowering stream of water". The beaches to the west of here are good and are the location of several resorts. **Fuju Beach** can be easily reached from Bububu village, and is a great place to take a relaxing swim if you've been exploring the area. There is a disco on the beach every Friday. Any *dala-dala* with the letter B from the main road will get you to Fuji beach.

Mangapwani slave caves

ⓘ *US$1. If you want to get there independently the caves can be reached by taking bus number 2 from Creek Rd opposite the market. It's best to take a torch.*

About 20 km north of Stone Town, these were used to hide slaves in the times when the slave trade was illegal but still carried on unofficially. One particular trader, Mohammed bin Nasser, built an underground chamber at Alwi that was used as well as the naturally formed cave. The cave itself is said to have been discovered when a young slave boy lost a goat that he was looking after. He followed its bleats, which led to the cave containing a freshwater stream (a blessing for the illegally confined slaves). You may well see women carrying water from this very same stream today.

Tumbatu Island

ⓘ *The White Sands Hotel in Kendwa organizes trips here.*

Northwest of Zanzibar, the island of Tumbatu is the third largest island in the archipelago and despite being only 8 km long by 3 km wide, it has a very individual history. The island contains Shirazi ruins of a large ancient town dating from the 12th century and about 40 of the stone houses remain. The Mvuleni ruins are in the north of the island and are the remnants of the Portuguese attempt to colonize Zanzibar.

The island's people, the Watumbatu, are distinct from the people of Unguja. They speak their own dialect of Kiswahili and are fiercely independent, renowned for their aloofness and pride rather than their hospitality. They are strictly Muslim and generally do not welcome visitors to the island. They also have the reputation of being the best sailors on the East Coast of Africa.

Kendwa

South of Nungwi (see below), about 20 min walk (3 km) along the beach, is the small resort of Kendwa. It is reached by the same minibuses that transport visitors to Nungwi or by boat from Nungwi. The beach is especially known as a good place to swim (as is Nungwi, see page 168) because the tide only retreats about 6 m at low tide, so swimming is possible at any time of day. A band of coral lies about 20 m off shore which offers interesting snorkelling, and trips can be organized by the hotels.

Nungwi

ⓘ *Tourist minibuses go from Stone Town throughout the day, take approximately 1 hr, and cost about US$10 each way, ask from any hotel or tour operator. There are also local dala-dala and the number 16 bus from Creek Road also goes to Nungwi. These take about 2 hrs and cost less than US$1 each way.*

At the north tip of the island is Nungwi, about 56 km from Zanzibar town. It's a pleasant fishing village surrounded by banana palms, mangroves and coconut trees with a local population of around 5,000. However, don't come to Nungwi expecting a quiet beach holiday – over recent years tourism has rapidly expanded in this area, large new resorts are going up at the time of writing, and Nungwi and nearby Kendwa Rocks have firmly established themselves as the party destination of the island. As well as resorts, there are a number of good beach-side bungalows, a short line of lively outdoor bars and restaurants known as the 'Nungwi Strip', and a few dive schools. The accommodation is of a good standard and most of Nungwi's cottages are built in a traditional African style with *makuti* thatched roofs to blend in with the natural surroundings. The bars are fantastically rustic and you'll find beautifully carved Zanzibari furniture sitting right on the beach.

As in other parts of the island, beach robberies have been reported.

Down on the beach, you'll often see local men working in groups to build dhows or dhow fleets heading out to fish in the mid-afternoon. Boat building here has been a traditional skill for generations using historic tools and a 12-m boat takes approximately six months to build. Goats are slaughtered when certain milestones are reached (eg raising the mast) and verses and prayers are read from the Koran. Upon completion a big ceremony is organized and all the villagers are invited. Before the launch the boat builder hammers the boat three times in a naming ceremony.

The name of the village is derived from the Swahili word *mnara*, referring to the 70-ft lighthouse built here 1886 by Chance and Brothers. Currently it's in a

Nungwi

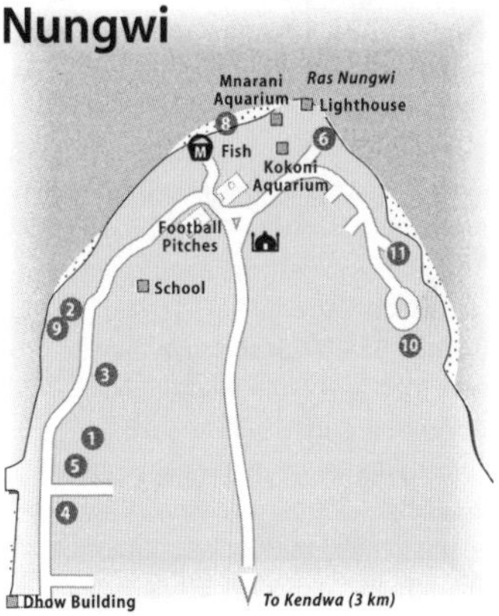

Sleeping
Amaan Bungalows **1**
Baraka Bungalows **2**
Baobab Beach Bungalows **4**
Kigoma Guest House **5**
Langi Langi **3**
Mnarani Beach Cottages **6**
Nungwi Village Beach Resort **8**
Paradise Beach Club **9**
Ras Nungwi Beach **10**
Sazani Beach **11**

 restricted area, with access permitted only by special request and photography is prohibited. Nearby, there are two natural aquariums. **Mnarani Aquarium** ⓘ *US$2*, was established in 1993 by a local resident in an attempt to help restore the local turtle population. Four varieties of turtle are endemic to Zanzibar; the hawksbill (*Ng'amba*); the green turtle (*Kasakasa*); the leatherback turtle (*Msumeno*) and the loggerhead turtle (*Mtumbi*). The aquarium has green turtles, which have a light grey/yellowish shell and hawksbill turtles, which have a yellowish/red shell. Their diet is seaweed and the hawksbill also eats fish. Any turtles hatched at the aquarium are released into the sea. Wild vervet monkeys live in the trees surrounding the rockpool.

Turtles in optimum conditions have a life expectancy of upto 100 years. To discourage the illicit trade in turtle products, do not to buy anything on offer.

You can buy basics at the small shops along the beach front but it is much cheaper to go into the village where water, bread and other items are available. Remember to respect local custom if you go into the village. Women should cover their arms, shoulders and thighs. There are several places to check email in Nungwi at the resorts or at the small shopping centre on the Nungwi strip. However, the best place to get online is at the school; it's US$1 per hour but the proceeds go back into the school.

Sleeping and eating

Mtoni and Bububu *p163*

L-A Mtoni Marine Centre, between the ruined palace of Maruhubi and the Mtoni ruins to the north, 8 km from Stone Town, T024-2250140, www.mtoni.com. Set in a large palm tree garden, the centre has a range of accommodation from shared bungalows to club rooms and suites. The newly finished Palm Garden apartments have private verandas, are traditionally furnished and have views of the beach. The bungalows have 1-3 bedrooms and are ideal for families. The restaurant is open air and has barbecue buffets and themed nights with live jazz or *taarab* music. There's also a beach cocktail and snack bar, and a sushi restaurant.

L-A Salome's Garden, Fuji Beach, reservations online or through Italian agent, T+39-051-234974, www.salomes-garden.com. Lovely early 19th-century restored royal house surrounded by 18 acres of walled private orchards and tropical gardens running down to the beach full of bougainvillaea. Refurbished in 1997 as a luxury guesthouse or you can rent the whole house. There are 4 bedrooms sleeping a maximum of 10, with traditional Zanzibari four-poster beds with mosquito nets, fans, and beautiful antique decor. US$540 a day for the whole house, or US$140 for a double.

B Imani Beach Villa, Bububu Beach, T024-2250050, www.imani.it. Only 7 clean, comfortable rooms with a/c, own bathrooms and traditional-style furniture. Breakfast is served in pleasant gardens that run down to the beach, other meals are a fusion of Mediterranean and African influences. The quality and presentation of food is very high and you eat Swahili-style, seated on cushions around low tables. Restaurant open to non-residents. Recommended.

C Kibweni Beach Villa, 4 km north of Stone Town, T024-2233496, www.geocities.com/kibwenibeach. Simple and friendly accommodation in singles, doubles or triples (US$20/35/50), in a double story whitewashed building with tiled roof. Some rooms have sea views, all have a/c and en suite bathrooms. Restaurant serves local and Oriental food. Can organize all tours.

C Bububu Beach Guest House, Bububu Beach, T024-2250110, www.bububu-zanzibar.com. Rooms with en suite bathrooms for US$25, hot water, nets, fans, also laundry, fax and email services available. Free shuttles to and from Stone Town on request. There's also a whole house that can be let out to a group of up to 8. The owner Omar Kilupi is the current chess master of Zanzibar and is always up for a game. He also arranges transfers and tours.

For an explanation of the sleeping and eating price codes used in this guide, see inside the front cover. Other relevant information is found in Essentials pages 31-34.

Kendwa *p165*

B-C La Rosa Dei Venti, T024-2411314, www.rosazanzibar.com. Bungalows overlooking the beach or self-contained rooms in the main guest house with wooden furnishings, fans and mosquito nets. It is run by Italians, so there is very good Italian, as well as local, cuisine in the restaurant.

C Amaan Bungalows, T024-2240026, www.amaanbungalows.com. 17 rooms in cottages with mosquito nets and balconies, some with en suite bathrooms, no electricity but a generator is used at night. Breakfast served on the hill near the rooms, the main restaurant is on the beach with tables in the sand, cocktail bar. Also has lots of hammocks to lounge around in.

C Kendwa Rocks Hotel, T0747-415474 (mob), www.kendwarocks.com. This was the original backpackers' lodge at Kendwa and the accommodation will appeal to people who are laid back enough to not worry about the rather variable levels of service. Accommodation is in basic, but pretty, thatched bandas on the beach for US$25, fish and Indian food is available. Sometimes the music pumps out late into the night, which may or may not be your thing.

C Kendwa Sunset Bungalows, T0747-413818 (mob), sunsetbungalow@hotmail.com. Has some nice standard rooms and some smart new bungalows, perched on top of a small cliff above the beach. There is a very good bar and restaurant and you can buy your own fish from a fisherman and ask them to cook it for you, they also do good pizzas. It has a slightly more organized feel to it, at least most of the time. There is a dive centre on site.

E White Sands Hotel, T024-2647620. 18 simple bandas or bungalows, basic food available in the bar. Boat rides to Tumbatu Island can be organized. Snorkel and kayaks can be hired. Rates are as low as US$10 per person sharing a banda.

Nungwi *p165, map p165*

The price of a hotel room in Nungwi varies from US$10-250 so the resort appeals to all budgets. At the time of writing a massive and tackily over-the-top Italian resort, *La Gemma Dell' Est*, was being constructed which will have an estimated 900 rooms. This will effectively join up Nungwi with Kendwa to the south and will perhaps irrevocably seal the stamp of mass tourism on the area.

A Nungwi Village Beach Resort, T0741-606701/2 (mob), www.nungwivillage.com. Beach cottages with thatched roofs, furnished with traditional-style Zanzibari wooden decor, en suite bathrooms, premium rooms have a/c. Bar, restaurant specializing in seafood, facilities for watersports including diving. Internet access, henna painting and massages also available.

A Ras Nungwi Beach Hotel, T024-2233767, www.rasnungwi.com. 19 lodge rooms, 36 beach chalets and 1 suite that is actually a huge detatched house with a plunge pool and total privacy from the rest of the hotel. All rooms have ocean views, four-poster beds and carved doors, en suite bathrooms, fans and balconies. The more expensive rooms have CD players and minibars. Restaurants and bars, pool, TV room, and lounge areas under thatched roofs. There's a full range of watersports on offer, mountain bikes can be hired, excellent dive centre with good diving on the reef, and deep-sea fishing. The hotel is closed for a few weeks in low season Apr-Jun. Mastercard and Visa attract a 10% surcharge.

B Mnarani Beach Cottages, T024-2240494, www.lighthousezanzibar.com. 12 self-catering cottages right by the sea. Friendly management, clean, comfortable and well maintained, great service and a good atmosphere. Reductions can be negotiated in low season. Sited up near the lighthouse, 20-min walk from the main strip and near enough to Nungwi to enable you to visit the bars and restaurants, but far enough away to let you get a decent night's sleep afterwards. Breakfast included, full and half-board accommodation available. Bar, seafront restaurant, international cuisine, laundry facilities, hot water, snorkelling, fishing and diving trips. Accepts major credit cards.

B Sazani Beach Hotel, near to Ras Nungwi, T024-2240014, www.sazanibeach.com. 10 rooms, with en suite bathroom, double or twin beds, veranda, electricity and fans, sea views. Tropical garden setting, quiet and well away from the 'strip'. The *Pweza Juma* bar and restaurant serves original dishes with local flavour, specializing in seafood and barbecues, morning tea brought to your room and buffet breakfasts are included in the price. There is a dive school on site offering PADI courses or snorkelling trips.

B **Langi Langi**, T024-2240470, langilangi@hotmail.com. 14 rooms in bungalows just across the track from the beach, a combination of singles, doubles and triples, all with en suite bathrooms, hot water, a/c, fan, veranda and hair dryer. You need to ask for mosquito nets. The lounge area has satellite TV, telephone and fax, and there's a rooftop restaurant with reasonably priced food including seafood.

C **Amaan Bungalows**, T024-2240026, www.amaanbungalows.com. Clean, basic, self-contained rooms or shared bathrooms, no fans, right on the beach, breakfast included. 3 bars and restaurant on site serve good quality food, and there's an internet café. Amaan is really the centre of the whole Nungwi strip and *Fat Fish* bar, with its thumping music is hugely popular, which means there is often a bit of a party scene. Nungwi Travel, who can organize tours, transfers and bicycle hire is based here.

C **Paradise Beach Club**, T0741-326574 (mob), run by *Dive Africa* (formerly Indian Ocean Divers), www.diveafrica.com. 8 double and 2 triple rooms, all with mosquito nets and sea view. Shared bathrooms, excellent and affordable food, pleasant beach bar that stays open 18 hrs a day. Can arrange PADI dive courses, windsurfing, snorkelling and sunset cruises.

C **Baraka Bungalows**, tucked away behind Paradise Beach, no phone. Has no direct sea frontage yet it is a beautiful little garden oasis with some of the best bungalows on this side of Nungwi. Rates included breakfast, communal showers, cheap restaurant with generous portions, mosquito nets, clean.

C **Baobab Beach Bungalows**, at the end of the south beach, away from the Nungwi 'strip', T024-2236315, www.baobabbeachbungalows.com. A fairly new complex of 50 rooms in bungalows set in spacious grounds, moderately priced with four-poster beds, fans and mosquito nets, deluxe rooms have a/c, simpler triple rooms work out to be very good value for 3 people. Bar and restaurant on a small rock directly above the sea, with à la carte, buffet or three courses set menus.

D **Kigoma Guest House**, next door to *Amaan*, no phone. Slightly more basic than *Baraka* and *Amaan* and serves as an overspill from the other two. The road runs right through its centre and there is building work going on everywhere. Sandwiched between the loud bar at *Amaan* and a busy local bar on the beach the other side. Rooms have nets, fans and en suite bathrooms.

Festivals and events

See page 156 for information on festivals which are held throughout the archipelago.

Activities and tours

Nungwi and Kendwa *p165, map p165*

Diving is good around Nungwi and Kendwa. 2 dive schools operate here: **Dive Africa**, at the Paradise Beach Club, www.diveafrica.com/zanzibar; and **Zanzibar Dive Centre-One Ocean Divers**, www.zanzibaroneocean.com. See page 159. Snorkelling equipment can be hired from local shops.

Nungwi has also become popular for **kite surfing**, www.kitezanzibar.com.

The beaches around Ras Nungwi are one of the few areas without a coral reef and you can **swim** at all tides here without walking out for miles to reach the sea, as is the case on the east coast.

A number of places organize '**sunset cruises**' on traditional dhows for US$15 per person.

To the northeast coast

The northeast part of the island is not too difficult to get to but nevertheless has a remote, 'get away from it all' feel. The villages are linked by a rocky high street that stretches right up the coast, fringed with shady palms. The local people live a peaceful existence making a living from farming seaweed or octopus fishing. An extensive coral reef runs down the whole east coast of the island, protecting a long, idyllic white sandy beach that runs for miles and is one of the Africa's most beautiful beaches. The only problem here is that the ocean is tidal, and during some parts of the day it's a very long walk over the tidal flats to reach the sea. There has been a mushrooming of fully inclusive resort properties on the northeast coast, many of them frequented by European package holiday makers. For the most part it is necessary to book these through a tour operator in Stone Town or in Dar es Salaam – or take a chance on getting a room when you arrive. This is particularly risky in high season from June to September and over the Christmas and New Year period. There is very little choice of budget accommodation along this stretch of coast. ▸▸ *For Sleeping, Eating and other listings, see pages 170-171.*

Ins and outs

Getting there Minibus transfers can be arranged in Stone Town and cost around US$10. Bus number 6 from the Mwembe Ladu station in Stone Town goes to Chakwa (1½ hrs), and then continues north to Uroa and Pongwe. The number 17 bus from the Creek Road station in Stone Town also goes along the better part of the beach road as far north as Kiwengwa. Both cost approximately US$1.

Dunga Palace

Just over 20 km down the road from Stone Town are the ruins of the Dunga Palace, which was built by Chief Mwinyi Mkuu Ahmed bin Mohamed Hassan. Legend has it that during the palace's construction slaves were killed in order that their blood could be mixed with the mortar to bring strength and good fortune to the building. During the 1920s a nearby well was found to be 'half full of human bones'. King Muhammad died in 1865 and was succeeded by his son Ahmed, who died without an heir in 1873, ending forever the line of the Mwinyi Mkuu. Unfortunately there is little left of the palace today beside bits of wall and arches, and the area has been taken over by a plantation.

Chwaka Bay

At the end of this road, 32 km from Stone Town via Dunga you will reach Chwaka Bay. On the way you will pass the small **Ufufuma Forest**, a home for Zanzibar red colobus monkey, impala and many bird species, and also the site of several caves. The forest has been actively conserved since 1995, and tourists are welcome, although there are no facilities at present. Chwaka is a quiet fishing village overlooking a broad bay of shallow water and mangrove swamps. Its history is evident from a line of fine but decayed villas, standing above the shoreline on the coral ridge, and it was once popular as a holiday resort with slave traders and their families in the 19th century. There is a lively open-air fish market but little accommodation and most visitors head north along the coast to the hotels.

North of Chwaka

The partly sealed road from Chakwa heads north through the coastal fishing villages where there are several accommodation options and watersports centres on what is a fantastic beach. **Uroa** is a lovely fishing village 10 km to the north of Chwaka, and is close to the Dongwe Channel, which offers suitable diving for novices. **Pongwe** is 5 km north of Uroa, and **Kiwengwa** another 10 km north of Pongwe. The coast road continues all the way up to **Matemwe**, a small village 45 km from Stone Town and 15 km north of Kiwengwa, but this last stretch of road is pretty rough. It is probably easier to take the inland route back to the north road and then back out to Matemwe. This inland route passes through some wide, flat agricultural land more reminiscent of the mainland. It is some of the most fertile land on the island and is a centre for rice, sugar and cassava production. About 1 km off the coast of Matemwe lies the small island of **Mnemba**. About 500 m in diameter, the island, surrounded by a circular coral reef, is renowned for its diving and game fishing. It is privately leased and to visit it is necessary to stay in the exclusive lodge (see below).

Chwaka Bay *p169*

C Chwaka Bay Resort, T024-2233943. Currently the only place to stay in the Chwaka Bay area, the simple bungalows occupy a huge area on the front of a deserted and sheltered beach, though the garden would benefit from maturing and the whole place has a pretty rundown feel. Curio shop, bar, relaxing atmosphere, good food. Can't pre-book accommodation.

North of Chwaka *p169*

Uroa

L Zanzibar Safari Club, Uroa, T024-2238553, wwwzanzibarsafariclub.com. A stunning newly refurbished resort on the beach, 50 luxury rooms in bands in the gardens, verandas with day couches, enormous four-poster beds with mosquito nets and very stylish brightly painted decor. Dive school, tennis courts, 3 bars, 1 of which is at the end of a wooden pier out to sea, 2 restaurants, disco, internet café and tours desk.

C Tamarind Beach Hotel, T024-2237194, tamarind@zanzinet.com. One of the oldest hotels on Zanzibar with a relaxed and informal atmosphere, simple bungalows near the beach with mosquito nets and ceiling fans. European-run, no pool, but pleasant restaurant and open-air bar. The dive centre offers fishing, snorkelling, game fishing, sailing, surfing and parasailing.

Pongwe

A Pongwe Beach Hotel, T0747-413973 (mob), www.pongwe.com. Nice stone and thatch beach bungalows with en suite bathrooms, Zanzibari beds with mosquito nets, and fans set in lovely relaxing gardens. The English chef used to work at the Dorchester Hotel in London. Can arrange snorkelling and game fishing.

Kiwengwa

A Bluebay Beach Resort, T2240240-4, www.bluebayzanzibar.com. An all round quality family resort on a lovely stretch of beach that opened in 1999, with 88 rooms with en suite bathrooms and sea views, four-poster beds, a/c, mosquito nets, satellite TV and minibar. 2 restaurants, disco, swimming pool, fitness centre, tennis court, children's club, watersports, *One Ocean Diving* have a base here. Reputedly there are over 1000 palm trees in the grounds.

A-C Shooting Star Inn, on headland at the north end of the beach, a 15-min walk along the road or beach from the village, T024-2232926, www.zanzibar.org/star. Family-run lodge with 6 luxury bungalows with Zanzibari-style beds and verandas overlooking the ocean. Also lodge rooms overlooking the garden and budget *makuti* bandas with shared bathrooms. Open-air bar and restaurant serving seafood, grills and traditional Zanzibari cuisine – some of the best food to be had on the east coast. Meals are included in the room rates. Bicycles for hire and there is a brand new salt water 'infinity' pool 10 m above the beach.

E Reef View, south of the village, no phone. Very simple accommodation in palm fronded shacks. You get the feeling that if there was a strong gust of wind the whole place could blown away without a trace. The restaurant serves simple, cheap and good food and caters for vegetarians. The bar is self service and has seating areas with views over the beach and headland below. US$10 including breakfast. You cannot make a reservation here, so it's first come first served.

Matemwe

L Mapenzi Beach Resort, 2 km south of Pwani Mchangani village, roughly half way between Matemwe and Kiwengwa, T0741-324985 (mob), www.planhotel.ch. Full-on all-inclusive resort with marine sports centre, good food, 87 a/c rooms, Swahili decor, set in 4 ha of gardens, swimming pool with jacuzzi, shops, internet café, and tennis courts. Rates include all meals and alcoholic drinks, activities such as windsurfing and canoeing, but diving and fishing are extra. Popular with Italians and Swiss.

For an explanation of the sleeping and eating price codes used in this guide, see inside the front cover. Other relevant information is found in Essentials pages 31-34.

B Matemwe Beach Guest Houses, T0747-425788 (mob), www.matemwe.com. To the north of the village, an exceptional small guest house out on its own on a long stretch of classic palm-lined, white sand beach. Many of the guests come here primarily for the diving at Mnemba Atoll, which is just offshore. The 16 bandas are built from local materials, coral stone walls and dried palm leaf roofs and all the bandas are surrounded by colourful flowers and have an ocean view. Bandas are self-contained and have solar powered lighting and hot water, verandas and mosquito nets. The food is the catch of the day and meat dishes are also available. The dive centre is run by *One Ocean Diving*.

★ Mnemba Island

L Mnemba Island Lodge, central reservations, CC Africa, Johannesburg, South Africa, T+27-11-8094300, www.ccafrica.com. Mnemba Island lies 4.5 km or 15 minutes by boat from northeast Zanzibar. This beautiful little private island has a reputation as one of the world's finest beach retreats and is impossibly romantic. Very stylish, very discreet and very expensive. The coral reef that circles the island is the finest in Zanzibar. 10 self-contained cottages, full board accommodation, includes most watersports and big game fishing. The US magazine, *Travel & Leisure* said of it, "It's the closest two people can get to being shipwrecked, with no need for rescue." If you can afford it, enjoy. Rates are over US$600 per person rising to over US$900 in high season.

❂ Festivals and events

See page 156 for information on festivals which are held throughout the archipelago.

Southeast Zanzibar → *www.zanzibareastcoast.com.*

To get to the southeast of the island leave Stone Town's Creek Road at the junction that leads out through the Michenzani housing estate. Eventually the houses begin to peter out and are replaced by small fields of cassava, maize, banana and papaya. The road continues via Tunguu and Bungi to the Jozani Forest near Pete, before joining the coastal road linking the resorts of Jambiani, Paje and Bwejuu, about 50 km from Stone Town. There is a magnificent beach here that runs for nearly 20 km from Bwejuu to Jambiani, with white sand backed for its whole length by palm trees, laced with incredibly picturesque lagoons. You will see the fishermen go out in their dhows, while the women sit in the shade and plait coconut fibre, which they then make into everything from fishing nets to beds. ▸▸ *For Sleeping, Eating and other listings, see pages 173-175.*

Ins and outs

Getting there Recently the road to Paje has been sealed, the trip there by minibus takes just over an hour and costs around US$10. Bus number 9 from the Creek Rd in Stone Town serves Paje and continues to Jambiani and Bwejuu. Bus number 10 from Creek Rd goes to Kizimkazi via Jambiani and Makunduchi.

Jozani Forest

ⓘ *Most people visit the reserve as part of a tour, usually combined with a dolphin tour, but you can get here independently by dala-dala and either bus 9 or 10 from Creek Rd in Stone Town. Going there by taxi will cost around US$25 (for four people in one car), which is competitive with the price of an organized tour.*

Most of Zanzibar's indigenous forests have been lost to agriculture or construction, but the Jozani Forest in the centre of Zanzibar has been declared a protected reserve. It covers 44 sq km, roughly 3% of the whole island. It is 24 km southeast of Stone Town, an easy stop-off en route to the southeast coast beaches. It is home to roughly one third of the remaining endemic Zanzibar red colobus monkeys, one of Africa's rarest primates. Only 1,500 are believed to have survived. In Zanzibar the Kiswahili name for the red colobus monkey is *Kima Punju* – 'Poison Monkey'. It has associations with the kind of poisons used by evil doers. Local people believe that when the monkeys have fed in an area, the trees and crops die, and dogs will lose their hair if they eat the colobus. Although legally protected the colobus remain highly endangered. Their choice of food brings them into conflict with the farmers, and their habitat is being destroyed due to demands for farmland, fuel, wood and charcoal. The monkeys appear oblivious to tourists, swinging above the trees in troups of about 40, babies to adults. They are endearing, naughty and totally absorbing. There is a **visitor centre** on the main road to the south where you pay US$10 per person for a guide for the 45 min nature trail through the forest. The reserve is completely managed by the local people who operate tree nurseries and act as rangers and guides. Stout shoes are recommended as there are some venomous snakes. Lizards, civets, mongooses and Ader's duiker are plentiful and easy to see, and there are also Sykes' monkey, bush babies, hyraxes, and over 50 species of butterfly and 40 species of birds. Unless you state otherwise you are unlikely to be taken into the reserve at all as the best place to get close to the monkeys is an area adjacent to farmland to the south of the road.

About 1 km south of the Jozani Forest Visitor Centre there is the **Pete-Jozani Mangrove Boardwalk**. From the visitor centre the walk takes you through coral forest to an old tamarind tree, which marks the beginning of the boardwalk. The transition from coral forest to mangroves is abrupt. The boardwalk, which is horseshoe shaped, takes you through the mangrove swamp. Mangroves anchor the shifting mud and sands of the shore and help prevent coastal erosion. There are 18,000 ha of mangrove forests along the muddy costs and inlets of Zanzibar. When the tide is out the stilt-like roots of the trees are visible. Crabs and fish are plentiful and easily seen from the boardwalk. The construction costs of the boardwalk were paid for by the government of The Netherlands, with local communities providing labour. Part of the profits made from tourists is returned directly to the local villagers.

ZALA Park

The road continues south to the village of Kitogani, and just south is **ZALA Park**, which is primarily a small educational facility set up in conjunction with the University of Dar es Salaam for Zanzibari children to help them learn about and conserve the island's fauna, (ZALA stands for Zanzibar Land Animals). Entry is free to local children if unable to pay, subsidized by the tourists' donations. The aim is to make it a self-funding enterprise in time. There is a small classroom where the children are taught. The adjacent **zoo** has a number of reptiles including lizards, chameleons and indolent rock pythons weighing up to 40 kg, Eastern tree hyrax, as well as Suni antelopes, an endemic Zanzabari subspecies. Donations to support this worthwhile enterprise are appreciated.

Paje

Paje is the first village on the coast you are likely to get to as it lies on the junction with the direct road from Stone Town. It has its share of guest houses and there is an old mausoleum, a long, low rectangular building with castellations and old plates and dishes set into the walls. This design, along with other reliefs and designs used in the villages are of typical Shirazi origin and indicate that this area was settled very early in Zanzibar's history.

Bwejuu

Bwejuu is best known for its proximity to 'the lagoon' and the Chwaka Bay mangrove swamps. The mangrove swamp at Chwaka Bay can be reached by a small road leading inland from the back of Bwejuu Village. It is possible to find a guide locally, who can navigate the way through the maze of channels and rivers in the swamps. Here you can stroll through the shallow rivers looking at this uniquely adapted plant and its ecosystem, there is also a good chance of seeing a wide variety of crabs that live in the mud-banks amongst the tangle of roots. The best snorkelling in the area is to be found at 'the lagoon', about 3 km to the north of Bwejuu, just past the pier at Dongwe. Bicycles and snorkels can usually be hired from any of the children on the beach.

Jambiani

The name Jambiani comes from an Arabic word for dagger, and legend has it that early settlers found a dagger here in the sand – evidence of previous visitors. These days the village spreads for several kilometres along the coast road and there are a number of resorts (see Sleeping below).

Kizimkazi

There is little of significance in this small fishing village, though this was once the site of a town built by King Kizi and his mason Kazi from whom the name Kizimkazi originates. Most people visit here as part of a tour to swim with the dolphins. The beach is attractive and there is a restaurant where those on dolphin tours from Stone Town are often taken to have a meal. The **Shirazi Dimbani Mosque ruins** are near Kizimkazi and contain the oldest inscription found in East Africa – from AD 1107. The mosque has been given a tin roof and is still used. However, its significance should not be underestimated for it may well mark the beginnings of the Muslim religion in East Africa. It was built by Sheikh Abu bin Mussa Lon Mohammed and archaeologists believe that it stands on the site of an even older mosque.

Sleeping and eating

Paje *p172*
D Paje by Night, T024-2230840, www.pajebynight.net. Very rustic verging on ethnic, run by an Italian. 20 self-contained thatched bungalows with ceiling fans and mosquito nets. Bar and restaurant with local and international food including good pizzas. An unashamed party place, bar stays open all night, hence the name.
D Paradise Beach Bungalows, 1 km north of the village, T024-2231387, paradisebb@zanlink.com. Run by a nice (but scatty) Japanese lady, Saora. There are 8 double rooms and 7 bungalows with roof balconies, a small restaurant and bar serving expensive Japanese meals that must be ordered in advance. No electricity so storm lanterns are the order of the day, which makes for a real campfire atmosphere.

Bwejuu *p172*
L The Palms, a few km north of Bwejuu towards Pingwe, T+254-20-272 9394 (Nairobi booking office), www.palms-zanzibar.com. This is a stunning resort, super-luxurious with attentive service. At US$365 you'd expect nothing less, but rates are inclusive of meals and some drinks and for your bucks you get a villa, with satellite TV, CD player, private terrace with jacuzzi, 2 bathrooms, living room, and bar. Facilities in sumptuous surroundings include tiered swimming pool, beauty spa, tennis court, elegant dining room, bars and lounge areas. The beach here is magnificent and there's a watersports centre and dive school.
L-A (depending on the season) **Breezes Beach Club**, 3.5 km north of the village, T0747-415049, www.breezes-zanzibar.com. Opened in 1998, this is a well-appointed resort. All 70 rooms have a/c, fans and en suite bathrooms. There are standard, deluxe and superior deluxe rooms, the latter have sea views, with either balconies or terraces. Shopping arcade, newly opened beauty spa, conference facilities, restaurants, bars, large swimming pool, fitness centre, watersports centre, tennis courts and disco. The *Rising Sun Dive Centre* is based here.

For an explanation of the sleeping and eating price codes used in this guide, see inside the front cover. Other relevant information is found in Essentials pages 31-34.

B Karafuu Hotel, 3 km north of the village before Michamvi, in Karafuu village, T0741-413647-8 (mob), www.karafuuhotel.com. The name means 'cloves' in Swahili. This is a large but quiet and professionally-run resort, with almost 100 a/c rooms with thatched roofs in spacious gardens. 3 restaurants, numerous bars, watersports, excellent food, swimming pool, tennis courts, nightclub, diving. The beach is good although watch out for the very sharp coral close offshore.
B Sunrise Guest House, 2 km north of the village, T0741-320206, www.sunrise-zanzibar.com. All bungalow rooms are self-contained with fans and nets and face towards the sea. Very good food, especially the chocolate mousse, courtesy of Belgian chef/owner. Bikes can be hired and there's a swimming pool. Standard rooms are US$75, bungalows are US$90.
C Andy's Karibuni, 3 km north of the village, T0747-472735 (mob), www.eastzanzibar.com (German website). Nicely decorated rooms in bungalows with four-poster beds and mosquito nets. Managed by friendly Germans who serve excellent home-cooked food including European dishes. Can organize dolphin trips and tours to the nearby mangrove swamps.
C Palm Beach Inn, T024-2233597. Simple and basic self-contained bungalows with a/c and hot water in the middle of the village, the food is fresh and good and the staff friendly, if you want to drink while you are there, take your own alcohol. Recommended if you want to meet local people, try local food and experience coastal village life.
C Sun & Sea View Resort, approximately halfway along the road between Bwejuu and Paje, T0747-420774 (mob), www.kulala bar.com. 10 attractive thatched bungalows with airy self-contained rooms with hot and cold showers, equipped with mosquito nets and fans. Good restaurant and bar on stilts with a *makuti* roof, and rates include breakfast.
C-D Evergreen Bungalows, www.evergreen-bungalows.com. 6 bungalows in a palm grove directly on the beach with 9 rooms, each with a different touch and very nicely decorated using local materials, with mosquito nets, solar power supply, balcony with chairs and a table. Some rooms are self-contained while others, including some dorm rooms, have shared bathrooms. Rates include breakfast and vary between US$45 for a room to US$15 for a dorm. Bar and restaurant offers a meat, fish and vegetarian dish each night for dinner. *Africa Blue Divers* offer single dives from US$45 to the PADI Open Water Course for US$350.
D Bwejuu Dere Beach Resort, T024-2231047. In the middle of the village, this is the largest, longest-established and best of the low cost accommodation on this coast. Facilities are pretty basic and the food is simpler still, but if you are on a tight budget, then this is the place. Rooms are self-contained or with shared bathroom and go for as little as US$10 per person. Bicycles and snorkelling equipment can be hired.
D-E Mustapha's Place, in the village, the number 9 bus will drop outside, T024-2240069, mustaphas@africamail.com. A chilled out, low budget hotel run by Mustapha, a friendly Rastafarian; lovely gardens with hammocks, reggae music, bar where you can play drums, good seafood. Prices range from US$10/15 for a room with shared bathroom to US$20/25 for a room with bathroom. Very relaxing, good reports.

Jambiani *p173*

B Sau Inn, T024-2240205, 2240169, sauinn@zanlink.com. The only guest house with a swimming pool. 35 rooms set in thatched cottages with fans and mosquito nets. Bar and good seafood restaurant, buffets on Fri evenings, sports facilities, volley ball, tennis, internet access, snorkelling and diving, B&B, half or full board rates.
C Blue Oyster Hotel, T024-2240163, www.zanzibar.de. Very congenial, Tanzanian owned, brand new hotel. Closer to the beach than *Sau Inn*. The 14 rooms have beautiful carved beds and mosquito nets, and are arranged around a serene ornamental pool and garden. Good food in the rooftop restaurant. Bike rental, watersports, their own dhow for fishing and snorkelling trips. A double is US$50 and the 4-bed rooms work out cheap for a group at US$70, including breakfast. Recommended.
C Coco Beach, T024-2240246, cocobeach@zitec.org. Self-contained rooms with hot water, fan and mosquito nets. Good restaurant serving reasonably priced seafood and bar. US$50 for a double including breakfast, add US$10 per person for full board. Can arrange tours and activities.

C **Kimti Beach Inn**, T024-2240212, www.ucpzone.com/kimte. Shady thatched huts in the gardens sleeping a total of 18 people, well decorated rooms with fans, mosquito nets and hot showers. Nice bar and restaurant with characterful wooden furniture, very good seafood buffets, long tables for everyone to eat together, lively cocktail bar on the beach with a fire in the evenings.

C **Mount Zion Bungalows**, T0747-439034 (mob), www.mountzion-zanzibar.com. 8 guest rooms in 4 stylish bungalows on a small rock just above the beach, with mosquito nets and ceiling fans, Zanzibari-style furniture and verandas overlooking the tropical garden and the ocean beyond. Daily fresh-caught fish is the specialty in the restaurant and bar, though there are also meat and vegetarian dishes. Rates drop to D in low season.

C **Visitor's Inn**, T024-2232283, www.visitorsinn-zanzibar.com. 39 basic but good value bungalows set in flowering gardens, each has hot water, a fan and a porch. A double with breakfast goes for US$25, TV room, restaurant and bar with fish, noodle and vegetarian dishes.

D **Horizontal Inn**, in the north end of the village, no phone. Owned by local Zanzibaris, simple and good value accommodation in shared rooms for just US$7 per night, but not much else.

Festivals and events

Mwaka Kogwa is the traditional Shirazi New Year on Zanzibar held in the **3rd week in July** and celebrated with traditional Swahili food, *taraab* music, drumming and dancing on the beach all night. Although the festival is celebrated around the island, the village of Makunduchi is the heart of the celebration. The men of the village have a play fight and beat each other with banana fronds to vent their aggressions from the past year. Then, the *mganga*, or traditional healer, sets fire to a ritual hut and reads which way the smoke is burning to determine the village's prosperity in the coming year.

See also page 156 for more information on festivals held throughout the archipelago.

Pemba Island

→ *Colour map 1, grid B6. 5°0'S 39°45'E.*

Unlike Unguja, which is flat and sandy, Pemba's terrain is hilly, fertile and heavily vegetated. The early Arab sailors called it 'Al Huthera', meaning 'The Green Island'. Today more cloves are grown on Pemba than on Zanzibar Island. Pemba has a wealth of natural resources ranging from beaches to mangrove ecosystems to natural forests. The coral reefs surrounding the island protect a multitude of marine species and offer some of the best scuba diving in the world. Zanzibar Island is connected to the African continent by a shallow submerged shelf. Pemba, however, is separated from the mainland by depths of over 1,000 m. During September and March the visibility around Pemba has been known to extend to a depth of 50m and there are great game fish such as sharks, tuna, marlin and barracuda. While much of the coast is lined with mangroves, there are a few good stretches of shoreline and attractive offshore islands with pure, clean beaches and interesting birdlife. There are also some important ruins and charming Swahili villages.The tourism industry here is still in its infancy and at any one time there is rarely more than a couple of dozen foreigners visiting the island. The infrastructure is therefore quite basic, although this is slowly beginning to change with a few exclusive resorts springing up. ▸▸ *For Sleeping, Eating and other listings, see pages 180-182.*

Pemba is known for its collective knowledge of traditional healing and witchcraft, and people have been known to come from as far away as Haiti to study the art of voodoo. Today people come from Uganda and the Democratic Republic of Congo to seek healing from the waganga (witch doctors) or to learn the ancient art of traditional medicine.

Ins and outs

Getting there

Air Pemba Airport is 7 km to the southeast of Chake Chake. The island can be reached by air either from Zanzibar Island or from Dar es Salaam, though most flights from Dar go via Zanzibar. **Coastal Air** have an additional direct flight between Tanga and Pemba. The airport tax for flights out of Pemba is US$2.50 but is payable in Tsh. Public transport to and from the airport only operates when there is a flight due.

Sea Nearly all ferries coming into Pemba arrive at the town of Mkoani, on the southwestern end of Pemba Island. Very few ships or dhows actually use Chake Chake anymore as the old harbour is silted up and only canoes can actually gain entrance. The journey between Zanzibar and Pemba can take between 3 and 6 hours depending on the company and boats used, and prices are about US$25 excluding Zanzibar's port tax of US$5. Dar es Salaam to Pemba via Zanzibar US$65. » *See Transport, page 181, for further details.*

Getting around

The island of Pemba is about 70 km long and 22 km wide. There is one bumpy main road in Pemba running from Msuka in the north to Mkoani in the south, which is served by public transport. There are buses or *dala-dala* along the main roads but these tend to operate in the mornings and early afternoons only and there are very few vehicles after 1500. *Dala-dala* no 606 runs between Chake Chake and Wete and the No 603 between Chake Chake and Mkoani. Each journey takes about 1 hr and costs US$0.30. Other less frequently run routes include the no 24 between Wete and Konde, (for the Ngezi Forest). Besides this, it is very difficult to get around on public transport and budget travellers will need to walk to get to the more out of the way places. It is possible to hire cars at around US$50 for a day, motorcycles for around US$20, and bicycles for around US$10 – ask at the hotels and remember that negotiation is necessary as ever. The motorcycle is the most comfortable form of transport on the island, more so than cars, as pot holes are more readily avoided, and it's a little too hilly in most places for cycling.

Background

There is nothing on Pemba that holds as much historical or cultural significance as Stone Town on Zanzibar Island, but it is the site of many historical ruins that bear testament to its role in the spice trade and early commerce with the other Indian Ocean dynasties. The major income for islanders is from cloves and the island actually produces about 75-80% of the archipelago's total crop. It is the mainstay of the island's economy.

Clove production

It has been estimated that there are about 6 million clove trees on the islands of Zanzibar and Pemba and they cover about one-tenth of the land area. The plantations are found mainly in the west and northwest of the islands where the soil is deeper and the landscape hillier. To the east the soil is less deep and fertile and is known as 'coral landscape'.

Cloves were at one time only grown in the Far East and they were greatly prized. On his first trip back from the East, Vasco da Gama took a cargo back to Portugal and they were later introduced by the French to Mauritius and then to Zanzibar by Sayyid Said who was the first Arab sultan. At this time all the work was done by slaves who enabled the plantations to be established and clove production to become so important to the economy of the islands. When the slaves were released and labour was no longer free, some of the plantations found it impossible to survive although production did continue and Zanzibar remained at the head of the world's clove production.

Cloves are actually the unopened buds of the clove tree. They grow in clusters and must be picked when the buds are full but before they actually open. They are collected in sprays and the buds are then picked off before being spread on the ground to dry out. They are spread out on mats made from woven coconut palm fronds for about five days, turned over regularly so that they dry evenly – the quicker they dry the better quality the product.

There may be many clove trees on Zanzibar now – but there were even more in the past. In 1872 a great hurricane passed over the island destroying many of the trees and it was after this that Pemba took over from Zanzibar as the largest producer. Zanzibar, however, has retained the role of chief seller and exporter of cloves so the Pemba cloves first go to Zanzibar before being sold on.

Also, unlike Zanzibar, production is largely by individual small-scale farmers who own anything from 10 to 50 trees each. Most of the trees have been in the family for generations and clove production is very much a family affair, especially during the harvest when everyone joins in the picking. Harvest occurs about every five months and everything is worked around it – even the schools close. The cloves are then laid out in the sun to dry and their distinctive fragrance fills the air.

The island is overwhelmingly Muslim, with more than 95% of the population following Islam. But the island is tolerant of other cultures, and alcohol is available at hotels, some guest houses and in the police messes (where visitors are welcome). Local inhabitants do, however, like to observe modest dress and behaviour.

An unusual quirk of the island is the fact that bull-fighting takes place in October and November at the end of the cool season. It is thought that it was introduced by the Portuguese during the 16th and 17th centuries when they established forts and settlements in the Indian Ocean, most notably at Mombasa, Lamu and Zanzibar. Why the practice endured in Pemba and not elsewhere remains a mystery, however. It is a genuinely sporting event in that there is sparring between the bull and the fighter, but the bull is not weakened with lances or killed at the end – the pragmatic Pembans consider the animal too valuable to be sacrificed in this way. You can see fights at Wingwi in the northeast and Kengeja in the south.

Around the island » pp180-182

Mkoani

Mkoani is Pemba's third largest town and the port of entry for ferries from Zanzibar and Dar es Salaam. The town is set on a hill overlooking a wide bay and comprises a mix of palm-thatch huts and rundown multi-storey apartment buildings. The landing stage is a modern jetty which projects out from the shallow beach on either side, where fishermen load their daily catch into ox-carts for the short trip to market. The main road runs directly from the port up the hill and most of this distance is rather surprisingly covered by a dual carriageway, complete with tall street lights on the central reservation. This, along with the ugly apartment blocks around town is evidence of the East German influence in Tanzania during the 1970s, which is also present at Chake Chake and Wete, and in the concrete estates on the edge of Stone Town on Zanzibar Island. Following the winding road up the hill from the port, the old colonial District Commissioners Office is on the right, where there is a bandstand in front of the compound. On the left is Ibazi Mosque, with a fine carved door. South of the dock there are steep steps down to the market by the shore.

Chake Chake → *Phone code: 024. Colour map 1, grid B6. 5°15'S 39°45'E.*

This is Pemba's main town, about halfway up the west coast of the island. The town sits on a hill overlooking a creek and is fairly small. The oldest surviving building in the town is the **Nanzim Fort,** which is thought to date back at least to the 18th century and possibly as far back as the Portuguese occupation (1499-1698). Records dating back to the early 19th century describe the fortress as being rectangular, with two square and two round towers at the corners, topped by thatched roofs. Round towers are typical of the Arab and Swahili architecture of the time, but the square towers are unusual and indicate possible Portuguese influence. Construction of the old hospital destroyed all but the eastern corner and tower which now houses the Ministry of Women and Children. A battery, dating from the same period, overlooked the bay to the west, but only two cannons remain to mark the site. There are some handsome Moorish-style

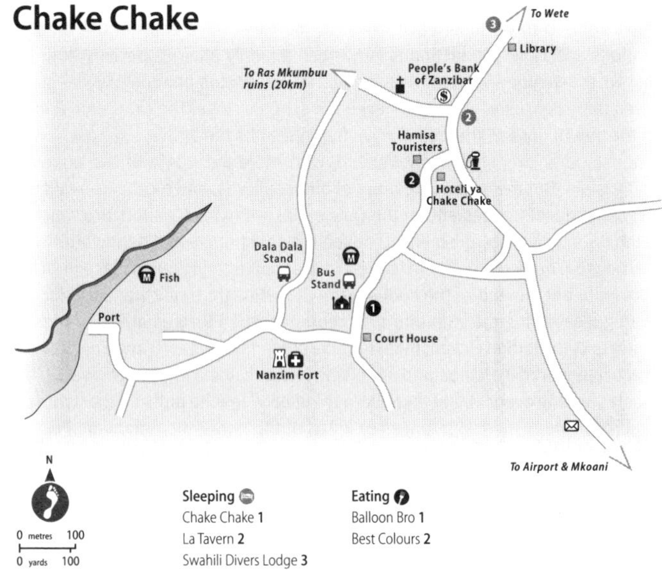

administrative buildings near the fort with verandahs, and a **Clocktower**. On the outskirts of town is a new hospital, built by the European Community overseas aid programme and a few kilometres past the old centre a huge new sports stadium, which is home to the local football team. The market and bus stand are both in the centre of town close to the mosque. There have been some strikes and riots during elections in recent years, as Pemba is the stronghold of the CUF opposition party.

Ruins at Pujini

About 10 km southeast of Chake Chake, this settlement is thought to date back to the 15th century. There was a fortified enclosure and rampart surrounded by a moat, the only known early fortification on the East Africa coast. It is believed to have been built by a particularly unpleasant character, nicknamed Mkame Ndume, which means 'a milker of men', because he worked his subjects so hard. He was known to order his servants to carry the large stones used to build the fortress whilst shuffling along on their buttocks. The memory remains and local people believe that the ruins are haunted. The settlement and the palace of Mkame Ndume were destroyed by the Portuguese when they arrived on the island in about 1520. Today the site is largely overgrown and there is little left of the fortications except for a crumbling staircase and some remains of 1 m thick walls. There is also the remnants of a two-chambered well that reputedly was used by the two wives of Ndume who lived in separate parts of the palace and never met. It is best to visit by hiring a bicycle (ask in Chake Chake).

Ruins at Ras Mkumbuu and Mesali Island

About 20 km west of Chake Chake, Ras Mkumbuu is probably Pemba's most important ruins, believed to date back about 1,200 years, the oldest settlement south of Lamu Island in Kenya. It is the site of a settlement originating in the Shirazi period (see page 95). The ruins include stone houses and pillar tombs and the remains of a 14th-century mosque. Of interest are the tombs decorated with pieces of porcelain that suggest an early connection with the Chinese. Most people visit by boat on the way to Mesali Island where the marine life on the reef make it excellent for diving and snorkelling and there is a fine beach. There are pleasant trails through the forest in the middle of the island which is rich in birdlife, and is also home to vervet monkeys and the Pemba flying fox (a large bat). Legend has it that the notorious 17th-century pirate Captain Kidd once had a hideout here and perhaps even buried some treasure during his stay. Apart from the dive schools who visit here on dives, the only licenced operator to offer boat trips to the island is **Mzee Island Shuttle**, T07747-458694 (mob).

Wete

This town is on the northwest coast of Pemba and serves as a port for the clove trade. It is a pleasant place on a hill overlooking the port with houses and small shops lining the main road down to the dhow harbour. Clustered close to the dock area is a pleasant group of colonial buildings. On the north side of the market a craftsman makes very fine carved doors. The town has a bank, post office and police station and the *dala-dala* station is about halfway up the hill.

The small island of **Mtabmwe Mkuu** opposite Wete, which means 'great arm of the sea', is linked to Pemba at low tide. It was once home to an 11th-century town and a number of silver coins have been discovered at the site, though there is nothing to see today and a small fishing village stands on the spot.

Tumbe and Konde

Tumbe is at the north end of Pemba and is a busy fishing village with a market where people from all around buy their fish in the mornings. Local fishermen contract to provide catches for firms, which chill the fish and export it to the mainland. At the end of the cool season in October, there is a boat race here. Teams of men compete, paddling dug-out canoes and the day is completed with a feast provided for contestants and onlookers. Konde is to the northeast of the island and is at the end of the tarmac road and the furthest most point of the *dala-dala* network. Access to the Ngezi Forest is from here. There is no accommodation in either Tumbe or Konde but both can be reached by *dala-dala* from Chake Chake.

Ngezi Forest Reserve

Ngezi Forest Reserve covers 1,440 ha and compromises ancient coastal forest that once covered all of Pemba. The area was declared a reserve in the 1950s after much of the island had been cleared for clove production. This is a thick blanket of forest with vines and creepers and a dense undergrowth that supports a variety of plants and wildlife. It has its own plant species and sub-species that are unique to this area. Most of the 27 species of bird recorded on Pemba have been spotted in the forest, some endemic to Pemba including hadada, the African goshawk, the palm-nut vulture, Scops owl, the malachite kingfisher and the Pemba white eye. Much of the ground is ancient coral rag, often sharp edged, containing pockets of soil. Mangrove forests grow on the tidal coastal creeks and the incoming tide sees seawater running deep upstream, forming brackish swampy areas. The central area contains heather dominated heathland where the soil is leached sand. The heather, *Philippia mafiensis*, is only found on Pemba and Mafia Islands.

Pemba's flying fox, a large fruit-eating bat, is found in Ngezi. Tree mammals include the Pemba vervet monkey and the Zanzibar red colobus monkey. Indolent-looking hyrax can also be seen climbing in the trees eating leaves. The Pemba blue duiker, an antelope about the size of a hare, is also here though it is very shy and is rarely spotted. Feral pigs, introduced long ago by the Portuguese, can be found along with the Javan civet cat, which was probably brought to the island by southeast Asian traders for the production of musk for perfume. The only endemic carnivore in Ngezi is the marsh mongoose, which normally lives by ponds and streams. There is a 2-km walking trail from the entrance that takes about an hour.

To the north of here is the secluded **Panga ya Watoro beach** on a peninsula that juts out from the island. At the end is the lighthouse at Ras Kigomasha, the far northwestern tip of the island; authorities are very sensitive so photography is not advised. The **Manta Reef Lodge** is on this beach and is one of the best places to stay on Pemba with excellent scuba-diving (see Sleeping below).

Sleeping and eating

Mkoani *p178*

L **Fundu Lagoon**, north of Mkoani across the bay near the village of Wambaa and reached by boat organized by the resort, T024-2232926, www.fundulagoon.com. Luxury British development opened in 2000 and the top place to stay on Pemba on a beautiful mangrove-fringed beach. Very stylish, with 20 bottle-green tents on stilts under thatched roofs, which are linked to the communal areas by decking walkways. Two suites have private plunge pools and decks and are perfect for honeymooners. All variety of watersports are available including diving, and there is a massage and treatment room. Restaurant, 2 bars, one of which is on a jetty overlooking a lagoon, dive centre and satellite TV available. Expect to pay around US$320 per person. Rates include all meals and drinks.

A **Manta Reef Lodge**, T0747-423930 (mob), www.mantareeflodge.com. Quiet and wonderfully remote location on a cliff overlooking a private beach in the extreme northwest of the island on Panga ya Watoro Beach, the lodge has a large central area with terrace, veranda, lounge, restaurant and snooker room, the wooden bungalows on stilts sleep up to 20 guests, with en suite bathrooms. There are also 2 family chalets which if not occupied can be let out as dormitories at a much cheaper rate. Food and service is excellent, rates are full board, which drop slightly out of season (Apr-Jun and Nov-Dec). There is snorkelling, kayaking, game fishing as well as diving, and a mini beauty spa for massages and facials.

C-E Jondeni Guest House, T024-2456042. In the small village of the same name, within easy walking distance from Mkoani, up on a hill and with no immediate neighbours. A tranquil spot, but unfortunately not on the beach. The accommodation is simple and Zanzibari in style, with single and double rooms with or without bathrooms and some dorm beds. There's a restaurant terrace out at the back from where you can watch over the forest and down to the sea below. The only option for budget travellers in the area.

Chake Chake *p178, map p178*

C-E Swahili Divers Lodge, 200 m north of *Hoteli ya Chake Chake* on the road to Wete, T024-2452786, www.swahilidivers.com. Housed in a renovated old Quaker mission house built in 1899 on small hill, often just referred to as the Mission. There are 7 simple rooms with fans and traditional Zanzibar-style beds, some rooms are a/c and have own bathrooms, also dormitory accommodation in two 6-bed dorms. Very good food and bar. With notice they will pick you up from the airport. Very good dive school with PADI instructors, and diving is from a dhow and rigid inflatable boats and a larger vessel allows for dive trips up the coast. Packages for a PADI Open Water Course and 6 nights dorm accommodation and all meals are US$650, slightly more to stay in a room, low season discounts in May and Sep.

D Hotel La Tavern, opposite the People's Bank of Zanzibar, T024-2452660. Only 4 rooms but spotlessly clean, mosquito nets and towels are provided, shared bathrooms, no other facilities.

Wete *p179*

E Sharook Guest House, near the market and bus stand, down the track that leads to the harbour, T024-2454386. Run by a friendly guy called Suleiman, it's very simple but reasonably clean, and has a restaurant with the best food in town, though it has to be pre-ordered. Own generator. Can arrange snorkelling trips to local islands and bicycle hire.

Eating

Chake Chake *p178, map p178*

Balloon Bros, just south of the market and bus stand and opposite the mosque on main street. Charcoal grill, cold drinks, pleasant patio with thatched bandas to sit under.

Best Colours, opposite *Hoteli ya Chake Chake*. Small but smart, friendly and good value, good filling local food.

Activities and tours

Diving

A Pemba Afloat, pembaafloat@pembaisland.com, www.pembaisland.com. Primarily a dive-base, Pemba Afloat consists of two or sometimes three decent-sized yachts, permanently moored in an absolutely idyllic setting by the Njao Inlet in northwest Pemba. The boats are fully equipped with scuba diving gear, guests sleep aboard the boats, spend their days diving and snorkelling, and also muck in and help prepare meals with the crew. The boats are owned and operated by Peter and Charlie Mason, experienced dive instructors. Rates are in the region of US$85 per day. See also box, page 182.

Hamisa Touristers, also near the *Hoteli ya Chake Chake*, T024-2452343, can help with local tours and ferry bookings.

Faizin Tours, near the bank in Mkoani, T024-2230705, can also organize ferry tickets and tours to most of the island.

Transport

Air

Coastal Air, T022-2117969-60, Dar es Salaam, www.coastal.cc, flies from **Dar** to Pemba via **Zanzibar** (50 min) daily at 1400 and returns to Dar at 1640, one way fare is US$85. The same flight from Zanzibar to Pemba (30 min) departs Zanzibar at 1430 and costs US$70, and returns at 1640. They also fly to Pemba from **Tanga** (20 min) daily at 1600, and to Tanga from Pemba at 1515; US$55.

Zanair, T022-2452990, Dar es Salaam, www.zanair.com, flies daily from **Zanzibar**

For an explanation of the sleeping and eating price codes used in this guide, see inside the front cover. Other relevant information is found in Essentials pages 31-34.

★ Dive Pemba

Pemba has some of the most spectacular diving in the world. The Pemba channel itself separates Shimoni in Kenya from Pemba Island. The channel runs deep until it approaches the Pemba coastline and then begins a dramatic rise creating a sheer wall off the coast. Diving is characterized by crystal clear, blue water drop-offs along with pristine shallow reefs. Hard and soft coral gardens abound with schools of coral fish, pelagic marine life, mantas and turtles. Here are a few of the more famous dive sites with their descriptions, although there are many more spectacular sites around Pemba's smaller offshore islands.

Fundu Reef The visibility ranges from 20-40 m and there is a large sheer wall with overhangs and caverns. The coral is remarkable, especially the large rose coral and red and yellow sea fans. You can see many types of fish here including kingfish, triggerfish and wrasse. The reef is relatively shallow and therefore Fundu is a good spot for a first dive.

Kokota Reef An ideal site for night diving, the waters are shallow and generally calmer, ranging from between 8-20 m. Of all the creatures that come out after dark, the Spanish dancer is a particular attraction.

Manta Point Visibility averages from between 20-40 m. Manta Point is one of the best sites in the world for close encounters with the giant manta rays that inhabit this area. The rays can be seen in groups of up to 15 and rise to depths as shallow as 9 m. The enormous variety of coral, fish and other marine life is so concentrated here you should try and include at least 2 dives. This is truly one of the finest dive sites in the region.

Mesali Island Visibility averages between 40-50 m. This is a wall dotted with small caves and ridges. Large rivers of sand run off the top of the reef to form wide canyons that enter the wall at approximately 25 m. Gorgonian fans are in abundance below 20 m and on a turning tide the marine life is exceptional and the currents strong. Giant grouper drift lazily through the reef and hundreds of surgeonfish cruise below divers.

Njao Gap Njao Gap is well known for its amazing wall diving. Mantas can be seen here in season and the coral is spectacular, but what distinguishes this particular location is the profusion of titan triggerfish. Visibility varies from day to day, but is usually good to 30 m.

See *Pemba Afloat*, *Swahili Divers* (page 181) and *Manta Reef Lodge* (page 180).

to Pemba at 0945 and 1600, returning at 1030 and 1645, US$70.

Sea

Azam Marine, T024-2123324, www.azam-marine.com, operates a service from **Dar** to Pemba via **Zanzibar** at 0730 which arrives in Zanzibar at 0855, departs again at 1000 and arrives in Pemba at 1205. The return boat is also on Tue and Fri and departs Pemba at 1230, arrives in Zanzibar at 1435, departs again at 1630 and arrives in Dar at 1755.

Sea Express, T024-2110217, www.sea-express.net, operates a daily ferry from **Dar** at 0730 which arrives in **Zanzibar** at 0915. On Mon, Wed, Fri and Sun the ferry continues from Zanzibar (departing at 1000) to Pemba where it arrives at 1200, beginning its return from Pemba at 1300, though this service is reported to be very irregular.

(See also Dar es Salaam transport, page 77.)

North to Kilimanjaro and Moshi

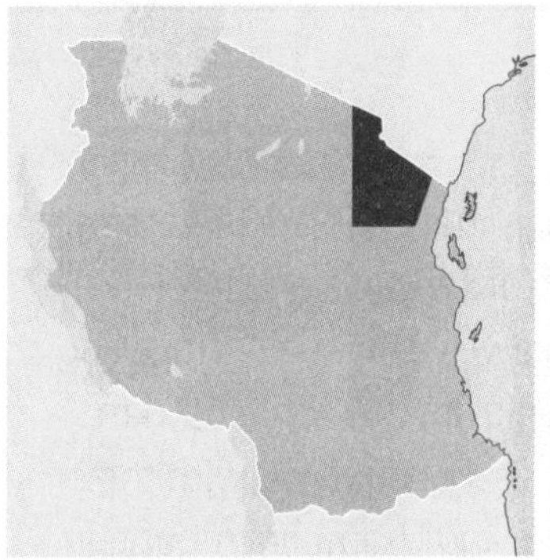

Footprint features

Introduction

The main road out of Dar es Salaam travels inland and joins the highway that runs the length of Tanzania and effectively links Kenya to the north with Malawi to the south. Travelling north from Dar to Arusha is a scenic drive of some 650 km, through extensive farmland and sisal plantations with the ever-present backdrop of the Pare and Usambara mountain ranges to the east. The main road is very busy, with a steady stream of buses linking Dar with Arusha, and the small regional towns offer petrol stations and services for bus passengers and drivers wishing to take a break from their journey. Away from the main road is the small mountain town of Lushoto, which is very attractive and a recommended spot for some good hiking in the hills. The forests and mountain scenery of the Usambara are not what is normally expected by visitors to Tanzania. Moshi is the town at the foot of Kilimanjaro and climbs start just a few kilometres away at the entrance of the Kilimanjaro National Park. On the approach to Moshi you may well be rewarded with a glimpse of the snow-capped top of Kili when the mists lift off the summit in the late afternoon. Climbing Mount Kilimanjaro is an adventurous break from game viewing and reaching the 'Roof of Africa' is one of the continent's greatest challenges. It is the highest mountain in the world that can simply be walked.

★ Don't miss...

1 **Usambara Mountains** Hike through these mountains around the German colonial hilltown of Lushoto where the air is refreshingly cool and the surroundings lush and green, page 186.

2 **Irente Viewpoint** Take a picnic of homemade bread, jam and cheese from Irente Farm near Lushoto to this viewpoint with its spectacular views over the Masai Steppe below, page 188.

3 **A nice cup of coffee** Enjoy the fresh coffee grown in the coffee plantations on the lower slopes of Kilimanjaro in the hotels and restaurants around Moshi, page 193.

4 **Kilimanjaro** Climb to the roof of Africa; Mount Kilimanjaro is the highest free-standing mountain in the world and the only one that you can walk up, page 205.

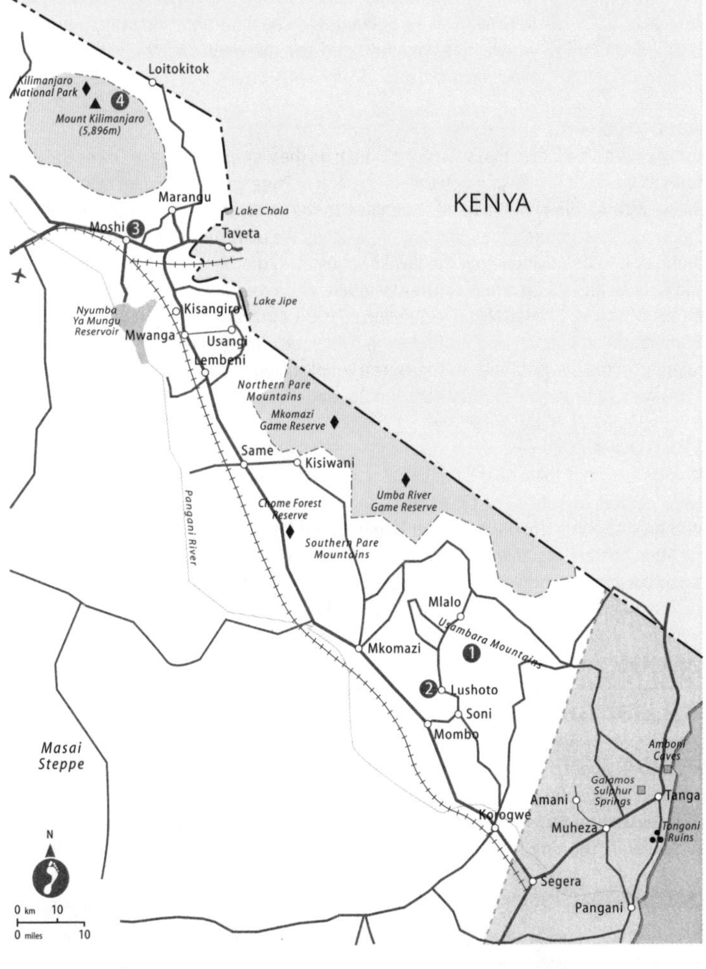

The road from Dar to Moshi

From Dar es Salaam, the main road goes 109 km to the west to Chalinzi and the junction with the main north-south road. North from Chalinzi it passes through the regional centres such as Karogwe, Mombo and Same before reaching Moshi at the foothills of Kilimanjaro. This is where climbers begin their ascent of the mountain. The road will not hold your attention long: the small towns that you pass through are fairly nondescript, but they do provide facilities such as petrol stations and shops and access to the Usambara Mountains to the east, which are worth a detour for the good hiking opportunities and country lodges, and the attractive town of Lushoto. Further north closer to Moshi are the Pare Mountains and Mkomazi Game Reserve. ▸▸ *For Sleeping, Eating and other listings, see pages 190-193.*

Although listed in this section because of their proximity to the main Dar/Arusha road, the towns of Korogwe, Mombo and Lushoto are administered from the Tanga Region.

Ins and outs

The driving time between Dar and Moshi is roughly 7-8 hr and there are scores of buses each day that ply this route. From Moshi it is a further 80 km to Arusha. There are daily flights between Dar es Salaam and Zanzibar and **Kilimanjaro airport**, which lies roughly midway between Moshi and Arusha. ▸▸ *See Transport, page 193, for further details.*

Korogwe → *Phone code: 022. Colour map 1, grid B5. 5°0'S 38°20'E.*

Korogwe is a small town that you pass through on the way from Tanga or Dar es Salaam north to Moshi. It lies at 52 m, on the north bank of Pangani/Ruvu Rivers, whose fertile valley, with its many settlements, stretches to the west. The local people are of the Zigua and Wasambaa tribes but call themselves Waluvu. It is a local administrative centre due to its position near the local sisal estates, the Dar es Salaam-Nairobi road and railway and its proximity to the Usambara and Pare Mountains. There are a few shops, a market, a hospital and a Christian mission. Most buses stop here at one of the many petrol stations in and around town, which also feature restaurants and shops catering for the bus passengers. There are a couple of reasonable places to stay and eat if you want to break the journey between Dar and Moshi.

Mombo → *Colour map 1, grid B5.*

Mombo is a small town on the Dar es Salaam to Moshi highway. There's little of interest here, its main activity is the provision of services for travellers and again lots of buses stop here at either the oddly-named **Liverpool Hill Breeze**, 1.5 km north of Mombo, or the **Manchester Executive Inn** in town, which have petrol stations and serve fast food. It is worth a mention, however, as this is the junction with the road to Soni and Lushoto in the Usambara Mountains (see below). You can jump off the bus here and switch to one of the many *dala-dala* that climb the mountain road the 33 km from Mombo to Lushoto.

★ Usambara Mountains ▸▸ *pp190-193.*

Lushoto is about 1½ hours or 33 km off the main Korogwe-Moshi road where the turnoff is at Mombo. The road up to Lushoto via the small town of **Soni** is spectacular as it twists and turns through the mountains, with glimpses of small waterfalls in Mlalo River. The tiny market town is reminiscent of an Indian hill station and the

Soni is close to the capital of the Shambaa people at Vugu. The Shambaa were well organized militarily, and supported Bushiri in the 1888-1889 Arab revolt (see page 83).

country lodges in the region have a charming colonial atmosphere. The climate changes quickly as you rise up into the mountains. Sunny days are warm but cloudy and windy days get very cool throughout the year and it is comfortable to sit around a fire in the evening throughout the year. The big pull here is exploring the Usambara Mountains, dotted with streams and waterfalls and rural villages. There is plenty of opportunity for hiking or mountain biking through the deep forests and green hillsides and this is a part of Tanzania a long way from the scorched plains of the game parks. From *Hotel Falls View* you can hire a guide for walks into the forest and up the peak of Kwa Mongo, a hike of 3-4 hours.

Lushoto → *Phone code: 027. Colour map 1, grid B5. Altitude: 1,500 m. 4°4'S 38°20'E.*

Lushoto, at an elevation of around 1500 m, was the town chosen by early German settlers to escape from the heat and dust of the plains for the holidays. Back then it was called Wilhemstal and the cool, fresh air and lush, green surroundings were greatly appealing. It was even once thought that it might develop into the capital of the colonial administration. It can get quite cold from June to September so take warm clothes.

Many of the surrounding farms and government buildings are originally German. There is a very fine Dutch-style **Governor's House**, just out of town on the road going north. Other reminders of the colonial connection are the horse riding arenas and the red tiles on some of the roofs of the buildings. There is a group of **German Alpine-style buildings** with flat red, rounded end tiles, chimney stacks and shutters on the east side of the main road near the Mission Hospital. The British changed the town very little. Their main contribution was to lay out a **cricket ground** just to the west of the town centre. Although football is played here now and not cricket, it is still possible to see the old weather-boarded cricket pavilion with a veranda, albeit in poor repair. East of the main road, near the Catholic church, is the **Parade Ground**. Horseriding was a favourite recreation of the Germans, and this was where the mounted officials were paraded, in front of the timber review stand. The **Lutheran church**, just west of the centre, is an attractive building, with blue window frames, black and white walls, Mangalore tile roof, a front stone arch and a free-standing bell in a wooden tower. The **market** is lively with several small, inexpensive eating places, hair salons, tailors and a maize mill making *posho* (maize flour).

Lushoto

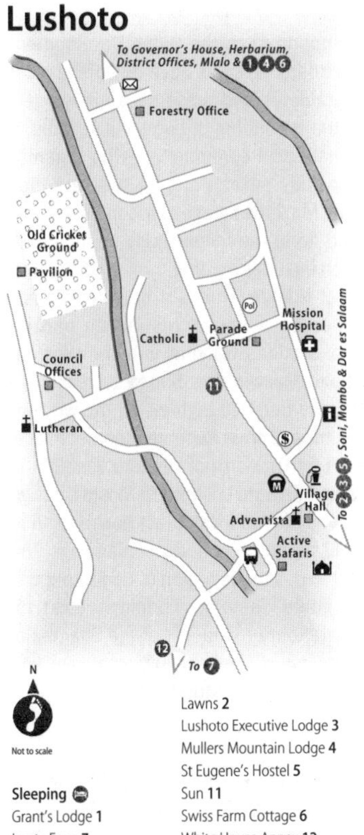

The **herbarium** on the slope to the north of the town dates from the German colonial period and has thousands of pressed plants from all over Tanzania – ask for Mr Msangi or Mr Mabula if you would like to see the collection. The town also holds a fine **market** (close to the bus station) that is very colourful and lively. Among the many products on sale is the locally produced pottery, with a variety of pots for cooking, storage or serving. One of the ancient beliefs of the Shambaa people is that Sheuta, their God or Supreme Being, made people from a handful of soil in the manner of a potter. In the Usambaras, potters are traditionally women, with the skills passed on from mother to daughter. Men are discouraged from participating in any stage of the potting process, as it is believed that to do so brings great misfortune including sterility. There is good fishing in the mountain streams, one of which runs through the centre of the town.

The views on the southern and western side of the Usambaras are spectacular vistas of the plains of Mkomazi and Handeni. Kilimanjaro can be seen on the horizon and at the end of the day the sun turns the land an unforgettable colour.

This area is a place to enjoy the views and countryside. It is fertile and verdant and there are plenty of tracks to **walk** along. One such walk takes about 45 minutes from Lushoto to reach ★ **'Irente viewpoint'** 5 km away, from where the view of the hills and the Masai Plain below really is breathtaking. Take the road out of town towards Irente and head for the children's home. Ask around and you'll be shown the track. On the way is **Irente Farm**, where fresh fruit, vegetables, preserves, bread and cheese are sold – the large garden is an excellent picnic spot, see page 192.

Usambara Mountains Cultural Tourism Programme

ⓘ *Guides are available from the information centre just off the road opposite the bus station, open daily 0800-1800, which is run by the Friends of Usambara Society, T027-2640060. Here there are details and photographs of each tour offered and you can discuss with the staff exactly what you would like to do. Further details from the Tanzanian Tourist Information Centre in Arusha, T027-2503840-3, www.infojep.com/culturaltours. Brochures for each project can be downloaded from the website.*

This is a local tourism initiative advised and supported by the Dutch Development Organisation (SNV) and the Tanzanian Tourism Board. This has been one of the most successful of Tanzania's cultural tourism programmes and these days runs largely self-sufficiently. It has already contributed to the rebuilding of two local schools. It aims to involve and ultimately benefit the small local communities who organize tourist projects off the usual circuits. These include several one-day walking trips from Lushoto to the Irente viewpoint overlooking Mazinde village 1,000 m below (see above), a walking tour of Usambara farms and flora, the increasingly popular rock tour from Soni and the Bangala River tour, which includes wading through the water. You can also visit and stay in *Carters Camp* at **Ndekia**. This is a hut precariously perched on a rocky outcrop, built by an American writer as his launch pad for hang-gliding. There are also longer 3-5-day excursions walking into the Western Usambara Mountains via the villages of **Lukozi**, **Manolo** and **Simga** to reach the former German settlement of **Mtae**, a small village perched high up on the western rim of the escarpment, and the tour to the **Masumbae Forest Reserve**. Another hike is to **Mlalo** and **Mount Seguruma** (2,218 m) about 25 km north of Lushoto. One of the more ambitious tours offered is a seven-day bike ride from Lushoto to Moshi through the mountains. On overnight hikes and rides, you stay in local guest houses and in some cases local homes, or the tourist office will supply tents and sleeping bags. The costs for all these trips varies greatly but expect to pay in the region of US$10 per day per group and US$3 per day per person for a guide. There are additional costs for accommodation and food. Most of the guides are former students of the Shambalai secondary school in Lushoto, speaking fair to good English, and can give you information on the history of and daily life in the Usambara Mountains.

Lushoto is one of only two places in the world where you will find the endangered Usambara/African Violet Saintpaulia ionantha (its other habitat is in Mexico). It was discovered in the Usambara Mountains in 1892 by Baron von Saint Paul, hence the name.

Back on the road to Moshi » pp 190-193

Same → *Colour map 1, grid A5.*

A small town 126 km north of Korogwe and 103 km south of Moshi, Same is a base for a visit to Mkomazi Game Reserve (see below). The market has covered and open sections, with a good selection of earthenware pots and bowls, baskets and mats. The bus station is particularly well organized with bus shelters clearly displaying the destinations and routes of the various buses. A feature of the area is the hollowed-out honey-logs hanging from the trees.

Mkomazi Game Reserve → *Colour map 1, grid A5. 4° S, 38° E.*

ⓘ *Entry into the reserve is US$20 per day. Access to the reserve is from Same. There is very little tourist development in the reserve, there are few places to stay and it is well off the normal safari circuit. If you have your own camping and cooking equipment and food, it is possible to walk from Same (5 km, there are no buses), and camp at the main gate at Zange. From here you can hire an armed guide to escort you into the park during the day. There is a small airstrip inside the reserve used by chartered planes.*

This national park of 3,600 sq km lies about 100 km north of Tanga and is contiguous with Kenya's Tsavo National Park. In the rainy season herds of elephant, zebra and oryx migrate between the parks. The **Mkomazi Rhinos Resettlement Project**, coordinated by the Tanzania Wildlife Protection fund, has taken a lead role in relocating black rhino from South Africa to Mkomazi Reserve and Ngorongoro. The released rhino are kept in intensive protection zones and it is hoped that they will breed, after which they will be relocated within Tanzania to other traditional natural habitats. It is an expensive programme. The cost of transferring 10 rhinos is put at over US$1 million.

African hunting dogs, the endangered wild dog and other big mammals such as zebra, giraffes and gazelles have also been reintroduced. The reserve is home to about 400 bird species including falcons, eagles, hawks, hornbills, barbets, starlings, weavers and shrikes. As it is a game reserve and not a national park, walking is permitted but there is dense vegetation and an armed guard is needed if hiking.

Southern Pare Mountains Cultural Tourism Programme

ⓘ *To get to Mbaga there are very infrequent buses from Same, usually one a day that operates on a return journey that departs from Mbaga very early in the morning and returns from Same back to Mbaga mid-morning. Further details from the Tanzanian tourist information centre in Arusha, T027-2503840-3, www.infojep.com/culturaltours.*

About 150 km southeast of Moshi and 35 km or a two-hour drive from Same is the small town of Mbaga in the **Mbaga Hills** and the Southern Pare Mountains Cultural Tourism Programme, supported by the Dutch Development Organization (SNV). From here local people will take you hiking to **Mghimbi Caves**, hiding places for the people during slave raids in 1860, or to **Malameni Rock**, where until 1930, in order to appease evil spirits, children were sacrificed to the gods, and to **Mpepera Hill**, from where there are fine views over the expanse of Mkomazi Game Reserve. Longer treks are possible, to the forest and peak of **Shengena**, the highest point of the Eastern Arc Mountains (Pare and Usambara Mountains), or up the mountains to **Mhero Village** and through **Chome Forest Reserve**.

Tours begin from *Hilltop Tona Lodge* in Mbaga on a hill just outside Mkomazi Game Reserve. The local guides, who have a reasonable standard of English, are well informed about the area's irrigation, soil conservation and afforestation development projects, and will be happy to take you to see them. Income generated helps to support these projects and to subsidize energy-saving stoves and educational scholarships to the local vocational training centre.

Mwanga and Usangi → *Colour map 1, grid A5.*

Mwanga is the district capital and is approximately half-way between Same and Moshi. Huge palm trees grow abundantly in the water that streams downhill from the Northern Pare Mountains. From here it is 50 km to Moshi and buses take around 1½ hours. From Mwanga there is a good sand road that winds upwards to **Usangi**, the centre of the Northern Pare Mountains. The little town is surrounded by 11 mountain peaks and is an important economic centre producing beer, bricks, stoves, pottery and clothing. There is a colourful market held on Mondays and Thursdays, where local farmers come to sell their produce. This is one of the most fertile regions in East Africa.

The **Northern Pare Mountains Tourism Programme** ⓘ *further details from the Tanzanian Tourist Information Centre in Arusha, T027-2503840-3, www.infojep.com/culturaltours,* is a cultural tourist programme supported by the Tanzanian Tourist Board and the Dutch (SNV) and German (GTZ) Development Organizations. The scheme is coordinated at Lomwe Secondary School, in the centre of Usangi, T7, by Mr Kangero. Local people take you on a walking tour of the area, you stay in locals' homes and eat outstandingly good food. In the mountains there are areas suitable for camping. The guides speak reasonable English; most of them are farmers or local craftsmen. Profits from these tourist projects are used to buy energy-saving stoves to reduce deforestation (they use only one third of the firewood) and to help reduce the workload of women. The walking tours from Usangi include the **Mangata view tour**, from where you have excellent views of Lake Jipe and Mount Kilimanjaro. The **Goma Caves** can be visited, where a century ago the Pare chiefs dug deep caves to hide from rival tribes and, later, the colonial rulers. Here the skulls of former chieftains killed in battle are preserved. The 2,000-m high table mountain **Kindoroko** and its forest reserve at the top can be reached from the Goma Caves. On the other side of the forest the stone terraces and irrigation systems of Kisangara Juu village can be seen before returning to Usangi via a route across the moorland. Another one-day tour is a steep climb up the moorland of **Kamwala Mountain** for the views of the surrounding plains. Longer hikes through the forests and mountains can be organized on request. There is no formal accommodation here, and this is a destination only suitable for self-sufficent campers with their own vehicles.

Sleeping and eating

Korogwe *p186*

C **Motel White Parrot**, opposite the post office, T022-2641068, motelwhiteparrot@yahoo.com. By far the best place to stay in Korogwe, and brand new. The white double-storey building has 22 small but smart a/c rooms with hot showers, satellite TV and phones. There is a separate thatched restaurant and bar.

D **Korogwe Transit Hotel**, on the main road, T022-2640640. Mosquito nets, private bath but cold water most of the time, some rooms have a/c, overpriced for what you get, front rooms have a balcony but are very noisy because of the traffic. With the amount of people around security could be an issue.

D-F **Segera Highway Motel**, at Segera, the junction with the turnoff for Tanga, 17 km south of Korogwe, T022-2640815. For motorists this is a useful stop en route to Tanga or Moshi, either overnight or just for a cup of tea at the Engen petrol station on this busy junction. The thatched roadside restaurant has a surprisingly large menu of steaks, salads, breakfasts, pizza and pastas, plus shakes and juices. Out back you can camp for US$5 or there are 23 very smart new motel-style chalets for US$20 a double.

E **Sunrise Guest House and Bar**, Main Rd, 100 m from post office, T022-2640967. Best of the budget options, clean with toilet and shower, fan and mosquito net, basic food available.

For an explanation of the sleeping and eating price codes used in this guide, see inside the front cover. Other relevant information is found in Essentials pages 31-34.

F Green Hills Restaurant, 10 km north of Korogwe. New and friendly set-up with a large thatched restaurant and bar serving soups, sandwiches, burgers, pizzas and fresh juice. Pretty setting beneath the picturesque mountains, although you still get the trucks and buses rumbling past on the road. Camping US$4, good ablution block.
F Korogwe Travellers' Inn, main road, T022-2640564. Bar, restaurant, fans, very basic, only baths with cold water, no showers or toilet seats. Only stay if other places are full.
E Pangani River Campsite, 47 km north of Korogwe, 65 km south of Same, clearly signposted 1.5 km off the main road, T0744-095515, panganirivercampsite@yahoo.com. Lovely spot on the banks of the picturesque river for self-sufficient campers in a vehicle, a fair amount of wildlife around including monkeys and hippos in the river, hot showers, restaurant and bar.

Soni *p186*

C Maweni Farm, 2km from Soni up a good dirt road, at the foot of a large rockface, T027-2640426, www.maweni.com. This guest house on a farm has 1 single and 7 double rooms, 4 with en suite bathrooms. Lovely restaurant with veranda, organic locally grown food and homemade bread, bar serving local wine, lounge with fire place, established gardens, sauna and swimming pool, internet access. A very pretty setting next to a small lake, lots of nature trails through the forest. En suite rooms are US$45, those with a shared bathroom are US$35. Rates are full-board. Pick ups can be arranged from the bus in Mombo.
D Hotel Falls View (formerly *Soni Falls Hotel*), about 1 km from town, a 5-min walk from the bus stand, no phone. Orignally built in the 1930s and recently refurbished, there are 10 double rooms with nets and en suite bath, shower and flush toilet facilities and hot water. Restaurant has a mixed local and European menu (meals US$2-5), well-stocked bar offers wine made by the local Benedictine monks. From the veranda there are good views of the river and falls and the peak of Kwa Mongo. Space for parking. Excellent value, price includes breakfast. Camping in the grounds, from where you can hear the waterfall, US$3.50.

E Hotel Kimalube, on the hill coming up into Soni before reaching the bus stand, no phone. 4 rooms with mosquito nets and bucket showers, very basic, warm beers, and sporadic electricity. Expensive at US$8.

Lushoto *p187, map p187*

There are a number of basic guest houses around the market in Lushoto itself, but by far the best places to stay to enjoy the mountain scenery are the country lodges on the outskirts of Lushoto. All of these provide restaurants and bars, and in town itself are a number of cheap food stalls and local bars, again around the bus stand and market.
B Grant's Lodge, Mizambo, Lushoto, T027-2642491, www.grantslodge.com. 15 km from Lushoto along a road that is rough in places; signposted from Lushoto, start by heading north on the road that passes the post office and district offices. Lovely brick house, 5 rooms, a welcoming atmosphere, open fireplace, games are organized on the lawn, lots of classic movies to watch. Generous helpings of tasty home-cooked food – soups are excellent as is the hot chocolate. Can organize short or long walking safaris with photocopied instructions. Car safaris can also be arranged. Range of bird reference books in the library. Highly recommended. Payment can be made in US$ or TSh. TCs accepted.
B-C Lushoto Executive Lodge, 1.5 km from town T027-2640076, 0748-360624. Relatively new with a 6-hole chip and putt golf course and swimming pool (though it can get freezing up here). Comfortable self-contained rooms are in single-storey brick buildings, some with thatched roofs, restaurant and bar, meals are prepared from local farm produce. A gym and sauna are planned.
C Muller's Mountain Lodge, 13 km from town on the road to Migambo, on the same road as *Grant's Lodge*, so follow their signs, T027-2640204, mullersmountainlodge@yahoo.com. Built in 1930 in the style of an English country home, it has brick gables, attractive gardens and orchards and lovely views. 7 bedrooms, shared dining and living rooms with outsized fireplaces, large camping area on the hill above the house, plus very good food and service; they offer guided walks. Pick ups can be arranged from town.

C St Eugene's Hostel, 2 km before Lushoto on the Soni Rd, T027-2640055. Run by the Usambara Sisters, plain but comfortable 14 self-contained rooms in a double-storey building decked with vines, hot water and phones. Serves food including delicious home-made ice cream, and in the farm shop you can buy homemade jam and marmalade made from various fruits such as passionfruit and grapefruit, herbed cheeses, and banana wine. This is a convent and a Montessori teacher training centre with modern buildings in gardens well tended by the sisters. Beer and the rather potent banana wine is available to drink.

C Swiss Farm Cottage, 500 m before Muller's Mountain Lodge, T027-2640161, or reservations through Muller's. 2 double rooms in a brick cottage with tin roof on a working farm, very peaceful retreat, good home cooking using organic farm produce, lounge and dining room with cosy fireplace. Free coffee, tea and cakes.

C-D Lawns Hotel, 1 km before town on Soni Rd, T027-2640005, www.lawnshotel.com. Old colonial-style hotel, has wonderful views with fireplaces in the rooms plus a veranda, restaurant and lively bar. Rates include a very good breakfast. Some rooms are self-contained, the cheaper ones have shared facilities. Run by a football-loving Cypriot who is quite a character and a good source of information about Tanzania. From here you can organize hikes to 'Viewpoint'. Camping possible, US$3.50 per person, new ablutions block with hot water.

E-F Irente Farm, 5 km from town southwest towards Irente viewpoint, T027-2640089. Run by the Evangelical Lutheran Church. Has a wonderful cheese factory. You can buy a picnic lunch from the farm to take with you to climb to the viewpoint, including rich brown bread, several types of jam, fresh butter, cheese and fruit juice. Campsite with ablutions block and watchman, can rent tents.

E White House Annex, in town near the market, T027-2640177, whitehouse@raha.com. Self-contained singles and doubles in a tidy one-storey white house near the tourist office and bus stand, TV room, bar and small restaurant, local food but good and big portions, sitting room. There is also an adjoining internet café here.

E Sun Hotel, Boma Rd near the police station, T027-2640082. Popular, has a restaurant and large double rooms for US$9.

Same *p189*

D Elephant Motel, simple but adequate, double rooms with mosquito nets, bathroom and hot water. Staff are helpful. Also has a restaurant and bar.

Mkomazi Game Reserve *p189*

L Mkomazi Camp, 8 km from the entrance gate of Zange, swala@habari.co.tz, www.swalasafaris.com. Not as luxurious as the usual tented camps, but simple and comfortable, and the only accommodation within the reserve. Tents are spacious and have attached bathrooms with shower and long drop toilet. Rates are US$190 for a double full board. Activities include night game drives, US$15 per person, a day safari to see the rhino, US$20 and an overnight rhino excursion that involves sleeping in a hide, US$110 per person (sleeping bag and mattress provided). Transport into the reserve is usually organized when you make a reservation.

Mbaga *p189*

D Hilltop Tona Lodge, in Mbaga on a hill just outside Mkomazi Game Reserve. It has 5 brick cottages, one of which has excellent views over the reserve, with electricity and running water, and meals can be prepared with advance notice. You can swim in a pool in a nearby river.

Local homestays are also possible and there are a number of suitable sites for camping along the tour routes but you must bring all your own equipment.

Activities and tours

Lushoto *p187, map p187*

Apart from the Tourist Information Office, there is also another private operator with an office near the market, next to the bus stand, **Active Safaris**, T0748-696731. They offer guided walks and mountain bike tours and part of their profits go towards helping the local disabled people.

Transport

Lushoto *p187, map p187*

Road

The roads to Lushoto are excellent, all sealed, even the 33-km gradual climb up from Mombo, which was resurfaced by the Germans in 1989 and is still in good repair. Public transport is frequent and hitching is possible as there are plenty of 4WDs who will give lifts in this area. Buses and *dala-dala* from **Mombo** take about 1½ hrs and costs US$1. You can also get a direct bus from **Tanga**, but it is slow, 6 hrs, and costs US$2. There are also slow buses between Lushoto and **Arusha** (6 hrs) and **Moshi** (5½ hrs). Direct buses from **Dar es Salaam** leave the stand on Mafia St in the Kariakoo area throughout the morning and take 6 hrs.

Directory

Lushoto *p187, map p187*

Banks National Microfinance Bank, on the main road opposite the bus station which changes money but at poor exchange rates. **Post** Post office at the northern end of main street. There is internet access at White House Annex but it is slow and expensive at US$2 per hr.

Moshi and Marangu

→ *Colour map 1, grid A5.*

Moshi is the first staging post on the way to climbing Mount Kilimanjaro and a pleasant place to spend a few days organizing your trip. It's an unusual African town in that it has very few European or Asian residents, unlike Arusha. Climbing expeditions depart from the town into Kilimanjaro National Park early each morning. The two peaks of this shimmering snow-capped mountain can be seen from all over the town and it dominates the skyline except when the cloud descends and hides it from view. Moshi means 'smoke' – perhaps a reference to the giant volcano that once smoked. Marangu is 23 km from Moshi and is the closest village to Kilimanjaro National Park, the entrance to which is 5 km away. Accommodation here is more expensive than Moshi, and if you're on a tight budget you should plan your assault on the mountain from Moshi. ›› *For Sleeping, Eating and other listings, see pages 195-200.*

Phone code: 027
Population: 200,000
Altitude: 890 m
3°22'S 37°18'E

Background

The area around Moshi is particularly fertile due to the volcanic soils and there are lots of melt-water streams fed by the snow. This is where Arabica coffee, the premium quality of the two coffee varieties, is grown by the Chagga people, helping them to become one of the wealthiest of the Tanzanian groups. All around the town, and on the lower slopes of Kilimanjaro, vast plantations of coffee blanket the area. The first coffee grown in Tanzania was planted at the nearby Kilema Roman Catholic Mission in 1898. Growth was steady and, by 1925, 100 tons were being produced each year. The Chagga people are particularly enterprising and formed the Kijimanjaro Native Cooperative Union (KNCH) to collect and market the crop themselves.

Moshi is the centre of Tanzania's coffee industry; the Coffee Board is located here and coffee from all over Tanzania is sold at auction to international buyers. However, apart from the coffee produced in the immediate locality, the crop does not pass through Moshi, it is auctioned on the basis of certified type, quality and grade, and then shipped directly from the growing area to the buyer. Not all of the wealth generated by the sale of coffee makes its way back to the growing community. Local small farmers have been known to receive only half the Moshi export price. By the time the coffee is sold in London their purchase price amounts to only one-tenth of the London price. Moshi was the site of the signing of the Moshi Declaration after the war with Uganda in February 1979.

★ Moshi » pp195-199

Moshi is a pleasant town with the former European and administrative areas clustered around the Clocktower, and the main commercial area southwest of the market. Despite being an attractive town, there are few places worth visiting in Moshi itself, and many visitors stay here just long enough to arrange their trek up the mountain and to enjoy a hot shower when they get back. The limited sights include the **Railway Station** southeast of the Clocktower, a two-storey structure from the German period, with pleasing low arches, a gabled roof with Mangalore tiles and arched windows on the first floor. On the corner of Station Road and Ghalla Road is a fine Indian shop building dating from the colonial period, with wide curved steps leading up to the veranda, tapering fluted stone columns and a cupola adorning the roof. In southeast Moshi is a leathercraft workshop, which also makes pressed flower cards and jewellery, batik and carvings. *Shah Industries Ltd* employ many disabled workers producing high-quality goods, which are available at *Our Heritage*, Hill St, T027-2753786. The shop takes credit cards.

Moshi is safe by day, but use taxis at night and don't walk around after dark without a local escort.

Excursions

West Kilimanjaro The road running in a northerly direction from Boma ya Ngombe on the Moshi-Arusha road passes through Sanya Juu and Engare Nairobi to reach Olmolog. This was the main area for European farming in northern Tanzania prior to independence. The boundaries of the old estates are marked on the existing Kilimanjaro Ordnance Survey map. After independence most estates were nationalized. However, lack of capital and management skills has now forced the Tanzanian government to invite foreign commercial interests back, in the hope of increasing production of cereals, seed beans, beef and dairy products.

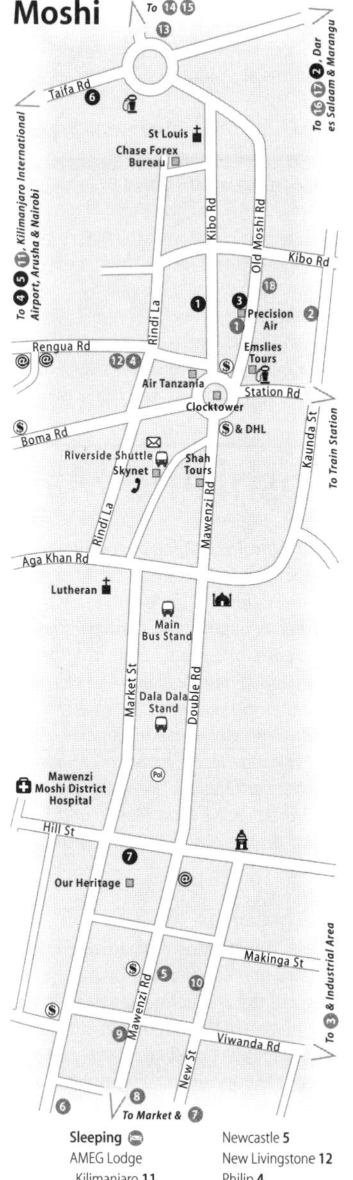

Sleeping
AMEG Lodge Kilimanjaro **11**
Buffalo Inn **10**
Coffee Tree **1**
Da' Costa **7**
Haria Palace **9**
Horombo Lodge **18**
Keys **14**
Kilemakyaro Mountain Lodge **15**
Kilimanjaro Crane **2**
Kindoroko **8**
Leopard **6**
Mountain Inn **16**
Newcastle **5**
New Livingstone **12**
Philip **4**
Rombo Cottage **17**
Springlands **3**
YMCA **13**

Eating
Chrisburger **1**
Coffee Shop **7**
El Rancho **5**
Golden Shower **2**
Ice Cream Parlour **3**
Pagoda **6**
Panda **4**

A drive in this area can include estate visits and a trip through the **Londorossi forest** glades. Most estate managers are happy to receive visitors. Of particular interest is the parastatal owned Rongai ranch, where African 'cowboys', mounted on horseback, herd Boran cattle and Persian black-headed sheep in Texas style. There is a very good lodge in this region hosted by *Hoopoe Safaris*.

Marangu

» *p197*

Most people visit Marangu only to attempt the climb to the summit of Mount Kilimanjaro. However, Marangu and nearby **Machame** are excellent centres for hiking, bird-watching and observing rural Africa. Marangu is 11 km north of Himo, a village 27 km east of Moshi on the road to the Kenya border.

The Ordnance Survey map of Kilimanjaro (1:100,000) is an essential guide for walks. The main tracks in the region radiate from the forest boundary, through the cultivated belt of coffee and bananas, to the road that rings the mountain. Other maps are less accurate but widely available at about US$10. For full details of climbing Kilimanjaro see page 205.

Foothill walks

The **Marangu/Mamba Cultural Tourism Programme** ⓘ *further details from the Tanzanian tourist information in Arusha, T027-2503840-3, www.infojep.com/culturaltours*, supported by the Dutch Development Organisation SNV, arranges guided walks through the attractive scenery of the valleys near Marangu and Mamba. **Mamba** is a small village 3 km from Marangu. From here you can also visit caves where women and children hid during ancient Masai-Chagga wars or see a blacksmith at work, using traditional methods to make Masai spears and tools. From Marangu there is an easy walk up Ngangu hill, a visit to a traditional Chagga home, or a visit to the home and memorial of the late Yohano Lawro, a local man who accompanied Dr Hans Meyer and Ludwig Purtscheller on the first recorded climb of Mount Kilimanjaro in 1889. He is reputed to have guided Kilimanjaro climbs until he was 70 and lived to the age of 115. Profits from the programme are used to improve local primary schools.

Sleeping

Most of the hotels offer arrangements to climb Kili, or at the least will recommend a tour operator. Without exception they all offer a base from which to begin your climb. Ensure that the hotel will store your luggage safely whilst you are on the mountain. Facilities to consider include hot water and a comfortable bed, and of course cold beer and a good hot meal on your return from the climb. Some establishments also offer saunas and massages. The Marangu hotels are better located on the lower slopes of Kilimanjaro but are considerably more expensive. Almost all hotels have restaurants.

Moshi *p194, map p194*

B AMEG Lodge Kilimanjaro, off Lema Rd, near the Moshi International School, Shantytown, T027-2750175, www.ameglodge.com. Very new, set in 4-acre garden, 20 rooms with en suite bathrooms with lovely modern, bright furniture, satellite TV, phone, and fan. The more expensive suites have a/c and internet access for laptops. Good value in this price range with the cheapest double only US$55. Swimming pool and pool bar, good restaurant, gym and business centre.

B Kilemakyaro Mountain Lodge, 7 km from Moshi, take the Sokoine road out of town, T027-2754925, www.kilimanjarosafari.com.

For an explanation of the sleeping and eating price codes used in this guide, see inside the front cover. Other relevant information is found in Essentials pages 31-34.

Perched on a hill above Moshi, set in a 600-acre coffee plantation at an altitude of 1450 m, a stay here will very much help climbers with acclimatization. The reception, bar and dining room are in the main house, a restored 1920s farmhouse, while rooms are in chalets dotted throughout the garden. Can organize climbs of Kilimanjaro and also Meru, and quite uniquely organize weddings at Uhuru Peak at the top of Kili.

C **Keys**, Uru Rd, just north of the town centre, T027-2752250, www.keys-hotels.com. This hotel functions primarily as a base for budget climb operations. Accommodation is in simple round huts and there is a restaurant and bar. The location itself is not particularly interesting and probably not as pleasant as basing yourself out in the more rural locations but nevertheless a firm favourite. Special rate for residents, food and rooms OK, but some rooms over the rear entrance can be noisy at night because of late returners or early starters for climbing. Single/double/triple are US$30/40/50, with breakfast, and camping is available in the grounds.

C **Kilimanjaro Crane**, Kaunda St, T027-2751114, www.kilimanjarocranehotels.com. 30 simple but neat rooms with mosquito nets and TV, en suite bathrooms, some singles and triples. Swimming pool, sauna, fitness centre, gardens, good views, pizza kitchen, several bars including one on the roof with fantastic views of the mountain. There is a very good bookshop in the lobby. A good mid-range option. Can organize transfers from Kilimanjaro Airport.

C **Horombo Lodge**, Old Moshi Rd, above the Tanzania Postal Bank, T027-2750134, horombolodge@kilionline.com. 33 rooms with en suite bathroom, TV and phone. Small restaurant downstairs serving drinks and affordable meals for guests only, reasonably new so still fairly smart, hot water all day, doubles from US$25.

C **Kindoroko**, Mawenzi Rd, close to market, T027-2754062, www.kindoroko.com. One of the best mid-range options in the middle of town, very organized and friendly, and fantastically decorated. 46 rooms which are on the small side but have satellite TV, some also have fridges and bathrooms have plenty of hot water. Rates include a hot breakfast. Downstairs is a restaurant and bar, internet café and tour booking office, upstairs is the rooftop restaurant and bar with excellent views of Kili. The menu's very good and includes authentic Indian dishes and 3-course set meals. A great place to meet other travellers even if you are not staying here. They operate their own Kili climbs on all routes from US$650 pp which includes a night before and after the climb in the hotel. Recommended.

C **Leopard Hotel**, Market St, T027-2750884, www.leopardhotel.com. This small centrally-located hotel claims to have received an award for good service from Bill Clinton when he visited Tanzania…a fact which makes the mind boggle. 16 clean but cramped rooms, with balconies, a/c, satellite TV and en suite bathrooms, half of which have a view of Kilimanjaro. Passable bar and restaurant serving buffet meals downstairs, and a bar with nice views on the roof.

C **Mountain Inn**, 6 km from Moshi on the road to Marangu, T027-2752370, www.kilimanjaro-shah.com. 35 comfortable rooms, a dining room with a veranda, set meals and an a la carte menu, Indian food at the pool bar, lush gardens, swimming pool, sauna. Doubles are a good value US$45. This is the base for *Shah Tours*, a quality operator for Kilimanjaro climbs.

C **Philip Hotel**, at the corner of Rindi Lane and Rengua St (formerly Chancery Lane and Wells Rd respectively), T027-2754746, www.africaonline.co.tz/philip. An old hotel with 28 rooms with bathrooms in a smart white double-storey block, some have balconies. Bar and dining room, limited parking on the street, fairly good service.

C **Springlands Hotel**, T027-2753581, www.zaratravel.com Set in large, attractive gardens, this place offers all sorts of treats that are ideal to recover from a Kili climb. 37 rooms with bathrooms. Restaurant, bar, swimming pool, TV room, massages, sauna, manicures and pedicures, bicycle hire, conference room, internet and fax services. A double room is US$50 with breakfast. Base for *Zara Travel*, a recommended operator for climbs.

D **Newcastle**, close to the market on Mawenzi St, T027-2750853. 51 rooms on 5 floors, 36 with bathrooms, the rest with shared bathrooms, good views from the top, hot water, rooms are well kept though all the dark wood makes the place a little gloomy. Rooftop bar with pool table.

D YMCA, Uhuru Highway, to the north of the Clocktower, T027-2751754. Facilities include gym, shop, several tours desks, bar, restaurant and swimming pool (non-guests can use the pool for US$2). An old favourite for budget travellers, some rooms with en suite bathrooms others with shared bathrooms, hot water. Very bare bedrooms but clean with spotless sheets and mosquito nets and recently repainted. A double is US$13 and one with a bathroom US$23.

D-E New Livingstone Hotel, corner of Rindi Lane and Rengua St near the Clocktower, T027-2666504. Suites and cheaper dormitory-style accommodation, but very basic, from US$10 pp with breakfast.

E Buffalo Inn, 2 blocks south and east of the bus station, T027-2550270. Clean budget hotel, very friendly, hot water with/without bathroom. Good restaurant and bar. Will store your luggage if you are going on safari.

E Coffee Tree Hotel, town centre (2 floors of a large office block), T027-2755040. Good views of Kilimanjaro, ideal for the bus station, communal cold showers, some rooms have bathroom. Wonderful views, will store rucksacks and baggage, restaurant, rundown but cheap.

E Hotel Da' Costa, T027-2755159, hotelda costa@yahoo.com, and **Haria Palace**, T027-2751128, hariapalce@yahoo.com, cheaper sister hotels of the Kindoroko (see above). You cannot argue with the price at either of these, the Da' Costa charges US$8 for a double, US$5 for a single, and the Haria Palace, US$4 for a double and US$9 for a triple. Both have shared bathrooms that are kept spotlessly clean, though there are few bathrooms to the amount of rooms. Rooms are simple but adequate. Guests can use the facilities at the Kindoroko.

E Rombo Cottage, off road to Marangu, T027-2757198. Hot water, own bathroom, bar and restaurant, good value and atmosphere. Safe parking for cars and motorcycles.

Camping

There is camping at the **Golden Shower Restaurant**, 2 km from Moshi on the road to Marangu (see Eating). It is also possible to camp at the **Keys Hotel**.

West Kilimanjaro *p194*

L West Kilimanjaro Camp, reservations, Arusha T027-2507011/2507541, Hoopoe Safaris, www.kirurumu.com. The 5 tents are spacious with en suite bathrooms and fully and tastefully furnished, set under the spreading branches of an acacia tree. Views of Kilimanjaro are superb and there is game in this region. Game drives, night drives, walks with the Masai and fly camping away from camp are possible. High season rates are US$420 per person full board.

Marangu *p195*

A Aishi Hotel, T027-2754104, www.protea hotels.com. This is one of the most luxurious hotels in the region and is an ideal base to conquer Kili. The hotel arranges mountain climbing and safaris. The 14 rooms, with private facilities, have recently been completely refurbished to the highest standard, set in well-kept gardens, spotlessly clean and very well furnished.

A Capricorn Hotel, T027-2751309, www.africaonline.co.tz/capricornhotel. Established country hotel with 24 standard and superior double rooms all with en suite bathrooms. Internet access, good restaurant, bar, lovely gardens, arranges climbs.

A **Marangu Hotel**, 5 km back from Marangu towards Moshi, T027-2756594, www.maranguhotel.com. Long-established, family-owned and run country-style hotel, warm and friendly atmosphere, self-contained cottages with private baths and showers, hot water, set in 12 acres of gardens offering stunning views of Kilimanjaro, swimming pool, croquet lawn, one of the original operators of Kilimanjaro climbs with over 60 years' experience. Can arrange treks on all the routes. Also permits camping (**E**).

B **Ashanti Lodge**, close to the Marangu Gate, T027-2756443, www.ashantilodge.com. Old-style country hotel. Spacious but rather plain rooms with en suite bathrooms, in thatched bungalows in the garden. Bar, restaurant, can organize local cultural tours and safaris. There is ample parking so if in your own vehicle, and climbing Kili, you could negotiate to leave your car here.

B **Babylon Lodge**, 500 m from the post office on the Jarakea Rd, T027-2751315, www.babylonlodge.com. Clean and comfortable, sited in well kept gardens, built into the hillside, all 18 rooms have private facilities, there's also a 3-bed bungalow for families, bar and restaurant with a set 4-course meal each evening, owner Mr Lgimo is very helpful and can organize climbs.

B **Nakara Hotel**, T027-2756571, www.nakara-hotels.com. Fairly new establishment 2 km before the park gate, plain but functional rooms with en suite bathrooms, in a modern whitewashed block though with little character. Bar and restaurant, gardens with wooden barbecue area, friendly and helpful staff, can arrange climbs.

B-F **Kibo Hotel**, about 1 km from Marangu village, T027-2751308, www.kibohotel.com. Recently revamped under new management, old German building, 45 rooms, restaurant, bar, swimming pool, fine gardens, well organized. Evelyn Waugh stayed here in 1959 and found it "so comfortable" with its "cool verandah". You can also camp here for US$5. Climbs can be organized.

Eating

Moshi *p194, map p194*

🍴🍴 **El Rancho**, off Lema Rd, Shanty Town, T027-2755115. Northern Indian food, good choice for vegetarians, very authentic and full range of curries, each dish is prepared from scratch so it can take a while. However, there are plenty of diversions in the garden to keep you occupied including table football, a crazy golf course and a pool table. There's a full bar with 16 brands of whisky. Open 1230-2300, closed Mon.

🍴🍴 **Golden Shower**, 2 km from Moshi on the road to Dar. The owner, John Bennet, is the son of the legendary character 'Chagga' Bennet, ex-First World War Royal Flying Corps ace, and economic adviser to the former Kilimanjaro Native Co-operative Union. He is a wonderful source of local information. Excellent restaurant serving continental food and friendly bar. Disco at weekends that goes on until the early hours.

🍴🍴 **Panda**, off Lema Rd, Shanty Town, just south of the Impala Hotel, T0744-838193. Good Chinese food served by ladies in Chinese clothes, tables set up in a house, very good seafood including king size prawns and sizzling dishes. Open daily 1200-1500, 1800-2200.

🍴 **Chrisburger**, close to the Clocktower. Has a small veranda at the front and sells cold drinks and snacks including very good fruit juice, closes mid-afternoon though.

🍴🍴 **Coffee Shop**, Hill St, near the bus station. Lovely food using fresh produce from Irente Farm in Lushoto, cakes homemade jam, cheese and tea. Healthy breakfasts, and light meals include omelettes, carrot and lentil soup and quiche. Try the cheese platter with apple, pickle and brown bread. Open 0800-1800, 1630 on Sat, closed Sun. Garden to sit in at the back. Outlet of St Margaret's Anglican Church. Across the road from here is the Tanzania Home Economics Association craft shop, a non-profit organization for mostly women and children.

🍴🍴 **Ice Cream Parlour**, Old Moshi Rd, north of the Clocktower, cold drinks and ice cream.

🍴 **Pagoda**, near CCM HQ. Basic Chinese dishes in bamboo hut in the garden, also a takeaway, not as good as the Panda restaurant.

Activities and tours

Moshi *p194, map p194*

It is cheaper to book tours for Kilimanjaro from Moshi than it is from either Arusha or Marangu. Like booking an organized safari in

Arusha for the game parks (see box on page 232) give youself a day or two in Moshi to talk to a couple of the tour operators that arrange Kilimanjaro climbs. Find one that you like, does not pressure you too much, and accepts the method of payment of your choice. Ignore the touts on the street. You may find if it is quiet that the tour companies will get together and put clients on the same tour to make up numbers. All tour operators below offer Kili climbs on most of the routes, some offer additional tours. This is a far from comprehensive list.

AfriGalaxy Tours & Travel Ltd, CCM Regional Building, Taifa Rd (near YMCA), T027-2750268, www.afrigalaxytours.com.

Akaro Tours Co Ltd, ground floor of NSSF House on Old Moshi Rd, T027-2752499, www.akarotours.com. Kilimanjaro climbs with local guides that include visit to small village among the coffee plantations. Specializes in tours to the Masai Plain, North and South Pare Mountains and to the foothills of Mt Kilimanjaro, for insights into the way of life of the indigenous peoples and appreciation of the plants and animals.

Emslie's Tours, Old Moshi Rd, T027-2506097, www.emsliestravel.biz. Also general travel agent for booking car hire, hotels, flights etc, business orientated.

Kibo Safari Adventure, Oloro Rd, T027-2750367, www.kibo-safaris.com. Weekly departures for northern circuit using Serena lodges, comprehensive 11-day tented camp safari to all the major parks for a cool US$4100 per person, professional and knowledgable guides.

Kilimanjaro Crown Birds Agency, based in the *New Kindoroka Hotel*, T027-2751162, T0744-285122 (mob), www.kilicrown.com. Offers a good, friendly service. Can arrange a 5-day Kilimanjaro climb by the Marangu route for US$620 and a 6-day climb for US$700.

Kilimanjaro Guide Tour Safaris, opposite (closed) *Moshi Hotel*, T027-2751220, www.kigusatours.com. Also offer Ngorongoro Highlands trekking.

Kilimanjaro Serengeti Tours & Travel Ltd, Old CCM Building, Mawenzi Rd, T027-2751287, www.kilimanjaroserengeti.com.

Kilimanjaro Travel Services Ltd, THB Building, Boma Rd, T027-2752124, www.kilimanjarotravels-tz.com. Meru and Kilimanjaro climbs, budget camping safaris to Ngorongoro, Serengeti and Manyara.

Laka Tours & Car Hire, Lutheran Building, 2nd Floor, Market St, T027-2751510.

Mauly Tours & Safaris, Mawenzi Rd, opposite Moshi post office, T027-2750730, www.mauly-tours.com.

MJ Safaris International, CCM Building, Taifa Rd, T027-2752017, www.habari.co.tz/mjsafaris. Climbing and trekking and tailor-made safaris to the northern and southern circuit parks.

Moshi Expedition & Mountaineering, Kaunda St, T027-2754574, www.memtours.com.

Shah Tours and Travel, Mawenzi Rd, T027-2752370, www.kilimanjaro-shah.com. There is also an office at the Mountain Inn Hotel where all tours start. A recommended operator with lots of experience.

Snow Cap, CCM Building, Taifa Rd, T027-2754826, www.snowcap.co.tz.

Trans-Kibo Travels Ltd, YMCA Building, T027-2751754/2752017, www.transkibo.com. All Kilimanjaro routes, one of the oldest operators in existence, also Meru and Mount Kenya.

Zara Tanzania Adventure, at Springlands Hotel, T027-2753581, www.zaratravel.com, www.kilimanjaro.co.tz. Kilimanjaro climb US$690 for 5-day 'Coca-Cola route' or Marangu route, US$890 for Machame and US$780 for the Umbwe route, the safari charges are US$100 per person per day for a tour of Serengeti/Ngorongoro but these drop considerably for 4 or more people, as does the Kili climb. Recommended for groups as prices are very good. There are also discounts of up to US$50 per day in low season (Apr-Jun). Zara takes thousands of people up the mountain each year, recommended as one of Tanzania's best budget operators.

Transport

Air

Kilimanjaro International Airport, is halfway between Moshi and Arusha, for flight details, see **Arusha** page 237. In Moshi the **Air Tanzania** office is on Rengua Rd near the clock tower. A shuttle bus leaves from here 2 hrs before the scheduled flight departure, cost US$3, and the buses meet the incoming flights. If you are using one of the other airlines, the only option is to take a taxi between Moshi and the airport, which should cost around US$12 or arrange for one of the tour operators to meet you. The **Precision Air** office is at KNCU building, Old Moshi Rd, T027-2753498, www.precisionairtz.com. Moshi also has its own small airfield. **Kilimanjaro Aero Club** based at Moshi Airport, T027-2750555, www.kilimanjaroaeroclub.com, can arrange charter flights, sightseeing flights and flying lessons.

Road

Moshi is 580 km from Dar es Salaam, 79 km from Arusha and 349 km from Nairobi. Local buses and *dala-dala* to nearby destinations like **Marangu** and **Arusha** cost little more than US$1 and go from the stand just to the south of the main bus stand, which are both on Market St. There are daily buses to and from **Dar**, US$20 'luxury', US$16 'semi-luxury' and US$9 'ordinary' which take about 7 hrs. The road has improved considerably. For **Tanga** the bus takes 4-6 hrs and costs US$4. It is possible to get a direct bus to **Mombasa**, cost approximately US$13, 7-8 hrs. These go through the Taveta border, on to **Voi** in Kenya where they join the main road from Nairobi to Mombasa. There are also private shuttle services to **Nairobi** via the Namanga border. **Impala Shuttle**, T027-2751786, Impala Hotel, departs daily for Nairobi at 0630 and 1200, US$25. **Riverside Shuttle**, THB House, T027-2750093, www.riverside-shuttle.com, departs daily at 1130 to Nairobi, US$25.

Regular *dala-dala* from **Marangu to Moshi** and back take 45 mins and cost US$1. A taxi will cost in the region of US$15, whilst those who organize a climb in Moshi will be transferred to the park gate by their tour operator.

Directory

Banks and foreign exchange bureaux Standard Chartered Bank on Rindi Lane, and the **National Bank of Commerce** on the Clocktower roundabout have ATM facilities. **Chase Forex Bureau**, Rindi Lane, T027-2755220, will advance money on Visa and Mastercard. **Courier services** DHL, Kahawa House on the Clocktower roundabout, T027-2754030, www.africa.dhl.com. **Skynet** is in the THB building, T027-2753590. **Internet** There are several places around Moshi to check email. These include **Dot Café**, Rengua Rd, **Duma** and **Fahari**, both on Hill St, next door to the Coffee Shop, and **M-Net Café** also on Rengua Rd. **Post** Post office can be found in the centre of town near the Clocktower. **Telephone** International calls can be made from the post office. **Medical services** Hospitals: Moshi is home to what is said to be the best hospital in Tanzania, the **Kilimanjaro Christian Medical Centre (KCMC)**, which is a few km out of town, T027-2754377. **Mawenzi Moshi District Hospital**, in town. **Useful addresses** The **Library**, Kibo Rd, just north of *Chrisburger*. **Police**, Market St, T027-2755055.

African Wildlife

Introduction

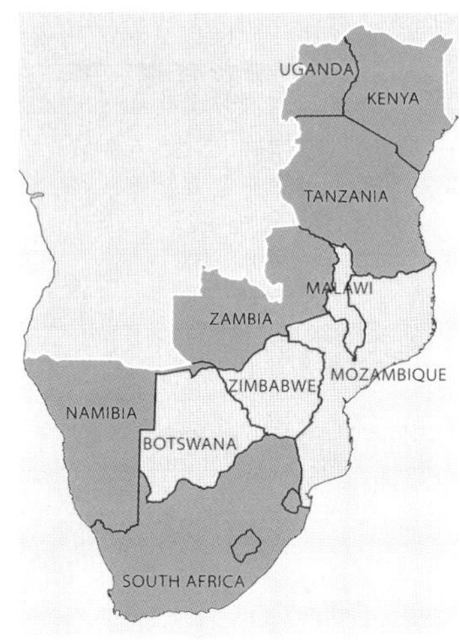

A large proportion of people who visit Africa do so to see its spectacular wildlife. This colour section is a quick photographic guide to some of the more spectacular mammals found in east and southern Africa (it covers the countries shown on the map here). From the 'Big Nine', once thought by hunters to be the ultimate 'trophies' on safari and now most prized of all by those who shoot with their cameras, to the more everyday warthog, and from the wildebeest to the tiny Kirk's Dikdik antelope, which stands at a mere 40 cm at the shoulder, here we give you pictures and information about habitat, habits and characteristic appearance to help you when you are on safari. It is by no means a comprehensive survey and some of the animals listed may not be found throughout the whole region (where this is the case, we have listed the areas where they occur). For further information about the wildlife of the country, see the Land and environment section of the Background chapter.

The Big Nine

Hippopotamus *Hippopotamus amphibius* (below). Prefers shallow water, grazes on land over a wide area at night, so can be found quite a distance from water, and has a strong sense of territory, which it protects aggressively. Lives in large family groups known as "schools".

Black Rhinoceros *Diceros bicornis* (bottom right). Long, hooked upper lip distinguishes it from White Rhino rather than colour. Prefers dry bush and thorn scrub habitat and in the past was found in mountain uplands. Males usually solitary. Females seen in small groups with their calves (very rarely more than four), sometimes with two generations. Mother always walks in front of offspring, unlike the White Rhino, where the mother walks behind, guiding calf with her horn. Their distribution has been massively reduced by poaching and work continues to save both the Black and the White Rhino from extinction. You might be lucky and see the Black Rhino in: Etosha NP, Namibia; Ngorongoro Crater, Tanzania; Masai Mara, Kenya; Kruger, Shamwari and Pilansberg NPs and private reserves like Mala Mala and Londolozi, South Africa.

White Rhinoceros *Diceros simus* (bottom right). Square muzzle and bulkier than the Black Rhino, they are grazers rather than browsers, hence the different lip. Found in open grassland, they are more sociable and can be seen in groups of five or more. More common in Southern Africa due to a successful breeding program in Hluhluwe/Umfolozi NP, South Africa.

Reticulated Giraffe *Giraffa reticulata* (right). Reddish brown coat and a network of distinct, pale, narrow lines. Found from the Tana River, Kenya, north and east into Somalia and Ethiopia. Giraffes found in East Africa have darker coloured legs and their spots are dark and of an irregular shape with a jagged outline. In southern Africa the patches tend to be much larger and have well defined outlines, although giraffes found in the desert margins of Namibia are very pale in colour and less tall – probably due to a poor diet lacking in minerals.

Leopard *Panthera pardus* (below). Found in varied habitats ranging from forest to open savanna. They are generally nocturnal, hunting at night or before the sun comes up to avoid the heat. You may see them resting during the day in the lower branches of trees, see picture page ii.

Common Zebra (Burchell's) *Equus burchelli* (right). Generally has broad stripes (some with lighter shadow stripes next to the dark ones) which cross the top of the hind leg in unbroken lines. The true species is probably extinct but there are many varying subspecies found in different locations across Africa, including: Grant's (found in East Africa) Selous (Malawi, Zimbabwe and Mozambique) and Chapman's (Etosha NP, Namibia, east across Southern Africa to Kruger NP).

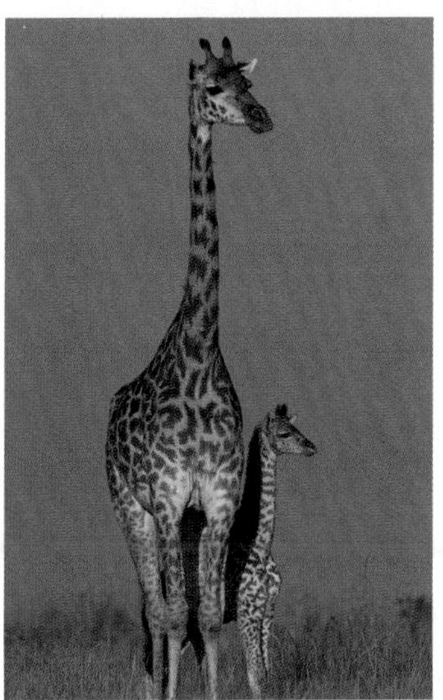

Common/Masai Giraffe *Giraffa camelopardis* (left). Yellowish-buff with patchwork of brownish marks and jagged edges, usually two different horns, sometimes three. Found throughout Africa in several differing subspecies.

Cheetah *Acinonyx jubatus* (below). Often seen in family groups walking across plains or resting in the shade. The black 'tear' mark is usually obvious through binoculars. Can reach speeds of 90 km per hour over short distances. Found in open, semi-arid savanna, never in forested country. Endangered in some parts of Africa, Namibia is believed to have the largest free-roaming population on the continent. More commonly seen than the leopard, they are not as widespread as the **lion** *Panthera leo* (see picture on front page of this section).

Grevy's Zebra *Equus grevyi* (left). Larger than the Burchell's Zebra, with bigger and broader ears and noticably narrower white stripes that meet in star above hind leg. Lives in small herds. Generally found north of the equator. A further zebra species, the **Mountain Zebra** *Equus zebra zebra*, is found in the Western Cape region of South Africa on hills and stony mountains. It is smaller than the two shown here and has a short mane and broad stripes.

Lion *Panthera leo* (page i). The largest (adult males can weigh up to 450 pounds) of the big cats in Africa and also the most common, lions are found on open savanna all over the continent. They are often not at all disturbed by the presence of humans and so it is possible to get quite close to them. They are sociable animals living in prides or permanent family groups of up to around 30 animals and are the only felid to do so. The females do most of the hunting (usually ungulates like zebra and antelopes).

Buffalo *Syncerus caffer* (below). Were considered by hunters to be the most dangerous of the big game and the most difficult to track and, therefore, the biggest trophy. Generally found on open plains but also at home in dense forest, they are fairly common in most African national parks but, like the elephant, they need a large area to roam in, so they are not usually found in the smaller parks.

Elephant *Loxodonta africana* (bottom and page xvi). Commonly seen, even on short safaris, throughout east and southern Africa, elephants have suffered from the activities of war and from ivory poachers. It is no longer possible to see herds of 500 or more animals but in southern Africa there are problems of over population and culling programmes have been introduced.

Larger antelope

■ **Gemsbok** *Oryx gazella* 122cm (below). Unmistakable, with black line down spine and black stripe between coloured body and white underparts. Horns (both sexes) straight, long and look v-shaped (seen face-on). Only found in Southern Africa, in arid, semi-desert country, though the very similar **Beisa Oryx** *Oryx beisa* occurs in East Africa. ■ **Nyala** *Tragelaphus angasi* 110cm (bottom left). Slender frame, shaggy, dark brown coat with mauve tinge (males). Horns (male only) single open curve. The female is a different chestnut colour. They like dense bush and are usually found close to water. Gather in herds of up to 30 but smaller groups more likely. Found across Zimbabwe and Malawi. ■ **Common** *Kobus ellipsiprymnus* and **Defassa** *Kobus defassa* **Waterbuck** 122-137cm (bottom right). Very similar with shaggy coats and white marking on buttocks. On the common variety, this is a clear half ring on rump and round tails; on Defassa, the ring is a filled in solid white area. Both species occur in small herds in grassy areas, often near water. Common in east and southern Africa.

Greater Kudu *Tragelaphus strepsiceros* 140-153cm (right). Colour varies from greyish to fawn with several vertical white stripes down the sides of the body. Horns long and spreading, with two or three twists (male only). Distinctive thick fringe of hair running from the chin down the neck. Found in fairly thick bush, sometimes in quite dry areas. Usually live in family groups of up to six, but occasionally larger herds of up to about 30. The **Lesser Kudu** *Strepsiceros imberis* 99-102 cm, looks similar but lacks the throat fringe and has two conspicuous white patches on the underside of the neck. Unlike the Greater Kudu, it is not found south of Tanzania.

Topi *Damaliscus korrigum* 122-127cm (below). Very rich dark rufous, with dark patches on the tops of the legs and more ordinary looking, lyre-shaped horns.

Sable Antelope *Hippotragus niger* 140-145cm (right) and **Roan Antelope** *Hippotragus equinus* 127-137cm. Both similar shape, with ringed horns curving backwards (both sexes), longer in the Sable. Female Sables are reddish brown and can be mistaken for the Roan. Males are very dark with a white underbelly. The Roan has distinct tufts of hair at the tips of its long ears. Found in east and southern Africa (although the Sable is not found naturally in east Africa, there is a small herd in the Shimba Hills Game Reserve). Sable prefers wooded areas and the Roan is generally only seen near water. Both species live in herds.

Hartebeest. In the Hartebeest the horns arise from a boney protuberance on the top of the head and curve outwards and backwards. There are 3 sub-species: **Coke's Hartebeest** *Alcephalus buselaphus* 122cm, also called the **Kongoni** in Kenya, is a drab pale brown with a paler rump; **Lichtenstein's Hartebeest** *Alcephalus lichtensteinii* 127-132cm, is also fawn in general colouration, with a rufous wash over the back and dark marks on the front of the legs and often a dark patch near shoulder; the **Red Hartebeest** *Alcephalus caama* (left), is another subspecies that occurs only throughout Southern Africa, although not in Kruger NP. All are found in herds, sometimes they mix with other plain dwellers such as zebra.

Brindled or **Blue Wildebeest** or **Gnu** *Connochaetes taurinus* (above) 132cm is found only in southern Africa; the **White bearded Wildebeest** *Connochaetes taurinus albojubatus* is found in central Tanzania and Kenya and distinguished by the white 'beard' under the neck. Both often seen grazing with Zebra.

Eland *Taurotragus oryx* 175-183cm (left). The largest of the antelope, it has a noticeable dewlap and shortish spiral horns (both sexes). Greyish to fawn, sometimes with rufous tinge and narrow white stripes down side of body. Occurs in groups of up to 30 in both east and southern Africa in grassy habitats.

Smaller antelope

Bushbuck *Tragelaphus scriptus* 76-92cm (top). Shaggy coat with variable pattern of white spots and stripes on the side and back and two white, crescent-shaped marks on front of neck. Short horns (male only) slightly spiral. High rump gives characteristic crouch. White underside of tail is noticeable when running. Occurs in thick bush, especially near water. Either seen in pairs or singly in east and southern Africa.

Thomson's Gazelle *Gazella thomsonii*, 64-69cm (above) and **Grant's Gazelle** *Gazella granti* 81-99cm. Superficially similar, Grant's, the larger of the two, has slightly longer horns (carried by both sexes in both species). Colour of both varies from bright to sandy rufous. Thomson's Gazelle can usually be distinguished by the broad black band along the side between the upperparts and abdomen, but some forms of Grant's also have this dark lateral stripe. Look for the white area on the buttocks which extends above the tail on to the rump in Grant's, but does not extend above the tail in Thomson's. Thomson's occur commonly on plains of Kenya and Tanzania in large herds. Grant's Gazelle occur on rather dry grass plains, in various forms, from Ethiopia and Somalia to Tanzania. Not found in southern Africa.

Kirk's Dikdik *Rhynchotragus kirkii* 36-41cm (top left). So small it cannot be mistaken, it is greyish brown, often washed with rufous. Legs are thin and stick-like. Slightly elongated snout and a conspicuous tuft of hair on the top of the head. Straight, small horns (male only). Found in bush country, singly or in pairs. East Africa only.

Steenbok *Raphicerus campestris* 58cm (top right). An even, rufous brown colour with clean white underside and white ring around eye. Small dark patch at the tip of the nose and long broad ears. The horns (male only) are slightly longer than the ears: they are sharp, have a smooth surface and curve slightly forward. Generally seen alone, prefers open plains, often found in more arid regions. A slight creature which usually runs off very quickly on being spotted. Common resident throughout southern Africa, Tanzania and parts of southern Kenya.

Bohor Reedbuck *Redunca redunca* 71-76cm (bottom left). Horns (males only) sharply hooked forwards at the tip, distinguishing them from the Oribi (see next page). It is reddish fawn with white underparts and has a short bushy tail. They usually live in pairs or otherwise in small family groups. Found in east and southern Africa. Often seen with Oribi, in bushed grassland and always near water.

Klipspringer *Oreotragus oreotragus* 56cm (bottom right). Brownish-yellow with grey speckles and white chin and underparts with a short tail. Has distinctive, blunt hoof tips and short horns (male only). Likes dry, stony hills and mountains. Only found in southern Africa.

Common (Grimm's) Duiker *Sylvicapra grimmia* 58cm (below). Grey fawn colour with darker rump and pale colour on the underside. Its dark muzzle and prominent ears are divided by straight, upright, narrow pointed horns. This particular species is the only duiker found in open grasslands. Usually the duiker is associated with a forested environment. It's common throughout southern and eastern Africa, but difficult to see because it is shy and will quickly disappear into the bush.

Oribi *Ourebia ourebi* 61cm (bottom left). Slender and delicate looking with a longish neck and a sandy to brownish fawn coat. It has oval-shaped ears and short, straight horns with a few rings at their base (male only). Like the Reedbuck (see previous page) it has a patch of bare skin just below each ear. They live in small groups or as a pair and are never far from water. Found in east and southern Africa.

Suni *Nesotragus moschatus* 37cm (bottom right). Dark chestnut to grey fawn in colour with slight speckles along the back, its head and neck are slightly paler and the throat is white. It has a distinct bushy tail with a white tip. Its longish horns (male only) are thick, ribbed and slope backwards. This is one of the smallest antelope, lives alone and prefers dense bush cover and reed beds in east and southern Africa.

Springbuck *Antidorcas marsupialis* or **Springbok**, 76-84cm (below). The upper part of the body is fawn, and this is separated from the white underparts by a dark brown lateral stripe. It is distinguished by a dark stripe which runs between the base of the horns and the mouth, passing through the eye. This is the only type of gazelle found south of the Zambezi River and you will not see this animal futher north. You no longer see the giant herds the animal was famous for, but you will see them along the roadside as you drive between Cape Town and Bloemfontein in South Africa. They get their name from their habit of leaping stiff-legged and high into the air.

Impala *Aepyceros melampus* 92-107cm (bottom). One of the largest of the smaller antelope, the Impala is a bright rufous colour on its back and has a white abdomen, a white 'eyebrow' and chin and white hair inside its ears. From behind, the white rump with black stripes on each side is characteristic and makes it easy to identify. It has long lyre-shaped horns (male only). Above the heels of the hind legs is a tuft of thick black bristles (unique to Impala) which are easy to see when the animal runs. There's also a black mark on the side of abdomen, just in front of the back leg. Found in herds of 15 to 20 in both east and southern Africa, it likes open grassland or sometimes the cover of partially wooded areas and is usually close to water.

Other mammals

There are many other fascinating mammals worth keeping an eye out for. This is a selection of some of the more interesting, or particularly common, ones.

■ **African Wild Dog** or **Hunting Dog** *Lycacon pictus* (right). Easy to identify since they have all the features of a large mongrel dog: a large head and slender body. Their coat is a mixed pattern of dark shapes and white and yellow patches and no two dogs are quite alike. They are very rarely seen and are seriously threatened with extinction (there may be as few as 6,000 left). Found in east and southern Africa on the open plains around dead animals, they are not in fact scavengers but effective pack hunters.

■ **Brown Hyena** *Hyaena brunnea* (above). High shoulders and low back give the hyena its characteristic appearance. The spotted variety, larger and brownish with dark spots, has a large head and rounded ears. The brown hyena, slightly smaller, has pointed ears and a shaggy coat, and is more noctural. The spotted hyena is only found in east Africa and the brown hyena is only found in southern Africa. Although sometimes shy animals they have been know to wander around campsites stealing food from humans.

■ **Spotted Hyena** *Crocuta crocuta* 69-91cm (middle right).

■ **Warthog** *Phacochoerus aethiopicus* (left). The warthog is almost hairless and grey with a very large head, tusks and wart-like growths on its face. It frequently occurs in family parties and when startled will run away at speed with its tail held straight up in the air. They are often seen near water caking themselves in thick mud which helps to keep them both cool and free of ticks and flies. They are found in both east and southern Africa.

■ **Chacma Baboon** *Papio ursinus* (opposite page bottom). An adult male baboon is slender and weighs about 40 kg. Their general colour is a brownish grey, with lighter undersides. Usually seen in trees, but rocks can also provide sufficient protection, they occur in large family troops and have a reputation for being aggressive where they have become used to man's presence. Found in east and southern Africa.

■ **Gorilla** *Gorilla gorilla* (left) are not animals you will see casually in passing – you have to go and look for them. They are sociable animals living in large family groups and have a vegetarian diet. Gorillas are the largest and most powerful of the apes. Adult males reach an average height of 150-170 cm and weigh from 135 to 230 kg. They occur only in the forests in the west of the region in Uganda, Rwanda and DR Congo.

Kilimanjaro National Park → *Colour map 1, A5.*

In 'The Snows of Kilimanjaro', Ernest Hemingway described the mountain: "as wide as all the world, great, high, and unbelievably white in the sun, was the square top of Kilimanjaro". It is one of the most impressive sights in Africa, visible from as far away as Tsavo National Park in Kenya. Just 80 km east of the eastern branch of the Rift Valley, it is Africa's highest mountain with snow-capped peaks rising from a relatively flat plain, the largest freestanding mountain worldwide, measuring 80 x 40 km and one of earth's highest dormant volcanoes. At lower altitudes, the mountain is covered in lush rainforest, which gives way to scrub – there is no bamboo zone on Kilimanjaro – followed by alpine moorland until you get to the icefields. Try to see it in the early morning before the clouds mask it. Despite its altitude even inexperienced climbers can climb it, provided they are reasonably fit and allow themselves sufficient time to acclimatize to the elevation. ▸▸ *For Sleeping, Eating and other listings, see page 195-200.*

Altitude: 1,829 m at Marangu Gate; 5,895 m at Kibo Peak
3°7'S 37°20'E

Ins and outs

Getting there

There are a number of ways of getting to Mt Kilimanjaro. The easiest is to fly to **Kilimanjaro International Airport** – during your approach you will get a magnificent view of the mountain if it is not covered by cloud. The park entrance is about 90 km from the airport, which takes about 1½ hours by road. Alternatively by road go to Moshi and from there to Marangu, the village at the park entrance at the base of the mountain. Many *dala-dala* go from Moshi to Marangu each day; they take 45 minutes and cost US$1. It is also cheap and easy to get to Kilimanjaro from Kenya by taking a *dala dala* from Nairobi to the border (about 4 hrs) and from there another *dala dala* to Marangu Gate. ▸▸ *See Transport page 199 for further details.*

Climate

Kilimanjaro can be climbed throughout the year but it is worth avoiding the two rainy seasons (late Mar to mid-Jun and Oct to beginning of Dec) when the routes become slippery. Best time to visit is Jan-Feb and Sep-Oct when there is usually no cloud.

Information

Anyone planning to climb Mount Kilimanjaro is advised to buy the *Kilimanjaro 1:50,000 Map and Guide* (1977) by Mark Savage. This is difficult to obtain in Tanzania but you can get it in Kenya, in England from **Executive Wilderness Programmes**, 32 Seamill Park Crescent, Worthing, BN11 2PN, or from **Kilimanjaro Adventure Travel**, 1770 Massachusetts Av, Suite 192, Cambridge, MA 02140, USA. It is not currently available from **Amazon**. Another guide that is particularly useful if you want to climb the mountain (rather than walk up) is the *Guide to Mount Kenya and Kilimanjaro* edited by Iain Allan and published by the Mountain Club of Kenya. There are other locally produced maps and coffee table books available in both Moshi and Arusha. Useful websites include **Kilimanjaro Adventure Travel**, www.kilimanjaro.com; **Africa Park East**, www.africaparkeast.com; **Terra Ferma**, www.terraferma.com; **Zara Tanzania Adventure**, www.kilimanjaro.co.tz.

It is assumed that the mountain got its name from the Swahili word 'kilima' which means 'top of the hill'. An estimated 20,000 tourists attempt the climb to the top each year.

Altitude sickness

Altitude sickness is often a problem while climbing Kilimanjaro. If you know you are susceptible to it you are advised not to attempt the climb. Symptoms include bad headache, nausea, vomiting and severe fatigue. It can be avoided by ascending slowly – if at all possible, spend an extra day half-way up to help your body to acclimatize. Mountain sickness symptoms can often be alleviated by descending to a lower altitude. The drug Diamox helps if taken before the ascent. Other more serious conditions include acute pulmonary oedema and/or cerebral oedema. In the former, the sufferer becomes breathless, turns blue in the face and coughs up froth. The latter is even more serious – symptoms are intense headache, hallucinations, confusion and disorientation and staggering gait. It is caused by the accumulation of fluid on the brain and can cause death or serious brain damage. If either of these conditions are suspected the sufferer should immediately be taken down to a lower altitude to receive medical care. It is, however, normal to feel breathless and fatigued at high altitudes and these are not always precursors to the more serious conditions.

Guides

A guide is compulsory on all routes and it essential to go with a tour operator who will supply not only guides but porters and relevant equipment (see Moshi tour operators, page 198). Do not be tempted to go it alone to avoid paying the park and guide fees – above the tree line the path is not always clear and you will be in big trouble if you are caught. Marangu is the usual route for tourists and only experienced hikers or climbers should use the other routes.

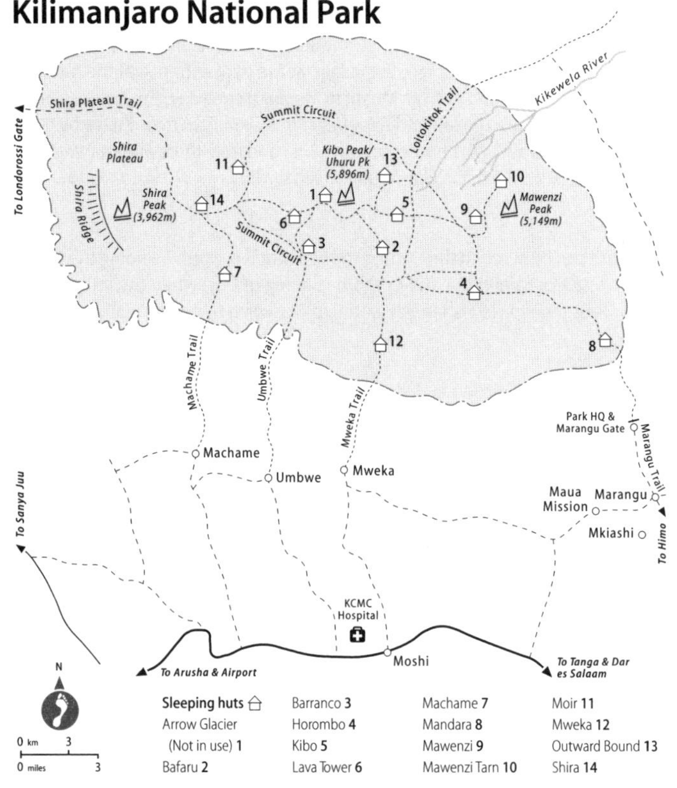

Equipment

Being well equipped will increase your chances of reaching the summit. In particular be sure you have a warm sleeping bag, insulating mat, warm rainproof jacket, thermal underwear, gloves, wool hat, sun-glasses or snow goggles, sun cream, large water bottle and first-aid kit. Some of these are available to buy or hire in Moshi from the tour operators; at the park gate for example is a shop that sells thick socks amongst other items. However, the quality is variable and it is best to come fully prepared.

Costs

Climbing Mount Kilimanjaro is an expensive business, though everyone who makes it to the summit agrees that it is well worth it. The costs are much higher than those in the Alps or the Andes. Park fees alone, charged by Tanzania National Parks are US$30 per person per 24 hours, camping or hut fees US$50 per person per day (whether you use the huts or not), a rescue fee insurance of US$20 per person, and guides at US$10 per guide per day. These are the set fees that the tour operator must pay on your behalf to the national park and can amount to almost US$500 for a 5-day trip. On top of this, other costs for the tour operators include the salaries of the guides and porters, the additional 20% VAT on the total invoice, 10% commission if booking through a third party travel agent, transport to the start of the trail, food, and the costs of equipment. The absolute cheapest you will probably manage to do it for will be around US$650 for the five-day Marangu Route. For a reputable operator with good guides and equipment, and perhaps an extra day's acclimatization on the mountain, expect to pay USS$700-750. The other more technical or longer climbs are US$800-900 or more.

At the time of writing, Tanzania National Parks proposed an increase of the park entry fee to US$60, *see page 40.*

Tipping On the last day of the tour your guide will request a tip for himself and his porters. The guide may try to negotiate a daily rate of US$15 for the guide, US$10 daily for the assistant guide, US$8 daily for the cook and US$5 for each porter. A reasonable tip for the whole trip is in the region of US$30 for a single guide, and US$10 for each porter. Even this amount is very high in comparison to the local income.

Background

Formation

Kilimanjaro was formed about 1 million years ago by a series of volcanic movements along the Great Rift Valley. Until this point, the area was a flat plain at about 600-900 m above sea level. About 750,000 years ago volcanic activity forced three points above 4,800 m – Shira, Kibo and Mawenzi. Some 250,000 years later Shira became inactive and collapsed into itself forming the crater. Kibo and Mawenzi continued their volcanic activity and it was their lava flow that forms the 11-km saddle between the two peaks. When Mawenzi died out, its northeast wall collapsed in a huge explosion creating a massive gorge. The last major eruptions occurred about 200 years ago and Kibo now lies dormant but not extinct. Although Kibo appears to be a snow-clad dome, it contains a caldera 2.5 km across and 180 m deep at the deepest point in the south. Within the depression is an inner ash cone that rises to within 60 m of the summit height and is evidence of former volcanic activity. On the southern slopes the glaciers reach down to about 4,200 m, while on the north slopes they only descend a little below the summit.

Vegetation and wildlife

Kilimanjaro has well-defined altitudinal vegetation zones. From the base to the summit these are: plateau, semi-arid scrub; cultivated, well-watered southern slopes; dense cloud forest; open moorland; alpine desert; moss and lichen. The slopes are home to elephant, rhino, buffalo, leopard, monkey and eland. Birdlife includes the enormous

The meaning of Kilimanjaro

Since the earliest explorers visited East Africa, people have been intrigued by the name Kilimanjaro and its meaning. The Chagga people do not have a name for the whole mountain, just the two peaks: *Kibo* (or kipoo) means 'spotted' and refers to the rock that can be seen standing out against the snow on this peak; *Mawenzi* (or Kimawenze) means 'having a broken top' and again describes its appearance.

Most theories as to the origin of the name Kilimanjaro for the whole mountain break the word down into two elements: *kilima* and *njaro*. In Swahili the word for mountain is *mlima* while *kilima* means hill – so it is possible that an early European visitor incorrectly used *kilima* because of the analogy to the two Chagga words Kibo and Kimawenzi.

The explorer Krapf said that the Swahili of the coast knew it as Kilimanjaro 'mountain of greatness', but he does not explain why. He also suggests it could mean 'mountain of caravans' (*kilima* = mountain, *jaro* = caravans), but while *kilima* is a Swahili word, *jaro* is a Chagga word. Other observers have suggested that *njaro* once meant 'whiteness' and therefore this was the 'mountain of whiteness'. Alternatively *njaro* could be the name of an evil spirit, or a demon. The first-known European to climb Mount Kilimanjaro mentions 'Njaro, the guardian spirit of the mountain' and there are many stories in Chagga folklore about spirits living here – though there is no evidence of a spirit called Njaro, either from the Chagga or from the coastal peoples.

Another explanation suggests that the mountain was known as 'mountain of water', because of the Masai word *njore* for springs or water and because all the rivers in the area rose from here. However, this theory does not explain the use of the Swahili word for 'hill' rather than 'mountain', and also assumes that a Swahili word and a Masai word have been put together.

The final explanation is from a Kichagga term *kilelema* meaning that 'which has become difficult or impossible' or 'which has defeated'. Njaro can be derived from the Kichagga words *njaare*, a bird, or else *jyaro*, a caravan. Thus the mountain became *kilemanjaare, kilemajyaro* or *kilelemanjaare*, meaning that which defeats or is impossible for the bird or the caravan. This theory has the advantage of being composed entirely of Chagga elements.

It seems possible either that this was the name given to the mountain by the Chagga themselves, or by people passing through the area, who heard the Chagga say *kilemanjaare* or *kilemajyaro*, meaning that the mountain was impossible to climb. Over time the name was standardized to Kilimanjaro.

lammergeyer, the scarlet-tufted malachite sunbird as well as various species of starlings, sunbirds, the silvery-cheeked hornbill and the rufous-breasted sparrowhawk.

History

When, in 1848, the first reports by the German missionary Johannes Rebmann of a snow-capped mountain on the equator arrived in Europe, the idea was ridiculed by the Royal Geographical Society of Britain. In 1889 the report was confirmed by the German geographer Hans Meyer and the Austrian alpine mountaineer Ludwig Purtscheller, who climbed Kibo and managed to reach the snows on Kilimanjaro's summit. At the centenary of this climb in 1989, the Tanzanian guide was still alive and 115 years old. Mawenzi was first climbed by the German Fritz Klute in 1912.

The mountain was originally in a part of British East Africa (now Kenya). However, the mountain was 'given' by Queen Victoria as a gift to her cousin, and so the border was moved and the mountain included within German Tanganyika. The national park was established in 1973 and covers an area of 756 sq km.

★ Routes up the mountain

Officially anyone aged over 12 may attempt the climb. The youngest person to climb the mountain was an 11 year old, while the oldest was 74. However, it is not that easy and estimates of the number of people who attempt the climb and do not make it to the top vary from 50-80%. The important things to remember are to come prepared and take it slowly – if you have the chance, spend an extra day half-way up to give you the chance to acclimatize.

There are a number of different trails. The most popular is the Marangu trail, which is the recommended route for older persons or younger people who are not in peak physical condition. The climbing tends to be much more strenuous than anticipated, which when combined with lower oxygen levels accounts for a 20-50% failure rate to reach the summit.

Marangu trail

Day 1 The national park gate (1,830 m) is about 8 km from the *Kibo Hotel*. This is as far as vehicles are allowed. From here to the first night's stop at **Mandara Hut** (2,700 m) is a walk of 3-4 hours. It is through *shambas* – small farms – growing coffee as well as some lush rainforest and is an enjoyable walk although it can be quite muddy. On the walk you can admire the moss and lichens, the vines and flowers including orchids. There is an alternative forest trail, which branches left from the main track a few minutes after the gate and follows the side of a stream. It is a little slower than the main track, which it rejoins after a walk of about three hours. The Mandara Hut, near the Maundi Crater, is actually a group of huts that can sleep about 200 people. Mattresses, lamps and stoves are provided but nothing else. The complex was built by the Norwegians as part of an aid programme. There are piped water, flushing toilets and firewood available, and a dining area in the main cabin.

This is probably the least scenic of the routes but being the gentlest climb and having a village at the start and accommodation on the way up means that it is the most popular.

Day 2 The second day will start off as a steep walk through the last of the rainforest and out into tussock grassland, giant heather and then on to the moorlands, crossing several ravines on the way. There are occasional clearings through which you will get wonderful views of Mawenzi and Moshi far below. You can also enjoy the views by making a short detour up to the rim of Maundi Crater. You will also probably see some of the exceptional vegetation that is found on Kilimanjaro, including the giant lobelia, Kilimanjaro 'everlasting flowers' and other uncommon alpine plants. The walk to **Horombo Hut** (3,720 m) is about 14 km with an altitude gain of about 1,000 m and will take you 5-7 hours. This hut is again actually a collection of huts that can accommodate up to 200 people. There are flushing toilets and plenty of water but firewood is scarce. Some people spend an extra day here to help get acclimatized and if you are doing this there are a number of short walks in the area. It is a very good idea to spend this extra day here – but there is the extra cost to be considered.

Day 3/4 On the next day of walking you will climb to the **Kibo Hut** (4,703 m), which is 13 km from Horombo. As you climb, the vegetation thins to grass and heather and eventually to bare scree. You will feel the air thinning and will probably start to suffer from altitude sickness. The most direct route is the right fork from Horombo Hut. It is

The snow sepulchre of King Solomon

Legend has it that the last military adventure of King Solomon was an expedition down the eastern side of Africa. Exhausted by his battles the aged king was trekking home with his army when they passed the snow-covered Mount Kilimanjaro. Solomon decided this was to be his resting place. The next day he was carried by bearers until they reached the snows. As they steadily trudged up to the summit they saw a cave glittering in the sunlight, frost sparkling in the interior, icicles hanging down to close off the entrance. As they watched, two icicles, warmed by the sun, crashed to the ground. They carried the old king inside and placed him on his throne, wrapped in his robes, facing out down the mountain. Solomon raised a frail hand to bid farewell. The bearers left with heavy hearts. The weather began to change and there was a gentle fall of snow. As they looked back they saw that icicles had reformed over the entrance.

stony and eroded, a climb of 6-7 hours up the valley behind the huts, past **Last Water** and on to the **saddle**. This is the wide, fairly flat, U-shaped desert between the two peaks of Mawenzi and Kibo and from here you will get some awe-inspiring views of the mountain. After **Zebra Rocks** and at the beginning of the saddle, the track forks. To the right, about three hours from Horombo Hut, is Mawenzi Hut and to the left across the saddle is Kibo Hut. The left fork from Horombo Hut is gentler, and comes out on to the saddle 1 km from Kibo Hut. Kibo Hut is where the porters stay and from here on you should just take with you the absolute bare essentials. It is a good idea to bring some biscuits or chocolate with you for the final ascent to the peak, as a lunch pack is not always provided. Kibo Hut sleeps about 120 people. There is a stone-built main block with a small dining room and several dormitory rooms with bunks and mattresses. There is no vegetation in the area and no water unless there has been snow recently, so it has to be carried up from Last Water. Some people decide to try and get as much sleep as possible before the early start, while others decide not to sleep at all. You are unlikely to sleep very well because of the altitude and the temperatures anyway.

Day 4/5 On the final day of the climb, in order to be at the summit at sunrise, and before the cloud comes down, you will have to get up at about midnight. One advantage of beginning at this time is that if you saw what you were about to attempt you would probably give up before you had even begun. You can expect to feel pretty awful during this final five-hour ascent and many climbers are physically sick. You may find that this climb is extremely slippery and hard going. The first part of the climb is over an uneven trail to **Hans Meyer Cave**. As the sun rises you will reach **Gillman's Point** (5,680 m) – it is a wonderful sight. From here you have to decide whether you want to keep going another couple of hours to get to **Kibo Peak** (5,896 m). The walk around the crater rim to Kibo Peak is only an extra 200 m but at this altitude it is a strenuous 200 m. At the peak there is a fair amount of litter left by previous climbers. You will return to **Horombo Hut** the same day and the next day (**day 5/6**) return to Marangu where you will be presented with a certificate.

Mawenzi Peak

This peak is accessible from Mawenzi Hut and Mawenzi Tarn Hut, but only experienced rock climbers should attempt any of the difficult routes to the top. **Mawenzi Hut** (4,600 m) sleeps five people. There is a stream nearby, but no toilets. **Mawenzi Tarn**

Hut (4,330 m) is a metal and wooden construction with bunk beds and mattresses, and a small dining room, sleeping six. There is a second hut, also for six people.

Umbwe trail

The climb is hard, short and steep but is a wonderfully scenic route to take to reach **Uhuru Peak** and as a result is becoming increasingly popular. However, it is not recommended for inexperienced climbers. Many climbers descend this way after climbing up by a different route. To get to the start of the trail take the turning off the Arusha road about 2 km down on the right. From there it's 14 km down the Lyamungu road, right at the T-junction towards Mango and soon after crossing the Sere River you get to **Umbwe** village (1,400 m). Ask at the mission school to leave your vehicle here.

Day 1 Umbwe to Bivouac 1, 4-6 hours' walk. From the mission the former forestry track continues through rainforest for about 3 km up to **Kifuni** village. From there it's another 6 km before you get to the start of the trail proper. There is a sign here and the trail branches to the left and climbs quite steeply through the forest along the ridge between the Lonzo River to the west and Umbwe River to the east. In several places it is necessary to use branches to pull yourself up. You will reach the first shelter, a cave, about 6-8 hours' walk from Umbwe. This is **Bivouac I** (2,940 m), an all-weather rock shelter formed from the rock overhangs. It will shelter about six or seven people. There is firewood nearby and a spring about 15 m below under a rock face.

If you made an early start and are fit and keen you can continue on to Bivouac II on the same day. However, most climbers take an overnight break here, camping in the forest caves.

Day 2 Bivouac 1 to Barranco Hut, 5 km, 4-5 hours' walk. From the caves, continue up, past the moorland and along the ridge. It is a steep walk with deep valleys on each side of the ridge and this walk is magnificent with the strange 'Old Man's Beard' – a type of moss – covering most of the vegetation. The second set of caves is **Bivouac II** (3,800 m), 3-4 hours from Bivouac I. There are two caves – one about five minutes further down the track – and both sleep 3-4 people. There is a spring down the ravine about 15 minutes to the west.

From the second set of caves the path continues less steeply up the ridge beyond the tree line before reaching **Barranco** or **Umbwe Hut** (3,900 m). Barranco Hut is about five hours away from the first caves or two hours from Bivouac II. The path is well marked. The hut is a metal cabin with a wooden floor, which sleeps 6-8 people. About 200 m beyond the hut is a rock overhang, which can be used if the hut is full. There is one pit latrine, water is available about 250 m to the east and firewood is available in the area. Some people may choose to spend an extra day at Barranco Hut to acclimatize to the altitude.

Day 3/4 Barranco Hut to Lava Tower Hut, 3-4 hours. Just before reaching Barranco Hut the path splits in two. To the left, the path goes west towards Shira Hut (5-6 hours) and the northern circuit, or you can climb the west lateral ridge to the **Arrow Glacier Hut** (now defunct after it was buried in an avalanche) towards the new **Lava Tower Hut** (4,600 m) about 3-4 hours away. Up this path the vegetation thins before disappearing completely on reaching the scree slopes. Lava Tower Hut is a round metal hut that sleeps 8. There are no toilets, but water is available in a nearby stream.

Day 4/5 Lava Tower Hut to Uhuru Peak, 4-6 hours. Having spent the night at Lava Tower Hut you will want to leave very early for the final ascent. Head torches are imperative and if there is no moonlight the walk can be quite difficult. Climb up between **Arrow Glacier** (which may have disappeared completely if you are there towards the end of the dry season) and **Little Breach Glacier** until you get to a few small cliffs. At this stage the course follows the Western Breach summit route and turns to the right heading for the lowest part of the crater rim that you can see. This part of the walk is really steep on scree and snow, and parts of it are quite a scramble. From December to February, crampons and ice axes are recommended. Having reached the crater floor, cross the **Furtwangler Glacier** snout to a steep gully that reaches the summit plateau about another 500 m west of **Uhuru Peak** (5,895 m), returning to **Mweka Hut**, among the giant heathers, for an overnight stop.

Day 5/6 Descent from Mweka Hut to Mweka Gate, 14 km, 5-7 hours. The return journey can be achieved in approximately half the ascending time.

Umbwe trail – alternative route

Day 3/4 Barranco Hut to Bafaru Hut, 5 km, 4-5 hours. The route is well marked at lower levels but not at higher altitudes. If you take the path to the right from **Barranco Hut** (eastwards on the Southern Circuit) you will cross one small stream and then another larger one as you contour the mountain to join the **Mweka trail**. The path then climbs steeply through a gap in the **West Breach**. From here you can turn left to join the routes over the south glaciers. Alternatively, continue along the marked path across screes, ridges and a valley until you reach the **Karangu Campsite**, which is a further 2-3 hours on from the top of the Breach. A further couple of hours up the **Karangu valley** (4,000 m) will come out at the **Mweka-Barafu Hut** path (part of the Mweka trail). If you go left down along this you will get to the **Barafu Hut** after 1-1½ hours. If you go straight on for about three hours you will join the Marangu trail just above the **Horombo Hut**.

Day 4/5 Barafu Hut to Uhuru Peak to Mweka Hut, 5-6 hours' walk to crater rim plus another hour to Uhuru Peak. Parties heading for the summit set off around midnight to 0100, reaching the crater at Stella Point. If the weather conditions are favourable, **Uhuru Peak** (5,895 m) is normally reached by first light. From here it is often possible to see the summit of Mount Meru to the west. Descend to **Mweka Hut** for an overnight stop.

Day 5/6 Descent from Mweka Hut to Mweka Gate, 14 km, 5-7 hours.

Machame trail

This trail is considered by some to be the most attractive of the routes up Kilimanjaro. It is between Umbwe trail and Shira trail and joins the latter route at Shira Hut. The turn-off to the trail is to the west of Umbwe off the main Arusha-Moshi road. Take this road north towards Machame village and leave your vehicle at the school or hotel there.

! This route is not suitable for older people or those of any age who aren't very fit.

Day 1 From the village to the first huts takes about 9 hours so be sure to start early. Take the track through the *shambas* and the forest to the park entrance (about 4 km), from where you will see a clear track that climbs gently through the forest and along a ridge that is between the Weru Weru and Makoa streams. It is about 7 km to the edge of the forest, and then 4-5 hours up to the **Machame Huts** (3,000 m). The two round metal huts, on the edge of the forest, will sleep about 7 people each. There are pit latrines and plenty of water down in the valley below the huts and firewood available close by.

Day 2 From the Machame Huts go across the valley, over a stream, then up a steep ridge for 3-4 hours. The path then goes west and drops into the river gorge before climbing more gradually up the other side and on to the moorland of the Shira Plateau to join the Shira Plateau trail near the **Shira Hut** (3,800 m). This takes about 5 hours. From the Shira Plateau you will get some magnificent views of Kibo Peak and the Western Breach. The area is home to a variety of game including buffalo. The Shira Hut sleeps about 8 people and is used by people on the Shira Plateau trail as well as those on the Machame trail. There is plenty of water available 50 m to the north and firewood nearby, but no toilets.

Day 3 onwards From here there are a number of choices. You can go on to the **Barranco Hut** (5-6 hours, 3,900 m) or the **Lava Tower Hut** (4 hours, 4,600 m). The path to **Arrow Glacier Hut** is well marked. The ascent includes scrambling over scree, rocks and snow fields – tough at times and probably only suited to experienced hikers. It goes east from Shira Hut until it reaches a junction where the North Circuit route leads off to the left. The path continues east, crossing a wide valley before turning southeast towards the Lava Tower. Shortly before the tower a route goes off to the right to Barranco Hut and the South Circuit route. To the left the path goes to Arrow Glacier Hut and the Western Breach.

Shira Plateau trail

This route needs a 4WD vehicle and so for this reason is little used. The road can be impassible during wet periods. However, if you do have access to such a vehicle and are acclimatized you can get to the **Arrow Glacier Hut** in one day.

The drive is a complex one and you may need to stop and ask the way frequently. Pass through West Kilimanjaro, drive for 5 km and turn right. At 13 km you will pass a small trading centre on the left. At 16 km you will cross a stream followed by a hard left. At 21 km you will enter a coniferous forest which soon becomes a natural forest. The plateau rim is reached at 39 km. Here the track continues upwards gently and crosses the plateau to the roadhead at 55 km. Just before the roadhead, about 19 km from **Londorossi Gate**, is a rock shelter. This site is suitable for camping and there is a stream nearby. From the roadhead you will have to walk. It is about 1½ hours to **Shira Hut** (3,800 m). From here you continue east to join the Umbwe trail to the **Lava Tower Hut**. The walk is fairly gentle and has magnificent views.

Mweka trail

This trail is the most direct route up the mountain. It is the steepest and the fastest. It begins at Mweka village, 13 km north of Moshi, where you can leave your vehicle at the College of Wildlife Management with permission.

Day 1 The first day's walk takes 6-8 hours. The trail follows an old logging road, which you can drive up in good weather, through the *shambas* and the forest, for about 5 km. It is a slippery track that deteriorates into a rough path after a couple of hours. From here it is about 6 km up a ridge to the **Mweka Huts** (3,100 m), which are some 500 m beyond the tree line in the giant heather zone. There are two unfurnished metal huts here that each sleep about 8 people. Water is available nearby from a stream in a small valley below the huts 5 minutes to the southeast and there is plenty of firewood. There are no toilets.

Day 2 From the Mweka Huts follow the ridge east of the Msoo River through heathland, open tussock grassland and then on through alpine desert to the **Barafu Huts** (4,400 m), a walk of 6-8 hours. These metal shelters sleep about 16 people. There are no toilets, and no water or firewood available – you will need to bring it up from Mweka Huts.

Day 3 From the Barafu Huts the final ascent on a ridge between **Rebmann** and **Ratzel** glaciers takes about 6 hours up to the rim of the crater between **Stella** and **Hans Meyer Points**. From here it is a further hour to **Uhuru Peak**. At the lower levels the path is clearly marked, but it becomes obscured further up. It is steep, being the most direct non-technical route. Although specialized climbing equipment is not needed, be prepared for a scramble. To catch the sunrise you will have to set off no later than

0200 from Barafu Huts. You return to the huts the same day, and (**Day 4**) make the final descent the next day.

Loitokitok trail

This approach from Kenya is closed to the public and is not recommended. However, you may be able to obtain special permission from the park's department to climb it. See the warden who is based in Marangu. You may have problems getting porters to go up this route. This, and the Shira Plateau trail, both come in from the north unlike the other trails.

From the Outward Bound School take the path towards the border road and on reaching it turn left down it. Cross the bridge over the Kikewela River and go a further 150 m. Here you will see a rough track leading through the plantations. Take this track, along which you will recross the Kikewela and continue up through the forest, and on to the heather and moorlands until you reach the caves. It is a total of approximately 5-6 hours to the caves.

From these caves follow the path that heads towards a point just to the right of the lowest point on the saddle. You will pass **Bread Rock** after about 1½ hours. The track then divides. To the right is the **Outward Bound Hut** that you will almost certainly find locked. The path continues upwards to the saddle towards the **Kibo Huts** – a climb of 3-4 hours. To the left another path crosses towards the **Mawenzi Hut**.

The Summit Circuit

A route around the base of Kibo, the Summit Circuit links Horombo, Barranco, Shira and Moir Huts. The southern section of the circuit is most spectacular, as it cuts across moorland, in and out of valleys and under the southern glaciers.

Arusha

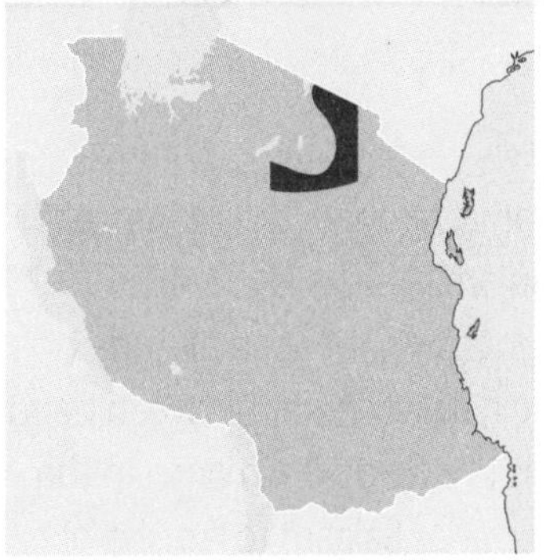

Footprint features

Introduction

In the northern highlands of Tanzania, beneath the twin peaks of Mount Meru and Mount Kilimanjaro, Arusha is the safari capital of the country. It is a pleasant town set at an altitude of 1,380 m above sea level, and is the halfway point between Cairo and Cape Town (the actual point is in a field 20 km or so to the south of town). The drive up from Dar es Salaam to Arusha passes through the semi-arid grass plains, gradually becoming greener, more cultivated and more heavily populated; Mount Meru, in the Arusha National Park appears on the right with its fertile, cultivated slopes. Built by the Germans as a centre of colonial administration in the early 20th century, Arusha was a sleepy town with a garrison stationed at the old boma and a few shops around a grassy roundabout. But from its backwater status amidst the farmlands and plantations of northern Tanzania, today Arusha been transformed into one of the busiest Tanzanian towns after Dar es Salaam. Its prominence has particularly increased in recent years since becoming the headquarters of the East African Community and being the host town for the Rwandan War Crimes Tribunals. The International Conference Centre here has witnessed the signing of some of the most important peace treaties and international agreements in modern African history. It is also the starting place for safaris in the north of Tanzania – the Serengeti, Ngorongoro, Lake Manyara, Tarangire, Olduvai Gorge and Arusha National Parks. It can be very busy with tourists, mostly either in transit to, or returning from, these attractions. The dusty streets are filled with four-wheel drive game-viewing vehicles negotiating the potholed roads and Masai warriors in full regalia mingling with tourists clad in crisp khaki. There are lots of good hotels and restaurants, and tourism has made Arusha a very prosperous town.

★ Don't miss...

1 **Masai** Meet the Masai at the Meserani Snake Park, where there are not only a number of snakes to get wrapped up in, but also a Masai Musuem, or take a camel out to the nearby Masai village, page 218.
2 **Arusha National Park** One of the few parks where you can walk. Explore the pretty lakes and hiking trails at the base of Mount Meru, page 221.
3 **Mount Meru** For a different view of Kilimanjaro, climb Mount Meru; from the top of each mountain you can see the other's peaks way above the clouds, page 224.
4 **Coffee plantation lodges** Stay in these lodges on the lower slopes of Mount Meru, page 227.
5 **Nightlife** Enjoy Arusha's cosmopolitan range of restaurants, bars and lively party spots, page 230.

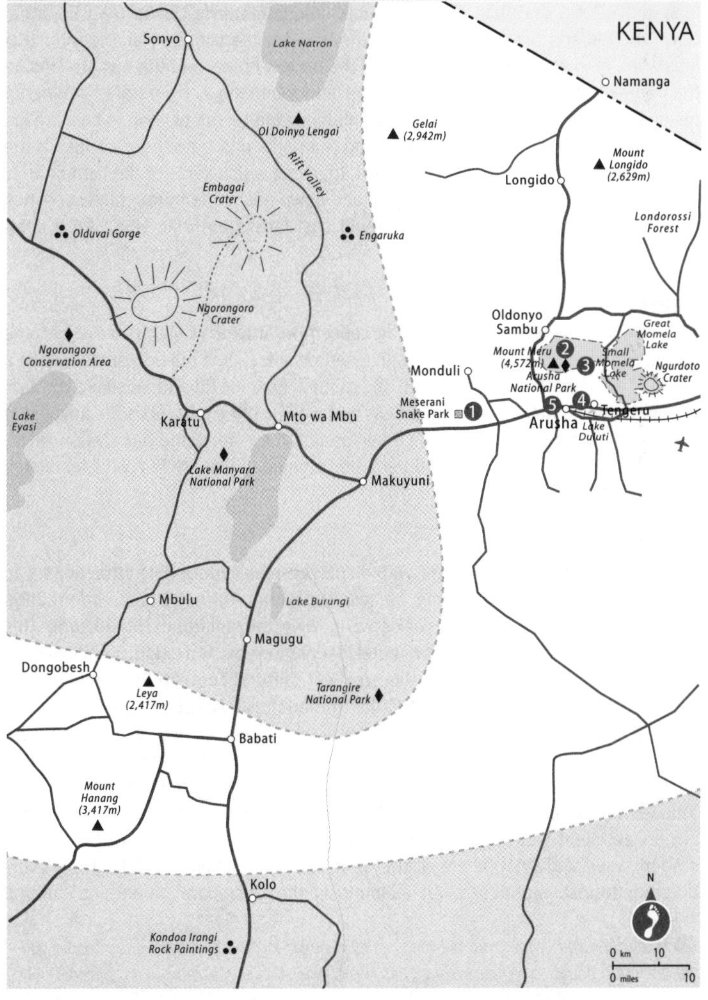

Ins and outs → *Phone code: 027. Colour map 1, grid A4. Population: 350,000.*

Altitude: 1,380 m
3°20'S 36°40'E

Getting there

Arusha is 50 km from Kilimanjaro International Airport, which is well served by international flights, 79 km from Moshi, and 650 km from Dar es Salaam. The road between Dar es Salaam and Arusha has recently been upgraded and is now smooth tar all the way. The journey by bus takes 8-9 hrs. It is also only 273 km south of Nairobi, with the Namanga border with Kenya being roughly halfway. The two cities are linked by regular shuttle buses and the journey takes around 4 hrs. ▸▸ *See also Transport, page 237, for further details.*

Getting around

The town is in two parts, separated by a small valley through which the Naura River runs. The upper part, to the east, contains the government buildings, post office, immigration, most of the top-range hotels, safari companies, airline offices, curio and craft shops, and the huge Arusha International Conference Center (AICC). Further down the hill and across the valley to the east are the commercial and industrial areas, the market, small shops, many of the budget hotels and the bus stations. In the middle of the centre is the Clocktower and roundabout. From here Sokoine Rd neatly bisects the town to the west and continues further out of town to become the main road that goes to both Dodoma and the parks of the northern circuit. To the southeast of the Clocktower is Old Moshi Rd, along which some of the better hotels are located. *Dala-dala* run frequently up and down the main throroughfares, costing US$0.20, taxis are everwhere and should cost little more than US$2 for a short journey around town.

Safety

Alas safety is becoming an increasing concern in Arusha. Muggings have become more common, and in 2004 there was a serious attack just outside Arusha when a group of 32 tourists were ambushed and robbed. Sokoine Rd and Moshi Rd towards Impala Hotel are unsafe at night, unless you are in a big group. Taxis are advised at night, and extra caution should be taken around the market and bus station where pickpockets (especially street children) are common. If you are in a vehicle, ensure that it is securely locked.

Tourist information

Information for tourists in Arusha, with displays on the surrounding attractions, can be obtained from the following places. **Tanzanian Tourist Board**, Information Centre, 47E Boma Rd, T027-2503840-2/3, www.tanzaniatouristboard.com. This office does not arrange bookings or hotel reservations but is a useful source of local information, including details of the excellent **Cultural Tourism Programmes** that were set up in conjunction with **SNV**, the Netherlands Development Agency. In the office are all the leaflets outlining these tours, which directly involve and benefit the local people. It is best to make reservations and arrangements here before going out to the individual locations. To date this initative has involved 32 villages around Arusha, Kilimanjaro, Iringa, Pangani, Mbeya and other regions. These programmes are an excellent way to experience traditional customs, music and dance, and modern ways of life in rural areas. They tend to be off the beaten track, giving a very different tourist experience. An example is the Usambara Mountains Cultural

Many of Arusha's wide roads are lined with flame trees, jacaranda and bougainvillaea. If you are lucky enough to be here in spring or summer when they are in bloom, it is a splendid sight.

Tourism Programme or the Northern Pare mountains walking tours (see page 190). The tours offered by each programme have been described by one traveller as relatively expensive but worth the cost. More information can be found at **www.infojep.com/culturaltours**, from which you can download each of the programme's brochures. See Excursions from Arusha below for the ones in the immediate region. The TTB office also holds a list of registered tour companies as well as a 'blacklist' of rogue travel agencies (see page 237). The office is open Mon-Fri, 0800-1600, Sat 0830-1330, Sun, closed. **Ngorongoro Information Office**, Boma Rd, T027-2544625, is a couple of doors along from the tourist information office. There's not much to pick up here in the way of leaflets, but it does sell some books and maps of the national parks and there is an interesting painting on the wall that shows all the parks in the northern circuit, which gives a good idea where they all are in relation to each other. There is also a model showing the topography of the Ngorongoro Crater. **Tanzania National Parks (TANAPA) head office**, Dodoma Rd, T027-2503471, tanapa@habari.co.tz, www.tanzaniaparks.com stocks booklets on the national parks at much more competitive prices than elsewhere, and is a useful resource if you require specialist information. It also provides information about the accommodation options in the more remote national parks. There are also a couple of **notice boards** with feedback bulletins from travellers at **Dolly's Patisserie** on Sokoine Rd (see page 230) and the **Jambo Makuti Garden** on Boma Rd. There is a superb colour map of Arusha and the road to Moshi by Giovanni Tombazzi, which can be obtained from bookshops (see page 231) or **Hoopoe Safaris** on India St (see page 234).

Sights

Centre

The centre of town is the **Clocktower**, which was donated in 1945 by a Greek resident, Christos Galanos, to commemorate the Allied victory in the Second World War. The German Boma now houses the **National Natural History Museum**, opened in 1987 ⓘ *at the north end of Boma Rd, www.habari.co.tz/museum. Open daily 0900-1700. Entry US$2.* The building was constructed by the Germans in 1886 and it has an outer wall, with block towers at each corner. Inside the fortifications are a central administrative building, a captain's mess, a soldiers' mess, a guard house and a large armoury. A laboratory has been established for paleoanthropological research (the study of man's evolution through the record of fossils).

The museum contains the celebrated **Laetoli Footprints**, dating back 3,500,000 years, set in solidified volcanic grey ash. Three hominids walking on two legs have left their tracks. The discovery was made at Laetoli, about 30 km southwest of Olduvai Gorge, by Andrew Hill, who was visiting Mary Leakey's fossil camp in 1978. Another display of interest is the tracing of the evolution of man based on the findings at Olduvai Gorge (see page 257).

North of the museum, the huge **Arusha International Conference Centre (AICC)**, www.aicc.co.tz, is made up of three main blocks – the Kilimanjaro, Ngorongoro and Serengeti wings. It has been an important centre for international deliberations, with recent events such as the Rwandan War Crimes Tribunal and the Burundi peace negotiations taking place here. The centre also has within it a bank, post office, foreign exchange bureau and cafeteria as well as various tour operators and travel agents.

On the east side of Simeon Road, just north of the AICC complex, is **State House**, a small but handsome building with double gables and a green tin roof. This was the residence of the provincial commissioner in the colonial period. Nowadays the president stays here when he is in Arusha. There is no sign announcing that it is State House – and it is best not to take photographs.

Old Moshi Road

In the colonial period Europeans settled in the area adjacent to the River Themi, along Old Moshi Road, and to the north and south of it. The Asian community lived near their commercial premises, often over them, in the area between Boma Road and Goliondoi Road. Africans lived further to the west on the far side of the Naura River. On the north side of the Old Moshi Road is **Christ Church Anglican Cathedral**, built in the 1930s in traditional English style of grey stone with a tiled roof and a pleasant interior. The

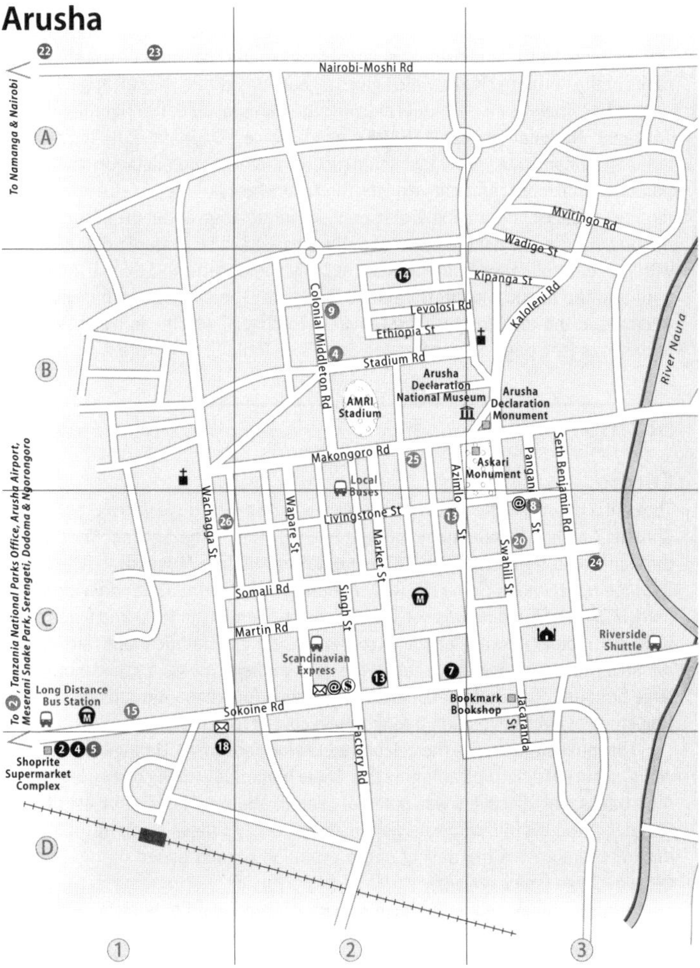

Arusha

Sleeping
Arusha by Night Annexe **4** *B2*
Arusha Coffee Lodge **2** *C1*
Arusha Crown **25** *B2*
Arusha Naaz **18** *C4*
Arusha View Campsite **28** *B5*
Fort des Moines **8** *C3*
Golden Rose **9** *B2*
Herbs & Spices & Ethiopian Restaurant **10** *D6*
Ilboru Safari Lodge **7** *A6*
Impala **11** *D6*
Karama Lodge **5** *D6*
Kilimanjaro Villa **13** *C2*
Klub Afriko **16** *A6*
Le Jacaranda **12** *D6*
L'Oasis Lodge **14** *A6*
Masai Camp **3** *D6*
Meru House Inn **15** *C1*
New Arusha **19** *C4*
New Safari **21** *C4*
Outpost **23** *D5*
Palm Court **26** *C1*
Sinka Court **20** *C3*

cathedral is surrounded by a vicarage and church offices. Further along the road there are several bungalows with red tile roofs and substantial gardens. These housed government servants. One building in particular, the **Hellenic Club** (or Greek Club), stands out with its classical porticos, on the corner of Old Moshi Road and Njiro Road.

Makongoro Road

The **Arusha Declaration Monument** is set on a roundabout past the police station on the Makongoro Road. Also commonly referred to as the Uhuru (Freedom) Monument,

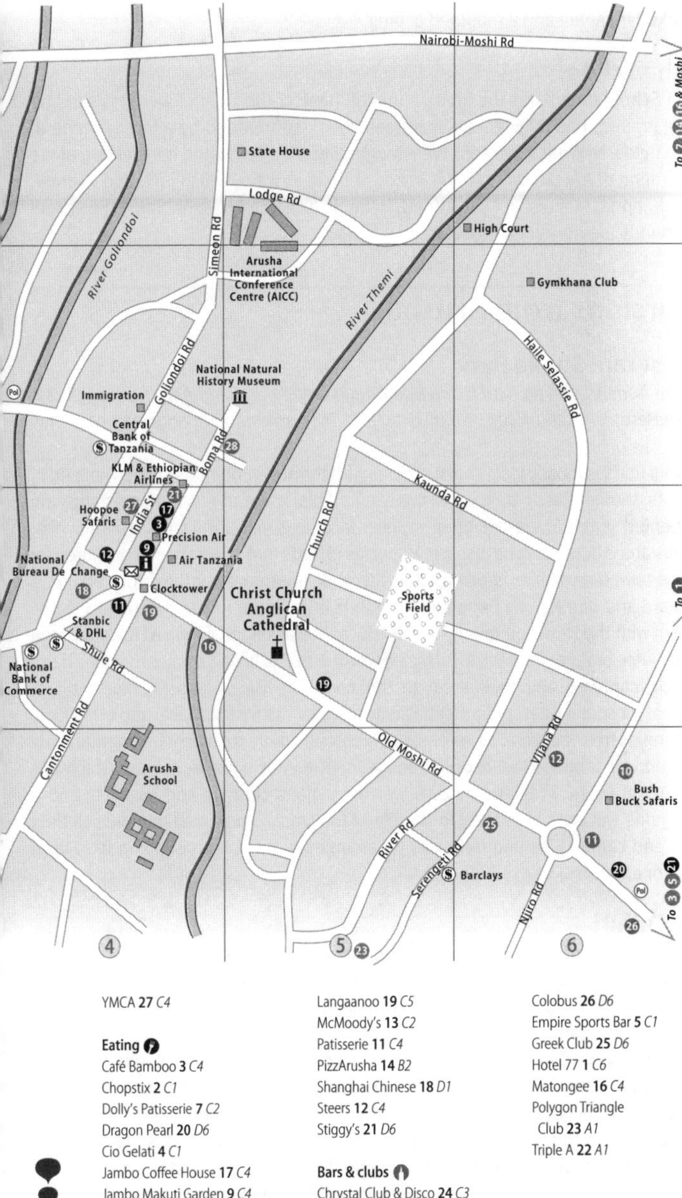

YMCA **27** *C4*

Eating

Café Bamboo **3** *C4*
Chopstix **2** *C1*
Dolly's Patisserie **7** *C2*
Dragon Pearl **20** *D6*
Cio Gelati **4** *C1*
Jambo Coffee House **17** *C4*
Jambo Makuti Garden **9** *C4*
Langaanoo **19** *C5*
McMoody's **13** *C2*
Patisserie **11** *C4*
PizzArusha **14** *B2*
Shanghai Chinese **18** *D1*
Steers **12** *C4*
Stiggy's **21** *D6*

Bars & clubs

Chrystal Club & Disco **24** *C3*
Colobus **26** *D6*
Empire Sports Bar **5** *C1*
Greek Club **25** *D6*
Hotel 77 **1** *C6*
Matongee **16** *C4*
Polygon Triangle Club **23** *A1*
Triple A **22** *A1*

it has four concrete legs that support a brass torch at the top of a 10-m column. Around the base are seven uplifting scenes in plaster. The Declaration of 1967 outlined a socialist economic and political strategy for Tanzania. The nearby **Arusha Declaration National Museum** is dedicated to this landmark in Tanzania's history, outlining the evolution of Tanzania's political and economic development. It also has historic photographs of the German period and a display of traditional weapons including clubs, spears and swords. South of the museum is a small park containing the **Askari Monument**, dedicated to African soldiers who died in the Second World War. On the east side of Azimio Street is an interesting **Temple** with a portico, fretworked masonry and a moulded coping.

Arusha School

Arusha School dominates the area on the left bank of the Themi River. It is sited on sloping ground, has huge eucalyptus trees and is surrounded by a large swathe of playing fields. Nyerere's two sons were taught there. It also hosted the meeting of the Organization of African Unity (OAU) Heads of State in 1966, which included Nyerere, Obote, Kaunda, Moi (as vice president), Haile Selassie and Nasser. Sadly the school and grounds are now very neglected.

Excursions from Arusha

★ Meserani Snake Park

ⓘ 25 km from Arusha on road to the Ngarongoo Crater and Serengeti, T027-2538282, www.meseranisnakepark.com. Small entry fee. *See also camping, page 227.*

Meserani houses mostly local snake species with the non-venomous snakes housed in open pits, though the spitting cobras, green and black mambas and boomslangs are kept behind glass. There are other reptiles including monitor lizards, chameleons, tortoises and crocodiles, and also a few species of birds that are orphaned or injured for whom a temporary home is provided at the park. There are gardens, a campsite, a restaurant and bar. Run by Barry and Lynn Bale from South Africa, this project works very well with the local community and the local Masai village. Some of the snakes in the park were brought in by the local Masai who instead of killing snakes that may harm livestock, captured and took them to the park. The Bales also provide antidote treatment for snake-bites and other basic health services for the Masai and other local communities free of charge, as well as providing antivenom for most of Tanzania. Barry has recently established an excellent museum of the local Masai culture, which has mock-ups of Masai huts and models wearing various clothing and jewellery and a Masai guide will explain the day-to-day life of the Masai. Local craftspeople sell their goods, and camel rides and treks can be arranged to meet the people in the Masai village for about US$10.

Lake Duluti

Just south of *Mountain Village Hotel*, about 15 km from Arusha along the Moshi road, this small crater lake, fringed by forest, provides a sanctuary for approximately 130 species of birds, including pied and pygmy kingfishers, anhinga, osprey, and several species of buzzards, eagles, sandpipers, doves, herons, cormorants, storks, kingfishers and barbets. Reptiles including snakes and lizards are plentiful too. The pathway around the lake starts off broad and level, but later on it narrows and becomes more difficult to negotiate. There are wonderful views of Mount Meru and occasionally the cloud breaks to reveal Mount Kilimanjaro. 'Ethno-botanical' walks are available, starting from the hotel through the coffee plantation and circumnavigating the lake. The walks are accompanied by guides who are knowledgeable about the flora and birds.

Cultural tourism programmes

Several villages on the lower slopes of Mount Meru, north of Arusha, have started cultural tourism programmes with help from the Dutch development organization, SNV, and the Tanzanian Tourist Board. Profits from each are used to improve the local primary schools. Further details of the programmes described below can be obtained from the Tanzanian tourist information centre in Arusha.

Ng'iresi village ⓘ *7 km from Arusha north of the Moshi Rd, transportation by pick-up truck can be arranged at the Arusha tourist centre.* Offers half-day guided tours of farms and local development projects such as irrigation, soil terracing, cross breeding, bio gas and fish nurseries. Longer tours can involve camping at a farm and a climb of **Kivesi**, a small volcano with forests where baboons and gazelle live. The Wa-arusha women will prepare traditional meals or a limited choice of western food. Profits go towards enlarging the local school.

Ilkiding'a village ⓘ *7 km north of Arusha along the road signposted to Ilboru Safari Lodge from Moshi road.* You will be welcomed in a traditional boma, be able to visit craftsmen and a traditional healer, and walk through farms to one of several viewpoints or into **Njeche** canyon. The guides of both this and the Ng'iresi programme are knowledgeable and have a reasonable standard of English.

Mulala village ⓘ *Set at 1,450 m above sea level on the slopes of Mount Meru about 30 km from Arusha, the turnoff is just before Usa River, follow signs for the Dik Dik Hotel, after the hotel the road climbs for about 10 km.* This programme is organized by the Agape women's group. There are walks through the coffee and banana farms to Marisha River, or to the top of Lemeka hill for views of Mounts Meru and Kilimanjaro, and on to the home of the village's traditional healer. You can visit farms where cheese- and bread-making and flower-growing activities have been initiated. The women speak only a little English but interpreters can be arranged.

Mkuru camel safari ⓘ *North side of Mount Meru, the camp is 5 km from Ngarenanyuki village, which is 5 km beyond the Momela gate of Arusha NP.* The Masai of this area began keeping camels in the early 1990s and there are now over 100 animals. Camel safaris of half a day or up to one week, towards Kilimanjaro, further to Mount Longido, or even further to Lake Natron can be arranged. Alternatively there are walks through the acacia woodland looking for birds, or up the pyramid-shaped peak of Ol Doinyo Landaree. In the camel camp itself, it is possible to see the Masai carry the new-born camels to their overnight shelters and watch them milk the camels. The guides are local Masai who have limited knowledge of English, communicating largely by hand signals – another guide to act as translator can be arranged with advance notice. There are three cottages at the camel camp, meals can be prepared if notice is given. Profits are used to support the village kindergarten, which was established because the nearest schools are too far for young children to walk to.

Mount Longido → *Colour map 1, grid A4. Altitude: 2,629 m.*

ⓘ *100 km north of Arusha on the road to Namanga on the border with Kenya. The town of Longido lies on the main road, at the foot of the mountain. To get here by public transport from Arusha take one of the shuttle buses or dala-dala that go to Namanga or on to Nairobi; the journey to Longido should take about 1½ hours. The tours are co-ordinated locally by Mzee Mollel, a local Masai who studied in Zambia and Australia. Mzee is happy to answer any enquiries about the Masai way of life.*

Mount Longido rises up steeply from the plains 100 km north of Arusha on the border with Kenya and forms an important point of orientation over a wide area. To climb Mount Longido is an excellent preparation for Mount Meru or Mount Kilimanjaro. The **Longido Cultural Tourism programme**, is an excellent way of supporting the local Masai people and learning about their lifestyle and culture. There are several walking tours of the environs, including a half-day 'bird walk' from the town of Longido across the Masai plains to the bomas of Ol Tepesi, the Masai word for acacia tree. On your return to Longido you can enjoy a meal cooked by the FARAJA women's group. The one-day walking tour extends from Ol Tepesi to Kimokonwa along a narrow Masai cattle trail that winds over the slopes of Mount Longido. On clear days there are views of Kilimanjaro and Mount Meru and from the north side there are extensive views of the plains into Kenya. The tour includes a visit to a historic German grave. There is also a more strenuous two-day tour climbing to the top of the steep Longido peak, following buffalo trails guarded by Masai warriors armed with knives and spears to protect you. Accommodation is in local guest houses or at campsites. Part of the money generated by this cultural tourism project goes to the upkeep of the cattle dip in Longido. The Masai lose about 1,500 head of cattle per annum, mainly because of tick-borne disease. Since Masai life is centred around their livestock this creates serious problems as reduced herd size means less work, income and food. Regular cattle dipping eradicates tick-borne diseases.

Babati and Mount Hanang → *Colour map 1, grid A4.*

ⓘ *Kahembe's Trekking and Cultural Safaris, T027-2531088, 0748-397477 (mob), is a local company whose owner, the enterprising Joas Kahembe, has been the pioneer for tourism in this otherwise rarely visited but rewarding area. There are regular bus services from Arusha to Babati (172 km) starting from 0730. Once there ask for Kahembe's Guest House, a 5-min walk from the main bus stand.*

Mount Hanang is the ninth-highest peak in East Africa, and the fourth highest in Tanzania, with an altitude of 3,417 m, and a challenge for more adventurous trekkers. It lies to the southwest of Babati, a small town approximately 170 km southwest of Arusha on the road to Dodoma. Here ethnic commercial and farming groups co-exist with conservative cattle herders and provide a distinguished cultural contrast. Amongst these people the Barbaig's traditional culture is still unchanged and unspoiled. The women wear traditional goatskin dresses and the men walk around with spears. English-speaking guides who know the area will help you around, and a Barbaig-born guide will tell you about Barbaig culture. **Kahembe's Trekking and Cultural Safaris** offers a gentle four-day trek up Mount Hanang using the easy Gendabi route for US$160 per person or a two-day trek along the steeper Katesh route for US$80 per person. The Katesh route can be completed in one day with the ascent and descent taking up to 12 hrs in total. They also have a number of imaginative local tours at US$40 per person per day (US$30 each for three or more people). These include 3-5-day walking safaris that explore the still largely intact traditional culture of the semi-nomadic pastoralist Barbaig people, and other longer cultural safaris, which have visits to and stays with several different local ethnic groups. There is the chance to participate in local brick- and pottery-making and beer brewing, and visit development projects like cattle, dairy farming, or piped water projects. Independent exploration of the area is possible but not common. Joas Kahembe arranges full board accommodation in local guest houses and in selected family homes.

★ Arusha National Park → *Colour map 1, A4. 4°0'S 36°30'E.*

The compact Arusha National Park is remarkable for its range of habitats. It encompasses three varied zones: the highland montane forest of Mount Meru to the west, where black and white colobus and blue monkeys can be spotted; Ngurdoto Crater, a small volcanic crater inhabited by a variety of mammals in the southeast of the park; and, to the northeast, Momela Lakes, a series of seven alkaline crater lakes, home to a large number of water birds. On a clear day it is possible to see the summits of both Mount Kilimanjaro and Mount Meru from Ngurdoto Crater rim. There are numerous hides and picnic sites throughout the park, giving travellers an opportunity to leave their vehicles and this is one of the few of the country's parks where walking is permitted. Climbing Mount Meru or enjoying the smaller trails that criss-cross its lower slopes is a popular activity for visitors to the park. The three-day trek to reach the crater's summit is a quieter, and some say more challenging, alternative to the famous peak of nearby Mount Kilimanjaro. Along the lower slopes, paths through ancient fig tree forests, and crystal clear cascading rivers and waterfalls make a relaxing day's hike for visitors who don't want to attempt the longer and more arduous climb. ▸▸ *For more information on national parks and safaris, see page 39.*

Ins and outs

Getting there Arusha NP is about 25 km east of Arusha and 58 km from Moshi. The road is a good one and the turning off the main road between Arusha and Moshi, about 35 km from Kilimanjaro International Airport, is at Usa River and is clearly signposted. From the airport the landscape changes from the flat dry and dusty Sanya Plain, gradually becoming greener, more fertile and more cultivated. Take the turning (on the right if you are heading towards Arusha) and follow the gravel road for about 10 km until you reach the **Ngurdoto Gate**. This is coffee country and you will see the farms on each side of the road. On reaching the park entrance this changes to dense forest.

The best time to visit is Oct-Feb. There are several excellent lodges around Usa River and on the lower slopes of Meru.
Entry to park: US$35

There's a second gate, **Momela Gate**, from which you access Mount Meru, to the north of the park. There are two routes leading to Momela Gate, starting near the village of Usa River, close by the Arusha/Moshi road. From here it is 8 km to Ngurdoto Gate. A single road enters the park, dividing near Serengeti Ndogo. The road to the northwest is known as the Outer Road (25 km) and NP fees are not payable if in transit. The only available transport are pick-up trucks, which take a few passengers and go the village of Ngare Nanyuki, beyond the Momela Gate. It is permissible to walk this route too. The right fork takes you to the road that runs northeast towards Ngurdoto Crater, before turning north (18 km) beside the Momela Crater Lakes, and this route attracts the NP fee. These roads through the park meet up again at the Momela Gate. If you do not have your own vehicle many of the safari companies offer day trips to Arusha NP.

Tourist information

At the main entrance a small museum provides information for the visitor on the bird, animal and plant life of the park. Park accommodation can be booked in advance through **Tanzania National Parks (TANAPA)** head office, Dodoma Rd, Arusha, T027-2503471, www.tanzaniaparks.com.

The vehicle used by John Wayne in the film Hatari was at one time on view in Arusha National Park. It had a metal seat over the inside front mudguard from which the 'Duke' lassoed rhino in Ngorongoro.

Background

The Arusha National Park, which contains within its boundaries Mount Meru, was established in 1960. The film *Hatari* was made here in 1962 by Howard Hawks, starring John Wayne, Elsa Martinelli, Red Buttons and Hardy Kruger. The park has actually changed its name a number of times from *Ngurdoto Crater National Park* to *Mount Meru National Park* and finally to *Arusha National Park*. It covers an area of 137 sq km and rises from 1,524 m at the Momela Lakes (also spelt Momella) to 4,565 m at the peak of Mount Meru. Although it is only small, because of this gradation there is a variety of landscapes, a variety of ecosystems and therefore a wide variety of flora and fauna. Within the park are the Ngurdoto Crater and the Momela Lakes.

Mount Meru is believed to have been formed at around the time of the great earth movements that created the Rift Valley, about 20 million years ago. The crater was formed about 250,000 years ago when a massive explosion blew away the eastern side of the volcano. A subsidiary vent produced the volcano of Ngurdoto, which built up over thousands of years. In a way similar to Ngorongoro, when the cone collapsed the caldera was left as it is today. Ngurdoto is now extinct, while Meru is only dormant, having last erupted about 100 years ago. The lava flow from this eruption can be seen on the northwest side of the mountain. It was at around this time in 1872 that the first European, Count Teleki, a Hungarian, saw the mountain.

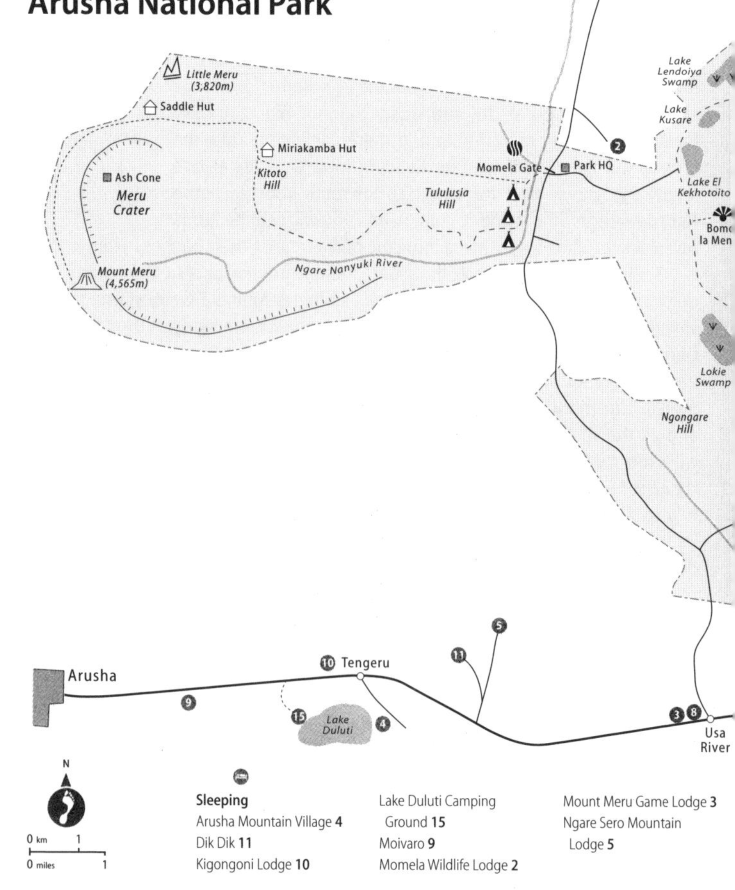

Arusha National Park contains many animals including giraffe, elephant, hippo, buffalo, rhino (if you're lucky), colobus monkey, bush buck, red forest duiker, reed buck, waterbuck and warthog and reportedly the highest density of giraffes in the world. There are no lions but you may see leopard. Birds include cormorants, pelicans, ibis, flamingos and grebes.

Ngurdoto Crater

Within the park there are over 50 km of tracks but no roads have been built into the Ngurdoto Crater in order to protect and preserve it. From the Ngurdoto Gate a road leads off towards the Ngurdoto Crater. This area is known as the 'connoisseur's park' – rightly so. The road climbs up through the forest until it reaches the rim. At the top you can go left or right, either going around the crater clockwise or anti-clockwise. The track does not go all the way round the rim of the crater so you will have to turn round and retrace your tracks back to the main road. You will be able to look down on to the animals in the crater below but will not be able to drive down. The crater is about 3 km in diameter and there are a number of viewing points around the rim from which you can view the crater floor, known as the 'park within the park'. These include Leitong Point (the highest at 1,850 m), Glades Point, Rock Point, Leopard Hill, Rhino Crest and Mikindani Point. From this latter point you will be able to see Mount Kilimanjaro in the distance.

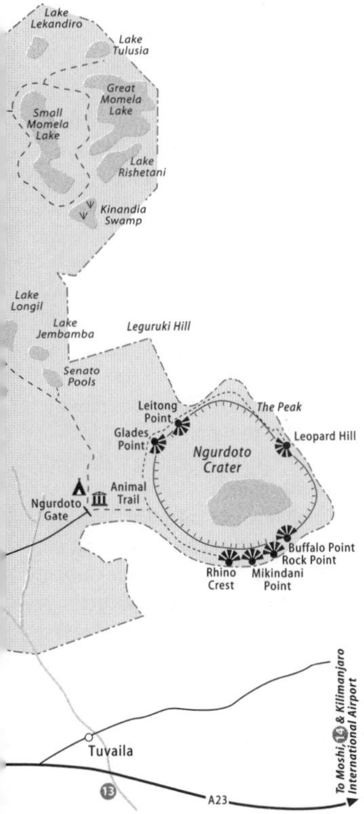

Momela Lakes route

From Ngurdoto Gate, if you take the left track you will reach the Momela Lakes. This track goes past the Ngongongare Springs, Lokie Swamp, the Senato Pools and the two lakes, Jembamba and Longil. At the peak of the dry season they may dry up but otherwise they are a good place to watch the animals and in particular the birdlife. At various spots there are observation hides. At **Lake Longil** there is a camping and picnic site in a lovely setting.

From here the track continues through the forest, which gradually thins out and through the more open vegetation you will be able to see Mount Meru. The Hyena Camp (Kambi ya Fisi) is reached at the point where you will probably see a pack of spotted hyenas. Beyond this there is a small track leading off the main track to **Bomo la Mengi** – a lovely place from which to view the lakes. Unless the cloud is down you will also be able to see Kilimanjaro from here. The main track continues past two more lakes – Lake El Kekhotoito and Lake Kusare – before reaching the Momela Lakes.

The **Momela Lakes** are shallow alkaline lakes fed by underground streams. Because they have different mineral contents and different algae their colours are also different. They contain few fish but the algae attracts

Ngurdoto Mountain Lodge **14**
Rivertrees Country Inn **13**
Tanzanite **8**

Climbing Mount Meru

The walk up Mount Meru involves a 3,500-m altitude hike, frequently climbed up and down within three days. The last section of the walk to the summit is very steep. It is easy to underestimate what are common problems associated with this walk – altitude sickness and frostbite. Snow is not unknown at the summit. On the ascent you will pass through the changing vegetation. The first change is to lower montane forest at about 2,000 m, then to higher montane forest. The road climbs up the mountain up to the heath zone at about 2,439 m from where you can climb to the peak. From the road and the park headquarters a track leads up to the **Miriakamba Hut**, which takes about three hours. The trail continues as a steady climb through montane forest, where there is an abundance of birds and black and white colobus monkeys. The first mountain hut sleeps about 48 people, while the second, **Saddle Hut**, sleeps about 24. Both huts provide firewood. It is a three-hour walk between the two huts but is a steep climb and having reached Saddle Hut you can spend the afternoon climbing **Little Meru** (3,820 m), which takes about 1½ hours. From Saddle Hut the climb up to the rim of the mountain and around to the **summit** usually starts at 0200 in order to to see the sunrise from the top. It's a steep climb to Rhino Point (3,800 m), before continuing along an undulating ridge of ash and rock to reach Cobra Point (4,350 m). The final ascent from Saddle Hut is difficult, cold and can be dangerous, but the views of the cliffs and crater rim are stunning: you can see the ash cone rising from the crater floor and Kilimanjaro floating on the morning clouds. Most of the tour operators in Arusha, and some in Moshi, can arrange climbs. Like the Kilimanjaro climb there are a number of park fees to climb the mountain that are paid to the Tanzania National Parks. Though these are not quite as expensive as for Kili, nevertheless expect to pay in the region of US$300-50 for a package including park fees, guide, porters, food and accommodation in the mountain huts.

lots of birdlife. What you see will vary with the time of year. Flamingos tend to move in huge flocks around the lakes of East Africa and are a fairly common sight at Momela Lakes. Between October and April the lakes are also home to the migrating waterfowl, which are spending the European winter in these warmer climes.

The track goes around the lakes reaching the **Small Momela Lake** first. This lake often has a group of hippos wallowing in it. Follow the road anti-clockwise and you will pass **Lake Rishetani**, which is a fantastic emerald green colour. Along this route you will be able to stop off at the various observation sites. The next lake that you will get to is the **Great Momela Lake**, which has a huge variety of birdlife and is a lovely spot. The last two lakes are **Tulusia** and **Lekandiro** where you may see animals grazing.

★ Mount Meru → *Colour map 1, grid A4.*

The other major attraction of Arusha National Park is Mount Meru (4,565 m), the second highest mountain in Tanzania and also the fifth highest in all Africa. The mountain lies to the west of the Ngare Nanyuki road in the western half of the park. There is a road that leads up the mountain to about 2,439 m from the **Momela Gate**, passing through an open space called **Kitoto** from where there are good views of the mountain, but vehicles are no longer allowed to pass this way.

Sleeping

The best hotels in the Arusha area are out of town in the foothills of Mt Meru. They have fine gardens, good standards and charming atmosphere. They are recommended above similar priced hotels in Arusha or its outskirts. If you do not have your own transport most will offer transfers from town and many are used as part of a safari package. At the budget end of the market there are a number of cheap hotels around the stadium and market, that cost as little as US$10 and are good value. If using a hotel's 'safe', you are advised to check your money when deposited and on collection. There are reports of false receipts being issued and less money being returned on collection.

Arusha *p214, map p216*

L Arusha Coffee Lodge, a few km from town on the road to the crater on a working coffee estate, T027-2500630-9, www.arushacoffeelodge.com, www.elewana.com. One of the most luxurious options in Arusha, with 18 stunning spacious chalets with balconies, fireplaces, facilities to make coffee, enormous beds with mosquito nets, hardwood floors and wooden decks, Zanzibar-style furniture and Persian rugs. Very elegant lounge and restaurant for fine dining (see Eating) with dressed up tables and leather sofas, swimming pool.

A Karama Lodge, 3 km from town off the Old Moshi Rd, turn off just past Masai Camp, T027-2500359, www.karama-lodge.com. Here are 12 delightful thatched stilted log cabins built on the hillside in a pretty tract of forest. Close enough to town but a very peaceful location with good views of Meru and Kilimanjaro. Beds have mosquito nets and there are hanging chairs on the balcony. Rustic bar on a deck and the restaurant uses ingredients from the garden.

B Arusha Crown Hotel, Makongoro Rd, T027-2544161, www.arushacrownhotel.com. A newly constructed modern hotel and very centrally located. 38 rooms on 6 floors, stylish decor throughout (though very much a business travellers' hotel with 24 single rooms), internet access, CCTV security cameras. Very good restaurant open to non-residents (see Eating). Won an award in 2005 for international quality. A single is US$60, a twin US$65 and a double US$70, excellent value in this price range. The rooms facing north overlook Meru and directly into the stadium – if there's a match on you can watch the football from bed!

B Impala, 500 m down Old Moshi Rd from the Clocktower, T027-2502962, www.impalahotel.com. 160 rooms in an ultra modern block with TV and phone, pleasant garden and patio, swimming pool, rates include breakfast, several good restaurants including an excellent Indian one and coffee shops, 24-hr room service, gift shop, bureau de change, arranges tours and safaris through *Classic Tours*, www.classictours.com. Run their own shuttle bus to and from Kilimanjaro airport and Nairobi.

B Ilboru Safari Lodge, 2 km west from town towards Mt Meru off the Nairobi Rd, T027-2577834, www.habari.co.tz/ilborulodge. Beautiful gardens that attract a lot of birds, very friendly, 20 large rooms in thatched rondavaals, Masai blankets on the beds, both international and local food in the restaurant (eating is a very social affair), tour desk for booking local acitivities.

B New Arusha, near the Clocktower, T027-2548541/3, www.newarushahotels.com. Formerly the site of the old German hotel built in 1903, of which the splendid restaurant is the only surviving feature. Completely refurbished in 2003, 65 elegantly decorated rooms, with a/c, phone and internet access. Behind the hotel is a beautiful garden running down to the Themi River. Facilities include a swimming pool, gym, snack bar, restaurant serving international food, Italian and Indian dishes and the bar downstairs leads to the garden. Also a good bookshop, gift/craft shop and a foreign exchange bureau.

B New Safari, Boma Rd, T027-2503261, www.newsafarihotel.co.tz. This used to be

For an explanation of the sleeping and eating price codes used in this guide, see inside the front cover. Other relevant information is found in Essentials pages 31-34.

down the road, but has moved into the newly built New Safari complex which not only houses the hotel but a number of offices and businesses such as internet cafes and bureaux de change. Very smart modern building, restaurant, bar, nice terrace café on the first floor with good views of Meru, conference facilities, 48 rooms with TV, internet connection for laptops, and minibar.

B-C **Outpost**, Serengeti Rd, off the Old Moshi Rd, near *Impala Hotel*, T027-2548405, www.outposttanzania.com. Run by a Zimbabwe couple, Kathy and Steve Atwell, who are wonderful hosts, staff superb, very welcoming, popular with expats. Accommodation either in spacious rooms in the main house or in bandas, the family unit can sleep 6, full English breakfast included. Manicures, pedicures and massages also on offer. Highly recommended, winners of a local competition for Best Guest House in Arusha.

B-D **L'Oasis Lodge**, 2 km out of town, in the quiet residential area of Sekei, signposted from the Novetel Hotel, T027-2507089, www.loasislodge.com. 22 rooms have en suite facilities, and there are 13 smaller twin budget rooms with shared bathrooms. A double room starts from US$65, while the budget rooms go for US$15. Good food, extensive menu including Thai, Indonesian, Greek, seafood and vegetarian dishes, breakfast included in the price, full and half-board rates also available, rates are significantly lower Apr-Jun. Pool with fish and wading birds, a charming dining area, bar, internet services. Highly recommended.

C **Klub Afriko Hotel and Safaris**, 3 km from town on the Moshi Rd, T027-2548878, www.klubafriko.com. Set in tropical gardens in a quiet neighbourhood just outside of Arusha town. 7 airy bungalows, with en suite bathrooms, decorated with local artwork. Excellent food and friendly bar with satellite TV. Breakfast set lunch and dinner costs US$7.

C **Arusha Naaz Hotel**, near Clocktower on Sokoine Rd, T027-2502087, www.arusha naaz.com. Once you get through the bizarre shopping centre entrance and head up the small staircase, the 21 rooms are centred around a little internal courtyard. Clean, newly decorated with modern furniture, en suite bathrooms, 24 hr hot water, fans and mosquito nets, restaurant with good food (closed in evening), internet access. Single/double/triple rooms are US$25/35/45. You can also hire cars from here.

C **Golden Rose**, Colonel Middleton Rd, Arusha, T027-2507959, www.goldenrose hoteltz.com. Comfortable, good value, self-contained rooms with hot water, telephones, balconies. Bar and restaurant, internet café and bureau de change. Price (doubles from US$48) includes English breakfast, they accept Visa and Mastercard though charge 10% more. Reported to have rather noisy generator at back. Can arrange car hire.

C **Le Jacaranda**, Vijana Rd, T027-2544624, www.chez.com/jacaranda. A nice house in a quiet garden suburb with 7 simple rooms with large bathrooms and hot water. A double goes for US$45, breakfast included. The hotel is best known for its restaurant and bar (see Eating).

C **Sinka Court**, near the market, T027-2504961, sinkacourthotel@hotmail.com. New hotel in a very modern block, 29 rooms with built-for-hotel furniture and excellent bathrooms, a/c, cable TV, mosquito nets, the larger rooms have fridges and floor to ceiling windows, though the view is not up to much as the hotel overlooks an ugly block of flats. Underground parking, restaurant and bar.

D **Arusha by Night Annexe**, on corner of Colonel Middleton Rd and Stadium Rd, T0741-654538. Very basic rooms with bathrooms and hot water, though the plumbing is leaky, and mosquito nets. Small restaurant and courtyard bar, where friendly ladies cook up Tanzania staples plus a stab at something international such as spag bol.

D **Herbs & Spices**, a few metres north of the *Impala Hotel* off Old Moshi Rd, T027-2542279, axum_spices@hotmail.com. Well appointed, with a garden and veranda in front leading to the restaurant which specializes in Ethiopian cuisine (see Eating). The 19 rooms are set around a courtyard to the rear, small but comfortable with hot showers, some are adjoining for families. In the middle of the courtyard are some chairs and a satellite TV.

D **Hotel Fort des Moines**, Livingstone St, T027-2500277, www.bimel.co.tz. Modern, a little gloomy, well maintained, fairly good restaurant with some Indian dishes, 23 s/c rooms, garish bedspreads and curtains, hot water, price includes continental breakfast.

D **YMCA**, India St, T027-2544032. Very central, the 10 rooms have new bedding, sinks in the corner and mosquito nets, clean, hot water mornings and evenings in the shared bathrooms, cheap restaurant downstairs for basic stews and soups and cold beers and soft drinks.

D-E Meru House Inn, western end of Sokoine Rd just past Wachagga St, T027-2507803, www.victoriatz.com/office.htm. Clean, friendly staff, hot water, nets, 52 rooms. Own generator. Rates are a very reasonable US$9 for a double with shared bathroom, and US$14 with an en suite. The attached restaurant and juice bar is canteen-style but fairly smart and offers good breakfasts, Indian dishes and ice cream.

E Kilimanjaro Villa, Azimio St, T027-2508109. 9 very clean and bright rooms with mosquito nets, shared bathrooms, western toilets, hot water, very pleasant and well maintained, friendly manager. Price includes breakfast. Has a walkway on 1st floor around courtyard. A good budget option.

E Palm Court Hotel, 500 m from the bus station off Wachagga St, T027-2572309. Double rooms US$7, singles US$6 including breakfast. Shared hot showers, laundry service, small restaurant, bar, tea and coffee, lounge with satellite TV, friendly set up, exceptionally good value.

Camping

E Arusha View Campsite, next to the Equator Hotel, Boma Rd, T027-2463391, www.blackmambatravels.com. Very central camping. Only US$1.50 (tent hire US$3). You will need a sleeping bag, grassy sites next to a small river, mosquitos love it.

E-F Masai Camp, 3 km along Old Moshi Rd T027-2500358, www.masaicamp.com. Fantastic restaurant, serving Tex Mex, burgers and pizzas, best nachos in East Africa, spotless ablutions with steaming hot water, shady camping spots on grassy terraces, some budget rooms in huts, lively bar with frequent party nights and live music, also new cocktail bar. Highly recommended for backpackers. The excellent safari company, *Tropical Trails* is also based here.

F Meserani Snake Park, 25 km out of town on the road towards the Ngorongoro Crater and Serengeti, T027-2538282, www.meseranisnakepark.com. A hugely popular spot with backpackers, independent overlanders and overland trucks, and just about any safari company on the way to the parks will stop here. A lively atmosphere and friendly hospitality, the bar serves very cold beers. The campsite has hot showers and vehicles are guarded by Masai warriors. Meals from simple hamburgers to spit roast impala are on offer (see also page 218).

★ Mountain lodges

L Arusha Mountain Village, 20 km out of town along the Moshi Rd, T027-2553313 (direct lodge number), for reservations go to www.serenahotels.com. Quality lodge in an old colonial homestead with 46 thatched bomas, distinguished by hand-carved African animals on the doors, nestled within a coffee plantation. Excellent gardens, splendid location, overlooking the forest-fringed Lake Duluti. A very good restaurant, a relaxed open bar and impeccable service.

L Dik Dik, about 20 km from Arusha off the Moshi Rd near Usa River, T027-2548110. Swimming pool, good restaurant, pleasant grounds, set on the slopes of Meru, very proficiently run by Swiss owners, though lacks African atmosphere, concentrates on running upmarket Kilimanjaro climbs, rooms are expensive at US$212 for a double with breakfast, but more reasonable rates are available if you are buying accommodation as part of a climb package.

L Ngurdoto Mountain Lodge, 27 km from Arusha, 3 km off Moshi Rd, T027-2555217-26, www.thengurdotomountainlodge.com. Very smart lodge in beautiful grounds with a range of facilities on a 140-acre coffee estate. Accommodation is 60 rooms in double-storey thatched rondavaals, 72 rooms in the main building, and 7 suites, some rooms have disabled access, satellite TV, most with bathtubs with jacuzzis. Good views of Kilimanjaro and Meru, 3 restaurants, 2 bars, a coffee shop, 18-hole golf course, health club and fully equipped gym, 2 tennis courts, badminton court, swimming pool, toddlers' pool, children's play area, tour desk that can arrange all safaris. Children under 6 go free and under 12s are half price. An excellent base in the region especially for families.

L-A Mount Meru Game Lodge, 20 km from Arusha off Moshi Rd near Usa River, T027-2553643, www.mountmerugamelodge.com. Small, well run, high-standard establishment in splendid garden setting, charming atmosphere, very good restaurant, rooms have 4-poster beds swathed in mosquito nets. Has an impressive animal sanctuary, which includes baboons, vervet monkeys and probably the only Sanje mangabey, *Cercocebus sanjei*, in captivity. A large paddock is home to zebra, waterbuck and eland, as well as saddle-billed and yellow-billed storks, sacred ibis and ostrich. Rates differ by US$100 per room between high and low seasons.

A **Kigongoni Lodge**, 10 km east of Arusha, 1 km before Tengeru, 1 km off the Moshi Rd, T027-2502799, www.kigongoni.net. On a 70-acre coffee farm with good views of Kilimanjaro and Meru, the lodge has 14 cottages, built with local materials, with fireplaces and verandas, 4-poster beds with mosquito nets and en suite bathrooms. Some rooms have internet access, restaurant serving a set 3-course meal each night, cocktail lounge, swimming pool on top of a hill with fantastic views. Revenues from the lodge support a local foundation for mentally disabled children and their families. Guided walks available.

A **Moivaro**, 7 km from Arusha off the Moshi Road, T027-2553326, www.moivaro.com. 26 lovely double- or triple-bed cottages with verandas and en suite bathrooms. Set in pretty gardens in a coffee plantation, swimming pool, good restaurant and bar, children's playground, massages, jogging or walking trail through the plantation, internet access, operated by a Dutch family, recommended by recent travellers.

A **Momela Wildlife Lodge**, about 50 km from Arusha, just outside Arusha NP, 3 km to the northeast of the Momela Gate, T027-2548104, www.lions-safari-intl.com/momella.html. Made famous by the 1960 movie *Hatari* starring John Wayne, which was filmed in the area. The formidable actor stayed here and the hotel was the production base. The lodge will screen the film on request for guests. Beautiful gardens, with a swimming pool, 55 rondavaals with private bathrooms, excellent views of Meru and Kilimanjaro. The lodge is well placed for visits to the Momela Lakes, and nearby are many plains animals and a huge variety of birds.

B **Ngare Sero Mountain Lodge**, 20 km east of Arusha on the Moshi Rd, T027-2553638, www.ngare-sero-lodge.com. Just 1.5 km from the main road is a jacaranda avenue leading to a footbridge. You reach the lodge by crossing the lake by the footbridge and climbing steps up through the gardens or by driving around the forest reserve to reach the car park. 8 garden rooms and 2 suites, pool and sauna in the garden, horse riding, trout fishing and trekking on Mount Meru can all be arranged, and you can play croquet on the lawn. Formerly the farm of Hauptmann Leue, a colonial administrator from the German period, the name means 'sweet waters' and there are magnificent gardens with an estimated 200 species of birds.

B **Rivertrees Country Inn**, 20 km from Arusha, off the Moshi Rd, near Usa River, T027-2553894, www.rivertrees.com. Set in natural gardens along the picturesque Usa River, this is a very elegant country lodge with excellent farm cuisine and personal service. There are 6 individually decorated rooms with bathrooms in the farmhouse and 2 garden cottages with additional decks and fireplaces. Swimming pool, and horse riding can be arranged with notice.

B-F **Tanzanite**, about 22 km along road to Moshi, near Usa River, T027-2553867. Popular with locals at the weekend, chalets set in verdant gardens, swimming pool, tennis, restaurant, small animal sanctuary, child friendly, nature trail, lovely surroundings, good value. Camp for US$5.

Camping

D **Arusha National Park Campsites**, there are 4 sites in the park, 3 are at the base of Tululusia Hill, the other in the forest near Ngurdoto Gate; another is proposed at the edge of Lake Kusare. All sites have water and toilets and provide firewood, book through Tanzania National Parks (TANAPA) head office, Dodoma Rd, Arusha, T027-2503471, tanapa@habari.co.tz, www.tanzaniaparks.com.

F **Lake Duluti camping ground**, 11 km from town toward Moshi, turn right at the sign and follow the road through a coffee plantation. Secure camping and parking is in a grassy yard around the jetty and bar, though ablutions are basic. There is a basic restaurant here, but it has limited choice of food and you may have to wait a while for something to materialize from the kitchen. However, cold beers and sodas are available and you can pay to get your laundry done.

Eating

Arusha *p214, map 216*

TTT **Arusha Coffee Lodge**, a few km from town on the road to the crater, T027-2500630-9. Fabulous setting in a luxurious lodge, lovely wooden building surrounded by decks and overlooking the swimming pool, fine china and crystal, very elegant, big fireplace in the bar area, superb service. At lunch there are set menus with at least 4 main courses to choose from, plus a snack menu. At dinner choose steak, pork, chicken or fish, and then choose a marinade and accompanying sauce, with a wide choice of veg and salad. Wines are from South Africa and Chile. Recommended for a splurge.

TTT **Arusha Crown Hotel**, Makongoro Rd, T027-2544161. The downstairs restaurant in this smart new hotel is very modern with excellent service and prices are surprisingly cheap for what you get. Starters are from US$2.50, try asparagus with crispy bacon and runny poached egg, main courses from US$5, pizza, steaks, seafood and fish including red snapper and king fish, lamb chops, curries and schnitzels, and a full Indian menu, good choice of wine and flavoured coffees. Recommended.

TTT **Dragon Pearl**, just off the roundabout near *Impala Hotel*, T027-2544107. Newer sister restaurant of *Shanghai*, different menu, good food and pleasant outdoor setting in lovely gardens. Wines from South Africa, very good vegetarian dishes, full range of Chinese, some Thai, specialities include fried wonton and sizzling dishes, try the crispy chilli prawns. A Korean chef will grill meat at your table and serve it with a range of sauces, similar to a fondue. Open Mon-Fri 1100-1500, 1800-2230, Sat-Sun 1230-2245.

TTT **Herbs & Spices Ethiopian Restaurant**, a few metres north of the *Impala Hotel* off Old Moshi Rd, T027-2542279. Simple, informal, Ethiopian place with good vegetarian options made from lentils, peas and beans, very good lamb, and continental food (steaks, chops and ribs). Set in a beautifully landscaped garden full of birds. Good service, full bar and live music Thu-Sat. Open daily 1100-2300. Some accommodation at the back (see Sleeping).

TTT **Jambo Makuti Garden**, Boma Rd just south of the *New Safari Hotel*, T0744-305430. Superb breakfasts, baguettes and stuffed chapatis, burgers, juices and shakes during the day, and afternoon tea from 1400-1700 with cakes and muffins. Dinner from 1930 of fish, steaks, ribs and vegetarian dishes and a good wine list. The art on the walls is for sale.

TTT **Le Jacaranda**, Vijana Rd, T027-2544624. At the hotel of the same name, restaurant and bar on an attractive upstairs wooden deck, lounge area downstairs, surrounded by very pretty gardens. French, Thai and some Dutch dishes, lots of lamb and seafood. Excellent but fairly pricey with even pasta dishes not coming in below US$6-7, and a simple Greek salad US$3, plus all vegetables and salads are extra to the main dishes.

TTT **Shanghai Chinese Restaurant**, Sokoine Rd near the bridge, beside the Meru post office, T027-2503224. Extensive menu, fairly authentic, quick service, the hot and sour soup is highly recommended. Open daily 1200-1500, 1830-2230.

TTT **Stiggy's**, Old Moshi Rd near *Impala Hotel*, T0744-895525. Wide range of food, good quality Asian meals, steaks from US$7, seafood from US$10, also cheaper snacks, lively bar with a very good atmosphere, run by a talkative Australian. 1200-2400, closed Mon.

TT **Chopstix**, in the shopping centre to the left of Shoprite, T027-2548366. Quality Chinese takeaway, also does pizzas, same chain as Dragon Pearl above.

TT **Masai Camp**, 3 km west on the old Moshi Rd, T027-2548299. Good food and bar, excellent place to meet other travellers, frequent party nights, cocktail bar, serves hamburgers, chips, pizzas and Mexican food on tables in a thatched boma around a roaring fire. Recommended.

T **Café Bamboo**, Boma Rd, near the main post office, T027-2506451. Very pleasant, bright and airy atmosphere, light pine tables and chairs, blue tablecloths, wicker-shaded lights over each table. Serves good value tasty food, including excellent salads, burgers, juices, fruit salad and ice cream. Fairly busy at lunchtime, closed evenings.

For an explanation of the sleeping and eating price codes used in this guide, see inside the front cover. Other relevant information is found in Essentials pages 31-34.

Y **Cio Gelati**, in the Shoprite complex on Sokoine Rd. Snacks, samosas, extremely cold orange juice, 14 flavours of ice-cream, sundaes, milkshakes, cappuccino, espresso, fresh ingredients, using no eggs.

Y **Dolly's Patisserie**, Sokoine Rd, south of the market. Very smart with modern counters and spotless tiles, fantastic freshly baked French bread, cakes and sweets, excellent biryanis, kormas and masalas for US$3.50, hot and cold drinks. Open daily from early morning to 1930.

Y **Jambo Coffee House**, Boma Rd just south of the *New Safari Hotel*. Has reasonable snacks and grills, toasted sandwiches, cakes, and excellent coffee (you can also buy coffee beans here).

Y **Langaanoo**, Old Moshi Rd, 5 mins' walk from the Clocktower. Veranda with thatched dining area, though spartan with only a few tables. Cheap Ethiopian food and beer, fairly authentic lamb, chicken and vegetarian dishes serves with *njera*, Ethiopian flat bread for around US$3 a plate.

Y **McMoody's**, on the corner of Sokoine and Market St, T027-2503791/2. McDonald's-inspired fast food for those hankering after fries and milkshakes. It has a peculiar circular staircase and mirrored walkway that goes absolutely nowhere. There is an internet café next door and you can take in your drinks.

Y **Naaz**, Sokoine Rd, 150 m from the Clocktower. Celebrated snack bar at the end of an arcade serving meat chop, egg chop, samosas, kebabs, tea and coffee, excellent juices, buffet lunches with lots of options for vegetarians. Spotless surroundings.

Y **Patisserie**, Sokoine Rd, just down the hill from the Clocktower. Freshly baked breads, pies, cakes, cookies, croissants, Indian snacks, fresh juices, cappuccino, espresso and hot chocolate. Open Mon-Fri 0715-1930, Sun 0800-1400. Also internet café.

Y **PizzArusha**, Levolosi Rd to the north of the market. Superb pizzas, curries and steaks, big cheap portions, one of the best budget places to eat in town. Superb service too.

Y **Steers**, near the Clocktower. Quality South African fast food chain selling ribs and burgers, sodas and shakes, in a/c and spotless environment.

Bars and clubs

★ Bars

Almost all the hotels and many of the restaurants already mentioned have bars; if you are looking for a party with other travellers the best places to go are the **Meserani Snake Park** and the **Masai Camp**. There are a number of popular bars in town including the **Empire Sports Bar**, in the arcade behind the Shoprite supermarket, off Sokoine Rd. It's a new spot, large and modern, with high ceiling and mezzanine floor, pool tables, dart board, long bar, large TVs for watching sport, some tables outside in the courtyard, popular with expats.

Greek Club, Old Moshi Rd. Set back from the road in a large white house with Grecian pillars out front, spacious sports bar with large TVs for crucial football matches, darts board and pool table, and outdoor tables on a terrace or in the garden.

Matongee, Old Moshi Rd. Outside tables in a spacious garden with *nyama choma* barbecues and plenty of cold beer. Relaxed and good value. Popular with local people.

Nightclubs

Colobus, Old Moshi Rd just past the *Impala*. A popular disco in town, open every night.

Chrystal Club & Disco, Seth Benjamin Rd, open most nights of the week from 2200. Large dance floors with 2 rooms (techno and African/trance), pool tables, very lively at weekends, has a wide selection of drinks.

Hotel Seventy Seven, off Moshi Rd, about 2 km to the east of the centre, T027-2503800, T0744-381047 (mob). Discos on Fri and often live music at weekends, which attract mostly locals. Good music including Congolese *soca*.

Poloygon Triangle Club, Nairobi Rd. New brick building, disco is upstairs, open Wed, Fri and Sat, 2100-0530.

Triple A, Nairobi Rd. This is easily the largest and most popular nightclub in Arusha with a big range of music including R&B and hip hop, enormous dance floor, pool tables, 2 bars, gets completely packed, also runs its own FM radio station. Open Wed, Fri and Sat, 2100-0500, entry is US$3, ladies free on Wed. Also open on Sun afternoons to allow the kids to get down and boogie!

Shopping

Bookshops

There is a bookshop at the *New Arusha Hotel* that sells international newspapers and magazines as well as books.

Bookmark, just off Sokoine Rd behind the BP garage. The best bookshop in Arusha by far. Fairly new and stocks a wide range of up to date novels, coffee table books on Africa, guide books, maps, intelligent Africana titles, as well as trendy wrapping paper and greeting cards. Prices are steep as everything is imported, but nevertheless one of the best ranges of books in Tanzania. There's also a small juice bar and 1 internet terminal.

Kase Stores, Boma Rd. Also has a good selection of books, stationery and postcards.

Crafts

There are some good craft shops on Goliondoi Rd and near the Clocktower with some very good examples of carvings. The curio markets crammed between the Clocktower and India Rd are brimming with carvings, masks, beads and some unusual antique Masai crafts including masks, drums, headrests, and beaded jewellery.

Cultural Heritage Centre, 3 km out on the road towards Dodoma and the crater. A massive structure on several floors showcasing some of the finest of African art, though of course it is very expensive. The items are of very high quality and there are carvings, musical instruments, cloth, beads, and leatherwork from all over the continent. They can arrange shipping back to your home country and there is a DHL branch office on site. Many of the safari companies stop here en route to the parks. Tingatinga paintings (see box page 60) are for sale at various outlets including the *Jacaranda Hotel* and at a gallery opposite the Meserani Snake Park 25 km from town towards the crater.

Markets and shops

The main market is behind the bus station along Market St and Somali Rd. It is very good for fruit, locally made basketware, wooden kitchenware and spices and is very colourful. The range of fresh produce is very varied and you can buy just about every imaginable fruit and vegetable. If you are shopping, then be prepared to haggle hard and visit a variety of stalls before deciding on the price. Market boys will help carry goods for a fee. In the rainy season watch where you are stepping – it becomes a bit of a quagmire. There are lots of shops along Sokoine Rd. Small supermarkets are found along Sokoine Rd, Moshi Rd and Swahili St. These sell imported food and booze as well as household goods. The brand new **Shoprite**, a South African supermarket chain which is beginning to feature in most African cities, is at the end of Sokoine Rd, beyond Meru Post Office and opposite the long distance bus station. This is an enormous supermarket selling just about anything you might be looking for with most items imported from South Africa. Next door is a wholesale food outlet, and outside towards the back on the left is a small arcade of new shops including a jeweller's, a Kodak film processing shop, a place to get a massage, a western-style hairdresser and 3 coffee shops.

Activities and tours

Sports

The Mount Meru Marathon is held yearly in Arusha and attracts competitors from all around the world.

Golf Gymkhana Club, Haile Selassie Rd out towards the High Court. 9-hole golf course at US$12 a day. Temporary membership available. Also has facilities for tennis and squash at US$1.50.

Horse and camel riding Horse safaris are increasingly popular and can be arranged through the tour operators in Arusha. Most of these begin from Usa River, which is 22 km from Arusha on the Moshi road. For camel rides see Mkuru Camel Sarfari, page 219.

Equestrian Safaris, T0744-595517 (mob), www.safaririding.com. Based on a farm on the slopes of Mount Meru and offer day rides, and 3-14 day horse safaris around Kilimanjaro, Meru and Lake Natron. These are for experienced riders as several hours a day are spent in the saddle. A real opportunity to explore terrain where vehicles cannot go. Full board rates inclusive of meals and fly camping are US$2-300 per day.

How to organize a safari

- Figure out how much money you are willing to spend, how many days you would like to go for, which parks you want to visit and when you want to go.
- If you have the time before arriving in Arusha, check out the websites and contact the safari operators with questions and ideas. Decide which ones you prefer from the quality of the feedback you get.
- Go to the Tanzania Tourist Board at the Clocktower and ask to see the list of licensed tour operators. Also ask to have a copy of the companies that are blacklisted and that are not licensed to operate tours.
- Pick 3-4 tour operators in your price range.
- Shop around. Talk to the companies. Notice if they are asking you questions in order to gain an understanding of what you are looking for, or if they are just trying to book you on their next safari (regardless of what would be the best for you). Also, are they open about answering your questions and interested in helping you get the information you need. Avoid the ones that are pressuring you.
- Make sure you understand what is included in the price, and what is not. Normally, breakfast on the first day and dinner/accommodation on the last day is not included.
- Listen to the salesperson and guide. They have current news about which parks are best at the moment. If they recommend you a different itinerary than you originally planned, it is probably the best itinerary for game viewing. They know the best areas to visit depending on the time of year and where the animals are in their yearly migrations.
- Get a contract with all details regarding itinerary, conditions and payment.
- Ask what kind of meals you can expect. If you are on a special diet, confirm that they can accommodate your needs.
- Ask how many people will be on the safari. Make sure there is enough room in the vehicle for people and equipment.
- Talk to the guide. Make sure that he is able to communicate with you, and that he is knowledgeable.
- If possible, inspect the vehicle you will be using beforehand. If you are going on a camping safari or trek, ask to see the equipment (tents, sleeping bags etc.).

Meserani Snake Park (see page 218). Ride a camel to a nearby Masai village. See also page 219 for camel safaris guided by local Masai.

Swimming Available at the pool at the **Novotel Mount Meru**, open to non-residents for a temporary membership fee.

Tour operators

Note: The cost of taking foreign-registered cars into the national parks in Tanzania means that it is usually cheaper to go on a safari in a Tanzania-registered vehicle.

There are over 100 tour operators and safari companies based in Arusha who organize safaris to the different national parks in the Northern Circuit (see next chapter). Most also offer Mount Kilimanjaro and Meru treks, beach holidays in Zanzibar, hotel and lodge reservations, vehicle hire, charter flights, cultural tours, and safaris to the other parks. The list below is far from comprehensive. It is just a matter of finding one you like and discussing what you would like to do. (See box, 'How to organize a safari'.) Many of them have also adopted cultural or environmental policies – supporting local communities, schools or empowerment projects – worth thinking about when choosing a safari operator. On the downside, travellers have reported that rival tour companies sometimes double up, with 2 or 3 groups sharing the same cars and other facilities – all paying different amounts. As a result, itineraries are changed without agreement. It is a good idea to draw up a comprehensive written contract of exactly what is included in the price agreed before handing over any money. Sometimes touts for rival tour companies are very persistent and this can be very frustrating. To get them off your back, tell them you have already booked a safari even if you haven't. Once in Arusha, give yourself at least a day or two to shop around and organize everything. Likewise, allow for at least one night back in Arusha on the final day of your safari as you will usually arrive back in town quite late.

Abercrombie & Kent, Njiro Hill, T027-2508347, www.abercrombiekent.com. Quality operator with years of experience in East Africa, not cheap but they use the best local guides and have a variety of tours in the region, online reservations.

Active Africa, T0744-282771 (mob), www.activeafrica.com. Relatively new upbeat operator offering Kili climbs, mountain biking, trekking with the Masai, cultural tourism, safaris with other activities including abseiling, no scheduled departures, all tailor-made trips.

Adventureland Safaris, Sokoine Rd, T0744-886339 (mob), www.adventurelandsafari.com. All safaris, Kilimanjaro and Meru climbs, cultural tours to the Lake Natron and Lake Eyasi regions, Zanzibar, budget operator.

Africa Royal Trekking, based at the Arusha View Campsite, Boma Rd, near *New Arusha Hotel*, T027-2463391, www.africa-royal- trekking.com. Safaris, Meru and Kilimanjaro climbs.

African Adventures, Arusha International Conference Centre (AICC), Suite 10527, T0744-263147 (mob), www.africanadventures.com. Camping and lodge safaris to the northern circuit, climbing and Zanzibar add-ons.

African Trails Ltd, New Safari Hotel Complex, Boma Rd, Second Fl, T027-2504406, www.africantrails.com. Mid-range and budget tours to the major parks.

Akorn, T027-2506190, www.akorn.com. Well established operator that has been running safaris for over 40 years, aimed at the upper end of the market, has over 200 vehicles.

Angoni Safaris, in the AICC complex. www.angoni.com. Safaris throughout Tanzania, cultural tours that include trekking and donkey rides, also car hire.

Arusha Sunrise Safaris, T0727-2544102 (mob), www.sunrisesafaris.com. Specialist in luxury and camping safaris, Mountain Meru and Kilimanjaro climbs, walking safaris, and Zanzibar arrangements.

Bobby Tours, Goliondoi Rd, T027-2403590, www.bobbytours.com. Good value camping safaris, expect to pay around US$250 for a 3 day/2 night safari to the crater and Serengeti, established operator but reports of poor camping equipment.

Bush Buck Safaris, T027-2507779, www.bushbuckltd.com. An established operator with 20 years experience, all safaris, hotel reservations, special arrangements for honeymooners, all the vehicles are 4WD landrovers, not minibuses.

Cappello Adventures and Safaris, T0748-452346 (mob), www.cappelloadventures.com. Budget camping and mid-range safaris using Sopa and Seronera lodges, Kilimanjaro and Mount Kenya climbing.

Classic Tours and Safaris, at *Impala Hotel*, T027-2508448, www.theclassictours.com. Safaris to northern circuit plus mountain climbs, Gombe, Usambara Mountains, all budgets. Recommended.

Duma Safaris, T027-2500115, www.duma safari.com. We get consistently good feedback from readers for this company. Kilimanjaro climb US$850, 6-day northern circuit US$900, some of their profits support a local school, excellent guides and food.

Easy Travel & Tours Ltd, *New Safari Hotel*, Boma Rd, T027-2503929, www.easy travel.co.tz. Budget tours to all the Tanzanian parks, from US$180 for 2 days, mountain trekking for Kilimanjaro and Meru, travel agent with representation of Air Zimbabwe and Air Mauritius.

Equatorial Safaris, Ngorongoro Wing, AICC, T027-2502617, www.equatorialsafaris.co.tz. Kilimanjaro climbs and northern circuit parks.

Fly-Catcher Safaris, Serengeti Rd, T027-2503622, www.flycat.com. Safaris to Rubondo Island, Serengeti, Kitavi and

Mahale, Dutch speaking.

Fortes Safaris, T027-2506094, www.fortes-safaris.com. Run trips to Lake Eyasi where they have an upmarket tented camp.

Good Earth Tours and Safaris, T027-2508334, www.goodearthtours.com. Toll free (USA) T877-265-9003. Mount Kilimanjaro climb, safaris and Zanzibar beach holidays, standard and luxury lodges.

Hima Tours & Travel, Shule Rd, T027-2507681, www.himatours.com. A variety of tours, helpful staff.

Klub Afriko Safaris, at the *Klub Afriko Hotel*, T027-2548878, www.klubafriko.com. Various safaris, specializing in Serengeti, Tarangire, Zanzibar and Kilimanjaro.

Hoopoe Safaris, India St, T027-2507011, UK address: PO Box 278, Watford WD19 4WH, T+44-(0)1923-255462, www.hoopoe.com. This company has been consistently recommended by a number of travellers and Conde Nast Traveler (USA) magazine voted Hoopoe Safaris the best Eco-tourism Operator in the World for 2004. They have an excellent commitment to the local communities and to conservation. They offer a range of safaris and climbs and unusual trekking itineraries including a 5-day trek with donkeys and the Masai. Also run exclusive safaris using their **Kirurumu Tented Camps and Lodges**, www.kirurumu.com. Some of the permanent camps are listed in the relevant chapters, but they also have camps that move seasonally. Check out the website for information. Highly recommended.

JMT African Heart, just outside town, in the Ilboru area, not far from Ilboru Safari Lodge, T027-2508414, www.africanheart.com. Luxury and budget safaris from US$105 per person per day. Horseback and mountain bike safaris, cultural trekkings, Kilimanjaro climbs from US$710.

JM Tours Ltd, Plot 15, Olorien, T027-2548801, www.jmtours.co.tz. Specializing in travel planning for disabled travellers, school exchange programs, and cultural tourism.

Kearsley Travel & Tours, next to *Golden Rose Hotel*, T027- 2508043/4, www.kearsley.net. Established safari operator with over 50 years experience.

Laitolya Tours and Safaris, Meru Plaza, Esso Rd, T027-2509536, www.laitolya.com. Northern circuit, also Mikumi, Udzungwa, and Bagamoyo coast. Scheduled and custom-made safaris.

Lions Safari International, Sakina/Nairobi Rd, T027-2506423, www.lions-safari-intl.com. Good, professional company operating camping and lodge 3-11 day safaris.

Malaika Tours, Ngaramtoni Rd, off Nairobi-Arusha Rd, T027-2601587, www.malaika.com. Package tours and tailor-made safaris, climbing, trekking and culture tours, northern and southern circuits including cultural tours in Pare Highlands and Mkomazi Game Reserve.

Moon Adventure Tours & Safaris, Seth Benjamin Rd, opposite Meru School, T027-2504462, www.moon-adventure.com. Low cost camping safaris, Ngorongoro Highlands trekking, birdwatching safaris.

Nature Beauties, Old Moshi Rd, T027-2548224, www.naturebeauties.com. Alternative routes and trekking safaris with a strong focus on the philosophy of sustainability of environment.

Peacock Tours and Safaris, Regional CCM Bldg, Makongoro Rd, T027-2507884/2501539, www.peacocksafaris.com. Mixed reports. Some travellers who had booked in advance were very happy with this company, including the drivers and cooks but problems seem to arise if tours are arranged at short notice, when they are subcontracted to other inferior operators.

Predators Safari Club, Namanga Rd, Sakina, T027-2506471, www.predators-safaris.com. A wide range of safaris from luxury lodges to camping all over Kenya and Tanzania, good national park combination packages, professionally run. Recommended.

Ranger Safaris, T027-2544994, www.rangersafaris.com. This is easily one of the biggest safari operators in Tanzania with a wide choice of lodge and camping safaris from 3-10 days and regular departure dates.

Roy Safaris Ltd, new office is near the Outpost Lodge, T027-2502115/2508010, www.roysafaris.com. Good value short camping safaris to the crater and Serengeti, plus more upmarket safaris, though have received poor reports from some travellers.

Shah Tours & Travels Ltd, PO Box 1821, Moshi, T027-2752370/2998, F027-2751449, www.kilimanjaro-shah.com. Specialists in mountain treks on Kilimanjaro and Meru and safaris to national parks and beaches of Zanzibar. Provide efficient and reliable service of high standard .

Shidolya Safaris, AICC, T027-2548506, www.shidolya-safaris.com. Drivers/cooks/ guides are excellent, recommended for lodge/camping safaris but not the Kilimanjaro climb, specialized bird watching safaris in the Arusha National Park.

Silver Spear Safaris, *New Safari Hotel*, Boma Rd, T027-2548885. Good value camping safaris, lodge upgrades on request.

Simba Safaris, between Goliondoi Rd and India St, T027-2503509, www.simba safaris.com. Kilimanjaro climbs, reservations for Pemba and Mafia, safari packages with lots of departure dates.

Skylink Travel & Tours, Bushbuck Building, T027-2509108, www.skylinktanzania.com. Quality travel agent for flights, also has offices in Dar and Mwanza, agent for Avis Rent-a-Car.

Sunny Safaris Ltd, T027-2508184, www.sunnysafaris.com. Recent travellers report excellent service. A very good fleet of game viewing vehicles, lodge and camping safaris, mountain trekking, mountain bike and walking safaris.

Tanganyika Film & Safari Outfitters, T027-2502713, www.tanzania-safari.com. Specializing in top-of-the-range tailor-made safaris for individuals, private groups, professional photographers, and filmmakers.

Takims Holidays Tours and Safaris, Room 422, Ngorongoro Wing, AICC, T027-2508026, www.takimsholidays.com. An established operator with over 20 years' experience offering photographic safaris to all Tanzanian national parks, including Serengeti, Kilimanjaro, Selous, and Ruaha. Recommended.

Tanzania Serengeti Adventure, Sokoine Rd, T027-2508475/2504069 www.habari.co.tz. Range of tented lodge or budget camping

safaris and lodge bookings.
Tropical Trails, Masai Camp on Old Moshi Rd, T027-2500358, www.tropicaltrails.com. Experienced operator offering northern circuit safaris aimed at the budget and mid-range traveller, Lengani, Meru and Kilimanjaro climbs, cultural tours and crater highland trekking. Recommended.
Victoria Expeditions and Safaris, at the Meru House Inn, T027-2500444, www.victoriatz.com. Professionally-run safaris and trekking, northern circuit parks from 2-7 days camping, can accommodate disabled clients.
Wildersun Safaris and Tours, Joel Maeda Rd, T027-2548847, www.wildersun.com. All standard safaris and an unusual half-day trip to Lake Manyara National Park for canoeing on the lake, US$120 including park fees.
WS Safaris Ltd, India St, T027-2544004, www.wssafari.com. French/Tanzanian team offering a range of safaris, offer good tours for a fair price of US$90 per day per person camping safari to Serengeti and Ngorongoro.

For details of other safari companies, both within Tanzania and overseas, see page 14

Blacklist At the tourist office there is a blacklist of rogue travel agencies, unlicensed agents and the names of people who have convictions for cheating tourists. It is recommended that you cross-check before paying for a safari. In addition, when going on safari check at the park gate that all the fees have been paid, especially if you plan to stay for more than a day in the park. Also check that the name of the tour company is written on the permit. Sadly there is a lot of cheating going on at present, and many tourists have fallen victim to well-organized scams. The tourist office also has a list of accredited tour companies in Arusha.

Transport

Air

Kilimanjaro International Airport, T027-2502223, is half way between Arusha and Moshi. It is served by international flights including **Ethiopian Airlines**, T027-2506167, www.flyethiopia.com, and **KLM**, T027-2508062-3, www.klm.com, who have offices on Boma Rd in the New Safari building. It is also served by **Air Tanzania**, Boma Rd, T027-2503201, www.airtanzania.com, who fly to **Dar es Salaam** and back once or twice a day (booking in advance is essential). Flights to Dar (55 min) depart Kilimanjaro on Wed, Thu, Sat, Sun; 0900, Mon; 1430, Tue, Thu, Fri, Sun; 1725. There are connections in Dar for **Zanzibar**. **Precision Air**, New Safari Hotel Building, Boma Rd T027-2506903/2502836, www.precisionairtz.com. Have a daily flight that departs from **Nairobi** at 0800, arrives in Kilimanjaro at 0850, before departing again for **Dar** at 0915, where it arrives at 1030. On the return leg it departs Dar at 1800, arrives at Kilimanjaro at 1915, departs at 1940 and arrives in Nairobi at 2030. Other flights to Nairobi are daily at 0835 and 1615, which return from Nairobi at 1000 and 1600. There are flights to and from **Mombasa** on Mon, Tue, Wed, Sat and Sun, which depart Mombasa 1250, and return from Kilimanjaro at 1440, and take 1 hr. There is also a daily flight to **Shinyanga** (1½ hr) and **Mwanza** (2 hr) at 1120, which returns from Mwanza at 1405.

To get to the airport you can get the Air Tanzania shuttle bus, which costs US$3 and leaves about 2 hrs before flight departure. Buses also meet incoming flights. Passengers with other airlines will have to get a taxi, about US$40, or can arrange to be picked up by one of the hotels and lodges or safari companies.

Closer to town is **Arusha Airport**, 10 km west along the road to Dodoma. This is mostly used for charter flights and scheduled services operated by **Coastal Air**, T027-2117969-60, www.coastal.cc. Flights go from Arusha to **Dar** (2 hr) daily at 1215 which continue on to the **Selous**, **Kilwa** and **Mafia Island**. To **Mwanza** (3 ½ hr) daily 1230 via **Grumeti** and the other airstrips in the **Serengeti** (2 ½ hr). To **Ruaha** (3 ½ hr) Tue, Fri, Sun 0800.

Road

There are now 2 bus stations in Arusha. The first is on Zaramo St just to the north of the market and buses from here mostly go to places not too far away. Buy your ticket from the driver on the day of travel. There are regular buses and *dala-dala* to and from **Moshi**. Trips cost US$1 and take 1½ hrs. You can also get a shared taxi, which will be more expensive. Long distance buses go from the new bus station opposite the Shoprite Supermarket at the western end of Sokoine Rd. There are reported to be thieves operating around the Arusha bus stations and there are certainly many persistent touts. Go directly to the bus companies' offices and make sure there is the company's stamp on the ticket. There are daily departures to **Tanga** and **Mwanza**: via both the **Serengeti** and **Singida**, (see **Mwanza** for details of these services). There are countless departures each day to **Dar es Salaam**: fare is around US$20 'luxury', US$16 'semi-luxury' and US$9 'ordinary' and takes about 8-9 hrs. The road has improved considerably and journey times are shortening. Taqwa offers a fast, reliable service, Fresh ya Shamba and Royale are also very good, while Scandinavian Express Services Ltd are recommended for reliablility and safety, T027-2500153, www.scandinaveangroup.com. The office is on Kituoni St near the police mess just south of the bus station on Zaramo St.

Nairobi: *dala-dala* only take 4 or 5 hrs from here, depart regularly through the day, and the border crossing is efficient. There are several through shuttle services to Nairobi including Riverside Shuttle, ACU Building, Sokoine Rd, T027-2502639, www.riverside-shuttle.com, departs at 0800 and 1400 daily, US$20.

Car hire Available from most tour companies and also Avis, in the Bushbuck Building, T027-2509108, www.avis.com. Angoni, office in the Arusha International Conference Centre, T027-2508498, www.angoni.com. Car hire and shuttle services. Cars can also be hired at the Arusha Naaz Hotel, Meru House Inn, Golden Rose Hotel and the Novotel, the latter is the agent for Hertz.

Directory

Banks Barclays, Sopa Plaza, Serengeti Rd. Standard Chartered, Goliondoi Rd. Central Bank of Tanzania, Makongoro Rd near the roundabout with Goliondoi Rd. National Bank of Commerce, Sokoine Rd down towards the bridge. Stanbic Bank, next to the National Bank of Commerce. CRDB, further west along Sokoine Rd, on the corner with Singh St. Almost all the town centre banks now have ATMs. There are now many Forex offices in town. Some will change both cash and travellers' cheques as well as give cash advances in local currency against credit cards. Others will not change travellers' cheques – cash only. Most of the bureaux are open 0900-1700, including weekends. Good exchange rates at National Bureau de Change opposite the post office at the Clocktower. The *Impala Hotel* will give cash advances but there is a large fee – approximately 25%. **Courier Services** DHL, Sokoine Rd next to the Stanbic Bank, T027-2506749. **Internet** There are places to check your email all over town including The Patisserie, near the clock tower, an internet café next to *Meru House Inn* on Sokoine Rd, and at McMoody's, Sokoine Rd – typical cost US$0.50 per hr. It can be worth looking around as there are differences in charges. **Post** The main post office is by the clocktower opposite the *New Arusha Hotel*, open Mon-Fri, 0800-1230, 1400-1630, Sat 0800-1230. Meru post office is at the other end of Sokoine Road beyond the market. There are 3 other post offices around town. **Telephone** The cheapest place to make calls or send faxes is from the Telephone House on Boma Rd, opposite the tourist office. Very efficient service, open Mon-Sat, 0800-2200, Sun, 0900-2000. **Medical services** Mount Meru Hospital, opposite the AICC, Simeon Rd, T027-2503352-4. AICC Hospital, Old Moshi Rd, T027-2502329. X-Ray Centre, near the tourist office, T027-2502345. The Flying Doctors, at Wilson Airport in Nairobi covers Tanzania. For an annual tourist fee of US$50, it offers free evacuation by air to a medical centre or hospital. You can contact them in advance; membership/information on T+254 (0)2-501301-3, www.amref.org. **Useful addresses** Arusha International Conference Centre (AICC), T027-2503161, www.aicc.co.tz Immigration office is on Simeon St, T027-2503569, open Mon-Fri, 0730-1530 for visa extensions.
Police Station, Makongoro Rd, T111/112.

Northern Circuit Game Parks

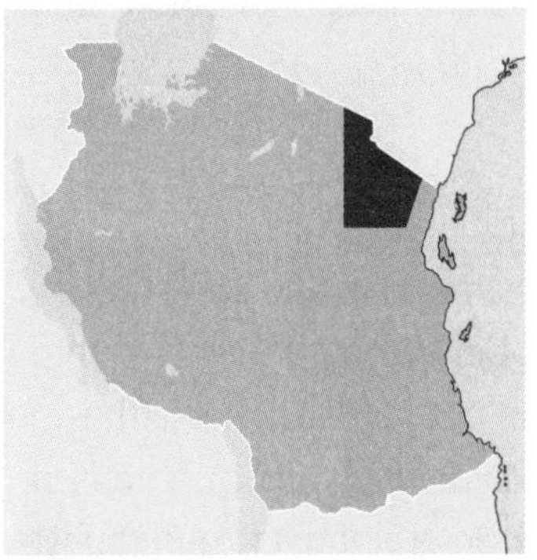

Footprint features

Introduction

The parks and game reserves that make up Tanzania's northern circuit are easily the most popular and accessible attractions in the country. All the big names of mainstream Tanzanian safari are located in the north. From Arusha the road runs southwest across the Masai Plains and hundreds of minibuses and landrovers a week drive along it taking tourists on safari. Immediately around Arusha the countryside is heavily cultivated and you will pass maize, coffee and banana plantations but before long the plains begin to unfold, acacia trees start to appear and you will probably see groups of Masai grazing their herds along the road. Lake Manyara National Park and Tarangire National Park are little more than two hours away and both are parks often overlooked in favour of the other two big names, but are well worth exploring and each is a unique habitat. Also in this region are the little visited Ol Doinyo Lengai volcano and Lake Natron, which offer a glimpse into the rural lives of the local Masai. The Ngorongoro Crater is the most visited part of the northern circuit where wildlife grazes and hunts in one of the largest volcanic calderas in the world. The legendary Serengeti National Park is to the far west of the crater and deservedly earns its name which means 'endless plains'. Here are vast herds of plains game that continuously wander around East Africa's largest ecosystem with the predators in their wake. If you are travelling from December to April, the annual wildebeest migration in Serengeti is definitely not to be missed.

★ Don't miss...

1 **Tarangire National Park** Famous for its dry season herds of game and distinctive baobab trees, page 242.
2 **Lake Manyara** From the Rift Valley escarpment, see the flocks of thousands of flamingos that tinge the edge of the lake shore pink, page 248.
3 **Ngorongoro Crater** An unmissable, World Heritage Site; packed with African game, page 253.
4 **Wildebeest migration** Witness the annual trek between the Serengeti National Park and Kenya's Masai Mara Game Reserve, one of the largest movements of animals on earth, page 264.
5 **Ballooning** Silently float over the endless plains of the Serengeti; an expensive but hugely memorable experience, page 270.

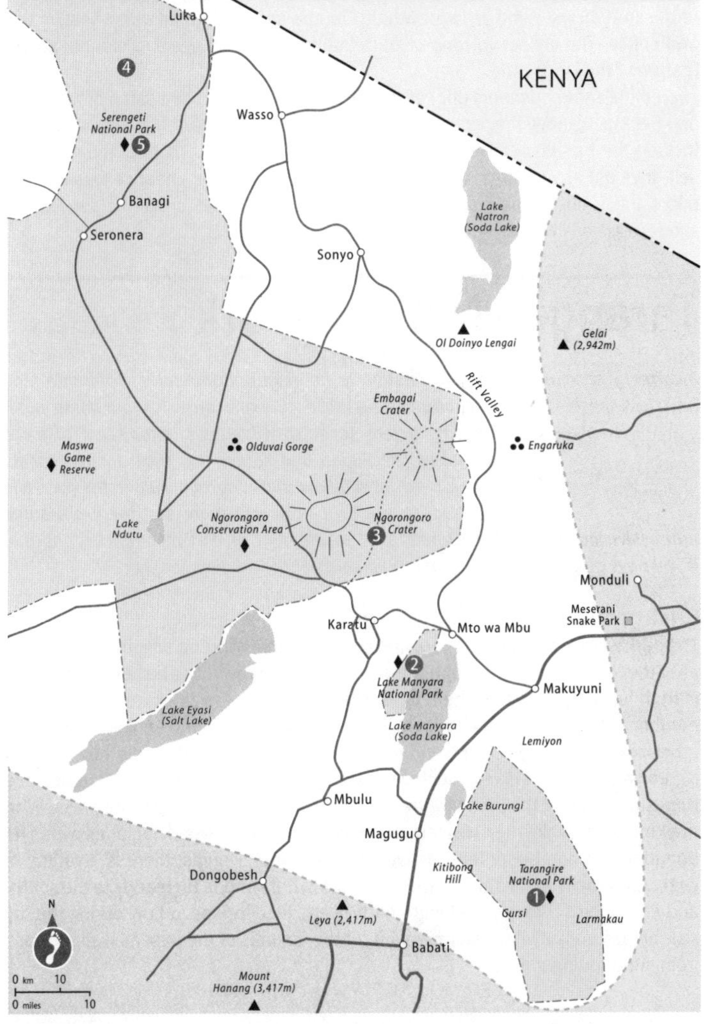

Ins and outs

About 80 km west from Arusha on the road towards Dodoma, there is a T-junction at Makuyuni. The entrance to the Tarangire National Park is 40 km to the south of this junction off the Arusha-Dodoma road whilst the road that heads due west goes towards Lake Manyara, the Ngorongoro Crater and the Serengeti. This road used to be notoriously bad, with deep ruts and potholes, but it has recently been upgraded to smooth tar all the way to the gate of the crater, thanks to overseas funding from Japan. The drive to the gate of the Ngorongoro Crater Reserve, takes about 4 hrs and is a splendid journey and if it's clear with a view of Mount Kilimanjaro all the way, arching over the right shoulder of Mount Meru. You will go across the bottom of the Rift Valley and at the small settlement of Mto wa Mbu, pass the entrance to the Lake Manyara National Park at the foot of the Great Rift Escarpment. Just beyond the entrance to the park the road climbs very steeply up the escarpment and there are wonderful views back down onto Lake Manyara. From here the country is hilly and fertile and you will climb up to the Mbulu Plateau which is farmed with wheat, maize and coffee. The extinct volcano of Ol Deani has gentle slopes and is a prominent feature of the landscape.

All the safari operators offer at the very least a 3 day/2 night safari of the crater and Serengeti, most offer extended tours to include Tarangire or Manyara, and some include the less visited Ol Doinyo Lengai and Lake Natron. There is the option of self-drive but as non-Tanzanian vehicles attract much higher entrance fees into the parks, this is not normally cost effective. » *For more information on national park fees and safaris, see page 39. For safari tour operators in Arusha, see page 232.*

Tarangire National Park

→ *Colour map 1, grid A4.*

Altitude: 1,110 m.
3° 50'S, 35° 55' E
Entry to park: US$35

Incorrectly considered the poor relation to its neighbouring parks, Tarangire may have less spectacular landscape and does make you work harder for your game, but it also retains a real sense of wilderness reminiscent of more remote parks like Ruaha and Katavi. It is most famous for its enormous herds of elephant that congregate along the river. It is not unusual to see groups of 100 more and there are some impressive old bulls. The gate opens at 0630, although an earlier entrance is possible if you have paid the fee in advance. » *For camp and lodge listings, see page 246.*

Background

The park was established in 1970, and covers an area of 2,600 sq km and is named after the river that flows through the park throughout the year. The best time to visit is from July to September when, being the dry season, the animals gather in large numbers along the river. Although you may not see as many animals here as in other places, Tarangire is a wonderful park. There are fewer people here than in Ngorongoro and that is very much part of the attraction. One of the most noticeable things on entering the park are the baobab trees that rise up from the grass. With their massive trunks they are instantly recognizable. As the park includes within its boundaries a number of hills, as well as rivers and swamps, there is a variety of vegetation zones and habitats. The river rises in the Kondoa Highlands to the south, and flows north through the length of the park. It continues to flow during the dry season and so is a vital watering point for the animals of the park as well as those from surrounding areas.

★ Wildlife

The Tarangire National Park forms a 'dry season retreat' for much of the wildlife of the southern Masailand. The ecosystem in this area involves more than just Tarangire National Park. Also included are the Lake Manyara National Park to the north and a number of 'Game Controlled Areas'. The largest of these are the Lake Natron Game Controlled Area further north and the Simanjiro Plains Game Controlled Area towards Arusha. The Mto wa Mbu Game Controlled Area, the Lolkisale Game Controlled Area and Mkungunero Game Controlled Area are also included. The key to the ecosystem is the river and the main animal movements begin from the river at the beginning of the short rains around October and November. The animals moving north during the wet season include wildebeest, zebra, Thompson's gazelles, buffalo, eland and hartebeest. The elephant population in this park was estimated at around 6,000 in 1987 but numbers are believed to have fallen since then because of poaching. At the height

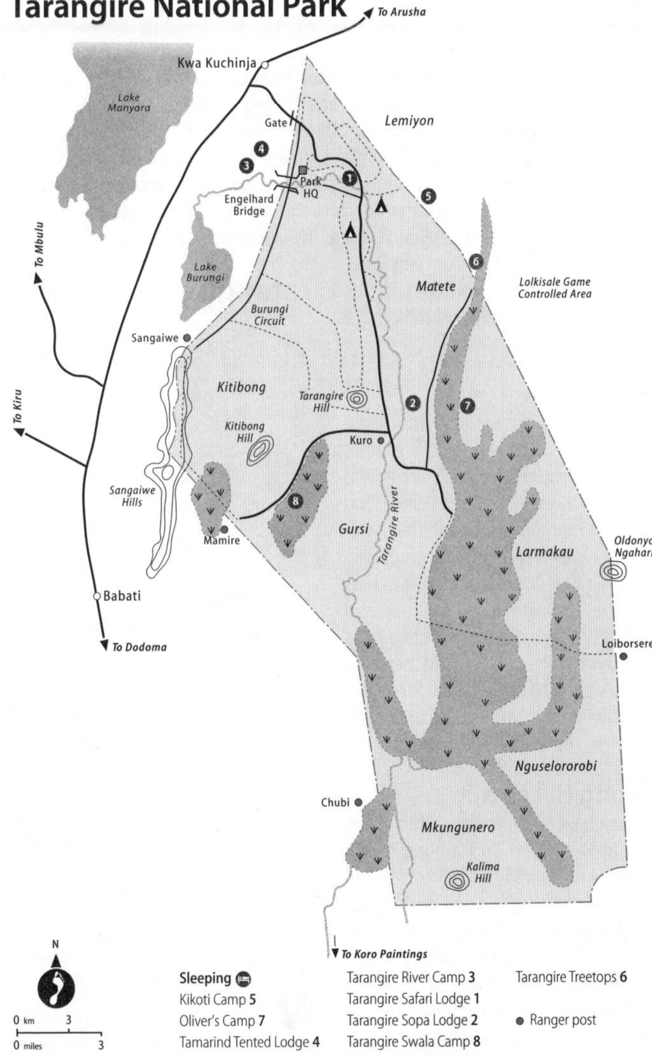

of the rainy season the animals are spread out over an area of over 20,000 sq km. When the wet season ends the animals begin their migration back south and spend the dry season (July-October) concentrated around the River Tarangire until the rains begin again.

The number of species of birds recorded in Tarangire National Park has been estimated at approximately 300. These include migrants that fly south to spend October-April away from the winter of the northern hemisphere. Here you may spot various species of herons, storks and ducks, vultures, buzzards, sparrowhawks, eagles, kites and falcons, as well as ostrich.

Routes

The park is large enough for it not to feel crowded even when there are quite a few visitors. There are a number of routes or circuits that you can follow that take you to the major attractions.

Lake Burungi circuit

Covering about 80 km, this circuit starts at the Engelhard Bridge and goes clockwise, along the river bank. Continue through the acacia trees until about 3 km before the Kuro Range Post where you will see a turning off to the right. Down this track you will pass through a section of Combretum-Dalergia woodland as you head towards the western boundary of the park. The route continues around and the vegetation turns back to parkland with acacia trees and then back to Combretum as the road turns right and reaches a full circle at the Englehard Bridge. The lake water levels have fallen and Lake Burungi is almost dry. If you are very lucky you may see leopard and rhino in this area although the numbers of rhino have reportedly decreased.

Lemiyon area

This circuit covers the northern area of the park bound on each side by the eastern and western boundaries of the park and to the south by the river. This is where you will see the fascinating baobab trees with their large silvery trunks and gourd-like fruits. Their huge trunks enable the trees to survive through a number of rain failures and they are characteristic of this type of landscape. Also found here are acacia trees, which provide food for giraffe. Other animals that you expect to see are wildebeest, zebra, gazelles and elephant.

Kitibong Hill circuit

This track covers the west section of the park and is centred on Kitibong Hill. It includes acacia parkland in the east and Combretum-Dalbergia woodland in the west, the Gursi floodplains to the south and the foothills of Sangaiwe Hills, which are along the western boundary of the park. This area homes a variety of plains animals including buffalo and elephant.

Tarangire migrations

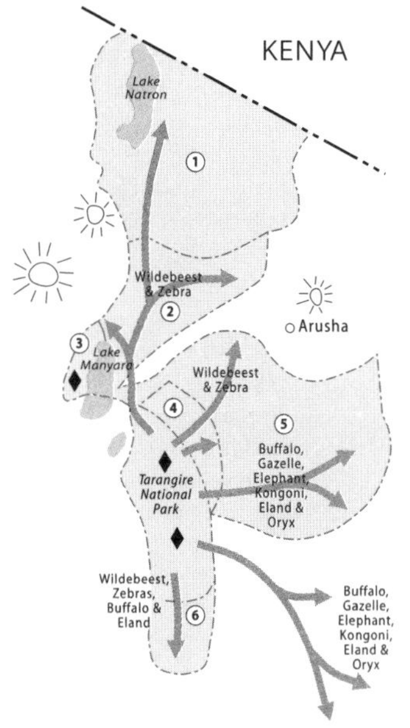

Lake Natron Game Controlled Area **1**
Mto wa Mbu Game Controlled Area **2**
Lake Manyara National Park **3**
Lolkisale Game Controlled Area **4**
Simanjiro Game Controlled Area & Plains **5**
Mkungunero Game Controlled Area **6**

Tsetse fly

The tsetse fly is a little larger than the house fly and is found over much of East Africa including Tanzania. It is a carrier of the disease known as 'sleeping sickness' or African trypanosomiasis, known as *nagana* among the people of Tanzania. This disease can be deadly to cattle and is therefore of great economic concern to large rural areas of Africa. The presence of the tsetse fly has meant that large areas of Tanzania are uninhabitable by cattle and consequently human beings, as farmers need to live where their livestock grazes. Instead these regions are left to the wild animals, as interestingly, the tsetse fly does not affect them. Since the colonial era, the areas have been gradually designated as national parks and game reserves. Tanzania is probably the worst affected by tsetse fly of all the countries of East Africa, which goes some way to explain why 23% of the country is in designated parks and reserves. Tsetse flies can also infect humans with sleeping sickness – the disease affects the central nervous system and does indeed make you sleepy during the day – but cases in humans are very rare. Occasionally there have been endemics of sleeping sickness in East Africa, but these usually occur when large groups of people are dispersed, refugees for example, into an infected area. Tsetse flies, however, do administer a wicked bite so try and steer clear of them. They are attracted to large objects and certain smells and dark colours – like cows. If you are riding a horse a tsetse fly is more likely to bite the horse than you.

The Gursi and Lamarkau circuit

The grasslands found in the south of the park are home to many plain-grazing species. You are also likely to see ostrich here. During the wet season a large swamp forms in what is known as Larmakau – a corruption of the Masai word *'o'llakau'*, meaning hippo, which can be seen here.

Without a four-wheel drive vehicle you will not be able to see much of the southernmost section of the park and during the wet season it is often impassable to all vehicles. There are two areas in the south – Nguselororobi to the east and Mkungunero in the southwest corner. The former is mainly swamp, with some plains and woodland, and if you are lucky you might see cheetah here. Mkungunero has a number of freshwater pools that serve to attract many different species.

The Tarangire Conservation Area is a 585 sq km area on the eastern boundaries of the park set aside by the local villages. The region comprises four distinct areas, the Lolkisale Conservation Area, the Naitolia Concession Area, the Makuyuni Elephant Dispersal Area, and the Lolkisale Livestock and Wildlife Zone. The Conservation Area was established to protect the main wet-season migration route from the park and provide the animals with a natural sanctuary from the demands of modern farming methods such as extensive deforestation by illegal charcoal collectors and years of indiscriminate poaching. What makes this whole project unique is that revenue goes directly into the local community and members of these same communities are being employed by tourism-based services within the area. The local craftsmen have been involved in building the new lodges in the area using local renewable materials from the surrounding regions; the village councils sit on the board of directors; and women empowerment projects and local schools have received funding from the project. For more information visit www.tarangireconservation.com.

Sleeping

Tarangire National Park *p242, map p243*

L **Kikoti Camp**, in the conservation area adjoining the park, reservations, Arusha, T027-2508790, www.tzphotosafaris.com. A small luxury tented lodge built amongst a landscape of ancient boulders, baobab, mopane and fig trees, with 10 spacious tents with grass roofs and wooden decks. Large eating boma with outside campfire and comfortable deck chairs, bush breakfast and lunches are served in secluded areas, sundowners on Kikoti Rock, bush walks as well as game drives on offer and visits to the local Masai village. Rates US$410 per person.

L **Oliver's Camp**, in the eastern part of Tarangire National Park, T027-2502799, www.oliverscamp.com. Intimate small luxury camp with 5 tents, a library and drinks tent, open air dining with the manager and guides who offer walking safaris and game drives during the day, stone fire place, one tent is in a secluded location in the bush for honeymooners, carefully designed to blend into the landscape.

L **Tamarind Tented Lodge**, reservations, Arusha T027-2507011/2507541, www.kirurumu.com. A luxury tented camp on a private concession just beyond the actual boundaries of the park, sitting snugly in a clearing surrounded by dense bush surrounded by acacia trees. Recently renovated, 5 immaculately decorated tents, dining room and bar, very intimate, special romantic dining tent for couples, closed during wet season, walking with the Masai and short night game drives on offer. Rates are from US$250 for a double full board.

L **Tarangire Sopa Lodge**, central reservations: T+254-2-336088, Nairobi, www.sopalodges.com. Luxury all-suite lodge with 75 suites, opened in 1995, opulent lounges, bars and restaurant, excellent food and barbecues, large landscaped swimming pool on the edge of a rocky gorge, shop and and conference facilities. There are however less impersonal choices of accommodation in the park. Rates are US$330 per person.

L **Tarangire Swala Camp**, reservations, Arusha, T027-2509816/2509817, www.kusini.com. On the edge of the Gursi swamp, which makes the camp a first-class site for birdwatching. Comprises 8 extremely comfortable guest tents raised on a wooden deck above the ground under acacia trees, with en suite facilities. Silver service dining. Camp closed during the rainy season Apr-Jun. The staff and management team at Swala have initiated a conservation project that has recently led to the building of a school for the children of a village that borders Tarangire. Rates US$550 per person.

L **Tarangire Treetops**, in the conservation area, T027-2500630-9, www.elewana.com, www.tarangiretreetops.com. The 20 enormous rooms at this lodge take the form of stilt houses, constructed 3-5 m up in huge baobab and marula trees on a wooded hillside overlooking the park. It really is a very pleasant and luxurious lodge, but its weakness lies in its location; it's a considerable distance on rough roads from the main game-viewing areas in Tarangire. Nevertheless excellent food and service, plunge pool, walking safaris, mountain biking, mobile camping and night drives on offer. Rates in the region of US$430 per person.

A **Tarangire River Camp**, T074-8593008 (mob), www.africawilderness.com. This camp is within a concession area set aside for conservation by the local Masai community of Minjingu, which borders Tarangire in the northwest, 3.5 km from the main gate. Shaded by a giant baobab tree, the 18 tents have wooden decks and en suite bathrooms, and the main building is an elegant elevated thatch and timber structure comprising a main lounge, wildlife reference library, dining room and cocktail bar.

B **Tarangire Safari Lodge**, 10 km into the park from the gate, lodge T027-2531447/8, reservations, Arusha, T027-2544222, www.tarangiresafarilodge.com. Tents and stone bungalows, sleeps 70, good restaurant and bar though meals are on the expensive side, US$10 for breakfast and US$20 for

For an explanation of the sleeping and eating price codes used in this guide, see inside the front cover. Other relevant information is found in Essentials pages 31-34.

dinner, large swimming pool, children's pool with slide, considerable discounts for children, overlooking the Tarangire River – wonderful setting, this area is relatively free of tsetse flies which are a problem in other areas of the park.

Camping

The National Park's public campsite is 10 minutes into the park from the gate and set amongst a grove of impressive baobab trees. Toilet and shower facilities are simple but above average. US$20. There are also 6 special campsites, water and firewood are provided but there are no other facilities. Nor have they been sympathetically located in decent positions with nice views. They are, however, generally pleasant and pretty remote, US$40. These are used by the safari operators on camping tours. Further information from Tanzania National Parks (TANAPA), head office, Dodoma Rd, Arusha, T027-2503471, tanapa@habari.co.tz, www.tanzaniaparks.com.

Mto wa Mbu to Lake Natron

From the turn off on the Arusha-Dodoma road, the road heads through the small town of Mto wa Mbu, home to many distinctive red-clad Masai. This used to be a popular stop for safari-goers who wanted to rest and have a break from the bumpy road, but these days the smooth tarmac carries vehicles straight through town. It is, however, the closest town to Lake Manyara National Park gate and from here is another road that goes north to Lake Natron. There are fabulous views over Manyara from the road that climbs up this escarpment from Mto wa Mbu towards the crater. In contrast to Kenya, here there is no eastern wall to the Rift Valley which flattens out as the fault continues south. ▸▸ *For lodges, camps and other Sleeping listings, see pages 251-253.*

Ins and outs

Getting there There are community initiatives using the local Masai people as guides who can arrange a visit to this region, for example the **Mkuru Camel Safari Cultural Tourism Programme** (see page 219) or the **Engaruka Cultural Tourism Programme** (see below). Several tour operators also offer cultural tours in this region using the local people as guides. These include Hoopoe, Roy Safaris, Takim's Holidays, and Klub Africo Safaris (see Tour operators in Arusha, page 232). For example Klub Africo Safaris offer a 7-day Ngorongoro Highlands hike that starts at the rim of the Ngorongoro Crater. One night is spent camping on the rim of the Empakaii Crater and one at the base of Ol Doinyo Lengai, including a climb to the summit at 0200. There is also the opportunity to visit a Masai village, before the tour ends at Lake Natron. Horseback treks can be arranged with Equestrian Safaris (see page 231).

Mto wa Mbu → *Colour map 1, grid A4.* ▸▸ *p251*

Mto wa Mbu (meaning Mosquito Creek) is a small, busy market town selling fruit and vegetables grown by the fertile surrounding farms. It is on the route from Arusha to the northern safari circuit of Ngorongoro and Serengeti and only 3 km away from the gate of Lake Manyara National Park. You are likely to be welcomed to the town by being surrounded by people, including some rather aggressive children, trying to sell the arts and crafts on display in the Masai central market, a cooperative of about 20 curio sellers, behind which is a fresh food market. However, all curios offered here seem to be more expensive than those in Arusha.

The area around Mto wa Mbu was dry and sparsely populated until the irrigation programmes begun in the 1950s which transformed the area into an important fruit and vegetable growing region. (Look out for the distinctive red bananas for sale.) The accompanying population growth turned Mto wa Mbu into a melting pot of cultures. There is greater cultural diversity in this area than elsewhere in Tanzania, so in one day you can sample Chagga banana beer, or see a farmer from the Kigoma region make palm oil. The Rangi use papyrus from the lakes to make beautiful baskets and mats, and the Sandawe continue to make bows and arrows, which are used to hunt small game. On the surrounding plains the Masai tend their cattle, and there are occasional Masai cattle markets. Seeing so many red-robed Masai men all together is quite a striking sight.

The **Mto wa Mbu Cultural Tourism programme** ⓘ *further information: Tanzanian Tourist Information Centre, Arusha, T027-2503840-3, www.infojep.com/culturaltours,* supported by the Tanzanian Tourist Board and SNV, the Dutch Development Organization, offers an opportunity to support the local inhabitants and learn about their lifestyle. Walking safaris with Masai guides through the farms in the verdant oasis at the foot of the Rift Valley can be arranged. There are walks to Miwaleni Lake and waterfall where papyrus plants grow in abundance, or an opportunity to climb **Balaa hill**, which overlooks the whole town. The Belgian Development Organization ACT has enabled locals to grow flowers commercially for export and there are colourful flower fields, with the wonderful backdrop of the Rift Valley. Alternatively you can rent a bicycle and cycle through the banana plantations to see the **papyrus lake**. The landscape is awe inspiring with the escarpment rising vertically up into the sky on the one side and the semi-desert stretching away to the horizon on the other. The guides are all former students of Manyara secondary school and they have a reasonable standard of English. Profits from the tours are invested in development projects and for the promotion of energy-saving stoves.

★ Lake Manyara National Park » p252

On the way to Ngorongoro Crater and the Serengeti, Lake Manyara is well worth a stop in its own right. Set in the Great Rift Valley, Lake Manyara National Park is beneath the cliffs of the Manyara Escarpment, and was established in 1960. It covers an area of 325 sq km, of which 229 sq km is the lake. The remaining third is a slice of marshes, grassland and acacia woodland tucked between the lake and the escarpment whose reddish brown wall looms 600 m on the eastern horizon. » *For more information on national parks and safaris, see page 39.*

Ins and outs → *Colour map 1, grid A4.*

Getting there There is an airstrip near the park gate, and **Coastal Air** T022-2117969-60, www.coastal.cc, flies daily from Arusha at 1230 to Manyara (25 min); on Tue, Fri, and Sun there is an additional flight at 0800. It returns to Arusha daily at 1120, and on Mon, Thu, Sat at 1530. The flight continues on from Manyara and stops at all the Serengeti airstrips before arriving in Mwanza. From Mwanza it returns daily 0900 and stops in the Serengeti and Manyara en route to Arusha. By road the park, 130 km west of Arusha, is reached via the Arusha-Serengeti road. The drive from Arusha takes about 1½ hrs. The main road through the park is good enough for most vehicles although some of the tracks may be closed during the wet season.

Best times to visit: Dec-Feb and May-Jul.
3° 40' S, 35° 50' E
Entry to park: US$35

Background

The lake is believed to have been formed two to three million years ago when, after the formation of the Rift Valley, streams poured over the valley wall. In the depression

The word 'Manyara' is derived from 'emanyara', the name of a plant (Euphorbia tirucalli) used by the Masai in the building of their kraals. Look out for a specimen next to the park gate.

below, the water accumulated and so the lake was formed. It has shrunk significantly and was probably at its largest about 250,000 years ago. In recent years it has been noted that lake levels are falling in several of the lakes in the region, among them Lake Manyara. This trend often co-exists with the development of salt brines, the rise of which are anticipated.

Wildlife

The park's ground water forests, bush plains, baobob strewn cliffs, and algae-streaked hot springs offer incredible ecological variety in a small area. Lake Manyara's famous tree-climbing lions make the ancient mahogany and elegant acacias their home during the rainy season, and are a well-known but rather rare feature of the northern park. In addition to the lions, the national park is also home to the largest concentration of baboons anywhere in the world. Other animals include elephants, hippo, plains animals as well as a huge variety of birdlife, both resident and migratory. At certain times of the year Lake Manyara feeds thousands of flamingos, which form a shimmering pink zone around the lake shore. Other birds found here include ostrich, egrets, herons, pelicans and storks. Also seen are African spoonbills, various species of ibis, ducks and the rare pygmy goose. As with all the other parks poaching has been a problem in the past and has affected the elephant population in particular. It was a shock when the census of 1987 found that their population had halved to under 200 in just a decade. At the gate of the national park is a small museum displaying some of the bird and rodent life found in the park.

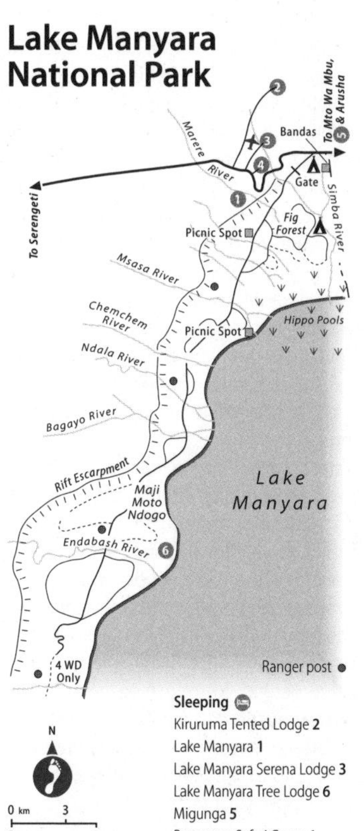

Routes

A road from the park gate goes through the ground water forest before crossing the Marere River Bridge. This forest, as its name suggests, is fed not by rainfall, but by ground water from the high water table fed by seepage from the volcanic rock of the rift wall. The first animals you will see on entering the park will undoubtedly be baboons. About 500 m after this bridge the road forks. To the left the track leads to a plain known as **Mahali pa Nyati** (Place of the Buffalo), which has a herd of mainly old bulls cast out from their former herds. There are also zebra and impala in this area. This is also the track to take to the Hippo Pool. The pool is formed by the Simba River on its way to the lake and is home to hippos, flamingos and many other water birds.

Back on the main track the forest thins out to bush and the road crosses the Mchanga River (Sand River) and Msasa River. Shortly after this latter bridge there is a turning off to the left that leads down to the lakeshore where there is a peaceful picnic spot. Soon after this bridge the surroundings change to acacia woodland. This is where the famous tree-climbing lions are found, so drive through very slowly and look out for a tail dangling down through the branches.

Continue down the main road crossing the Chemchem River and on to the Ndala River. During the dry season you may see elephants digging in the dry riverbed for water. At the peak of the wet season the river may flood and the road is sometimes impassable as a result. Beyond the Ndala River the track runs closer to the Rift Valley Escarpment wall that rises steeply to the right of the road. On this slope are many different trees to those on the plain and as a result they provide a different habitat for various animals. The most noticeable are the very impressive baobab trees with their huge trunks.

The first of the two sets of hot springs in the park are located where the track runs along the wall of the escarpment. These are the smaller of the two and so are called simply **Maji Moto Ndogo** (Small Hot Water). The temperature is about 40°C, heated to this temperature as it circulates to great depths in fractures that run through the rocks that were formed during the formation of the Rift Valley. The second set of hot springs is further down the track over the Endabash River. These, known as **Maji Moto**, are both larger and hotter, reaching a temperature of 60°C. You are supposed to be able to cook an egg here in about 30 minutes. The main track ends at Maji Moto and you have to turn round and go back the same way. In total the track is between 35 and 40 km long.

North of Mto wa Mbu

Engaruka → *Colour map 1, grid A4.*

Engaruka, one of Tanzania's most important historical sites, is 63 km north of Mto wa Mbu on the road to Ol Doinyo Lengai and Lake Natron. Access along here is really only feasible by 4WD. The village lies at the foot of the Rift Valley escarpment. Masai cattle graze on the surrounding plains and dust cyclones often arise on the horizon. They are feared as the 'devil fingers' that can bring bad luck when they touch people.

In the 15th and 16th centuries the farming community here developed an ingenious irrigation system made of stone-block canals with terraced retaining walls enclosing parcels of land. The site included seven large villages. Water from the rift escarpment was channelled into the canals that led to the terraces. For some unknown reason the farmers left Engaruka around 1700. Several prominent archaeologists, including Louis Leakey, have investigated these ruins but to date there are many questions left unanswered about the people who built these irrigation channels, and why they abandoned the area. The ruins are deteriorating because, with the eradication of the tsetse fly, Masai cattle now come to graze in this area during the dry season, causing extensive damage.

The **Engaruka Cultural Tourism Programme** ⓘ *further details: Tanzanian Tourist Information Centre, Arusha, T027-2503840-3, www.infojep.com/culturaltours,* is supported by the Tanzanian Tourist Board and SNV, the Dutch Development Organization. In half a day you can tour the ruins or visit local farms to see current farming and irrigation methods. A Masai warrior can also guide you up the escarpment – from where there are views over the ruins and surrounding plains – pointing out trees and plants the Masai use as food and medicine along the way. In one day you can climb the peak of **Kerimasi** to the north of the village and there is a two-day hike up Kerimasi and then **Ol Doinyo Lengai** volcano (see below). The sodium-rich ashes from the volcano turn the water caustic, sometimes causing burns to the skin of the local Masai's livestock. Moneys generated are used to exclude cattle from the ruins and start conservation work, and also to improve the village primary school. There is no formal accommodation but it is possible to camp.

Ol Doinyo Lengai → *Altitude: 2,886 m.*

ⓘ *As the mountain lies outside the conservation area no National Park fees are payable.*

Ol Doinyo Lengai, the 'mountain of God', is Tanzania's only active volcano. It is north of and outside the Ngorongoro Conservation area in the heart of Masailand, to the west of the road to Lake Natron. This active volcano is continuously erupting, sometimes explosively but more commonly just subsurface bubbling of lava. It is the only volcano in the world that erupts natrocarbonatite lava, a highly fluid lava that contains almost no silicon, and is also much cooler and less viscous than basaltic lavas.

The white deposits are weathered natrocarbonatite ash and lava and these white-capped rocks near the summit are interpreted by the Masai as symbolizing the white beard of God. The last violent eruption was in 1993 and lava has occasionally flowed out of the crater since late 1998. The summit is frequently wreathed in clouds.

It is possible to climb the mountain but the trek up to the crater is an exceptionally demanding one. In parts of the crater that have been inactive for several months the ground is so soft that one sinks into it when walking. In rainy weather the light brown powdery surface turns white again because of chemical reactions that occur when the lava absorbs water. Climbs are frequently done at night as there is no shelter on the mountain and it gets extremely hot. The gradient is very steep towards the crater rim. A guide is required and you are strongly advised to wear sturdy leather hiking boots to protect against burns should you inadvertently step into liquid lava. Boots made of other fibres have been known to melt. Another safety precaution is to wear glasses to avoid lava splatter burns to the eyes.

Lake Natron → *Colour map 1, grid A4.*

This pink, alkaline lake is at the bottom of the Gregory Rift (part of the Great Rift Valley), touching the Kenyan border and about 250 km from Arusha. It is surrounded by escarpments and volcanic mountains, with a small volcano at the north end of the lake in Kenya, and the much larger volcano, Ol Doinyo Lengai, to the southeast of the lake (see above). The lake is infrequently visited by tourists because of its remoteness but numerous Masai herd cattle around here. The route from Arusha is through an area rich with wildlife, depending on the season, particularly ostriches, zebra and giraffe.

The lake measures approximately 56 km long by 24 km wide but its size varies according to rainfall.

The lake has an exceptionally high concentration of salts and gets its pink colour from the billions of cyano-bacteria that form the flamingo's staple diet. There are hundreds of thousands of lesser flamingos here as this lake is their only regular breeding ground in East Africa. Often more of the birds are found here than at either Lake Magadi in Kenya or Lake Manyara. Lake Natron is also an important site for many other waterbird species, including palearctic migrants. A few kilometres upstream to the Ngare Sero River there are two **waterfalls**. Follow the river from the campsite: with the occasional bit of wading, it is a hike of about an hour.

Sleeping

Mto wa Mbu *p247*

L-A (depending on season) **E Unoto Retreat**, 14 km from Mto wa Mbu on the road to Lake Natron, T074-436 0908 (mob), www.maasaivillage.com. A totally Masai-inspired lodge that resembles an authentic Masai Village and blends into the surroundings. The luxurious rooms are in separate bandas with nice views over Lake Miwaleni which is home to many hippo, 4 of the bandas are designed for wheelchair users, the honeymoon suite has a personal butler and luxurious heavy wood furniture. Bikes can be hired, and guests are encouraged to interact with the local Masai on guided walks to villages and there is cultural entertainment. Restaurant and bar, pool. Full or half board rates.

C-E Kiboko Bushcamp, 2 km before town on the Arusha Rd, 2 km from the main road,

T027-2507006, www.equatorialsafaris.co.tz. 12 self-contained permanent tents in a lovely tract of acacia forest, set well apart under thatched roofs, though sparsely furnished and with unattractive concrete showers and toilets. Also has a large campsite. No electricity but a generator operates in the evening. Restaurant and bar in a new and rather impressive thatched building, can organize Masai dancing.

C-E **Twiga Campsite and Lodge**, 1 km from Mto wa Mbu towards the gate of Lake Manyara National Park, T027-2539101, twigacampsite@hotmail.com. There are some decent tent pitches at the back with plenty of shade, hot showers, curio shop, and a reasonable covered bar and restaurant area serving chicken, beef and rice and the like and plenty of cold beer. The 10 double or triple rooms are very basic and leave a little bit to be desired. New additions to the facilities include a small but nice swimming pool and a mini-supermarket.

Lake Manyara National Park

p248, map p249

L **Lake Manyara Tree Lodge**, central reservations, CC Africa, Johannesburg, South Africa, T+27-11-8094300, www.ccafrica.com, www.lakemanyaralodge.com. Set in the heart of a mahogany forest in the remote southwestern region, this is the only lodge within the park and is nicely designed to exert minimal impact on the environment. The 10 luxurious treehouse suites are crafted from local timber and makuti palms, with en suite bathroom and outside shower, deck, fans, mosquito nets, and butler service. Dining boma where guests can watch what is going on in the kitchen, breakfast and picnics can be organized on the lake shore. Swimming pool. Game drives and bird watching safaris included in the price. Rates in the region of US$675 per person, but for this you get an impeccable safari experience.

L **Kirurumu Tented Lodge**, reservations, Hoopoe Safaris, Arusha T027-2507011/ 2507541, www.kirurumu.com. Built on the escarpment in a stunning location overlooking the lake, 20 well appointed tents on solid platforms under thatched roofs, with splendid views, excellent service and meals, horse riding, fly camping and mountain biking on offer. Rates from US$250 for a double full board.

L **Lake Manyara Serena Lodge**, T027-2539160 direct lodge number, reservations www.serenahotels.com. Set on the edge of the eastern Rift Valley's Mto wa Mbu escarpment overlooking the lake. Offers 'soft adventures' – mountain biking, hiking, nature and village walks, abseiling and rock climbing, canoe safaris and children's programmes. Available to everyone, not just staying guests. Manyara is perhaps the weaker of the 3 Serena lodges in the area, but remains a good and reliable option with fantastic views. Rates from US$350 per person.

A **Lake Manyara Hotel**, a member of the South African Three Cities hotel group, Arusha reservations, T027-2544595, www.threecities.co.za. 10 km from the park gate, 300 m above the park on the escarpment overlooking the lake and park – wonderful views. 100 rooms in a rather ugly 1970s building but inside it's very nicely furnished, swimming pool, established garden, TV room, babysitting service, restaurant and bar. Can arrange village walks and guided mountain bike trails.

B **Migunga**, outside the park, just a couple of km before the gate, swala@habari.co.tz, www.swalasafaris.com. Set in 35 acres of acacia forest in a secluded part of Migungani Village. Bushbuck and other antelope are sometimes seen on the property. 9 self-contained tents, hot water, dining room and bar under thatch. A lot less luxurious than the normal tented camps, but much more affordable and rates include meals. Game drives into the park can be arranged, there is a short 30-min nature trail from the camp, and longer hikes/camping tours are on offer to the region around Lake Natron.

C-F **Panorama Safari Camp**, T027-2539286, www.panoramasafari.com. A very good budget option run by Hungarians on the escarpment overlooking the lake, 500 m from the main road. 6 large standing pre-erected tents with thatched roof, veranda and proper beds go for US$40, small tents with mattress are US$10 or camping with

For an explanation of the sleeping and eating price codes used in this guide, see inside the front cover. Other relevant information is found in Essentials pages 31-34.

your own equipment is US$5. There's a new ablution block with hot water, a bar and restaurant and a new swimming pool. A good option for independent travellers.

National Parks accommodation
There are 10 bandas just before the park entrance in a pretty tract of forest, though mosquitos are an enormous problem here. Each has an en suite bathroom, sleeps 2, and costs US$40 per person. There is also a youth hostel at park headquarters that sleeps 48 people, facilities basic, normally used by large groups only.

Camping There are 2 public campsites at the entrance to the park. Both have water, toilets and showers and camping costs US$20. There are 3 special campsites inside the park itself, all of which must be pre-booked as part of a safari and can only be used by one group at a time, US$40. Bookings through Tanzania National Parks head office, Dodoma Rd, Arusha, T027-2503471, tanapa@habari.co.tz, www.tanzaniaparks.com.

Lake Natron *p251*
B-C Lake Natron Camp, southwest of the lake, the only local accommodation near Lake Natron, operated by **Swala Safaris**, swala@habari.co.tz, www.swalasafaris.com. 9 self-contained spacious tents with showers and flush toilets, thatched dining room and bar, swimming pool, solar power in all tents and dining room. US$55 per person full board. You can also camp here if you have your own tent. The camp is an excellent base to explore the surrounding area on hikes and from which to climb Ol Doinyo Lengai. The camp can organize the climb and can offer transfers from and to Arusha if you have no transport.

Camping
Independent overlanders report that it is possible to bush camp reasonably close to the lake, or near the waterfalls on the Ngare Sero River, if fully self-sufficient, although it should be remembered that lions may visit the area to drink.

Ngorongoro Conservation Area

The Conservation area encompasses Ngorongoro Crater, Embagai Crater, Olduvai Gorge – famous for its palaeontological relics – and Lake Masek. Lake Eyasi marks part of the southern boundary and the Serengeti National Park lies to the west. The Ngorongoro Crater is often called 'Africa's Eden' and a visit to the crater is a main draw for tourists coming to Tanzania and a definite world-class attraction. A World Heritage Site, it's the largest intact caldera in the world, containing everything necessary for the 30,000 animals that inhabit the crater floor to exist and thrive. Karatu, the busy town known as 'safari junction', 25 km south of the conservation area, is often used by budget travellers who want to visit the Ngorongoro Crater without spending money on a full-on safari from Arusha. You can catch public transport to Karatu, stay overnight and then take a half day safari to the crater the next morning. ▸▸ *For lodges and camps and other listings, see pages 259-262.*

Ins and outs → *Colour map 1, grid A4. 3°11'S 35°32'E.*

Getting there Ngorongoro is 190 km west of Arusha, 25 km from Karatu and 145 km from Serengeti and is reached via the Arusha-Serengeti road. At Karatu (known as Safari Junction), is the turning off to Gibb's Farm, 5 km off the main road. From this junction you turn right towards the park entrance and on the approach to **Lodware Gate**; as the altitude increases the temperature starts to fall. Your first view of the crater comes at **Heroes' Point** (2,286 m). The road continues to climb through the forest to the crater rim. It is sometimes possible along this road to spot leopard that inhabit the dense forests at the top of the crater. ▸▸ *See also Ins and outs for the crater itself, page 255.*

Entry fees and information On top of the daily park entry fee of US$30 to enter the Ngorongoro Crater Reserve, there is an additional US$10 fee per half day excursion to enter the crater itself. The cost of a vehicle to go down into the crater has recently risen from US$30 to US$100. At the time of writing, unlike the entry fees to the Serengeti and Kilimanjaro national parks, the entry fee to the crater had not gone up. Tanzania National Parks wanted to wait and see what the impact of the price rises on these other parks are when the fees go up in 2006, before deciding whether to put up the entry fee of the crater as well. However, the amount of people and vehicles that go down into the crater each day has been under scrutiny for some time and the decision is likely to be that fees will go up considerably to encourage a high-price, low-impact policy. For more information: www.ngorongoro-crater-africa.org. The best times to visit are Dec-Feb and Jun-Jul. During the long rains season (Apr-May) the roads can be almost impassable, so access to the crater floor may be restricted.

Background

The Ngorongoro Conservation Area was established in 1959 and covers an area of 8,288 sq km. In 1951 it was included as part of the Serengeti National Park and contained the headquarters of the park. However in order to accommodate the grazing needs of the Masai people's livestock it was decided to reclassify it as a conservation area. In 1978 it was declared a **World Heritage Site** in recognition of its beauty and importance. Where the road reaches the rim of the crater you will see memorials to Professor Bernhard Grzimek and his son Michael. They were the makers of the film *Serengeti Shall Not Die* and published a book of the same name (1959, London, Collins). They conducted surveys and censuses of the animals in the Serengeti and Ngorongoro Parks and were heavily involved in the fight against poachers. Tragically Michael was killed in an aeroplane accident over the Ngorongoro Crater in 1959 and his father returned to Germany where he set up the Frankfurt Zoological Society. He died in 1987 requesting in his will that he should be buried beside his son in Tanzania. Their memorials remain as a reminder of all the work they did to protect this part of Africa.

Karatu → *Phone code 027.* ▸▸ *pp259-262*

The small but burgeoning town of Karatu is 25 km from the gate of the Ngorongoro Crater Reserve, 25 km from Lake Manyara, and 140 km from Arusha. The new road from Arusha to the gates of the Ngorongoro Crater which was completed in 2003 was sponsored by the Japanese government. With completion of this road, Karatu has come into its own and now spreads for several kilometres along the highway. It is locally dubbed 'safari junction' and for good reason. All safaris vehicles en route to the parks in the northern circuit pass through here. Because of its proximity to the crater more and more lodges and campsites are springing up. Some offer a very good and in some cases much cheaper alternatives to staying within the confines of the Ngorongoro Crater Reserve. However, the disadvantage is not having the views that the lodges on the rim of the crater afford. As well as the accommodation options listed below, those on an organised camping safari may find themselves staying at one of the many other campsites around Karatu as the cheaper companies use these instead of the more expensive campsite at the top of the crater (which, incidentally, is overcrowded, has poor facilities and gets extremely cold). These cater exclusively to the groups who have their own cooks, though there are often also bars to buy beers and sodas. There is one bank in town, the National Bank of Commerce, on the main road next to the *Ngorongoro Safari Lodge* that changes cash and travellers' cheques and a very good restaurant, *Bytes* (see below). For those on self-drive safaris this is the last place to buy food and fuel before entering the Ngorongoro Crater Reserve. There's a market on the left hand side of the road if coming from Arusha which has a good variety of fresh food; meat can be bought from the small butcher at the back and bread from the kiosks. Petrol stations spread from one end of town to the other. There are plenty of buses throughout the day between Arusha and Karatu. One option here for budget travellers wanting to visit the Ngorongoro Crater, is to catch public transport as far as Karatu, stay overnight and then take a half day safari to the crater the next morning, and return to Arusha the following afternoon. This is considerably cheaper than booking a safari from Arusha.

★ Ngorongoro Crater → *Colour map A4.* ▸▸ *p260*

The crater has an area of 265 sq km and measures between 16 and 19 km across. The rim reaches 2,286 m above sea level and the crater floor is 610 m below it. The crater floor is mainly grassy plain interspersed with a few tracts of sturdy woodland. Scrub heath and remnants of montane forests cloak the steep slopes. There are both freshwater and brackish lakes, and the main water source is Lake Migadi in the centre of the crater; a soda lake that attracts flocks of pink-winged flamingos and plenty of contented hippos who remain partially submerged during the day and graze on grass at night. The views from the rim overlooking Ngorongoro Crater are sensational, and you can pick out the wildlife as dots on the crater floor.

Ins and outs

All the lodges and the public campsite are around the rim of the crater. The descent into it is by way of two steep roads, which are both one-way. You enter by the **Windy Gap** road and leave by the **Lerai** road. The Windy Gap branches off the Serengeti road to the right and descends the northeast wall to the floor of the crater 610 m below. The road is narrow, steep and twists and turns as it enters the crater, which is rather like a huge amphitheatre.

Most people go down into the crater on an organized safari from Arusha (see page 232), or join one in Karatu. Access into it and onto its floor is limited to half a day per visitor, and safaris enter either early in the morning or early in the afternoon. Access is restricted to registered tour operators in Tanzanian-registered vehicles, and for most of the year, only 4WDs are allowed. If you have your own vehicle, you are allowed to take it through the Ngorongoro Crater Reserve (and beyond into the Serengeti) but you are not allowed to take it down into the crater. However, there is the option to leave your own vehicle at the top and Land Rovers and drivers can be hired in Crater Village where you pick up the ranger, which is cheaper than hiring through the lodges.

Background

The name 'Ngorongoro' comes from a Masai word *Ilkorongoro*, which was the name given to the group of Masai warriors who defeated the previous occupants of the area, the Datong, around 1800. The sounds of the bells that the Masai wore during the battle that were said to have terrified their enemies into submission, was '*koh-rohng-roh*' and it is from this that Ngorongoro comes. The Masai refer to the Ngorongoro Southern Highlands as *'O'lhoirobi'*, which means the cold highlands; while the Germans also referred to the climate, calling these the 'winter highlands'. Ngorongoro is believed to date from about 2,500,000 years ago – relatively recent for this area. It was once a huge active volcano and was probably as large as Kilimanjaro. After its large major eruption, as the lava subsided its cone collapsed inwards leaving the caldera. Minor volcanic activity continued and the small cones that resulted can be seen in the crater floor. To the northeast of Ngorongoro crater are two smaller craters, Olmot and Embagai. From the crater on a clear day you should be able to see six mountains over 3,000 m.

The crater is home to an estimated 30,000 animals and visitors are almost guaranteed to get a good look at some or all of the Big Five. About half of this number are zebra and wildebeest. Unlike those in the neighbouring Serengeti, these populations do not need to migrate thanks to the permanent supply of water and grass through both the wet and the dry seasons. Thanks to the army of pop-up minibuses that go down each day the animals are not afraid of the vehicles and it's not unusual for a pride of lions to amble over and flop down in the shade of a minibus. The crater's elephants are mostly old bulls with giant tusks. The females and calves prefer the forested highlands on the crater rim and only rarely venture down into the grasslands. There are no giraffe. Because of the crater's steep sides they can't climb down, and there is a lack of food to munch on at tree level.

On the crater floor Lerai Forest is a good place for a picnic lunch and most safari operators stop here. Beware of dive-bombing kites snatching your lunch.

In early 2001 huge swarms of *Stomoxys* flies were harmful to many animals and particularly the lions, of which 6 died and 62 were seriously damaged. The lions apparently left the crater in an attempt to escape. In a previous outbreak of the flies, in 1962, the lion population was decimated, with only 8 lions surviving. Numbers have slowly increased since that time, but the Ngorongoro lions, generally bigger and stronger than lions elsewhere, are in danger of extinction, not least because the lack of genetic diversity within the population leaves it vulnerable to events such as *Stomoxys* attacks and disease. There have also been reports that since the middle of 2000 many other animals have died of unknown causes, including over 300 buffalo, 200 wildebeest, over 60 zebra and a few hippo and rhino.

Ngorongoro Conservation Area

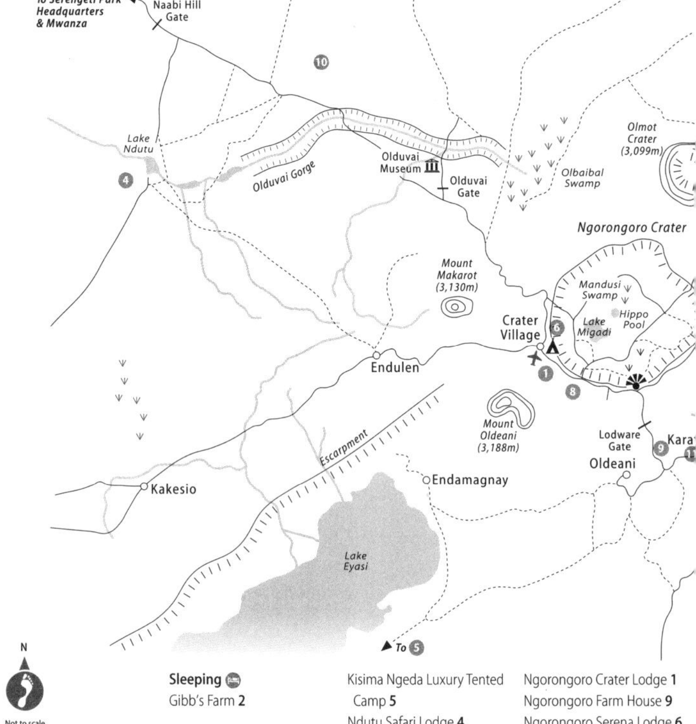

Embagai Crater → *Colour map 1, grid A4. 2°55'S 35°50'E.*

Embagai Crater (also spelt Empakaai) can be visited in a day from any lodge at the Ngorongoro rim. The caldera is approximately 35 sq km. You can walk down to the 80-m deep, alkaline Lake Emakat, which partly occupies the caldera floor. The vegetation is predominantly highland shrubs and grassland but there are small patches of verdant, evergreen forest in the southern part of the caldera. Buffalo, hyenas, leopards and various species of bats may be seen. Birdlife is prolific and includes the lammergeyer, Egyptian vulture, Verreaux's eagle, pelicans, storks, flamingos, duck, sandpiper, doves, kingfishers and ostrich. This is an isolated, beautiful place, accessible by four-wheel drive only. You need to be accompanied by a ranger because of the buffaloes.

Lake Ndutu is a soda lake in the Ndutu woodlands in the western part of the Ngorongoro Conservation Area. Rarely visited, it is home to many flamingo, plains game mammals and their attendant predators.

Olduvai Gorge → *Colour map 1, grid A4.*

» p261

Olduvai Gorge, a water-cut canyon up to 90 m deep, has become famous for being the site of a number of archaeological finds and has been called the 'cradle of mankind'. Lying within the Ngorongoro Conservation Area to the northwest of the crater, the site is about 10-15 minutes off the main road between Serengeti and Ngorongoro. The name Olduvai comes from the Masai word *oldupai*, which is the name for the type of wild sisal that grows in the gorge.

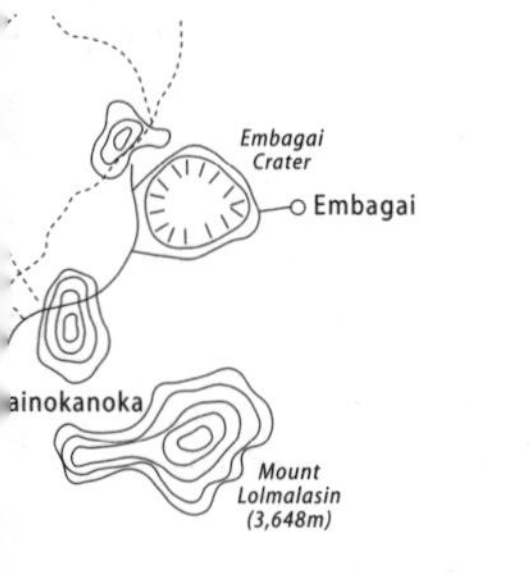

Ngorongoro Sopa Lodge **7**
Ngorongoro Wildlife Lodge **8**
Olduval Camp **10**
Plantation Lodge **11**

Archaeological finds

Olduvai Gorge first aroused interest in the archaeological world as early as 1911 when a German, Professor Katurinkle, while looking for butterflies in the gorge, found some fossil bones. These caused great interest in Europe and in 1913 an expedition led by Professor Hans Reck was arranged. They stayed at Olduvai for three months and made a number of fossil finds. At a later expedition in 1933 Professor Reck was accompanied by two archaeologists, Dr Louis Leakey and his future wife Mary.

The Leakeys continued their work and in July 1959, 26 years later, discovered 400 fragments of the skull *Australopithecus-Zinjanthropus boisei* – the 'nutcracker man' – who lived in the lower Pleistocene Age around 1,750,000 BC. A year later the skull and bones of a young *Homo habilis* were found. The Leakeys assert that around 1.8-2 million years ago there existed in Tanzania two types of man, *Australopithecus-Zinjanthropus boisei* and *Homo habilis*. The other two, *Australopithecus* africanus and *arobustus*, had died out. *Homo habilis*, with the larger brain, gave rise to modern man. *Habilis* was a small ape-like creature and, although thought to be the first of modern man's ancestors, is quite distinct from modern man. Tools, such as those used by *Homo erectus* (dating from 1-1½ million years ago), have also been found at Olduvai as well as at Isimila near Iringa. Other exciting finds in the area are the footprints found in 1979 of man, woman and child at Laetoli (a site near Olduvai) made by 'creatures' that walked upright, possibly dating from the same period as *Australopithecus afarensis*, popularly known as 'Lucy', whose remains were discovered near Hadar in Ethiopia in 1974. Dating back 3.6-3.8 million years they pushed back the timing of the beginnings of the human race even further. In 1986 a discovery at Olduvai by a team of American and Tanzanian archaeologists unearthed the remains of an adult female dating back 1,800,000 years. In total the fossil remains of about 35 humans have been found in the area at different levels.

Prehistoric animal remains were also found in the area and about 150 species of mammals have been identified. These include the enormous Polorovis with a horn span of 2 m, the Dinotherium, a huge, elephant-like creature with tusks that curved downwards and the Hipparion, a three-toed, horse-like creature.

At the site there is a small **museum** ⓘ *open until 1500, may be closed during the wet season (Apr-end Jun), entrance US$2.50*. The building was built in the 1970s by the Leakeys to house their findings. It holds displays of copies of some of the finds, a cast of the footprints and pictures of what life was like for Olduvai's earliest inhabitants. You can go down into the gorge to see the sites and there will usually be an archaeologist to show you around.

Nearby places of interest include **Nasera Rock**, a 100-m monolith on the edge of the Gol Mountain range – it offers stunning views of the southern Serengeti and is a great vantage point from which to watch the annual **wildebeest migration**. This is sometimes called the Striped Mountain, so named for the streaks of blue-green algae that have formed on the granite. **Olkarien Gorge**, a deep fissure in the Gol Mountains, is a major breeding ground of the enormous Ruppell's griffon vulture.

A geological feature of this area are shifting sand-dunes, or *barchan*, crescent-shaped dunes lying at right angles to the prevailing wind. They usually develop from the accumulation of sand around a minor obstruction, for example a piece of vegetation. The windward face has a gentle slope but the leeward side is steep and slightly concave. The *Barchans* move slowly as more sand is deposited; they range in size from a few metres to a great size, as seen in the Sahara or Saudi Arabia.

Lake Eyasi

→ *Colour map 1, grid A4.* ▸▸ *p261*

ⓘ *Access to Lake Eyasi is from the Kidatu-Ngorongoro road. The journey takes about 1½-2 hrs, driving southwest of Karatu and the Ngorongoro Crater. There are few tourist facilities here but in recent years it has been included in walking safaris by several companies. There are no set itineraries for the 5 day/4 night hiking and camping tours but they generally start at ChemChem Village from where the guides start their search for a Hadzabe camp. Once there, hikers can freely participate in the Hadzabe daily activities including mending of bows, collecting herbal poisons for the arrows, actual hunts, gathering of firewood, plants, water, etc.*

This soda lake, one of several lakes on the floor of the Rift Valley, is sometimes referred to as the 'forgotten lake'. It is larger than Lakes Manyara or Natron and is situated on the remote southern border of the Ngorongoro Conservation Area, at the foot of Mount Oldeani and the base of the western wall of the Rift Valley's Eyasi Escarpment. The Mbula highlands tower to the east. Seasonal water level fluctuations vary greatly and, following the trend in the region, the lake levels are falling and salt brines have developed. It is relatively shallow even during the rainy season. Lake Eyasi mostly fills a *graben*, or elongated depression of the earth's crust, areas that are commonly the sites of volcanic and/or earthquake activity. The Mbari River runs through the swampy area to the northeast of the lake known locally as **Mangola Chini**, which attracts much game.

Two ancient tribes inhabit this area. The **Hadzabe** people (also called the Watindiga) who live near the shore are hunter-gatherers, still live in nomadic groups, hunt with bows and arrows and gather tubers, roots and fruits. These people are believed to have their origins in Botswana, their lifestyle is similar to the San (of the Kalahari) and the Dorobo (of Kenya). It is estimated that they have lived in this region for 10,000 years. Their language resembles the click language associated with the San. Their hunting skills provide all their requirements – mostly eating small antelopes and primates. Their hunting bows are made with giraffe tendon 'strings', and they coat their spears and arrows with the poisonous sap of the desert rose. They live in communal camps that are temporary structures constructed in different locations depending on the season.

Nearby there is a village of **Datoga** pastoral herdsmen, also known as the Barabaig or Il-Man'ati (meaning the 'strong enemy' in the Masai language). The Datoga are a tall, handsome people who tend their cattle in the region between Lake Eyasi and Mount Hanang. The Masai drove them south from Ngorongoro to Lake Eyasi about 150 years ago, and remain their foes. They live in homes constructed of sticks and mud, and their compounds are surrounded by thornbush to deter nocturnal predators. Like the Hadzabe, the Datoga speak a click language and they scarify themselves to form figure of eight patterns around their eyes in a series of raised nodules.

The northeastern region of the lake is a swampy area fringed by acacia and doum palm forests. Nearby are some freshwater springs, and a small reservoir with tilapia fish. These springs are believed to run underground from Oldeani to emerge by the lakeshore. There are several *kopjes* (see page 265) close by the lake. Wildlife includes a profusion of birdlife including flamingos, pelicans and storks as well as leopards, various antelope, hippos and many small primates.

Archaeological excavations of the nearby **Mumba cave shelter** were undertaken in 1934 by Ludwig and Margit Kohl- Larsen, and their discoveries included many fossilized hominoid remains: a complete prehistoric skull, molars and prehistoric tools such as knives and thumbnail scrapers. Animal remains included rhino, antelope, zebra, hippo and catfish. The Mumba cave also contained ochre paintings. It is believed that the Mumba cave shelter was occupied over the years by various people.

Sleeping

Karatu *p254, map p256*

L Gibb's Farm, 4 km from Karatu, T027-2508930, www.gibbsfarm.net. At the edge of a forest facing the Mbulu Hills to the southeast. Original farm built by German settler in 1930s to cultivate coffee, sold to James Gibb in 1948 after the Second World War, and currently run by his widow, Margaret Gibb. Fine atmosphere, open log fires, excellent gardens, coffee is still grown on the farm, the meals in the restaurant are made from organic vegetables, and the 4-course dinners each evening are truly excellent. The 20 twin-bedded rooms with en suite bathroom are set in the grounds, whilst the dining, reading room and bar are in the old farmhouse. Rates US$330 per person. Discount between Easter and end June.

A Ngorongoro Farm House, on a 500-acre coffee farm 4 km from the Lolduare gate of the crater, T074-8593008 (mob), www.africawilderness.com. There are 3 separate camps of 9 comfortable bungalows, attractively built in the style of an old colonial farm. In the main thatched building is the bar, dining area, library and lounge with a fireplace. Excellent food using dairy food or products and fresh vegetables from the farm.

A Plantation Lodge, 4 km towards the crater, 2 km from the main road, badly signposted so look hard, T027-2534364/65, www.plantation-lodge.com. The Arusha booking office is in the arcade of shops behind Shoprite Supermarket, T027-2534364-5. Accommodation in exquisitely stylish rooms on a coffee estate. A huge amount of detail has gone into the safari-style decor. The 18 individual and spacious rooms are in renovated farm buildings throughout the grounds. There are several places to sit and drink coffee or enjoy a sundowner and you can choose to eat at grand dining tables on your veranda, in huge stone halls, in the garden, or in the main house with the other guests. The honeymoon suite has a vast bed, fireplace, jacuzzi and sunken bath, some units are whole houses which are ideal for families. Swimming pool.

A-E **Kudu Lodge and Campsite**, signposted to the left if going out of town towards crater, 600 m off the main road, T027-2534055, www.kuducamp.com. Established and popular lodge in mature gardens with experienced staff. Accommodation in comfortable rondavaals. There's a variety of options: doubles from US$100, triples US$120, brand new family cottages with kitchen from US$160. 50% discount in low season. A good option is to stay in the park lodges. The large shady campsite, often used by safari groups, has separate cooking shelters and good ablution blocks with hot water. Camping US$10, tents and sleeping bags for hire. Enormous bar with satellite TV, pool table, fireplace and lots of couches, internet café, gift shop, small restaurant presently being extended, safaris can be organized. Takes US$, GBP and Euros but no credit cards.

B-E **Ngorongoro Safari Resort**, on the main road in the middle of Karatu next to a petrol station and bank, T027-2534287/90, safariresort@yahoo.com. Well run by the affable manager Aloyce, this is a good mid-range option, with 12 neat and tidy double rooms with space for extra beds and good showers with plenty of hot water. Full breakfast included, cosy (though expensive) bar with fireplace and satellite TV, restaurant, supermarket. Room rates are overpriced at US$95 for a double but nevertheless a friendly and comfortable place to stay. Camping is available for US$5 pp but large groups will be directed to a larger purpose-built campsite on one of the back roads. Here there is a bar and kitchen area for the safari cooks. Safaris organized, especially good value are half-day crater tours for US$110 and full day for US$120.

D-F **Safari Junction**, 500 m from the main road, on the same road as Kudu Lodge, not clearly signposted, T074-5360704 (mob). One of the first camps to be established in town and now a little tatty, nevertheless it has functional but basic self-contained rooms for US$20, and a large shady campsite with thatched cooking shelters and fairly reliable hot showers for US$5 per person, a small dining room and a bar. The highlight here is the dancing. Not traditional dancing as such but the staff and local patrons put on a very good show of modern African dance with a local band if there are enough people in the bar. Very lively and good fun – and it often turns into an impromptu disco.

Ngorongoro Crater rim *p255, map 256*

For other accommodation options within 20 km of the Ngorongoro Crater, outside the conservation area's boundary, see Karatu, page 259.

L **Ngorongoro Crater Lodge**, central reservations, CC Africa, Johannesburg, South Africa, T+27-11-8094300, www.ccafrica.com. A lodge has been on this spot since 1934, but it was completely rebuilt in 1995, and the architecture and style is simply magnificent. It's the most luxurious lodge on the rim of the crater, very romantic individual cottages with views down into the crater even from the bathrooms. Member of Small Luxury Hotels of the World. Very expensive at US$625 per person per night, but fully inclusive of meals, drinks and game drives, discount between Easter and end of Jun.

L **Ngorongoro Serena Lodge**, T027- 2537050 direct lodge number, reservations www.serenahotels.com. Luxury development built to the highest international standards out of wood and pebbles. Stunningly perched on the rim of the crater and each of the rooms has its own rock enclosed balcony. Telescope provided on main balcony to view the crater. The centre of the public area is warmed by a roaring fire and lit by lanterns. Friendly staff, good food and has its own nursery in the gardens to plant indigenous plant species. Offers hiking and shorter nature walks. Local

Masai make up 25% of staff. Rates from US$350 per person.

L Ngorongoro Sopa Lodge, central reservations T+254-2-336088, Nairobi, www.sopalodges.com. Luxury all-suite lodge with 92 suites on the exclusive eastern rim of the crater, all enjoying uninterrupted views into the crater. Spectacular African rondavaal design with magnificent lounges, restaurant and entertainment areas, swimming pool and satellite TV. Most of the lodges are on the southern or western crater rim but the Sopa is on the unspoilt eastern rim, way off the beaten track. Unfortunately this involves an extra 45-50 km journey (one way) over poor quality roads.

A Ngorongoro Wildlife Lodge, a member of the South African Three Cities hotel group, Arusha reservations, T027-2544595, www.threecities.co.za. An ugly 1970s concrete block on the rim of the crater with wonderful views, the facilites are fine inside. 75 rooms with balconies overlooking the crater. Geared to fast throughput of tours. Bar with log fire, TV room with satellite TV, restaurant serving either buffets or à la carte. Zebra can be seen on the lawns here.

National Park campsites

Simba Campsite, about 2 km from Crater Village. The public campsite with showers, toilets and firewood, but facilities have deteriorated and water supplies are irregular – make sure that you have sufficient drinking water to keep you going for the night and the game drive the next day. Given that you are camping at some elevation at the top of the crater, this place gets bitterly cold at night so ensure you have a warm sleeping bag. It gets very busy with tour groups, with up to 200 tents at any one time. The hot water runs out quickly – so expect not to have a shower here. Many budget safari companies use this site, though Karatu is quite frankly a better option. If in your own vehicle, there is no need to book. Just pay for camping (US$30) along with park entry when you enter at the gate. Elsewhere in the reserve are 5 special campsites (US$50) usually used by the safari companies going off the beaten track.

Olduvai Gorge *p257, map 256*

L Olduvai Camp, just south of the Serengeti border, closest lodge to the Olduvai Gorge, reservations through UK T+44-(0)1306-880770, www.africatravelresource.com. The three head guides are all Masai warriors from the villages immediately around the camp and there is the opportunity to go walking with them in the Ngorongoro highlands. Facilities are simple, the 16 tents are of a modest size with thatched roofs and wooden floors, furnished with the basic essentials, en suite bathrooms with chemical toilets and bladder showers, public spaces are limited to two small thatched rondavaals and an open fire-pit. Has a generator, lanterns are provided at night. Rates US$300 per person. Compared to the other giant impersonal concrete lodges in the Ngorongoro Conservation Area, this is an intimate camp that offers the opportunity to sleep on the plains amongst the local Masai.

L Ndutu Safari Lodge, reservations, Arusha, T027-2502829, www.ndutu.com. Established in 1967 by professional hunter George Dove, Ndutu is one of the earliest permanent lodges in the Crater/Serengeti area and has become something of an institution over the years. On the southern shore of Ndutu soda lake, amongst acacia woodland, in a good position for the migration in the calving season, midway between the Ngorongoro Crater and Seronera Lodge in the Serengeti, 90 km to both and near to the Olduvai Gorge. Sleeps 70 in 32 stone cottages. Bar and restaurant, fresh ingredients from Gibb's Farm, restricted use of water as it is trucked in. Rates in the region of US$300 per person.

Ndutu was home for over 20 years to the famous wildlife photographer Baron Hugo van Lawick, one of the first filmmakers to bring the Serengeti to the attention of the world. He died in 2002 and was granted the honour of a full state funeral before being buried at Ndutu.

Lake Eyasi *p258, map 256*

L Kisima Ngeda Luxury Tented Camp, on the shores of Lake Eyasi, a remote southern corner of Ngorongoro Conservation Area, at the foot of Mount Ol Deani, reservations, Arusha, T027-2506094, www.fortes-safaris.com/kisng.htm. Tents with thatched roofs next to lake, en suite stone baths, wooden furniture, electric lights and plenty of space. Swimming in the lake, all activities on offer including meeting the Hadzabe people.

Eating

Karatu *p254*

🍴 **Bytes**, in the middle of town behind a petrol station. Very stylish café-bar with cane furniture, homemade cakes, good coffee, imported alcoholic drinks, delicious daily specials such as Mexican wraps and curries, expensive internet access for nearly US$4 an hour (Karatu does not have its own server). Next door is a shop selling local farm produce and coffee beans.

Serengeti National Park

The Serengeti supports the greatest concentration of plains game in Africa. Frequently dubbed the eighth wonder of the world, it was granted the status of a World Heritage Site in 1978, and became an International Biosphere Reserve in 1981. Its far-reaching plains of endless grass, tinged with the twisted shadows of acacia trees, have made it the quintessential image of a wild and untarnished Africa. Large prides of lions laze easily in the long grasses, numerous families of elephants feed on acacia bark, and giraffes, antelope, monkeys, eland and a whole range of other African wildlife is here in awe-inspiring numbers. The park is the centre of the Serengeti Ecosystem – the combination of the Serengeti, the Ngorongoro Conservation Area, Kenya's Masai Mara and four smaller game reserves. Within this region live an estimated three million large animals. The system protects the largest single movement of wildlife on earth – the annual wildebeest migration. This is a phenomenal sight: thousands upon thousands of animals, particularly wildebeest and zebra, as far as the eye can see. ▸▸ For more information on national parks and safaris, see page 39. For lodges and camps listings, see page 268.

Ins and outs

Getting there There are several airstrips inside the park used by charter planes arranged by the park lodges and by **Coastal Air** T022-2117969-60, www.coastal.cc, who have flights from the Grumeti and Seronera airstrips daily to Arusha (2 hr) at 0940 and to Mwanza (1 hr) daily at 1500 (stopping at the other lodge airstrips on demand). From Arusha the flight departs at 1230, from Mwanza at 0900.

By road, the Serengeti is usually approached from the Ngorongoro Crater Reserve. From the top of the crater the spectacularly scenic road with a splendid view of the Serengeti plains winds down the crater walls on to the grasslands below. Along here the Masai tribesmen can be seen herding their cattle in the fresher pastures towards the top of the crater. Shortly before the Serengeti's boundary there is the turning off to Olduvai Gorge where most safari companies stop. Then entry is through the **Naabi Hill Gate** to the southeast of the park where there is a small shop and information centre. From here it is 75 km to **Seronera**, the village in the heart of the Serengeti, which is 335 km from Arusha. Approaching from Mwanza or Musoma on the shore of Lake Victoria, take the road east and you will enter the Serengeti through the **Ndabaka Gate** in the west through what is termed as the Western Corridor to the Grumeti region. This road requires 4WD and may be impassable in the rainy season. There is a third, less frequently used gate in the north, **Ikoma Gate** that lies a few km from Seronera. This also goes to Musoma but again is not a very good road.

Colour map 1, grid A4
2°40'S 35°0'E
For more information: www.serengeti.org

Getting around Most tourists use a safari package from either Arusha or Mwanza but it is possible to explore in your own vehicle. However, the roads are quite rough and you can expect hard corrugations, (especially the road from Naabi Hill to Seronera) where there are deep ruts, and in many regions of the park there is a fine top soil known locally as 'black cotton', which can get impossibly sticky and slippery in the wet. This is especially true of the Western Corridor. The dry season should not present too many problems. The Park Headquarters are at Seronera and there are airstrips at Seronera, Lobo and Grumeti, and at many of the small exclusive camps. **Park entry fee**: US$50.

Climate The dry season runs from June to October, the wet between March and May and in between is a period of short rains, during which time things turn green. At this time of year there are localized rain showers but it's more or less dry. With altitudes ranging from 920 to 1,850 m, average temperatures vary from 15 to 25 degrees Celsius. It is coldest from June to October, particularly in the evenings.

Background

The name is derived from the Masai word '*siringet*' meaning 'extended area' or 'endless plains'. A thick layer of ash blown from volcanoes in the Ngorongoro highlands covered the landscape between 3-4 million years ago, preserved traces of early man, and

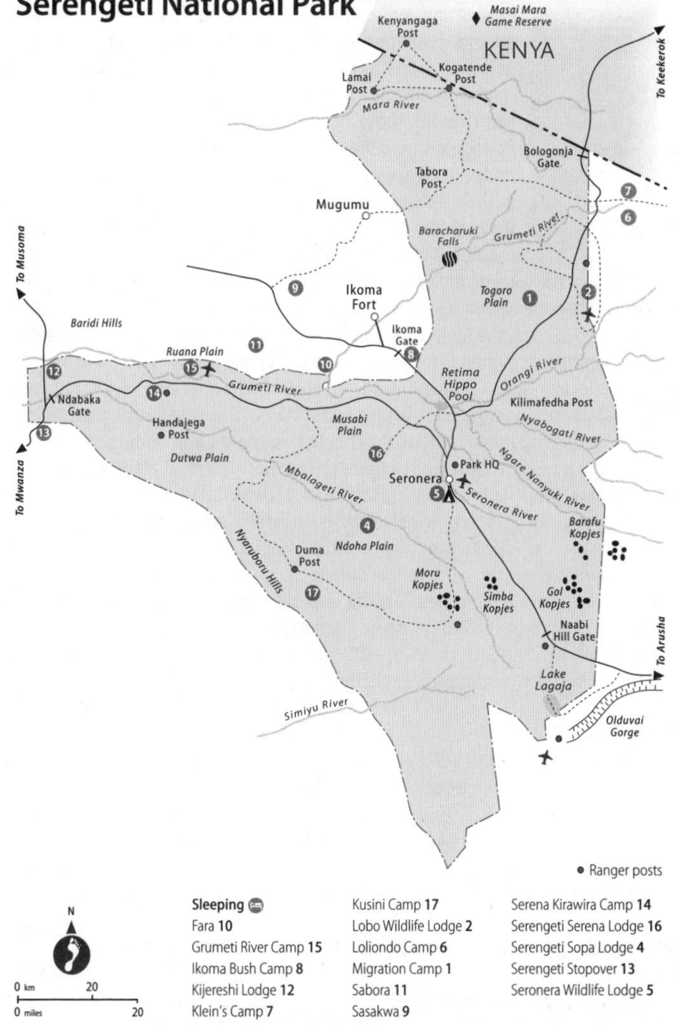

 enriched the soil that supports the southern grass plains. Avoided by the pastoralist Masai because the woodlands had tsetse flies carrying trypanosomiasis (sleeping sickness), the early European explorers found this area uninhabited and abounding with game. Serengeti National Park was established in 1951 and at 14,763 sq km is Tanzania's second largest national park (after Selous). It rises from 920-1,850 m above sea level and its landscape varies from the long and short grass plains in the south, the central savanna, the more hilly wooded areas in the north and the extensive woodland in the western corridor. The **Maswa Game Reserve** adjoins its western border.

★ Wildlife

During the rainy season the wildebeest, whose population has been estimated at around 1,500,000, are found in the eastern section of the Serengeti and also the Masai Mara in Kenya to the north. When the dry season begins at the end of June the annual migration starts as the animals move in search of pasture. Just before this, they concentrate on the remaining green patches, forming huge herds, the rutting season begins and territories are established by the males, who then attempt to attract females into their areas. Once mating has occurred, the herds merge together again and the migration to the northwest begins. The migrating animals do not all follow the same route. About half go west, often going outside the park boundaries, and then swing northeast. The other half go directly north. The two groups meet up in the Masai Mara in Kenya. To get to the west section of the Serengeti and the Masai Mara, where they will find pasture in the dry season, the wildebeest must cross a number of large rivers and this proves too much for many of them. Many of the weaker and older animals die during the migration. Needless to say predators follow the wildebeest on their great trek and easy pickings are to be had. The animals have to cross the Mara River where massive Nile crocodiles with thickset jaws lick their lips in anticipation of a substantial feed. For any visitor to Tanzania, the herds are a spectacular sight. They return to the southeast at the end of the dry season (October/November) and calving begins at the start of the wet season (March).

This migration to the Masai Mara and back again generally lasts 7-8 months and the biggest concentrations of wildebeest can be seen in the Serengeti between November and June before they begin to head north again.

The Serengeti is also famous for cheetah, leopards and lions, some of which migrate with the wildebeest while others remain in the central plain. Prides of lions are commonly seen, leopards are most frequently detected resting in trees during the daytime along the Seronera River, whereas cheetahs are usually spotted near the Simba Kopjes. The elephant population in Serengeti was estimated to have fallen fivefold during the mid 1970-1980s thanks to poaching, though since then the numbers have slowly increased. Birdlife is prolific and includes various species of kingfishers, sunbirds and rollers, ostrich, egrets, herons, storks, ibis, spoonbills and ducks. Birds of prey include Ruppell's vulture and the hooded vulture, several varieties of kestrels, eagles, goshawks and harriers.

Routes

If you are approaching the Serengeti from the southeast (from the Ngorongoro Crater Conservation Area), **Lake Ndutu**, fringed by acacia woodland, lies southeast of the main road. Lake Ndutu is a soda lake, with a substantial quantity of mineral deposits around the shoreline. It is home to many birds, including flamingos. During the rainy season it offers excellent opportunities to see a large variety of animals including predators. Next you will reach the **Short Grass Plains**. The flat landscape is broken by

In the space of 3-4 weeks 90% of the female wildebeest give birth. These new calves provide easy pickings for larger scavengers and cats – a very good reason why wildebeest calves are up and running within four minutes of birth.

the **Gol Mountains**, to the right, and by kopjes. The grass here remains short during both the wet and dry seasons. There is no permanent water supply in this region as a result of the nature of the soil. However, during the rains water collects in hollows and depressions until it dries up at the end of the wet season. It is then that the animals begin to move on.

The **Southern Plains** provide nutritious grasses for the wildebeest, and when the short rains come in November these mammals move south to feed. In February-March, 90% of female wildebeest give birth and the plains are filled with young calves.

Naabi Hill Gate marks the end of the Short Grass and beginning of the **Long Grass Plains**. Dotted across the plains are **kopjes**. These interesting geological formations are made up of ancient granite that has been left behind as the surrounding soil structures have been broken down by centuries of erosion and weathering. They play an important role in the ecology of the plains, providing habitats for many different animals from rock hyraxes (a small rabbit-like creature whose closest relation is actually the elephant) to cheetahs.

The kopjes that you might visit include the **Moru Kopjes** in the south of the park to the left of the main road heading north. You may be lucky enough to see the Verreaux eagle, which sometimes nests here. The Moru Kopjes have a cave with Masai paintings on the wall and a rock called **Gong Rock** after the sound it makes when struck with a stone. There are also the **Simba Kopjes** on the left of the road before reaching Seronera, which, as their name suggests, are often a hideout for lions.

Passing through the Long Grass Plains in the wet season from around December to May is an incredible experience. All around, stretching into the distance, are huge numbers of wildebeest, Thompson's gazelle, zebra etc.

The village of **Seronera** is in the middle of the park set in the **Seronera Valley**. It forms an important transition zone between the southern grasslands and the northern woodlands. The area is criss-crossed by rivers, and as a result this is where you are most likely to spot game. It is reached by a gravel road, which is in fairly good condition. Seronara is the best area to visit if you can only manage a short safari. It

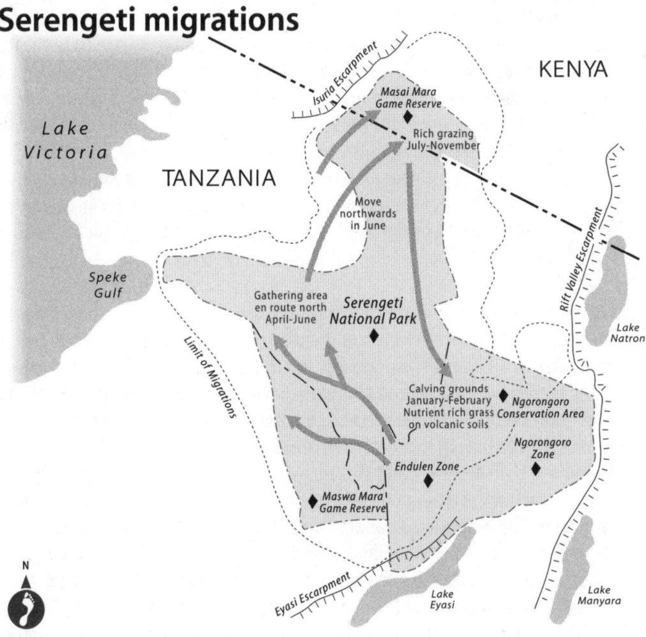

Grumeti Reserves

At the time of writing three new lodges were being built on the northern boundaries of the Serengeti to the north of the Grumeti River and not far from the Fort Ikoma Gate. During research we were lucky enough to visit the construction sites and by the time that this book comes out they should all be functional. The lodges are Sasakwa, Sabora and Fara.

During the 2-3 years of construction, the companies involved have made a concerted effort to maintain a good relationship with the local communities living to the north of the Serengeti's boundaries around the villages of Nata and Ikoma, and to contribute to the area's environment. Not only has the project provided thousands of jobs in construction, but a local quarry that has been opened to quarry stone used at the lodges will remain open for the benefit of the local economy after the lodges have been finished. By using the extensive building machinery brought in for construction, boreholes with handpumps have been dug and installed at 15 schools in the area; hi-tech machine-built bricks, which are more environmentally friendly than regular local bricks made from sand, have been made at the lodge sites and been used to upgrade and maintain these schools; and scholarships for secondary schools and universities have been offered to local children. In addition to this conservation officers have been employed on the construction sites to educate local people about the damaging affects of poaching so close to the Serengeti's boundary (this is a fairly poor rural area, and tradionally people hunt and eat livestock such as antelope). Previously the region was over-hunted which had an affect on the herds that migrated through the Serengeti, but in the two years since the project started, poaching has been dramatically reduced. As well as education, the project has implemented alternative sources of protein and vitamins for the local communities such as small scale fish and chicken farms, bee-keeping, and fruit and vegetable gardens. In addition, when the lodges become operational, these will be used to supply the lodge restaurants with fresh produce, and local people will be able to sell their livestock to the lodges' butcheries. The biggest conservation initiative plans to relocate up to 25 rhinos from Kenya into the Serengeti in the area directly south of the lodges. At present there are no rhino in this region of the park, and very few in the Serengeti at all. On our visit, the bomas to house the rhinos during the relocation process were being built.

All these efforts are largely down to a committed team headed by one man

has a visitor centre and the research institute is based here. It also contains a small museum noted for its giant stick insects (near the lodge). In the approach to Seronera the number of trees increases, particularly the thorny acacia trees. You can expect to see buffalo, impala, lion, hippo and elephant. If you are lucky you might see leopard.

About 5 km north of Seronera the track splits. To the right it goes to Banagi and Lobo beyond, and to the left to the Western Corridor, about 20 km north of Banagi Hill, which is home to both browsers and grazers. At its base is the **Retima Hippo Pool** about 6 km off the main track at Banagi. Banagi was the site of the original Game Department Headquarters before it became a national park. North of here the land is mainly rolling plains of both grassland and woodland with a few hilly areas and rocky outcrops.

In the northeast section of the park is the **Lobo Northern Woodland**. Wildlife remains in this area throughout the year including during the dry season. The area is characterized by rocky hills and outcrops, where pythons sunbathe, and woodlands (who shall remain anonymous). Suffice it to say he is an American billionaire, who came to the Serengeti several years ago and fell in love with it. (He and his family have a private house at Sasakwa which is on a hill with a panoramic view of the Serengeti plains.) The lodges will be run as commercial enterprises but it is expected that the money generated from them will only cover day-to-day expenses, and with all the conservation and community initiatives implemented in the region (it costs thousands of US$ to relocate a rhino), and the millions of dollars gone into construction, the project will not be profit-making.

Sabora is modelled on a classic 1920s safari camp with elegant furnishings, fine china and crystal in the restaurant. **Fara** will also be styled in a classic Africa safari theme with a large glass frontage overlooking a waterhole. Both will be luxury tented camps with no more than half a dozen tents. The piece de résistance will be **Sasakwa** which comprises 3 1-bed villas, 2 2-bed villas and 1 3-bed villa plus the owner's extravagant house. Each of the villas has its own living room, dressing room, veranda, all with fireplaces and claw foot baths in the bathrooms, and plunge pool right on the rim of the hill. The views from all rooms look down on to the plains of the Western Corridor of the Serengeti which, during the migration, is literally stuffed with animals. In the main building is a restaurant, billard room, gym, yoga room with heated floor, bar, entertainment area with TV, large rim flow swimming pool again on the lip of the hill, all decorated with 'distressed' antique furniture and elaborate curtains. Other facilities include an equestrian centre with around 20 horses with a jumping paddock and walled (because of the wild predators) riding course which can also be used for jogging. Guests will be able to get around the whole complex by golf cart and the camp will have its own helicopter to transfer guests from the airstrip at the bottom of the hill to the helipad near the lodge. They are also talking about buying their own hot air balloon.

Reservations and information from the office at the Burka Coffee Estates, in Arusha, a few kilometres out of town on the road to the crater, T027-2508976, administration@grumetireserves.com, www.grumetireserves.com. Prices at the time of writing had not been set but could be up to US$3000 per room per night at Sasakwa. Without doubt the most luxurious and attractive safari experience in Tanzania. Finally you will be able to watch the annual wildebeest migration whilst lying in the bath...

frequented by elephants fringe the rivers. Lobo is the site of the **Lobo Lodge**, 75 km from Seronera. Further north is the Mara River with riverine forest bordering its banks. This is one of the rivers that claims many wildebeest lives every year during the migration. You will see both hippo and crocodile along the river banks.

If you take the left-hand track where the road splits north of Seronera you will follow the **Grumeti Western Corridor**. The best time to follow this track is in the dry season (June-October) when the road is at its best and the migrating animals have reached the area. Part of the road follows, on your right, the Grumeti River, fringed by lush riverine forest, home to the black and white colobus monkey. On the banks of the river you will also see huge crocodiles basking in the sun. The Musabi and Ndoha Plains to the northwest and west of Seronera respectively can be viewed if you have a four-wheel drive vehicle. The latter plain is the breeding area of topi and large herds of up to 2,000 will often be found here. All but the main routes are poorly marked.

Inside the park *p262, map 263*

L **Grumeti River Camp**, Western Corridor, 93 km west of Seronera and 50 km east of Lake Victoria, central reservations, CC Africa, Johannesburg, South Africa, T+27-11-8094300, www.ccafrica.com. Overlooks a tributary of the Grumeti River teeming with hippo and crocodiles. The wildebeest migration also passes through. Real African bush country with an abundance of birdlife including Fisher's lovebird. Central bar/ dining area, 10 custom-made tents with private shower and WC, solar electricity minimizes noise and pollution. Expensive at US$590 per person but stylish and fantastic service.

L **Kusini Camp**, reservations, Arusha, T027-2509816/2509817, www.kusini.com. At the Hambi ya Mwaki-Nyeb Kopjes in the southwest, near the border with the Maswa Game Reserve, well off the usual tourist track, the camp is situated in a conchoidal outcrop of kopjes, offering superb views. Closes during the rainy season Apr-May. 9 stylish tents, one of which is a honeymoon suite, hospitable camp managers arrange sundowners on cushions up on the kopjes and candlelit dinners each evening. There's also a library and lounge. Rates US$550 per person.

L **Lobo Wildlife Lodge**, a member of the South African Three Cities hotel group, Arusha reservations, T027-2544595, www.threecities.co.za. Northeast of Seronera in the Lobo area, 45 km from the border with Kenya. The 75 rooms built entirely of wood and glass around clusters of large boulders remain almost invisible from distance. The swimming pool and bar, both dug into the rock, afford good views over the savanna.

L **Migration Camp**, T028-2500630-9, www.elewana.com, www.serengeti migrationcamp.com. Built within the rocks of a kopje in the Ndassiata Hills near Lobo, overlooking the Grumeti River, giving excellent views of the migration. Jacuzzi, swimming pool, restaurant. The 20 richly decorated tents include a secluded honeymoon tent and a family tent sleeping 6, each one is surrounded by a 360º veranda, and there are many secluded vantage points linked by timber walkways, bridges and viewing platforms. Resident game includes lion, leopard, elephant and buffalo. Rates in the region of US$430 per person.

L Serena Kirawira Camp, Western Serengeti, T028-2621518 direct lodge number, reservations www.serenahotels.com. A luxuriously appointed all-inclusive tented camp 90 km from Seronera in the secluded Western Corridor area. A member of Small Luxury Hotels of the World group. All the 25 tents have Edwardian decor and great views across the plains. The central public tent is adorned with exquisite antiques. Each tent has a personal valet and the colonial theme continues in the dining room with silverware, crystal and staff dressed in white turbans and Swahili robes. Rates US$550 per person.

L Serengeti Serena Lodge, T028-2622612/ 2621519 direct lodge number, reservations www.serenahotels.com. Another super-luxurious establishment in an idyllic central location with superb views towards the Western Corridor. Set high overlooking the plains, the lodge is constructed to reflect the design of an African village. Each of the 66 rooms are stone-walled and thatched rondavaals, with wooden balcony, natural stone bathrooms, a/c, central heating, carved furniture and decorated with Makonde carvings. Also has beauty centre. Rates US$350 per person.

L Serengeti Sopa Lodge, central reservations, Nairobi, T+254-2-336088, www.sopalodges.com. Luxury all-suite lodge with 75 suites in the previously protected area of Nyarboro Hills north of Moru Kopjes. Excellent views of the Serengeti plains through double-storey window walls in all public areas, multi-level restaurant and lounges and conference facilities, double swimming pool and satellite TV, way off the beaten track involving an extra 50 km drive over poor roads (one way).

L Sayari Camp, reservations through Asilia Lodges, Arusha, T027-2502799, www.asilialodges.com. A completely mobile camp that follows the migration; from Dec-Mar it operates on the southern plains and from Jun-Dec in the north of the park. 8 luxurious and comfortable tents with en suite bathrooms, the mess tent has a bar, lounge and restaurant, centred around a camp fire, attentive service, rates are full board and include all drinks, game drives, fly camping. High season rates US$400 per person.

L Seronera Wildlife Lodge, lodge number T028-2502711, book through any travel agent or tour operator. This large lodge really is at the heart of the Serengeti. Good game-viewing year round, but also significant visitor traffic. The public areas are very cleverly built into a rocky kopje, and the bar is especially nice, but the 75 rooms are in unattractive and old-fashioned accommodation blocks built in the 1970s. Restaurant, shop, electricity mornings and evenings, bar and viewing platform at the top of the kopje (beware the monkeys). Campers at the nearby public campsites are allowed into the bar in the evenings (suitably dressed) as driving around the immediate vicinity of Seronera is permitted until 2200.

L Serengeti Safari Camp, this is a Nomad's property, no direct bookings, email them for a list of the agents info@nomad.co.tz, www.serengeti-safari-camp.com. Seasonally mobile camp following the migration. Green canvas tents stand open to the savanna, decorated in suede, bark cloth and muslin in classic safari style. The bathrooms have reed mats, enamel basins and plenty of hot water. The mess tents are central and sociable.

A-D Kijereshi Lodge, T028-2621231, shares a website with www.hoteltilapia.com (a hotel in Mwanza) and is at the far end of the Western Corridor. Tents and bungalows, with en suite bathrooms, though not in the same class as some of the other tented camps. Excellent restaurant in an old homestead that sometimes has game meat on the menu, cosy lounge and bar with fire in winter, swimming pool, gift shop, TV room with wildlife videos. This is usually fairly quiet and convenient if you want to enter or exit the park at the Ndabaka Gate from Mwanza or Musoma. The **campsite** here is very basic with only a long drop loo and cold shower, but campers can use the other facilities at the lodge (see above). Be warned though – the campsite is a km or so from the lodge; exercise extreme caution if walking back in the dark, animals are present. Camping fees are paid directly to the lodge reception here and not on entry to the park.

National Park campsites

There are several public campsites around the Seronera. Be prepared to be totally self-sufficient and if you are self-driving bring food with you as there is little available in Seronera Village. It is not neccessery to pre- book the public campsites; you simply pay for camping when you enter the park. Facilities vary but most have nothing more than a long drop loo and are completely unfenced. The animals do wander through at night so ensure that you stay in your tent. Camps are regularly visited by hyenas each night scavenging for scraps and lions have also been known to wander through in the middle of the night.

Outside the park *map p263*

L **Klein's Camp**, on a private ranch on the north eastern boundary of the park just south of the Kenyan border, central reservations, CC Africa, Johannesburg, South Africa, T+27-11-8094300, www.ccafrica.com, www.kleinscamp.com. Named after the American big game hunter Al Klein, who in 1926 built his base camp in this valley. The ranch is located between the Serengeti and farmland, which forms a natural buffer zone for the animals. 10 stone cottages each with en suite facilities, the dining room and bar are in separate rondavaals with commanding views of the Grumeti River Valley, swimming pool, solar power electricity. Rates US$590 per person per night.

L **Loliondo Camp**, in the 200 sq km Loliondo Concession, which borders the northeastern boundary of the Serengeti and is close to the south eastern side of the Masai Mara, reservations through Hoopoe Safaris, Arusha T027-2507011/2507541, www.kirurumu.com. Open Oct-Mar. The tented accommodation is luxuriously comfortable and spacious and tastefully furnished. The 5 tents are spread out throughout a kopje area with the dining tent at the base of the main kopje rock. Resident game is plentiful in the area, drawn during the dry seasons by the nearby waterhole, and the migration passes through the concession on its way to/from the Mara area. Activities include walking with the Masai, fly camping and game drives. High season rates US$420 per person.

A **Ikoma Bush Camp**, 2 km from Ikoma Gate, swala@ habari.co.tz, www.swalasafaris.com. Has the concession for the area to operate game viewing drives and walks and works in close collaboration with the local villages. This is considerably cheaper than some of the more luxurious tented camps above, and rates start from US$80 per person full board. The camp is small, comfortable and secluded. Tents are spacious with their own bathroom. There is hot and cold running water and flush toilets. Electricity is provided by solar power as is hot water. There is a dining room and bar under thatch.

C-E **Serengeti Stopover**, along the Mwanza-Musoma Road on the western edge of Serengeti, 141 km east of Mwanza and 1 km west of Ndabaka Gate, T028-2537095, www.serengetistopover.com. Lake Victoria is within walking distance. 16 self-contained chalets, some with verandas and lounge areas, and a campsite. Swimming pool, shop, a bar built in the trees with good views into the Serengeti, a collection of snakes. Its proximity to the park means that game can be present and you could avoid park entrance fees. Unlike safaris from Arusha, the lodge can arrange day trips into the park that can be very good value. It is run as a community initiative with the local Sukuma people, and tours can be arranged to the local villages. Recommended for budget travellers, you can jump off any of the buses that go between Mwanza and Musoma.

Activities and tours

★ Serengeti National Park *p262, map p263*

Balloon Safaris, US$399 per person available at *Seronera Lodge*, 1-hr balloon flights at sunrise, champagne breakfast and transport to and from your lodge. The desk is in reception T027-2508578, www.balloon safaris.com. Especially during the months of the migration, this is often the highlight of visitors' trips to Tanzania. The journey takes a little over an hour and sets off before dawn, flying low over the plains as the sun comes up and turns the grasslands from blue to gold. After landing, guests have a champagne breakfast complete with crystal glasses and white linen tablecloths in the middle of the African bush, as zebra and antelope graze nearby. Although expensive, the experience is well worth the treat. Given that there are only two balloons, it is essential to pre-book this excursion

Around Lake Victoria

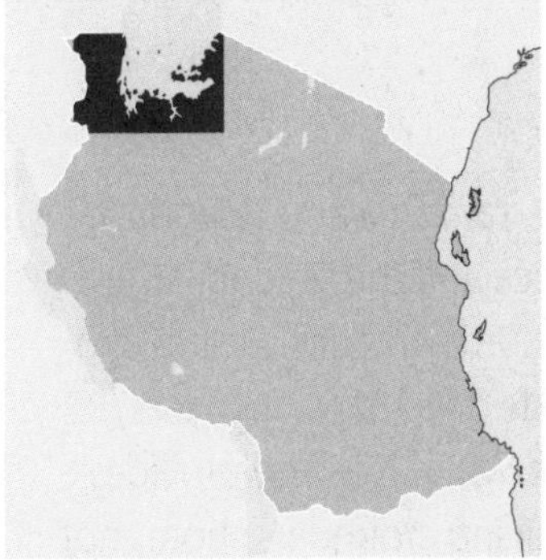

Footprint features

Introduction

Lake Victoria, bordered by Kenya, Tanzania and Uganda, is the largest freshwater lake in Africa and the second largest in the world after Lake Superior in North America. Occupying a shallow depression at an altitude of 1,135 m, it covers 69,490 sq km, is the source of the White Nile and provides a livelihood for millions of people living around its shores not only in Tanzania but in Kenya and Uganda too. This area is a long way from the coast and transport links leave much to be desired. The road to Mwanza through central Tanzania is in a poor state, and better (albeit slow) access is by train, or by air (though services can be erratic) or by road through Kenya. Mwanza is a busy city, and surprisingly, given its location, the second largest in Tanzania, and there is much activity in exporting fish from Lake Victoria. It is the terminus of a branch of the central railway line from Dar es Salaam, and has trade links with nearby Kenya. Bukoba, on the west side of the lake, is in a very attractive setting. But none of these places feature high on the usual tourist itinerary, though the western section of the Serengeti National Park can be accessed from this region, and the most notable attraction on the lake is the Rubondo Island National Park.

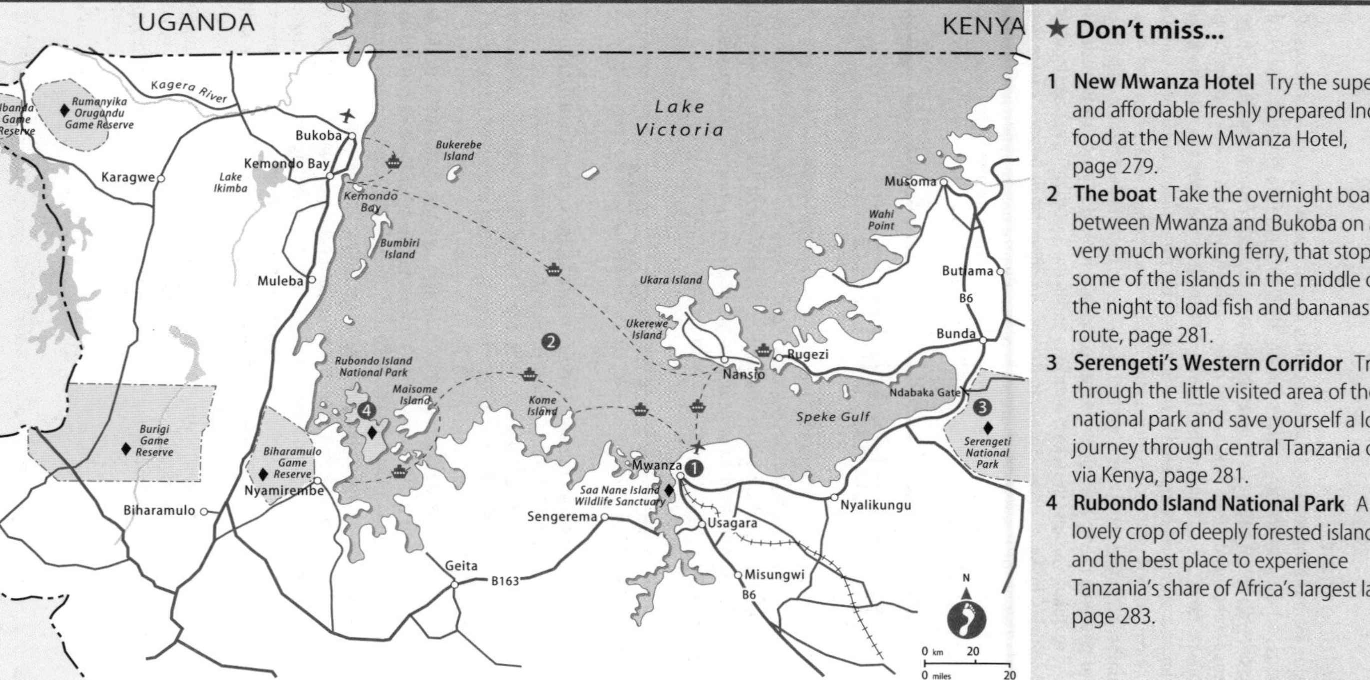

★ Don't miss...

1 **New Mwanza Hotel** Try the superb and affordable freshly prepared Indian food at the New Mwanza Hotel, page 279.

2 **The boat** Take the overnight boat between Mwanza and Bukoba on a very much working ferry, that stops at some of the islands in the middle of the night to load fish and bananas en route, page 281.

3 **Serengeti's Western Corridor** Travel through the little visited area of the national park and save yourself a long journey through central Tanzania or via Kenya, page 281.

4 **Rubondo Island National Park** A lovely crop of deeply forested islands and the best place to experience Tanzania's share of Africa's largest lake, page 283.

Ins and outs

Getting there

Aside from the major tarred road that links Mwanza with the border of Kenya, the roads in the region are very poor, especially after rain. There are frequent buses to the border with Kenya and beyond and long distance buses to Arusha and Dar es Salaam usually take the route via Kenya. Most people arrive in Mwanza by train on the Central Railway from Dar es Salaam. The railway line, built in the 1920s during the British administration, was completed in 1928. It forms the extension of the Central Line and was considered vital for the development of the northwest area. There are also a number of ferry services operating on Lake Victoria, notably the Mwanza-Bukoba car and passenger ferry which is the only reasonable method of reaching Bukoba. The road to Bukoba around the lake is atrocious and in the past there have been incidents of vehicles being hijacked. This was the region where many refugee camps were located along the Rwanda and Burundi borders. Mwanza has an airport and there are regular flights from both Dar es Salaam and Nairobi. There are also flights to Rubondo Island National Park.

Eastern Lake Victoria

The Tanzania towns of Musoma and Mwanza and the nearby islands offer the opportunity to witness the majesty of Lake Victoria. Mwanza, the second largest town in Tanzania, is the spring board for the ferry across the lake to Bukoba on the western side, easily the best method of getting to the other side, and the terminus for the Central Railway. » *For Sleeping, eating and other listings, see pages 278-282.*

Musoma → *Phone code: 028. See map page 278.* » *pp278-282*

Colour map A3. Population: 150,000. 1°50'S 34°30'E.

This small port is set on the east shores of Lake Victoria close to the border with Kenya. It's close to the Western Corridor of Serengeti National Park and so should be one of the centres for safaris to the park. However, because the Kenyan border was closed for several years, and because of its general inaccessibility, it has not developed as such. There is little reason to come here although the views over the lake are very good and it is a bustling and friendly town and capital of Mara Region. Visitors usuallly pop in on their way to or from Kenya. The weekday market, when women bring their crops of mangoes and green leafy vegetables, ripe avocados and bunches of bright yellow bananas to sell is worth seeing; as are the many varieties of boats on the lake, from large ferries and transport barges to *ngalawa* fishing boats and dugout canoes. Small boats can be taken across the bay and to the little islands nearby for around US$1 per person. They leave from the fish market and harbour on the north shore, not far from the *Afrilux Hotel*.

The town has a climate of hot days and cool nights. Electricity and water supplies can be erratic, and the small hotels will not have generators. None of the hotels currently take credit cards, only the banks will change travellers' cheques, and there are no internet cafés.

Haya men from this region are tall and the women have a reputation throughout the country for great beauty.

Lake Victoria

Lake Victoria is one of the most important natural water resources in the sub-Saharan region of Africa. It is has a surface area of approximately 69,500 sq km with an adjoining catchment area measuring 184,000 sq km. The Tanzania share of the lake is 49%, Kenya's share is 6% and Uganda has 45%. The surrounding lake communities in all three countries equal approximately 30 million people, a large proportion being totally dependent on the lake for water, food and economic empowerment. Despite its vast size, Lake Victoria remained one of the last physical features in Africa to be discovered by the 19th-century explorers from Europe. Early charts depict a vague patch of water lying to the north and east of the 'Mountains of the Moon' (today's Rwenzori Mountains in Uganda), but it was not until 1858 that explorers Speke and Burton stumbled on to its southern shore near Mwanza in Tanzania. Speke later wrote that he felt no doubt that the lake gave birth to the River Nile, the source of which had been the subject of so much speculation and the object of many explorers' expeditions. He said "the lake at my feet is the most elusive of all explorers' dreams, the source of the legendary Nile".

Lake Victoria is relatively shallow and has a gentle slope to the shores, so any slight change in water level affects a large land area. It's mean depth is 40 m, the deepest part is 82 m. The water balance is dominated by evaporation and rainfall in the lake, with contributions from river inflow and outflow. The outflow of water, into the River Nile through the Owen Falls Dam in Uganda, accounts for only 20% of water loss from the lake. The remaining 80% is taken by evaporation. Similarly, the inflow through the many rivers from the catchment area only contributes 15-20% while rainfall on the lake accounts for 80-85%. Of the inlets, the River Kagera, which flows from Rwanda, contributes about 46%, Kenya's Nzoia and Sondu/Miriu rivers about 15% and 8% respectively and Tanzania's Mara River about 10-15%.

There is a wide variety of fish in the lake. Scientifically, it is puzzling that so many diverse species unique to these waters could evolve in so uniform an environment. Biologists speculate that hundreds of thousands of years ago, the lake may have dried into a series of smaller lakes causing these brilliantly coloured cichlids to evolve differently. These fish are greatly sought after for aquariums. One unique characteristic for which cichlids (tilapia being the best known) are noted for is the female's habit of nursing its fertilized eggs and young in its mouth. To the people of Lake Victoria, the cichlids have been their livelihood – the catch, preparation (sun-drying) and sale of these fish are an important resource for them. Lake Victoria is also a home to a predator fish, the Nile perch, introduced into the lake some 20 years ago as a sport fish.

Note: Lake Victoria is infected with bilharzia (Schistosomiasis) so swimming close to the shore is not recommended.

Excursions

Butiama The home village of Julius Nyerere (see box, page 359) is 48 km from Musoma. The village has a museum that commemorates Nyerere's life and work ⓘ *entrance US$2*. Exhibits document the rise of nationalism, the independence movement, and the early history of Tanzania, as well as displaying various items of interest that belonged to the late leader, including a copy of Plato's Republic translated into Kiswahili by hand. Tanzania's first president was buried here, not far from the humble dwelling where he was born 77 years before. The bus ride is through pleasant scenery and costs US$1.

Mwanza → *Phone code: 028.* ▸▸ *pp280-282*

Colour map 1, grid A2 2°30'S 32°58'E.

Mwanza is the largest Tanzanian port on Lake Victoria and with a population of roughly 3 million it is Tanzania's second-largest town. It lies on a peninsula that juts into the lake. It is surrounded by rocky hills and the land is dominated by granite outcrops some of which are very impressive and look as if they are about to topple. The road approach is spectacular, tunnelling through some of the great boulders on the route. As the railway terminus and major lake port, Mwanza is a bustling and lively town. Fishing is a major commercial activity in this area, though tea, cotton and coffee plantations around here produce large volumes of cash crops that pass though Mwanza on their way to market. The produce from the lake region is gathered here and is then transported to the coast by rail. Recently the town has received a major economic boost with the South African takeover of the Mwanza Brewery, and the substantial mining developments in Shinyanga and around Geita. For visitors, the city makes a good base from which to explore nearby Rubondo Island National Park and the western parts of the Serengeti.

Ins and outs

Getting around Taxis can be found near the bus and train stations or outside the New Mwanza Hotel. Commuter buses, locally known as 'express', are well distributed throughout the town and are the most popular and cheapest means of transport. ▸▸ *See page 281 for further details on transport to and from Mwanza.*

Sights

The colonial centre of Mwanza was around the port on the west side of the town. Among the historic buildings in this area are the **Primary Court**, dating from the German period, and the **Mahatma Ghandi Memorial Hall** from the British period. The **Clocktower** has a plaque recording that on 3 August 1858, on Isamilo Hill, a mile away, John Hanning Speke first saw the main water of Lake Victoria, which he later proved to be the source of the Nile.

The colonial residences spread over **Capri Point** and social life centred on the **Mwanza Club** and its golf course and the **Yacht Club**. One of the celebrated sights is **Bismark Rock**, which appears precariously balanced, just south of the main port.

Excursions

Saa Nane Island ⓘ *Boats from Mwanza depart from the jetty 1 km south of the centre off Station Rd just before the Tilapia Hotel, at 1100, 1300, 1400, 1500 and 1600. Combined boat and entry fee about US$1.50*. This wildlife sanctuary is not far from Mwanza, on the lake. It has hippo, zebra and wildebeest, as well as various caged animals, including some very unhappy-looking hyenas, although it is reported that the number of animals has fallen. It gets very busy at the weekends and despite its location, with rocky outcrops appearing out of a grassy landscape, it is not a particularly pleasant place to visit and is not much more than a glorified zoo with cramped enclosures.

Bujora Sukuma Village Museum ⓘ *18 km from Mwanza on the Musoma road, reached by taking a local bus from the bus station near the market in Mwanza to Kisessa, then walking the remaining 2 km*. Originally set up by missionaries from

Quebec in 1952, the museum celebrates the traditions and culture of the Sukuma who make up one of the largest tribal groups in Tanzania. Exhibits include an unusual two-storey royal pavilion in the shape of the royal stool, shrines, and traditional instruments, including a drum collection. Traditional dances are held when the museum is busy, usually on a Saturday, and include the impressive Sukuma snake dance or *Bugobogobo*, which is performed with a live python. It is best to be shown around by a guide, cost US$2.

Ukerewe, Kome and Maisome Islands These three islands on Lake Victoria are very pretty, but there is little else to attract the tourist. Ukerewe Island to the north of Mwanza can be reached by ferry, (2 hrs 30 min), leaving Mwanza at 0800 and 1200, and returning at 1600, US$3. It is also possible to go by road – east round the lake to Bunda and then west along the north shore of Speke Gulf, crossing by ferry to Ukerewe Island. There are no regular buses on the last leg of this route so it is necessary to hitch. There are some small hotels and a number of cheap restaurants.

Kome and Maisome islands are served by the ferries to Myamirembe, which leave Mwanza on Monday (0800) and Thursday (2100). Kome takes about three hours to reach and Maisome about seven hours. Ferries return from Nyamirembe on Tuesday (0800) and Friday (1900).

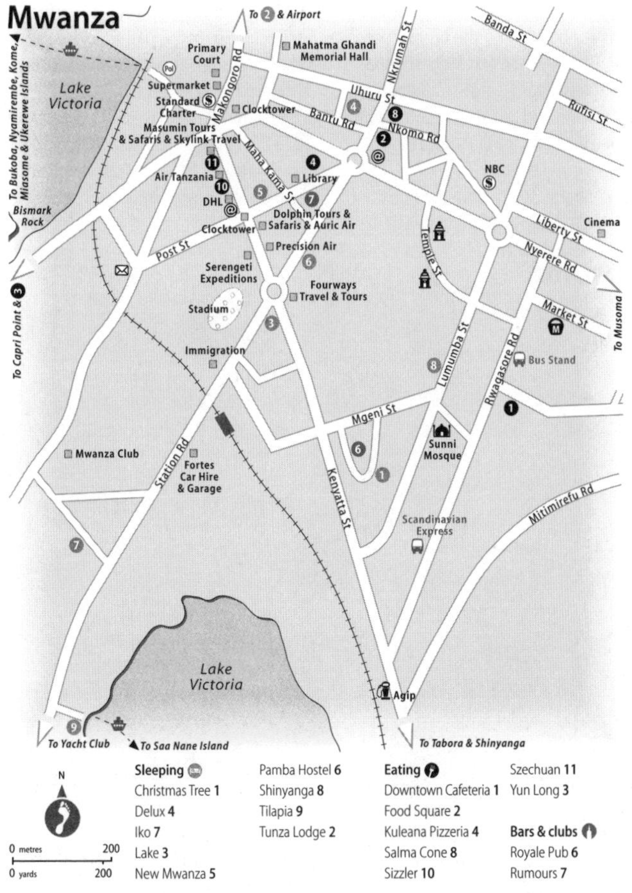

Sleeping

Musoma *p274, map below*

L **Lukuba Island**, reservations, Arusha, T027-2548840, www.lukubaisland.com. This is primarily a fishing lodge on Lukuba Island on Lake Victoria, and guests are transferred from Musoma by boat which takes around 45 min. 5 grass thatched buildings nestle in the island's forest with lake views, good cuisine of understandably mostly fish, managed by a friendly couple. Fishing excursions by dhow and motor boat with fish-finding equipment and all the gear from US$25-50 per hour. It is possible to catch Nile perch in these waters and otters and monitor lizards are frequently seen around the island. Room rates US$230 per person.

C **Penninsula**, 2 km south from town towards the pleasant suburb of Makoko, south of the airstrip, T028-2642546. Smart whitewashed building on the beach, rooms have a/c, TV, hot water, and fridges, good value for the standard. Large restaurant serving western and Indian dishes, separate beach area with a swimming pool (not always open) and boats.

D **Afrilux**, central, 500 m from the bus stand, T028-2620031. Newly constructed and very good value, self-contained rooms with hot water, fans, and satellite TV. Restaurant serving filling local and Indian meals and a large garden bar area.

D-F **Tembo Beach**, at Old Musoma Pier, 2 km west of town, T028-2622887. Hotel with private beach on a peninsula. Variety of accommodation from self-contained units with porches and hot water to camping. Good bar and restaurant facilities, a little dilapidated, but very peaceful, with wonderful views of the lake.

E **Orange Tree**, in town centre, 1 block back from the Afrilux, T028-2622651. Basic and rundown self-contained double rooms, but fairly friendly with a reasonable bar and restaurant.

E **Catholic Conference Centre**, town centre, close to the bus stand, T028-2620168. Secure and clean, 30 rooms, bathrooms are shared. Good restaurant and bar, with a satellite TV. Recommended for value.

F **Silver Sands**, 1 km west of town centre, T028-2622740. More than a little rundown, rooms are very basic and not too clean. Shared cold shower, a big garden bar, but no food.

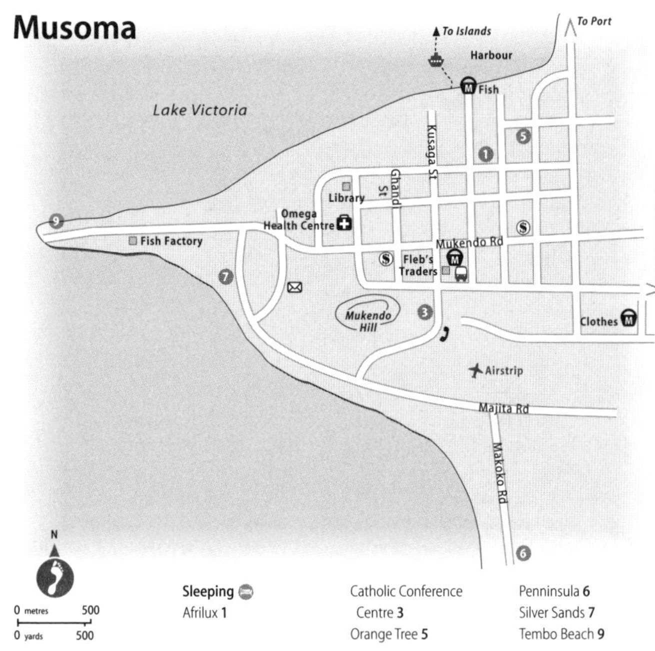

See also **Serengeti Stopover**, south of Musoma near the Ndabaka Gate of the Serengeti National Park, page 270.

Mwanza *p276, map p277*

A-B Tilapia, Station Rd near ferry to Saa Nane Island, 1 km southwest of town, T028-2500517, www.hoteltilapia.com. Chalet-style accommodation, in 40 self-contained rooms with a/c or fans, TV, fridge, there is also some accommodation on a houseboat moored on the lake by the hotel. Lovely swimming pool, non-guests can swim for US$4 per day, small gym. Has Indian, Thai and Japanese restaurants and a decking bar overlooking the lake. Fax and internet services, can arrange car hire. A vintage box-body Ford and an old Rolls Royce have been restored and are on display next to reception. The facilities here are superb but some reports from readers say it is a glorified brothel.

★ **B New Mwanza**, central on Post St, T028-2501070, www.newmwanzahotel.com. Has recently undergone a major refurbishment, which has introduced plenty of marble and gilt. Well run with attentive and helpful staff and management. The 54 rooms have en suite bathrooms, a/c, satellite TV, and internet access for laptops. Extensive facilities include *King's Casino* with a number of tables and slots, 24-hr coffee shop and room service, Blue Moon disco, bar and restaurant. The Indian food here is superb and very authentic, cooked by Indian chefs. Eat here even if you are not staying. Also has good buffet breakfasts. Swimming pool, gym, sauna and steam room are currently being built.

B Tunza Lodge, Ilemela Beach, near the village of Hemla, 10 km north of town and 3 km from the airport, T028-2562215, www.renair.com. A fairly new beach resort and the only one of its kind on Lake Victoria, 5 doubles, 5 twins and 3 single rooms, all with en suite bathrooms. Nice gardens leading down to the beach but remember Lake Victoria has got bilharzia and swimming close to the shore is not recommended. Can arrange fishing trips, waterskiing and wind surfing. Good bar and restaurant in pleasant thatched building.

D Iko Hotel, close to the Tilapia Hotel, T028-2540900. 52 a/c rooms, prices vary depending on the size, a little tatty but comfortable and good value with a double going for US$15. Reasonable restaurant with main dishes for US$3 and a bar.

D Christmas Tree, Karuta St, just off Mgeni St, T028-2502001. Modern 3-storey block, simple rooms with hot water in bathrooms. Restaurant good value.

E Lake Hotel, Fourways junction, off Station Rd close to stadium, T028-2500658. Restaurant, outdoor bar, parking space, noisy and busy. Lots of rooms (but fills up quickly) with fans, mosquito nets, bathrooms. Good value, rates include a very basic breakfast (pineapple sandwiches?!).

E Pamba Hostel, Station Rd near roundabout, T028-2502697. Central location, a bit rough and ready, shared facilities, squat WCs, noisy, especially at the weekends when there is a disco. Continental breakfast, restaurant, rooftop bar. Owned by the company that does the catering for all the ferries and trains in Tanzania.

F Hotel Delux, Uhuru St, T028-2500831. Newly painted, white 5-storey block with shabby rooms, but reasonable for the price. Downstairs restaurant serves huge plates of steaming stews and curries for next to nothing. Rates include basic breakfast.

F Shinyanga, Lumumba St. Just off centre, rundown tall blue block with 108 rooms, very basic, mosquito nets, shared bathrooms, no restaurant or bar though there is a fridge in reception selling water and soft drinks.

Eating

Musoma *p274, map opposite*

There are a few basic food canteens around town, and most of Musoma's hotels provide food, the **Penninsula** and **Afrilux** are particularly recommended.

Mwanza *p276, map p277*

Hotel Tilapia, Station Rd, near ferry to Saa Nane Island, 1 km southwest of town, T028-2500517. Good standard and popular, restaurants inside in basement and outside on roof serving Chinese, Japanese and Indian food, and a decking bar overlooking the lake.

For an explanation of the sleeping and eating price codes used in this guide, see inside the front cover. Other relevant information is found in Essentials pages 31-34.

Set courses in the Japanese restaurant are not unreasonable at US$14 and saki is US$7 a flask. Main dishes in the other restaurants go for around US$6.

Yun Long, 5-min walk along the lake road, T0744-609790 (mob). Fantastic setting in lovely gardens, with all the tables right on the edge of the lake. There's a large bar under thatch with a full range of imported drinks, 2 pool tables, TV. Starters from US$3, main courses from US$5. Try the Chinese-style tilapa fillet with chilli or sweet and sour sauce. Open daily 1200-midnight.

Sizzler, Kenyatta St, T0741-341118 (mob). Good quality international, Chinese and Indian food, especially the Indian dishes, but perhaps a little pricey. Does not sell booze. Open daily 1100-1500, 1800-2230.

Szechuan, Kenyatta St. Better than Sizzler above, reasonable quality Chinese food and very authentic Indian food from talented chefs served with roti and naan bread, a wide range of dishes and good for vegetarians, main courses are around US$6.

Kuleana Pizzeria, Post St, near the *New Mwanza Hotel*. Promises cappuccino and the like but doesn't always deliver and some of the menu items are downright strange (avocado gravy?). The pizzas and homemade bread are very good though and they support street kids. Open daily until 1700.

Salma Cone, corner of Barti St and Nkrumah St. Coffee, snacks and ice cream. There are other cheap restaurants at this junction serving up barbecued meat, fried chicken and stews, including: **The Food Square**, which is clean and smart.

Downtown Cafeteria, opposite the bus stand. Very busy with market traders and people waiting for buses, clean and bright with good buffet breakfasts, fresh juices and coffee, satellite news on the TV.

Bars and clubs

Mwanza *p276, map p277*

Rumours, Station Rd. New bar with a modern interior and mirrored glass on the exterior, satellite TV and big screen, pool tables, dance floor very popular.

Royale Pub, just off Mgeni St. A big outdoor bar under a large canopy, most of the awnings are made from UN tarps, barbecued meals, busy all day, friendly service.

Entertainment

Mwanza *p276, map p277*

There is a **cinema** on Liberty St – look out for the billboard on the corner of Nyerere/ Station road for details of films.

King's Casino is on the first floor of the New Mwanza Hotel. Open every evening until very late, roulette and black jack, slot machines and bar, free drinks to players, no entry fee. The **Blue Moon** disco is also in the hotel.

Shopping

Musoma *p274, map p278*

Flebs' Traders, Kusaga St, has a good range of imported items.

Mwanza *p276, map p277*

There is an excellent supermarket on the site of the previous *U Turn Restaurant*, corner of Nkrumah and Hospital St. This sells frozen meat, toiletries, canned drinks including Diet Coke, English biscuits and chocolate bars, English choc ices, fairly expensive but has an impressive range of products. There is another supermarket at the Clocktower roundabout next to Standard Charter Bank.

Activities and tours

Mwanza *p276, map p277*

Tour operators

Dolphin Tours & Safaris, Kenyatta St/ Post St corner, T028-2500096 (in the same office as Auric Air, an air charter company, www.auricair.com). Car hire and tailor-made safaris.

Fourways Travel & Tours, corner of Station and Kenyatta Rds, T028-2502620, fourways.mza@mwanza-online.com. Very helpful agency, managed by Sharad J Shah. Fishing and wildlife safaris, airport pick ups, and flight tickets.

Masumin Tours & Safaris and Skylink Travel, Kenyatta St, T028-2500233, www.masuminsafaris.com. Safaris to the parks in the northern circuit from Mwanza, also offers short/long term car hire. Shares an office with Skylink who also have offices in Dar and Arusha, www.skylinktanzania.com. Agents for Avis Car Hire.

Serengeti Expeditions, Kenyatta St, opposite the New Mwanza Hotel, T028-2500061, www.serengetiexpedition.com. Safaris to the northern circuit, car hire, agents for most of the major airlines including British Airways and KLM.

Yachting

Yacht Club, Station Rd, southern end. Offers sailing on the lake. Well-appointed premises with restaurant, bar and a billiards table. US$4 entrance fee payable for non-members.

Transport

Musoma *p274, map p278*

Bus Musoma lies 18 km from the main road that goes from Mwanza to the Kenya border and through buses do not stop here. However there are direct regular buses to **Mwanza** leaving from the bus station, which is behind Kusaga St in the centre. The trip takes 3 hrs, and costs US$4. **Arusha** buses go through the **Serengeti** and the **Ngorongoro Crater Reserve** to **Karatu** and then along the new road to Arusha. This journey takes just about all day and the bus leaves Musoma very early in the morning.

Mwanza *p276, map p277*

Air

Air Tanzania, Kenyatta Rd, T028-2500368, www.airtanzania.com. There are 2 daily flights from **Dar es Salaam** (90 min) at 0700 and 1600, which return at 0900 and 1800. **Precision Air**, Kenyatta Rd, T028-2500819, and at the airport, www.precisionairtz.com. There are daily flights between **Dar** and Mwanza (2 hr) that leave from Dar at 0715 and 1400, and from Mwanza at 1100 and 1645. One way is US$150, return US$240. Also daily is a flight to **Nairobi** in Kenya (1 hr 40 min) at 1350, which returns at 1555. One way US$193, return US$285. On Mon, Wed and Fri, there are flights to **Bukoba** (55 min) at 0800, 1110 and 1755, which return at 0700, 0915 and 1240. One way US$65, return US$106. **Coastal Air**, T022-2117969-60, www.coastal.cc, flies from Mwanza daily at 0900 to **Arusha** (2 hr 15 min) via the camps in the **Serengeti** and the flight returns to Mwanza from Arusha at 1230. There is also a flight from Mwanza to **Rubondo Island National Park** (40 min) on Tue and Fri at 1620 if there is the demand. **Auricair**, T028-2500096, www.auricair.com. Air charter company based at Mwanza Airport. Runs regular charters between Mwanza and **Kampala** in Uganda. The office is at Dolphin Tours (see above).

★ Ferry

This is easily the most reliable, enjoyable and comfortable way to travel on to **Bukoba**. The boats, the **MV Serengeti** and the **MV Victoria**, though old, have recently been refitted. There is a ferry on Sun, Tue and Thu from Mwanza to Bukoba, and from Bukoba to Mwanza on Mon, Wed and Fri, both leaving at 1800 taking 10 hrs. Fares are US$15, US$13 and US$9. 1st class provides a berth in a 2-person cabin, 2nd in a 4-person cabin, 3rd is seating or deck space. Earplugs can be a boon. **Nyamirembe** is served by 2 ferries a week, from Mwanza at 0800 on Mon and 2100 on Thu and from Nyamirembe at 0800 on Tue and 1900 on Fri. The journey takes 10 hrs. Ferries call at **Kome** and **Miasome Islands** and cost US$5 (2nd class) and US$3 (3rd). **Ukerewe Island** has a daily ferries (2 hrs 30 min), leaving Mwanza at 0800 and 1200, and returning at 1600, US$3.

Road

Bus The large bus stand is off Pamba Rd and is fairly organized with kiosks around the edge selling tickets. Locally, there are plenty of buses to **Musoma** costing little more than US$2.50 and taking 3 hrs. Further afield buses go to **Dar** and **Arusha** via **Nairobi**, 30 hr, US$36. The buses go north across the Kenya border, then to Nairobi via **Kisii**, **Kericho** and **Nakuru**, then south to cross the **Namanga** border into Tanzania again, and onward to Arusha and Dar. These do not run every day. There is at least 1 bus a day to **Kisumu** in Kenya, leaving at around 0700. There is another service to **Dar** via **Singida**, 27 hr, US$27. Though the roads are not in great condition and the ride is bumpy, the roads in the central region are improving. A couple of times a week there are also buses to **Kigoma** but this is a very poor road and the train is advised for this journey. Buses also go to **Arusha** through the **Serengeti National Park** and **Ngorongoro Crater Conservation Area**, 12-15 hrs,

US$25. This service leaves very early in the morning and goes via **Bunda** on the road to the Kenyan border which is tar sealed, then branches off on a horrendously bad dirt road to the Serengeti's Ikoma Gate, or via the Serengeti's Ndabaka Gate 10-15 km south of Bunda on the main road from Musoma towards Mwanza. It then goes through the park via **Seronera** and out again into the Ngoronogro Conservation Area at Naabi Hill Gate. It does not stop to look at any animals and takes a little under 2 hrs to cross the Serengeti. The bus continues past the crater (though of course does not go down into it) to **Karatu** and then on to Arusha, arriving there late at night. Although this service is the quickest method of getting between Mwanza and Arusha, foreigners will have to pay the US$30 entrance fee for both the Serengeti and the crater, which means another US$60 is added to the US$25 bus ticket. This makes it an expensive option with the added disadvantage of speeding past the animals in a crowded bus without being able to stop. An alternative is to arrange a safari of the Serengeti and the crater with one of the tour operators in Mwanza and asked to be dropped off at the end in either Karatu or Arusha. Scandinavian Express, Rwegasore St, T028-2503315, www.scandinaviangroup.com.

Car hire Avis, Kenyatta Rd, opposite Kenya Central Bank, T028-2500233, www.avis.com, run by Skylink, www.skylinktanzania.com. Fortes, just south of the railway station, T028-2500700, fortes@thenet.co.tz, also has a garage.

Train

The train from **Dar** to **Mwanza** (1227 km) leaves Dar on Sun, Tue and Fri at 1700. Trains go to **Dar** from Mwanza 5 days a week on Sun, Tue, Thu, Fri, Sat at 1800. Double check departure times. The journey takes roughly 36 hrs. The trip may involve changing trains at **Tabora** (10 hrs from Mwanza). You can also get to **Kigoma** by train from Mwanza (via Tabora). See Tanzania Railways Corporation www.trctz.com for full details of timetables and fares.

Directory

Musoma *p274, map p278*

Medical services Omega Health Centre, in the town centre, is recommended. Musoma Hospital is next to the market, T028-2622111. **Telephone** Telecoms on Kusaga St have international call facilities and will send faxes.

Mwanza *p276, map p277*

Banks National Bank of Commerce, Liberty Rd. Trust Bank, Station Rd. Standard Chartered Bank, Kenyatta Rd, north of the Clocktower. All have ATMs. Stanbic Bank is on Nyerere Rd. Victoria Travels in the arcade of shops in the New Mwanza Hotel is a general travel agent but also offers a bureau de change with competitive exchange rates. Can also buy US$ cash here. **Courier services** DHL, Kenyatta Rd, T028-2500910, www.dhl.co.tz. SkyNet has an office in the New Mwanza Hotel. **Internet cafés** Karibu Corner Internet Café, corner of Kenyatta Rd and Post St, US$1 for 1 hr. Several others too. **Post** Post office on Post St. The quickest and cheapest place to send a fax is across the road from the post office at the Fax Centre. **Medical services** The Bugando Hospital, on a hill about 1 km southwest of town, T028-240610-5. Hindu Union Hospital, Belewa Rd, Mwananchi Hospital, Station Rd behind Tanesco. Aga Khan Clinic, Wurzburg Rd. **Useful addresses** Immigration office, opposite the railway station, T028-2500585. Open Mon- Fri, 0730-1530. Police station, Kenyatta Rd near the ferry terminal.

Western Lake Victoria

The western shores of Lake Victoria are little visited and the principal town of Bukoba, best reached by ferry from Mwanza, is little more than a sleepy backwater in this far north western corner of Tanzania. The roads are so bad in this region that even sodas and beers are delivered to Bukoba by ferry. But the town is relaxed and in a scenic position on the lakeshore, and it provides an unusual access route to Uganda a little way to the north. Further south the highlight of the region is the Rubondo Island National Park where the forests harbour a number of species of game and birds.
▸▸ *For Sleeping, Eating and other listings, see pages 287-290.*

★ Rubondo Island National Park

→ *Colour map A2.* 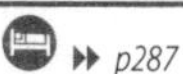 ▸▸ *p287*

ⓘ Coastal Air, T022-2117969-60, www.coastal.cc, has a service that arrives from Mwanza on Tue and Fri and departs on Wed and Sat. The fare is US$70 one way. This flight connects with a service from Mwanza to the camps in the Serengeti, so a visit to Rubondo can be combined with a safari of the parks in the northern circuit. Alternatively you could catch the ferry to Maisome Island (see page 277) just east of Rubondo, and from Maisome arrange a boat transfer to Rubondo. You can also drive the 10 hrs to Nyamirembe (via Gieta) from where the boat journey is about 30 mins. But this doesn't work out much cheaper than the flight and will take considerably longer. No vehicles are allowed on the island although there is a lorry that can be hired to drive visitors around.

> The best time to visit: November-February. Park entry fee: US$20 US$50 sport fishing per day. (see page 39). 2° 30' S, 31° 45' E.

Rubondo National Park is an island northwest of Mwanza and directly south of Bukoba. The park encompasses Rubondo Island as well as several smaller islands nearby. It was gazetted in 1977 with a total area of 460 sq km, about 240 sq km of which is land.

Rubondo Island National Park

Chitebe Island
Chitende Island
Rubiso Island
Kageye & Park HQ
Kalela Island
Miso Island
Ibozya Bay
Mlaga
Iloba Island
Chambuzi Island
Manyila Island
Mamba Island
Lake Victoria
Chitoma Bay
Lukaga
Lukukuru
Izilamouda Island
N
0 km 2
0 miles 2

Sleeping
Rubondo Island Tented Lodge 1

Ranger post ●

There are a number of different vegetation types on the island providing differing habitats for a variety of animals. With a high water table the island is able to support dense forest. Other vegetation includes more open woodland, savanna grassland and swamps. There is little 'big game' on the island although some has been introduced, including giraffe, elephant and rhino. Many of the animals were relocated here in the 1970s when the island was identified as a safe haven in the fight against poaching and land encroachment. Other animals include crocodile, hippo, bushbuck, sitatunga (a swamp-dwelling antelope only found here and in Selous), vervet monkeys and mongoose. The park is good for hiking and has wonderful birdlife. You are likely to spot fish eagle, martial eagle, sacred ibis, saddle-billed stork, kingfishers, water fowl, cuckoos, bee eaters and sunbirds. There are animal hides for viewing the wildlife.

The Hen and the Hawk: a Bukoba Fable

Once upon a time a hen and a hawk who were friends lived together in the same hut. One day, during a great famine the hen went off in search of food. She was successful for she met a man who had some bananas. As she was carrying her load home she met the hawk who asked her how she had got the bananas. The hen, standing on one leg and hiding the other in her feathers, replied that she had paid for them with her foot. The hen told the hawk that he must also buy some food with his foot.

The hawk agreed that this was indeed fair and went off in search of some food. He met a man and offered his leg in return for some food. The man agreed, cut off the hawk's leg and then gave him some food. The hawk had great difficulty walking home with only one leg, trying to balance the load.

When the hawk eventually reached home he saw the hen standing on two legs. He was extremely angry with the hen, saying that although the hen was supposed to be his friend she had cheated him. The hawk told the hen that he could not forgive her and would kill her. The hen replied that he would never succeed in killing her for she would run away. Sure enough the hen ran away and lived with man, while the hawk and all his descendants remain determined to kill the hen and its offspring. This is why the hawk will always try to kill any hen that it sees.

Bukoba

→ *Phone code: 028. Colour map A2.*  ›› pp289-290

Although it receives few visitors, Bukoba, set in a bay between lush hills, with a population of 81,000 and a university, is now is Tanzania's second largest lake port. But for several centuries, until Bukoba was established at the end of the 19th century, Karagwe, some 100 km inland, was the principal centre. The Bahinda, a cattle-herding people from the interior, operated a feudal system where chiefs took tributes from their subjects and the wealth of the area was based on cattle that were raised successfully despite problems with tsetse flies (see box, page 245). It was founded for the Germans in 1890 by Emin Pasha. It is a lovely part of Tanzania – green and fertile and with a very relaxed way of life.

1°20'S 31°59'E
Bukoba is only 1 degree south of the equator.

The major food crop here (as in much of the area around the lake) is *matoke*. This is the green banana you will see grown everywhere. It is peeled, wrapped in banana leaves and cooked very slowly by steaming. Vanilla is another recently introduced cash crop. The major commercial crop is coffee, which has contributed significantly to the wealth of the area. There is a coffee factory near the jetty. Unfortunately the world price has fallen in recent years with notable effects on the people of this district. There are quite a few aid projects in this area so a number of expatriate aid workers live here. Huge deposits of nickel and cobalt have been discovered in the area, and there are plans to exploit these.

Sights

Near the lake shore is a group of buildings from the German period. **Duka Kubwa**, the first general store in the town and the first stone building in Bukoba, is on the corner of Jamhuri Road and Aerodrome Road. Originally the market was in this area but during the British period it was moved about a kilometre inland. When the British took the town in 1914 during the First World War, in their excitement they blew up the German Boma (which was on the site of Holy Trinity Church) and the German Post

Office (set under the heliograph – a device for sending messages by mirrors – along the lake shore, of which only the concrete feet still remain). Later the British regretted their impetuosity – they had no administrative centre – and they used the German Hospital (now called the **Old Boma**, and currently housing part of the University of Bukoba). Across the road from the *Lake View Hotel* is a **German cemetery**. Further west is the area with European housing up in the hills. Beyond the aerodrome runway to the east is **Nyamukazi** fishing village. Between Lake View Hotel and the lake shore is the former Gymkhana Club where there was a cricket pitch, a golf course and tennis courts, now called the **Bukoba Club** (see page 289). The centre of town has many Asian-style buildings, now very shabby.

The **Mater Misericordia Cathedral** (Roman Catholic) is an extraordinary building on a huge scale in spectacular style. When it was originally constructed the dome began to subside. All the cladding was removed, new foundations inserted under the building, and the whole shebang raised 3 m on hydraulic jacks. The levitation was done a millimetre at a time and took 10 weeks.

The **Lutheran Cathedral** is an altogether more modest and practical construction in modern style. The Evangelical Lutheran Church of Tanzania (ELCT) has a large presence in Bukoba, including the main office, conference and training centre, Huyawa Orphans Project (all near the Lake View Hotel), the Nyumba ya Vijana Youth Centre (near the government hospital) and a bookshop and internet café (on Market street).

Coffee has long been the economic mainstay of the region and there is a **coffee factory** on the lake shore by the wharf, south of the administrative centre, and it is usually possible to be shown round. Continuing southwest from the wharf is the **Bunena Roman Catholic Mission** buildings with a spire, gardens and a cemetery.

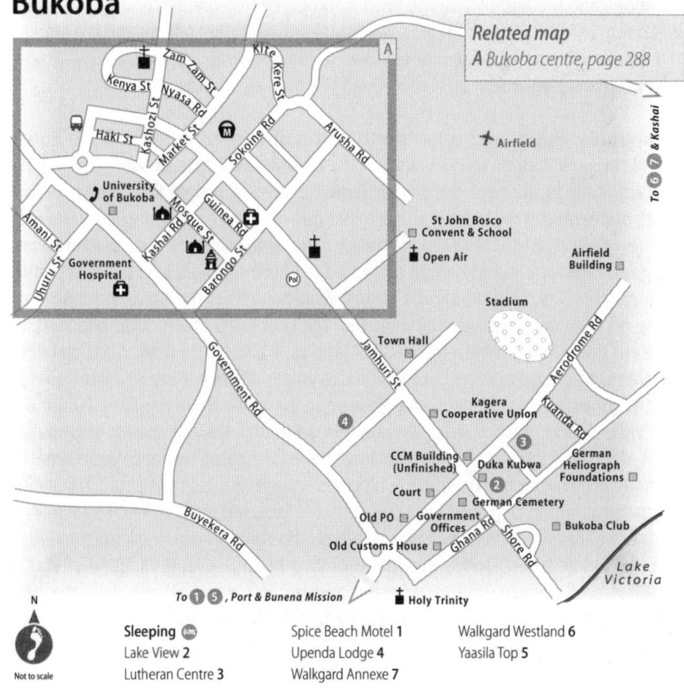

Karagwe → *Colour map 1, grid A2. 2° 0s, 31° 0' E.*

ⓘ *Buses run daily except Sun from Bukoba, taking about 4 hrs to cover the distance of about 100 km, and cost around US$2.50.*

Located inland, this was an important centre until Bukoba came to prominence with the introduction of access by steamer across Lake Victoria to Mwanza and the rail link to the coast. The surrounding area is rich and fertile and cattle thrive here. The town hosts a sombre reminder of the war with the war with Uganda: a bombed-out and ruined church high atop the hill overlooking the town. In the past few years Karagwe has served as a base for the non-government organizations coping with the exodus of refugees from Rwanda. The refugee camps were to the west of the border, but supplies come through Bukoba and then Karagwe. There are several small hotels charging less than US$5 per night. They are very basic, with shared bathrooms and no running water.

South from Bukoba  ›› pp288-290

Kemondo Bay port is about 18 km south of Bukoba. On the ferry you don't get a chance to appreciate the attractiveness of the bay entrance to the port as it is usually dark when the boat docks and departs. The quayside is a grand sight when the lake steamers, en route from Bukoba and Mwanza, are in – bags of charcoal and coffee being loaded, great bunches of bananas are piled on deck, joyful reunions at homecomings and tearful partings as relatives and work mates come to bid travellers farewell.

Biharamulo → *Colour map 1, grid A2. 2° 25' S, 31° 25' E.*

Continuing south from Muleba, skirting the edge of Biharamulo game reserve (not much wildlife visible from the road), is Biharamulo, a well laid out town that served as an administrative centre during the German period. There are some fine colonial buildings and the entrance to the town is through a tree-lined avenue. The **Old Boma** has been restored. At present the town houses government offices and is a market for the surrounding area; is the nearest town to the eponymous game reserve. There's a large market, a bank and post office with telephones and fax.

Biharamulo, Burigi and other northwest game reserves Adjacent to Rubondo Island National Park on the mainland is the **Biharamulo Game Reserve** (1,300 sq km), and adjoining to the west the **Burigi Game Reserve** (2,200 sq km). These are to the south of Bukoba on the main Mwanza to Bukoba road but have no facilities and receive very few visitors. Because of the proximity of the large numbers of displaced Rwandan refugees who were put in camps on the edge of the reserves in the Ngara District of northwestern Tanzania during the 1990s Rwandan crisis, the flora and fauna of the game reserve have been greatly depleted. Many of the animals were poached, trees were cut down for fuel and large tracts of land were cleared for the cultivation of crops. Biharamulo Reserve borders Lake Victoria, at an altitude of between 1250-2000 m, and is contiguous with the Burigi Game Reserve to the west. There are north/south ridges and valleys, and much of it is swampy with a healthy, thriving mosquito population. Most of the larger mammals numbers have been decimated by poaching. Animals that formerly lived in the reserve include hippo, elephant and zebra. A small population of sitatunga antelope also lived here and primates included the red colobus monkey. The birds are believed to have been less adversely affected by human encroachment. They include saddle-billed storks, the rufous-bellied heron, several varieties of starlings, sunbirds and weavers, the grey kestrel and the fish eagle. These days the park is notably good for roan antelope, klipspringer, dik-dik, oribi and impala, but sadly it is mostly used as a hunting concession. There are no visitor facilities and the old guest house at Biharamulo has fallen into disrepair.

Other game reserves in northwest Tanzania were also adversely affected including **Moyowosi Game Reserve, Ibanda Game Reserve** and **Rumanyika Game Reserve.** The Kagera Kigoma Game Reserve Rehabilitation Project (KKGRRP) is seeking to reverse the extensive damage done to these game reserves, which cover a total area of 14,500 sq km. It is estimated that the mammal population decreased by 90% after the arrival of the refugees. There are plans to rehabilitate the roads and coordinate anti-poaching enforcement strategies.

Sleeping

Rubondo Island National Park

p283, map p283

B-D There are camping facilities and basic banda accommodation at the National Park's rest camp on the island but they are very basic so you are advised to take all your own equipment. All food supplies must be taken with you. The basic bandas are US$20 with shared bathroom, and the newer chalets with bathrooms are US$50 per person. Camping also costs US$30 per person. The park headquarters are at Kageye. The rest camp is 1 km from here and about a similar distance to the upmarket tented camp (below). You are permitted to walk from the rest camp to enjoy a meal or a drink at the tented camp, though you need to give some notice for them to prepare food. Further information from Tanzania National Parks (TANAPA), head office, Dodoma Rd, Arusha, T027-2503471, tanapa@habari.co.tz, www.tanzaniaparks.com.

L Rubondo Island Tented Lodge, T027-2544109 (Arusha), www.flycat.com. Run by Flycatcher Safaris, there is just one luxury camp on Rubondo Island, in a shady tract of forest along the lake shore. 20 tents on concrete bases under thatch, set apart from each other with lovely views overlooking the lake and beach. Gardens still need to mature, rustic central area with dining room, bar, lots of lounging space, and small swimming pool set in an outcrop of rock. Walking and fishing safaris can be arranged. Most people visit here as part of a package that includes flights.

Bukoba *p284, maps p285 and p288*

C Walkgard Westland Hotel, 3 km from Bukoba on the slopes of the Kashuru Hills, overlooking the lake, T028-2220935, www.walkgard.com. Brand new hotel, opened in 2004, comfortable rooms with en suite bathrooms, satellite TV, balconies with great views, but old-fashioned furnishings. Very nice swimming pool with sun loungers. Rates include full English breakfast. Friendly staff can organize boat trips and tours to the local sites. Good restaurant, pool café and bar. Easily the best place to stay in the area.

C Walkgard Annex Hotel, along Uganda Road, 1.5 km from the airport, T028-2220626. 13 spacious and comfortable rooms with a/c, TV, phone, fridge. Reasonable food with barbecues, buffets, and bar.

C-D Kamachumu Inn, around 30 km south of Bukoba, the turning for Kamachumu is at Muhutwe, T028-2222466, www.kamachumuinn.com. A fairly remote, but cosy country inn on the 1800-m plateau of Kamachumu, about 50 min drive from Bukoba. Rooms with bathrooms are US$30 and those with shared bathrooms US$15, all have satellite TV. The gardens are very pleasant with rondavaals. They grow their own vegetables for the restaurant. Beer is available.

C-D Yaasila Top Hotel, next to Spice Beach on the lakeshore. New hotel in a nice location, with 15 rooms of which 10 rooms have bathrooms (US$24 a double), and 5 budget rooms with shared bathroom (US$8 a double). Big difference in price though the better rooms have a balcony facing Lake Victoria together with a king size bed, a fridge, TV and phone.

D Lake View Hotel, T028-2220232. Imposing building on the lake shore, comfortable accommodation, some rooms with bathroom and fans, TV and hot water. Moderate food, good terrace bar, hotel has bureau de change. Has recently been refurbished, good view of the lake. Camping possible for US$4.

For an explanation of the sleeping and eating price codes used in this guide, see inside the front cover. Other relevant information is found in Essentials pages 31-34.

D **New Banana**, Zam Zam St, east of the Market, T028-2220861. Restaurant, central and well run, outside area with tables, reasonable food and quite popular bar. Simple rooms some with a/c and hot water.

D **Spice Beach Motel**, on the lake shore, on the lower road to the port, T028-2220142. Modern bungalow, rooms have TV, hot water and a/c. Very good bar and restaurant. Good place for waiting for the evening ferry to Mwanza even if not staying here.

D **Upenda Lodge**, Rwaijumba street, off Jamhuri St, T028-2220620. Courtyard with bar, 16 rooms, 3 are larger with extra sitting room, all are s/c with hot water, cable TV and large beds, modern kitchen serving Tanzanian and European dishes.

E **Lutheran Centre**, off Shore Rd towards the lake, T028-2220027, elct-nwd@africa online.com. Very comfortable, clean and safe, rooms have TV, a/c and hot water. No alcohol is served, but there is basic and cheap food.

Biharamulo *p286*

F **Sunset Inn**, opposite the bus stand. One of the best of the basic guest houses in town. Spartan rooms with communal bathrooms, US$5 for a double. Serves food all day, one reader has reported it to be clean and functional but very boring.

Eating

Bukoba *p284, maps p285 and p288*

Lake View Hotel, moderate food and a good variety, including many Western dishes, excellent barbecued kebabs, though overpriced and slow service. Nice atmosphere in the outside terrace beer garden with a view of the lake, gets busy especially at the weekends.

Kopling Café, across from the Kahawa Guest House near the cathedral. Inexpensive fish, meat, rice and *matoke*, TV.

Pizza Restaurant, just off Jamhuri St in commercial centre. Small restaurant with very good pizzas, sausage and chips, samosas and juices. Only open in the mornings, and not all mornings at that.

Rose Cafe, Jamhuri St. Serves local food like *matoke*, beans, *sambusas*, *mchicha*, and fruit juice.

Soft Rock Café, off Karume St on Kashai Rd. Established by a German guy working in Bukoba. A sports bar with an outside patio bar with satellite TV. Serves tasty grilled chicken and fish with chips.

Spice Beach, Lower Port Rd on the beach. Good grills and kebabs; if you order the day before they will lay on an Indian meal. Pool table and TV. Particularly charming at night when ferry boats are docked at the port.

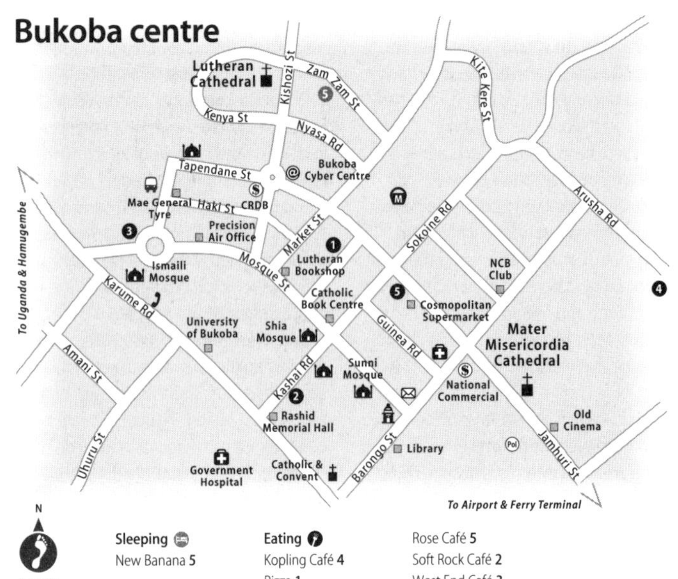

West End Café, on roundabout at northwest end of town. Serves mostly simple grills, and is quite popular with TV and music.

Bars and clubs

Bukoba *p284, maps p285 and p288*
Garden View Bar, in Hamugembe, on road to Uganda, about 1 km. Disco on Fri and Sat, US$1.
NBC Club, just to west of Jamhuri St. Owned and run the employees of the National Bank of Commerce, sometimes has a disco on Fri and Sat, and also serves cold beer.

Shopping

Bukoba *p284, maps p285 and p288*
Cosmopolitan Provision Store, also known as 'Mama Cosmo', sells many imported western items, including cheese and and wine. A good place to stock up on snacks for the ferry, open daily, though closes for lunch.

Activities and tours

Bukoba *p284, maps p285 and p288*
Bukoba Club has tennis, snooker, table tennis and darts. Indians sometimes play cricket on the open grassy area near the club. The **Kaitaba Stadium** hosts football matches of the home Kagera Sugar team, and **Walkgard Hotel** has a swimming pool which non-guests can use for a small fee.

Transport

Bukoba *p284, maps p285 and p288*
Local Bicycle taxis can be found around the market in Bukoba; they are widely used for short journeys, which are as cheap at US$0.20. Local buses west to **Bugene** and **Kaisho** US$4 and south to **Biharamulo** US$9.

Air

Transport to and from Bukoba is fitful. Buses, ferries and flights are all rescheduled on a regular basis, depending on demand, and you must check before you travel. **Precision Air**, near the bus stand, T028-2220545, Dar office T022-2130800, www.precisionairtz.com. On Mon, Wed and Fri, there are flights from **Mwanza** to Bukoba (55 min) at 0800, 1110 and 1755, which return to Mwanza from Bukoba at 0700, 0915 and 1240. One way US$65, return US$106.

Road

Bukoba is a long way from anywhere else by bus and the roads in this region, although improving slowly, are rough and remote. It is recommended you travel to Bukoba by ferry from Mwanza and link up with the slightly better bus services from there. However, Bukoba does offer a useful service between Tanzania and **Uganda**. The bus stand is in the centre of Bukoba town near the clock tower. **Jaguar/Gateway/Dolphin Bus Services**, T0744-786364 (mob) runs from Bukoba to **Kampala** everyday at 0700, US$9, 6-8 hrs. The bus from Kampala to Bukoba returns at 1100. The border crossing is fairly efficient and the road from Bukoba is in a reasonable condition. Visas for most nationalities for Uganda cost $30. Remember, because of the East Africa customs agreement, you are permitted to travel between Tanzania, Kenya and Uganda on single entry visas without getting re-entry visas for each of these countries as long as the visas you have are valid. **Tashrif**, T028-2220427, kiosk at the bus stand, have a bus that does the central line route to **Dar** on Tue, Thu and Sat via **Nzega**, **Singida**, **Dodoma**, and **Morogoro**, up to 24 hrs, US$32. Services go to **Kigoma** though these are rough rides on poor roads and each journey can take days rather than hours. These depart very early in the morning at about 0500, generally only go twice a week and in wet season less so, US$13.

Ferry

Easily the most reliable and comfortable way to travel to **Mwanza**. The boats, the *MV Serengeti* and the *MV Victoria*, though old, have recently been refitted. There is a ferry on Sun, Tue and Thu from Mwanza to Bukoba, and from Bukoba to Mwanza on Mon, Wed and Fri, both leaving at 1800 taking 10 hrs. Fares are US$15, US$13 and US$9. 1st class provides a berth in a 2-person cabin, 2nd in a 4-person cabin, 3rd is seating or deck space. The ferry makes a stop in **Kemondo Bay** an hour after departure from Bukoba Port.

Biharamulo *p286*
Buses from **Bukoba**, leave when full, usually around 1100, take about 6 hrs to cover about 200 km, and cost around US$5. The road is unsealed and in poor shape. Also buses to **Mwanza**, about 3 hrs and US$3.

Directory

Bukoba *p284, maps p285 and p288*
Banks CRDB, near the market, Kashozi Road. National Bank of Commerce, near the Catholic Cathedral on Jamhuri Rd, has ATM. **Post** Post office is near the NBC bank and also has an attached internet café which is open Mon-Fri, 0800-2000, Sat 0800-1800, and Sun 1030-1600. **Internet** Bukoba Cyber Centre, opposite the CRDB bank, both US$0.50 per hr. **Hospitals** Bukoba Medical Centre, T028-2220510, Zam-zam St off Kashozi Rd.

Central Region

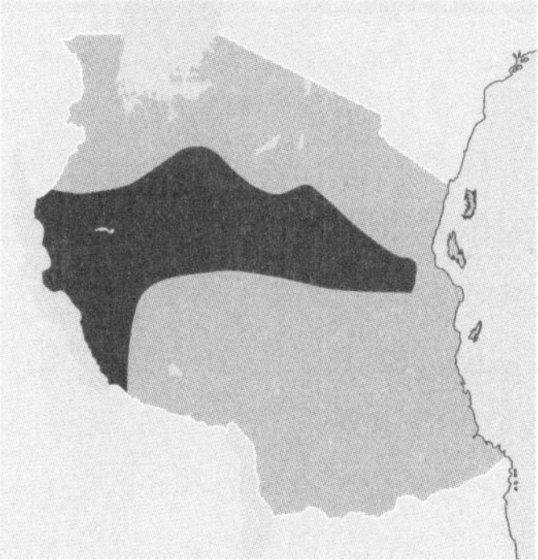

Footprint features

Introduction

The central route from Dar es Salaam to Kigoma in the far west passes through a number of different landscapes and vegetational zones. The distance between the towns is large and much of this route is sparsely populated. The major towns that you pass through are Morogoro, Dodoma and finally Tabora before reaching Kigoma. The Central Railway line is the focus of this route, and it follows the old slave and caravan trail from the coast to Lake Tanganyika. The road is good only as far as Dodoma, just over a third of the distance to Kigoma, though there are currently major road building projects going on in the central region. On the shores of Lake Tanganyika are Mahale and Gombe Stream National Parks, both famous for their substantial chimpanzee populations. Also to the west of the region is the Katavi National Park which is so remote it only receives a handful of visitors each year. These parks are not easy to get to but nevertheless offer safari experiences away from the hordes of pop-up minibuses of the Northern Circuit in landscapes that are more wild and untouched.

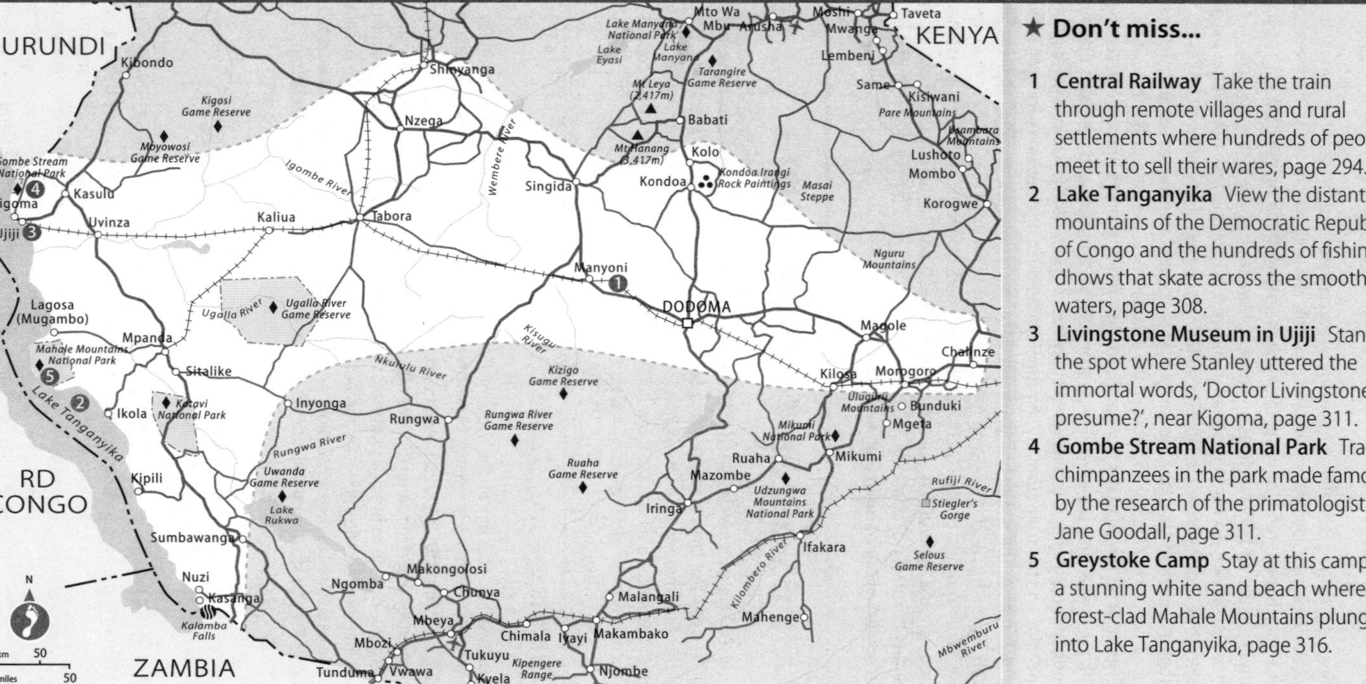

★ Don't miss...

1 **Central Railway** Take the train through remote villages and rural settlements where hundreds of people meet it to sell their wares, page 294.

2 **Lake Tanganyika** View the distant mountains of the Democratic Republic of Congo and the hundreds of fishing dhows that skate across the smooth waters, page 308.

3 **Livingstone Museum in Ujiji** Stand on the spot where Stanley uttered the immortal words, 'Doctor Livingstone I presume?', near Kigoma, page 311.

4 **Gombe Stream National Park** Track chimpanzees in the park made famous by the research of the primatologist Jane Goodall, page 311.

5 **Greystoke Camp** Stay at this camp on a stunning white sand beach where the forest-clad Mahale Mountains plunge into Lake Tanganyika, page 316.

Ins and outs

For access to the destinations in the central area and for budget travellers not wanting to take the expensive flights to Kigoma, the only real option is the train. The ★ **Central Line** goes from Dar to Morogoro, then heads northwest through Dodoma to Tabora, where it splits and the two lines go either to Mwanza on Lake Victoria or Kigoma on Lake Tanganyika. To either destination this is a lengthy journey, but the train is an interesting experience and relatively comfortable, especially if you travel first class. It stops at dozens of stations en route through the central area (hence the 36-hr journey time from Dar to Kigoma) and at each the villagers meet the train to sell their wares – anything from live chickens to wooden spoons. Although there are some buses that link the towns, they are infrequent, uncomfortable and slow and the roads are very poor, especially after the rains when many become impassable. However, things are changing and there are currently some major road-building operations going on in the central region. The Nzega-Shinyanga-Mwanza road is now tarred. The Japanese are working on the Singida-Dodoma road, the Chinese on the Nzega-Singida road, and the South Africans on the Tabora-Shinyanga road. By the end of 2006, these new roads should make the region much more accessible. The only feasible option for getting to Katavi National Park is by flying, and safaris here are usually arranged with an additional trip by air to Mahale National Park.

Dar es Salaam to Dodoma

From Dar the road heads inland to Morogoro where another road and the railway veer off to cross the largely empty expanses of rural central Tanzania. The towns in the region have little to offer the visitor, but Morogoro is a lively centre surrounded by attractive mountains and Dodoma holds the inauspicious title of being the capital of the country. ⏩ *For Sleeping, Eating and other listings, see pages 298-301.*

Chalinze → *Colour map 1, grid B5.*

Chalinze lies 100 km to the west of Dar es Salaam, a small town, essentially a truckstop, and the main fuelling centre for travellers to north and south Tanzania (it's also a big HIV/AIDS centre). There are six petrol stations and hundreds of little bars – everyone's accommodated for. This makes Chalinze a buzzing place in the evenings, and a good place to break a journey for 30 minutes. Look out for the young men who sell little homemade toy trucks and buses on the roadside – replicas of the passing vehicles painted in the same colour and complete with company logos. About 200 m along the Dar road from the junction is a petrol station with a good restaurant, just look for the thatched roof. Most of the buses stop here for a quick break.

Morogoro → *Phone code: 023. Colour map 1, grid B5.* ⏩ *pp 298-301*

Population: 250,000
Altitude: 500 m
6°50'S 37°40'E

Morogoro lies in the agricultural heartland of Tanzania, and is a centre of farming in the southern highlands. Tobacco is grown in the region and accumulated here before going on to market, and fruit and vegetables from here are transported the 195 km to Dar es Salaam. In addition to its agricultural importance, Morogoro is also the centre for missionary work that goes on in the country, and the various missions and their schools and hospitals are a central feature of the town. Morogoro is based at the foot of the Uluguru Mountains, which reach a height of 2,138 m and provide a spectacular backdrop to the town; the peaks are often obscured by dramatic, swirling mists. It was here that Smuts was confident he would confront and destroy the forces of von Lettow in the First World War – only to be bitterly disappointed (see page 356).

Morogoro has been particularly unlucky in that the two main enterprises that were expected to provide substantial employment in the area, the Groundnut Plantation at Kongwa on the road to Dodoma (see page 358) and the state-owned Morogoro shoe factory, have been failures. However, the countryside is green and fertile, large sisal plantations predominate, and the market is probably the largest in the country and worth visiting to soak up the atmosphere. Just about anything that grows and can be eaten can be bought here. It's a good place to stock up on fresh produce if heading south to Malawi and Zambia.

Morogoro is also the largest town near the **Selous Game Reserve** (see page 322), which lies to the south of Mikumi National Park (100 km further down the road), along the most frequently used road route. It was en route to Morogoro that Edward Sokoine, the Prime Minister, widely expected to be Nyerere's successor, was killed in a road accident in October 1984. The Agricultural University in Morogoro has been named after him.

Sights

The old German **Boma** is to the south of the town in the foothills of the **Uluguru Mountains**, along Boma Road. The mountains dominate Morogoro, with a range of impressive summits, and the lower slopes are densely cultivated and terraced. Higher up they are forested and there are some splintered rock bastions. Further back they rise to over 2,438 m. There are three birds endemic to the Ulugurus, the Loveridge sunbird, the black cap shrike and Mrs Moreau's warbler.

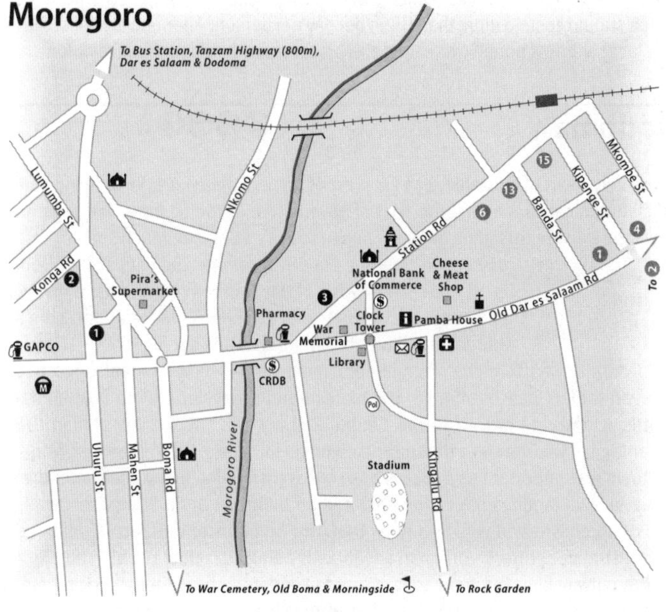

Sleeping
Hilux **4**
Kola Hill **2**
Mama Pierina **6**
New Acropol **1**
New Savoy **15**
Oasis **13**

Eating
1 High Classic **2**
Chipukizi Club **1**
New Green **3**

At the top of Kingalu Road there is a pretty **rock garden**, laid out around a mountain stream with a café.

The **War Cemetery** ⓘ *locked although it is reasonably easy to obtain a key from Dimitri at Mama Pierina's (see page 298)*, south on Boma Road and then turn west, is interesting in that it records the deaths in both the German and the British and Empire Forces. There are two graves of Germans from before 1914, a postal officer and a train driver. Also here is the grave of Kannanpara John, born in Kerala, India, and the first Asian priest of the Diocese of Central Tanganyika. The involvement of the British Empire in the First World War is apparent with 49 graves for troops and support service personnel of regiments from South Africa, Gold Coast, West Africa and the British West Indies, as well as East Africa. There is a special plinth to the 'Hindus, Mohammedans and Sikhs' who died in Imperial Service. These troops were accompanied by 'followers', including their families, traders and craftsmen, and three of these – 'Jim', 'Aaron' and 'Harr' – are recorded as having died in the fighting around Morogoro. The plinth for the Germans records about 180 dead, a mixture of German officers and African soldiers of the Schuztruppe (see box page 357).

Further along Boma Road, well into the Ulugurus, is **Morningside**, one of the summits above Morogoro and a relatively popular climb. The area, with its pretty valleys and good fishing in the mountain streams, is reminiscent of Switzerland. Morningside is almost 10 km from the centre of Morogoro, and whilst you could walk alone it is advisable to take a local guide as there may be opportunist thieves on the road. Morningside is a 15-minute walk from the village of Ruvuma which can be reached by car or bicycle by following the Boma road out of Morogoro. However, before you go you are likely to spend a number of hours traipsing around various offices in Morogoro to obtain the necessary 'thumbs up' and obligatory yellow receipt of permission which must be obtained prior to climbing the summit. Go to the Uluguru Information Office in Pamba House, opposite the post office, who will direct you to the Catchment Forest Officer, who in turn will help you get an official receipt which should cost no more than US$5 per day per person. Alternatively enlist the help of a local or guest house owner and the process may become much simpler.

Dodoma → *Phone code: 026. Colour map 1, grid B4.*  » *pp298-301*

In the very heart of Tanzania, 453 km west of Dar es Salaam, Dodoma is the nation's official political capital and the seat of government in the country. The government legislature divide their time between here and Dar es Salaam. Much smaller and less developed than the country's commercial centre, Dar, Dodoma is on the eastern edge of the southern highlands; a dry, windy and some say desolate place to choose for a capital, lying at an altitude that gives it warm days and cool nights.

Population: 150,000
Altitude: 1,113 m
6°8'S 35°45'E

Dodoma was formerly a small settlement of the semi-pastoral Gogo people. Caravan traders passed through the plateau and it developed into a small trading centre. It owes its growth to the Central Railway and the Germans' plan to take advantage of Dodoma as a trading and commercial centre. During the First World War the town was important as a supply base and transit point. In the years after the war, however, two famines struck the area and an outbreak of rinderpest followed. The British administration was less keen than the Germans to develop Dodoma as the administrative centre, its only real advantages being its central position and location on the railway line. But from 1932, Cape to London flights touched down here and Dodoma received all Dar es Salaam's mail, which was then transferred by rail.

As it is in the very centre of the country, Dodoma was designated the new capital by the former president Nyerere. However the process of transfer has never fully taken off and today only one government ministry has its permanent base in Dodoma. The area's water shortage and poor road network are important contributing factors, and thus the city functions as a capital only when parliamentary sessions are held. On the approach road from Dar is a sprawling housing estate of unfinished and empty houses – a one-time, unsuccessful, effort to move civil servants here. Besides this, and being the CCM party political headquarters, the most notable thing about Dodoma is probably that it is the only wine-producing area in the country and the Tanganyika Vineyards Company is active in promoting its products. It is also an important beef producing area and delicious roasted meat can be found in the many open bars scattered around town. A cattle **market** (*mnada*) takes place each Saturday on Kondoa Road, 5 km from the centre. It is an important event for many locals and is an interesting spectacle. All in all, Dodoma is a peaceful town surrounded by a large number of missions. Few tourists stay long here, although as the designated administrative centre the city is becoming fairly important for foreign businesses. Opposite the *Aladdin's Cave* shop in town a tourist information centre has been built and a sign put up. It is, however, completely empty.

Excursions → *Colour map 1, grid B4.*

Kondoa Irangi Rock Paintings About 180 km down the Great North Road to Arusha in the Great Rift Valley, these are the nearest attraction to Dodoma and are among the finest rock paintings in the world. They are a fine example of ancient art and a further reminder of the existence of ancient humanity in this part of Africa (the rock shelters were used in the later Stone Age by the Bushmanoid tribes who were mainly hunters). The paintings vary in quality, size, style and colour. The most important are from the pre-agriculturalist period, red pigment outlines in streaky and silhouette styles more than 3,000 years old. There are patterned designs, human and animal figures, mainly giraffe, eland and elephant, and hunting scenes. 'Late whites' from a later period are mostly abstract finger paintings. More than 100 sites were described by Mary Leakey

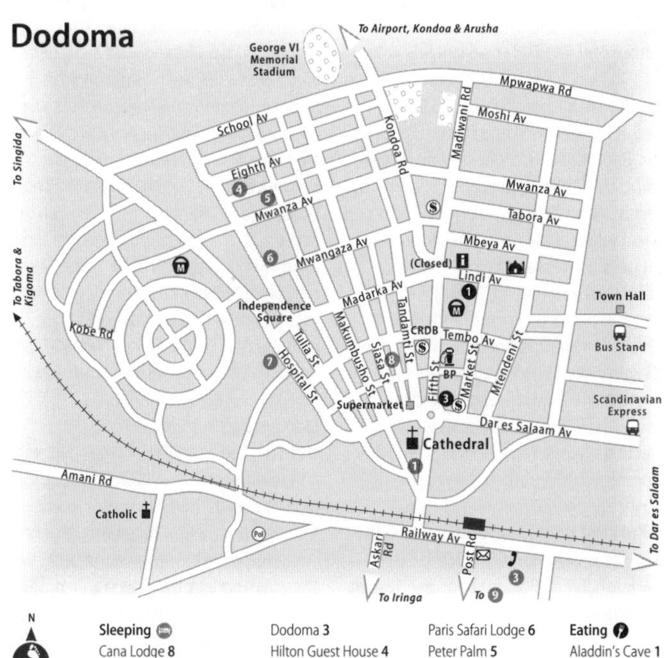

Sleeping
Cana Lodge **8**
Christian Council of Tanzania Guest House **1**
Dodoma **3**
Hilton Guest House **4**
Kilimanjaro Villa **9**
Kilondoma Inn **7**
Paris Safari Lodge **6**
Peter Palm **5**

Eating
Aladdin's Cave **1**
Wimpy **3**

 in the 1950s but only recently have efforts been made to preserve and promote them, and they are currently nominated for designation on the World Heritage List. At **Kolo** where interesting paintings are most accessible, guides must be hired from the visitors' centre office run by the Department of Antiquities. Other sites include **Kinyasi, Pahl, Swera** and **Tumbelo.** Many of the shelters have fantastic views over the plains for miles around. » *See Sleeping, below.*

Mount Hanang, sometimes called the forgotten mountain and East Africa's ninth highest, rises some 1,828 m above the Mangati Plain and is accessed off the road from Dodoma to Arusha, southwest of Babati, northwest of Singida, see page 220.

Sleeping

Morogoro *p294, map p295*
There is a dense crop of cheap guest houses on the streets around the market where you will get a bed and a mosquito net, and not much else, for around US$5.
B-C **The New Acropol**, Old Dar es Salaam Rd, T023-2603403, newacropolhotel@morogoro.net. Canadian-run hotel set in very pretty gardens. Verandas, lovely furnishings, efficient and professional staff, excellent food and comfortable surroundings. A double room with a/c, TV, hot water and mosquito nets costs around US$50, single and family rooms also available. Varied menu with main dishes from around US$4, bar snacks, burgers and pizzas, and a selection of puddings, cakes and ice cream.
C **Hilux Hotel**, Old Dar es Salaam Rd, T023-2603946, hiluxhotel@yahoo.com. Smart, functional hotel with good facilities aimed at businessmen and conference-goers. Rooms have a/c, satellite and en suite bathrooms with hot water, and include a full breakfast. A busy lively covered outdoor bar and restaurant offers good value food. Pasta, meat grills and seafood from US$4.
C **Hotel Oasis**, Station Rd, T023-2604178, hoteloasistz@morogoro.net. Efficient and well run, clean rooms, outdoor swimming pool with mountain views. The large restaurant offers a wide range of Indian, Chinese and European dishes, as well as a buffet at the weekends, and this is probably the best food in Morogoro. There is also a fantastically stocked bar.
C-D **Kola Hill Hotel**, 3 km from town on the Old Dar es Salaam Rd, T0744-388013 (mob), www.kolahill.com. Efficient and very clean in a peaceful out of town location with excellent views of the mountains. Single storey chalet-style accommodation laid out in attractive gardens, each with en suite bathroom, a/c and TV, (rooms with fans are cheaper). Rates include breakfast. Bar in thatched banda with pool table. Restaurant has meat dishes and bar snacks. A taxi here costs very little or you can get a *dala-dala*.
E **The New Savoy Hotel**, just opposite the railway station, T023-2603041. This was the former *Banhof Hotel* built in the German period by the Greeks and the scene of an elaborate prank by von Lettow in the First World War (see page 356). It is now rather run down and shabby, but the buildings are impressive and set in attractive gardens. Rooms are spacious and provide functional accommodation for those on a budget who enjoy 'character' (such as the original Armitage Shanks sinks and plastic flowers). Food is available and there's a lively bar offering a disco at the weekends.
E **Mama Pierina**, Station Rd next to *Hotel Oasis*, T0741-786913 (mob). Family-run guest house with comfortably furnished veranda, run by Dimitri a friendly Italian/ Greek. Worn but comfortable rooms with fan, mosquito net and hot water, breakfast included. Probably best known for its good food, Greek, Indian and Italian dishes including pizzas.

Dodoma *p296, map p297*
The town can be very busy when parliament is in session or there is a CCM meeting, so try to book ahead. There has been a recent mushrooming of new hotels though, rather oddly, many are hidden away on back streets. These are modern, featureless and mostly aimed at visiting civil servants. They usually

For an explanation of the sleeping and eating price codes used in this guide, see inside the front cover. Other relevant information is found in Essentials pages 31-34.

offer single or very small double rooms. You will find all of them empty at the weekends when the town is exceptionally quiet.

B Dodoma Hotel, close to the railway station, T026-2321641, dodomahotel@kicheko.com. Old German Hotel, now extended and completely refurbished, opened by the Vice President in 2004. Easily the best place to stay and it is deservedly popular. The 91 rooms are on the small side but are of a good standard with new furniture, café, shop, hair salon, internet café, small swimming pool, restaurant and bar. Everything is centred around an attractive courtyard, a good place to come for a drink even if you are not staying. Food here includes steak, chicken, Indian and Chinese, and main dishes go for around US$6.

C Kilondoma Inn, Hospital St, south of Independence Sq. Tiny, tiny rooms really only suitable for 1 person though they do have double beds, with fans and mosquito nets, spotless bathrooms with long drop loos. Breakfast included.

D Paris Safari Lodge, Tulia St, T026-2352990. Rooms with reliable hot water, clean but not as modern as some of the other places.

D Peter Palm, Mjimpya St, T026-2320154, 0744-265224 (mob). Very new block with miniscule rooms and only just enough room for the bed and bathroom. Cool white tiles throughout. Basic breakfast included.

C-D Cana Lodge, 9th St, T026-2321199. 17 rooms of various size which is reflected in the price, with fans, cable TV, hot water and mosquito nets. Small restaurant serving soups, snacks, a stab at Western pasta dishes for no more than US$3 a plate. Modern block but old fashioned chunky furniture.

C-D Hilton Guest House, off Tulia St, to the northeast of the market, T026-2321831. Brand new with ornate pillars outside and mirrored windows. Smart but small rooms go for a little under US$20 (hot water in new shiny tiled bathrooms). Breakfast included.

E Kilimanjaro Villa, 500 m from the railway station. Basic but affordable and clean though a little way out in a residential area, run by a friendly group of women though English is a problem here. Rooms with cold water go for US$6 double or single, rooms without bathrooms are a little cheaper. Sells beer and you can get tea in the morning.

E Christian Council of Tanzania Guest House, 5th St, next to the cathedral, T026-2321682. Extremely basic with canteen, cold showers, water supply from petrol barrels, refilled every 3-4 days, off-putting toilets and mosquito nets. Food not recommended. No booze but there's a bar across the road.

Kondoa Irangi Rock Paintings *p297*

You can camp near the visitors' centre but there is no other accommodation near the paintings. The closest guest houses are in Kondoa, a small town 20 km south of Kolo on the Arusha-Dodoma road, 5 hrs by bus from Dodoma or 9 hrs from Arusha.

E New Planet, near the bus stand. The best guest house in Kondoa has clean single and double rooms with basic private bathrooms and a reasonable restaurant.

Eating

Morogoro *p294, map p295*

There are few restaurants in Morogoro and the best eating is to be found at the hotels. Food stalls on the street offer chips and meat, the market has an excellent variety of fresh fruit, and some of the shops offer soft drinks and tinned food.

TT New Green Restaurant, Station Rd. An established restaurant that has been closed for a while. The daughter-in-law of the original owner now has the business up and running again. Excellent Indian dishes, a favourite haunt amongst ex-pats in town, bar. Open daily 1100-1600, 1900-2230.

T 1 High Classic, Konga Rd. Fairly central, bright and well maintained, has satellite TV, grills, chips, omelettes, pilau and local dishes. Good value.

T Chipukizi Club, central location. A typical local bar with a pool table, satellite TV, and barbecued food.

Dodoma *p296, map p297*

It might have been expected that the transfer of the seat of government would have seen the emergence of some reasonable restaurants but this doesn't appear to have been the case at all. The best place to eat by far is the Dodoma Hotel. There are several places in the back streets north of Mwangaza Av where you can get a whole chicken, chips and salad on a large plate to share for around US$3. There is a supermarket a few metres to the northwest of the roundabout near the cathedral that sells imported items such as Pringles and Weetabix, and booze.

Aladdin's Cave, on Market St near the corner with Lindi Av. An Indian-run shop selling lots of sweets and chocolate, ice cream and juice, foreign magazines and there is an internet café. Closes for a few hours in the afternoon.

Wimpy, on the corner of the roundabout opposite the Anglican Church, though is nothing like any Wimpy in the western world. There are tables outside, stools around a bar, and food includes small snacks such as greasy donughts but not much else.

Shopping

Morogoro *p294, map p295*

Although at one time there was a shop run by the German Mission which used to sell pastries, cheesecake and ice cream, these days it has closed. However, you can still order meats and cheeses and other specialized food items from the same building. Turn right after passing the cathedral on your right off the Dar es Salaam Road and the building is easily identified as it is an all-white multi-storeyed building on the left. To the left of the building are two large wrought-iron gates, enter here and you will see a doorway on your right in a basement – ring the bell at the top of the steps and ask for Papa Joe. If in doubt chat to the askaris outside who will be very helpful. Conflicting information suggests you may or may not need to order a day in advance.

Pira's Supermarket, Lumumba St, T023-2604594. A wide range of items including wines, cheeses, and meat including pork.

The GAPCO petrol station, near the market. Also sells wide range of goods but no alcohol.

Transport

Morogoro *p294, map p295*

Air Morogoro has an airstrip, but there are no regular flights.

Road The 196-km road to Morogoro from **Dar** is tarmac. At Morogoro the road divides northwest to Dodoma and southwest which passes through the Mikumi National Park, and then on to Iringa and Mbeya and, ultimately, the Zambian border. Buses leave from the Ipogoro Stand a couple of km out of town on the main road. This enormous new bus stand was recently built with a donation from the World Bank and has space for over 85 buses. A taxi from the centre will cost US$1.50. There is a good choice of buses, and it is safest (the road is busy and notorious for accidents) and most comfortable to opt for a large coach rather than a minibus. There are numerous buses making the trip to **Dar**, about 2 hrs, and the fare is around US$3. Buses from Dar to **Mbeya** pass through Morogoro until mid- day arriving in Mbeya about 2000-2100 (US$ 13, depending on how pushy you're feeling – because of competition amongst the bus companies there is room for negotiation here) and to **Iringa** (US$6). Buses also go to **Dodoma**, roughly 3 hrs (US$4). **Note** At the bus stand be very careful with your luggage and don't be fooled by young men posing as ticket collectors. Don't part with your ticket at any time and only show it to a conductor once your journey has started. You should not pay for a normal or average amount of luggage, so ignore anyone who tries to charge you extra for luggage.

Train It's not really worth getting the train from Dar to Morogoro (or vice versa), you are better off taking the bus, but if you really want to, see **Tanzania Railways Corporation** www.trctz.com for full details of timetables and fares and for other routes west from here.

Dodoma *p296, map p297*

Air Despite it being the capital, there are very few flights to and from Dodoma and most of the government people drive here from Dar. **Coastal Air**, T022-2117969-60, www.coastal.cc, flies from **Arusha** to Dodoma (2 hrs) on Tue, Fri, and Sun at 0800, and from Dodoma to Arusha Mon, Thu and Sat 1300. This flight only runs if there are enough takers.

Train The train from Dar leaves at 1700 and takes 14½ hrs on Sun, Tue and Fri. Overnight trains to **Dar** leave at 1840 on Sun, Tue, Thu, Fri, Sat. See **Tanzania Railways Corporation** www.trctz.com, for full details of timetables and fares, see also Kigoma Transport, page 317.

Bus The main bus stand is opposite the town hall two blocks up from Dar es Salaam Av. The **Scandinavian Express** terminal is on Dar es Salaam Av, T026-2322170, www.scandinaviangroup.com. Buses go to **Arusha** via **Chalinze** daily taking 12-15 hrs (US$11). They can fill up so it's advisable to book a seat a day in advance. A journey to Arusha via Konoa takes 2 days on a largely unsurfaced road. The road to **Dar** is surfaced all the way. Buses go daily and take about 4-6 hrs (US$8).

Directory

Morogoro *p294, map p295*
Banks National Bank of Commerce, just off Machupa Rd opposite the post office. CRDB is just past the war memorial on the left hand side of the Dar es Salaam Rd before crossing the river into the centre of town. Both have ATM machines that accept Visa.
Internet There are a number of internet cafés in the town centre. The regional library just past the post office offers reliable internet connection at US$0.50 per hour.
Hospitals The **Aga Khan Hospital** and dispensary are suitable for minor ailments. Pharmacy opposite the CRDB bank on the Dar es Salaam Rd.

Dodoma *p296, map p297*
Banks CRDB, Bank St has ATM.

Tabora and around

The region around Tabora was once frequently crossed by Livingstone on his quest to explore central Africa but few people visit today and there is little of interest for the visitor to Tanzania. However, the Central Railway splits at Tabora and anyone riding the train will spend either a few hours or a whole day here depending on what direction they are travelling, to Mwanza via Shinyanga, Kigoma or Dar. ▸▸ *For Sleeping, Eating and other listings, see pages 306-307.*

Tabora → *Phone code: 026. Colour map 1, grid B2.* ▸▸ *pp 306-307*

Population: 100,000
5°25'S 32°50'E.

The railway continues along the old caravan trading route to Tabora, founded in 1820 by Arab slave traders and of enormous historical interest. During the German occupation, Tabora was one of the most populated and prosperous towns in the whole of East Africa. From 1852 Tabora was the Arab's slaving capital (*Kazeh*) in Unyanyembe, the kingdom of Nyamwezi (Tanzania's second-largest tribe) with famous chieftains Mirambo and Isike. Ivory and humans were bartered in exchange for guns, beads and cloth. Its heyday was in the 1860s when 500,000 caravans annually passed through the town and many trade routes converged here. The Germans realized this and constructed a fort. (Isike later fought the Germans here in 1892, and the Germans captured the town in 1893.)

The building of Mittelland Bahn (the Central Railway) in 1912 increased the town's importance. It fell to Belgian forces from the Congo after 10 days' fighting on 11 September 1916. Tabora was a 'railway town' by the time the British took over. The explorers Burton, Speke, Livingstone and Stanley all used the town as an important base for their journeys into more remote areas. Tabora School (1925) was important for nurturing future leaders including Nyerere. However, these days not much happens here and it's little more than a collection of dusty streets. But it is here that

The region around Tabora is famous for its honey. Large jerry cans and bottles of it can be bought in the local markets and from the train when it stops at the smaller stations.

The Miombo Woodland of Tanzania

A type of woodland called miombo is found in large parts of south, central and western Tanzania. At a glance these areas appear to be ideally suited for agricultural and other development. However, this area is infected with the tsetse fly (see page 245), which is a serious hindrance to settlement and so parts of it are very thinly populated.

If you are visiting miombo country around the rains it is a very colourful sight – all reds, pinks and browns – and plenty of shade. However, in the dry season all the leaves fall and bush fires are common. There is little shade and the slate grey bark of the trees seems to shimmer in the heat. One of the most successful economic activities in areas of miombo is the cultivation of tobacco. This has been introduced in the Urambo area and is ideal as tsetse fly make the area unsuitable for livestock.

happens here and it's little more than a collection of dusty streets. But it is here that the railway divides, one line going on to Kigoma, the other north to Mwanza and for this reason people often stay a night here in order to change trains.

Sights

Tabora is dominated by the **Fort** (or Boma) on a hill overlooking the town built by the Germans at the turn of the century. This is southeast of the town centre along Boma Road at the junction of Boma Road and School Street. Do not take pictures as it is a military building. The **central market** is worth a wander around and has an excellent second-hand clothing section, which is cheaper than in some of the other cities.

Kwihara Museum ⓘ *to get there follow the road out of town past the fort, after the roundabout take the right-hand fork, a taxi there and back will cost in around US$9,* about 10 km outside the town, this is probably one of the major attractions of Tabora. It is dedicated to Dr Livingstone. The museum is in the house that he occupied for

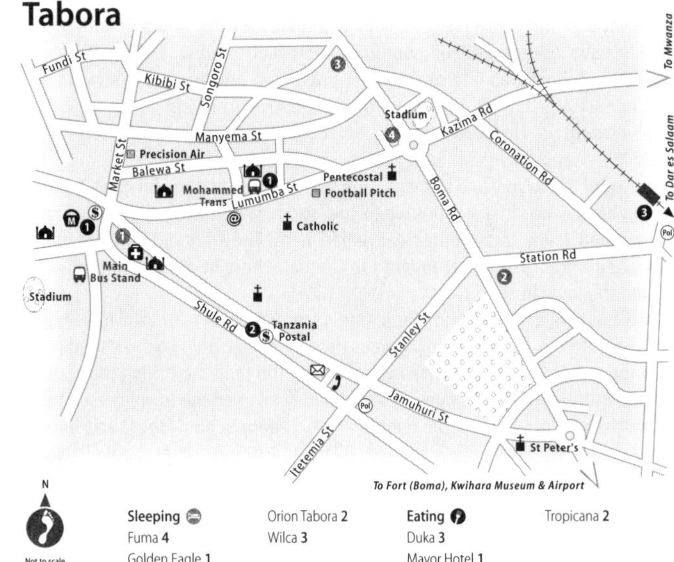

about 10 months before setting off on the final leg of the journey in 1872 that was to be his last. He died less than a year later at Chitambo, Zambia. The museum, although rundown, is interesting and contains various letters, maps, pictures etc associated with the man, as well as with other early missionaries and explorers.

Ugalla River Game Reserve → *Colour map 1, grid B2. 6° 30' S, 32° E.*

ⓘ *There is no formal entrance into the park but the Ugalla River is around 40 km south of the central railway. From Tabora follow the road along the railway to Usoke from where there is a track heading south to the village of Sire, but you will need to ask locally which this is.*

The Ugalla River Game Reserve, to the west of Tabora, is approximately 5,000 sq km. Its inaccessibility and lack of facilities mean that is rarely visited by tourists. It is between Tabora and Lake Rukwa, approximately 100 km north east of Mpanda, well off the beaten track. It consists of miomba woodlands, and is home to the rare sable antelope, lion, leopard and cheetah, elephant, buffalo and waterbuck. West of the Ugalla River there are chimpanzees living in the riverine forests. There is abundant birdlife with over 300 different species recorded, including the pygmy goose, various herons and the glossy ibis. If you do manage to get there be aware that there are no tourist facilities and you must bring all your own supplies. Be prepared to be totally self-sufficient.

Shinyanga → *Phone code: 028. Colour map 1, grid A3.* ▸▸ *pp 306-307*

Shinyanga is a large, sprawling town with buildings and roads in poor condition, mostly built in the 1940s and 1950s when the area was thriving on gold, diamonds and cotton. During that time a large number of Europeans lived here and many vets from the UK were employed at a research station involved in eradicating rinderpest.

Mosquitos are a major problem here – the region is known for having drug-resistant malaria strains. Report unusual symptoms to a doctor immediately.

The region is known for its cattle production and African dew-lapped cows can be seen everywhere. Some gold is still found in the area and mined in open-cast pits with the ore broken with large mortars and pestles. There's still a lot of cotton here too and it's brought to the area's ginneries for processing. Rice is also grown and just outside town are several large, circular, covered stores where the surplus is kept to be distributed in the event of crop failure. The area has been deforested, the timber being used for firewood and now the region is hot, dry and dusty.

The inhabitants are very friendly and there is no problem walking around, especially in the day time. Education has always been very important in Shinyanga and now there is a big college on the road to Kamborage Stadium. There is a sizeable Indian community and also many Africans of Arab descent, hence the large number of Muslims.

There are no large shops, but a great number of stores selling only a few items – many with a dressmaker and sewing machine outside. Every day there is a busy market selling just about everything.

Electricity and water supply is unreliable and when there is water (not every day)

Shinyanga has many birds of all types and sizes. In particular there are a large number of Marabou storks and during the breeding season these huge birds have nests on most of the acacia trees in town. During the heat of the day the adult birds shade the young with their vast wings. Kites also frequently swoop down to pick something off the road and large eagles can be seen on the plains around here; they feed on some of the many snakes.

Shinyanga witches

Shinyanga has attracted an unenviable reputation for its appalling treatment of elderly women. Years of cooking over open cow dung fires have caused many of the women to develop red, inflamed eyes. This feature has been interpreted as a sign that the elderly person is a witch and therefore responsible for all manner of ills from crop failures, to ill health or other misfortunes. In recent years, many elderly women have been killed, usually by machete blows to their heads, but their possessions left untouched. In the two-year period up to October 1999 it was reported that 168 women and 17 men had been killed after being accused of witchcraft.

Some of the killings have been attributed to polygamous males moving on to younger wives and using accusations of witchcraft to incite vigilantes to kill their elderly spouses. Sometimes the motive is acquisition of property owned by the elderly. Another theory is that the reason these poor women are killed is as human sacrifices, offered up to bring good luck to people prospecting for diamonds and gold. Finally, there are the irresponsible activities of soothsayers. Soothsayers are asked to identify enemies, who are accused of perpetrating evil spells against the client. Over half the population of Shinyanga follow traditional religions that recognize witchcraft and condone the killings.

The situation is complicated by the activities of a local enforcement group known as SunguSungu. Their founder decreed that they should go about their work bare-chested, and this rules out the participation of women. SunguSungu claim to apprehend the perpetrators of witchcraft killings, extracting confessions by beatings. When SunguSungu thugs are handed over to the police, it has been difficult to secure prosecutions because people are unwilling to testify as they fear reprisals from the witch-killers and their families.

The police say that more secure dwellings need to be provided for the elderly and that they should live with their families and not alone, as has been the custom in Shinyanga region.

it is so muddy it has to be filtered as well as boiled. The water treatment works built by the Germans in the mid-1980s is no longer in use.

Sights

About 15-20 minutes along the road to the southeast of Shinyanga, on the right you come to a turning for **Mwadui Mine**, where there is a tree-lined road leading up to the compound. In the 1960s it was a flourishing diamond mine with its own hospital, churches, supermarket and schools. A Dakota flew weekly to Nairobi from the on-site airstrip for shopping trips. (The same Dakota still flies to Dar es Salaam and onward to South Africa, with diamonds.) The Mwadui diamondiferous kimberlite pipe was one of the largest in the world but a combination of flooding and exhaustion of the ore reserves have led to a reduction in the output. The most famous stone mined here was the 'Williamson pink' diamond found in October 1947, given to Princess Elizabeth as a wedding gift. It weighed 23.6 carats after cutting and polishing, and was a beautiful rose colour.

This Williamson diamond mine is part-owned by the Tanzanian Government (30%) and De Beers (70%), who are refurbishing the mine, but only industrial diamonds are now found. It covers a huge area and sometimes it is possible to get a

Dr Livingstone

David Livingstone was born on 19 March 1813 in Blantyre in Scotland. He had a strict Scottish upbringing, and his first job was in a factory. He studied during the evenings and at the age of 27 finally qualified as a doctor. In 1840 he joined the London Missionary Society, was ordained in the same year and set off for Africa. On the voyage out he learnt to use quadrants and other navigational and mapping instruments, which were to prove vital skills during his exploring of uncharted parts of Africa. In 1841 he arrived in South Africa and journeyed north from the mission in search of converts.

In his first few years as a missionary Livingstone gained a reputation as a surveyor and scientist. His first major expedition into the African interior came in 1853, lasted three years, and included in 1855 the discovery of the Victoria Falls. When he returned to England in 1856 he was greeted as a national hero, was awarded a gold medal by the Royal Geographical Society, and made a Freeman of the City of London.

He returned to Africa in 1858 and began his quest for the source of the Nile in 1866. This trip was funded by a grant from the British government, which enabled Livingstone to be better equipped than during his previous expedition. During this journey little was heard of him and rumours reached Britain of his apparent death. Henry Morton Stanley, a newspaper reporter for the New York Herald, was sent by James Gordon Bennett, his publisher, to find Livingstone. On 1871 Stanley found Livingstone's camp at Ujiji, a small town on the shores of Lake Tanganyika, greeting him with the now legendary, 'Dr Livingstone, I presume?' At the time of the meeting Livingstone had run short of supplies, in particular quinine, which was vital in protecting him and his companions from malaria.

Livingstone set out on his last trip from near Tabora and continued his explorations until his death at Chitambo in what is now Zambia. His heart was buried at the spot where he died, his body embalmed and taken by Susi and Chumah, his two servants, to Bagamoyo (see page 87) from where it was shipped back to England. He was buried at Westminster Abbey and a memorial was erected at Chitambo.

permit to look around. Many people dig up their own land in areas close to the Mwadui Mine in the hope of discovering the precious stones. The Sukuma people of this region have always strongly believed in the power of witchcraft. Offerings of grain and domestic animals are made on the advice of the witch doctors to enhance their chances of successful prospecting.

Within a few kilometres of leaving Shinyanga going south to Nzega, houses give way to plains and baobab trees. To the left is a vast open area and the smoke of the engine at **Manonga Ginnery** in Chomachankula village can be seen way off in the distance with large blue hazy hills behind. Further along the main road is a strange sight – an **oasis** with a group of palms providing Shinyanga with a good supply of dates. The baobabs have a crop of heavy seed pods, which the children harvest to sell in the market. They are popular and taste similar to sherbet.

Further on is a large area used as paddy fields during the rains and you can often see oxen working. Away to the left on the plains is the main **gold region** where settlements have sprung up.

Sleeping

Tabora *p301, map p302*

C **Orion Tabora** (formely Railway Hotel), T026-2604369, oriontbrhotel@spidersat.net. Completely refurbished in 2003 this is an historic old German Hotel (there once used to be a sign here warning that the hotel did not permit black people or dogs), close to the station, with sweeping steps up to the outside terrace. The more modern rooms are around the back of the main building. There's a bar and restaurant serving good food, and an extensive buffet breakfast is included in the price. Easily the best option.

D-E **Golden Eagle**, Songeya Rd, T026-2604623. Reasonable value rooms with or without bathrooms, fans, mosquito nets and spotless white sheets, are upstairs around a bright, freshly painted, courtyard. A good location for early morning buses. Simple food and beer in the restaurant.

D **Wilca**, Boma Rd, T026-2604105. Comfortable and well run, friendly staff, very nice bar, *nyama choma* grill and good restaurant, the rooms have satellite TV and hot water in the bathrooms. There are only 10 rooms so you may need to get here early to get one. This is by far the best of a whole bunch of guest houses in this area, most of which are very basic. Avoid the *Wild Roses* nearby, it's not nice at all.

E **Fuma Hotel**, off Lumumba Rd, T026-24657260. 12 spotless rooms around a small courtyard, each one is named after a month of the year, mosquito nets, some with bathrooms for not much more. Good value and secure parking behind a locked gate. Small restaurant and bar near the entrance.

Shinyanga *p303*

C **Mwoleka**, T028-2762249. En suite facilities, mosquito nets and fans, it is clean, has quite good food and a locked compound for cars.

C **Shinyanga Motel**, T028-2762458. Has been refurbished with en suite bathrooms, but close to railway, so noisy. African and some Indian dishes can be made on request.

Eating

Tabora *p301, map p302*

TTT **Orion Tabora**, T026-2604369. The best food in town is to be found at the Tabora Hotel, there's a formal dining room or you can eat in the comfy bar in front of the enormous satellite TV. Snacks such as fish fingers, chicken bites or sandwiches, or main meals of curries and grilled fish or chicken. If you arrive early in the morning off the train, you can come and eat breakfast here for US$4.

T **The Mayor Hotel**, behind Market St near the National Bank of Commerce. Excellent breakfasts available, buffet-style canteen, surprising variety of food including lots of vegetables, plastic seats overlooking the bicycle-mending stalls, clean kitchen. There is another branch on Lumumba St.

T **Tropicana Restaurant**, next to the Tanzania Postal Bank on Shule Rd. High ceilings with fans, lots of fake flowers, good for breakfast, snacks and grills, a big urn is on the go all day for tea and coffee.

T **Wilca**, simple menu but food is well prepared and served in a nice outdoor bar area with pool table.

Duka Bar, opposite the station, garden bar with pool table and TV, good place to wait for the train; watch the mosquitos though.

Shinyanga *p303*

T **Green View Bar**, on road to Mwanza. Serves chargrilled chicken in the evening. An attractive place under thatched rondavaals. Masoi, the owner, makes you welcome. To one side of the road leading to the bar there is a football pitch used by the locals and most evenings the teams of shirts versus no-shirts can be seen playing.

T **Mama Shitta's Café**, in the centre of town. Serves excellent local dishes cooked over charcoal – beef, roast potatoes with crispy onions, rice, and many vegetables. Cold sodas are available and the staff will bring back cold beer from the nearby bar.

For an explanation of the sleeping and eating price codes used in this guide, see inside the front cover. Other relevant information is found in Essentials pages 31-34.

Transport

Tabora *p301, map p302*
Air There is an airport at Tabora and there are regular flights by **Precision Air**, T022-2130800/2121718, www.precisionairtz.com, daily except Thu. The office is on Market St to the north of the National Bank of Commerce, T023-2604818. A taxi to the airport costs US$5-6 and taxis go out there to meet the incoming flight. The flight leaves Dar at 1335, arrives in Tabora at 1525, departs Tabora at 1550, arrives in **Kigoma** at 1645, departs Kigoma at 1710 and arrives in **Dar** at 1950. Fares: Dar-Tabora US$155 one-way, and US$245 return (via Kigoma). One way to Kigoma US$85.

Bus The new Tabora bus stand is off Market St with a huge football stadium behind. It is fairly well organized with the bus company kiosks around the perimeter. Buses go daily to **Mwanza**, 8 hrs; US$8, **Dar**, 16 hr; US$20, **Dodoma**, 11 hrs; US$11, and **Arusha**, 15 hrs; US$18. Most of these services leave very early in the morning. Buses also serve closer destinations such as **Shinyanga**, **Ngeza** and **Singida**. Another bus depot away from the station is **Mohammed Trans Ltd**, on Lumumba Rd next to the Mayor Hotel, T0748-566505, www.mtlid.com. The road from Tabora west to **Kigoma** is impassable in places during the rainy seasons. There is, however, talk about upgrading it.

Train Both the **Kigoma** and **Mwanza** services stop at Tabora. The railway station is 3 km outside the town. A taxi there costs US$1-2. If it is on time the train from Dar arrives about 2100. The train from Mwanza usually arrives earlier in the day. Then the trains are split and the carriages shunted around, which takes around 2 hrs during which you may have to swap trains depending in what direction you are going. Both trains then depart again to Kigoma and back to Mwanza respectively and arrive at each of these destinations the following morning. See **Tanzania Railways Corporation** www.trctz.com for full details of timetables and fares and see Kigoma Transport, page 317.

Shinyanga *p303*
Air There is a grass airstrip a few km out of town toward Mwanza. When the cows are shooed off, a joint **Air Tanzania/Precision Air** T022-2130800/2121718, www.precisionairtz.com, flies from **Dar** to Shinyanga (2 hr) and **Mwanza** (3 hr) on Mon, Wed, Thu, Fri, and Sun 1330. From Shinyanga to Dar via Mwanza the flight departs at 1550.

Road Shinyanga is 162 km from **Mwanza**, and the road between the two has recently been tarred and the journey takes a little over 2 hrs. There are a great number of buses in every direction daily.

Train Shinyanga is on the Central Line railway on the branch line between Mwanza and Tabora. See Tabora above.

Directory

Tabora *p301, map p302*
Banks The National Bank of Commerce on Market St has an ATM. **Internet** There is an internet café on Lumumba Rd near the Catholic Cathedral. However Tabora does not have its own server and is expensive.

Shinyanga *p303*
Medical services On the main Shinyanga/Mwanza road about 20 mins out of town is **Kalandoto Hospital**, run by the African Inland Church, T028-228627. Several American doctors and nurses work here, some for over 30 years. It is the best place to go if taken ill in the region. The state-run **Shinyanga Hospital** is in the centre of town, T028-22235/6.

Lake Tanganyika

Despite its remote location in the extreme north west of Tanzania, Lake Tanganyika has a number of attractions. Here are the attractive lakeside national parks of Mahale and Gombe famous for their chimpanzee populations, and further south is the wild and scenic Katavi National Park. A safari here gives you the feeling of having the park to yourself. The region is an adventurous destination to get to and explore for the budget traveller by train or ferry, though reasonably accessible for those who can afford to visit by plane. ▸▸ *For Sleeping, Eating and other listings, see pages 315-318.*

Kigoma → *Phone code: 028. Colour map 1, grid B1.* ▸▸ *pp315-318*

Population: 80,000
Altitude: 800 m
4°55'S 29°36'E

Capital of the Western Region of Tanzania, Kigoma is a small, sleepy town 1,254 km west of Dar es Salaam with one tree-lined main road. It overlooks the picturesque Lake Tanganyika on its western side and has scenic rolling hills to the east. It is the main railway terminus in the west of the country for the Central Railway that was built in the early 20th century to transport agricultural goods from the African hinterland to the coast. Just a few km to the south is the old Arab slave trading settlement of Ujiji (see below), the famous meeting place of Stanley and Livingstone. Most people come here on their way to Burundi or Zambia across the lake on the

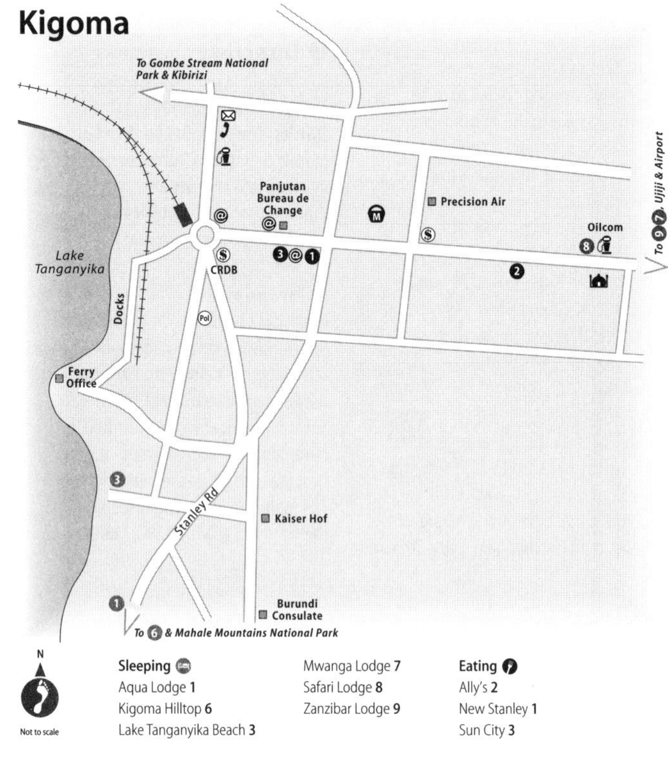

The graveyard at Kigoma

At the graveyard at the top of the hill in Kigoma there are three gravestones dating back to the late 19th century. Two of them belong to members of the London Missionary Society (LMS) – Rev J B Thompson and Rev A W Dodgshun.

The LMS had sent an expedition of four ministers and two laymen to establish a mission on the shores of Lake Tanganyika under the leadership of Rev Roger Price. Following the death of the bullocks used to carry their equipment inland – they were struck down by tsetse fly – Price returned to the coast to try to persuade the missionary authorities to establish a string of mission stations along the road heading into the interior. The expedition that continued on to the Lake divided into two, with Thompson – who had had seven years' experience as a missionary in Matabeleland – taking the forward party with Dodgshun, who had only recently left training, following on behind.

The advance party reached Ujiji on 23 August 1878. Thompson, who had been seriously ill during the early part of the journey, again fell ill and died on 22 September. Meanwhile Dodgshun was having many problems of his own and did not reach Ujiji until 27 March 1879, by which time he was very unwell. He died just one week later on 3 April.

A third gravestone belongs to Michel Alexandre de Baize (known as Abbé de Baize), who had gone out to Africa under the auspices of the French government. He was a young man, with no experience of Africa or of exploration. He had been generously equipped with a large sum of money by the French government and had a huge array of supplies and equipment, including such things as rockets, fireworks, coats of armour and a barrel organ. He planned to travel across Africa from east to west and set off from Bagamoyo with a small army of about 800 men. However, he was beset by troubles. He was attacked at night, many of his porters deserted and so much of his equipment had to be abandoned, and many of his supplies were stolen.

When he reached Ujiji he apparently became upset that the White Fathers failed to come out to greet him. He is said to have paraded through Ujiji firing his revolver. He received assistance from the LMS before setting off for the north shores of Lake Tanganyika. During that stretch of the journey he offended a local chief and set fire to a number of huts and had to be rescued by the LMS at Ugaha. He then fell ill and the LMS again came to his aid. When he was well enough he returned to Ujiji where he again fell ill. He died on 12 December 1879. The LMS finally abandoned their station at Ujiji in 1884.

The graveyard has fallen into disrepair and it is difficult to find. Walk in the direction of Ujiji, after the CCM building turn to the right.

steamer *MV Liemba* (see page 310) or else on their way to **Gombe Stream National Park** (see page 311). The **Mahale Mountains National Park,** also famous for chimpanzees, lies to the south of Kigoma but is very remote and is accessed most easily by plane from Kigoma (see page 313).

There are still a large number of refugee camps close to Kigoma following the unrest in DR Congo, Burundi and Rwanda. UN offices and landcruisers can be spotted all over town.

MV Liemba

The steamer Liemba, originally named Gotzen, was built in Germany in 1913 and transported at great expense to Kigoma where it was reconstructed. Its first trial runs took place in June 1915 and average speeds of around 8 knots were reached. It was the flagship of the German flotilla on Lake Tanganyika and was used during the First World War as armed transport, particularly to carry troops down the lake from Kigoma to Kasanga. The Gotzen was the largest ship on the lake at this time and could carry about 900 men in a quarter of the time that it took the dhows to do the same journey.

In June 1916 the Gotzen was attacked by Belgian planes but was not too seriously damaged. In July of the same year, when the railway to Kigoma was captured, the Germans scuttled her.

After the war, the Gotzen was raised from the deeps and refitted. On 16 May 1927 the ship was rechristened Liemba, the name by which Lake Tanganyika had originally been known by local people, and in trials that month managed an average speed of 8.5 knots – not bad for a ship that had spent from 26 July 1916 to 16 March 1924 at the bottom of the lake. It is still in operation today.

Since then the Liemba has steamed the lake from end to end almost continuously, for a period of over 80 years (however, see page 318). She has probably completed the nearly 1000 km, week-long round trip between Kigoma and Mpulungu in Zambia over 4000 times, perhaps steaming over 4 million kilometres. She is generally believed to be the oldest operational passenger vessel in the world.

The **railway station** is a very imposing building built before the First World War by the Germans. The nearby **Kaiser Hof**, another German building, was built for the Kaiser and today is used as the State House (do not take photographs). Intruiguingly there is a tunnel between this house and the railway station which was a secret escape route for the Kaiser. The major industry in Kigoma is fishing and this is mostly done in the afternoon when hundreds of dhows set sail across the lake from **Kibirizi** village, 3 km north of Kigoma. In this village you can see the fishermen building dhows or stringing fishing nets together. There is also a large depot here for the petrol companies that transport fuel across the lake.

Fossilized fish remains in the extensive sedimentary deposits of Lake Tanganyika are currently being examined as part of the **Nyanza Project** in Kigoma. Lake Tanganyika is considered to be an evolutionary 'hot spot' due to its lengthy, complex geological history. Over 1,500 species of animals and plants have been identified in this biologically diverse lake. Cichlid fish, gastropods and crustaceans account for most of the endemic species.

Ujiji

This small market village 10 km south of Kigoma has a thriving boat-building industry. It used to be the terminus for the old caravan route from the coast and the resulting Arab influence is clear to see. The houses are typical of the coastal Swahili architecture and the population is mainly Muslim. The post office on Kigoma Road is a substantial structure dating from the German period. It is, however, most famous for being the place where the words 'Dr Livingstone, I presume' were spoken by Henry Morton Stanley (see page 305). The two men met on the 10th November 1871. The site where this is thought to have occurred is marked by a plaque, between the town and what used to be the shore, on Livingstone Street. The original mango tree under which the two gentlemen met died in the 1920s, but there are two very large mango trees that are supposed to have been grafted from the original one. After the meeting Livingstone left Uijiji and went to Tabora with Stanley. The site is now the ★ **Livingstone Museum** and the museum curator will show you around for a small tip and tell you the story. He will also proudly tell you about the day he met Michael Palin when he visited here during the making of *Pole to Pole*. In the main building of the museum are some faded drawings and books and rather comical brightly painted, full size papier mâché figures of the two men shaking hands. There is also a small plaque in the grounds to Speke and Burton, the first Europeans to set eyes on Lake Tanganikya on Feb 14th 1858. There are regular *dala-dala* to and from Kigoma, ask to be dropped off at Livingstone St and the museum is a few minutes' walk towards the lake.

★ Gombe Stream National Park → *Colour map B1.*  ▸▸ *p316*

In the extreme northwestern corner of Tanzania on the shore of Lake Tanganyika and sharing a border with Burundi, Gombe Stream National Park is one of Tanzania's most remote. The park is most famous for the work of Jane Goodall, the resident primatologist who spent many years in its forests studying the behaviour of the endangered chimpanzees. Guided walks deep into the forest to observe and sit with the extraordinary primates for an entire morning are possible and an incredible experience. Aside from chimpanzee viewing, many other species of primates and mammals live in Gombe Stream's tropical forests, as well as a wide variety of tropical birdlife.

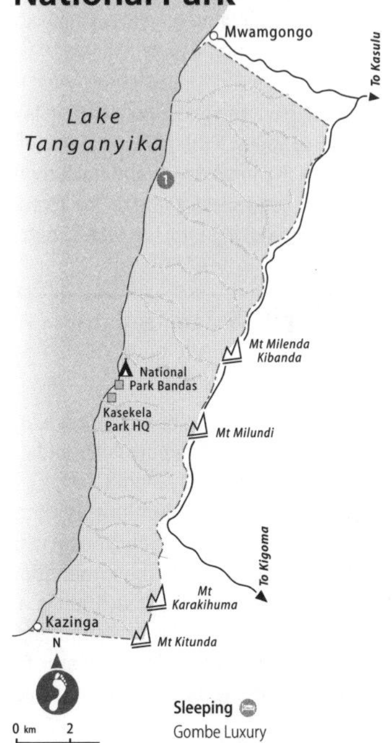

Ins and outs

Getting there You can get a boat fairly easily from Kigoma (16 km south of the park). They normally leave around 1400-1500, the trip takes about 3 hrs and costs about US$3. Arrange with the boatman what time you want to return the next day. As the boats only leave in the afternoon it is essential to spend at least one night in the park. You can also organize a transfer by motor boat from the *Tanganikya Beach Hotel* or *Aqua Lodge* in Kigoma. Motor boats cost around US$150 per return trip, can carry up to 20 people and take 2-3 hrs each way. The hotels will organize for a cook to go with you if you are staying in the park's bandas. You can also arrange a tour through **Chimpanzee Safaris** at the *Kigoma Hilltop Hotel*, see page 315.

4°38'S 31°40'E. The park can be visited all the year around.

Park information The main purpose of the park is research rather than tourism and the facilities there are minimal. The park headquarters is at Kasekela.

The entrance fee is US$100 per person per 24-hour period. Obligatory guide US$10 per trip for up to 5 people. Note that children under 7 cannot go chimp-tracking in either Gombe or Mahale.

Background

In 1960 Jane Goodall set up the area as a chimpanzee research station. She wrote a book on the findings of her research called *In the Shadow of Man*. Her work was later filmed by Hugo van Lawick, the wildlife photographer. This attracted much publicity to the reserve and in 1968 the Gombe Stream National Park was established. It covers an area of 40 sq km, making it the smallest park in Tanzania. It is made up of a narrow, mountainous strip of land about 16 km long and 2.5 km wide that borders Lake Tanganyika. The mountains, which rise steeply from the lake to 681-1,500 m, are intersected by steep valleys, which have streams running in them and are covered in thick gallery forest (that is, the river banks are wooded, but beyond is open country).

Wildlife

There are approximately 90 chimpanzees in the park divided into two family troops. They each guard their territory fiercely. One of the groups often goes down to the valley so you can see them from there. Alternatively there are a number of observation points around the park and the wardens usually know where to go to see them. However, there is no guarantee that you will see the chimpanzees during your visit. They are less visible here than at Kibale Forest in western Uganda. Other primates include red-tailed and blue colobus monkeys. Birdlife is also prolific and includes various barbets, starlings, sunbirds, kingfishers, the palm-nut vulture, crowned eagle and the rufous-bellied heron. Recently, problems have been reported at Gombe. It is thought that the chimps have got far too used to humans and in 2002 an adult male called Frodo actually ripped a human baby off the back of its mother (a park ranger's wife) and ate it. Gombe has also lost at least four chimps since 2002 to disease suspected to be human-borne. As chimpanzees can catch many of our diseases, you will not be allowed to visit Gombe if you have a cold or any other infectious illness.

Routes

It is compulsory to take a guide with you to the forest. From the guest house there is a trail leading to a lovely waterfall just over 2 km away in a valley. If there are no chimps in this valley, one of the guides will take you further into the forest to try and track them down. It can be hard, slippery walking up and down the valleys through the forest. Another route you can take (which does not require a guide) is along the lake shore.

Mahale Mountains National Park → *Colour map 1, grid B1.*

▸▸ *p316*

This is another chimpanzee sanctuary established in 1985 as a national park covering an area of 1,577 sq km, and lying at an altitude of over 1,800 m. The park is about half way down the eastern shore of Lake Tanganyika, 120 km south of Kigoma. Although Gombe is more famous, the primate population in Mahale Mountains is more numerous and sightings more regular and prolonged (reputedly, the only person who stayed in Mahale and didn't see chimps, was Bill Gates!). Hikes to their habitation areas are accessible and not strenuous. As well as being the premium location in all Africa for viewing chimpanzees in the wild, Mahale Mountains is also in a stunningly beautiful lakeshore setting, with superb white sand beaches and clear water for swimming (though check with the lodge staff before swimming as some parts of Lake Tanganyika are affected by bilharzia).

Ins and outs

Getting there There are no roads running into the park and the only access is by boat or plane. The most practical, though most expensive, way of getting there is by charter flight direct to the park's landing strip. Return flights from Kigoma cost in the region of US$300 per person and return flights from Arusha around US$600 per person. These can be organized as part of a package through the operators who run the luxury lodges or from the *Hilltop Hotel* in Kigoma (see Sleeping page 315). Many of the packages also include stays in Katavi National Park (see below) and flights go via Katavi en route between Mahale and Arusha. A cheaper though more difficult alternative is organizing a boat transfer from the *Tanganikya Beach Hotel* or *Aqua Lodge* in Kigoma. Motor boats cost in the region of US$800 per return trip, can carry up to 20 people and take 6-8 hrs each way. The hotels will organize for a cook to go with you if staying in the park's rest house. In theory it is also possible to take the lake ferry *(MV Liemba* or *MV Mwongozo)* to the park from Kigoma, though this is an adventurous option, see page 318. You get to Lagosa (also known as Mugambo) after about 6 hrs at about 0300 and will have to get a small boat to take you to the shore. From Lagosa you will have to hire another boat to take you the 3-hr journey to the park office at Bilenge. As you are relying on the lake ferry you will have to stay until the next ferry comes through on the way back to Kigoma, which is usually about a week later although it is not very reliable.

The best time to visit is May-Sep during the drier months.

Park information The park office is at Bilenge where all fees are paid. From here there is a boat transfer to Kasiha village 10 km south of Bilenge, where the chimp walks go from, which is also the location of the national park rest camp. Entrance fee: US$80 per person per 24-hr period. Obligatory guide US$10 per forest walk.

Wildlife

The park is largely made up of montane forests and grasslands and some alpine bamboo. The eastern side of the mountains is drier, being in the rain shadow, and the vegetation there is the drier miombo woodland (see box, page 302), which is found over much of west Tanzania and east DR Congo. The highest peak reaches 2,460 m and the prevailing winds from over the lake, when forced up to this level, condense and ensure a high rainfall. The wildlife found here is more similar to that found in western Africa than eastern. Other than the chimpanzees, it includes porcupine, colobus monkeys (both red and the Angolan black and white), and elephant, although there are also giraffe, zebra, buffalo and roan antelope. The range and numbers of animals has increased since the *Ujaama* villagization programme of the 1970s. Indeed animals such as the leopard and lion have reappeared in the area. Birdlife includes the fish eagle, kestrel, kingfisher, barbet and starling, similar to those found at Gombe Stream. The chimpanzee population has been the focus of much research by scientists from around the world. According to a recent census there are now more than 700 individuals in

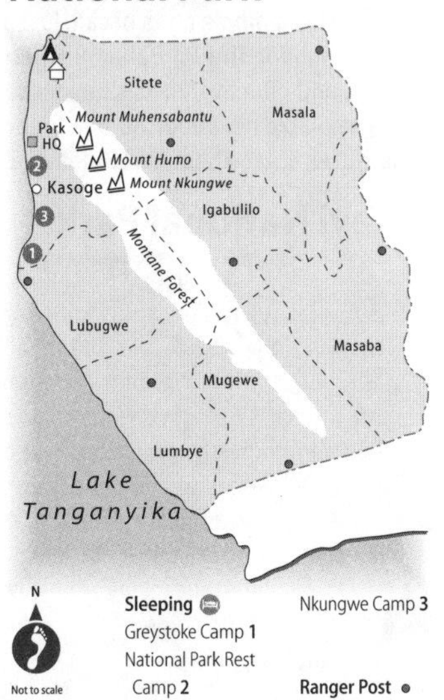

 about 15 communities. Some of these groups are accessible to visitors, others are the subject of research studies, but most live undisturbed deep inside the forest.

Katavi National Park

→ Colour map 1, grid B2.  » p317

7°S, 31°E
Best time to visit: Jul-Oct
Perk entry fee: US$20

Katavi National Park is 40 km southeast of Mpanda town astride the main Mpanda-Sumbawanga road. It was upgraded to a national park in 1974 and now covers an area of 4,471 sq km. Travelling south from Mpanda or north from Tunduma (the border town of Tanzania and Zambia), the road passes through the park. However, like the Ugalla River Game Reserve, its isolation and lack of facilities has meant that it receives few tourists (about 200 a year). It offers unspoilt wildlife viewing in what is the country's third largest national park, in a remote location far off the beaten track.

The scenery is as varied as it is pristine. Flood plains of thick reeds and dense waterways are home to a huge population of hippo, and in the woodlands to the west, forest canopies shelter herds of buffalo and elephant. Seasonal lakes fill with dirt-coloured water after the rains and animals from all corners of the park descend on them to drink. The park is characterized by miombo woodland (see box, page 302), and acacia parkland as well as some water-logged grassland plains. There is a large swampy area around the Katuma River, which joins the two lakes in the park – Lake Katavi and Lake Chada. The park is famous for its sable and roan antelope, rarely found in other Tanzanian parks, and also for its large amounts of buffalo which can be seen in herds 1500 strong. It also has a high density of crocodiles, Defassa water buck, topi, eland, hartebeest and greater kudu. Other large mammals seen here include hippo, crocodile, zebra, elephant, various antelope as well as lion and, if you are lucky, leopard. Over 400 species of birds have been identified. The park has many waterbirds and birds of prey including the black heron, Dickinson's kestrel, bee-eaters, strikes, weavers, nightjars and the Go-away bird.

South to Mbeya

» pp315-318

Kipili and Kirando

→ Colour map B2.

On the shores of Lake Tanganyika, Kipili is one of the *MV Liemba*'s ports of call. Just a few kilometres north is a very pretty town called Kirando. The (E) Bahama Guest House on the main road in Kipili is near the bus stop and offers very basic but cheap accommodation (no mosquito nets). Tasty food is available next door. To link to the road to Mbeya take a bus to Sumbawanga. The buses (cost about US$8) leave at 0700 and just after arrival of the ferry. The roads are poor and it is a very slow journey taking about 24 hours.

Sumbawanga

→ Phone code: 025. Colour map B2.

This is a lovely large town with some impressive buildings, in particular the Roman Catholic church. There is a large market selling second-hand clothes, and a separate one selling a wide range of fruit, vegetables and fish. The town is very clean, with a newly laid tarmac road and its name is said to mean 'witch people'.

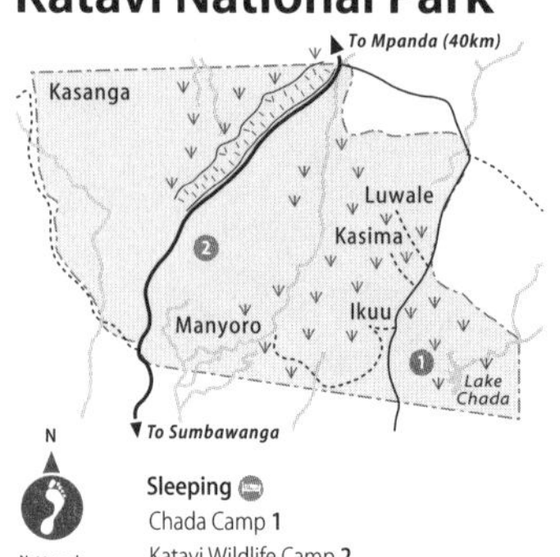

The **Rukwa Rift Valley** is currently being investigated in several sites by archaeologists. Near Sumbawanga is the **Milanzi Rockshelter** dating from the Upper Palaeolithic period. It is still used today as an ancestor shrine. **Chamoto Hill**, north of the village of Igurusi, was discovered by E. Haldemann during the 1950s and many artefacts were identified. Northeast of Sumbawanga on the shores of Lake Rukwa is the village of **Mkamba**, identified as an **Early Iron Age site** where a virtually complete pot was found in the sediment in 1989 by researchers from the University of Alberta.

In October 2000 an earthquake destroyed several houses in Nkasi District, part of the Kipili-Sumbawanga area. One person was killed and several injured.

Nuzi and Kasanga → *Colour map C2.*

Southwest of Sumbawanga on Lake Tanganyika is the charming, unspoilt village of Nuzi, surrounded by palm trees. There's no electricity or piped water and only one very basic hotel – bucket shower, no mosquito nets (but lots of mosquitoes). Transport by truck from Sumbawanga will cost US$5 and take eight hours on a very poor road.

Nuzi is a short walk (5 km) away from the next, larger village of Kasanga Bismarck. It is possible to arrange for a local fisherman to take you by boat from Nuzi to Kasanga. The trip takes about 30 mins and costs about US$1 per person. The *MV Liemba* also calls here. Shopping is very expensive and it is difficult to buy mineral water, toilet paper, fresh fruit and snacks. There are 2-3 local restaurants serving local food – the fish is cheap and very good. Kasanga has one guest house. If waiting to board the lake ferry one can visit the nearby ruins of the German Fort Bismarckburg.

Kalamba waterfalls Close by, near the border with Zambia, are the Kalamba waterfalls, which merit a visit despite the poor road. They are said to be the second highest in Africa and there are many crocodiles there. They are 211 m high and the width varies between 3-15 m seasonally. If you don't fancy riding in the back of a truck for several hours it is possible to organize a trip from *Upendo Hotel* in Sumbawanga. A car and driver will cost just under US$100 but it will still take 5 hours each way. It is not clear whether the falls lie in Tanzania or Zambia in this border region so it is best to go with a guide who has been arranged in Kasanga.

Sleeping

Kigoma *p308, map p308*

B Kigoma Hilltop Hotel, T028-2804435-7, or through Dar es Salaam: T022-2337181, www.kigoma.com. Luxurious resort on headland overlooking the lake. 30 a/c cottages with colonial-style furnishings, TV, fridge and balcony, suites also available. Restaurant, swimming pool, gym, tennis courts. The facilities are there but when it comes to service, food and style the Hilltop falls short. No alchohol is served though you can bring your own and drink in your room. It is, however, still the best place to stay in Kigoma. **Chimpanzee Safaris** has an office here, www.chimpanzeesafaris.com, and can arrange tours to their luxury camps at Gombe and Mahale by motor boat and private plane. Transfer rates start from US$300 per person for the return flight to Mahale and US$300 for the return boat ride to Gombe, though this takes several people.

C Lake Tanganyika Beach Hotel, T028-2802694. Overlooking the lake with beautiful views, very clean, 24-hr water, toilet and shower in room. Price includes breakfast. Bar and restaurant, lake-shore walks south (past the power station and local prison that resembles a medieval fort), disco on Sat. Like the *Hilltop* can arrange private boat trips to Gombe Stream or Mahale Mountains NPs.

D Aqua Lodge, on lake shore (no phone). 9 comfortable rooms with bathroom.

Sumbawanga attracted some notoriety in 1998 when the owner of a dog called 'Immigration' was given a six-month suspended sentence and ordered to kill the animal because the dog's name offended immigration officials at Kasanga.

The only trouble is that TANESCO have built their diesel generator (which supplies electricity to the whole of Kigoma) right across the road and the thundering noise is constant. Despite this the beach is lovely here with palm trees and umbrellas, food is available but you need to pre-order it, no alcohol, can arrange boat trips to Gombe.

E Zanzibar Lodge, Mwanga, on the Ujiiji road about 2 km from Kigoma, T028-2803306. Nowhere near the lake, but handy if catching buses (which depart from Mwanga). Good smart option with a restaurant and bar. Rooms with or without bathrooms are neat and surround a courtyard.

E-F Mwanga Lodge, close to the Zanzibar Lodge in Mwanga, and very similar, though not as smart. Rooms with shared bathroom are under US$5.

F Safari Lodge, next to Oilcom petrol station on the main street. Very basic, plain and bare rooms, mosquito netting on the windows, shared toilet and sink.

Gombe Stream National Park

p311, map 311

L Gombe Luxury Tented Camp, T028-2804435-7, www.chimpanzeesafaris.com. Near the Mitumba Stream at the northern end of the park on the lakeshore, on a spacious beach. All the tents are under big shady trees. There is a small reception area made out of local wood with a thatched roof and wooden deck, where there is a library, a curio shop, a bar and lounge. Power from a generator (lights off at 2245). The tents face the lake on raised wooden platforms. Meals either in the main mess tent or on the beach.

National park accommodation

There is a hostel that sleeps 12 people but this can only be used for organized groups. Beds and mattresses are provided but all cooking equipment and food should be brought with you. The Tanzania National Parks Authority (TANAPA) operates simple bandas with 4 beds in each, bookings: **Tanzania National Parks**, head office, Dodoma Rd, Arusha, T027- 2503471, tanapa @habari.co.tz, www.tanzaniaparks.com. The park bandas here are rather grim blocks, the verandas of which are caged in to protect you from baboons and chimpanzees. Facilities are basic. You can stay in the bandas in one of two ways: either be completely self-sufficient and bring everything with you, or come on a package trip from Kigoma, bringing a cook, food and bedding. Camping is allowed with permission. Camping and banda accommodation is US$20, hostel US$10.

Mahale Mountains National Park

p312, map p313

★ **L Greystoke Camp**, info@nomad.co.tz, greystoke-mahale.com. Operated by **Nomad Safaris** who do not take direct bookings, email them and they'll send a list of their agents. In a stunning spot, on a white sand beach where the forest-clad Mahale Mountains plunge into Lake Tanganyika. Established in 1992, Greystoke, which also goes under the name of Zoe's Camp, was the 1st accommodation in Mahale and remains the best place to stay by some considerable margin. The 6 suites are open-fronted, with adjoining bathrooms and upstairs decks. Apart from trekking to see the chimps, kayaking and snorkelling is on offer, they have their own dhow for fishing trips, the staff will arrange intimate dinners on the beach for couples, there's a fantastic bar on a rocky headland very good food and service. One of the finest safari camps in Tanzania with a price tag to match at over US$500 pp.

L Nkungwe Camp, T028-2804435-7, www.chimpanzeesafaris.net. This simple camp is on a sandy beach near to the ranger post. It is of a reasonable standard but not significantly cheaper than Greystoke Camp at US$400 per person. The 8 tents are raised on wooden platforms overlooking the lake, with toilet and hot shower and a veranda; there's a communal lounge, dining area, curio shop, library and beach hut complete with chunky cushioned lounge beds.

C National Park Rest Camp, at Kasiha village 10 km south of the park office at Bilenge. Further information from Tanzania National Parks (TANAPA), head office, Dodoma Rd, Arusha, T027-2503471, www.tanzania parks.com. Facilities are minimal, bring all food, drinking water and cooking equipment from Kigoma. There are 4 rooms with shared

For an explanation of the sleeping and eating price codes used in this guide, see inside the front cover. Other relevant information is found in Essentials pages 31-34.

bathrooms and 6 newer rooms with bathroom, though there is no running water or electricity so bucket showers and paraffin lamps are provided. Costs US$20 per person.

Katavi National Park *p314, map p314*
The nearest hotels and other facilities are at Mpanda, which is 40 km away.
L **Chada Camp**, operated by Nomad Safaris, info@nomad.co.tz, www.chada-katavi.com. They do not take direct bookings, email them and they will send a list of their agents. Only accessed by private plane, this is a superb bush camp in the heart of the park offering unsterilized safaris for people who really want to get out in the wilds. 6 luxury tents, excellent food, game drives, guided walks, fly camping safaris, elegantly hosted but still refreshingly simple and earthy. Rates US$465 per person.
A **Katavi Wildlife Camp**, Foxes of Africa, Dar es Salaam, T022-2440194, www.tanzania safaris.info. Another luxury tented camp camouflaged from the animals in a clump of trees, hosted by a zoologist who takes guests on game drives and walks. Only accessed by private plane, usually from Ruaha.

Sumbawanga *p314*
D **Moravian Centre**, Nyerere Rd, central, T025-2802853. Rooms with or without bathrooms, breakfast included, nothing remarkable but fairly new and very clean. Canteen serving basic local dishes.
Of the number of very basic guest houses around the bus stand, the better ones are:
F **Zanzibar Guest House**, clean, communal bath facilities, mosquito nets; and
Upendo Hotel, double rooms with bathroom, and reasonable bar and restaurant attached.

Eating

Kigoma *p308, map p308*
ΨΨ **Lake Tanganyika Beach Hotel**, probably the best place to eat and drink in town with tables right next to the lake, very good views, bar in main building and another on the lake-shore. The staff are very friendly and there is a lot on the menu such as curries, fish and steak.
Ψ **Ally's**, along Ujiji Rd going east. Quite reasonable, closed during Ramadan, serves stews and kebabs and is consistently busy.
Ψ **New Stanley Restaurant**, the best of the cheap options in town along the main street, opposite the *dala-dala* stand. Several outside terraces including one with a pool table. Fish or chicken and chips is US$2 while a daily set meal of soup, curry and fruit is US$4.
Ψ **Sun City**, on the main road. Has a pool table and slot machines and also sells popcorn and ice cream. There are also a number of food stalls around the station.

Transport

Kigoma *p308, map p308*
Air Precision Air, T022-2130800/2121718, www.precisionairtz.com, flies between **Dar** and Kigoma daily except Thu. The flight leaves Dar at 1335, arrives in **Tabora** at 1525, departs Tabora at 1550, arrives in Kigoma at 1645, departs Kigoma at 1710 and arrives in Dar at 1950. Kigoma-Dar, one way US$175, return US$272. The Precision Air office T028-2804720, is just off the main street opposite the market. It is closed in the afternoon when the man in the office goes to the airport to meet the flight.

Bus Long-distance bus services go from **Mwanga**, 2 km from Kigoma on the Ujiji road, where there are several bus company kiosks. Services go to **Mwanza** and **Bukoba** though these are rough rides on poor roads and each journey can take days rather than hours. These depart very early in the morning (about 0500) and generally only go once a week and in wet season less so. If running, the bus to Bukoba goes on Fri and to Mwanza on Sat, each costs US$13.

Train The journey from Kigoma to **Dar es Salaam** is 1,254 km and it takes about 36 hrs although it may be worth getting on or off at **Morogoro** or **Dodoma** and doing the last stretch to or from Dar by road, saving a few hours. In 1st class there are only 2 beds in the compartment, in 2nd class there are 6.
It is easy to buy fruit and small meals at the stations along the way. There is also a reasonable restaurant car, which offers beef or chicken with rice or chips for US$3, and warm drinks including beer; book ahead if at all possible. Local people fear theft on the train, especially at stations. The women frequently lock themselves inside their compartment and don't go out at night. Police ride on the train. 1st/2nd/3rd class tickets are

Dar-Kigoma US$38/30/14, Dodoma-Kigoma US$34/21/10, and Tabora-Kigoma US$17/14/7. See **Tanzania Railways Corporation** www.trctz.com for full details of timetables and fares.

Ferry The famous ferry on Lake Tanganyika, the *MV Liemba*, was at the time of the writing out of service and awaiting new parts to be sent from Europe. A smaller boat the *MV Mwongozo* is running instead although it is not operating a service to Burundi. The ferry leaves Kigoma at 1600 on Wed for **Mpulungu** (Zambia), arriving there at 0800 on Fri morning, a 40-hr journey. It stops at lots of small ports on the way. If travelling to **Mbeya**, and wanting to remain in Tanzania, it may be worth disembarking at **Kasanga**, or **Kipili** (journey time 24 hrs) or at the town of **Kirando** just north of Kipili. Kirando may be preferable to Kipili because you arrrive while it is still daylight, there is no port but small boats take passengers to the shore for approximately US$0.60. Buses to **Sumbawanga** will be waiting. On the return leg it departs Mpulungu at 1600 on Fri and reaches Kigoma at 1100 on Sun. Kigoma-Kipili and Kigoma-Kirando 1st class US$37, 2nd class US$32, 3rd class US$26; Kigoma-Kasanga 1st class US$52, 2nd class US$43, 3rd class US$32; Kigoma-Mpulungu (Zambia) 1st class US$55, 2nd class US$45, 3rd class US$40; Kigoma-Bujumbura (Burundi) 1st class US$30, 2nd class US$25, 3rd class US$20 (though boats are not presently running to Burundi). Plus US$5 port tax. The journey can be very crowded and rowdy at times. 3rd class are benches or deck space, 2nd class cabins are small, hot and stuffy with 4 or 6 bunks. 1st class cabins have 2 bunks, a window, fan, and meals and drinks are available. Book and pay for your ferry at least 1-3 days in advance. For information phone the booking office in Kigoma, T028-2802811. The port in Kigoma is fairly organized and there is a large seating area under a tin roof for waiting ferry passengers. There is also an immigration and customs post for passengers arriving from Zambia. These are also found on arrival at Mpulungu in Zambia, and at Kasanga the Tanzania immigration and customs officials come on board the boat.

At Kibirizi, village 3 km north of Kigoma, down at the boat yard, local motor boats depart for **Burundi** about twice a week when there is a demand. There is an immigration, customs and police post just to the back of the boats.

Gombe Stream National Park can be reached by lake taxis (small boats with an outboard motor), which are hired at Kigoma (ask around for the best price). The journey takes about 3 hrs. A passenger boat heads north from Kibirizi at around 1500 and a trip to Gombe will cost approximately US$3. The boat returns the next day, passing Gombe at about 0730. You can get to Kibirizi by walking north along the railway track from Kigoma; any hotel should be able to provide further details.

Sumbawanga *p314*
Regular bus service to **Mbeya** via **Tunduma**. Be warned of serious competition from ticket sellers – there is room to bargain. Expect to pay around US$7. Buses leave at 06-0700 and take around 8 hrs. In the morning several 4WDs leave from the petrol stations for the Zambian border or to **Kasanga** on Lake Tanganyika. The journey takes the best part of the day.

Directory

Kigoma *p308, map p308*
Banks National Bank of Commerce, next to the market and has an ATM. As does the CRDB, on the roundabout next to the police station. Panjutan Bureau de Change, on the main road up from the station, has erratic opening hours but changes a surprisingly wide range of currencies. **Embassies and consulates** Burundi Consulate, in a house just out of town on the road to the Hilltop Hotel, T028-2802865. **Internet** There are a couple of internet places in town on the main road up from the railway station. They are expensive at US$3 an hour. **Medical services** Maweni Hospital, T028-2802671, 1 km or so down the road towards Ujiji. **Post** Post office is about 500 m to the north of the main roundabout past the *Caltex* station. **Useful addresses** Mahale Mountains Wildlife Research Centre, T028-2802072, has an office in Kigoma on the road to the Hilltop Hotel but the staff here are not terribly informative and can only show you a dusty old brochure.

Southwestern Tanzania

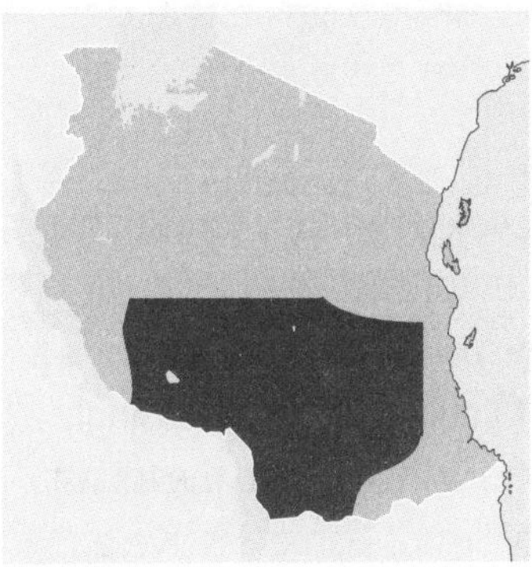

Footprint features

Introduction

The southwest, only recently discovered by many tourists, has much to offer in the form of huge untouched areas of great beauty and fascinating wildlife. The parks in this area are frequently dubbed the 'Southern Circuit' and are increasingly popular, particularly with those who want to avoid the tourist trails. The parks include the mighty Selous Game Reserve, a World Heritage Site and the largest game reserve in Africa, though little of its vast plains and forests have been developed for tourism and not much has changed here for hundreds of years when vast herds of game roamed East Africa undisturbed. The other smaller parks are Mikumi and Ruaha, which offer interesting safari experiences away from the hordes. The major towns in the southwest are Iringa and Mbeya. Mbeya is on the railway that links Tanzania with Zambia. Road communications are good, and the main road that cuts through southwest Tanzania is the extension of Zambia's Great North Road and the continuation of the road that runs down the length of Lake Malawi in Malawi to the south.

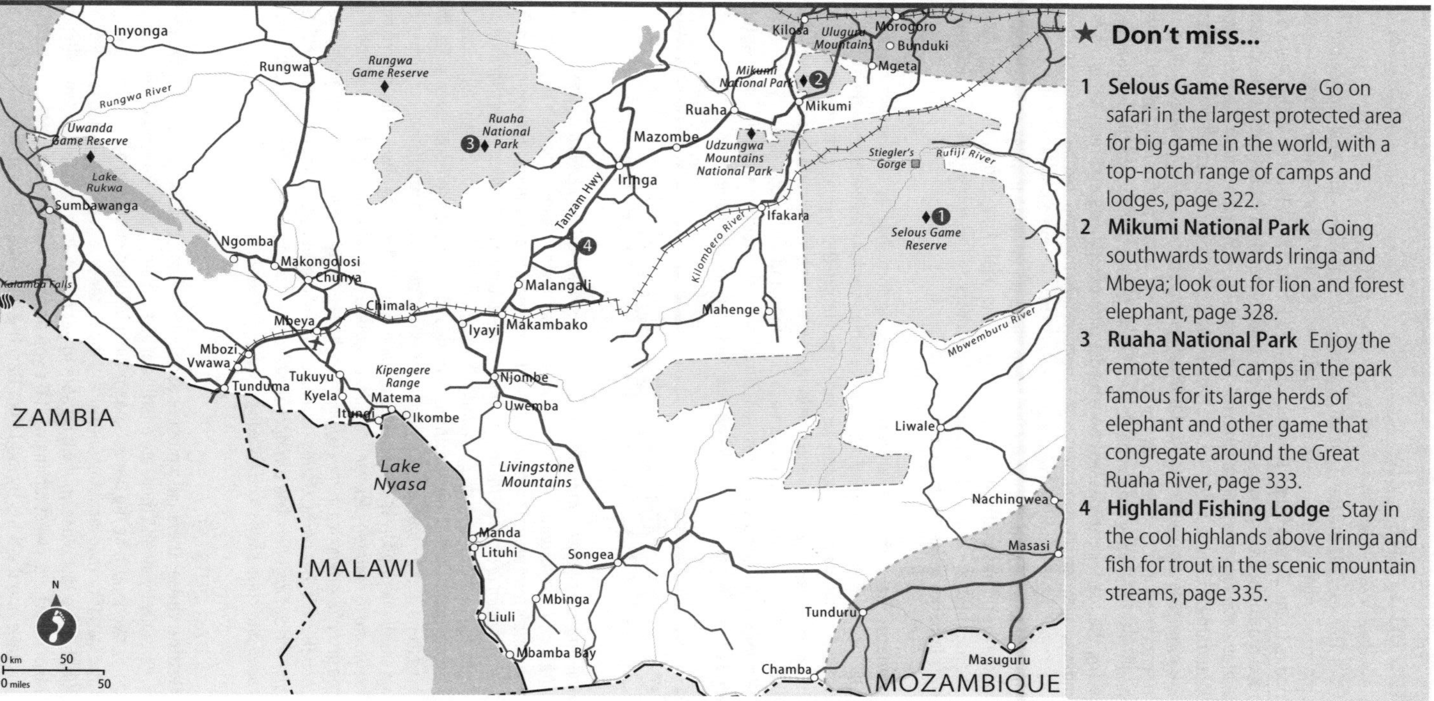

★ Don't miss...

1 **Selous Game Reserve** Go on safari in the largest protected area for big game in the world, with a top-notch range of camps and lodges, page 322.

2 **Mikumi National Park** Going southwards towards Iringa and Mbeya; look out for lion and forest elephant, page 328.

3 **Ruaha National Park** Enjoy the remote tented camps in the park famous for its large herds of elephant and other game that congregate around the Great Ruaha River, page 333.

4 **Highland Fishing Lodge** Stay in the cool highlands above Iringa and fish for trout in the scenic mountain streams, page 335.

Ins and outs

From Dar es Salaam the Tanzam Highway through the southwest heads out to Chalinze and Morogoro (see page 294). To the south of it are the limited road access points to the **Selous Game Reserve** whilst 70 km to the southwest of Morogoro the road runs through a 50-km stretch of the **Mikumi National Park**. Beyond the Mikumi National Park the road climbs into the Kitonga Hills, which are part of the **Udzungwa Mountains**. It is quite a journey, with sharp bends, and dense forest all around. Part of the road runs alongside the **Ruaha River gorge**, often dubbed 'Baobab Valley' by veteran overlanders. Eventually the road levels out to the plateau and **Iringa**. To the northwest of Iringa is the **Ruaha National Park**. **Mbeya** lies 390 km to the southwest along the road which passes though vast pine plantations and rural farms. About midway between the two towns is the junction with the road that heads due south to the little-visited extreme southwest of Tanzania around **Songea** and the eastern shore of **Lake Nyasa**. Except for the steep climb up to Iringa through Baobab Valley where the tar has melted, the Tanzam Highway is in fairly good condition. From Dar es Salaam there are regular buses linking the towns on this route. The TAZARA railway runs from Dar to Mbeya and on to Zambia.

Climate The southern highlands of Tanzania form one of the largest blocks of highland in East Africa. They mostly have a high rainfall and because of their altitude are cool. Like the rest of south Tanzania (and unlike the highlands to the north) they have one long wet season and one long dry one. High rainfall and rich soil mean that this area is agriculturally productive in both food and cash crops (tea and coffee). As with most highland areas in East Africa they are associated with the Rift Valley system and there has been much volcanic activity in the area over the years.

Selous Game Reserve

→ *Colour map B5. 9° S, 38° E.*

This enormous reserve in south Tanzania, first established in 1922, is the largest park in Africa and the second largest in the world, covering an area of 45,000 sq km, or 5% of Tanzania's total area. This makes it about twice the size of Denmark. However, from the visitor's point of view, all these facts and figures are a bit misleading given that they are restricted to the area north of the Rufiji River. South of here is completely forbidden to visitors, undeveloped, and much more heavily forested with series of steep cliffs. The landscape in the north is largely open grassland and acacia woodland, cut across by slivers of riverine forest and patches of miombo woodland. Its rivers, hills, and plains are home to roaming elephant populations, the area's famous wild dogs, and some of the last black rhino left in the region, though the density of animals in the park is lower than that of other parks. During a game drive you are unlikely to see any other vehicles and the Selous offers you a chance to see a wild and expansive Africa far from paved roads and curio shops. ⏩ *For Sleeping and other listings, see pages 326-327.*

Ins and outs

Getting there There are a number of approaches to the park. The most convenient is certainly by air and there are airstrips at all the camps (see Transport, page 327). If going overland, take the Dar es Salaam-Kibiti-Mkongo road. The road to Kibiti (145 km from Dar) is tarmac for about one third of the distance, after that the road is very poor. Kibiti is the last place you will be able to get petrol. It is then 30 km from Kibiti to Mkongo, where a west turning will take you on to the final 75 km to **Mtemere Gate**. It will take about 7-8 hrs by road from Dar. The other road you can take is the Dar es

Salaam-Morogoro-Matombo-Kisaki road, which will take you into the north section of the park – from Kisaki it is 20 km to **Matambwe Gate**. This route is a total of 350 km and will take 8-9 hrs. The road from Morogoro is rough, should only be attempted in the dry season and will require a 4WD vehicle. You will have to bring plenty of fuel from Dar es Salaam, Morogoro or Kibiti for your whole stay in the reserve. There are no car repair facilities here and drivers are advised to carry essential items such as tools, spare tyre, tyre repair kit, shovel and drinking water. Getting the train is another option. Take the **TAZARA**, www.tazara.co.tz, railway as far as Fuga. From here, by prior arrangement, the lodges will collect you. This may be expensive unless you get a group together to share the cost. The train to the Selous from Dar es Salaam is fairly reliable, but not so from the Selous back to Dar as the train comes from Zambia and there are often several hours' delay.

There are no buses to the Selous and hitching is almost impossible. Because of the problem of accessibility most people go to the Selous on organized safaris from Dar es Salaam, see page 74.

Park information Park fees for the reserve are US$30 per person per day. Part of the reason for the lack of human habitation in this area is that it is infested with the tsetse fly (see page 245). Use insect repellent on exposed areas of your body. Although sleeping sickness is rare, the flies do administer a nasty bite.

Climate The best time to visit is Jul-Oct. The camps and lodges are closed at the peak of the wet season from Easter-Jun when the rains render many of the roads impassable, but check as they have been known to stay open in drier years.

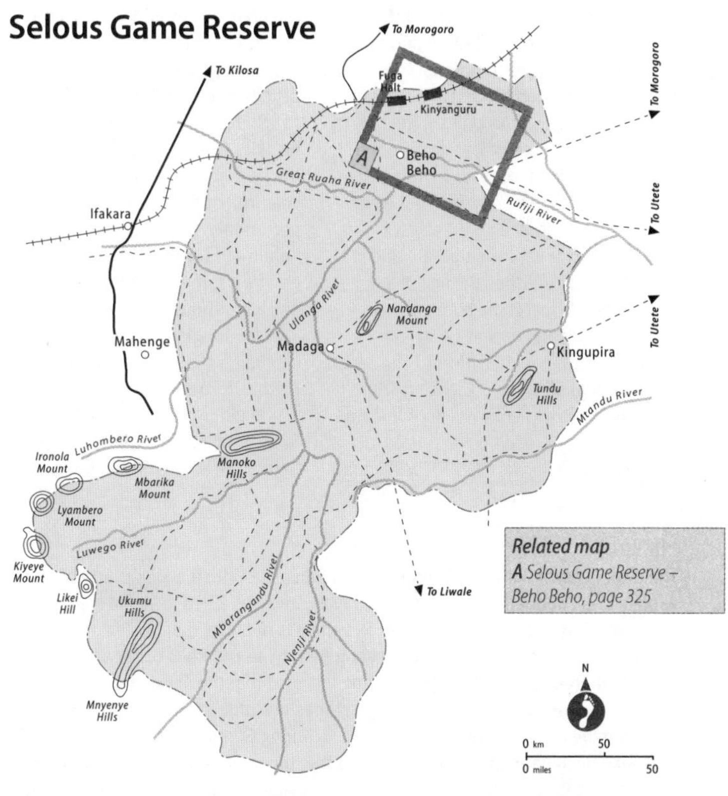

Frederick C Selous: Greatest of the White Hunters

Born in 1852 in London, the young Selous went to Rugby school. An early expedition saw him trek to a lake 25 km from Rugby, strip off, swim through the icy water to a small island and shin up a tree to collect eight blue heron's eggs. On returning to school he was rewarded by being made to copy out 63 lines of Virgil for each egg. Undeterred, and inspired by the writings of Livingstone, Selous wanted to visit Africa. After toying with the idea of becoming a doctor, he travelled to South Africa in 1871, and rapidly established himself as a supreme tracker and hunter.

Hunting was tough. The rifles were heavy muzzle-loaders, and powder was carried loose in one pocket, ignition caps in another and a supply of four ounces of lead bullets in a pouch. It was not uncommon for a hunter to be knocked out of the saddle by the gun's recoil and accidents were common.

Selous killed much game in his early years, partly for trophies in the case of lion and rhinoceros, for ivory in the case of elephants, and anything else as meat for his party. His skills were based on absorbing the skills of African hunters and trackers, and in 1881 he published the first of a series of highly successful books on his methods and exploits, *A Hunter's Wanderings in Africa*. In 1887 he began a career of paid work leading safaris for wealthy clients, which culminated in a huge expedition organized for President Roosevelt in 1909. (A young British diplomat in South Africa, H. Rider Haggard, based his character Allan Quatermain on Selous and his adventures in his novel *King Solomon's Mines*, published in 1895.)

During one visit to England, Selous took delivery of a new .450 rifle at his hotel an hour before he was due to catch the boat train from Waterloo to return to Africa. There was no time to test the sights and alignment on a rifle range, so Selous ordered a cab to stand by, flung open his bedroom window, squeezed off five shots at a chimney stack, checked that the grouping was satisfactory with his binoculars, swiftly packed the rifle and skipped down to the cab, pausing only to remark that he had heard shots on his floor and that the manager had better look into it.

By 1914, Selous, now married, had retired to Surrey and busied himself with running his own natural history museum. At the outbreak of war, despite being 63, he was determined to serve in East Africa, where he felt his skills would be useful. He joined the Legion of Frontiersmen, a colourful outfit that included French Legionnaires, a Honduran general, a handful of Texan cowboys, Russian émigrés, some music hall acrobats and a lighthouse keeper.

In January 1917, scouting in the campaign against General von Lettow Vorbeck (see page 356), he was killed by a German sniper at Beho Beho on the Rufiji River (now part of the Selous Game Reserve).

History

The park is named after Captain Frederick Selous, a British explorer and hunter who wrote a book about the region and his travels, and was killed in action in January 1917 while scouting in the area (see box). His grave is near Beho Beho.

The game reserve has an interesting history. In the days of the slave trade the caravan routes passed through the park. It is said that the occasional mango groves that can be seen grew from the mango stones discarded from the caravans on their way from the coast. In the early 20th century during German colonial rule some of this area was designated as game reserves but in those days big game hunting was the most significant activity. In 1910 Kaiser Wilhelm gave part of the reserve to his Kaiserin as an anniversary gift. This is how the nickname 'Shamba la Bibi', meaning 'The Woman's Field' and referring to the section of the present Selous north of the Rufiji River, came to be. In 1922, the land area was increased and named after Frederick Selous. From then until 1975, when the current boundaries were delineated, the reserve's size increased steadily to today's present 45,000 sq km.

Wildlife

There are supposed to be over a million animals in the park, which is probably best known for its large numbers of elephant. However, poaching has been an enormous problem in the past and the numbers have been reduced substantially in recent years. A very disturbing report that came out in 1988 estimated that the elephant population had fallen by 80% in the Selous in just 10 years, from 1977 (census estimated population at 22,852) to 1987 (population estimated at 3,673). However, more recent estimates of the numbers of elephant show an increase. Rhino have also been seriously affected and their population in the Selous is estimated to have fallen from 2,500 in 1976 to fewer than 50 in 1986. Numbers are still low but thought to be increasing slowly. Other animals you may see include lions, buffalo, hippo, African wild dogs and crocodile, while over 400 species of birds have been recorded (including herons, fish eagles, kingfishers, and other various waterfowl and birds of prey). The overall population of African wild dogs is greatly depleted in East Africa. The canines living in the Selous Game Reserve and Mikumi National Park are one of the largest remaining viable wild dog populations in Africa. The proximity of areas for trophy hunters exacerbates the difficulty of viewing the animals here.

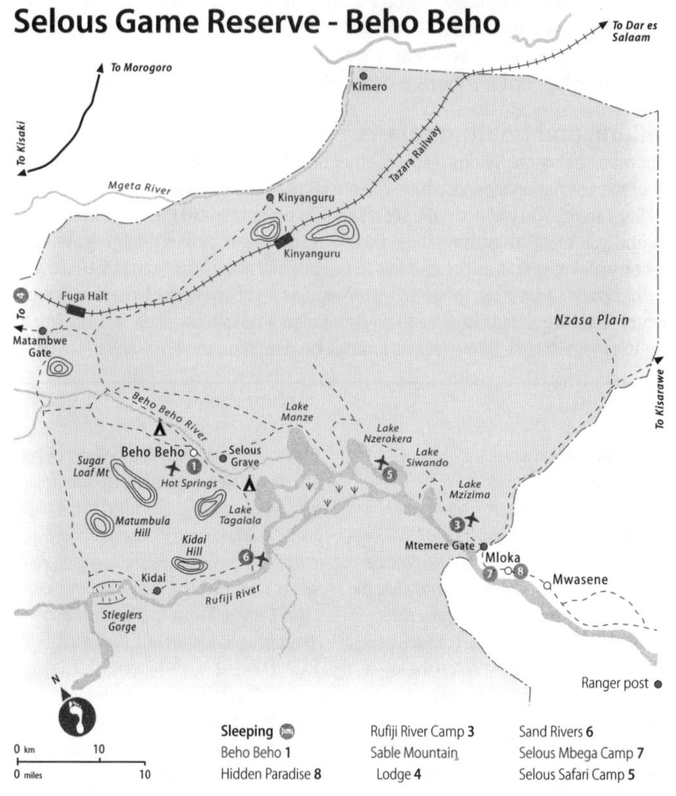

Routes

Great Rufiji River

Central to the park is the Great Rufiji River. This river and its associated water system has the largest catchment area of any river in East Africa and is probably the most significant feature of the park. It rises from the south and becomes the Rufiji where the Luwegu and Mbarangandu join together. Other rivers join it and further north it swings east before it is forced through Stiegler's Gorge. At its delta, opposite Mafia Island, millions of tonnes of silt are deposited every year during the wet season. During this season it swells to such an extent that it renders much of the park inaccessible. During the dry season it subsides and the sand banks are revealed.

Stiegler's Gorge

Named after a German explorer who was killed here by an elephant in 1907 and in the north of the reserve at the junction of the Rufiji and Ruaha rivers, Stiegler's Gorge is a 40-km, two-hour drive from Matambwe. It is a bottleneck as the water from this huge catchment area is forced through the narrow gorge. The gorge is about 7 km long, 100 m wide and deep. If you have a head for heights there is a cable car that spans it.

Beyond the gorge the river widens again and splits to form a number of lakes – Tagalala, Manze, Nzerakera, Siwando and Mzizima. The swampy area is home to many animals that congregate here especially when water is scarce during the dry season, in particular elephant, buffalo and, of course, hippo, sometimes in large numbers.

Other attractions in the park include the hot springs known simply as **Maji Moto** (hot water in Kiswahili). These are on the eastern slopes of Kipalala Hill and the water flows down into Lake Tagalala. You get to them by walking (with a ranger at all times) up the ravine. The water emits a strong smell of sulphur. The highest springs are the hottest, while further down they are sufficiently cool for you to be able to swim in them.

Walking and boating safaris

Apart from seeing the Selous by road, other popular ways are by foot or by boat. This is one of the few national parks where you are allowed to walk and all camps can arrange walking safaris. You will normally set off early in order to avoid the worst of the midday sun and you must be accompanied by an armed ranger. Animal sightings tend to be rarer on walking safaris as the animals frequently shy away from humans. However, it is very pleasant to be able to stretch your legs and get a different perspective of the country. Trekking safaris of several days are also a possibility as is fly camping away from the main lodges. Some lodges arrange boat trips up the Rufiji River.

Sleeping

Selous Game Reserve

p322, maps p323 and p325

L **Beho Beho**, bookings are made in the U.K. through **Bay Travel**, T+44(0)20-8897 9991, www.behobeho.com. (Confusingly, *Beho Beho* used to be called *Selous Safari Camp*, while the former *Mbuyuni Tented Camp* is now called *Selous Safari Camp*). Expensive (US$400 per person sharing) resort perched on the lower slopes of Namikwera Hill overlooking Kipalala Hill. From the spacious verandas are panoramic views over the Rufiji river flood plain. 10 thatched a/c stone cottages have flush toilets and open-air showers. Lounge and dining area, billiards room, swimming pool, all completely revamped to the highest luxury in 2004. Rates include full board and all activities – game drives and boat and walking safaris. Children under 12 years not allowed.

L **Rufiji River Camp**, bookings through **Hippotours & Safaris Ltd**, Dar es Salaam, T022-2128662, www.hippotours.com. Overlooking the Rufiji River, this is the oldest camp in the reserve. 20 tents with bathrooms, electricity and mosquito nets, spaced out along the river in an attractive tract of woodland. Restaurant, bar and swimming pool. Rates US$250 per person, inclusive of park fees, full board and 2 excursions per day, from a choice of fishing, boat safaris, game drives or walking safaris.

L Sand Rivers, info@nomad.co.tz , www.sand-rivers-selous.com. A **Nomad Safaris** property: email them and they will send a list of their agents. 16 cottages offer comfortable but expensive accommodation, overlooking the Sand River, with many hippo and crocodiles. The most luxurious and isolated of the lodges, with superb food and service. Walking safaris and fly camping (sleeping out in the bush). A stunning swimming pool set in rocks right next to the river, and a library. US$465 pp.

L Sable Mountain Lodge, bookings through **A Tent With a View Safaris**, Dar es Salaam, T022-2110507, www.selouslodge.com. Just outside the reserve, 10 km along the road from Kisaki, a 20-min drive from the airstrip at Matembwe. 8 comfortable stone cottages, the honeymoon cottage overlooks a small waterhole, plus 4 new luxury bandas, 2 of which have got private plunge pools. Swimming pool constructed over a natural spring and treehouse overlooking a waterhole. Rates US$125-175 per person full board, fly camping is US$295 per person. Game drives are additional, US$60 for a full day game drive and US$15 for a game walk.

L Selous Mbega Camp, bookings through **Baobab Village Co Ltd**, Dar es Salaam, T022-2650250, www.selous-mbega-camp.com, www.baobabvillage.com. Newish tented camp just outside Mtemere Gate. There are 8 tents on raised platforms overlooking the river and a simple central bar and restaurant with a good varied menu and excellent service. Offers game drives and half-day boat safaris and walks. Not as luxurious as the other camps and at US$190 per person full board, a little over-priced for the standard.

L Selous Safari Camp (previously *Mbuyuni Tented Camp*), bookings through **Selous Safari Co**, Dar es Salaam, T022-2134802, www.selous.com. A luxury development with views overlooking the lakes. 12 individual huts, WCs, showers, solar electricity and swimming pool, impeccable and attentive service. Animals wander freely in the camp at night (visitors include elephant and hippo). Boats and fishing equipment available and morning and evening game drives included. Rates are US$365 per person full board. May remain closed longer than other camps because of its location on the floodplain.

C Hidden Paradise, T022-2772215, ftts@raha.com. In the village of Mloka, about 7 km from Mtemere Gate. Sleep on mattress in basic tent. Has a restaurant (no beer) and can organize game drives and boat safaris, US$30 each. No running water.

Camping

You can camp beside the bridge over the Beho Beho River a few kilometres northwest of Beho Beho itself, and at a site beside Lake Tagalala. There are no facilities apart from a pit latrine, so bring everything with you. Small fires made with dead wood are permissible and rainwater can be collected nearby. Camping fees must be paid in advance at one of the gates, and are US$30 per person. No camping is permitted outside of the official camping sites, but arrangements can be made for special campsites in the Mtemere-Manze zone for US$40. Further information from **Tanzania National Parks** (TANAPA), head office, Dodoma Rd, Arusha, T027-2503471, tanapa@habari.co.tz, www.tanzaniaparks.com.

Transport

Selous Game Reserve

p322, maps p323 and p325

There are airstrips at all the camps. The flight takes about 35 mins from Dar es Salaam and costs about US$120. **Coastal Air** T022-2117969-60, www.coastal.cc, flies daily from **Dar** at 1500 and on Mon, Thu and Sat there is an additional flight at 0830. The return flight to Dar is daily at 1515 and on Tue, Fri and Sun another at 1325. Both flights continue on to **Zanzibar**. On Mon, Thu and Sat there is also a flight between the Selous and **Ruaha** (2 hr) at 0930, which returns at 1145, and a flight from Selous to **Mafia Island** (50 min) daily at 1400, which returns at 1500. **Zan Air**, T022-2843297, www.zanair.com, has daily flights from Zanzibar/Dar at 0700/0730 and 1600/1630, which return at 0830 and 1715.

For an explanation of the sleeping and eating price codes used in this guide, see inside the front cover. Other relevant information is found in Essentials pages 31-34.

Mikumi National Park → *Colour map B5.*

Between the Uluguru Mountains and the Lumango range, Mikumi is the fourth largest park in Tanzania and has a wide variety of wildlife that is easy to spot and well used to game viewing (the park is popular with weekend visitors as it only takes about four hours on a good road to drive the 300 km from Dar es Salaam). It borders the Selous Game Reserve and Udzungwa National Park, and the three locations make a varied and pleasant safari circuit. Mikumi has a pretty, undulating landscape with good resident game, but it is not as spectacular as the other parks. ▸▸ *For Sleeping, Eating and other listings see pages 329-330.*

Altitude: 549 m
7°26'S 37°0'E

Ins and outs

Getting there From Morogoro the main Tanzania-Zambia road travels through cultivated land for about 100 km before reaching the boundary of the park. The national park is on both sides of the road so drive with care. The speed limit along this stretch is 50 km per hr and the road has recently been given speed bumps – animals have been killed before by speeding vehicles. There is an airstrip near the park headquarters suitable for light aircraft; a flight from Dar es Salaam will take approximately 45 mins.

Park information Park entry fee is US$20 per 24 hrs. The best time to visit is Sep-Dec. Take a guide for a short time when you first arrive. it isn't expensive (about US$10) and can greatly improve chances of seeing the rarer types of game. ▸▸ *For more information on national park fees and safaris, see page 39.*

Background

The park was gazetted in 1964 during the construction of the Morogoro-Iringa highway, and is set in a horseshoe of the towering Uluguru mountain range, which rises to 2,750 m and covers an area of 3,230 sq km. It lies between the villages of Doma and Mikumi from which it takes its name. 'Mikumi' is the Kiswahili name for the borassus palm found in the area.

Wildlife

The landscape is typically woodland and grassy plains, which are fed by the Mkata River flood plain, an area of lush vegetation that attracts a number of animals throughout the year. These include lion, eland, hartebeest, buffalo, wildebeest, giraffe, zebra, hippo and elephant. Up to 300 species of birds stop over on migratory routes over Tanzania. Birdlife is particularly abundant here with many species present which are seen infrequently in other game parks of northern Tanzania. They include the violet turaco and the pale-billed hornbill, along with various species of storks, pelicans, herons, ibis, kestrels, kites and eagles. The Mikumi forest elephants are much smaller than their big game park counterparts and are mainly grazers so they do not cause as much damage to the trees. It's not unusual to see them, and sometimes lion, from the main road, especially in the evening or night. They seem quite accustomed to the traffic that rumbles past.

Routes

From the park gate the road leads to the floodplain of the Mkata River, which is particularly important for the wildlife. To the north the floodplain remains swampy throughout the year, while in the south water channels drain to the Mkata River. Here you will see, among other animals, elephant, buffalo and hippo. About 15 km northwest of the park gate there are some hippo pools where there are almost always a number of hippos wallowing in the mud.

Other areas worth visiting are the Choga Wale area and Mwanambogo area – the latter can only be reached in the dry season. The track is to the east of the flood plain and heads north towards the Mwanambogo Dam. The Kisingura circuit is another popular drive, as is the Kikoboga area where you are likely to see elephant, particularly during December and January.

The road that goes along the river is a good one to take for viewing. It passes through a patch of woodland and some swampy areas before coming on to the grasslands of the Chamgore. Chamgore means 'place of the python' and here there are two waterholes that are always ideal for spotting game. Hill Drive leads up the foothills of the Uluguru Mountains and from here you will get wonderful views all around. The vegetation is miombo woodland and the ebony tree grows here.

To get to the south part of the park take the track that branches off opposite the park entrance, which heads towards an area called Ikoya. Here you will see sausage trees, *Kigelia africana*, with their distinctive pods hanging down. This is also where you may see leopard.

Sleeping

Mikumi National Park *map p328*
The small village of Mikumi has a number of cheap hotels and guest houses.

L Foxes Safari Camp, Foxes of Africa, Dar es Salaam, T022-2440194, www.tanzaniasafaris.info. Luxury tented camp raised on wooden decks overlooking the Mkata River floodplain. 8 large thatched tents with bathrooms and 2 double beds, scattered around a granite kopje. The central boma

For an explanation of the sleeping and eating price codes used in this guide, see inside the front cover. Other relevant information is found in Essentials pages 31-34.

area for eating is perched on top of a hill.

L **Mikumi Wildlife Camp**, also known as Kikoboga, about 300 m off the main road to the right, near the park headquarters. Reservations Dar es Salaam, T022-2600352, obhotel@acexnet.com. 12 very comfortable stone bandas, some with 3 or 4 beds in 1 or 2 rooms – good value for families or groups. Bar and lounge under a huge fig tree, dining room in a rondavaal. Small stone swimming pool, good views from the sun deck and there is an observation tower for game viewing.

L **Vuma Hills**, Foxes of Africa, Dar es Salaam, T022-2440194, www.tanzaniasafaris.info. 16 luxury tents with bathrooms and private verandas and colonial decor. The dining area and bar overlook the swimming pool. Slightly more luxurious than the Safari Camp.

C-F **Genesis Hotel**, Mikumi village on the Iringa side, T023-2620466. Very comfortable banda accommodation with satellite TV, bathroom. Breakfast included. Camping costs US$2 per person. Restaurant with reasonable menu, nice bar, secure. There is also a snake park attached.

E-F **Mikumi Medical Centre Guest Cottages**, if driving from the park entrance to Mikumi, keep going until you cross the railway, the centre is on the left a few hundred metres on. Excellent place to stay, run by a Dutch organization who have funded the building of the guest cottages as a continuing source of income for the medical centre. Facilities include fully equipped kitchen (take own food), shower room with hot water, lounge/dining room and a number of rooms with fans and nets. Camping is also possible.

D **National Park Campsite**, about 4 km into the park from park entrance gate. Water and firewood usually available, otherwise it's very basic.

Udzungwa Mountains National Park

→ *Colour map B4.*

The Udzungwa Mountains rise up from the western edge of the Selous Game Reserve. Botanical diversity is exceptional, and the park is host to a large number of endangered bird species as well as forest antelope and vervet monkeys. This is a forest area and covers approximately 1,990 sq km lying between 250-2576 m (on the highest peak, Luhomero). Views from the peaks of the mountains, towards the Selous Game Reserve and the distant Indian Ocean coast are incredible and well worth the effort. Recently classified as a national park, where previously it was a national forest reserve, the conservation programme is designed to benefit the local people and improve their social amenities of health and education, water supplies and transport and to encourage them to cooperate fully in the conservation programme with the National Park Management. ▸▸ *For Sleeping, Eating and other listings, see pages 331-332.*

Ins and outs

7° 50′ S, 37° E
Best time to visit: Sep-Dec

Getting there By car the park is about 6 hrs drive from Dar es Salaam and 75 km from the Mikumi National Park. To reach the park headquarters, turn south off the main Dar-Mbeya highway at Mikumi and follow the signs to Ifakara. The tarmac road continues to Kidatu where you cross the Ruaha River. Follow the gravel road another 24 km and you will reach Manug'ula, the signposted turning for the park headquarters is on the right. Buses to Ifakara can drop off here. Charter flights can be arranged from Dar to nearby airstrips at Msolwa and the Kilombero Sugar Company. By train, the **TAZARA** trains stops in Manug'ula. ▸▸ *See Transport, page 331.*

Park information Permits are valid for 24 hrs and are available at the park headquarters; US$20. A guide/ranger costs US$10 per group. Park Warden in Charge, T023-2620224, udzungwa@inafrica.com, www.udzungwa.org.

Wildlife

The Udzungwa Mountains are part of the Eastern Arc Range of mountains which stretch from southern Kenya to southern Tanzania. The Eastern Arc are small and fragmented mountains, each block having a patchwork of dense tropical forests with high rainfall. River catchments protected within the park boundary are important for hydroelectricity production, local communities' water supply and agriculture. The national park protects more than 2500 plant species of which 160 are used locally as medicinal plants. Over 300 animal species have been recorded, including 18 vertebrate species found only in the Eastern Arc Mountains. The recently discovered Sanje mangabey and the Iringa red colobus are thought to be endemic to the region, and there are also elephant, buffalo, lion and leopard present. Birds found here include sunbirds, shrikes and the Iringa akalat. To the south lies the green Kilombero Valley, with the jagged slopes of the Mbarika Mountains, 100 km away, clearly visible rising out of the lowlands. There are no roads or tracks through the park but guided walks are available, so hikers have the park to themselves. A variety of trails are available to suit different abilities, including short half-day trails, mountain climbing trails with overnight camping and long-range wilderness trails taking several days.

Ifakara → *Colour map B4.*

For those with a penchant for getting off the beaten track, a visit to this isolated central Tanzanian town southeast of Iringa and 100 km from Mikumi is recommended. Ifakara is a verdant, tree-dotted old trading station close to the Kilombero River in a highly fertile area. The most important crop of the local Pogoro people is rice and there is thriving trade in this commodity between Ifakara and Dar es Salaam. Tropical hardwoods (from the rainforests north of Ifakara) are also being sent from here to the coast for export.

To get the most out of this remote area, you should visit with a tour operator familiar with the area. Wild Things Safaris, see page 74, are recommended.

The countryside surrounding Ifakara is very attractive and is ideal for cycling (bikes can be hired from the town centre); it is also rich in birdlife. The Kilombero River flows past about 10 km to the south of the town and supports a large seasonal wetland in the Kilombero Valley. The area has several species of endemic birds including the Kilombero weaver the only sustainable population in Tanzania of the very rare puku antelope and a fair amount of lion and elephant. At Kivukoni there is a ferry crossing for the road to Mahenge. There are hippos in the river here and it is possible to arrange a trip in a dug-out canoe to see them.

Sleeping

Udzungwa Mountains National Park

E Goa Guest House, 100 m from the market on Uhuru Rd. The best of the local lodges. Clean, simple doubles with fan and bathroom. There are designated campsites (US$30) with basic facilities. Bring your own equipment.

Ifakara *p331*

E Diamond Guest House and the **E Kayuga Guest House**. Confusingly, there are two Diamond Guest Houses in Ifakara but each offers pretty much the same: a simple bed with shared washing facilities for under US$5.

Transport

Ifakara

Take the ordinary TAZARA train (not the international train that arrives at 0100) from Dar. Booking in advance is essential (in Dar, T022-2865187, www.tazara.co.tz). The station is 11 km north of the town centre.

For an explanation of the sleeping and eating price codes used in this guide, see inside the front cover. Other relevant information is found in Essentials pages 31-34.

Buses also go from **Kariakoo** to Ifakara daily. Leaving Ifakara, the trains depart at rather inconvenient times, but there are several companies running buses. By far the best of these is **Zanil's**, which has daily buses leaving at 1000 for **Morogoro** and **Dar**. Book a seat on the left-hand side for good views of the Udzungwa Mountains. For the more adventurous there are also daily bus services to **Mahenge** and **Malinyi** (towns to the south and west of Ifakara).

Iringa and around

→ *Phone code: 026. Colour map 1, B4.*

Up in the chilly highlands, Iringa, set on a plateau 502 km from Dar es Salaam on the main Tanzania-Zambia road beyond Mikumi National Park, commands a panoramic view over the surrounding boulder-strewn countryside. Maize, vegetables, fruits and tobacco are grown in the fertile soil around here and consequently the safe and welcoming town has an excellent market, where you can barter for almost every vegetable under the sun. About four hours' drive and 130 km west of Iringa, Ruaha National Park is a huge undeveloped wilderness, whose ecology is more like that of southern Africa. ▸▸ *For Sleeping, Eating and other listings, see pages 335-338.*

Sights

On the drive to Iringa you are likely to see giraffe, elephant, zebra and baboons close by. If travelling by bus avoid sitting at the rear as there are a number of speed bumps on this stretch of road. From Mikumi the road steadily climbs upwards to the chilly highlands of Iringa. On arrival you will notice the distinct drop in temperature and vendors on the roadside arranging rows of welly-boots and jackets to sell. Be sure to take some warm clothes. During German occupation, the German military constructed the town as a fortified defence against marauding Hehe tribal warriors intent on driving them out of the region. **Gangilonga Rock**, a site just outside the town, is a legendary spot where the Hehe chief at that time, Chief Mkwawa, met with his people and decided how to fight the Germans in an uprising of 1894. He was finally defeated in 1898 but, refusing to be captured by the Germans, he committed suicide.

Population: 90,000
Altitude: 1,635 m
Position: 7°48'S 35°43'E

The pleasant albeit slightly chilly climate attracted settlers and there is an impressive legacy of German colonial architecture, including the old **Boma**, the **Town**

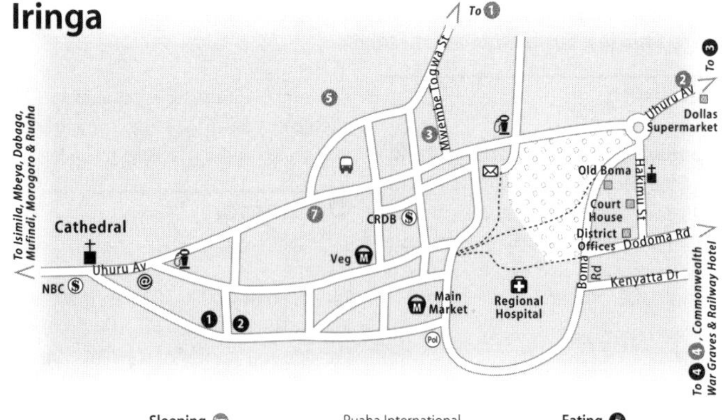

Sleeping
Banker's Acadamy 2
Huruma Baptist Conference Centre 1
MR 3
Ruaha International Lodge 4
Staff Inn Annex Lodge 7
White House Lodge & Restaurant 5

Eating
Aashiana 1
Bottoms Up Pub 2
Hasty Tasty Too 3
Lulu's 4

Hall, the **Hospital** and **Post Office**. Iringa was also the site of several battles during the First and Second World Wars, and **Commonwealth War Graves** are just outside town.

Isimila Stone Age site ⓘ *About 20 km from town. Can be reached by buses going to Mbeya, then a walk to the site of about 2 km. A taxi from Iringa will cost US$20. Entry to museum US$2.* This is considered to be one of the finest stone age sites in East Africa. Once a shallow lake, now dried up, the site was discovered in 1951 by a South African, D Maclennan, and excavated in 1957-1958 by Dr Clark Howell and G Cole, sponsored by the University of Chicago. Soil erosion in a *korongo* (a watercourse, which is dry for most of the year) exposed a great number of Acheulian stone tools, including pear-shaped axes, cleavers and spherical stones, which had been artificially shaped. They are believed to date from 60,000 years ago. Also among the finds were fossilized animal bones, including a now extinct form of hippopotamus (*H Gorgops*), whose eyes protruded like periscopes and a short-necked giraffe (*Sivatherium*). It is believed that early hominoids used this area as both a watering place and to hunt the animals that came to drink there. A small museum was built on the site in 1969 and displays some of the tools, fossils and bones found during excavations.

Isimila Gully is upstream from the site and is a spectacular natural phenomenon. Erosion over the millennia has left standing several pillars that tower above you.

Ruaha National Park and Rungwa Game Reserve

▸▸ *pp336-338*

Ruaha National Park is one of the most remote parks in Tanzania, and visitor numbers reflect that: 2,500 per annum to Ruaha, compared to 250,000 to the Serengeti. Yet it is Tanzania's second largest national park, with vast concentrations of buffalo, elephant, gazelle, and over 400 bird species. Elephants are found here in some of the highest concentrations in the country, travelling in matriarch-led herds through ancient grazing lands and seasonal supplies of water. The Ruaha River is the main feature of the park, and meanders through its borders. Most of the national park is on the top of a 900-m plateau whose ripples of hills, valleys, and plains makes the game viewing topography uniquely beautiful. Small mountains run along the southwest borders of the park and their tree-covered slopes are visible in the distance. During the rainy seasons, dry river beds swell with the biannual deluge and within days, a thin coat of green covers all the land in sight.

Ins and outs

Getting there From Iringa the road passes through densely populated countryside until the development gradually thins out. The vegetation becomes miombo woodland and about 60 km from Iringa the turning off to the right to the park is indicated. It is another 50 km down this road to the park boundary and from there about 10 km to Ibuguziwa where you pay the park entrance fees and cross the Ruaha River. About 1 km beyond the river there is a junction. To the right the track goes to Msembe and the park headquarters and to the left to Ruaha River camp. There is an airstrip at the park headquarters for light aircraft. ▸▸ *See Transport, page 338.*

Park information Entry fees are US$20 per 24 hrs. A 2-hr foot safari with an armed ranger can be arranged at park headquarters. ▸▸ *For more information on national park fees and safaris, see page 39.*

Background

Ruaha National Park was classified a national park in 1964. The area was a part of Sabia River Game Reserve, established by the German colonial government in 1911, and later renamed the Rungwa Game Reserve. It covers an area of 12,950 sq km which is the size of Belgium and ranges from 750 m to 1,900 m above sea level. The park gets its name from the river that forms part of its boundary. The name *Ruaha* is from the word *Luvaha*, which means 'great' in the Hehe language and the river certainly is that. It is vital to the economy of the country for it supplies much of Tanzania with electricity through hydroelectric power from the dam at Kidatu. Further downstream the Ruaha joins the Ulanga to form the Rufiji River.

Visiting is possible during both the dry 'yellow' season and the wet 'green' season, even in January when the rain is heaviest because the rains are short and most of the roads are all-weather. However, in the wet season the grass is long and game viewing is almost impossible, so it's best to visit from July-December.

Wildlife

There is a wide variety of wildlife in this park, largely due to the different vegetation types found here. There are four major vegetation zones: the river valleys, the open grassland, the miombo woodland (see page 302), and undulating countryside where baobabs dominate. Animals include elephant, lion, zebra, giraffe, Cape hunting dogs, ostrich, greater and lesser kudu, gazelle (and other antelope) and, in the river, hippo and crocodile. There are over 480 recorded species of bird in the park. The rare Eleonora's falcon may be sighted here, as well as the pale-billed hornbill and violet-crested turaco. Pel's fishing owls are also seen, as well as several species of bat. Unfortunately poaching here is a serious problem and the animal population has suffered enormously from this. In particular rhinos, which were once found here, are probably now extinct. The elephant population also fell tremendously from over 22,000 in 1977 to under 4,000 in 1987. In 1988 the government instigated the Selous Conservation Programme with support form WWF which, with new manpower resources, considerably helped guard the reserve from poaching. This coincided with

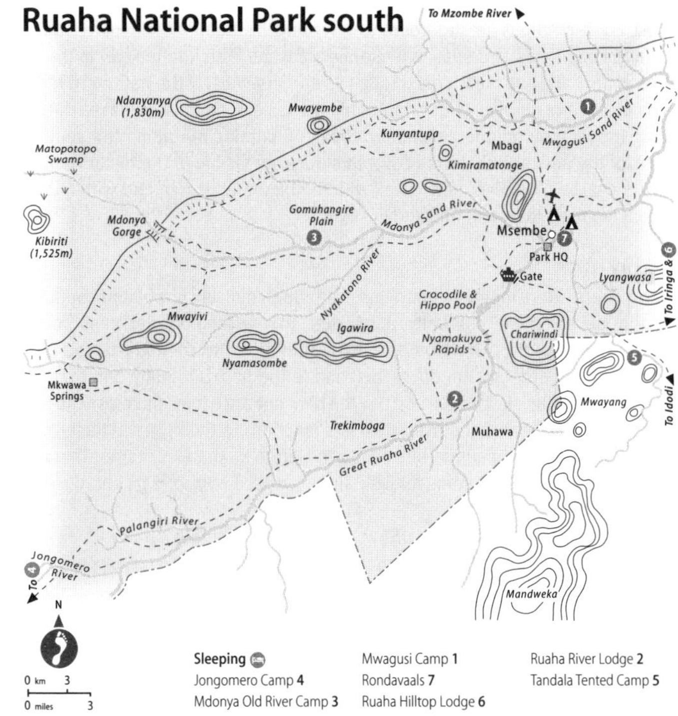

the international ban on ivory in the early 1990s and since then elephant numbers have climbed quickly and there are now thought to be about 70,000.

Routes

Around Msembe is bush country, with acacia and baobab trees, and elephants are often found here. Along the river, particularly during the dry season, many animals congregate and you may see confrontations between lion and buffalo. You can expect to see elephant, giraffe, baboon, warthog, buffalo, zebra, all sorts of antelope and if you are lucky leopard and cheetah. In the river itself are both hippo and crocodile.

The Mwagusi Sand River joins the Ruaha about 10 km from Msembe. If you cross this river and follow the track you will get to Mwayembe Hill and the escarpment where there is a salt lick often frequented by elephant and buffalo.

The Mdonya Sand River joins the Ruaha between the ferry and the park headquarters. From the ferry a drive southwest will take you past the Nyamakuyu Rapids and Trekimboga to where the Jongomero joins the Ruaha, about 40 km upriver. This is a good place to see hippo and crocodile. Roan and sable antelopes, which are difficult to see elsewhere, can also been seen here. There are supposed to be rhino in the western part of the park, but the location is kept secret.

Sleeping

Iringa *p332, map p332*

The oldest hotel in town, the **Railway Hotel**, which was built by the Germans in anticipation of the arrival of a railway line that never materialized, is currently closed. Only remnants of its former grandeur remain, though it may reopen in the future after restoration.

★ **A Highland Fishing Lodge**, Mufindi, **Foxes of Africa**, Dar es Salaam, T022-2440194, www.tanzaniasafaris.com. Above the Great Rift Valley, south of Iringa, in the scenic southern highlands and set among the tea plantations is this fishing lodge, whose 8 well appointed log cabins command fine views across the valley. The cabins have bathrooms and private verandas, while there is also a TV room with pool table, living room with large log fires, and dining room serving meals cooked using fresh produce from the farm. Full board. Activities include: mountain biking, horse-riding, birdwatching, walking, canoeing and swimming in dammed pools. Trout fishing available at extra cost (this is thought to be the only place where naturally-bred rainbow trout are found in Tanzania). The farm is off the sealed road to Mbeya. Go past Kisolanza Farm (see below) and turn off at Mafinga, the junction just past a Total petrol station (about 45 mins from Iringa). Head towards Sawala along this unsurfaced road for 30 km until a signposted turning to the left. Follow signs for a further 11 km. There are buses to Sawala from Mafinga, pre-arrange for someone to meet you at the lodge sign.

B-F The Old Farm House, Kisolanza Farm, T0744-306144 (mob, they reply to texts 3 times per day), kisolanza@bushlink.co.tz, www.kisolanza.com. Charming old house with new thatched guest cottages, 50 km southwest of Iringa adjacent to the Dar es Salaam-Mbeya Rd. The home of the Ghaui family for over 70 years. Pleasant climate at an altitude of over 1,600 m, large freshwater dam offers excellent swimming and fishing, nearby golf at Mufindi. A separate site for **campers** and overlanders is available in a secluded area away from the main house. Site has showers, WC, stone-built barbecue and plenty of shade. Fresh food, including bread, meat and eggs available to buy from the farm, and all meals. Very friendly management, beautiful site. From Iringa (travelling towards Mbeya) pass by Ifunda (on your right), and when you reach Ulete Mission (again on your right) Kisolanza Farm is shortly after on the left.

C Comfort Kitonga Hotel, 60 km north of Iringa towards Morogoro on the main highway, T0744-372371 (mob). Roadside hotel and conference venue, rooms (with bathrooms) are old fashioned but comfortable and have big beds and mosquito nets. Bar and 2 restaurants. Not a bad place to break from driving even if not staying.

C MR Hotel, off Uhuru Av, near bus station, T026-2702779, www.mrhotel.co.tz. Popular with expats and Japanese, this is the best hotel in town. Big rooms have hot showers and satellite TV. Excellent restaurant with American diner-style interior, which unusually offers a separate vegetarian menu, but slow service. Many of the staff speak good English. There are executive suites, a conference centre and a shop. Price includes breakfast.

D-E Huruma Baptist Conference Centre, Mkwawa St,1 km north of centre, T026-2701532, reservations@baptist-conference hotel.com. In pleasant, walled grounds, very good value, very clean, good food. The garden and main driveway have benches and bandas from where you can enjoy the views of the surrounding countryside. All 24 rooms are US$20, including breakfast. **Camping** also available. Can arrange transport to Ruaha and Mikumi national parks, and also has an excellent value Swahili language school which runs 1-month courses at US$450 full board.

E **White House Lodge & Restaurant**, T026-2700161, behind the bus stand. Double or single rooms with mosquito nets and hot water. The restaurant at the front has local, Chinese and western dishes from US$3. Convenient for those who are late arriving or starting early, however, it's rather run down and grubby.

E **Staff Inn Annex Lodge**, off the main Uhuru Rd. Double rooms with bathrooms, TV, clean, comfortable and modern if a little small. A bustling friendly environment with welcoming staff but often full. Great value for money. Restaurant and bar serves local and Indian dishes in a modern diner-style restaurant and veranda. A good place for single travellers to stay and eat.

E-F Bankers' Academy, Uhuru Av. The previous Bankers' Academy is still used for educational and training purposes although involves lesser numbers of students than in the past, and college rooms are available for visitors. Simple accommodation with dated decor though very clean and well maintained, about US$10. There are cheaper rooms for US$4 at the back, just past the main gates (take the left turn and follow the drive up to the back gates and security desk). These are double rooms with communal bathroom in a hall of residence. The guards at the gate will find the appropriate lady to administer keys etc. No hot water, fans or nets but very cheap.

F **Ruaha International Lodge**, about 10 min walk from the bus stand. Not quite in keeping with its grand title, a local guest house with simple rooms, shared bathrooms, a bit worn and weary, deserted during the week but busy at the weekends when there's a disco on.

Camping

Riverside Campsite, at an attractive site on the Little Ruaha River, 15 km southeast of Iringa, 2 km off the road to Dar es Salaam (the Tanzam Highway), T026-2725280. Friendly, hot showers, toilets, cold drinks, barbecue under a large tree, fresh farm produce and other food supplies if requested in advance, separate area for overlanders, US$3 per person. Horse riding can be arranged at the nearby farm, mountain bikes for hire, birdwatching, cold but refreshing swimming in the river. There are regular *dala-dalas* along the Tanzam Highway to Iringa, a taxi from town may cost up to US$7.

Ruaha National Park *p333, map p334*

L **Jongomero Camp**, bookings through the **Selous Safari Co**, T022-2135638, www.selous.com. A luxury tented lodge set under shady acacia trees on the banks of the Jongomero Sand River in the remote southwestern sector of Ruaha. 8 large and well appointed en suite tents under enormous thatched roofs with spacious private verandas, comfortable dining and living areas, natural rock pool for swimming, excellent food and good service, airstrip for direct access, full board rates and game drives included. Walking safaris can also be organized with prior notice. Rates in the region of US$350 per day.

L **Mdonya Old River Camp**, reservations through **Rove Africa Safaris**, South Africa, T+27-(0)11-4532790, www.roveafrica.com. Near Mdonya Falls, a 2-hr drive from the airstrip, a rustic tented camp with 8 twin-bedded tents with verandas, open air showers and toilets in reed walls, centred around a large lounge/dining/bar tent. All game drives and meals included in rates. Attentive staff.

L **Mwagusi Camp**, owned and run by Chris Fox and managed separately from the other Foxes' lodges, reservations through **TropicAfrica** in the UK, T+44-(0)20-8846

9363, www.ruaha.org. Without doubt the best safari camp in the park. It is in a better position than other lodges, is more stylish and luxurious and more professional and competent about its game-viewing. The site overlooks the Mwagusi Sands River, which does not dry up and so attracts all kinds of wildlife to drink there. It's a tented camp with en suite showers, hot water in the morning, evening and on request. The site has 12 luxury thatched tented rooms, and is 30 mins away from the airstrip. As soon as you disembark from the plane you are among the wildlife. The owner will take you on game drives and is very experienced, alternatively short guided walking tours are available, giving you an opportunity to 'touch the wild'. Animals wander freely through the camps. All-inclusive rate, US$300 per person per night.

L **Ruaha River Lodge**, booking through **Foxes of Africa**, Dar es Salaam, T022-2440194, www.tanzaniasafaris.info or www.ruahariverlodge.com. US$250 per person full board. Banda accommodation in one of 3 sites, 18 km south of Msembe on and around a kopje overlooking the Ruaha River. In wonderful settings, each camp has a restaurant and bar. Peter and Sarah Fox, who have lived in Ruaha for decades, are your hosts. During the dry season (Oct) the animals remain around here. Vehicle hire available. Excellent value.

L **Tandala Tented Camp**, just outside the park before the park gate, T026-2703425, tandala@iwayafrica.com. Walking safaris are permitted here as it is outside the park. Tents are built on elevated platforms, bathrooms in thatch and stone, solar power, leather sofas in the lounge area, nice bar with pool table crafted out of old railway sleepers, French and Greek cuisine in the restaurant, lovely swimming pool surrounded by wooden deck.

C **Ruaha Hilltop Lodge**, outside park, 5 km from the entrance, T0748-726709, 0744 489 375, ruahahilltoplodge@yahoo.com. A beautifully designed, outstandingly run safari lodge overlooking miombo woodland and views of Ruaha. A family business set up by two brothers from Iringa. Accommodation in comfortable cottages each with own balcony and bathroom. The spacious bar and restaurant offer amazing views at sunset and superb food. At US$80 per night for a double full board, this is the cheapest option around Ruaha and the management are very accommodating, flexible and keen for business. Transport from Iringa can be arranged through the owner.

C **Rondavaals and campsite**, at the park headquarters. Hot showers, pit latrines, very basic banda accommodation and camping. US$40 for the huts and US$30 camping. There are also two campsites inside the park, bring everything you need with you (firewood is supplied). **Tanzania National Parks (TANAPA)**, head office, Dodoma Rd, Arusha, T027-2503471, tanapa@habari.co.tz, www.tanzaniaparks.com.

Eating

Iringa *p332, map p332*

¥¥ **Bottoms Up Pub**, Majumba St. Pub serving Chinese, Indian and local dishes, including seafood and pizzas. Good value and friendly service. Has a well stocked bar and is a favourite with ex-pats at weekends, although looking a bit worn and grubby. Closed Mon.

¥ **Aashiana**, central, between Uhuru Av and the market, a huge variety of predominantly Indian foods, snacks and beverages such as fresh juices and milkshakes, great food and fantastic value for money.

¥ **Hasty Tasty Too**, Uhuru Av, opposite *Hoteli ya Kati*. Indian run café serving a good variety of meals and snacks including wraps, burgers, cakes, hot chocolate, milkshakes and toasted sandwhiches. A relaxed yet busy café with outdoor seating, again popular with the ex-pat community.

¥ **Lulu's**, Dodoma Rd. A pleasant place with garden seating and picnic umbrellas. Meals and light snacks including take away cheese toasted sandwiches. Clean and friendly. Open 0830-1500, 1830-2100, closed Sun.

¥ **White House Restaurant**, behind the bus station, good range of local and Chinese meals and snacks, outside seating, good place to wait for buses.

Shopping

Iringa *p332, map p332*

The **market** offers a huge variety of fresh foods and a number of grocery shops around the side of the market sell packaged European foods. **Dollas** supermarket recently opened opposite the Banker's Academy on Uhuru St, and sells a wide range of imported goods although at foreign prices.

Transport

Iringa *p332, map p332*
Bus If travelling on a bus which is not terminating in Iringa you may find yourself getting off at the bus stand on the main road at the bottom of the hill a few km outside Iringa town. Taxis into town cost US$1.50 or there are regular *dala-dala*. Buses leave from the main bus stand in the centre of town. The bus offices all have kiosks here. Scandinavian Bus Service, T026-2702308, www.scandinaviangroup.com. Buses to **Dar** 7 hrs, US$9; **Morogoro** 5 hrs, US$6; **Mbeya** 5 hrs, US$6; **Songea** 10 hrs, US$12. The Supa Bus leaves the main stand at 0600 daily; **Dodoma** 10 hrs, US$8, departs daily at 0800.

Ruaha National Park *p333, map p334*
The scheduled air service by Coastal Air, T022-2117969-60, www.coastal.cc, costs US$300 each way to both **Dar** and **Zanzibar**. It departs Dar at 0830 (having previously departed Zanzibar at 0800) on Mon, Thu and Sat, goes via **Selous** and arrives at 1450. The return to Dar and Zanzibar departs only 5 minutes after arrival.

Directory

Iringa *p332, map p332*
Banks CRDB Bank near the Post Office, Uhuru Av. National Bank of Commerce, Uhuru Av near the cathedral. Both have ATMs. **Internet** There are internet places, try at the side of the *MR Hotel*, US$1 per hr, or at the Post Office (often busy). Iringanet Internet Café opposite the GAPCO petrol station offers great service and plenty of terminals, US$0.50 per hr. You can also make international telephone calls from here.

Tanzam Highway to Lake Nyasa

On its way to Mbeya, the Tanzam Highway from Iringa cuts through mixed woodland and savanna as well as cultivated land. Towards the end of the rainy season the scenery looks almost Mediterranean with its cultivated rolling hillsides flecked with the yellow of sunflower crops and wild flowers. Gradually it opens up to more open savanna and various roads off the main road will lead you into the Usangu Plains. Roughly midway between Iringa and Mbeya is the junction town of Makambako. Heading south from here through fertile, rolling hills leads down to the eastern side of Lake Nyasa and Mbamba Bay via the towns of Njombe and Songea. The road is in good condition as far as Songea but then it deteriorates considerably for the 170 km from Songea to Mbamba Bay on the eastern shore of Lake Nyasa. ▸▸ *For Sleeping, Eating and other listings, see pages 340-341.*

Makambako → *Colour map C4.*

About halfway between Iringa and Mbeya, Makambako developed because of its station on the Tanzania-Zambia Railway and because it is a stop for road traffic passing through from Zambia. It is also at the intersection with the road to Njombe and Songea. It is not a pleasant place to stay, however, and the much more friendly and amenable Njombe is only 60 km to the south on a good surfaced road. If you do stay, there are several cheap hotels and a Lutheran church hostel, but only the comfortable *Uplands*

Lake Nyasa (known as Lake Malawi in Malawi) is 580 km long and, at the widest point, 80 km wide. Some 300 km of the northwestern lakeshore belongs to Tanzania. It is over 700 m deep and lies in the East Africa Rift Valley System at a height of 500 m above sea level.

Hotel offers a good degree of safety and food. The railway canteen also offers good food during the day and there are other cheap local restaurants.

Njombe → *Phone code: 026. Colour map C4. 9°20'S 34°50'E.* ▸▸ *pp340-341*

Set among attractive green rolling highlands, Njombe is an undistinguished Tanzanian town in a wonderful location. The surrounding hills are excellent walking country and are easily accessible from the town. Being 1,859 m above sea level the climate here is cool all year round. There are several wattle and tea plantations in Njombe district, some of which can be seen on the road between Iringa and Mbeya. The town was set up in rich farming country of the Southern Highlands, possibly because of the aerodrome, an early refuelling point en route to South Africa. Nearby is a spectacular **waterfall**, within an easy walking distance north on the road to Makambako, and wattle estates and a tanning factory on the hill opposite (Kibena). The Anglican Universities' Mission to Central Africa (UMCA) Diocesan HQ, Bishop's House and cathedral are worth a visit – Njombe is very much the centre of missionary activity and the old town hotel was bought by the mission. There is a single high street with a few shops and not much else.

Songea → *Phone code: 025. Colour map C4. Altitude: 4,000 ft. 10°40'S 35°40'E.*  ▸▸ *pp341-341*

The provincial headquarters of Southern Province, Songea, northeast of Mbamba Bay on Lake Nyasa and 540 km south of the Makambako junction, was comparatively isolated until the construction of the sealed road. Tobacco is the main cash crop in the area, although Mbinga, to the south, is an important centre for coffee growing. It was named after the Ngoni chief of the same name. It's a pleasant enough place, although there is little to keep you in the town itself, but it is surrounded by attractive rolling countryside and hills, which are good for walking in. Matogoro peak, in part of the **Matogoro forest reserve**, is within easy reach to the southeast of the town – take one of the tracks leading off the road to Tunduru. There are fine views from the top.

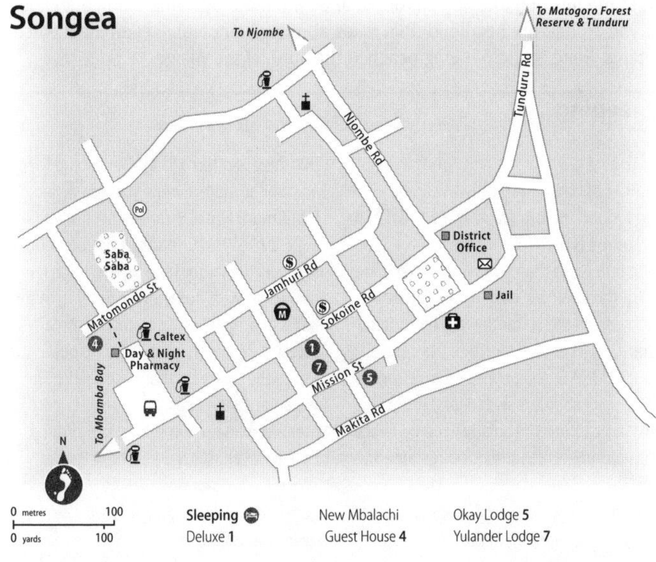

Songea and the surrounding area is home to the Ngoni, a group descended from an offshoot of the Zulus who came from South Africa in the mid-19th century fleeing the rule of King Chaka in about 1840. The Ngoni had to fight several tribes in the area to establish a foothold. They were hunters and farmers and later on strongly resisted the German colonial settlement. From 1905-1907, there was an extensive two-year insurgence against the Germans, triggered by the harsh working conditions in the cotton plantations. It was known as the **Maji Maji Rebellion** and was led by a witch-doctor named Kinjekitile, who told his followers that with the help of his magic potion, which could transform bullets into water, they would be invincible. Warriers shouted '*maji maji*' (meaning 'water water'), while going into battle armed only with swords, pangas and clubs, convinced that in doing so they would disable the German arms. The rebellion was finally suppressed locally when the Ngoni chiefs were all hanged in Songea by the Germans in 1907. The tree used to execute the local chieftains survives.

Mbamba Bay → *Colour map C4. 11°13'S 34°49'E.*  ▸▸ *pp341-341*

The route from Songea to Mbamba Bay is very scenic, passing up, down and around the green hills and mountains surrounding Mbinga before descending to Lake Nyasa. The road is bad, however, and the journey is pretty awful in the rainy season. Mbamba Bay (known in the German colonial period as Sphinxhaven) is a modest village on a glorious bay surrounded by hills on the eastern shore of Lake Nyasa (to Malawians, Lake Malawi). Most people coming to Mbamba Bay will be here to connect with (or arriving on) the ferries (Swahili = '*ëmeli*') going north to Itungi or across the lake to Nkhata Bay in Malawi and will probably only stay overnight. The scenic surroundings of Mbamba Bay, however, may well entice you into waiting for a later ferry. Many of the houses here are made in the traditional style with sun-dried, baked bricks, topped with thatch made from a long grass called *nyasi*. There's nothing much to do but what a setting for doing nothing! If Mbamba Bay was in Malawi the place would be heaving with tourists, as it is you're likely to have the place to yourself. The magnificent **Mohalo Beach**, reportedly over 20 km in length, lies 4-5 km south of Mbamba Bay. It can be reached by walking along the road to Mbinga and taking a right at the junction after 1.5 km or so, or alternatively by hiring a dug-out canoe to take you around the headland (this takes about 45 minutes). It is an ideal place for camping. There is another long beach to the north of the village.

Sleeping

Njombe *p339*
A number of basic guest houses can be found around the bus stand. For a town of its size Njombe is particularly poorly served for restaurants – but then you won't have come here for the cuisine. Good simple meals are available from the restaurants at the hotels.

D **Chani**, 10 mins walk north of the centre, T026-2782357. 8 double and 4 single rooms with en suite showers and toilets, some rooms are carpeted, regularly used by Peace Corps volunteers. Bar and good restaurant, but there is often a long wait for the food, an hour or more, even if you pre-order.

E **Milimani Hotel**, near the post office, T026-2782408. 20 spacious double rooms, some a little larger than others, each has a bathroom with hot shower. Seating in the bar is arranged like a cinema, facing a satellite TV screen, popular with locals especially when football is showing. The restaurant serves tasty, generously portioned meals but again you should pre-order. Excellent value.

For an explanation of the sleeping and eating price codes used in this guide, see inside the front cover. Other relevant information is found in Essentials pages 31-34.

Sailing schedule for MV Ilala

	Arrive	Leave
Mbamba Bay	Tuesday 0430	Tuesday 0730
Nkhata Bay (Malawi)	Tuesday 1100	Tuesday 1300
Monkey Bay (Malawi)	Thursday 0600	Sunday 1130

Note The boats are subject to delays.

Songea *p339, map p339*
Again, there are few accommodation options in Songea and these are limited to half a dozen nondescript basic local guest houses. The best of the bunch are listed below. Most have small restaurants but the best is probably the restaurant at the *Okay Lodge*, which does decent simple meals such as fish and chips or *ugali* and stew.
D Okay Lodge, 1 block south of the market, T025-2602640. Good doubles with bathrooms. Food and beer is available.
D Yulander Lodge, opposite Okay. Spotless, spacious double rooms, with bathroom.
F New Mbalachi Guest House, very close to the bus stand (go to the back of the bus stand and walk down the passageway between the Caltex pumps and Day & Night dispensary). Very clean rooms with mosquito nets.
F The Deluxe Hotel, Sokoine Rd opposite the market. Cheap and not so cheerful rooms on 2 storeys with mosquito nets.

Mbamba Bay *p340*
Accommodation and food is very limited. There are a few basic lodging houses offering very ordinary rooms for under US$5 including the **Satellite** and the **Mabuyu** guest houses, and only one restaurant at the **Nema** which isn't bad, but it's inconvenient if you're not staying there.
E Nema Beach Guest House, on its own beach about 1.5 km from the centre of the village. The best place for longer stays but inconvenient for overnights. Very good clean rooms with bathrooms. There is also a bar restaurant and pharmacy here.

Transport

Njombe *p339*
Bus To **Dar**, two direct buses daily leaving 0500-0600, journey time 9-10 hrs. Fare US$15. To **Songea, Iringa and Mbeya**: there are numerous buses daily, they all take around 3-4 hrs and cost around US$4. The bus stand is very busy, watch out for theft.

Songea *p339, map p339*
Bus There are several buses leaving daily to **Dar** all leaving early. The journey takes around 12 hrs and costs US$15. Three buses a day go to **Mbeya** costing around US$6 and taking 6-7 hrs. Buses to **Njombe** are numerous, costing US$4 for the 3-4 hr ride. On both of these routes buses go when full. To **Mbamba Bay** (outside the rainy season) there are two daily buses leaving between 0600-0700. The journey takes 8-10 hrs, US$10. Book a seat the day before. There is at least one bus leaving Songea for **Tunduru** leaving early every other morning, costing US$10. Try to book a seat in front of the back axle in view of the appalling state of the roads. (See page 125 for details of transport between Songea and Mtwara).

Mbamba Bay *p340*
Bus The 170 km road to Songea is very rough in parts and the bridges are occasionally severely damaged. It is very slow and becomes treacherous in the wet. In the dry season there are sometimes buses from **Songea** that leave very early in the morning, the journey takes 8-10 hrs, US$10. But mostly local landrovers make the journey, and then only sporadically so. The only option is to get as far as Songea and wait for transport.

Boat The ferry journey up the lake to **Itungi**, cruises along the eastern shore of Lake Nyasa with the impressive Livingstone Mountains looming in the background. For details of ferries on Lake Nyasa see box above.

Mbeya and around

→ *Phone code: 025. Colour map C3.*

Near the Zambian border deep in the southern highlands, the city of Mbeya is the major agricultural capital in the country's southwest region. The Mbeya mountain range lies to the north, and the Poroto mountain range lies to the southeast. Large coffee and tea plantations, banana farms, and fields of cocoa are all grown around the region and come to Mbeya for packaging and transport. Mbeya's location also makes it an ideal transit point for good travelling by road and rail between Tanzania and neighbouring Zambia and Malawi. Other towns in the Mbeya region worth heading for are Tukuyu, on the road to the border with Malawi, which offers good trekking in the surrounding hills, and Matema, on the shores of Lake Nyasa, a remote and traditional settlement with spectacular lakeside scenery. ▸▸ *For Sleeping, Eating and other listings, see pages 346-350.*

Population: 160,000
Altitude: 1,737 m
8°54'S 33°29'E

Mbeya →

▸▸ *pp346-350*

The town was founded in the late 1920s when the gold mines at Lupa became active, and continued to grow after they closed in 1956. However, recent international exploration of five licensed sites of an 150-sq km area near the town of Makongolosi, to the north of the old **Lupa Goldfields**, have indicated that there are

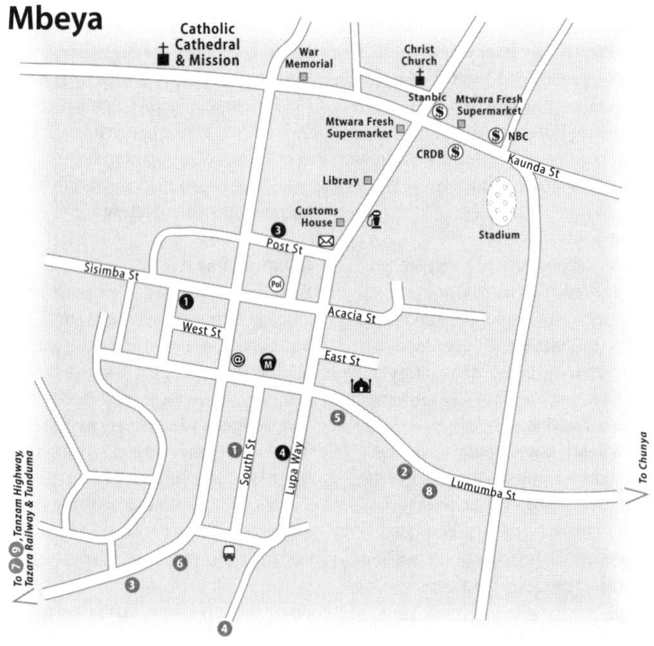

Sleeping
Dandho Highway Complex **7**
FM Guest House **1**
Karibuni Centre **9**
Moravian Church Hostel **4**
Mount Livingstone **5**
New Holiday Lodge **2**
New Millennium Inn **6**
Nkwenzulu Guest House II **3**
Rift Valley **8**

Eating
Baba Kubwa **4**
Eddy Coffee Bar **1**
Sombrero **3**

Tazara Railway

The Tazara (Tanzania and Zambia Railway Authority) railway runs from Dar es Salaam to Kapiri Moshi in Zambia. It was built by the Chinese between 1970-1975 and is an impressive feat of engineering. The track covers 1870 km, and it passes over 300 bridges, through 23 tunnels and past 147 stations. At a cost of US$230 million, this was the largest railway project at the time since the Second World War. The railway was Zambia's answer to the closure of its routes to Southern African ports as a result of Rhodesia's Unilateral Declaration of Independence in 1965. Initially, it was meant to handle all of landlocked Zambia's freight, and it did. But since the reopening of the southern routes following independence in Mozambique in 1975 and the coming of majority rule in Zimbabwe in 1980, Zambia's dependency on the Dar es Salaam port has lessened. As a result, the volume of cargo along the railway has been considerably reduced. However, its passenger trains, built to carry 600-plus people, are almost always full to capacity, and for people living along the route, the train is the cheapest and most convenient link to the rest of Zambia or Tanzania. The railway is also a lifeline to villagers living along its route. When they hear the train coming, people bearing baskets full of red onions, potatoes, rice, bananas, tomatoes, plantains and oranges rush to meet it.

still significant deposits of gold, silver, copper and diamonds, which it may prove economically viable to extract.

Mbeya has developed into a bustling, if a little rundown, town and is an ideal base from which to explore the Southern Highlands. Being only 114 km from the Zambian border and the last main station on the TAZARA railway line makes it a popular overnight stop and important trading centre. However, remember that it's still 875 km from Dar es Salaam and was rather isolated until the construction of the railway and the sealed road.

Excursions and walking

Although there is little of interest in Mbeya itself, it is an excellent point from which to make excursions into the outstanding beautiful surrounding countryside. There are endless options, particularly for hikers and cyclists. Tourism is still a micro industry in this region which may explain the laid-back and unobtrusive approach of the available tour guides. ▸▸ *To organize a guide, see Activities, page 348.*

Recent travellers report that there are security concerns for walkers, and that the environs of Mbeya are no longer considered to be safe for tourists unless accompanied by a guide.

Between Mbeya and Lake Rukwa is the small town of **Galula**, at the northern end of the Songwe River Valley. Galula has an imposing Catholic church built by the French White Fathers. Nearby are lake deposits indicative of a previously much larger lake and evidence of **Iron Age** and **Late Stone Age** sites have been found on the river terraces. At **Mapogoro**, northeast of the Lupa Goldfields, close to the village of Njelenje, volcanic **rock shelters** were identified in 1990 by researchers from the University of Alberta. Many artefacts of the Late Stone Age were found.

About 37 km before Mbeya on the Tanzam Highway from Irniga is the Mlowo River and the Kimani Falls; 25 km before Mbeya on the right hand side of the road is the Mwambalisi River, which is also fairly spectacular during the rainy season.

The **Mbozi Meteorite** is a 12-tonne mass, believed to be the eighth largest in the world and to have landed over 1,000 years ago. The meteor is roughly rectangular in shape and approximately 5 m in diameter. There is evidence that many small samples have been removed for analysis judging from what appear to be saw indentations in several places. It is 40 km southwest of Mbeya, along the road to Zambia; take the turning off just after Mbowa, it's a good 10-15 km from the highway.

The **Ngozi Crater Lake**, 38 km south of Mbeya, is worth a visit but you will need a guide to get there, see page 345.

Walking This is walking country and you will be able to get some tremendous views of the surrounding countryside. The mountain to the north of the town and part of the Mbeya Range is **Kaluwe** (known as Loleza Peak) and rises to 2,656 m. It can be reached in about two hours and is well worth it if you have a spare afternoon. The view from the summit is breathtaking and if you enjoy a good romp the pathway is quite rugged and steep. The hillsides are dotted with wild flowers and the peace is only disturbed by the bells of cattle and birdsong. From Mbeya turn right just after the Catholic cathedral and mission and head straight – find the path that leads up a slope and follow it (it passes a number of Christian monuments and crosses along the way). This leads to the summit.

Mbeya Peak, rising to 2,826 m, is the highest peak in the range and looms to the north above the town. There are two possible routes, one harder than the other. The first is down a track about 13 km down the Chunya Road. From the end of this track the climb will take about one hour, including a walk through eucalyptus forest and high grass. The second, and more difficult route, is only recommended for those prepared for a steep climb and, in parts, a real scramble. This begins from the coffee farm at Luiji. There is very good accommodation here at the *Utengele Country Hotel* (see Sleeping). At the top you can catch your breath and admire the view for miles around.

Another worthwhile, but also energetic trek is to **Pungulume** (2,230 m) at the west end of the range. It is approached from the road at its base near Njerenji. Alternatively follow the ridge from Mbeya Peak. (Avoided this trek in the wet season.)

Probably one of the best viewpoints in the Mbeya Range is known as **World's End**. From here you will see the Usangu Flats and the Rift Valley Escarpment; the view is really quite breathtaking. To get to it go about 20 km down the Chunya Road, due north of Mbeya beyond World's End to a forest camp and take the track off to the right.

The **Poroto Mountains**, southeast of Mbeya, are home to a wide variety of birdlife, including Livingstone's turaco and the green barbet. There are also several species of kingfishers, woodpeckers and eagles (see below.)

Tukuyu » *pp347-350*

This is a small town about 40 km south of Mbeya, on the road to Lake Nyasa. It was an administrative centre for the Germans and there is a group of colonial buildings to the southeast of the town, but all in all it's a pretty dreary place and appears quite bleak when hidden under swirling mists. On the other hand it has a glorious location in the scenic **Poroto Mountains**. There's nothing to keep you in the town itself but a great deal to see in the surrounding countryside. The dark volcanic soils provide a fertile productive region swathed in banana trees and fresh mountain air. Tukuyu is an important tea-growing area and the road to Kyela is lined with the picturesque fields of plantations.

Altitude: 1,615 m
9°17'S 33°35'E.

Trekking

Tukuyu is a good centre for trekking but it is necessary to engage a guide (the *Langiboss Hotel*, see page 347, can arrange one). Among the local attractions are **Mount Rungwe**, the most important mountain in this area, and at 2,961 m the highest mountain in southern Tanzania. Its slopes are vast and wild with over 100 sq km of uninhabited forest, upland scrub and rock terrain. It is accessed from Isangole, 10 km north of Tukuyu, and will take at least a full day to climb. Other attractions are the **Masoko Crater Lake** 15 km to the southwest and the **Kapalogwe Falls**, south of Tukuyu, which are around 40 m high and in an attractive lush setting. Halfway down there is a cave behind the falls, which it is possible to enter. There's good swimming at the bottom in the pool the falls cascade into. To reach them go about 6 km down the main road towards Kyela to the Ushirika village bus stop. From there it's about 2½ hours to walk or it's possible to hire a bicycle at the main road (with or without rider!).

Ngozi Crater Lake about 20 km north of Tukuyu in the Poroto Mountains, is a beautiful lake lying in the collapsed crater of an extinct volcano the sides of which plunge down steeply from a rainforest-covered rim. The forest is home to colonies of colobus monkeys. Witch-doctors are said to call upon ancestral powers here and local legend claims that there is an underwater snake-like monster hidden deep in the waters of the lake, causing the surface waters to change colour from time to time. To get there catch a *dala-dala* going to Mbeya up to Mchangani village (this takes 1-1½ hours). It's advisable to arrange for a guide at Mchangani to take you up to the lake as the route is by no means obvious. It's a two-hour walk from the main road to Ngozi. The second half of the walk entails a steep climb through rainforest before you emerge at the crater rim. From here the views across the lake are spectacular. You could camp at the top, in which case you would be there for sunset and dawn.

Daraja la Mungu (Bridge of God), also known as Kiwira Natural Bridge, is an unusual rock formation spanning a small river close to Tukuyu. To get there take a *dala-dala* going to Mbeya and get off at Kibwe (12 km north of Tukuyu). Here change to one of the Land Rovers waiting at the beginning of the road branching off to the left (ask for Daraja la Mungu). It's a further 12 km down this rough road. There are apparently also hot springs (*maji ya moto*) a little further on and nearby is Kijunga waterfall.

Kyela » pp347-350

Kyela is a small commercial centre northwest of Lake Nyasa and the nearest town to the Malawi border. The surrounding countryside is fertile, abounding with banana plants, mango trees, maize, bamboo and also rice, particularly prized throughout Tanzania and much of it being transported to Dar es Salaam after harvest. Unfortunately the town itself doesn't match its attractive surroundings; it is dusty and characterless and on arrival you'll probably be keen to get out as soon as possible. However, if you're hoping to catch the ferry to Mbamba Bay or Nkhata Bay (in Malawi) at least one night in Kyela is necessary, as this is the access town for the ferries that leave from Itungi.

Matema » pp347-350

Matema is the secret paradise of the southwest of Tanzania and a walk along the lakeshore here will simply take your breathe away. The slopes of the Livingstone Mountains – vertiginous rock, meadows and plunging waterfalls – provide a backdrop for the blue waters and sandy beaches of the lakeshore. Although not the easiest place to reach don't be put off by tales of woe – it is well worth the trip. To get there, turn off to the left just before the Malawi border where a gravel road takes you to Matema. The village itself is very friendly, with banana trees and flowers and pigs, dogs and chickens milling around. In the market bamboo wine is drunk literally by the bucket load, and grilled meat (especially pork) is offered by the vendors.

A walk along the mountainside to the village of **Ikombe**, the site of a former mission, is a highly recommended excursion. The mountainside comprises steep slopes and deep valleys which are home to fresh mountain streams, butterflies and wild flowers. Ikombe can be reached by a rough cliff top path which is currently being dynamited in an attempt to build an adjoining road. This makes the path almost impassable at points. Alternatively, it is possible to hire a dugout canoe which takes 30 min each way between Matema and Ikombe depending on the wind. Ask locally about making excursions and you will be sure to find a willing and helpful guide who will ensure that the relevant permission is sought. The beach is safe for swimming, and reportedly clear of bilharzia, but check locally. There are supposed to be hippos and crocodiles in the river that flows into the lake about three kilometres or so west of the village. It is a pleasant walk along the beach.

The **Wakisi**, one of the peoples who make up the population of the surrounding area, are well known throughout Tanzania for their pottery skills. The role of the Wakisi women is not only to raise and rear children, farm, and look after the home but also to make the pots – a woman's skill affects her ability to marry. In the market in Matema large piles of Wakisi pots can be seen bound up awaiting transportation to Mbeya, Iringa and even as far away as Dar es Salaam. The Saturday market in the village of Lyulilo attracts buyers from all over the region.

Sleeping

Mbeya *p342, map p342*

B **Utengule Country Hotel**, 20 km south of Mbeya on a coffee estate beneath Mbeya Peak and 90 km from the Zambian border, T025-2560100, www.utengule.com. The signposted turning is roughly 12 km south of Mbeya on the main road, it is then about another 8 km to the hotel. A charming country hotel, with restaurant, bar, comfortable rooms, and very good food, it has a swimming pool and tennis court, and hires out mountain bikes. Refurbished in 1998. A good base for excursions into the mountains.

B **Mount Livingstone**, opposite mosque on Lumumba St, T0741-350484, mtlivingstone@hotmail.com. Possibly Mbeya's most established hotel, centrally located, private drive and pleasant gardens. All rooms have bathrooms with hot water and TV. Clean, comfortable and professionally run, though the decor is looking a little dated. The bar has an extensive wine and cocktail list, good food in the restaurant with meat and fish grills, and pasta dishes from US$5. Double rooms US$60. **Camping** also available. Accepts Euros and £GB as well as US dollars.

D **Rift Valley**, town centre, T0744-641666 (mob), info@twiga.ch. Functional multi-storey hotel with 75 rooms with bathrooms, doubles with TV are US$10 more than those without TV. Restaurant and bar with reasonably priced main courses. Rates include breakfast.

D **Nkwenzulu Guest House II**, Set back from the main road close to the bus stand, T025-2502225. A little more secure and exclusive than the other nearby guest houses, with high walls and iron gates and garden with seating and umbrellas. All rooms have bathrooms, hot water and mosquito nets. Breakfast included in the price, good variety of food available.

D-E **Karibuni Centre**, 500 m off the Tanzam highway at the Mbalizi Evangelical Church, T025-2503035, mec@atma.or.tz. Run by a Swiss missionary in a forest area. Accommodation in a clean and peaceful setting, good simple food, restaurant closed Sun, safe car parking. Also has a small guesthouse with rooms for less than US$10 and **camping** facilities (US$3 per tent). The church also runs a school for mechanics and is a good place for vehicle repairs.

D **New Millennium Inn** (formerly the *Central Tourist Lodge*), T0744-885265 (mob). A very smart Greek-style villa with secure private parking. Opposite the main bus stand so very convenient for early starts/late arrivals. Rooms have hot water, mosquito nets and the promise of TVs in the near future. Friendly staff and beautifully tended garden, no bar or restaurant, though this shouldn't pose a problem as the *Nkewezulu* is next door.

E-F **New Holiday Lodge**, central, near *Rift Valley Hotel*, T025-2502821. Doubles only with or without bathrooms, TVs available for extra. Clean, a little old-fashioned but pleasant with friendly staff, restaurant and veranda at the front.

F **Moravian Church Hostel**, from the bus

station, head up the hill directly opposite and follow the path round, T025-2503263. Very clean and friendly, twin rooms only, good security with safe parking for vehicles. If you are catching an early bus you can pay an askari to accompany you.

F **FM Guest House**, T0745-075552 (mob). Locally-run guest house which gets very busy, worth pre-booking. Clean but simple double rooms with shared bathrooms, hot water available. Lounge area with TV, veranda and local food available from nearby stall. Has a very friendly atmosphere. Because it's Muslim-run, couples must present a marriage certificate. Also the office for Peter's Walking Tours (see page 348).

Tukuyu *p344*

C **Landmark Hotel**, T025-2552450. This impressively smart modern hotel is an unexpected find in the town, with large manicured garden, mirrored windows and shining granite-topped reception desk. Friendly and professional staff who speak a wide range of European languages. Modern rooms with satellite TV, phones, and hot water. Bar, large restaurant with a reasonable menu, private car park. We especially liked the men's loos, 'gentle toilets'. Breakfast included.

E-F **Langiboss Hotel**, about 1 km from the town centre on the road to Masoko. Basic accommodation but in a stunning location. Rooms with or without bathrooms, clean and simple, food can be arranged with notice, well stocked bar not to mention the year round Christmas decorations. Staff also arrange tours in the local area.

Kyela *p345*

There are several basic guest houses in the centre offering a bed in a bare room and shared bathroom for around U$5. These include: **Bikutuka Guest House**, **Kilimanjaro Guest House**, and **Livingstone Cottage**.

E **Pattaya Central**, opposite the bus stand, T025-2540015. The best of all. Has spotless rooms, all with fans and hot water but no mosquito nets. The only drawback may be the noise resulting from its central location.

E **Gwakisa Guest House**, on the same road near the market, T025-2540029. Clean and efficiently family-run guest house which offers secure, pleasant rooms with mosquito nets and fans. Double US$5, single US$3.

Matema *p345*

C-E **Matema Lutheran Guest House**, in the centre of the village, T2025-504178, www.twiga.ch. Run by the Mbalizi church, guest house in superb location with 8 good rooms, some have up to 5 beds in them and are ideal for families. Also has good value accommodation in bandas. Simple, spotlessly clean, possible to **camp**. Rates US$10 pp and upto US$30 for a double, breakfast included.

C-E **Lake Shore Resort Evangelical Church Hostel**, signposted from the village, on the beach. Popular with expats, spotlessly clean and well run, offers a variety of accommodation, from beachfront chalets sleeping up to 5 with private verandas (US$25), to double rooms with shared bathrooms (US$7). The beach is raked and cleaned daily with palms planted to create some privacy for sunbathing. Good restaurant that serves food to order. No alcohol available.

E **Roman Catholic Guest House**, on beach, a little more tricky to find but just a 2-mins walk from the bus stand. A well-kept clean and functional guest house which you will most probably have to yourself. 6 rooms with or without bathrooms, each with views and the front doors open on to the beach. The manager, BaBa Pascal and his family are extremely welcoming. They will prepare food if you order in advance and sell bottled beers.

Eating

Mbeya *p342, map p342*

🍴🍴 **Dandho Highway Complex**, outside of town on the highway to the east of the turn off to Mbeya, T025-2500838. A recent large-scale project started by a local businessman although far from completion. A variety of buildings built around a central thatched banda with restaurant and bar, swimming pool and in the future accommodation. Use of swimming pool is US$1.50. Food includes meat and fish dishes and bar snacks. Also live music and disco.

🍴🍴 **Mount Livingstone Hotel**. The best place to eat in town with a great choice of seafood, meat grills and Mediterranean dishes. Extensive wine and cocktail menu suggest that there's potential for a fun night out.

🍴 **Baba Kubwa**, just off Lupa Way. Indian-run café with a wide variety of Indian and African dishes and snacks, also cold beers. The outside area is popular in the evenings.

Eddy Coffee Bar, near the market in Sisimba St. Reasonably priced local dishes, licensed restaurant, satellite TV, some outdoor seating.

Sombrero, just off Post St near customs house and library. Diner-style restaurant with fixed seats. Whilst waiting for food you can admire the peculiar tardis-like glass locked bar. A variety of Indian and African dishes.

Kyela *p345*

New Steak Inn. A fairly new and surprisingly plush restaurant for a Tanzanian town of this size. It does good basic dishes like chicken and chips and a variety of snacks. Very popular with locals and has a healthy buzz.

Shopping

Mbeya *p342, map p342*

Mtwara Fresh, is a locally run supermarket with two outlets in the centre of town. Packed and fresh produce including brown bread and cheese, friendly staff and open until late. Worth a visit if planning a picnic. For souvenirs there are a variety of craft stalls on the walk from the main bus stand to the town and on Kaunda Street near the banks.

Activities and tours

Mbeya *p342, map p342*

Sisi Kwa Sisi Society, near the Memorial of Friendship with Japan on the walk from the bus station towards town, T0744-463471 (mob), sisikwasisi@hotmail.com. Set up 7 years ago and literally meaning 'Us for Us', it is an affiliated partner of the Cultural Tourism Programmes of the north of Tanzania. Like those programmes, Sisi Kwa Sisi offers tours of the area and uses profits to help the local community, in this case through agricultural projects. Tours offered include visits to all attractions in the Mbeya, Tukuyu and Matema areas, with the chance to experience the traditional local cultures. The guides speak good English, and some speak French and German. Theoretically open from 0800-1800 every day although during the 'low season' the hours may be revised. The office provides a variety of information with maps, and book-swap library. The staff are a wealth of local information. Depending on transport an average day trip costs US$15 per person. Further details can also be obtained from the Tanzanian tourist information centre in Arusha, T027-2503840-3, www.infojep.com/culturaltours.

Peter's Walking Tours, FM Guest House on South St, T0745-075552 (mob), peterwalkingtour@hotmail.com. Peter Nsopela is a highly enterprising and enthusiastic local guide who has set up business on his own. Occasionally Peter takes on work for Sisi Kwa Sisi and although his business is as yet unlicensed he has been recommended by Sisi Kwa Sisi, amongst many others, as a reputable and fun guide. He offers guided trips to all sites of local interest. A one-day trip costs between US$15-25.

Transport

Mbeya *p342, map p342*

Bus Buses are very regular to **Dar** via **Morogoro** (around US$17 luxury, US$13 semi-luxury and US$9 ordinary, take 10-12 hrs). **Scandinavian Express**, T025-2504305, www.scandinaviangroup.com. Fixed departure times are 0630 and 0700. The road goes through the **Mikumi National Park** (see page 328). There are 2 buses a week to **Tabora** on a poor road, (US$10, 24 hrs). There are frequent small buses to the **Zambian border** at **Tunduma** (US$2.50, 2 hrs). Through buses for Zambia pass through Mbeya at around 1500, having come from Dar, and head on through to **Lusaka** arriving there at 0600 the following morning. However, the large buses can get stuck at the border for a considerable time and there are often delays. There are also frequent buses to **Kyela** (US$3, 3 hrs) close to Lake Nyasa for the **Malawi border**, although few travel all the way to the Malawi border. Ask to be dropped off at the turn-off to the border before you reach the town of Kyela. From there it is about 5 km to the border and you should be able to get a lift or a bicycle taxi. Locals will be clamouring to carry your luggage, change your money and show you the way although there is often a price to pay. After Tanzanian immigration formalities you cross the bridge over the Songwe River to the Malawi immigration on the other side. It's a friendly border. Your yellow fever card may be checked. A few mins' walk from the immigration office is a bus stand where you

Ferries on Lake Nyasa

There is a ferry service of sorts between Itungi and Mbamba Bay and Nkhata Bay in Malawi on Lake Nyasa. The boats are run by TAZARA whose office is opposite the post office in Kyela, although it is not glaringly obvious. However, the best source of information regarding sailing times are the local businessmen and traders who use the ferries regularly. If you can afford the time, take a trip to the port at Itungi itself, 10 km from Kyela on the lakeshore where the ferries go from, and ask there.

In theory, the *MV Songea* runs weekly, leaving Itungi port on Thu at 1300. It travels around the lake, stopping frequently, as far as Mbamba Bay arriving on Fri at 1530, where it then supposedly* crosses to Nkhata Bay in Malawi and begins the return journey on Sun arriving in Itungi on Mon. Tickets can be bought on the day of travel – although the office advises booking in advance for first class tickets. However, the unreliable nature of services would suggest that you don't part with any money until the day of travel is a dead cert. Tickets can be bought at the port and arriving several hours before estimated time of departure will ensure that you have time to buy tickets and read several novels before there's even a hint of movement. A first class ticket to Mbamba Bay will cost about US$18. 1st class cabins are for 2 people and are small but comfortable. Try to get a cabin facing the lake-shore. In 3rd class you get a wooden bench and plenty of company. (2nd class seems to have disappeared!) Food is available on board.

(*At the time of writing, despite assurances in Tanzania that the *MV Songea* runs to Nkhata Bay, the residents of Nkhata Bay in Malawi swore that the service was not running and hadn't been for some time although there are rumours that it might start again in mid-2005. It seems likely, however, that the *MV Songea* does run as far as Mbamba Bay on a weekly basis.)

If the services are resumed to Malawi then access to Nkhata Bay across the lake from Itungi and via Mbamba Bay would be available weekly. In its absence crossing the lake is not easy (private boats cross very infrequently), so it is not advisable to rely on boat travel between Tanzania and Malawi. If you do get across the lake then there is an immigration office in Mbamba Bay where you can get an exit stamp from Tanzania or buy an entry visa.

Becky Stickland

can pick up a bus to **Karonga** (approx 2 hrs, US$1, paid in Malawi Kwacha). From Karonga public transport continues on to Mzuzu, Lilongwe and Blantyre. Malawi is 1 hr behind Tanzanian time.

There are 3 buses daily to **Songea** (US$6.50, 6-7 hrs). To **Njombe** buses leave several times a day (US$5, 3-4 hrs). To **Iringa** (US$5, 4-5 hrs) several times a day. To **Tunduma** frequently (US$1.70, 1-2 hrs).

Train The TAZARA railway station is outside the town on the Tanzam highway. The ticket office at the rather impressive glass station is open until 1700 every day. Trains are often full and booking in advance is advised through the Tanzanian-Zambia Railway Authority in Dar, T022-2865187, www.tazara.co.tz for online reservations. In Mbeya, try and purchase tickets the day before travel as although it is possible on the day of travel the queues are long and chaotic. Currently the ordinary train to **Dar** departs on Tue at 1200 and arrives 24 hrs later. The express train departs on Wed and Sat at 1300 and arrives in Dar the following morning at 1000. Fares; 1st class US$18/22, 2nd Class US$13/17, 3rd Class US$11/13 for ordinary/express trains respectively. Heading into **Zambia** there are 2 express trains per week which terminate in **Kapiri Moshi**, departing on Wed and Sat at 1300 arriving the following day at 1130. Passports and immigration matters are dealt with on the train. Fares vary from US$15-26 depending on which class you choose to travel in. At least 2nd class is advisable. Although the above are official departure times, after the multitude of children, boxes, chickens and associated needs of train travel are boarded, departure is usually delayed by a few hours. In 1st and 2nd class, bunks are provided, and there is a buffet carriage which provides reasonable food and beers etc, though it is advisable to take along some basic provisions. The route between Dar es Salaam and Mbeya passes through lovely countryside. However, the frequent stops and jerky motions involved in braking and acceleration, mean that the journey is quite a tiring experience.

Tukuyu *p344*
Bus From **Mbeya** buses run regularly to **Kyela** and the Malawi border passing through Tukuyu. The 1 ½ hr journey from Mbeya costs US$1. Both **Scandinavian Express** and **Kilimanjaro Express** services run buses to **Dar** daily, reporting time is 0600, journey time around 11 hrs, and the fare is US$16. Ticket offices are found at the bus stand just off the main Mbeya-Border road.

Kyela *p345*
Bus You have to be an early riser to catch a bus going to **Dar** (US$17, 13 hrs). They leave between 0440-0500 and pick up passengers at **Tukuyu** and sometimes **Mbeya** too. There are numerous minibuses going to **Mbeya**, which if you're very lucky will take 3 hrs, but normally more like 4 hrs, and can take up to 6 hrs or more. Most buses pass by the border and wait to fill up which can be a time-consuming process. Be prepared! It costs US$2.50. For **Tukuyu**, catch a bus going to Mbeya (US$1.50, 2-3 hrs). The bus to **Itungi** for the Nyasa ferry (US$0.60, 30 mins).

To the **border with Malawi**: some of the minibuses to Mbeya go via the border (US$0.60, 30 mins). It is far more convenient to take a taxi, which only takes 5-10 min. Private taxis cost US$3.50, or there are shared taxis which squeeze 6 passengers and associated luggage into a 5-seater vehicle for US$0.50 per person. Shared taxis leave from the corner opposite the *Pattaya Guest House* on the right hand side (as if you're heading for the TAZARA office).

Matema *p345*
Matema is little visited largely because of the difficulty in getting there by public transport. Vehicles to Matema are painfully slow, uncomfortable and extraordinarily over-crowded. Vehicles depart from **Kyela** at 0600, and the later you leave it the less chance you have of arrival on the same day due to scant transport for the last leg of the journey between **Ipinda** and Matema. From Kyela pick-up trucks run from the stand opposite the *Gwambuzi Guest House*. This can be quite adventurous (clinging to fellow passengers is necessary to avoid involuntarily ejection). The Kyela pick-ups drop off in the small town of **Ipinda** and cost US$0.60. From here buses leave for Matema, 1-2 hrs, US$1 but are irregular and tend not to run after mid-day – aim to arrive early morning to ensure a link to Matema. On the return journey from Matema to Kyela, transport is again scarce and there is just one bus leaving the stand for Ipinda each day at 0600 which occasionally continues to Kyela. Once in Ipinda there are plenty of pick-ups to Kyela.

Directory

Mbeya *p342, map p342*
Banks National Bank of Commerce, on the corner of Kaunda St, opposite the stadium, has reasonable rates and is the best place to cash TCs; they will change most major currencies (taking about 10 mins). It also has an ATM that accepts Visa cards. CRDB, also with an ATM which tends to offer slightly better rates of exhange. Stanbic Bank, on the corner with Lupa Way. **Post** Office near the library at the end of Post St. **Internet** Available next to the Safari Hotel down from the Aga Khan Dispensary (US$0.50 per hr). **Medical services** Mbeya Medical Centre, the main state hospital in the region, T025-2503571/3351. For malaria testing and other minor ailments the Aga Khan Dispensary, Post St opposite the post office, provides an efficient service.

Tukuyu *p344*
National Bank of Commerce on main St.

Background

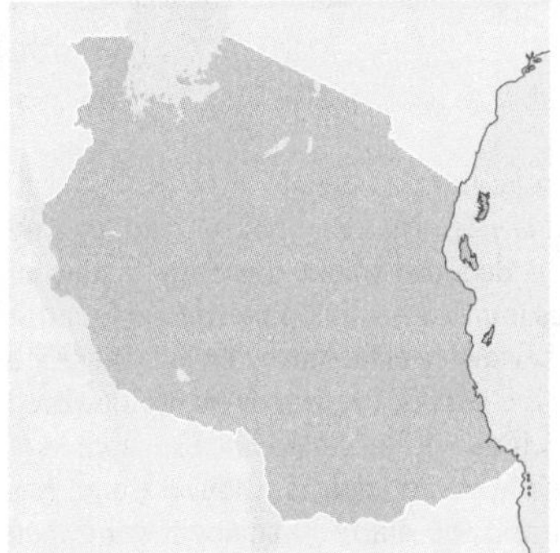

Footprint features

History

Earliest times

From oral history, archaeology, linguistic analysis and anthropology (although no written records), a certain amount can be deduced about the early history of Tanzania. The bones of two types of hominids from the Australopithecine era found at Olduvai Gorge (see page 257) have provided evidence of human evolution. These are *Zinjanthropus*, the 'Nutcracker Man' and *Homo habilis*, the 'Handy Man'. They lived together about 2 million years ago and it is thought that *Homo habilis*, capable of using tools, is the ancestor of modern man – *Homo sapiens*. Olduvai Gorge has become known as the cradle of mankind and the era of Australopithecine man probably lasted several million years.

By about 500,000 years ago *Homo erectus* was on the scene (somewhere between the Australopithecine and *Homo sapiens* eras). The brain was larger and the hands more nimble and therefore better at making tools. The development of tool-making is clearly seen at Olduvai Gorge. The different layers of rock contain tools of different ages, which show the development from crude tools to more efficient and sharper implements. Another collection of such tools can be found at Isimila near Iringa (see page 333).

The Middle Stone Age saw the further development of tools, advances in human ingenuity and craftsmanship and the use of fire. Progress accelerated in the Late Stone Age, which began about 100,000 years ago, and there are a number of sites from this era in Tanzania, particularly well known because they are the locations of rock painting. The hunter-gatherers were probably related linguistically and racially to the San and Khoikhoi of South Africa. (Interestingly the Sandawe who now live in the area of the rock paintings speak a form of the Khoisan or 'click' language, which otherwise is not spoken in East Africa and which is characteristic of the San.)

The virtual disappearance of these people was a result of the migration and expansion of other people who were more numerous and more advanced. The most significant factor about these migrating people was that instead of being hunter-gatherers they were food producers – either by agriculture or by keeping livestock. They spoke the language of the Cushitic group (legendary biblical descendants of the Cush in Ethiopia, Somalia and north Sudan) and came from the north from around 1,000 BC onwards. They did not have iron-working skills and this meant that the efficiency of their agriculture was limited.

Bantu migration

Later still, during the past 1,000-2,000 years, two other groups migrated into the area. These were both Negroid but were of different linguistic groups – the Bantu from the west and the Nilo-Hamite pastoralists from the north. A process of ethnic assimilation followed and the Cushitic intermarried with the newcomers and adopted their languages. The Bantu possessed important iron-processing skills, which greatly improved agricultural efficiency and this enabled population growth. There was not one single migration but a series of waves of various groups, expanding and contracting, assimilating and adapting. The present ethnic mix is as a result of this process over many centuries.

The most recent of the Nilotic migrations was by the Masai. By about the year 1800 they had reached the area around Dodoma where their advance was stopped by the Gogo and the Hehe (see page 366). Their reputation as a warrior tribe meant that the north part of Tanzania was largely avoided by slave traders and caravan routes.

As a result of these migrations north and central Tanzania has great ethnic diversity. In this part of the country there are Khoisan, Cushitic, Nilotic and

Bantu-speaking peoples. The rest of the country is entirely Bantu speaking; indeed about 95% of Tanzanians born today are born into a family speaking one of the Bantu dialects. Swahili itself is a Bantu tongue and this has developed into the national language and as such is a significant unifying force.

Arab traders

Initially Swahili was a coastal language and developed as the language of trade. The earliest visitors to Tanzania were Arab traders who arrived on the coast, and their influence can be seen in the coastal settlements such as Kilwa (see page 108). By the 13th century there was a bustling trade on the coast. Initially the trade was dominated by the Persians, Arabs, Egyptians, Indians and Chinese but the Arab influence began to dominate and with it the spread of Islam. The major trading objects were gold, ivory and rhino horns, exchanged for guns, textiles and beads. These coastal towns were very much orientated towards the sea and away from the interior until the beginning of the 16th century when the development of long-distance trade led to more integration. Caravan routes began to extend from the coast to the Congo and Buganda.

Portuguese seafarers

By the mid-15th century the Portuguese had arrived on the scene. Vasco da Gama noted the beauty of Kilwa, and attempted to take control of the gold trade. The Portuguese were later expelled by the Arabs and the influence of the Arabs increased again. A period of reduced trading activity followed until the latter half of the 18th century when it flourished again, this time the commodity being slaves. Around 1776 the only trading route inland went southwest from Kilwa to the area around Lake Nyasa and this became increasingly important through the slave trade. During the 18th century Kilwa became East Africa's major slave-trading port, drawing first on the peoples of southeast Tanganyika and then on the Lake Nyasa area.

During the 19th century the trade pattern shifted as a result of the changes in the supply of ivory. During the first half of the century, most of the ivory had come from within what was to become Tanganyika. However, as Tanganyika's elephants were destroyed, so the price of ivory rose. Prices at Tabora are reported to have increased tenfold between 1846 and 1858 and the hunters began to look further afield, eventually leaving Tanganyika altogether. As the hunters moved away the chiefs in these areas lost their major source of revenue and it was this that led some of them to look to the new trade in slaves.

The slave trade

Caravan routes into the interior developed in the 19th century and trade centres developed at places such as Ujiji and Tabora. Humans and ivory were exchanged for guns, beads and cloth. The slaves were largely obtained by bartering with the local chiefs rather than by force. Some of the more militarized tribes raided their neighbours and 'prisoners of war' were then sold on to the Arabs as slaves. Convicted criminals were often sold as slaves and this penalty was sometimes extended to include their families.

The size of the slave trade remains a matter of speculation. However, it has been estimated that approximately 1,500,000 slaves from the interior reached the coast and 10 times that number died en route. Bagamoyo was a terminus of the trade and from there they were taken to Zanzibar, which developed into an important trading centre. The slaves were either put to work in the plantations of Pemba and Zanzibar or were shipped to the Middle East.

By the 1830s Zanzibar had become sufficiently prosperous from the sale of slaves and spices for the Omani Sultan Seyyid Said to move his capital from Muscat to Zanzibar. For some time Britain tried to suppress the slave trade by signing various agreements with the Omani Sultans but it was not until 1873 that the trade was officially abolished when an agreement was signed with Sultan Barghash (Seyyid Said's successor). However, this prohibition was implemented only slowly and the practice continued on the mainland for some years. By the 1880s the internal market for slaves had become more important than the external.

The first Europeans

The first Europeans in this part of Africa (since Vasco da Gama) were missionaries and explorers. In 1844 John Krapf, a German working for the Church Missionary Society of London, arrived in Zanzibar. He was joined by John Rebmann who was to become the first European to set eyes on Mount Kilimanjaro in 1848. The two British explorers Burton and Speke, sent by the Royal Geographical Society, arrived in Zanzibar in 1856 and journeyed along the caravan routes into the interior. In 1858 Speke came across the huge expanse of water, which he named Lake Victoria. Dr Livingstone was perhaps the most celebrated of all the missionaries, being found, after no news of him for several years, by HM Stanley, a newspaper reporter (see box, page 305).

By the 1880s considerable numbers of Europeans were arriving in East Africa as missionaries, big game hunters, traders and adventurers. Some had political ambitions, including two Germans, Carl Peters and HH Johnson, who wanted to see this part of Africa under the control of Germany. They formed the Society for German Colonization from which emerged the German East Africa Society. Emissaries of the Society signed 'protective treaties' with unsuspecting and often illiterate chiefs from the interior. These so-called treaties of friendship were then used by the German East Africa Company to exploit the areas that they covered with the apparent agreement of local authorities.

Both Germany and Britain made claims over East Africa, which were resolved by a series of agreements. The Berlin Conference of November 1884 to February 1885 was convened by Bismarck and was important in demarcating European spheres of influence in Africa. This saw the recognition of the German 'protective treaties' and by early 1885 several chiefdoms were formally placed under the control of the German East Africa Company. Three years later the Germans were shaken by an uprising of both Arabs and Africans and the German government took control in 1891. The Anglo-German Agreement of November 1886 defined the north boundary from the coast inland to Lake Victoria. A month later another agreement saw the defining of the boundary with Mozambique. These and various other treaties saw Zanzibar, Pemba and a 16-km coastal strip go to the Sultan under British Protectorate rule in 1890, while what is now mainland Tanzania, Rwanda and Burundi became German East Africa. But it was not until 1898 that German rule was secured and consolidated with the death of Mkwawa, chief of the Hehe who had resisted German domination.

Mount Kilimanjaro

While Germany and Britain were deciding the north boundary, Kaiser William I insisted that Mount Kilimanjaro should be German because it had been discovered by a German, John Rebmann. Queen Victoria generously 'gave' the mountain to her grandson, the future Kaiser William II, on his birthday in 1886, reportedly explaining, by way of justification, that 'William likes everything that is high and big'. The boundary was thus moved so that Kilimanjaro is now found within Tanzania. As can be seen on the present map, instead of marking the boundary by pencilling it in with a ruler from the coast to Lake Victoria in one go, a freehand detour was made when the ruler hit the mountain, before carrying on again with the ruler and pencil on the far side.

The German colonial period

There were a number of phases of German colonial rule. The first, around the turn of the century, saw attempts at establishing a settler economy. This was to be based in the north highlands and agriculture was to be the mainstay of the economy. It was initially not a great success. Revolts occurred in Bagamoyo, Pangani and Tanga,

Central and northern railways

The first railway to be constructed in Tanganyika was the Tanga (Northern) line which began when the German authorities decided in 1891 that a metre-gauge line should be built from Tanga to Muheza, and then on to Korogwe. Eventually this line would be continued on to Moshi and Arusha. A small port was built at Tanga to land equipment and material and the construction of the line began in 1893. Labour was scarce and at times had to be imported from Mozambique making progress slow. It took two years for the laying of just 40 km as far as Muheza. Financial difficulties caused construction to be halted periodically and the line finally reached Korogwe in 1902 and Moshi in 1911. Unfortunately much of this line, built at great expense over a long period of time, was destroyed by the Germans as they retreated in 1914.

Meanwhile the central route of the old slave trail to Lake Tanganyika was receiving attention. Dar es Salaam had been made the capital of the German protectorate in 1891 and talk of the construction of a railway began soon after. However, delays again ensued and it was not until 1905 that construction began on a line from Dar es Salaam to Morogoro. This was to be built by a private company with a grant from the Imperial German Government. The Maji Maji rebellion created problems with the supply of labour, but the line reached Morogoro in December 1907. By 1914 the line had been extended as far as Kigoma although it was clear that it had little commercial value and traffic was extremely light.

Planning continued for other lines but the First World War intervened and much of the work already carried out was destroyed. Most of the bridges between Dar es Salaam and Kigoma were blown up, and the rolling stock destroyed. A line was built during the war, linking the Tanga line to the Kenya railway system which facilitated the advance and occupation of Tanga by the British.

Following the war many repairs were carried out so that the goods traffic on the railways increased. However, the problems returned with the depression of the 1930s which severely affected revenues. The non-metre gauge lines were closed and about 40% of the staff were laid off. The Second World War saw an increase in the activities of the railways, and following the war the 'Groundnut Scheme' (see box, page 358), involved the hasty construction of a branch line from Lindi on the coast to Nachingwea, one of the areas where groundnuts were to be grown. The scheme was a monumental failure, the expected traffic never materialized, and the line was abandoned.

In 1948 the railway and port services in Tanganyika were amalgamated with the Kenya and Uganda railways under the East Africa High Commission. A regional authority, East African Railways & Harbours (EAR&H), ran the railways until 1977 when the East African Community collapsed, severing the rail link through Taveta to Kenya, with Tanzania assuming responsibility for its own network.

which were all crushed. The best-known uprising was the Maji Maji rebellion (*maji* means water in Swahili), which occurred in the south of the country from 1905 to 1906 (see page 340). Discontent was initially aroused over a cotton scheme that benefited the Africans little although they were obliged to provide all the manual labour. The uprising was unique in eastern Africa for it was cross-tribal and included a large area – almost the whole of the country south of Dar es Salaam.

The uprising led to a major reappraisal of German colonial policy. The administrators realized that development would be almost impossible without a contented local population. This period saw the building of the railway to Tabora to open up the area to commerce, and crops such as coffee and groundnuts were encouraged. Economic activity increased and a world boom led to the re-emergence of a settler cash crop economy as the most significant part of colonial policy. In particular the boom saw prices of sisal and rubber soar. Most farming took place along the coast and on the slopes of Mount Kilimanjaro and Mount Meru. Inland the threat of the tsetse fly hindered development as domestic animals could not be raised in affected areas. Missionary activity led to the growth of clinics and schools.

First World War

With the outbreak of hostilities in Europe, the German commander General Paul von Lettow Vorbeck realized that his meagre forces could not defeat the British but he resolved to aid Germany's efforts in the European theatre of war by tying up as many British military resources as possible. Von Lettow, his German officers and African troops conducted an astonishing rearguard campaign, retreating from Kenya through what is now Tanzania and Mozambique, as was undefeated when Germany surrendered in Europe.

Von Lettow arrived in Dar es Salaam at the start of 1914 to take command of the German forces. He was 44 years old, son of a general, a professional soldier and experienced in bush warfare from service in German South West Africa (now Namibia). His forces consisted of around 2,500 Schutztruppe (see box, page 357) askaris in 14 field companies, and he promptly signalled his intentions by capturing Taveta across the border in Kenya. The British assembled a force of 5,000 mainly British, South African and Indian troops and von Lettow withdrew to begin his epic, 4,000-km, four-year campaign. When faced by overwhelming odds von Lettow fell back, but at defendable positions, although always hopelessly out-numbered, he inflicted fearful losses on his adversaries, most notably at Tanga and Kibata (see page 91).

The British fared better when commanded by the South African, Jan Christian Smuts, for 11 months in 1916. A rare combination of intellectual, politician and soldier, he later became Prime Minister of South Africa. During the war, however, found himself pursuing an infuriatingly elusive, and surprisingly humorous, foe. He was convinced that he would trap and destroy von Lettow's troops in Morogoro, where retreat to the south was blocked by the Ulunguru Mountains. But as his forces marched into the town they heard a mechanical piano playing *Deutschland Uber Alles* in the *Bahnhof Hotel* and, in the empty Schutztruppe barracks, on every item of furniture, was a piece of human excrement.

Never defeated, at the end of the campaign von Lettow and his force numbered 155 Germans 1,156 Schutztruppe askaris and about 3,000 camp-followers made up of porters and askari wives and children, many of the latter born during the campaign. Over 250,000 Allied troops had been thrown against them at one time or another during the four years. But with their ultimate defeat in the First World War, the Germans lost control of German East Africa. The northwest, now Rwanda and Burundi, went to the Belgians. The rest was renamed Tanganyika, and the British were allocated a League of Nations mandate.

Von Lettow returned to Germany, in 1920 entered politics and for 10 years was a Deputy in the Reichstag. In 1930 he resigned and in 1935 Hitler suggested he become Ambassador to Britain. Von Lettow declined. It is said he told Hitler to 'go fuck himself', but von Lettow subsequently denied he had ever been that polite. In 1958, at the age of 88, von Lettow returned to Dar es Salaam. He was met at the dockside by a crowd of elderly Schutztruppe askaris who carried him shoulder-high to an official reception at Government House. In 1964 the German Bundestag finally voted the funds to settle the back-pay owing to the Schutztruppe at the surrender in 1918. Over

Schutztruppe – an African fighting elite

It was recognized by the Germans from the start that white troops in East Africa would be nothing more than a 'walking hospital'. So, under German officers, an African fighting force of askaris was recruited, thoroughly drilled, trained, disciplined and well paid – 30 rupees a month for privates (about US$80 in present-day values) and 150 rupees for non-commissioned officers.

The Shutztruppe became an elite. The uniform was a khaki jacket, trousers and puttees and a black leather belt with ammunition pouches. Head gear was a kepi – rather like a khaki fez with a chin-strap and a gold Imperial eagle on the front. The non-commissioned officers decorated their kepis with feathers. Each soldier had his own servant (an askari-boy). When travelling, a Schutztruppe private would send his askari-boy ahead to a village with a cartridge. This was an order to the local headman to have ready four beds (one for the askari, one for his rifle, one for his ammunition pouch and one for his uniform) – and some 'blankets' – a selection of the village girls.

Tough, resilient, and brave, around 150 askaris made up a field company that included two machine-gun teams. With several hundred porters carrying food and ammunition, it was highly mobile. During the First World War, the British were contemptuous of these African troops, thinking they would collapse when faced with European and Indian forces. In the event, the Schutztruppe was never defeated, and inflicted fearful losses on the British and their allies.

300 veterans, some in faded and patched uniforms presented themselves at Mwanza. Only a handful had their discharge papers. Those who didn't were handed a broom and taken through arms drill, with the orders given in German. Not one man failed the test. The same year, at the age of 94, von Lettow died.

The British period

From 1921 Britain introduced the policy of Indirect Rule, which had proved effective in other parts of colonial Africa. This involved giving a degree of political responsibility to local chiefs and ruling through them. Economic development between the wars was negligible. Tanganyika had few exportable products – unlike Uganda, there was no major cash crop such as cotton suited to production by small African farmers. The most significant export was sisal, a spiky plant that yields fibres that can be made into ropes and twine, but this required long-term, large-scale, capital-intensive investment and was not suitable for small-scale African production. It was produced almost entirely by British and Asian companies with a local workforce. The most successful African cash crop was coffee grown by the Chagga on the slopes of Mount Kilimanjaro, and by the Haya west of Lake Victoria. Coffee growing was extended to Africans by the British in 1922. Previously only settlers were allowed to grow coffee on estates established by the Germans from 1910.

Most British settlers went to Kenya where there was already a sizeable settler community and the highlands provided an attractive climate. Moreover the British presence seemed more secure in Kenya, which was a colony. The League of Nations mandate required Britain to prepare Tanganyika for eventual self-government, and the British kept expenditure on administration, infrastructure and education to a minimum.

The 1920s saw the emergence of the first African political groups. In 1922 the African Civil Servants Association of Tanganyika Territory was formed in Tanga, and in 1929 the Tanganyika African Association (TAA). Throughout the 1930s and 1940s,

The Groundnut Scheme

Immediately after the Second World War there was an attempt by the British Labour government to grow groundnuts on an enormous scale. Three sites were chosen in the south, near Lindi at Nachingwea; just north of Morogoro at Kongwa; and at Urambo west of Tabora on the Central Railway line. The scheme aimed to alleviate the worldwide shortage of edible oils following the war. The operation was to be capital-intensive, with a military-style approach to planning, and there was immense enthusiasm among the British who went out to run the programme (and who became known as 'groundnutters'). It was thought that with modern methods and enough machinery it would be impossible for the scheme to fail. It was a complete disaster. When finally abandoned a total of £36.5 mn was written off. This huge sum was equal to a little less than the entire Tanganyikan government expenditure from 1946-1950.

The reasons for failure were numerous and included inadequate planning, which meant the environmental and climatic problems were not properly considered; unsuitable machinery (which meant that it was actually more efficient to clear the land by hand); and failure to test the scheme by way of a pilot project. Other difficulties included insufficient rain and inadequate capacity in the transport system to keep the tractors supplied with fuel.

The project is held up as an example of everything that was wrong with attempting to impose European agricultural techniques without adequate consideration of local African conditions.

Kongwa is now a ranch, Urambo has been given over to tobacco, and at Nachingwea oilseeds and cereals are grown.

unions and agricultural cooperatives developed. These were not primarily political associations although their formation obviously led to increased political awareness. The major issues were land-use policies, aimed in particular at soil conservation, and the eviction of Africans to make way for white settlers. The African population in 1950 was about 8 million, compared to an Asian population of 55,000 and European population of 17,000. However, Europeans and Asians dominated local government councils even in areas that were almost exclusively African. These were issues upon which the TAA focused. In 1953 Julius Nyerere became the leader of the TAA and the movement towards independence developed momentum. In July 1954, at a meeting of all political elements, the Tanganyika African National Union (TANU) was created with the slogan *Uhuru na Umoja* (Freedom and Unity).

There were two major strengths to this movement in comparison to other similar movements in other parts of Africa). Firstly, there was no dominating tribal group, and secondly, Swahili had developed into the major language, encouraged by German colonial policy, and this served as an important unifying force. A further point of relevance in the run-up to independence was that after the Second World War Tanganyika was given UN Trustee status in place of the mandate. Both the mandatory system and the trusteeship system were very important because they meant that controversial issues could be referred to the UN Council, unlike in other colonial territories. In December 1956 Nyerere addressed the UN General Assembly's Fourth (Trusteeship) Committee, which gave him a platform to present the views of Tanganyikans to the outside world.

The first elections were held in two phases, in September 1958 and February 1959, and TANU won a sweeping majority. These were multiracial elections but even

Julius Nyerere

Julius Kambarage Nyerere was born in 1922 in Butiama, east of Lake Victoria. He was the Roman Catholic son of a Zanaki chief. His father died having had 26 children by 18 wives. The name Nyerere means 'caterpillar' in the Zanaki language and was supposed to have been given to Nyerere's father because at the time of his birth (around 1860) the countryside was infested with them. Nyerere attended a boarding school in Musoma and, from 1937, the Tabora Government Secondary School. He was baptized in 1943 and the same year he entered Makerere College, Uganda. After Makerere he returned to Tabora where he taught history and biology at St Mary's Catholic Boys' School operated by the White Fathers. In 1949 he went to Edinburgh University and in 1952 obtained his Master of Arts. In 1953 he married Maria Gabriel Magigo who was also a Catholic of the Msinditi tribe and was to become its first woman teacher. He paid the traditional bride-price of six head of cattle for her and they had seven children.

Nyerere subsequently took a teaching post at the Catholic Secondary School of St Francis at Pugu a few kilometres west of Dar es Salaam and it was from here that he became involved in politics. In 1954 he became president of the Tanzania African Association and was instrumental in converting this into the political organization TANU. He was appointed a temporary member of the Tanganyika Legislative Council in 1954, and a full member of the Legislative Assembly in 1958 where he remained until his assumption of the Presidency in 1962. He resigned as President in 1985 and became known as 'Mwalimu', which means teacher. He was undoubtedly one of Africa's greatest statesmen, admired for his integrity, modest lifestyle and devotion to equality and human rights. On his death in October 1999, the ANC released a statement: "The organization weeps in memory of this giant amongst men...an outstanding leader, a brilliant philosopher and a people's hero – a champion for the entire African continent".

the European and Asian candidates owed their success to TANU. Tanganyika attained Independence on 9 December 1961 with Nyerere as the first Prime Minister. The constitution was subsequently changed, Tanzania becoming a republic with Nyerere as President.

Post-Independence Tanzania

In 1964 Zanzibar and Tanganyika merged to form Tanzania (see page 140). An awkward union has resulted in which Zanzibar has retained its own President, Parliament, a full range of Ministries and handles most of its own finances. The President of Zanzibar was, *ex officio*, one of the two Vice-Presidents of Tanzania until the multiparty elections in 1995. Despite having a population that is less than 5% of the total, Zanzibar has almost a third of the seats in the Tanzanian Assembly.

After Independence there was pressure to replace Europeans with Africans in administration and the business sector. There was also considerable demand for basic education and health services. Although economic progress was significant in these early years, there was an impatience at the slow pace of development, and Nyerere made plans for a bold, radical change.

This culminated in the 1967 Arusha Declaration, a programme of socialist development accepted by TANU and which was then amplified in a number of pamphlets by Nyerere. Its two main themes were egalitarianism and self-reliance and it was broadly based on the Chinese communist model. (It has been said that Tanzania took the Chinese model, mistakes and all and then added a few mistakes of its own.) Politicians were subject to a leadership code, which required that they had no private sources of income, and no more than one house or car. Banks, plantations and all major industries were nationalized. The cornerstone of the programme was the villagization and agricultural collectivization programme known as *Ujamaa*. This, and efforts in the rest of the economy, would, it was hoped, lead to the development of a just and prosperous society. Education was considered to be one of the most important aims of the programme and as a result Tanzania achieved some of the highest literacy rates in Africa. In the initial years there was success, too, in extending basic health care in the rural areas.

Ujamaa

Ujamaa, a programme for advancement in the rural areas, was an important element in post-independence Tanzanian philosophy. Intended to involve the voluntary movement of people into villages, its major objective was to raise output through collectivization and large-scale agricultural production. Emphasis was also on the social benefits – the provision of services such as piped water, electricity, schools and clinics. Self-reliance was the key and the villages were meant to be set up and run by the villagers themselves.

There were three phases of villagization in the decade from 1967. The first was voluntary movement on a locally selective basis combined with compulsory movement in Rufiji and Handeni, which were areas worst affected by drought and flood. From 1970 to 1973 this was replaced by a 'frontal approach' whereby incentives were given for people to move to villages, which included financial and technical assistance. The reluctance of people to move of their own accord meant the targets were not reached and after 1973 these methods were replaced by the use of force in support of rapid villagization. The results were dramatic. In 1970 the villagized population stood at about 500,000, or less than 5% of the population. After the first year of compulsory movement Nyerere claimed that there were over 9 million people – or about 60% of the mainland population, living in villages. Force was justified on the grounds that people could not always see what was best for them and had to be shown the way. As it is easier to provide amenities such as piped water and electricity to people grouped in villages, the *Ujamaa* did provide some benefits.

However, attempts to farm collectively were disastrous and agricultural output fell. The programme was vigorously resisted in the major coffee-growing areas of Kagera (west of Lake Victoria) and in Kilimanjaro region. By 1977 the *Ujamaa* programme was effectively abandoned, although considerable villagization remains.

Late 20th century to the present

In 1973 it was decided to move the capital city from Dar es Salaam on the coast to Dodoma in the centre. The position of this city is suitable in so far as it is on communication networks and is in the centre of the country about 320 km inland. However, it is also a dry and desolate area and the major problem with the plan has been the cost of moving. A Presidential official residence, the Prime Minister's office, and a National Assembly building have all been established there but the cost of relocation has forced the rest of central government to remain in Dar es Salaam for the time being.

In 1975 a law was passed that gave legal supremacy to TANU as the national political party, and in 1977 TANU and the Afro-Shirazi party (which had taken control in Zanzibar after the revolution) merged to form *Chama Cha Mapinduzi* (CCM) the 'party of the Nation'. The 1970s saw the gradual disintegration of the East Africa Community (EAC), which involved Kenya, Tanzania and Uganda in a customs union and provision of common services. Tanzania and Kenya had different ideological perspectives, and the three countries could not agree on the distribution of the costs and services of the EAC. Things came to a head over East African Airways. The failure of Tanzania and Uganda to remit funds to Kenya caused Kenya to 'ground' the airline (conveniently when all the planes were sitting on the tarmac in Kenya) and Tanzania reacted by closing the border with Kenya in February 1977. The border was only reopened in 1983 after the ownership of the EAC's assets was finally agreed.

In 1978 Tanzania's relations with neighbouring Uganda worsened and skirmishes on the border were followed by an announcement by Idi Amin that Uganda had annexed the Kagera salient. This is an area of about 1,800 sq km of Tanzanian territory west of Lake Victoria. The Organization of African Unity (OAU) applied pressure, which caused Uganda to withdraw, but fighting continued. In January 1979 a Tanzanian force of over 20,000 invaded Uganda, Amin's army capitulated and the Tanzanians rapidly took control of the southern part of the country. The invading force had withdrawn by 1981 having spent the interim period in Uganda overseeing the election of Milton Obote for the second time. A remarkable feature of this episode is that, despite being the only African country ever to win a war in the 20th century, this event is not celebrated in Tanzania. The only monument is a small pyramid on columns, located on the road from Bukoba to Masaka, just south of the border. It is dedicated to the 16 Tanzanian soldiers who died in the war.

In 1985 Nyerere decided to step down as President of Tanzania (the first President in post-independence Africa to retire voluntarily). He remained as Chairman of the party (CCM) before formally retiring from politics in 1990. Vice-President Sokoine, who had been widely thought of as Nyerere's successor, had been killed in a car crash in October 1984. Ali Hassan Mwinyi, who was then President of Zanzibar, was nominated to be the sole candidate for President and was elected in October 1985.

Throughout the early 1980s Tanzania had been put under pressure to accept economic reforms suggested by the World Bank and International Monetary Fund. These financial institutions, as well as western governments, aid donors and foreign investors argued that the socialist development strategy had led to a crisis involving falling incomes, decaying infrastructure, deteriorating health and educational provision and a climate of petty corruption. For many years Tanzania resisted changes, but eventually the climate of opinion changed in 1986, under Mwinyi, a market economy strategy was adopted, and Tanzania began an economic recovery.

In 1993, Tanzania allowed political parties other than CCM to form. In October 1995 there were elections in which CCM won a substantial majority of seats in the Union Assembly. The Presidency was won by the CCM candidate, Benjamin Mkapa, Mwinyi having retired after two terms in office. Mkapa and CCM were returned again in the 2000 elections.

In 1995, the main opposition in Zanzibar, the Civic United Front (CUF) ran CCM very close in both the Zanzibar Assembly and in the race for the Zanzibar Presidency. There were allegations of election fraud, supported by evidence from international observers. Nonetheless, CCM formed the administration in Zanzibar, and Salim Amour was installed as Zanzibar's President. In 2000, there were again allegations of election irregularities and administrative incompetence at the polls, but once more CCM were returned, and CCM's Amani Karume (son of Zanzibar's first President) secured the Presidency.

The current situation in Zanzibar is a cause for concern. It is argued in Zanzibar that the Union, created in 1964, although following constitutional procedures, has no political legitimacy as the Zanzibar party to the agreement seized power undemocratically after the 1964 revolution (see page 140). In addition, there are the cultural and religious differences with the mainland stemming from the population of Zanzibar being overwhelmingly Islamic. Zanzibaris feel the Union with the mainland has held back their development, and that they would have benefited in terms of aid and foreign investment if they had been able to forge stronger ties with Islamic states, particularly in the Gulf, where they have strong historical links (see page 136). In 1994 Zanzibar joined the Organization of Islamic States (OIS), which, although unconstitutional, as Zanzibar is not an independent state, appeared to be tolerated by the government. However, Nyerere, whose liberal and egalitarian philosophy was uncompromisingly secular, denounced the move, and Zanzibar was forced to withdraw.

Various Zanzibari separatist groups have formed in exile, some wishing merely for independence, others pressing for an independent Islamic state, but splits within the separatist movement have enabled the government to contain the problem so far. A former Chief Minister of Zanzibar, Shariff Hamad, who was suspected of sympathy to the separatist cause, was removed from office and detained.

For the multiparty elections in October 1995 13 opposition parties were formed. The strongest was NCCR-Maguezi led by a former Interior Minister from CCM, Augustine Mrema, who had considerable popular appeal. CUF, in which Shariff Hamad, the dismissed former CCM Chief Minister on the Isles, was the driving force, had little support on the mainland, but was very strong in Zanzibar. Prior to the election there was a good prospect that Zanzibar would elect a CUF president, and the CUF world have a majority of seats in the Zanzibar Assembly. The Assembly could then instigate a referendum on the separation issue, and most observers judged that this would be carried. Given the commitment of Tanzania to democratic self-determination in the past, it would be difficult to resist the break-up of the union. Indeed Tanzanians seemed to be preparing themselves to face up to such an eventuality – "let us end the Union, if that is what the Zanzibaris want, while we are all still smiling" – was a sentiment frequently heard on the mainland. Former President Nyerere, architect of the original Act of Union, observed that he felt Zanzibar would always be a headache, and that if he could have towed it away from the Tanzanian coast to the centre of the Indian Ocean, he would have done so.

Mkapa won comfortably with 62% of the vote, over Mrema with 28%, and the practice of having two Vice-Presidents (with one being the President of Zanzibar) was discontinued.

In the Union Assembly elections, run on a first-past-the-post-basis, CCM got 219 seats, NCCR-Maguezi 19, CUF 28 (mostly from Zanzibar), CHADEMA four, and UDP four. Some irregularities were reported, but the general impression of observers was that the election was a reasonable reflection of the nation's political preferences.

By contrast, the elections for the Zanzibar Assembly and President were a disaster as far as both credibility and the medium-term future of the Islands were concerned. CUF boycotted the Zanzibar Assembly, and the donor community exerted pressure for a re-run of the election under international control. Norway, Sweden and the EU suspended aid to Zanzibar.

Yet, aside from this, the Mkapa presidency began well with a determined stance over corruption. Three ministers (the Finance Minister, the Deputy Finance Minister and the Minister for Wildlife and Tourism) were forced to resign because of corruption allegations. The opposition fared less well. The major success was that the NCCR-Maguezi Presidential candidate, Augustine Mrema, won a by-election in a Dar es Salaam constituency. However, this was followed by an apparent split between the party General Secretary, Mabere Marondo and Mrema.

The 2000 election was fought by fewer parties, but the opposition was still divided, and CCM and Mkapa had comfortable victories. In Zanzibar the incumbent President, Salim Amour, having completed two terms, was prevented from running again. His successor as CCM candidate for the Presidency was Amani Karume, son of the former President. On election day there was chaos at the polls, and elections in 16 constituencies had to be re-run. Despite opposition claims of electoral fraud, the outcome was a victory for CCM and Karume. Seif Shariff Hamad, the CUF leader, got the remaining 33%. His party won 16 assembly seats on the island of Pemba. Both parties signed a reconciliation agreement in 2001 and Zanzibar is set to remain part of Tanzania. But the CUF, which enjoys strong support on Pemba, has called for greater autonomy and some CUF members have called for independence. In 2005, Zanzibar presented its new flag, the first time for over 40 years that the archipelago has flown its own flag since uniting with Tanganyika to form Tanzania in 1964, though Zanzibar's government has stressed the adoption of a flag does not mean that this is a move towards independence.

In April 2004 Tanzania celebrated its 40th birthday as an independent country. Overall, during this period Tanzania's political stability has remained excellent. The government has stayed secure in a period that has seen the advent of multiparty democracy and economic policies that have changed from socialism to capitalism. In 2004 the presidents of Tanzania, Uganda and Kenya signed a protocol in Arusha to establish a new customs union, intended to boost trade in East Africa. The next elections are due in Tanzania in October 2005, and as Mpaka has already served for two terms, the constitution does not allow him to stand for a third. The CCM are priming their replacement candidate, who at the time of writing was chosen as Jakaya Mrisho Kikwete the current deputy prime minister.

Economy

Economic strategy underwent a profound change in 1967 when financial and business enterprises were taken into public ownership and a major reorganization of the agricultural sector was introduced, involving collective production and relocating the population into villages. By 1977, the collectivization of agriculture had virtually been abandoned. In 1986 Tanzania signed an agreement with the IMF, which heralded the beginnings of a reversal of economic strategy to more encouragement for the private sector and reliance on market forces, rather than on planning and central control.

In the latter part of the colonial era (1960/1961) a waiter in a good hotel would earn TSh150 (US$10 per month) at a time when a bottle of beer cost TSh2.50 (US$0.20). In other words one day's pay was the equivalent of the price of two bottles of beer. In 2001 the same waiter would expect to earn TSh 60,000 (US$54 per month) while a bottle of beer now costs TSh1100 (US$1). A day's pay continues to equate to roughly the price of two bottles of beer.

Economic structure

Despite still being a third world country, Tanzania's economy has benefited from mining and mineral resource projects over recent years including the opening of gold mines in the interior and gas extraction plants along the coast. But Tanzania still only produces a modest output of around US$23.71 bn of GDP, converted to US$ using the exchange rate. Using a purchasing power parity conversion, GNP per head is US$700 a year. Both these measures put Tanzania among the very poorest countries in the world. However, over the last decade GDP growth has almost tripled from US$8 bn allowing living standards to show an improvement of more than 4% a year. Agriculture is the most important sector, producing 43% of GDP and, more importantly, providing the livelihood of 80% of the population. The industry sector is small and is mainly limited to processing agricultural products and light consumer goods and provides 17% of GDP and the services sector provides 39% of GDP, 23% in Tanzania's tourist industry (see box on page 15). Industry and services combined generate 20% of employment. The main commodity sources of export income which stands at about US$1.2 bn per year is agriculture, which accounts for 85% of all exports. The remaining 15% includes minerals and manufactures. New export crops include deluxe vegetables and cut flowers grown around Mount Kilimanjaro and shipped by air to European supermarkets. Mining has been an important factor in the industrial sector, with a series of new gold mines coming on stream. Over 30 million ounces of gold resources have been identified in Tanzania in the past five years, almost exclusively in the Lake Victoria region. The World Bank offers insurance for foreign investment in Tanzania, and these measures have assisted in attracting exploration capital to the country. Annual investment in mineral exploration has increased from US$500,000 to US$150 mn in less than a decade, and in the future the export of gold will contribute greatly to the county's GDP. Other resources that have been tapped into recently include gas and a gas field is now operational on the offshore island of Songo Songo. Services have also picked up to grow at more than 10% a year, driven by strong expansion in tourism, which is booming, with receipts rising at 25% a year, and visitors tripling since 1992. Export volumes have also recovered, and together with revenues from aid have allowed imports to rise steadily. There has been slow but steady improvement in inflation performance in recent years and, in 2000-2005, the rate was 5.5-6% a year.

Aid receipts at US$31 per head are a little below the African average, and total aid receipts are around US$1.3 bn a year.

People

In terms of both population and geographical area, Tanzania is a large country in the African context. The population has been growing rapidly at 2.8% a year, and in 2005 the population was estimated at 35 million people, 1 million of which live on Zanzibar, and 2.5 million in Dar es Salaam. This gives a population density of 3.5 persons per sq km, rather higher than the African average. However, the distribution is very uneven, with the areas around Mount Kilimanjaro and west of Lake Victoria heavily populated, while in the south and southwest there is much uncultivated fertile land. Urbanization is not as advanced as elsewhere in the continent, and only 23% live in the towns.

The population is largely made up of mixed Bantu groups but there are 129 recognized tribes. East Africans are frequently divided into 'tribes'; but exactly what makes a tribe is often difficult to define. A tribe usually refers to a group of people with a common language and culture. They possess a common name and recognize themselves to be distinct from their neighbours. Sometimes the group may be fairly distinctive and easy to define – but in other cases the divisions are much less clear. There are some observers who believe that the concept of 'tribe' is largely an artificial one imposed during the colonial period. The colonialists wanted identifiable groups with leaders through whom they could rule indirectly, and they were inclined to create such structures if they did not exist. Certainly there are some 'groups' who only attained full identity and unity after the arrival of Europeans. Putting this debate to one side, the term 'tribe' is used frequently and the people of Tanzania have been classified into such groups.

The 129 different tribal groups that have been distinguished in Tanzania vary from groups of over 1 million people to tribes of just a few hundred. It is obviously impractical to look at all these groups here so only the most important are examined. The largest ethnic groups are the Sukuma and the Nyamwezi, and although no group makes up more than 15% of the population, about a dozen of the largest groups make up about 50% of the population. Most of these are of Bantu origin (see page 352), although there are some Nilotic groups as well, and about 95% of the population is Bantu-speaking. The most important Bantu language is Swahili, a language which is the mother tongue of the people of Zanzibar and Pemba as well as some coastal people. Swahili became a *lingua franca* before the colonial period in some areas and this was encouraged by both the Germans and the British. It is very widely spoken and in 1963 it became Tanzania's national language.

Sukuma

This is Tanzania's largest ethnic group and makes up between 10 and 13% of the population. The name means 'people of the north' and the group lives just to the south of Lake Victoria. The ethnic consciousness of this group is fairly recent and is not entirely pervasive. In the pre-colonial period they were organized into a large number of small chiefdoms. They practise mixed agriculture, with both cattle-herding and cultivation. This is also an important cotton growing area.

Nyamwezi

The Nyamwezi people are found to the south of the Sukuma people in north Tanzania and in many ways are similar to them. Like the Sukuma they were formerly made up of a large number of very small chiefdoms. Some of these chiefs tried later to dominate wider areas. Their identity is fairly recent and rather fragile. They are primarily a cultivating people and have established a reputation as traders.

Makonde

These people are located in the southeast part of the country and are fairly isolated on the Makonde Plateau. Although they are one of the five largest groups the Makonde have been little affected by colonial and post-colonial developments. They are renowned for being a conservative people who are determined to defend their way of life. This is facilitated by the difficulty in reaching this part of Tanzania. Even today communications with the southeast are poor, particularly during the wet season. The Makonde are perhaps most famous for their beautifully crafted woodcarvings that are sold all over Tanzania. Makonde people are also found in Mozambique.

Chagga

The Chagga (or Chaga) are found around the south slopes of Mount Kilimanjaro and constitute the third largest group in Tanzania. They are greatly advantaged by living in a fertile and well-watered region, which is ideally suited to the production of coffee. They were also one of the first groups to be affected by the Christian missionaries, in particular the Roman Catholics and Lutherans, and this meant that the initial provision of education in the area was ahead of many other areas. The high level of education and opportunity of cash-cropping have resulted in a comparatively high level of income, and also a relatively high level of involvement in community activity. One example of the form that this has taken is through cooperative action in the production and marketing of coffee.

The Chagga believed that the god they called Ruwa was greater than all the other gods that they worshipped. They believed all men had their origin in him and that, as he did not trouble them with petty demands, unlike some other gods, he must love men. He lived in a place in the skies that they called *nginenyi*, which means blue skies. Sacrifices would be made to Ruwa when someone was ill or when there was a famine or epidemic. Usually prayers would be said and then a goat would be slaughtered. The goat should be a male of uniform colour without any spots, and it should not have had its tail docked. Sacrifices would also be offered to the spirits of the dead. When a person dies it is believed that they live in the new world but in a different form. The spirits of the dead are able to return to the world to demand what is due to them from their relatives. It is said that their physical presence is not noticed but they appear in dreams or through the noises made by animals.

Haya

The Haya people are different from most other ethnic groups in Tanzania. They live in the far northwest of Tanzania, to the west of the shores of Lake Victoria. Culturally and linguistically they are more closely related to the interlacustrine Bantu who are found to the north and west of the Haya. Like the interlacustrine Bantu they are organized into a few centralized states. Although they have common traditions, social system, culture and language as well as territorial identity, they are divided into several chiefdoms, which suggests that in this case political unity is not an essential part of tribal identity. The Haya are cultivators, growing coffee and plantains, and live in densely populated villages. Exactly similar to the situation in Kilimanjaro region, the high altitude of west of Lake Victoria provided a pleasant climate for missionaries and the Catholics and Protestants competed for converts by providing education here, and this, combined with the production of coffee, has had a significant beneficial effect on the economy of the area.

Hehe

The Hehe people live in the central south region of Tanzania around Iringa. They have a strong sense of being Hehe, and have their own more or less distinctive social system and culture with a unifying political system. However, within this group there are differences in the way of life and social systems between those who live in the drier eastern parts of the region and those in the wetter uplands to the west. These are caused by environmental factors as well as the effects of distance. Despite this, one observer has suggested that there is a greater unity and identity among the Hehe than there is with any other group of people.

Masai

The Masai inhabit the north border area with Kenya, but are found as far south as Morogoro and Tabora. They are a spectacular group of tall, slender cattle-herders, living off milk, blood and meat. Young men leave to become *moran* before returning to begin family life. As *moran* they carry spears, wear distinctive red garments and have elaborately decorated faces, bodies and hair. The women have shaven heads and often wear many coils of beads on their necks and shoulders.

Shirazi

The Shirazi is the name given to people who are a mixture of Africans and people who are said to have come at a very early time from the Shiraz area of Iran. They are divided into three 'tribes' called the Hadimu, Tumbatu and Pemba. The Africans are descendants of mainlanders who came to the islands of Zanzibar and Pemba, often as slaves although later of their own accord. Descendants of the Shirazis have intermixed with other Swahili people and have become more African in race, speech and culture.

Swahili

This is the general term given to the coastal people who have a Muslim-orientated culture. They are the descendants of generations of mixing of slaves, migrant labourers and Afro-Arabs.

Other African groups

The **Hi** people are a very small group of click-speakers. They are hunter-gatherers and live on the southwest shores of Lake Eyasi, in the central north part of Tanzania. Other click speakers found in Tanzania include the **Hadzabe** and the **Sandawe**. The Hadzabe live in the same area as the Hi and the groups are believed to be closely related. The Sandawe live in the interior central region of Tanzania to the north of Dodoma. The **Dorobo** are a small group of hunter-gatherers who are found throughout Masailand and also in Kenya.

Non-Africans

This group makes up under 1% of the population of Tanzania and comprises Europeans, Asians and Arabs.

Social development

In 2005 adult literacy was estimated at around 78%. Education in Tanzania was significantly improved when in 2000 the number of primary schools rose from 11,100 to 11,654, school fees were abolished for one year to encourage enrolment, which rose from 67% to 77%. Secondary education, however, has been very low priority and, with only 7% of students enrolling, is well below the African average of 14%. Though again like the primary schools, since 2000 the number of secondary schools in the country has increased significantly from 595 to 927. Tertiary education enrolment rates are less than 1%, slightly lower than Kenya, though again reforms in 2000 increased the number of accredited universities from 4 to 19.

Life expectancy, at 45 years, is about the African average, and provision of medical care, indicated by numbers of doctors per head, is slightly better than the average elsewhere on the continent. However, infant mortality rates are high, and are a reflection of the concentration of medical services in the urban areas and comparative neglect of the majority of the population in the countryside.

Despite being a fertile country with unused agricultural land, nutrition levels leave something to be desired with average daily calorie supply about 10% below the recommended daily minimum.

A big effort has been made to improve the status of women in recent years, and enrolment levels for females are only slightly below the rate for males at the primary level. However, at the secondary level, 25% fewer women are enrolled. Low income levels lead to many women needing to work outside the home (mostly on the family farm), and 87% are so engaged, compared to 60% in the rest of Africa. The burden of home-care and work are compounded by high fertility rates of close to six children per female. Only 10% of women are using contraceptives, and this rate of uptake is about half the African average.

Land and environment

Geography

Tanzania is a large coastal country (approximately 945,000 sq km) which lies just below the Equator and includes the islands of Pemba and Zanzibar between 1° S and 11° S latitude and 30° to 40° E longitude. It is bounded by Kenya and Uganda to the north, Rwanda, Burundi and DR Congo to the west, Zambia, Malawi and Mozambique to the south. Temperatures range from tropical to temperate moderated by altitude. Most of the country consists of high plateaux but there is a wide variety of terrain including mangrove swamps, coral reefs, plains, low hill ranges, uplands, volcanic peaks and high mountains, as well as depressions such as the Rift Valley and lakes. Dar es Salaam is the main port and there are hydro-electric schemes on the Rufiji and Pangani rivers. Mineral deposits include diamonds, gold, gemstones (tanzanite, ruby, emerald, green garnet, sapphire), graphite, gypsum, kaolin and tin.

Climate

There is a long dry season, June to October, followed by short rains in November and December. January to March can be very hot, and are followed by heavy rains in April and May. The timing of the rains has been less regular in recent years and the volume also varies from year to year, and from region to region. Short rains have tended to spread from November to May with a drier spell in January and February. In northeast Tanzania, the long rains are in March to June. A quarter of the country receives an annual average of 750 mm of rain, but in some areas it can be as high as 1,250 mm.

The central area of the country is dry with less than 500 mm per annum. In many areas two harvests can be grown each year.

Environmental problems

Tanzania has a large area of forest, about 35% of its total land area. However, a fast-expanding population has led to demands for more agricultural land. Poor provision of electricity, and inadequate income levels to allow purchase of bottled gas have led to a high demand for wood fuel. As a result the forest area has been declining at 1% a year, significantly higher than the African average.

In general there is adequate rainfall in Tanzania, although uneven distribution can lead to pockets of drought. Domestic usage per head is very low, and commercial usages are modest, and there is little strain on overall water availability, with only 0.6% of annual renewable freshwater supplies being utilized.

Wildlife

Mammals

Practically everyone travelling around East Africa will come into contact with animals during their stay. Of course there is much more than the big game to see and you will undoubtedly travel through different habitats from the coast to the tropical rain forests but the mammals are on the top of most people's 'to see' lists. » *See African Wildlife colour section in the middle of the guide.*

Big Nine The 'big five' **Elephant** (*Loxodonta africana*), **Lion** (*Panthera leo*), **Black Rhino** (*Diceros bicornis*), **Buffalo** (*Syncerus caffer*) and **Leopard** (*Panthera pardus*), was the term originally coined by hunters who wanted trophies from their safaris, but nowadays the **Hippopotamus** (*Hippopotamus amphibius*) is usually considered one of the Big Five for those who shoot with their cameras, whereas the Buffalo is far less of a "trophy". Equally photogenic and worthy to be included are: **Zebra**, **Giraffe** and **Cheetah** (*Acinonyx jubatus*). The Table 1 shows the major game areas where you might expect to see these larger and more spectacular animals, known here as the 'Big Nine'. Whether they are the Big Five or the Big Nine these are the animals that most people come to Africa to see, and, with the possible exception of the Leopard, you have an excellent chance of seeing all of them.

They are all unmistakable and when seeing them for the first time in the wild you will find that they are amazingly familiar and recognizable. The only two that could possibly be confused are the Leopard and the Cheetah. The **Leopard** is less likely to be seen as it is more nocturnal and more secretive in its habits than the Cheetah. It frequently rests during the heat of the day on the lower branches of trees, and, as you drive round the parks, your best bet is to look for the animal's tail, which hangs down below the branches, and can be quite easily spotted while the rest of the animal remains well concealed. If you are lucky you will see one with its kill, which it may have hauled up into the lower branches (see African Wildlife colour section, page ii).

Cheetahs are often seen in family groups walking across the plains or resting in the shade. They are slimmer and longer legged than Leopards, with a characteristic sway back. The black "tear" mark on the face is usually obvious through binoculars. (If all else fails you can identify Cheetahs by the accompanying mini buses.)

Lions (*Panthera leo*), usually found in open savanna in Africa, are, after tigers, the second largest carnivorous members of the cat family. They live in prides or permanent family groups, numbering up to around 30 animals, and are the only felid to do so. The prides are usually composed of a group of inter-related females and their cubs, led by a dominant male, or occasionally, a group of males. There is no dominant lioness. They communicate with one another with a range of sounds that vary from roaring, grunting

Tanzania The big nine	Lion	Leopard	Cheetah	Elephant	Buffalo	Black rhino	Zebra	Giraffe	Hippo
Arusha		●		●	●		●	●	●
Katavi	●	●		●	●		●		●
Kilimanjaro		●		●	●				
Lake Manyara	●	●		●	●		●	●	●
Mikumi/Selous	●	●	●	●	●		●	●	●
Ngorongoro Crater	●	●	●	●	●	●	●	●	
Ruaha/Rungwa	●	●	●	●	●		●	●	●
Serengeti	●	●	●	●	●		●	●	●
Tarangire	●	●	●	●	●		●	●	

and growling to meowing. Roars, more common at night, can reach sound levels of over 110 decibels and be heard from distances of up to 8 km. The females do most of the hunting (usually ungulates like zebra and antelopes), while the males are mostly involved in protecting their pride from other lions and predators. Lions are very sociable except when eating, when aggressive fighting can break out. Although the females kill most of the prey the males are first to feed, followed by the lionesses, the cubs just getting the leftovers. (The main cause of cub death is starvation.) Lions augment their diet by scavenging prey killed by other predators.

Elephants are awe-inspiring and it is wonderful to watch a herd at a waterhole. Although they have suffered terribly from the activities of poachers in recent decades they are still readily seen in many of the game areas.

The other animals which have suffered badly in recent times are the two Rhinos. The **White Rhino** (*Diceros simus*) is now probably extinct in much of its former range in eastern Africa though it flourishes in the southern part of the continent. The **Black Rhino** has also diminished in number in recent years. The two rhinos may be distinguished by the shape of their mouth. The White Rhino has a square muzzle, whereas the Black has a long upper lip (the difference is in fact quite easy to see). Their names have no bearing on the colour of the animals as they are both a rather nondescript dark grey. In some guide books the White Rhino is described as being paler in colour than the Black Rhino, but this by no means obvious in the field. The name White Rhino is derived from the Dutch word "weit" which means wide and refers to the shape of the animal's mouth. The Black Rhino on the other hand is a browser, that is to say it feeds usually on shrubs and bushes. It achieves this by using its long, prehensile upper lip which is well adapted to the purpose. If you see rhino with their young you will notice that the White Rhino tends to herd its young in front of it, whereas the Black Rhino usually leads its young from the front.

The **Buffalo**, considered by hunters to be the most dangerous of the big game, can be seen everywhere, sometimes in substantial herds in many areas. Beware: these animals, cut off from the herd, can become bad-tempered and easily provoked.

The **Hippo** is another animal which appears harmless, even comic (from a safe vantage point). During the day it rests in the water and you can get excellent views and interesting photographs, particularly if there are displaying males active in the area. These Hippos will "yawn" at each other and two animals will sometimes spar. At night the Hippo leaves the water and ranges very far afield to graze (a single adult animal needs up to 60 kg of grass every day). Should you meet a Hippo on land by day or night keep well away. If you get between it and its escape route to the water, it may well attack. (These animals are now considered as dangerous as buffalos, once thought to be the most dangersous of all the big mammals.)

In many ways the most stunning of the Big Nine is the **Giraffe**. It may not be as magnificent as a full-grown Lion, nor as awe-inspiring as an Elephant, but its elegance is unsurpassed. To see a small party of Giraffe galloping across the plains is seeing Africa as it has been for hundreds of years. Although the Giraffe itself is unmistakable and easily identified, there are in fact several sub-species which differ from each other. (Authorities, though, are not always agreed on the exact division into species and races, as there seems to be much overlap of the types.) Extending from about the Tana River northwards and eastwards into Somalia and Ethiopia is the almost chestnut coloured **Reticulated Giraffe** (*Giraffa reticulata*) which is sometimes considered a separate species. This is the most handsome of the various forms, its reddish brown coat being broken up by a network of pale, narrow lines, like the outlines of crazy paving stones. Found further south than the Reticulated Giraffe the **Common Giraffe** (*Giraffa camelopardalis*) which has two forms, or races: one is the **Masai Giraffe** which occurs in southwest Kenya and Tanzania. This has a yellowish-buff coat with the characteristic patchwork of brownish markings with very jagged edges. In most animals there are only two horns, though occasionally animals are seen with three horns. The other form of the Common Giraffe is known as **Rothschild's Giraffe** and accurs west and north of the Masai Giraffe and into Uganda as far west as the Nile. It is usually rather paler and heavier looking than the Masai Giraffe and can have as many as five horns, though more commonly three. Both male and female animals have horns, though in the female they may be smaller. The lolloping gait is very distinctive and it produces this effect by the way it moves its legs at the gallop. A horse will move its fore and hind legs diagonally when galloping, but the giraffe moves both hind legs together and both fore legs together. It achieves this by swinging both hind legs forward and outside the fore legs. It is not a dumb and voiceless animal as many believe but can produce a low groaning noise and a variety of snorts.

The **Zebra** forms herds, often large ones, sometimes with antelope. As with giraffe, there is more than one sort of zebra in eastern Africa, and, again, the relationship between the types is complex, but they can be considered as two main types: **Grevy's Zebra** (*Equus grevyi*) and the **Common** or **Burchell's Zebra** (*Equus burchelli*). Grevy's is the larger of the two and has much narrower white stripes which are arranged in such a way as to meet in a sort of star-shaped arrangement at the top of the hind leg. Burchell's, on the other hand, has broad stripes which cross the top of the hind leg in unbroken oblique lines. The ranges of the two animals overlap to a certain extent and they can be seen in mixed herds in some northern areas. Generally though, Grevy's Zebra prefers the more arid areas and seems less dependent on water, and occurs mainly north of the equator, whereas Burchell's ranges to the south.

Larger antelope The first animals that you will see on safari will almost certainly be antelope. These are by far the most numerous group to be seen on the plains. Although there are many different species, it is not difficult to distinguish between them. For identification purposes they can be divided into the larger ones which stand at 48 in (about 120 cm) or more at the shoulder, and the smaller ones at 36 in (about 90cm) or less.

For the record, it is worth pointing out here that antelope are not 'deer', which do not occur in Africa, except in parts of the very north, but you will undoubtedly hear many people refer to them as such. There are many differences between the two groups. For example, deer have antlers, which are solid, boney, branching outgrowths from the skull and which are shed annually. Antelope, on the other hand, have horns, which are hollow, unbranched sheaths made of modified skin, rather like finger and toe nails. They are not shed seasonally and if a horn is lost it is not replaced.

The largest of all is the **Eland** (*Taurotragus oryx*) which stands 175-183 cm (69-72 in) at the shoulder. It is very cattle-like in appearance, with a noticeable dewlap and shortish spiral horns, present in both sexes. The general colour varies from greyish to fawn, sometimes with a rufous tinge, with narrow white stripes on the sides of the body. It occurs, usually in small herds, in a wide variety of grassy habitats.

Not quite as big, but still reaching 140-153 cm (55-60 in) at the shoulder, is the **Greater Kudu** (*Tragelaphus strepsiceros*) which prefers fairly thick bush, sometimes in quite dry areas. Although nearly as tall as the Eland it is a much more slender and elegant animal altogether. Its general colour also varies from greyish to fawn and it has several white stripes running down the sides of the body. Only the male carries horns, which are very long and spreading, with only two or three twists along the length of the horn. A noticeable and distinctive feature is a thick fringe of hair which runs from the chin down the neck. Greater Kudu usually live in family groups of not more than half a dozen individuals, but occasionally larger herds of up to about 30 can be seen. Its smaller relative, the **Lesser Kudu** (*Strepsiceros imberis*), looks quite similar, with similar horns, but stands only 99-102 cm (39-40 in) high. It lacks the throat fringe of the bigger animal, but has two conspicuous white patches on the underside of the neck. It inhabits dense scrub and acacia thickets in semi-arid country, usually in pairs, sometimes with their young.

The **Roan Antelolope** (*Hippoptragus equinus*) and **Sable Antelope** (*Hippotragus niger*) are similar in general shape, though the Roan is somewhat bigger, being 140-145 cm (55-57 in) at the shoulder, compared to the 127-137 cm (50-54 in) of the Sable. In both species, both sexes carry ringed horns which curve backwards, and these are particularly long in the Sable. There is a horse-like mane present in both animals. The Sable is usually glossy black with white markings on the face and a white belly (the female is often a reddish brown in colour). The Roan can vary from dark rufous to a reddish fawn and also has white markings on the face. The black males of the Sable are easily identified, but the brownish individuals can be mistaken for the Roan. Look for the tufts of hair at the tips of the rather long ears of the Roan (absent in the Sable). The Sable is found in well wooded areas. The Roan generally is more widespread and is found in open grassland. Both the Roan and the Sable live in herds.

Another large antelope with a black and white face is the **Oryx** (*Oryx beisa*). This occurs in two distinct races, the **Beisa Oryx** which is found north and west of the Tana River, and the **Fringe-eared Oryx** which occurs south and east of this river. Both these animals stand 122 cm (48 in) at the shoulder and vary in colour from greyish (most Beisa Oryx) to sandy (most Fringe-eared Oryx), with a black line down the spine and a black stripe between the coloured body and the white underparts, rather like that on found on the much smaller Thomson's Gazelle. They both also have very long straight (not curving) horns, present in both sexes, and which make identification of this animal quite easy. The two races may be distinguished by the long dark fringe of hair on the tips of the ears in the Fringe-eared Oryx, absent in the Beisa Oryx. The Beisa Oryx is found in herds in arid and semi desert country and the Fringe-eared Oryx, also in herds, in similar habitat, but also sometimes in less dry habitats.

The two **Waterbuck** are very similar, both being about 122-137 cm (48-54 in) at the shoulder, with shaggy grey-brown coats which are very distinctive. The males have long gently curving horns which are heavily ringed. The two species can be distinguished by the white mark on the buttocks. In the **Common Waterbuck** (*Kobus ellipsiprymnus*) this forms a clear half ring on the rump and round the tail, whereas in the **Defassa Waterbuck** (*Kobus defassa*) this ring is filled in, forming a white patch. Both animals occur in small herds, in grassy areas, often near water. Solitary animals are also often seen. They are fairly common and widespread.

The **Wildebeest** or **Gnu** (*Connochaetes taurinus*) is well-known to many people from published photographs of the spectacular annual migration through Serengeti National Park. It is a big animal about 132 cm (52 in) high at the shoulder, looking rather like an American bison from a distance, especially when you see the huge herds straggling across the plains. The impression is strengthened by its buffalo-like horns (in both sexes) and humped appearance. The general colour is greyish with a few darker stripes down the side. It has a noticeable beard and long mane.

The four remaining large antelope are fairly similar, but, as there is not a lot of overlap in their ranges, it is not too difficult to identify them. Three of these four are **Hartebeest** of various sorts and the fourth is called the **Topi**. All four antelope have long, narrow horse-like faces and rather comical expressions. The shoulders are much higher than the rump giving them a very sloped back appearance, especially in the three hartebeest. Again all four have short, curved horns, carried by both sexes. In the three hartebeest the horns arise from a boney protuberance on the top of the head and curve outwards as well as backwards. One of the hartebeests, **Jackson's Hartebeest** (*Alcelaphus buselaphus*) (about 132 cm, 52 in) is similar in colour to the **Topi** (*Damaliscus korrigum*) (about 122-127 cm , 48-50 in) being a very rich dark rufous in colour. But the Topi has dark patches on the tops of the legs, a coat with a rich satiny sheen to it, and more ordinary looking lyre-shaped horns. Of the other two hartebeest, **Coke's Hartebeest** (*Alcephalus buselaphus*) (about 122 cm, 48 in), also called the **Kongoni**, is usually considered to be a race of Jackson's Hartebeest, but is a very different colour being a more drab pale brown with a paler rump. Finally **Lichtenstein's Hartebeest** (*Alcephalus lichtensteinii*) (about 127-132 cm, 50-52 in) is also fawn in general colouration, but usually has a rufous wash over the back. Also look out for dark marks on the front of the legs, and often, a dark patch on the side near the shoulder. All four of these antelope are found in herds, in the case of Topi quite large herds. Sometimes they mix with other plain dwellers such as zebra. The hartebeest has the habit of posting sentinels, solitary animals who stand on the top of anthills keeping a watch out for predators.

Smaller antelope The remaining common antelopes are a good deal smaller than those described above. The largest is the **Impala** (*Aepyceros melampus*) which is 92-107 cm (36-42 in) at the shoulder and a bright rufous in colour with a white abdomen. From behind, the white rump, with black lines on each side, is characteristic. Only the male carries the long, lyre shaped horns. Just above the heels of the hind legs is a tuft of thick black bristles, unique to the Impala, which are surprisingly easy to see as the animal runs. Also easy to see is the black mark on the side of abdomen, just infront of the back leg.

The **Uganda Kob** (*Adenota kob*), which is about 92 cm (36 in) at the shoulder, is superficially rather like the Impala as it is also usually a bright rufous colour. It may be distinguished by the white ring around the eyes and white mark on the throat, and the black marks on the front of the fore legs. Only the males carry horns, which are beautifully proportioned and lyre-shaped. Both Kob and Impala live in herds in grassy areas, but occasionally you may see solitary males. The Uganda Kob is most likely to be seen in western Uganda, whereas the Impala is most common in Kenya and Tanzania.

Two slightly smaller antelope are **Grant's Gazelle** (*Gazella granti*), about 81-99 cm (32-35 in) at the shoulder, and **Thomson's Gazelle** (*Gazella thomsonii*), about 64-69 cm (25-27 in) at the shoulder. They are superficially similar. Grant's, the larger of the two and has longer horns, but this is only a good means of identification when the two animals are seen together. The general colour of both varies from a bright rufous to a sandy rufous. In both species the curved horns are carried by both sexes. Thomson's Gazelle can usually be distinguished from Grant's by the broad black band along the side between the rufous upper parts and white abdomen, but not invariably, as some forms of Grant's also have this dark lateral stripe. If in doubt, look for the white area on the buttocks which extends above the tail on to the rump in Grant's, but does not extend above the tail in Thomson's. This is the surest way to distinguish them. The underparts are white. Thomson's Gazelle or "Tommies", are among the most numerous animals that inhabit the plains of Kenya and Tanzania. You will see large herds of them often in association with other game. Grant's Gazelle, occurs on rather dry grass plains, in various forms.

The **Bohor Reedbuck** (*Redunca redunca*) and the **Oribi** (*Ourebia ourebi*) are not really very similar, but they do both have a curious and conspicuous patch of bare skin just below each ear. The horns (carried only by males) are quite different being sharply hooked forwards at the tip in the Bohor Reedbuck, but straight in the Oribi and this is enough to distinguish them. There is a slight difference in size, the Bohor Reedbuck being about 71-76 cm (28-30 in) at the shoulder and the Oribi only about 61 cm (24 in). The Oribi is more slender and delicate looking than the Bohor Reedbuck, with a proportionally longer neck. Both animals are a reddish fawn, but the Oribi tends to be duller or more sandy in appearance. Both Oribi and Bohor Reedbuck are usually seen in pairs in bushed grassland, never far from water.

The last two of the common smaller antelopes are the **Bushbuck** (*Tragelaphus scriptus*) which is about 76-92 cm (30-36 in) at the shoulder, and the tiny **Kirk's Dikdik** (*Rhynchotragus kirkii*) only 36-41 cm (14-16 in). Both are easily identified. The Bushbuck's colour varies from chestnut (probably the most common) to a darkish brown. The coat has a shaggy appearance and a variable pattern of white spots and stripes on the side and back. There are, in addition, two white crescent shaped marks on the front of the neck. The horns, present in the male only, are short, almost straight and slightly spiralled. The animal has a curious high rump which gives it a characteristic crouching appearance. The white underside of the tail is noticeable when it is running. The Bushbuck tends to occur in areas of thick bush especially near water. They lie up during the day in thickets, but are often seen bounding away when disturbed. They are usually seen either in pairs or singly. Kirk's Dikdik is so small it can hardly be mistaken for any other antelope. In colour it is a greyish brown, often washed with rufous. The legs are noticeably thin and stick-like, giving the animal a very fragile appearance. The snout is slightly elongated, and there is a conspicuous tuft of hair on the top of the head. Only the male carries the very small straight horns.

Other mammals Although the antelope are undoubtedly the most numerous animals to be seen on the plains, there are others worth keeping an eye open for. Some of these are scavengers which thrive on the kills of other animals. They include the dog-like Jackals, of which there are three main species, all being similar in size, (about 86-96 cm, 34-38 in, in length and 41-46 cm, 16-18 in at the shoulder). The **Black-backed Jackal** (*Canis mesomelas*) , which is the most common and ranges throughout the area, is a rather foxy reddish fawn in colour with a noticeable black area on its back. This black part is sprinkled with a silvery white which can make the back look silver in some lights. In general colour the **Side-striped Jackal** (*Canis adustus*) is greyish fawn and it has a variable and sometimes ill-defined stripe along the side. It is most likely to be seen around Lake Victoria and in Tanzania.

The other well known plains scavenger is the **Spotted Hyaena** (*Crocuta crocuta*). It is a fairly large animal, being about 69-91 cm (32-36 in) at the shoulder. Its high shoulders and low back give it a characteristic appearance. It is brownish with dark spots and has a large head. It usually occurs singly or in pairs, but occasionally in small packs.

A favourite and common plains animal is the comical **Warthog** (*Phacochoerus aethiopicus*). This is unmistakeable being almost hairless and grey in general colour with a very large head with tusks and wart-like growths on the face. They are often seen in family parties. The adults will run at speed with their tails held straight up in the air, and followed by the young.

In suitable rocky areas, such as *kopjes*, look out for an animal that looks a bit like a large grey-brown guinea pig. This is the **Rock Hyrax** (*Heterohyrax brucei*), an engaging and fairly common animal that lives in communities in rocky places.

The most common and frequently seen of the monkey group are the Baboons. The most widespread species is the **Olive Baboon** (*Papio anubis*), which occurs almost throughout the area. This is a large (127-142 cm, 50-56 in), heavily built animal olive brown or greyish in colour. Adult males have a well-developed mane. In the eastern part of Kenya and Tanzania, including the coast, the Olive Baboon is replaced by the **Yellow Baboon** (*Papio cynocephalus*) (116-137 cm, 46-54 in) which is a smaller and lighter animal than the Olive Baboon, with longer legs and almost no mane in the adult males. The tail in both species looks as if it is broken and hangs down in a loop. Baboons are basically terrestrial animals, although they can climb very well. In the wild they are often found in acacia grassland, often associated with rocks, and are sociable animals living in groups called troops. Females are very often seen with young clinging to them. In parts of East Africa they have become very used to the presence of man and can be a nuisance to campers. They will readily climb all over your vehicle hoping for a handout. Be careful, they have a very nasty bite.

The smaller monkey that makes a nuisance of itself is the **Vervet or Green Monkey** (*Cercopithicus mitis*), which is the one that abounds at camp sites and often lodges. This has various forms, the commonest and most widespread having a black face framed with white across the forehead and cheeks. Its general colour is greyish tinged with a varying amount of yellow. The feet, hands and tip of the tail are black.

Chimpanzees (*Pan troglodytes*) are not animals you will see casually in passing, you have to go and look for them. They occur only in the forests in the west of Tanzania.

At dusk in Africa you'll notice many bats appearing. The most spectacular of them is the **Straw-coloured Fruit Bat** (*Eidolon helvum*) which has a wing span of 76 cm (30 in).

Birds

East Africa is one of the richest areas of birdlife in the world. The total number of species is in excess of 1300, and it is possible, and not too difficult to see 100 different species in a day. You will find that a pair of binoculars is really essential, and even a simple pair will make a lot of difference. The birds described here are the common ones and, with a little careful observation, you will soon find that you can identify them. They have been grouped according to the habitat in which you are most likely to see them. Remember that birds, on the whole, are creatures of habit, with likes and dislikes about habitat. For example, you will not see a Jacana far from water, nor will the Red-cheeked Cordon-bleu venture into the forest.

Urban birds The first birds that you will notice on arrival in any big city will almost certainly be the large numbers soaring overhead. Early in the morning the numbers are few, but as the temperature warms up, more and more are seen circling high above the buildings. Many of these will be **Hooded Vultures** (*Neophron monachus*) 66 cm, 26 in and **Black Kites** (*Milvus migrans*) 55 cm, 22 in. They are both rather nondescript brownish birds which are superficially similar. They are, however, easily distinguished by the shape and length of the tail. The tail of the Hooded Vulture is short and slightly rounded at the end, whereas the Black Kite (which incidently is not black, but brown) has a long, narrow tail which looks either forked when the tail is closed or slightly concave at the end when spread. The end of the tail never looks rounded. In flight the Kite looks very buoyant and uses its tail a lot, twisting it from side to side. Also soaring overhead in some cities (notably Kampala) you will see the **Marabou Stork** (*Leptoptilos crumeniferus*) 152 cm, 60 in. Although this bird is a stork it behaves like a vulture, in that it lives by scavenging. Overhead its large size, long and noticeable bill and trailing legs make it easily identified. The commonest crow in towns and cities is the **Pied Crow** (*Corvus albus*) 46 cm, 18 in. This is a very handsome black bird with a white lower breast which joins up with a white collar round the back of the neck. In towns along the coast you will see another member of the crow family the **Indian House Crow** (*Corvus splendens*) 38 cm, 15 in. This is not indigenous to Africa, but was introduced and is spreading along the coast. It is a slender, shiny black bird with a grey neck. In gardens and parks there are a number of smaller birds to look out for. The **Dark-capped or Common Bulbul** (*Pycnonotus barbatus*) 18 cm, 7 in, can be heard all day with its cheerful call of "Come quick, doctor, quick". It is a brownish bird with a darker brown head and a slight crest. Below, the brown is paler fading to white on the belly, and under the tail it is bright yellow.

There are a large number of Weaver birds to be seen, but identifying them is not always easy. Most of them are yellow and black in colour, and many of them live in large noisy colonies. Have a close look at their intricately-woven nests if you get the chance. The commonest one is probably the **Black-headed Weaver** (*Ploceus cucullatus*) 18 cm, 7 in, which often builds its colonies in bamboo clumps. The male has a mainly black head and throat, but the back of the head is chestnut. The underparts are bright yellow, and the back and wings mottled black and greenish yellow. When the bird is perched, and seen from behind, the markings on the back form a V-shape.

Also in parks and gardens, and especially among flowers, you will see members of another large and confusing bird family: the Sunbirds. The thickset and sturdy looking **Scarlet-chested Sunbird** (*Nectarinia senegalensis*) 15 cm, 6 in often perches on overhead wires allowing you to get a good look at it. The male is a dark velvety brown colour with a scarlet chest. The top of the head and the throat are an iridescent green. The tail is short. There are two common thrushes often seen in parks and gardens. They look rather similar, but they do not occur in the same areas. The **Olive Thrush** (*Turdus olivaceous*) 23 cm, 9 in is the common thrush of the highlands, where it is often seen in gardens. The very similar garden thrush of lower areas, especially in Uganda, is the **African Thrush** (*Turdus pelios*) 23 cm, 9 in. Both birds are basically brown, but the Olive Thrush is a much richer looking bird with a rufous belly and a bright orange bill. The African Thrush has a wash of rufous on the side and is duller looking altogether.

Birds of open plains Along with the spectacular game, it is here that you will see many of the magnificent African birds. In particular, there are two large birds which you will see stalking across the grasslands. These are the **Ostrich** (*Struthio camelus*) 2 m, 7 ft and the **Secretary Bird** (*Sagittarius serpentarius*) 101 cm, 40 in. The Secretary Bird is so called because the long plumes of its crest are supposed to resemble the old time secretaries who carried their quill pens tucked behind their ears. The bird is often seen in pairs as it hunts for snakes, its main food source. The Ostrich is sometimes seen singly, but also in family groups. There are other large terrestrial birds to look out for, and one of them, the **Kori Bustard** (*Otis kori*) 80cms, 35 in, like the Secretary Bird quarters the plains looking for snakes. It is quite a different shape, however, and can be distinguished by the thick looking grey neck (caused by loose feathers). It is particularly common in Serengeti National Park and in the Masai Mara. The other large bird that you are likely to see on the open plains is the **Ground Hornbill** (*Bucorvus cafer*) 107 cm, 42 in. When seen from afar, this looks for all the world like a turkey but close up it is very distinctive and cannot really be mistaken for anything else. They are very often in pairs and the male has bare red skin around the eye and on the throat. In the female this skin is red and blue.

Soaring overhead on the plains you will see vultures and birds of prey. The commonest vulture in game areas is the **African White-backed Vulture** (*Gyps africanus*) 81 cm, 32 in. This is a largish, brown bird with a white lower back, and it has, of course, the characteristic bare head of its family. Because they are commonly seen circling overhead the white rump is sometimes difficult to see. So look out for the other diagnostic characteristic – the broad white band on the leading edge of the undersurface of the wing. The **Bateleur** (*Terathopius ecaudatus*) 61 cm, 24 in, is a magnificent and strange looking eagle. It is rarely seen perched, but is quite commonly seen soaring very high overhead. Its tail is so short that it sometimes appears tailless. This, its bouyant flight and the black and white pattern of its underparts make it easy to identify.

Where there is game look out for the Oxpeckers. The commonest one is the **Red-billed Oxpecker** (*Buphagus erythrorhynchus*) 18 cm, 7 in. These birds are actually members of the starling family although their behaviour is not like that of other starlings. They associate with game animals and cattle and spend their time clinging to, and climbing all over the animals while they hunt for ticks, which form their main food. There are other birds which associate with animals in a different way. For example the **Cattle Egret** (*Bubulcus ibis*) 51 cm, 20 in, follows herds and feeds on the grasshoppers and other insects disturbed by the passing of the animals. Occasionally too, the Cattle Egret will perch on the back of a large animal, but this is quite different from the behaviour of Oxpeckers. Cattle Egrets are long legged and long billed white birds which are most often seen in small flocks. In the breeding season they develop long buff feathers on the head, chest and back

Birds of dry, open woodland The two habitats of open plain and dry open woodland form a vast area of Africa and most of the game parks come into these categories. As well as being quintessentially African, this dry open woodland with acacia thorn trees is an extremely rewarding area for bird watching. It supports an enormous variety of species and it is relatively easy to see them.

The Guinea Fowls live in flocks and if you suprise a group on the road they will disappear into the bush in a panic, running at great speed. There is more than one sort of Guinea Fowl, but they are rather similar, being a slaty grey with white spots. The **Vulturine Guinea Fowl** (*Acryllium vulturinum*) 59 cm, 22 in, is a most handsome bird with long blue, white and black feathers covering its neck and upper body. The rather small head itself is bare, hence the bird's name. The **Helmeted Guinea Fowl** (*Numida meleagris*) 55 cm, 21 in, is rather less handsome, but with its dark slaty and white spotted plumage and the boney "helmet" on its head, it is nonetheless a striking bird.

The tops of the thorn trees are used as observation perches by a number of different species. Specially noticeable is the **Red-billed Hornbill** (*Tockus erythrorhynchus*) 45 cm, 17 in, which has blackish-brown back, with a white stripe down between the wings. The wings themselves are spotted with white. The underparts are white and the bill is long, curved and mainly red. As the bird flies into a tree the impression is of a black and white bird with a long red bill and a long tail. Another striking bird which perches on tree tops is the **White-bellied Go-away Bird** (*Corythaixoides leucogaster*) 51 cm, 20 in. This gets its strange name from its call "Go-away, go-away". It is a basically grey bird with a very upright stance. The top of the head carries a long and conspicuous crest. The belly is white and the long tail has a black tip. It is usually seen in small family parties.

The strange looking, brightly coloured bird **d'Arnaud's Barbet** (*Trachyphonus darnaudii*) 15 cm, 6 in is quite common in the dry bush country. The impression you get is of a very spotted bird, dark with pale spots above, and pale with dark spots below. It has a long dark tail which again is heavily spotted. Its call and behaviour is very distinctive. A pair will sit facing each other with their tails raised over their backs wagging them from side to side, and bob at each other in a duet. All the while they utter a four note call over and over again. "Do-do dee-dok". They look just like a pair of clockwork toys. Another brightly coloured bird is the **Lilac-breasted Roller** (*Coracias caudata*) 41 cm, 16 in, which is very easy to see as it perches on telegraph poles or wires, or on bare branches. The brilliant blue on its wings, head and underparts is very eye catching. Its throat and breast are a deep lilac and its tail has two elongated streamers. It is quite common in open bush country. Also often seen sitting on bare branches is the **Drongo** (*Dicrurus adsimilis*) 24 cm, 9 in, but this is an all black bird. It is easily identified by its forked tail, which is "fish-tailed" at the end. It is usually solitary.

There are two common birds which in the field look rather similar, although they are not related at all. These are the **White-crowned Shrike** (*Eurocephalus rueppelli*) 23 cm, 9 in, and the **White-headed Buffalo Weaver** (*Dinemellia dinemelli*) 23 cm, 9 in. They both occur in small flocks in dry acacia country and are both thickset, rather chunky birds which appear basically dark brown and white. To distinguish between them look at the rump which is red in the White-headed Buffalo Weaver, but white in the White-crowned Shrike. This is usually easy to see as they fly away from you.

There are many different species of starling to be seen in eastern Africa, and most of them are beautifully coloured. Two of the most spectacular are the **Golden- breasted Starling** (*Cosmopsarus regius*) 32cms, 13in, and the **Superb Starling** (*Spreo superbus*) 18 cm, 7 in. Both are common, but the Superb Starling is the more widespread and is seen near habitation as well as in thorn bush country. Tsavo East is probably the best place to see the Golden-breasted Starling. Look out for the long tail of the Golden-breasted Starling, and the white under tail and white breast band of the Superb Starling. Both are usually seen hopping about on the ground. Another long- tailed bird quite commonly seen in bush country is the **Long-tailed Fiscal** (*Lanius cabanisi*) 30 cm, 12 in. Unlike the Golden-breasted Starling, however, it is a black and white bird which is usually seen perched on wires or bare branches. It can be identified by its very long all-black tail and mainly black upperparts, which are grey on the lower back and rump.

Finally look out for three birds which though small are very noticeable. The **Red-cheeked Cordon-bleu** (*Uraeginthus benegalus*) 13 cm, 5 in, is a lovely little blue bird with a brown back and bright red cheek patches. They are seen in pairs or family parties, and the females and young are somewhat duller in colour than the males. They are quite tame and you often see them round the game lodges. In the less dry grasslands you can see the beautiful red and black Bishop birds. There are two species both of which are quite brilliant in their colouring. The brightest is the **Red Bishop** (*Euplectes orix*) 13 cm, 5 in, which has brown wings and tail, and noticeable scarlet feathers on its rump. The almost equally brilliant **Black-winged Bishop** (*Euplectes hordeaceus*) 14 cm, 5.5 in, may be distinguished from the Red Bishop by its black wings and tail and rather less obvious red rump. Both species occur in long grass and cultivation, often, but not invariably, near water.

Birds of more moist areas Although so much of eastern Africa consists of grass plains, to the west of the area there are moist wooded grass lands which support a very different variety of bird species. The tall and elegant **Crowned Crane** (*Balearica pavonina*) 1 m, 40 in, is quite common near Lake Victoria, though it also occurs in much of the rest of the area as well. It cannot really be mistaken for anything else when seen on the ground. In flight the legs trail behind and the neck is extended, but the head droops down from the vertical. Overhead flocks fly in loose V-shaped formation. The curious **Hamerkop** (*Scopus umbretta*) 58 cm, 23 in, is another unmistakable bird. It is a rather dull brown in colour and has a stout, moderately long bill. Its most distinctive feature is the large crest which projects straight backwards and is, rather fancifully, said to look like a hammer. It is a solitary bird usually seen on the ground near water, sometimes even roadside puddles. It nests in trees, and builds an enormous nest, which is so large and strong that it can easily support the weight of a man. Another rather dull looking ground bird which is common is the **Hadada Ibis** (*Hagedashia hagedash*) 76 cm, 30 in. This is a greyish olive bird with a long down curved bill and a green wash on the wings. It is almost invariably seen in pairs and flies off with its characteristic loud call "Ha-da-da, Ha-da-da". It is one of Africa's most familiar birds, and walks about on lawns and open spaces. The **Black-and-white Casqued Hornbill** (*Bycanistes subcylindricus*) 70 cm, 28 in, is yet another loud and conspicuous bird, but it is always seen in trees, and is particularly common in moist woodland in the west. The similar **Silvery-cheeked Hornbill** (*Bycanistes brevis*) 70 cm, 28 in, replaces it to the east, though their habitat requirements are broadly similar. Both are basically black and white birds, but the wings of the Silvery-cheeked Hornbill are wholly black, whereas the Black-and-white Casqued Hornbill has a large white patch on the black wings. Look also at the casque on top of the bill, which is carried by both species. This casque is all pale in the Silvery-cheeked, but, as its name would suggest, black and white in the other bird. The moist forests and woodlands around Lake Victoria which are the home of the Black-and-white Casqued Hornbill, are also home to the **Grey Parrot** (*Psitticus erithacus*) 30 cm, 12 in. This bird is usually seen in flocks and is best distinguished both in flight and at rest, by its bright red tail. The **Paradise Flycatcher** (*Terpsiphone viridis*) male 33 cm, 13 in, female 20 cm, 8 in, is very easily identified by its very long tail and bright chestnut plumage. The head is black and bears a crest. The tail of the female is much shorter, but otherwise the sexes are similar. It is seen in wooded areas, including gardens and is usually in pairs. (In certain parts, noteably eastern Kenya its plumage is often white, but it still has the black head. Sometimes birds are seen with partly white and partly chestnut plumage.) Another long-tailed bird is the **Speckled Mousebird** (*Colius striatus*) 36 cm, 14 in. They are usually seen in small flocks and follow each other from bush to bush. The mainly brown plumage has a speckled appearance and the tail is long and graduated. It has a red rather parrot-shaped bill and a crest.

Water and waterside birds The inland waters of Africa form a very important habitat for both resident and migratory species. A lot can be seen from the shore, but it is especially fruitful to go out in a boat, when you will get quite close to, among others, the large and magnificent herons which occur here. The king of them all is the aptly named **Goliath Heron** (*Ardea goliath*) 144 cm, 58 in, which is usually seen singly on mud banks and shores, both inland and on the coast. Its very large size is enough to distinguish it, but the smaller **Purple Heron** (*Ardea purpurea*) 80 cm, 34 in, which frequents similar habitat and is also widespread, may be mistaken for it at a distance. If in doubt, the colour on the top of the head (rufous in the Goliath and black in the Purple) will clinch it, also the Purple is much more slender with a slender bill.

The Flamingos are known to most people and will be readily identified. However, there are two different species which very often occur together. The **Greater Flamingo** (*Phoenicopterus ruber*) 142 cm, 56 in, is the larger and paler bird and has a pink bill with a black tip. The **Lesser Flamingo** (*Phoenicopterus minor*) 101 cm, 40 in, is deeper pink all over and has a deep carmine bill with a black tip. They both occur in large numbers in the soda lakes of western Kenya, but are also seen in several lakes in Tanzania. The magnificent **Fish Eagle** (*Haliaeetus vocifer*) 76 cm, 30 in, has a very distinctive colour pattern. It often perches on the tops of trees, where its dazzling white head and chest are easily seen. In flight this white and the white tail contrast with the black wings. It has a wild yelping call which is usually uttered in flight. Try and watch the bird as it calls: it throws back its head over its back in a most unusual way.

There are several different kingfishers to be seen, but the most numerous is the black and white **Pied Kingkisher** (*Ceryle rudis*) 25 cm, 10 in. This is easily recognized as it is the only black and white kingfisher. It is common all round the large lakes and also turns up at quite small bodies of water. It hovers over the water before plunging in to capture its prey.

In quiet backwaters with lily pads and other floating vegetation you will see the **African Jacana** (*Actophilornis africana*) 25 cm, 10 in. This is a mainly chestnut bird almost invariably seen walking on floating leaves. Its toes are greatly elongated to allow it to do this. When flying away from you the legs dangle right down distinctively. Do not confuse this with the **Black Crake** (*Limnocorax flavirostra*) 20 cm, 8 in, which also frequents the quieter backwaters. This is an all slatey black bird with bright pink legs. It is rather shy and disappears into the vegetation at your approach. But if you wait quietly it will reappear.

Marine wildlife

To most visitors the East African beaches mean the reef. The fish and coral here are indeed wonderful, and can be observed without having to dive to see them. Many of the fish do not have universally recognized English names, but one that does is the very common **scorpion** or **lion fish** (*Pterois*), which is probably the most spectacular fish you can see without going out in a boat. It is likely to be wherever there is live coral, and sometimes it gets trapped in the deeper pools of the dead reef by the retreating tide. It can be up to 26 cm long and is easily recognized by its peculiar fins and zebra-like stripes. Although it has poisonous dorsal spines it will not attack if left alone.

While most visitors naturally want to spend time diving and snorkelling on the live reef and watching the brilliant fish and many coloured living corals, do not bypass the smaller, humbler creatures which frequent dead as well as living coral. These can be seen on most of the beaches, but one of the best places is Tiwi beach by Twiga Lodge in Kenya. Here a vast area of dead coral is partly exposed at low tide and you can safely paddle. Be sure to wear shoes though, because there are many sea urchins. These **sea urchins** (*Echinoidea*) are usually found further out towards the edge of the reef, but can be found anywhere. There are two forms, the more common **short-needled sea urchin** and the much less common **long-needled** variety. Their spines are very sharp and treading on them is extremely painful. Look out also for the common **brittle stars** (*Ophiuroidea*) which frequent sandy hollows. They vary considerably in size, but are usually 10 cm across. They are so called because the arms break off very readily, but they will grow again. These are not sea urchins, though they are related, and can safely be picked up for a closer look, but handle them carefully.

Other living creatures which can be seen crawling along in the shallows include the **sea slug** (*Nudibranchia*) and the **snake eel** (*Ophichthidae*). Both are quite common in sandy places. The unlovely sea slug is blackish brown and shaped a bit like the familiar garden slug, though much bigger. It often has grains of sand sticking to it. Don't be put off by the name of the snake eel, it is quite harmless. It looks a bit like a snake and has alternating light and dark bands on its body. What are beautiful, without doubt, are the **starfish** (*Asteroidea*) which are best seen by going out in a boat, but some can be seen nearer in shore.

The commonest shells are without doubt the **cowries**. Many dead ones can be found on the beach. The two most common are the **ringed cowrie** (*Cypraea annulus*) and the **money cowrie** (*Cypraea moneta*). Of these the ringed is especially plentiful and is a pretty grey and white shell with a golden ring. The money cowrie, once used as currency in Africa, varies in colour from greenish grey to pink according to its age. The big and beautiful **tiger cowrie** (*Cypraea tigris*) is also seen occasionally. This can be up to 8 cm in length. There is quite a lot of variation in colouring, but it is basically a very shiny shell with many dark round spots on, much more like a leopard than a tiger.

Freshwater fish

The king of the freshwater fish is without doubt the massive **Nile perch** (*Lates albertianus*). This huge predator lives on other fish, and originally came from the Nile below Murchison Falls, but was introduced into Lake Kyoga and the Nile above the Falls in 1955 and 1956. It has now spread to Lake Victoria itself, which has proved to be very much a mixed blessing. Weights of 20 to 40 kg are common and there are several records of over 100 kg. Also caught commonly in fresh waters is the **tilapia** (*Tilapia nilotica*), a much smaller, rather bony fish which makes good eating. Unlike the Nile perch this much smaller fish is herbivorous, and is now being farmed in fish ponds, where it is fed largely on the green leaves of the cassava plant.

Books

History

Millar, C *Battle for the Bundu*. Superbly readable account of the First World War in German East Africa.
Hibbert, C *Africa Explored: Europeans in the Dark Continent*. (Penguin, 1982). Fascinating detail on the early visitors and their motivations.
Packenham, T *The Scramble for Africa*. (Weidenfeld and Nicholson, 1991). The events that laid the foundations for the modern history of Tanzania.

Natural history

Grzimek, B *Serengeti Shall Not Die*. (Collins, 1959). Classic account of the unique character of this world-famous park.
Douglas-Hamilton, I *Among the Elephants*. (Collins, 1978). Interesting perspective on elephant conservation in Lake Manyara.
Goodall, J *In the Shadow of Man*. (Collins, 1971). Gives something of the flavour of what is involved in making a life's work of studying a particular species, in this case chimpanzees.

Field guides

Dorst, J and Dandelot, PA *Field Guide to the Larger Mammals of Africa*. (Collins, 1970).
Williams, J and Arlott, NA *Field Guide to the Birds of East Africa*. (Collins, 1980).
Larcassam, R *Hand guide to the Butterflies of East Africa*. (Collins, 1971).
Blundell, MA *Field Guide to the Wild Flowers of East Africa*. (Collins, 1987).
Hedges, NR *Reptiles and Amphibians of East Africa*. (Kenya Literature Bureau, Narobi, 1983).

Travellers' tales

Waugh, E *A Tourist in Africa*. (Chapman & Hall, 1960). A trip through Tanzania just prior to Independence.
Dahl, R *Going Solo*. (Penguin, 1986). Impressions of a young man sent out to work in the colonies.

Fiction

Boyd, W *An Ice-cream War*. (Penguin, 1982). Neatly observed, humorous and sensitive tale set against the First World War campaign in East Africa.
Boyd, W *Brazzaville Beach*. (Vintage, 1999). Although written as a West African story, it's clearly based on Jane Goodall and the chimps of Gombe Stream.

Other guides

Jafferji, J and Rees, B *Images of Zanzibar*. (HSP Publications, 1996). Superb photographs, good introduction to, and souvenir of, Zanzibar. Jafferi owns the The Gallery in Stone Town, a book and curio shop and among his many other titles are: *A Taste of Zanzibar*, a Zanzibar recipe book. *Historical Zanzibar – Romance of the Ages*, an illustrated account of Zanzibar's turbulent past with archive photographs of the slave and ivory trade. *Zanzibar Stone Town, An Architectural Exploration* (Professor Abdul Sheriff), examines the unique blend of architectural styles that make up Zanzibar's historic quarter, illustrated with sketches and colour photographs.
Spectrum *Guide to Tanzania and Pemba*. (Camerapix, Nairobi, 1992). Quite glorious photographs that serve to capture the special flavour of Tanzania and Zanzibar.

Magazines

Travel Africa Magazine, www.travelafricamag.com, makes for some inspiring and up-to-date reading if planning a trip to Tanzania or any other African country.

Footnotes

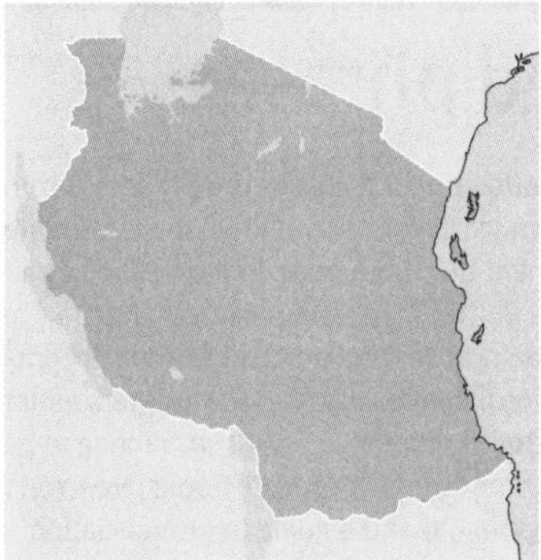

Footprint features

Swahili words and phrases

Swahili is not a difficult language but in *Shadows on the Grass* (1960) Karen Blixen called it "a primitive ungrammatical lingua franca", an observation that will infuriate Swahili scholars, particularly in Zanzibar where they take pride in the beautiful and pure form of the language spoken there. It is the main language of instruction in schools, everyone speaks it, and it is continually absorbing new words and concepts (see box). Those new to Swahili often have difficulty with the use of prefixes for plurals. Thus *mzungu* is a European, *wazungu* is Europeans. For those wanting to go further the *Swahili Dictionary* compiled by DV Perrot (Teach Yourself Books, New York: Hodder and Stoughton) contains a concise grammar and a guide to pronunciation.

Basics

Please	*Tafadhali*
Thank you	*Asante*
Good morning/ afternoon	*Habari ya asubuhi mchana/ jioni*
Good evening/ night	*Habari ya asubuhi usiku*
Sorry	*Pole*
Hello	*Jambo*
Goodbye	*Kwa heri*
Yes	*Ndio*
No	*Hapana*
Good	*Mzuri*
Bad	*Mbaya*
How much?	*Bei gani*
Where is?	*Wapi*
Why?	*Kwa nini*
Food	*Chakula*
Water	*Maji*
Room	*Chumba*
Bed	*Kitanga*
Toilet	*Choo*
One	*Moja*
Two	*Mbili*
Three	*Tata*
Four	*Nne*
Five	*Tano*
Six	*sita*
Seven	*saba*
Eight	*nane*
Nine	*tisa*
10	*Kumi*
100	*Mia*
1,000	*Elfu*
10,000	*elfu kumi*
100,000	*laki mmoja*
1,000,000	*milioni mmoja*

Useful phrases

A respectful greeting to elders, actually meaning "I hold your feet"	Shikamoo
Their reply: "I am delighted"	Marahaba
How are you?	Habari yako?
I am fine	Nzuri/Sijambo
I am not feeling good today	Sijiziki vizuri leo
How are things?	Mambo?
Good/cool/cool & crazy	Safi/poa/poa kichizi
See you later	Tutaonana baadaye
Welcome!	Karibu!
Welcome again!	Karibu tena!
Where can I get a taxi?	Teksi iko wapi?
Where is the bus station?	Stendi ya basi iko wapi?
When will we arrive?	Tutafika lini?
Can you show me the bus?	Unaweza ukanioyesha basi?
How much is the ticket?	Tiketi ni bei gani?
Is it safe walking here at night?	Ni salama kutembea hapa usiku?
I don't want to buy anything	Sitaki kununua chochote
I have already booked a safari	Tayari nimeisha lipia safari
I don't have money	Sina hela
I'm not single	Nina mchumba/siko peke yangu
Could you please leave me alone?	Tafadhali, achana na mimi
It is none of your business!	Hayakuhusu!
Chill out/relax/be cool	Poa

Swahili slang

Swahili, by origin a Bantu language, has been greatly influenced by Arabic and more recently further enriched by borrowing from other languages including English. There are several examples where are two Swahili words, each with the same meaning but with different origins. The origins of some words that have been adopted are very obvious. Modern transport has yielded, for example, *basi* (bus), *treni* (train), *stesheni* (station), *teksi* (taxi), *petroli*, *tanki*, *breki*. A rich man is *mbenzi* because he would be expected to drive a Mercedes. A traffic bollard is a *kiplefti*.

Other adoptions may not seem immediately obvious – for example, 'electricity' is sometimes called *elekrii* but more commonly *stimu* because the electricity generating stations used to be run by steam engines. In the same way the word for steamship, *meli*, derives from the fact that when the word was first used most of the ships would have carried mail. The dockyards are *kuli* because the dockyard workers were known as 'coolies'.

The Second World War also produced a number of words that were adopted into the Swahili language, many of them relating to animals: a submarine was *papa*, the word for shark, a tank was *faru*, for rhino, an aeroplane is *ndege ulaya*, which means white-man's bird.

Swahili, like all other languages, also has a large collection of slang. For example the period shortly before pay day when all the previous month's money has been spent is known as *mwambo*, which is derived from the word *wamba*, to stretch tight.

Coins have also been given a variety of nicknames. Examples include *ng'aru*, which derives from the word to shine, *ku-ngaa*. During the colonial era the shilling, which had a picture of the king's head on it, was known as *Usi wa Kinga* meaning the king's face. Five and 10 cent pieces, which used to have a hole in the centre, were nicknamed *sikio la Mkwavi* meaning 'the ear of the Mkwavi', after the Kwavi people who pierce their ear lobes and often used to hang coins from them as decoration. A slang phrase for bribery is *kuzunguka mbuyu*, which literally translated means to go behind a baobab tree, the implication being that behind such a wide tree as the baobab no one will see the transaction that takes place. The slang term for liquor is *mtindi*, which actually means skimmed milk – it was probably used to conceal what was really being drunk. A frequently-used term for drunk is *kupiga mtindi*, which translates as 'to beat up the liquor' and is used in the same way that we would use 'to go on a binge'. Someone who is drunk may be described as *amevaa miwani*, or 'wearing spectacles', suggesting that he can't see well as a result of the alcohol! A similar phrase is *yuko topu*, which translates to 'he is full right up to the top'.

Clothes have also attracted various nicknames. *Americani* was the name given to the cheap cloth imported from America during the colonial era. Drainpipe trousers were known as *suruwali ya uchinjo*, which means cut-off trousers – because being so narrow they look as if part of them is missing. Many of the names are derived from English words, such as *tai* (tie), *kala* (collar), and *soksi* (socks). The phrase used by off-duty policemen to describe their clothes also needs little explanation: *kuvaa kisivilyan*, which means 'to wear civilian clothes', while a fashionable haircut is known as *fashun*.

Many of the examples here were collected by R H Gower, a colonial administrator in Tanganyika.

Index

Footnotes Index

Map index

Advertisers' index

Credits

Footprint credits
Text editor: Sarah Thorowgood
Map editor: Sarah Sorensen
Picture editor: Claire Benison
Proofreader: Stephanie Egerton

Publisher: Patrick Dawson
Editorial: Alan Murphy, Sophie Blacksell, Claire Boobbyer, Felicity Laughton, Nicola Jones, Angus Dawson
Cartography: Robert Lunn, Claire Benison, Kevin Feeney
Series development: Rachel Fielding
Design: Mytton Williams and Rosemary Dawson (brand)
Sales and marketing: Andy Riddle
Advertising: Debbie Wylde
Finance and administration: Sharon Hughes, Elizabeth Taylor

Photography credits
Front cover: Photolibrary
Back cover: Superstock
Front colour section: Alamy, Images of Africa, Superstock
Wildlife colour section: NATUREPL (Karl Ammann, Ingo Arndt, Peter Blackwell, Nigel Bean, John Cancalosi, Philippe Clement, Richard Du Toit, Laurent Geslin, Tony Heald, Eliot Lyons, Pete Oxford, Andrew Parkinson, Constantinos Petrinos, T J Rich, Jose B Ruiz, Francois Savigny, Anup Shah, Mike Wilkes)

Print
Manufactured in Italy by LegoPrint
Pulp from sustainable forests

Footprint feedback
We try as hard as we can to make each Footprint guide as up to date as possible but, of course, things always change. If you want to let us know about your experiences – good, bad or ugly – then don't delay, go to **www.footprintbooks.com** and send in your comments.

Publishing information
Footprint Tanzania
1st edition

October 2005

ISBN 1 904777 49 X
CIP DATA: A catalogue record for this book is available from the British Library

Published by Footprint
6 Riverside Court
Lower Bristol Road
Bath BA2 3DZ, UK
T +44 (0)1225 469141
F +44 (0)1225 469461
discover@footprintbooks.com
www.footprintbooks.com

Distributed in the USA by
Publishers Group West

Acknowledgments

Lizzie would like to thank the following people in Tanzania for their exceptional hospitality. Sparky & Nic in Dar es Salaam, Ma & BJ at the Meserani Snake Park in Arusha, and Andy Nagy the construction manager and the Grumeti Reserves team of Sasakwa Lodge near the Serengeti. Thanks to the local headmaster of the school near the Serengeti's Ikoma Gate for the somewhat interesting lift he gave us through the Serengeti and the Ngorongoro Crater, when, after two blow outs we drove up the crater on three wheels and one rim! Thanks to Stu Lodge at Global Village, a leading travel agent in London specializing in Africa, for organizing flights. Thanks to the staff at the helpful Arusha Tourist Office and the staff at Hoopoe Safaris also in Arusha. For car hire thanks to Evergreen Car Rentals in Dar es Salaam and John and Debbie Adderson of Wild Frontiers in Johannesburg, an excellent African tour operator. Thanks also to Debbie for last minute advice on changing national park fees and policies. For additional research in the south of Tanzania thanks to Dave & Kat Horner for their invaluable information, especially about crossing the border with Mozambique – enjoy the rest of your trip! Also a big thank you to Becky Stickland for her detailed maps and information of southwest Tanzania and her excellent recommendations. Thanks to Simone Epting for assistance on Zanzibar and in Bagamoyo. Readers that found the time to write in to offer suggestions include: Josh Busby, Donna Stride and Linda Jensen. Thanks to the staff at Footprint for their back up and to Sarah Thorowgood for making it all make sense. The health section was written by Dr Charlie Easmon, MBBS, MRCP, Msc Public Health, DTM&H, DoccMed, Director of Travel Screening Services. Finally thanks to my good mate Simon Lewis, sales manager of Acacia Adventure Holidays, a leading tour operator for travel all over Africa, for travelling with me in Tanzania despite the cockroaches on the train. Simon contributed greatly to this book through his role of 'finding somewhere to watch sport' throughout Tanzania when his beloved Liverpool were in the run up and won the 2005 European championships. His enthusiasm was shared by many Tanzanians.

About the author

Originally from London, Lizzie Williams has worked and lived in Africa for 12 years, starting as an expedition leader on trips across the continent on overland trucks, including the Istanbul to Cape Town run. She is now something of an expert on border crossings and African beer, and has sat with a gorilla, slept amongst elephants, swum with a hippo and fed a giraffe. Lizzie has travelled independently to over 20 African countries and could feasibly have driven many hundreds of thousands of kilometres through Africa. She has spent lengthy periods working in Zimbabwe, running an overland stop and tour company specializing in Mozambique, and in South Africa as manager of a backpacker's lodge equipped to receive overland trucks. She is co-author of *Footprint South Africa*, author of *Footprint Kenya*, and has updated *Footprint Namibia*. She has written www.overlandafrica.com a leading website on the overland industry in Africa, contributed Africa destination guides to US websites including iexplore and yahoo, and written *Africa Overland*, a glossy look at the Kenya to Cape overland route. She is also the author of the first country-specific guidebook to Nigeria, the *Bradt Guide to Nigeria*. Lizzie writes full time and, when not on the road, lives in Cape Town.

Map symbols

Administration

- Capital city
- Other city/town
- International border
- Regional border
- Disputed border

Roads and travel

- Main road (National highway)
- Unpaved or *ripio* (gravel) road
- 4WD track
- Footpath
- Railway with station
- Airport
- Bus station
- Metro station
- Cable car
- Funicular
- Ferry

Water features

- River, canal
- Lake, ocean
- Seasonal marshland
- Beach, sand bank
- Waterfall

Topographical features

- Contours (approx)
- Mountain
- Volcano
- Mountain pass
- Escarpment
- Gorge
- Glacier
- Salt flat
- Rocks

Cities and towns

- Main through route
- Main street
- Minor street
- Pedestrianized street
- Tunnel
- One way street
- Steps
- Bridge
- Fortified wall
- Park, garden, stadium
- Sleeping
- Eating
- Bars & clubs
- Entertainment
- cp Casa particular
- Building
- Sight
- Cathedral, church
- Chinese temple
- Hindu temple
- Meru
- Mosque
- Stupa
- Synagogue
- Tourist office
- Museum
- Post office
- Police
- Bank
- Internet
- Telephone
- Market
- Hospital
- Parking
- Petrol
- Golf
- Detail map
- Related map

Other symbols

- Archaeological site
- National park, wildlife reserve
- Viewing point
- Campsite
- Refuge, lodge
- Castle
- Diving
- Deciduous/coniferous/palm trees
- Hide
- Vineyard
- Distillery
- Shipwreck
- Historic battlefield

Map 1
UGANDA
Rumanyika Orugundu Game Reserve
Lake Victoria
Ibanda Game Reserve
Karagwe
Bukoba
Kemondo Bay
Musoma
KAGERA
Muleba
Ukerewe Island
Nansio
Bunda
RWANDA
Burigi Game Reserve
Rubondo Island National Park
Saa Nane Island Game Reserve
Biharamulo Game Reserve
Ngara
Nyamirembe
Mwanza
Sengerema
Biharamulo
Geita
MWANZA
BURUNDI
SHINYANGA
Shinyanga
Kibondo
Kigosi Game Reserve
Moyowosi Game Reserve
Nzega
Wemberer River
Igombe River
Kasulu
Gombe Stream National Park
KIGOMA
Kigoma
Ujiji
Uvinza
Kaliua
Tabora
Malagarasi River
TABORA
RD CONGO
Lagosa (Mugambo)
Ugalla River
Ugalla River Game Reserve
Mpanda
RUKWA
Mahale Mountains National Park
Sitalike
Nkululu River
Inyonga
Lake Tanganyika
Ikola
Katavi National Park
Rungwa
Rungwa River
N
Uwanda Game Reserve
Kipili
Lake Rukwa (Salt Lake)
0 km 50
0 miles 50
Sumbawanga
Ngomba
Lake Rukwa (Salt Lake)
Makongolosi
Nuzi
Kasanga
Chunya
Kalamba Falls
Mbeya
Mbozi
Vwawa
Tukuyu
Tunduma
Kyela
Itungi
ZAMBIA
Altitude in metres
3000
2000
1500
1000
500
200
100
0
Neighbouring country
Principal highway, surfaced & unsurfaced
Provincial road, partly surfaced
Minor road, track
Rail
MALA
A
B
C
1
2
3

KENYA
Indian Ocean
MOZAMBIQUE
Lake Natron (Soda Lake)
Namanga
Mt Longido (2,629m)
Longido
Loitokitok
Ngorongoro Conservation Area
Eugaruka Ruins
Rift Valley
Kilimanjaro National Park
Arusha National Park
Olduvai Gorge
Ngorongoro Crater
Mt Meru (4,572m)
Mt Kilimanjaro (5,896m)
Taveta
Mto wa Mbu
Arusha
Moshi
Lake Manyara National Park
Mwanga
Lake Manyara (Soda Lake)
ARUSHA
Lembeni
KILIMANJARO
Tarangire National Park
Mkomazi Game Reserve
Same
Kisiwani
Mt Leya (2,417m)
Pangani River
Pare Mountains
Umba River Game Reserve
Babati
Usambara Mountains
Mt Hanang (3,417m)
Kolo
Lushoto
Soni
Mombo
Galamos Sulphur Springs
Amboni Caves
Pemba Island
Kondoa Irangi Rock Paintings
Masai Steppe
Tanga
Chake Chake
Kondoa
Korogwe
Muheza
Tongoni Ruins
TANGA
Pangani
Mkoani
Nguru Mountains
DODOMA
Zanzibar Island
Saadani National Park
Stone Town
DODOMA
Bagamoyo
Magole
Kaole
Kunduchi Beach
Mbezi Beach
Chalinze
DAR ES SALAAM
Kilosa
Morogoro
Kisarawe
Uluguru Mountains
Bunduki
Mgeta
Mikumi National Park
PWANI
Kisiju
IRINGA
Ruaha
Mikumi
Mafia Island
Kilondoni
Mafia Island Marine Park
Mazombe
Udzungwa Mountains National Park
Rufiji River
Iringa
Mohoro
Ifakara
Selous Game Reserve
Kilombero River
Malangali
Kilwa Kivinje
Kilwa Masoko
LINDI
Mahenge
Mbwemburu River
Makambako
MOROGORO
Tendaguru
Liwale
Litipo Forest Reserve
Lindi
Mingoyo
Mikindani
Mtwara
Nachingwea
RUVUMA
Makonde Plateau
Masasi
Songea
MTWARA
Newala
Ruvuma River
Mbinga
Lukwika-Lumesule Game Reserve
Tunduru
Mbamba Bay
Chamba
Masuguru
A
B
C
4
5
6

Map 2 National Parks & Game Reserves

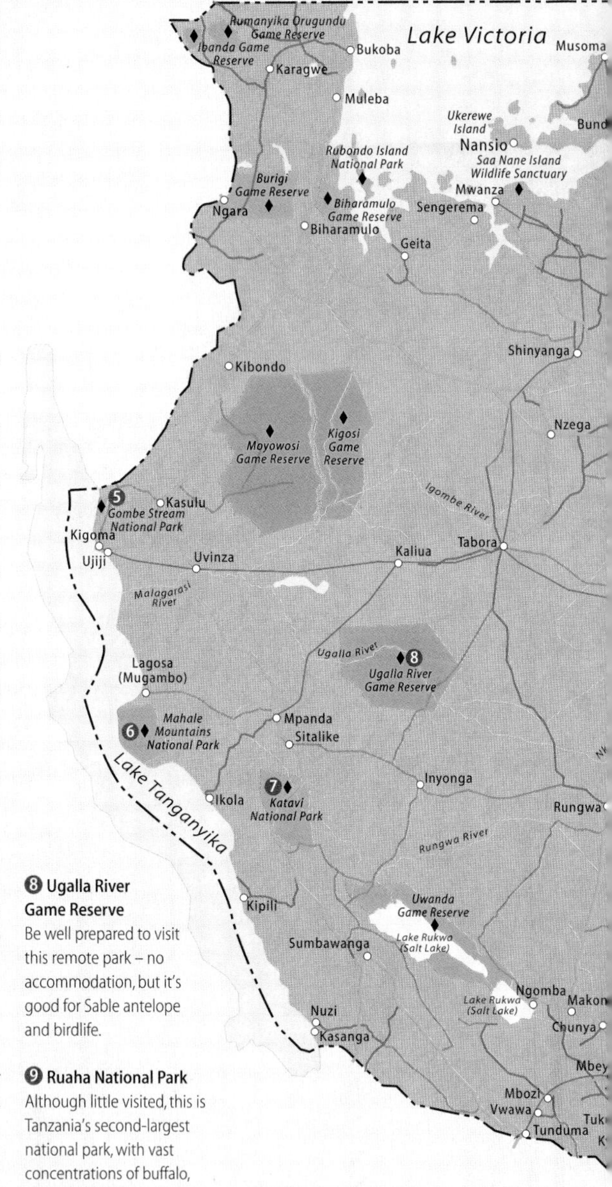

❶ Serengeti National Park
Far-reaching plains of endless grass, tinged with the twisted shadows of acacia trees, make this the quintessential image of wild, untarnished Africa. It supports the highest concentration of game in Africa.

❷ Ngorongoro Conservation Area
Often called 'Africa's Eden', Ngorongoro encompasses the volcanic Ngorongoro and Embagai craters, Olduvai Gorge – famous for its palaeontological relics – and Lake Masek. The crater is a world-class visitor attraction.

❸ Arusha National Park
In the shadow of mounts Kilimanjaro and Meru, this is a compact park with three varied habitats: the highland montane forest; a small volcanic crater inhabited by a variety of mammals; and a series of seven alkaline crater lakes.

❹ Kilimanjaro National Park
One of the most impressive sights in Africa, the highest mountain on the continent is visible from as far away as Tsavo National Park in Kenya. Kibo Peak rises to 5,895 m.

❺ Gombe Stream National Park
One of Tanzania's most remote parks and famous for its chimpanzee populations.

❻ Mahale Mountains National Park
Another chimpanzee sanctuary with a larger population so there's more chance of sightings here than at Gombe.

❼ Katavi National Park
A very isolated park less frequented by tourists, Katavi is famous for its Roan and Sable antelope and large herds of buffalo.

❽ Ugalla River Game Reserve
Be well prepared to visit this remote park – no accommodation, but it's good for Sable antelope and birdlife.

❾ Ruaha National Park
Although little visited, this is Tanzania's second-largest national park, with vast concentrations of buffalo, elephant, gazelle and over 400 bird species.

❿ Udzungwa Mountains National Park
Recently classified as a National Park, this forested area plays host to a large number of endangered bird species as well as forest antelope and vervet monkeys.

⓫ Selous Game Reserve
The largest park in Africa and the second largest in the world, Selous covers 5% of Tanzania's total area (although much is off limits to visitors). The area is famous for African wild dogs and some of the last black rhino left in the region.

⓬ Mafia Island Marine Park
The best deep-sea diving ir Tanzania in protected coral gardens. The island is the meeting place of large oceanic fish and the vast variety of fish common to th Indian Ocean coral reefs.

Serengeti National Park
1
Ngorongoro Conservation Area
2
Lake Natron (Soda Lake)
Namanga
Longido
Loitokitok
Kilimanjaro National Park
4
Arusha National Park
3
Mto Wa Mbu
Arusha
Moshi
Taveta
Mwanga
Lembeni
Lake Manyara National Park
Lake Eyasi (Salt Lake)
Lake Manyara (Soda Lake)
Mkomazi Game Reserve
Same
Kisiwani
Umba River Game Reserve
Pangani River
Tarangire National Park
Babati
Kolo
Singida
Kondoa
Lushoto
Mombo
Soni
Korogwe
Muheza
Tanga
Pemba Island
Chake Chake
Pangani
Indian Ocean
Manyoni
Zanzibar Island
Saadani National Park
Stone Town
DODOMA
Magole
Bagamoyo
Chalinze
DAR ES SALAAM
Kisugu River
Kilosa
Morogoro
Kisarawe
Bunduki
Mikumi National Park
Mgeta
Kisiju
Ruaha
Mikumi
Ruaha National Park
9
Mazombe
Udzungwa Mountains National Park
10
Mafia Island
Kilondoni
12
Mafia Island Marine Park
Rufiji River
Iringa
Mohoro
Ifakara
Kilombero River
11
Selous Game Reserve
Malangali
Kilwa Kivinje
Kilwa Masoko
Mahenge
Iyayi
Makambako
Matandu River
Njombe
Uwemba
Liwale
Litipo Forest Reserve
Lindi
Mingoyo
Mikindani
Mtwara
Nachingwea
Mnazi Bay Marine Reserve
Manda
Lituhi
Songea
Masasi
Newala
Ruvuma River
Mbinga
Lukwika-Lumesule Game Reserve
Tunduru
Liuli
Mbamba Bay
Masuguru
Chamba
N
0 km
50
0 miles
50

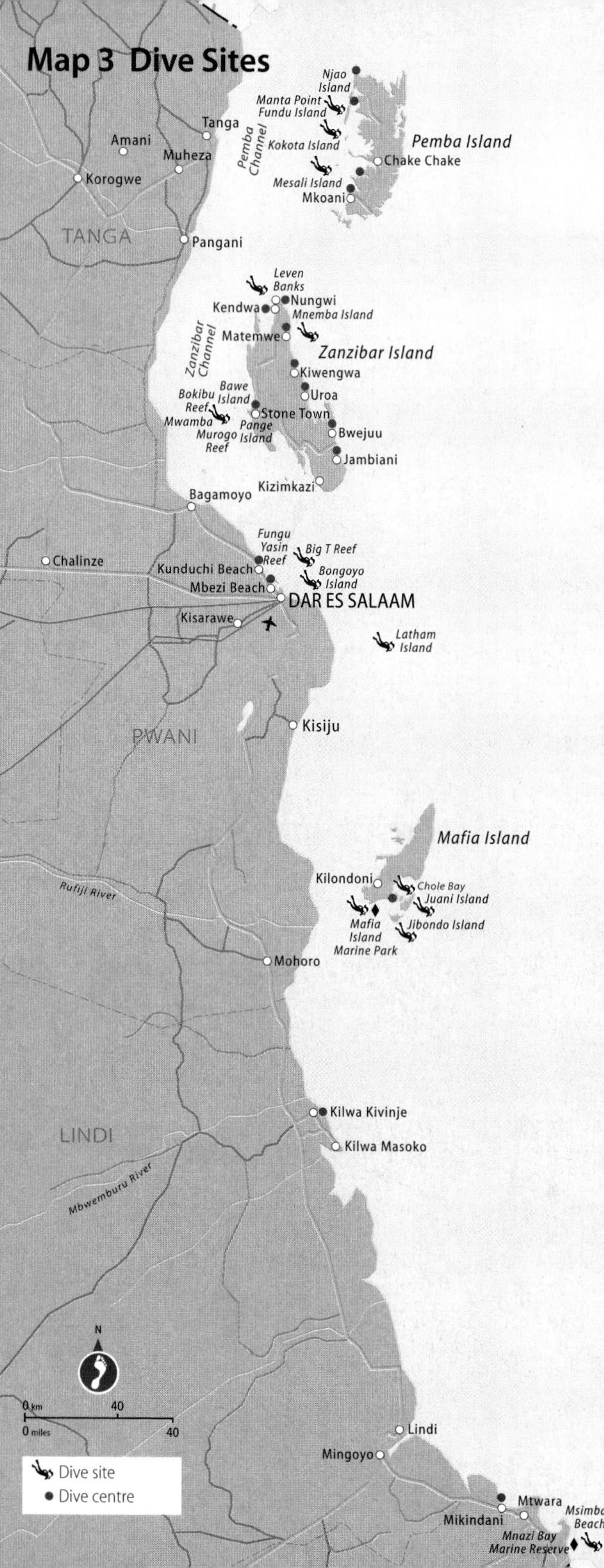

Pemba Island

Africa's 'Emerald Isle' is the jewel in Tanzania's dive-site portfolio and is considered a world-class diving destination. On the west coast the deep waters of the Pemba Channel create dramatic walls and drop-offs. You may see sharks, eagle rays, manta rays, Napoleon wrasse, great barracuda, tuna and kingfish.

Zanzibar

Near Stone Town there are pristine coral gardens and a proliferation of marine life. Murogo Reef has some beautiful coral. Leven Banks on the north coast is near the deep water of the Pemba Channel and you may see big shoals of jacks and trevally. The east coast has the most talked about diving on Zanzibar and is also great for snorkelling.

Mafia Island

"Shallow Pemba with more fish", according to one diver. Mafia has beautiful reefs and spectacular fish life. Jino Pass and Dindini Wall are two good reefs to the northeast of Chole Bay. Here you can see huge malabar, potato and honeycomb groupers, giant reef rays, green turtles, great barracuda, kingfish, bonito, shoals of bluefin trevalley and snappers in their thousands.

Mainland sites

If you are not visiting Pemba or Zanzibar, try a dive around Dar. Ferns Wall, on the seaward side of Fungu Yasin Reef has barrel sponges, gorgonian fans, 2-m long whip corals and reef sharks. Big T Reef is a must for the experienced diver but only on a calm day. Off Latham Island you can see big game fish and hammerheads. Mnazi Bay Marine Reserve also has superb snorkelling and diving. Fabulous coral reef and turtles are common.

The South American Handbook: 1924-2006

It was 1921

Ireland had just been partitioned, the British miners were striking for more pay and the federation of British industry had an idea. Exports were booming in South America – how about a Handbook for businessmen trading in that far away continent? The *Anglo-South American Handbook* was born that year, written by W Koebel, the most prolific writer on Latin America of his day.

1924

Two editions later the book was 'privatized' and in 1924, in the hands of Royal Mail, the steamship company for South America, became *The South American Handbook*, subtitled 'South America in a nutshell'. This annual publication became the 'bible' for generations of travellers to South America and remains so to this day. In the early days travel was by sea and the Handbook gave all the details needed for the long voyage from Europe. What to wear for dinner; how to arrange a cricket match with the Cable & Wireless staff on the Cape Verde Islands and a full account of the journey from Liverpool up the Amazon to Manaus: 5898 miles without changing cabin!

1939

As the continent opened up, *The South American Handbook* reported the new Pan Am flying boat services, and the fortnightly airship service from Rio to Europe on the Graf Zeppelin. For reasons still unclear but with extraordinary determination, the annual editions continued through the Second World War.

1970s

From the 1970s, jet aircraft transformed travel. Many more people discovered South America and the backpacking trail started to develop. All the while the Handbook was gathering fans, including literary vagabonds such as Paul Theroux and Graham Greene (who once sent some updates addressed to **"The publishers of the best travel guide in the world, Bath, England"**.)

1990s

During the 1990s Patrick and James Dawson, the publishers of *The South American Handbook* set about developing a new travel guide series using this legendary title as the flagship. By 1997 there were over a dozen guides in the series and the Footprint imprint was launched.

2000s

In 2003, Footprint launched a new series of pocket guides focusing on short-break European cities. The series grew quickly so that at the end of 2004 there were over 100 Footprint travel guides covering more than 150 destinations around the world. In January 2004, *The South American Handbook* reached another milestone: 80 annual editions. A memorable birthday party was held at Stanfords in London to celebrate. An Activity series was also launched in 2004, with the publication of *Surfing Europe*, packed with colour photographs, maps and charts. This was followed by a new full-colour Discover series in 2005.

The future

There are many more guides in the pipeline. To keep up-to-date with new releases check out the Footprint website for all the latest news and information, **www.footprintbooks.com.**